Psychodynamic Psychiatry in Clinical Practice

The DSM-IV Edition

Psychodynamic Psychiatry in Clinical Practice

The DSM-IV Edition

Glen O. Gabbard, M.D.

American Psychiatric Press, Inc.

Washington, DC
London, England

Note: The authors have worked to ensure that all information in this book concerning drug dosages, schedules, and routes of administration is accurate as of the time of publication and consistent with standards set by the U.S. Food and Drug Administration and the general medical community. As medical research and practice advance, however, therapeutic standards may change. For this reason and because human and mechanical errors sometimes occur, we recommend that readers follow the advice of a physician who is directly involved in their care or the care of a member of their family.

Books published by the American Psychiatric Press, Inc., represent the views and opinions of the individual authors and do not necessarily represent the policies and opinions of the Press or the American Psychiatric Association.

Copyright © 1994 American Psychiatric Press, Inc.
ALL RIGHTS RESERVED
Manufactured in the United States of America on acid-free paper
97 96 95 94   4 3 2 1
Second Edition

American Psychiatric Press, Inc.
1400 K Street, N.W., Washington, DC   20005

Library of Congress Cataloging-in-Publication Data
Gabbard, Glen O.
    Psychodynamic psychiatry in clinical practice / Glen O. Gabbard. —
    The DSM-IV ed.
        p.   cm.
    Includes bibliographical references and index.
    ISBN 0-88048-658-9
    1. Psychodynamic psychotherapy. I. Title.
    [DNLM: 1. Biological Psychiatry. 2. Mental Disorders—therapy.
    3. Psychoanalytic Therapy. 4. Psychotherapy. WM 400 G112p 1994]
    RC489.P72G33 1994
    616.89′1—dc20
    DNLM/DLC   93-27939
    for Library of Congress   CIP

British Library Cataloguing in Publication Data
A CIP record is available from the British Library.

To My Teachers, My Patients, and My Students

About the Author

Glen O. Gabbard, M.D., is Vice President for Adult Services, The
Menninger Clinic; Director, C. F. Menninger Memorial Hospital;
Training and Supervising Analyst, Topeka Institute for Psychoanalysis; and Clinical Professor of Psychiatry, University of Kansas School
of Medicine, Wichita.

Contents

Section I
Basic Principles and Treatment
Approaches in Dynamic Psychiatry

Section II
Dynamic Approaches to Axis I Disorders

Section III
Dynamic Approaches to Axis II Disorders

Foreword

The growth of biological psychiatry over the past two decades has effected an almost paradigmatic shift in the prevailing understanding of psychiatric illness, a shift back into a more "medical" illness model, more exactly akin to the natural science explanatory model of somatic medicine in general. This had been the model of the first scientific descriptive nosology of psychiatric illness devised by Kraepelin a century ago, from which the field was subsequently swung into the psychodynamically conceptualized psychological understanding of mental functioning and its disorders based on the theory of the psychoanalysis created and elaborated by Freud and his followers. This psychodynamic (and to some extent, psychoeducational) understanding held an almost exclusive sway throughout the middle decades of this century—until the recent knowledge surge in neurobiology and the growth of modern-day biological psychiatry under the attractive banner of "remedicalization."

A major reflection of this pendular to-and-fro in the conceptualization of psychiatric illness enterprise has been in the structure and the philosophic tenets of the official psychiatric nomenclature. The American Psychiatric Association's *Diagnostic and Statistical Manual of Mental Disorders* (DSM-I), which appeared in 1952, and even more so its successor, DSM-II, were both underpinned by the prevailing psychological paradigms of mental illness of the period. DSM-I contained a lingering reflection of Adolf Meyer's psychobiological view that mental disorders represented reactions of the total personality to the con-

verging relevant psychological, social, and biological factors; DSM-II
was more unreservedly psychoanalytic in its psychological framework.
It was within this predominantly psychoanalytic (euphemistically
called *psychodynamic*) understanding of mental health and illness and
the DSM-I and DSM-II nomenclatures that reigned for a combined
quarter century that the post–World War II generations of psychiatrists were taught the fundamentals of psychodynamic case formulation and treatment planning, the practice of psychoanalytically
oriented expressive and supportive psychotherapies based on those
case formulations, and the derived psychoanalytically informed treatment plans.

The major sea change embodied in DSM-III (approved by the
American Psychiatric Association in 1979) was both a major aspect and
a signal reflection of the concomitant shifting conceptual emphases im-
pelled by the rise of biological psychiatry and of modern psychopharmacology, with its proliferation of putatively specifically targeted
psychoactive drugs. The dissatisfactions with DSM-II had indeed been
serious. A psychoanalytically based nomenclature was imprecise, with
ambiguous and elastic diagnostic boundaries, and contained high levels of (often unspecifiable) inferential reasoning. Case formulations
were therefore notoriously unreliable, and professional disagreements
seemed often to be rather arbitrarily resolved simply by the weight of
authority or seniority. Questions of validity could hardly even be approached for purposes of research classification, medical record keeping, or reimbursement.

The intent of the creators of DSM-III was in the first instance to
enhance diagnostic reliability and precision; the guiding framework
was to be a closer modeling of the kinds of clearer delineations of medical somatic illness by symptom picture in the *International Classification of Diseases* (ICD). The path toward this goal was to classify only
descriptively, rigorously eschewing the levels of inference inherent in
the psychodynamic, or psychoanalytically based, viewpoint—that is, to
be specifically atheoretical and theory-neutral as far as human intention could ensure. The result has been a new nomenclature, with us
now for a decade, that is indeed more stable, more precise, and more
reliable across individuals and across time and space. For the purposes
of empirical research studies on the clinical trials model, for statistical,
epidemiological, and treatment reimbursement purposes, and for purposes of clinical treatment with the ever-widening array of psychoactive drugs, the gains have indeed been impressive. The thinking of

DSM-III (and its successors in the DSM-III-R and the presently in-process DSM-IV) is now the centerpiece of current academic psychiatric education and research. Within the governmental research grant-giving structure, it is currently extremely difficult to garner funding support for clinical psychotherapeutic *or* psychopharmacological treatment research unless that research is embedded within the specific nosological categories of DSM-III, the specific syndromes of Axis I, and the specific personality disorders as delineated by Axis II.

The gains that have accrued to psychiatry with the newer "atheoretical" nomenclature of DSM-III and its successors—and, specifically, the greatly enhanced gains in the understanding and treatment of many psychiatric illnesses that have derived from the burgeoning biological (including, of course, genetic) and epidemiological understandings of these disorders—have also unhappily had their price. Every swing of the pendulum in the historic unfolding of psychiatric understanding has brought important new emphases and new advances in relation to the fathoming of the ideally integrated overall "biopsychosocial" conceptual framework (to which we will all pay at least lip service). But with each swing there has been a concomitant unnecessary deemphasis and condoned neglect of the immediately prior dominant arm of the tripartite psychiatric explanatory structure—biological, psychological, and social. We are now solidly in an era in psychiatric education of deemphasis of psychodynamic understanding and case formulation and treatment planning, as if enhanced knowledge of the biological dimensions of mental disorders renders psychosocial and psychological approaches far less relevant—if not completely obsolete.

It is the implicit challenge, in this state of affairs, to accept the current "atheoretical" diagnostic framework of the DSM-III (and the DSM-III-R and the forthcoming DSM-IV) classification of psychiatric disorders by symptom cluster, and to demonstrate specifically, even within that framework, the continued usefulness of—or rather the continued necessity for—the fullest psychodynamic exploration and understanding in order to ensure the most comprehensive treatment— the continuingly relevant psychotherapeutic in proper interaction with the newly relevant psychopharmacological—for the array of defined psychiatric disorders. It is this formidable challenge that Glen Gabbard so successfully takes on. Briefly put, the intent of this book is to persuade the reader that psychoanalytically based understandings of the disorders of the mind and the paths toward their amelioration

must not be lost today in the illusory expectation that biological understanding and remediation is sufficient for the effective reversal of disordered mental functioning and behavior. It would be everyone's
loss—most directly, that of the patients—if this were allowed to happen. It is books like this one by Gabbard that will therefore play a vital
role in ensuring that the imbalances in our diagnostic understandings,
conceptual frameworks, and therapeutic armamentaria created by our
dramatic pendular paradigmatic swings are properly self-corrected—
in this particular case, to maintain the full value of the psychodynamic
orientation within the current house of psychiatry. No one book can be
completely successful in attaining so ambitious a goal, and each of us
will find our points of disagreement or disappointment with the
author's effort. What is more important is how much of the overall
message *does* get conveyed and *does* persuade.

Robert S. Wallerstein, M.D.

Source Acknowledgments

The author gratefully acknowledges permission to reprint portions of the following material:

American Psychiatric Association: Diagnostic and Statistical Manual of Mental Disorders, 4th Edition. Washington, DC, American Psychiatric Association, 1994. Portions reprinted with permission.

Gabbard GO: The exit line: heightened transference-countertransference manifestations at the end of the hour. J Am Psychoanal Assoc 30:579–598, 1982. Portions reprinted with permission.

Gabbard GO: The role of compulsiveness in the normal physician. JAMA 254:2926–2929, 1985. Copyright 1985, American Medical Association. Portions reprinted with permission.

Gabbard GO: The treatment of the "special" patient in a psychoanalytic hospital. International Review of Psychoanalysis 13:333–347, 1986. Portions reprinted with permission.

Gabbard GO: A contemporary perspective on psychoanalytically informed hospital treatment. Hosp Community Psychiatry 39:1291–1295, 1988. Portions reprinted with permission.

Gabbard GO: Patients who hate. Psychiatry 52:96–106, 1989. Portions reprinted with permission.

Gabbard GO: Splitting in hospital treatment. Am J Psychiatry 146:444–451, 1989. Copyright 1989, American Psychiatric Association. Portions reprinted with permission.

Introduction

When Carol Nadelson, editor-in-chief of American Psychiatric Press, first invited me to write a book that approached DSM-III-R from a psychodynamic perspective, I asked her why she had selected me for the task. She replied that she felt I was the logical person to do it. At that moment I was like the man who one day discovered that he had been speaking prose all his life. I realized that indeed I had been practicing psychodynamic psychiatry all my professional life. I had treated a broad array of outpatients and inpatients with individual psychotherapy, psychoanalysis, medications, family/marital therapy, and group therapy, but these therapeutic approaches had always been informed by psychodynamic understanding of the clinical situation.

After accepting the challenge, I set to work on a prospectus for the book. I originally proposed an edited volume with multiple authors. The APPI Board responded to the proposal by making a compelling case for a single-authored volume. The advantage of having one author, they argued, would be a cohesive and unified application of theory to diagnostic understanding and treatment from chapter to chapter. One author could lay down the theoretical principles at the beginning of the book and then proceed to demonstrate how those principles applied to DSM-III-R disorders. An edited volume would be prone to fragmentation of theory and practice because of the multiple perspectives and approaches of diverse authors.

Having been persuaded by the argument of the APPI Board, I developed a working outline for the book. I immediately confronted the fact that no one clinician could possibly be equally knowledgeable about the treatment of every major diagnostic entity. As a result, in some chapters involving disorders with which I have limited clinical experience, I have had to rely more on the experience and writings of others who are more expert than I. When writing about other conditions, I have drawn more from my own clinical experience. I also realized that my review of the relevant literature would have to be selective rather than comprehensive if I were to complete the task during my lifetime.

While in the process of writing this volume, I had the opportunity to lecture to residents, psychiatrists in private practice, and other groups of mental health professionals throughout the country. My interactions with these clinicians convinced me that a book such as this one was sorely needed. Residents repeatedly expressed concern that their programs were not providing an adequate foundation in psychodynamic psychiatry. They could diagnose a psychiatric disorder according to symptoms, course, and history, but they could not understand the person with the disorder. Psychiatrists in practice repeatedly complained of "getting stuck" when their patients would not respond to psychopharmacologic agents. I was also struck by the unnecessary polarization between biological and psychodynamic approaches within psychiatry. It had always seemed to me that medications were part of the dynamic psychiatrist's therapeutic armamentarium and that a sophisticated knowledge of transference, countertransference, and resistance was extraordinarily helpful in the practice of pharmacotherapy. This book is written in that spirit of integration, with the hope that biological psychiatrists will find it as useful as those who are more dynamically oriented. The audiences I have targeted are psychiatric residents and psychiatrists in clinical practice. Those involved in hospital work and the treatment of severely disturbed patients may find it useful as well.

The book is organized into three sections. Section I discusses the basic theoretical principles of dynamic psychiatry and the major treatment modalities, including individual psychotherapy, group psychotherapy, family/marital therapy, dynamic pharmacotherapy, and dynamically informed hospital treatment. Section II applies the theoretical principles and therapeutic approaches described in Section I to the major Axis I disorders of DSM-III-R. Since my goal was to produce a reasonably slender one-volume text that does not require a forklift to transport, I have not been able to include every Axis I disorder listed in the manual. Forced to be selective, I have focused on the most common Axis I disorders and those conditions for which a psychodynamic approach is most useful. To keep the scope of the book manageable for a single author, I have further limited myself to adult psychiatry.

Section III addresses Axis II disorders, with chapters subdivided according to the DSM-III-R clusters. One chapter each is devoted to Cluster A (comprising those personality disorders that appear "eccentric") and to Cluster C (subsuming personality disorders that share in common the feature of anxiety). Cluster B personality disorders— borderline, narcissistic, antisocial, and histrionic—are grouped together because of their more dramatic nature. Moreover, they are the personality disorders most commonly encountered in the practice of dynamic psychiatry and the Axis II conditions about which more is known. Accordingly, a separate chapter is devoted to each Cluster B personality disorder in order to cover the relevant literature and theoretical controversies more comprehensively.

All of us are shaped by our environments, and my 15 years of clinical work at the Menninger Clinic have profoundly influenced my perspective on psychiatric practice. To a large extent, the psychodynamic psychiatry described in this volume reflects the nature of Menninger practice. I must acknowledge a debt of gratitude to my teachers over the years who have taught me the importance of listening to and understanding patients. These mentors are too numerous to mention by name, and I would not want to run the risk of omitting someone in an attempt to list them. My psychoanalytic training at the Topeka Institute for Psychoanalysis was also of enormous value in my professional development. I am particularly grateful to my training analyst, Dr. Ramon Ganzarain, and to my teachers and supervisors: Drs. Ishak Ramzy, Irwin Rosen, Jack Ross, Jerome Katz, Stuart Averill, Alfredo Namnum, and J. Cotter Hirschberg.

Patients, of course, are our most important teachers, and I wish to acknowledge their contribution to my development as a clinician. The residents and other trainees I have taught during my years as a teacher and supervisor in the Karl Menninger School of Psychiatry have also been an important source of stimulation and education for me.

Writing a book of this nature is truly a team effort. Alice Brand Bartlett and Marcy Schott of the Menninger Professional Library were most helpful in their provision of up-to-date literature searches. Mary

Ann Clifft, Phil Beard, and Eleanor Bell spent many hours with early manuscript drafts meticulously copyediting and checking references. I am especially grateful to Faye Schoenfeld for patiently and enthusiastically typing many drafts of each chapter. I have also greatly appreciated the administrative support of my colleagues, Dr. Roy Menninger and Dr. Walt Menninger, without which the writing of this book would not have been possible. Other colleagues, including Drs. Donald Colson, James Eyman, Leonard Horwitz, Lisa Lewis, Donald Rinsley, and Kathryn Zerbe, graciously read portions of the manuscript and contributed constructive suggestions for revision. Several other colleagues—including Drs. Steve Katz, Joel Nance, Tom Picard, Victoria Spinazzola, Howard Rosenfield, and Mrs. Alice Brand Bartlett—provided clinical material for the book or added supplemental information to my own cases. Dr. Robert Wallerstein has been most generous in sharing a portion of his much-sought-after time to carefully read the manuscript and write a foreword.

The American Psychiatric Press staff were, as usual, a superb support system. Carol Nadelson provided encouragement and moral support from the project's inception right on through to its completion. Tim Clancy and Claire Reinburg efficiently kept the project on schedule and contained my anxieties when necessary. Karen Loper and Margaret Gore were involved in the planning of a marketing program far in advance of the book's completion. I am grateful to all of them.

Finally, I wish to thank my wife and best friend, Dr. Joyce Davidson Gabbard, who sustained me emotionally so I could face the challenge of this project with energy and enthusiasm.

Glen O. Gabbard, M.D.

Preface to the Second Edition

A major impetus for this second edition was the introduction of DSM-IV and the associated passing of DSM-III-R. Each of the chapters has been revised to include the DSM-IV criteria, the advances in understanding the various diagnoses that led to alterations in the criteria, and the psychodynamic implications of these changes. However, my goals for this new edition go well beyond the changes in official nomenclature. I have sought also to correct oversights and omissions from the first edition and to draw from the psychiatric and psychoanalytic literature of the past several years to produce an up-to-the-minute account of contemporary psychodynamic psychiatry.

The first edition was widely adopted by training programs around the country and abroad, resulting in a great deal of feedback from many enthusiastic students and an equal number of thoughtful faculty members. I have incorporated many of the constructive criticisms and suggestions from these colleagues in the pages that follow. One rather substantial omission from Volume I was any detailed discussion of dissociative disorders. To remedy that situation, I have included a brand-new chapter in this volume devoted to that subject. In addition, several careful readers of the text noted that I failed to cover the issue of termination in psychotherapy, so I have added a segment on termination to Chapter 4.

Attempting to keep up with the psychiatric and psychoanalytic literature on the major diagnostic entities represented in DSM-IV is a formidable task. No one person can be completely comprehensive in such an undertaking. However, in the years since the appearance of the first edition, I have maintained for each chapter a file in which I have systematically kept track of the major contributions that I felt needed to be included in the second edition. As a result, each chapter has been not only revised to illustrate DSM-IV changes, but also updated more generally to reflect advances in the field since 1990. In some chapters this effort has resulted in relatively minor changes; in others, substantial additions will be found. The burgeoning research literature on the role of childhood trauma in the pathogenesis of borderline personality disorder, for example, has led to a considerable expansion of Chapter 15.

These changes have made this volume a bit longer and perhaps a bit more unwieldy than the first edition. I trust that the reader will forgive me those inconveniences and take some solace in the knowledge that the book is more complete and more up-to-date. As always, my editorial assistant, Mrs. Faye Schoenfeld, was of enormous value in shaping the final product. I am also grateful for the assistance provided by Ms. Claire Reinburg of American Psychiatric Press. Drs. Jon Allen, Joyce Davidson, George Ganaway, and Richard Kluft were kind enough to review new material, and I appreciate their contributions as well. Finally, I wish to thank all the readers of the first edition who have made my textbook popular enough to warrant a second version.

Glen O. Gabbard, M.D.

Section I

Basic Principles and Treatment Approaches in Dynamic Psychiatry

Chapter 1

Basic Principles of Dynamic Psychiatry

It would be far easier if we could avoid the patient as we explore the realm of psychopathology; it would be far simpler if we could limit ourselves to examining the chemistry and physiology of his brain, and to treating mental events as objects alien to our immediate experience, or as mere variables in impersonal statistical formulae. Important as these approaches are for the understanding of human behavior, they cannot alone uncover or explain all the relevant facts. To see into the mind of another, we must repeatedly immerse ourselves in the flood of his associations and feelings; we must be ourselves the instrument that sounds him.

John Nemiah (1961, p. 4)

Psychodynamic psychiatry (used interchangeably with dynamic psychiatry in this volume) is celebrating its 100th birthday. Ellenberger (1970) has traced the first usage of the term to the period between 1880 and 1900. Leibniz originally used *dynamic* to emphasize the contrast with *static*. Herbart applied this distinction to states of consciousness. Fechner appropriated the term to refer to mental en-

ergy and probably influenced Freud in this regard. *Dynamic* then came
to be used by the French physiologists to connote *functional* as opposed
to *organic*. Eventually, the eminent neurologist Hughlings Jackson
borrowed the term to mean physiological as opposed to anatomic, functional as opposed to organic, and regressive as opposed to the status
quo. In fact, Jackson's notion of mental energy very likely caught
Freud's eye.

Dynamic psychiatry owes its greatest debt to Freud. Whatever else
it may be, this approach is steeped in psychoanalytic theory and knowledge. (While some would argue that dynamic psychiatry subsumes a
broader purview than that of psychoanalytic psychiatry, the predominant contemporary usage is to equate *psychodynamic* with *psychoanalytic*.) For much of this century, modern dynamic psychiatry has been
viewed as a branch of psychiatry that explains mental phenomena as
the outgrowth of *conflict*. This conflict derives from powerful unconscious forces that seek expression and require constant monitoring
from opposing forces to prevent their expression. These interacting
forces may be conceptualized (with some overlap) as 1) a wish and a
defense against the wish, 2) different intrapsychic agencies or "parts"
with different aims and priorities, or 3) an impulse in opposition to an
internalized awareness of the demands of external reality.

In the last couple of decades, psychodynamic psychiatry has come
to connote more than the conflict model of illness. Today's dynamic
psychiatrist must also understand what is commonly referred to as the
"deficit model" of illness. This model is applied to patients who, for
whatever developmental reasons, suffer from weakened or absent psychic structures. This compromised state prevents them from feeling
whole and secure about themselves, and as a result, they require inordinate responses from persons in the environment to maintain psychological homeostasis. Also contained within the purview of
psychodynamic psychiatry is the unconscious internal world of relationships. All patients carry within them a host of different mental
representations of aspects of themselves and others, many of which
may create characteristic patterns of interpersonal difficulties. These
representations of self and others reside in the patient's unconscious,
where they form the world of internal object relations.

Above all, psychodynamic psychiatry is a *way of thinking*—not only
about one's patients but also about oneself in the interpersonal field
between patient and treater. In fact, to characterize the essence of dynamic psychiatry, one might well use the following definition: *Psycho-*

dynamic psychiatry is an approach to diagnosis and treatment charac-terized by a way of thinking about both patient and clinician that in-cludes unconscious conflict, deficits and distortions of intrapsychic structures, and internal object relations.

Although dynamic psychotherapy is one of the foremost tools in the dynamic psychiatrist's therapeutic armamentarium, dynamic psycho-therapy is not synonymous with dynamic psychiatry. The dynamic psy-chiatrist uses a wide range of treatment interventions that depend on a dynamic assessment of the patient's needs. Dynamic psychiatry sim-ply provides a coherent conceptual framework within which all treat-ments are prescribed. Regardless of whether the treatment is dynamic psychotherapy or pharmacotherapy, it is *dynamically informed.* In-deed, a crucial component of the dynamic psychiatrist's expertise is knowing when to avoid exploratory psychotherapy in favor of treat-ments that do not threaten the patient's psychic equilibrium.

Psychiatry has grown beyond the era when typical practitioners passed their days in the privacy of their consulting rooms, seeing one neurotic patient after another in long-term, insight-oriented psycho-therapy. Just as psychiatry as a field has changed, so has dynamic psychiatry. Today's dynamic psychiatrist must practice in the context of impressive advances in the neurosciences, integrating psychoana-lytic insight with biologic understanding of illness. Nevertheless, the dynamic psychiatrist is still guided by a handful of time-honored prin-ciples derived from psychoanalytic theory and technique that provide psychodynamic psychiatry with its unique character.

The Unique Value of Subjective Experience

Dynamic psychiatry is further defined by contrasting it with descrip-tive psychiatry. Practitioners of the latter approach categorize patients according to common behavioral and phenomenological features. They develop symptom checklists that allow them to classify patients ac-cording to similar clusters of symptoms. The patient's subjective expe-rience, except as used to report items in the checklist, is less important. Descriptive psychiatrists with a behavioral orientation would argue that the patient's subjective experience is peripheral to the essence of psychiatric diagnosis and treatment, which must be based on observ-able behavior. The most extreme behavioral view is that behavior and mental life are synonymous (Watson 1924/1930). Moreover, the descriptive psychiatrist is primarily interested in how a patient is *similar to* rather than *different from* other patients with congruent features.

In contrast, dynamic psychiatrists approach their patients by trying to determine what is unique about each one—how a particular patient *differs* from other patients as a result of a life story like no other. Symptoms and behaviors are viewed only as the final common pathways of highly personalized subjective experiences that filter the biological and environmental determinants of illness. Furthermore, dynamic psychiatrists place paramount value on the patient's internal world—fantasies, dreams, fears, hopes, impulses, wishes, self-images, perceptions of others, and psychological reactions to symptoms.

Descriptive psychiatrists approaching an occluded cave nestled in the side of a mountain might well describe in detail the characteristics of the massive rock obstructing the cave's opening, while dismissing the interior of the cave beyond the rock as inaccessible and therefore unknowable. In contrast, dynamic psychiatrists would be curious about the dark recesses of the cave beyond the boulder. Like the descriptive psychiatrists, they would note the markings of the opening, but they would regard them differently. They would want to know how the cave's exterior reflected the inner contents. They might be curious about why it was necessary to protect the interior with a boulder at the opening.

The Unconscious

Continuing with our cave metaphor, the dynamic psychiatrist would figure out a way to remove the boulder, enter the dark recesses of the cave, and perhaps with a flashlight, illuminate the interior. Artifacts on the floor or markings on the wall would be of special interest to the explorer because they would shed light on the history of this particular cave. A steady gurgling of water coming up through the floor might suggest an underground spring applying pressure from below. The dynamic psychiatrist would be particularly interested in exploring the depths of the cave. How far into the mountainside does it extend? Is the back wall the true limit that defines the inner space, or is it a "false wall" that gives way to even greater depths?

As the cave metaphor suggests, a second defining principle of dynamic psychiatry is a conceptual model of the mind that includes the unconscious. Freud (1915/1963) recognized two different kinds of unconscious mental content: 1) the preconscious (i.e., mental contents that can easily be brought into conscious awareness by merely shifting one's attention) and 2) the unconscious proper (i.e., mental contents that are censored because they are unacceptable and therefore are repressed and not easily brought into conscious awareness). Throughout this book, *the unconscious* will be used to refer exclusively to those mental contents in this second category. The preconscious can be illustrated by a memory of your first-grade teacher—although not generally conscious of him or her, you can retrieve an image of the teacher simply by shifting your attention. A common example of unconscious thought is the murderous wish an older sibling directs at a new baby brother or sister. Because this wish is unacceptable, it is repressed and buried in the unconscious.

Together, the unconscious, the preconscious, and the conscious systems of the mind compose what Freud (1900/1953) termed the *topographic model*. He became convinced of the unconscious because of two major pieces of clinical evidence: dreams and parapraxes. Analysis of dreams revealed that an unconscious childhood wish was usually the motivating force of dreams (1900/1953). The dreamwork disguised the wish, so analysis of the dream was necessary to discern the true nature of the wish. Reflecting on the manifest or overt content of your own dreams should be enough to convince you that dreams provide a forum for ideas that are not acceptable during waking life.

Parapraxes consist of such phenomena as slips of the tongue, "accidental" actions, and forgetting or substituting names or words. A typist, for example, repeatedly typed "murder" when she intended to type "mother." The notion of the "Freudian slip" is now a thoroughly entrenched part of our culture that connotes the unwitting revelation of a person's unconscious wishes or feelings. Freud (1901/1960) used these embarrassing incidents to illustrate the breakthrough of repressed wishes and to demonstrate the parallels between the mental processes of everyday life and those of neurotic symptom formation.

The dynamic psychiatrist views symptoms and behaviors as reflections of unconscious processes that defend against repressed wishes and feelings, just as the boulder protects the contents of the cave from exposure. Moreover, dreams and parapraxes are like the artwork on the walls of the cave—communications, symbolic or otherwise, in the present that deliver messages from the forgotten past. The dynamic psychiatrist must develop sufficient comfort with this dark realm to explore it without stumbling.

Psychic Determinism

To assert that symptoms and behavior are external manifestations of unconscious processes is to touch on a third principle of dynamic psychiatry—psychic determinism. The psychodynamic approach asserts that we are consciously confused and unconsciously controlled. We go through our daily lives as though we have freedom of choice, but we are actually far more restricted than we think. In actuality, we are but characters living out a script written by the unconscious. Our choices of marital partners, our vocational interests, even our leisure-time pursuits are not randomly selected; they are shaped by unconscious forces in dynamic relationship with one another.

By way of example, one young woman learned in the course of her psychotherapy that her choice of medicine as a career was profoundly shaped by events in her childhood and her reactions to them. When she was 8 years old, her mother had succumbed to cancer. The little girl witnessing this tragedy felt helpless and powerless at the time, and her decision to be a physician was partly determined by an unconscious wish to gain mastery and control over disease and death. At an unconscious level, being a physician was an attempt to actively master a passively experienced trauma. On a conscious level, she simply experienced medicine as a fascinating and compelling field.

When human behavior becomes markedly symptomatic, the limits of free will become more obvious. An obsessive-compulsive patient who must retrace the route from the subway to the office three times a day is consciously aware of being out of control, but simply does not understand the nature of the unconscious forces at work. A man who can only reach orgasm during masturbation by imagining humiliation at the hands of a muscle-bound sadist has similarly lost the freedom to choose his sexual fantasies. The dynamic psychiatrist approaches these symptoms with the understanding that they represent adaptations to the demands of an unconscious script forged by a mixture of drives, defenses, object relations, and disturbances in the self. In short, behavior has meaning.

The meaning is rarely as simple and straightforward as the foregoing example involving the physician. More commonly, a single behavior or symptom serves several functions and solves many problems—a notion that Waelder (1930) referred to as the principle of multiple function. He developed the principle out of dissatisfaction with Freud's more restrictive concept of overdetermination, which implied that several intrapsychic factors must operate together to create sufficient cause for a specific effect (a behavior or symptom). As Sherwood (1969) pointed out, "Freud clearly held that the causes of behavior were *both* complex (overdetermined) and multiple (in the sense of their being alternate sets of sufficient conditions)" (p. 181). In other words, certain behaviors or symptoms are at times caused by a specific intrapsychic constellation of factors, but in other instances they are produced by a multitude of other etiological forces in the unconscious. Suffice it to say that the psychodynamic view of human behavior defines it as the end result of many different conflicting forces that serve a variety of different functions corresponding both to the demands of reality and to the needs of the unconscious.

The principle of psychic determinism, although certainly a bedrock notion, calls for two disclaimers. First, unconscious factors do not determine all behaviors or symptoms. When a patient with Alzheimer's disease forgets the name of his spouse, it probably is not a parapraxis. When a patient with partial complex seizures ritualistically buttons and unbuttons his shirt during the aura of his seizure, the symptom can likely be attributed to an irritable focus of the temporal lobe. The dynamic psychiatrist's task is to sort out which symptoms and behaviors can or cannot be explained by dynamic factors.

The second caveat derives from experience with patients who make no effort to change their behavior because they claim to be passive victims of unconscious forces. Within the concept of psychic determinism, there is room for choice. Although it may be more restricted than we like to think, conscious intention to change can be an influential factor in recovery from symptoms (S. A. Appelbaum 1981). The dynamic psychiatrist must be wary of the patient who justifies remaining ill by invoking psychic determinism.

Past Is Prologue

A fourth basic principle of dynamic psychiatry is that the experiences of infancy and childhood are crucial determinants of the adult personality. In the succinct words of William Wordsworth, "The child is father of the man." The dynamic psychiatrist listens intently when a patient speaks of childhood memories, knowing that these experiences may play a critical role in the current presenting problems. Indeed, etiology and pathogenesis are often linked to childhood events in the dynamic view. In some cases, overt trauma, such as incest or physical abuse, leads to disturbances in the adult personality. More often, the chronic, repetitive patterns of interaction within a family are of greater etiological significance.

The dynamic point of view also takes into consideration the fact that infants and children perceive their environment through highly subjective filters that may distort the real qualities of the figures around them. Similarly, certain children are constitutionally difficult to raise no matter how effective their parents may be. Research has revealed several discrete constitutional temperaments in newborn infants (Thomas and Chess 1984). The etiology of some psychiatric illness may be related to how good the "fit" is between the temperament of the child and the temperament of the parenting figure. The hyper-irritable child who does reasonably well with a calm and low-key mother may do poorly with a high-strung mother. This model of "goodness of fit" avoids blaming either parents or children for the latter's psychiatric problems.

The psychodynamic tradition has sometimes been regarded as overemphasizing environmental influences on psychiatric illness and neglecting constitutional factors. However, from the beginning of psychoanalysis, Freud always recognized the convergence of nature and nurture:

> Psychoanalysis has talked a lot about the accidental factors in aetiology and little about the constitutional ones; but that is only because it was able to contribute something fresh to the former, while, to begin with, it knew no more than was commonly known about the latter. We refuse to posit any contrast in principle between the two sets of aetiological factors; on the contrary, we assume that the two sets regularly act jointly in bringing about the observed result. (1912/1958, p. 99)

The process of development is an ongoing interplay between the inherited traits and the environmental factors that shape those traits. Indeed, twin studies (Bouchard et al. 1990) suggest that, in part, identical twins are so similar because they tend to elicit and seek out highly similar environments. Infants who are born with similar temperaments are likely to elicit similar parenting responses. Erik Erikson (1963) observed: "Babies control and bring up their families as much as they are controlled by them; in fact, we may say that the family brings up a baby by being brought up by him" (p. 69). Longitudinal studies have recently revealed that shyness, for example, is an inherited variation in the threshold of arousal in selected limbic sites in the brain (Kagan et al. 1988). The same research also suggests, however, that for shy behavior to be actualized, or for it to be transformed into a clinically significant anxiety disorder, some variety of chronic environmental stress needs to act on the basic temperamental disposition present at birth.

Theories of childhood development have always been central to dynamic psychiatry. Freud postulated that a child passes through three principal psychosexual stages on the road to maturity. Each of these—the oral, the anal, and the genital—is associated with a particular bodily zone where Freud believed that the libido, or sexual energy, of the child was concentrated. As a result of environmental trauma, constitutional factors, or both, a child may become developmentally arrested at the oral or anal phase, resulting in a fixation that is retained into adult life. Under stress, the adult may regress to this more primitive phase of development and manifest the mental organization of the instinctual gratification associated with that phase. Although Freud reconstructed childhood development retrospectively based on the reports of adult patients in psychoanalysis, subsequent psychoanalytic investigators have studied development prospectively through direct infant and child observation. These studies (Mahler et al. 1975; Stern 1985) have led to more elaborate developmental theories of normal and abnormal personality and to a greater emphasis on the nature of the child's relatedness to others as opposed to the vicissitudes of instinctual energies. These theories will be discussed in more detail in Chapter 2.

Transference

The persistence of childhood patterns of mental organization in adult life implies that the past is repeating itself in the present. Perhaps the most compelling example of this is the core psychodynamic concept of transference, in which the patient experiences the doctor as a significant figure from the patient's past. Qualities of that past figure will be attributed to the doctor, and feelings associated with that figure will be experienced in the same way with the doctor. The two outstanding characteristics of transference are that it is inappropriate to the current relationship and that it is a repetition of the past (Greenson 1967).

The patient unconsciously *reenacts* the past relationship, instead of remembering it, and in so doing introduces to the treatment a wealth of information about past relationships.

Although the concept of transference is generally associated with psychoanalysis or psychotherapy, the therapeutic relationship is merely one example of a more general phenomenon. As Brenner (1982) put it: "*Every* object relation is a new addition of the first, definitive attachments of childhood. . . . Transference is ubiquitous, it develops in every psychoanalytic situation because it develops in every situation where another person is important in one's life" (pp. 194–195). To be more precise, every relationship is a mixture of a real relationship and transference phenomena, since transference is superimposed on real characteristics.

The dynamic psychiatrist recognizes the pervasiveness of transference phenomena and realizes that the relationship problems of which the patient complains will eventually manifest themselves in the patient's relationship with the treater. What is unique, then, about the doctor-patient relationship in dynamic psychiatry is not the presence of the transference, but the fact that it represents therapeutic material to be understood. Dynamic psychiatrists do not respond to transference with the same actions as everyone else. When subjected to hateful invectives from their patients, they do not angrily reject them as others would. Instead, an attempt is made to determine what past relationship is being repeated in the present. In this sense, dynamic psychiatrists are defined by what they do *not* do as much as by what they do.

Countertransference

An overarching principle embraced by those of us who practice dynamic psychiatry is that we are basically more similar to our patients than we are different from them. The psychological mechanisms in pathological states are merely extensions of principles involved in normal developmental functioning. Doctor and patient are both human beings. Just as patients have transference, treaters have countertransference. Since every current relationship is a new addition of old relationships, it follows logically that countertransference in the psychiatrist and transference in the patient are essentially identical processes—each unconsciously experiences the other as someone from the past. The difference lies in how the feelings are handled in the therapeutic encounter (Brenner 1982). While transference is discussed and analyzed as part of the therapeutic process, countertransference is monitored by the constant internal vigilance of the psychiatrist, who notes the emergence of powerful positive and negative feelings toward the patient and reflects silently on the possible origin of those feelings in the context of past relationships. This monitoring process is a deliberate attempt to remember that helps avoid repeating or reenacting the old object relationship.

The concept of countertransference has undergone considerable evolution since its inception (Hamilton 1988; Kernberg 1965). Freud's (1912/1958) narrow definition referred to the analyst's transference to the patient or the analyst's response to the patient's transference. Implicit in this conceptualization is the emergence of unresolved conflicts from the analyst's unconscious. Winnicott (1949), however, in working with psychotic patients and those with severe personality disorders, noted a different form of countertransference. He termed the feeling *objective hate,* because it was not a reaction stemming from unresolved unconscious conflicts in the treater, but rather was a natural reaction to the patient's outrageous behavior. It is objective in the sense that virtually everyone would react similarly to the patient's provocative behavior.

As Kernberg (1965) pointed out, this broader definition of countertransference as the therapist's conscious and appropriate total emotional reaction to the patient is gaining greater acceptance, particularly because it helps characterize the work with severe personality disorders, which are an increasingly common segment of the dynamic psychiatrist's practice. This definition serves to attenuate the pejorative connotation of countertransference—unresolved problems in the treater that require more analysis—and to replace it with a conceptualization that views countertransference as a major diagnostic and therapeutic tool that tells the treater a good deal about the patient's internal world. In this volume I will attempt to clarify whether the narrower or broader sense of countertransference is being used in a given instance.

Resistance

The last major principle of dynamic psychiatry involves the patient's wish to preserve the status quo, to oppose the treater's efforts to produce insight and change. In his early papers on technique, Freud (1912/1958) had already noted these powerful oppositional forces: "The resistance accompanies the treatment step by step. Every single association, every act of the person under treatment must reckon with the resistance and represents a compromise between the forces that are striving towards recovery and the opposing ones" (p. 103). Resistances to treatment are as ubiquitous as transference phenomena and may take many forms, including being late to appointments, refusing to take medications, forgetting the psychiatrist's advice or interpretations, being silent in therapy sessions, focusing on unimportant material during the sessions, or forgetting to pay the therapy bill, to name only a few. Resistance may be conscious, preconscious, or unconscious. All resistance has in common an attempt to avoid unpleasant feelings, whether anger, guilt, hate, love (if directed toward a forbidden object such as the therapist), envy, shame, grief, anxiety, or some combination of these. The dynamic psychiatrist notes that treatment threatens the repression of unacceptable impulses, feelings, and thoughts, and so must expect to encounter resistance in the service of protecting repression.

Resistance defends the patient's illness. The patient's characteristic defense mechanisms designed to safeguard against unpleasant affects come to the fore during dynamic treatment. In fact, resistance may be defined as the patient's defenses as they manifest themselves in psychodynamic treatment (Greenson 1967). The difference between resistances and defense mechanisms is simply that the former can be observed, whereas the latter must be inferred (Thomä and Kächele 1987). The strength of the defense or resistance is necessarily proportional to the strength of the underlying impulse. As Ralph Waldo Emerson once observed, "The louder he talked of his honor, the faster we counted our spoons." Similarly, those who most speak out *against* sin may be struggling with powerful urges *to* sin, a conjecture amply supported by the fates of several prominent televangelists in the 1980s.

The dynamic psychiatrist expects to encounter resistance to treatment and is prepared to address this phenomenon as part and parcel of the treatment process. Whereas other treaters may get angry when their patients do not comply with prescribed treatments, dynamic psychiatrists are curious to know what this resistance is protecting and what past situation is being reenacted. Despite the connotation of resistance as an obstacle that must be removed to conduct the treatment, to a large extent, understanding the resistance *is* the treatment. Freud tended to use resistance to mean two different phenomena: 1) a stoppage of the patient's free associations and 2) a revelation of a highly significant internal object relationship from the patient's past transported into the present moment with the treater (Friedman 1991). The manner in which the patient resists is likely to be a re-creation of a past relationship that influences a variety of present-day relationships. For example, patients who spent their childhoods rebelling against their parents may unconsciously find themselves rebelling against their doctor as well as other authority figures. The dynamic clinician helps the patient understand these patterns so that they become fully conscious.

Mind and Brain in Psychiatry

One of the most unfortunate developments in contemporary psychiatry is the polarization between biologically oriented and dynamically oriented psychiatrists. At the root of this conflict lies the age-old mind-body problem. Is the etiology of mental illness in the brain or in the mind? Should the treatment of mental illness be somatic or psychotherapeutic? The main problem with the debate between these polarized factions is the questions posed. It is not a situation of "either-or," but "both-and." As Nemiah (1961) noted over 30 years ago, "For a practical understanding of the human being, sometimes it is the language of psychology and sometimes the language of physiology and biochemistry that is more apposite; and when we are lucky, we occasionally catch a glimpse of the complex interrelations between these modes of discourse" (p. 9). The dynamic psychiatrist who neglects the biological dimension of experience and the biologically oriented psychiatrist who neglects the psychological realm are both guilty of narrow-minded reductionism.

Putting aside the enormous philosophical literature on the mind-body problem, from the standpoint of hard science, any distinction between functional and organic psychiatric illness is somewhat artificial. In the words of Kandel (1979), "What we conceive of as our mind is an expression of the functioning of our brain" (p. 1037). In a series of highly creative experiments with the marine snail *Aplysia,* Kandel (1979, 1983) demonstrated that experiences with the environment alter the functional effectiveness of synaptic connections by modulating calcium influx in the presynaptic terminals. In this sense, disturbances of a psychological nature are reflected in specific changes in neuronal and synaptic function. Kandel shared Freud's view that all mental disturbances must fundamentally be biological in nature. Environmental factors, such as genetic/constitutional characteristics and infectious or toxic agents, affect the mind at the level of brain function.

Kandel (1979) extrapolated implications for psychotherapy from his molecular research. Since experience appears to modify brain function through altering synaptic strength and regulating gene expression, "it is only insofar as our words produce changes in each other's brains that psychotherapeutic intervention produces changes in patients' minds. From this perspective the biological and psychological approaches are joined" (p. 1037).

Despite this promising research, we are far from being able to make one-to-one correlations between mind and brain. As Reiser (1988) observed: "Even though the brain is the organ that subserves the function of the mind, brain and mind are not the same thing. Brain science does not yet, and probably never will, fully explain the mind or make mental functions fully understandable" (p. 149). Although we fully recognize the inseparability of mind and brain, we must also acknowledge that the two domains use different languages (Edelson 1984; Reiser 1985). The parlance of the brain and the parlance of the mind depend on different conceptual models and on different levels of abstraction as well. The language of dynamic psychiatry is the language of the mind, but we must not for a moment allow the semantic demands of communication to obscure the fundamental origin of that language in the brain.

This model of the interrelationship between mind and brain is best illustrated by a brief clinical example. In the language of the brain, the locus coeruleus is associated with anxiety and panic attacks (Charney et al. 1982). Certain drugs that stimulate the locus coeruleus produce panic in patients who suffer from panic disorder. Those drugs that have been found effective in treating panic attacks also quiet the firing of the locus coeruleus. In the language of the mind, patients who lack the ability to summon up a soothing mental image of their therapists over a long weekend will also undergo a panic reaction. However, when the locus coeruleus fires, a patient's subjective experience may be a sense of terror that the therapist has died and will never be seen again. The sound of the therapist's voice over the phone may immediately diminish that terror. Hence the locus coeruleus may be quieted with words as effectively as it is with medication.

Two levels of discourse describe the same physiological and psychological phenomenon. One involves the language of the brain, and one prefers the language of the mind. Dynamic psychiatry predominantly speaks the language of meanings, a realm of discourse foreign to the locus coeruleus. Meanings reside in the domain of the mind.

Much of the polarization between the biological and psychodynamic perspectives arises from a failure to appreciate the complex relationships between psychosocial and neurophysiological factors in the etiology and pathogenesis of psychiatric disorders. In clinical practice today, patients commonly report that they have been told they have a "chemical imbalance." This oversimplified and reductionistic explanation is problematic because it implies that biochemical processes are causal agents rather than mediating mechanisms (Lipowski 1989). Neurochemical and neuroanatomical changes in the brain may be causally related to psychosocial influences in the environment and to the meaning attributed to those influences. As a corollary to this point of view, psychotherapeutic interventions may result in permanent alterations in brain functioning.

The phenomenon of *kindling* may illuminate some of the processes involved in the triggering of neural mechanisms by psychological/environmental etiological factors. Gold et al. (1988a, 1988b), drawing on the work of Post et al. (1982), postulated that painful events such as separations or losses early in life may sensitize receptor sites, leading to a vulnerability to recurrent depression in adulthood. They pointed out that ideas and images associated with depressive states could ultimately act as conditioned stimuli capable of eliciting a major depressive episode even without a concrete loss or external stressor in the environment. This model is in keeping with the observation that chronic stress and loss early in life may leave people vulnerable to depression as adults. Their model is also consistent with psychoanalytic observations that an imagined loss or a perceived discrepancy between idealized expectations and reality may precipitate depression. Gold et al. (1988a, 1988b) concluded from this model that major depression is best treated with a combination of medication and psychotherapy because the inner conflict brought on by prior life events may increase the burden of stress unless addressed psychotherapeutically. They also pointed out that simple equations of depression with single neurotransmitters are no longer tenable as our knowledge of the complexity of the neurotransmitter systems has increased with more and more sophisticated neuroscience research.

Primate research has been of extraordinary heuristic value in demonstrating the impact of psychological trauma on brain functioning. Squirrel monkeys separated from their mothers experience elevated plasma cortisol levels. If the separations are repeated, these physiological changes become permanent (Coe et al. 1978, 1983). Primate research also suggests that the opioid system is intimately involved in the regulation of separation anxiety and that social isolation has a direct impact on the sensitivity and number of brain opiate receptors (van der Kolk 1987). Other long-lasting neurobiological changes resulting from early maternal separations include changes in adrenal gland catecholamine synthesizing enzymes (Coe et al. 1978, 1983) and hypothalamic serotonin secretion (Ciaranello 1988; Coe et al. 1985; Timiras 1982), as well as lasting alterations in the sensitivity of noradrenergic receptors (Kraemer et al. 1984). Imipramine and other agents that increase noradrenergic activity at the synapses alleviate the effects of separation and social isolation in monkeys (Suomi et al. 1978).

The psychodynamic notion that psychological trauma may be more or less damaging, depending on the critical developmental phase during which it is inflicted, is also supported in principle by primate studies. In Suomi's (1984) research on the impact of maternal deprivation, the effects of removing infant monkeys from their mothers were much more striking if the separation occurred at 90 days than if it occurred at either 60 or 120 days, possibly because of a link between myelinization of the nervous system and certain kinds of bonding behavior (van der Kolk 1987).

After an extensive review of the primate research, van der Kolk (1987) concluded:

> There may be actual morphological changes in the brain following social deprivation, or other disruptions of affiliative bonds. There also is evidence that the number and nature of brain receptors for particular neurotransmitters can continue to change throughout a person's lifetime, as illustrated by dopamine receptor alterations leading to the clinical symptoms of tardive dyskinesia. . . . Thus it is conceivable that receptor changes induced by early deprivation or trauma in the [central nervous system] can to some degree be modified by later life experiences. (pp. 50–51)

These primate studies not only support the kindling model based on psychological trauma, such as separations, but they also lend credence to the idea that the brain is possessed of remarkable structural plasticity. We now know that morphological changes in brain cells occur nearly every day and that massive trauma is not necessary to induce such changes (Levin 1991; Roose and Pardes 1989; Sacks 1990). The influence of psychosocial factors on neurobiological processes can be seen in changes that occur as a result of psychotherapy as well as in pathological states, such as posttraumatic stress disorder (PTSD), in which recurring intensive stimulation from the environment exceeds the capacity of the cortex to process what is happening and leads to permanent synaptic changes. The fact that one person will respond with PTSD to a situation that leaves no permanent mark on another reflects how the subjective meaning given to the environmental stimulus is critical in effecting synaptic changes.

Conversely, one can also observe the impact of biology on psychology in the aging process. As Roose and Pardes (1989) have suggested, the well-known "mellowing" phenomenon of middle age, associated with a shift to more mature defenses (Vaillant 1976), may well be linked to the dramatic drop-off in the amount of norepinephrine that occurs in the locus coeruleus between the ages of 40 and 60.

Psychiatry that loses the domain of meaning is mindless. The essential role that meaning plays, even in disorders with significant biological underpinnings, can be illustrated by examining in detail a case of obsessive-compulsive disorder (OCD). There is abundant evidence that OCD is an illness with a strong biological component. Monozygotic twins have a higher rate of concordance for the disorder than do their dizygotic counterparts, there is an increased prevalence in patients with Tourette's syndrome and in their families, and there is a dramatic response in some patients to psychosurgery and clomipramine (Elkins et al. 1980; Lieberman 1984; Turner et al. 1985). A quantitative study in which computed tomography was used also demonstrated a smaller caudate nucleus volume in patients with OCD than in healthy control subjects (Luxenberg et al. 1988). Finally, OCD patients show virtually no response to placebo, in contrast to patients with other anxiety disorders (Mavissakalian et al. 1990).

To provide a convincing case for the ongoing relevance of psychodynamic thinking in contemporary psychiatry, there must be a demonstrable advantage to a psychodynamic approach. However, there is little evidence in the literature to suggest that dynamic psychotherapy or psychoanalysis is effective in the treatment of OCD (Esman 1989). As the following case illustrates, however, dynamic principles are of great value even in the treatment of "biologically based" disorders, and the somatic therapies used to treat them are often imbued with psychodynamic meanings.

Case Vignette

Mr. A was a 29-year-old single man with OCD. At the time he presented for psychiatric hospitalization, he reported a 10-year history of obsessive-compulsive symptoms, and he complained of being totally housebound for the last 8 years because of constant incapacitating, "grotesque, horrific" thoughts that never ceased. Eight years before admission, when Mr. A became housebound, his mother retired from her job so she could take care of him at home and meet his demands for cleanliness. Her life revolved around him.

Mr. A was obsessed with the need to avoid contamination. He also worried about making women pregnant, because he feared he might have semen on his hands. Hence, he became a compulsive hand washer. He insisted that his mother be with him 24 hours per day. Although she did not sleep with him or go into the shower with him, she did help him dress so that he would not touch his clothes and become contaminated. He also required her to follow an elaborate 58-step ritual while cooking his food and placing it on the table. If she did not follow this ritual precisely, she had to discard the entire meal and start over again. She threw out thousands of dollars' worth of food each year in order to respond to these demands. Mr. A also insisted that his father had to either stay away from home or remain in another part of the house so he would not be contaminated by germs that his father brought home from work.

Mr. A's early childhood development was reportedly unremarkable, but he did recall a very unpleasant memory from when he was approximately 5 years old. He remembered seeing his father grab his mother by the breasts while she cried for the patient to rescue her. He tried to stop his father, but he was overpowered by the older man. He remembered feeling terrible about the incident, and he cried because he was unable to rescue his mother.

Although Mr. A had been to numerous psychiatrists, he always refused to go back after one visit. At one time, he agreed to take clomipramine, but he stopped after the first dose because he said the side effects bothered him. His parents felt they finally had to hospitalize him because he was incapacitated. When he came to the hospital, his doctor asked him why he was seeking treatment. He responded, "I'm determined to be dependent—I mean, independent." The doctor commented on the fact that he had first said "dependent," and inquired, "Is there perhaps a part of you that would like to be dependent?" Mr. A responded, "You mean on my mother?" His doctor replied that Mr. A would know better than he. Mr. A reflected a moment and said, "Well, she does take pretty good care of me."

Mr. A's slip of the tongue provided a glimpse into the unconscious motivations for his resistance to treatment. Any kind of successful treatment threatened his dependent relationship with his mother. If clomipramine were likely to help him, then he would not take it. Similarly, he would defeat all other outpatient or inpatient treatment efforts as well.

After about a week of hospitalization, Mr. A defied the staff members' expectations. He began to make dramatic improvements. He could touch doorknobs without fearing contamination, he could read magazines that others had touched, and he greatly decreased the time he spent washing his hands. This improvement occurred without medication. Mr. A commented that he felt "a lot less nervous" in the hospital than he had expected. As he explored how the hospital setting might have reduced his anxiety, it became apparent that he was increasingly worried about his sexual wishes toward his mother. He commented that when his mother dressed him, he felt that "there was something sexual about that." Removing him from the emotionally charged household made his sexual wishes toward his mother much less problematic for him. Similarly, aggressive wishes to keep his father out of his life were less troubling. Because his anxiety about both sexual and aggressive wishes had diminished, his obsessive-compulsive symptoms were not needed so extensively to bind his anxiety.

The case of Mr. A beautifully illustrates the interface between the psychodynamic and the biological. However biologically driven his obsessive-compulsive symptoms may have been, they also revealed a symbolic wish to win his mother's affection away from his father, as poignantly depicted in his early childhood memories. His symptoms reflected the core psychodynamic concept known as compromise formation; that is, they contained both the direct expression of an underlying wish and a defense against that wish (Brenner 1982). Mr. A's compulsive rituals served as a defense against his sexual longings for his mother by consuming all his time in hand washing and various other exercises. However, these symptomatic rituals also resulted in his being dressed by his mother and receiving all her attention while his father stayed away from home. Hence, the symptomatology had the dynamic meaning of fulfilling his childhood wish to steal his mother away from his father. Taking clomipramine or receiving any other form of treatment threatened this triumph by putting him in a position in which he no longer needed his mother. On the other hand, this oedipal victory created enormous anxiety and guilt, which increased his recourse to rituals and obsessions. When removed from the triangle he had established with his parents at home, Mr. A had much less need of his obsessive-compulsive symptoms to deal with the anxiety and showed remarkable improvement.

Consider an analogy: When a magnet is placed under a sheet of paper containing iron filings, the filings line up in formation and follow the movement of the magnet along the surface of the paper. In a similar manner, psychodynamic issues frequently appropriate the magnet-like biological forces for their own purposes. Thus, Mr. A's unconscious wishes and his defenses against them attached themselves to the biologically driven obsessive-compulsive symptoms and used them as a vehicle for their expression.

Although formal dynamic psychotherapy was not used in the treatment of Mr. A, the dynamic understanding of his resistance to pharmacotherapy and to treatment in general was essential in explicating Mr. A's refusal to take clomipramine and to otherwise cooperate with treatment. In fact, Mr. A's slip of the tongue led to his awareness that any improvement in his symptoms might cause him to lose his privileged position with his mother.

The case of Mr. A also underscores the importance of a psychodynamic approach to pharmacotherapy for cases in which compliance is a problem. Failure to comply with pharmacotherapeutic regimens often can be understood along conventional lines of transference, countertransference, and resistance issues. A considerable literature has accrued on the practice of dynamic pharmacotherapy (P. S. Appelbaum and Gutheil 1980; Book 1987; Docherty and Fiester 1985; Docherty et al. 1977; Gutheil 1977, 1982; Karasu 1982; Ostow 1983; Thompson and Brodie 1981; Wylie and Wylie 1987), and there has been a broad consensus that psychodynamic meanings of medications may pose formidable obstacles to compliance with medication regimens. In Chapter 5 I will consider dynamic approaches to pharmacotherapy in some detail.

Quite apart from examining problems with compliance, psychological interventions may also have direct effects on brain functioning. In a study that compared a group of patients with OCD treated with fluoxetine with a group treated with behavior therapy, a majority of both groups showed significant decreases in brain activity in the right caudate nucleus after 10 weeks of treatment (Baxter et al. 1992).

The Role of the Dynamic Psychiatrist in Contemporary Psychiatry

In an age when impressive advances in the neurosciences occur almost weekly, dynamic psychiatry has lost some of its luster. Only a generation ago, psychoanalysts and dynamic psychiatrists enjoyed unparalleled prestige. They have since been upstaged by biologically oriented researchers, whose contribution to the field is beyond question. However, above the din of optimistic proclamations about the genetic-biochemical basis of all mental illness, another cry can be heard, one that is growing in intensity. Groups of psychiatric residents in biologically oriented programs complain that they know all about neurotransmitters but do not know how to talk to their patients. Freshly trained private practitioners ask analysts for consultation and supervision when their patients fail to respond to medications. Even patients are beginning to demand that they be listened to rather than simply medicated.

Advances in any scientific field conform to a predictable pattern—an initial flurry of excitement is followed by sobering disillusionment. Our own field of psychiatry is no exception in this regard. The post–World War II enthusiasm for psychoanalysis as a panacea for a host of social problems led to a bitter disenchantment in the decade of the 1960s. American psychiatrists today are encountering the limitations inherent in the tools of biological psychiatry. The alarming prevalence of tardive dyskinesia has dampened the early enthusiasm for antipsychotics. The dexamethasone suppression test that was going to revolutionize psychiatric diagnosis only a few years ago is now mired in controversy about whether it has only limited clinical usefulness or none at all. Psychiatric clinicians are frustrated when certain patients do not respond to medications or to electroconvulsive therapy. Patients are frustrated when their hallucinations remit on medication but their lives remain miserable because of numerous interpersonal problems. The fanfare accompanying advances in neurochemistry has masked the fact that there is a formidable distance between the research laboratory and the psychiatrist's consulting room.

Training in dynamic psychiatry significantly broadens the scope of the clinician's expertise. The real advantage of the dynamic approach is its attention to the role of personality factors in illness. In fact, personality and its influence on the patient is a principal area of expertise for dynamic psychiatrists (Michels 1988). As Perry et al. (1987) persuasively argued, since every treatment involves therapeutic management and modification of the patient's personality, a psychodynamic evaluation is applicable to all patients, not simply those referred for long-term psychoanalytic psychotherapy. Characterological resistances to treatment frequently torpedo the medication program designed to maintain the patient in remission. A recent study of treatment-resistant hospitalized patients (Marcus and Bradley 1987) revealed that 71% of such patients had an Axis II diagnosis in addition to the more obvious Axis I diagnosis of depression, schizophrenia, or other psychosis. Symptoms are embedded in character structure, and the dynamic psychiatrist recognizes that in many cases one cannot treat the symptoms without first addressing the character structure.

A dynamic therapeutic approach is certainly not necessary for every psychiatric patient. Those who respond well to medications, electroconvulsive therapy, or behavioral desensitization do not require the services of a dynamic psychiatrist. A patient with dementia may be so cognitively impaired as to be unable to think in the language of psychodynamic treatment. As with all other schools of psychiatry, the dynamic psychotherapeutic approach cannot effectively treat all psychiatric illnesses or patients. It is particularly useful with personality disorders, the paraphilias, some anxiety disorders, most eating disorders, and with treatment-resistant Axis I patients who do not respond to conventional biological treatments. The patient with dual diagnoses on Axis I and Axis II is also in need of a dynamic approach.

A strictly dynamic therapeutic approach should probably be reserved for patients who most need it and who will not respond to any other interventions. However, a *dynamically informed* approach to most—if not all—patients will enrich the psychiatrist's practice and enhance the clinician's sense of mastery over the mysteries of the human psyche. Most importantly, it will help the dynamic psychiatrist identify and understand the daily countertransference problems that interfere with effective diagnosis and treatment. In a recent survey of private psychiatric practitioners and academic psychiatrists, Langsley and Yager (1988) found that the second most highly regarded skill was the ability to "recognize countertransference problems and personal idiosyncrasies as they influence interactions with patients and be able to deal with them constructively" (p. 471). The dynamic approach is the only one that systematically addresses the psychiatrist's conscious and unconscious contributions to the process of treatment and evaluation.

References

Appelbaum PS, Gutheil TG: Drug refusal: a study of psychiatric inpatients. Am J Psychiatry 137:340–346, 1980

Appelbaum SA: Effecting Change in Psychotherapy. New York, Jason Aronson, 1981

Baxter LR, Schwartz JM, Bergman KS, et al: Caudate glucose metabolic rate changes with both drug and behavior therapy for obsessive-compulsive disorder. Arch Gen Psychiatry 49:681–689, 1992

Book HE: Some psychodynamics of non-compliance. Can J Psychiatry 32:115–117, 1987

Bouchard TJ, Lykken DT, McGue M, et al: Sources of human psychological differences: the Minnesota study of twins reared apart. Science 250:223–228, 1990

Brenner C: The Mind in Conflict. New York, International Universities Press, 1982

Charney DS, Heninger GR, Sternberg DE: Assessment of alpha-II adrenergic autoreceptor function in humans: effects of oral yohimbine. Life Sci 30:2033–2041, 1982

Ciaranello RD: Neurochemical aspects of stress, in Stress, Coping and Development in Children. Edited by Garmezy N, Rutter M. Baltimore, MD, Johns Hopkins University Press, 1988, pp 85–105

Coe CL, Mendoza SP, Smotherman WP, et al: Mother-infant attachment in the squirrel monkey: adrenal responses to separation. Behavioral Biology 22:256–263, 1978

Coe CL, Glass JC, Wiener SG, et al: Behavioral, but not physiological, adaptation to repeated separation in mother and infant primates. Psychoneuroendocrinology 8:401–409, 1983

Coe CL, Wiener SG, Rosenberg LT, et al: Endocrine and immune responses to separation and maternal loss in nonhuman primates, in The Psychobiology of Attachment. Edited by Reite M, Field T. Orlando, FL, Academic Press, 1985, pp 163–199

Docherty JP, Fiester SJ: The therapeutic alliance and compliance with psychopharmacology, in Psychiatry Update: American Psychiatric Association Annual Review, Vol 4. Edited by Hales RE, Frances AJ. Washington, DC, American Psychiatric Press, 1985, pp 607–632

Docherty JP, Marder SR, Van Kammen DP, et al: Psychotherapy and pharmacotherapy: conceptual issues. Am J Psychiatry 134:529–533, 1977

Edelson M: Hypothesis and Evidence in Psychoanalysis. Chicago, IL, University of Chicago Press, 1984

Elkins R, Rapoport JL, Lipsky A: Obsessive-compulsive disorder of childhood and adolescence: a neurobiological viewpoint. Journal of the American Academy of Child Psychiatry 19:511–524, 1980

Ellenberger HF: The Discovery of the Unconscious: The History and Evolution of Dynamic Psychiatry. New York, Basic Books, 1970

Erikson EH: Childhood and Society, 2nd Edition. New York, WW Norton, 1963

Esman AH: Psychoanalysis and general psychiatry: obsessive-compulsive disorder as paradigm. J Am Psychoanal Assoc 37:319–336, 1989

Freud S: The interpretation of dreams (1900), in The Standard Edition of the Complete Psychological Works of Sigmund Freud, Vols 4, 5. Translated and edited by Strachey J. London, Hogarth Press, 1953, pp 1–627

Freud S: The psychopathology of everyday life (1901), in The Standard Edition of the Complete Psychological Works of Sigmund Freud, Vol 6. Translated and edited by Strachey J. London, Hogarth Press, 1960, pp 1–279

Freud S: The dynamics of transference (1912), in The Standard Edition of the Complete Psychological Works of Sigmund Freud, Vol 12. Translated and edited by Strachey J. London, Hogarth Press, 1958, pp 97–108

Freud S: The unconscious (1915), in The Standard Edition of the Complete Psychological Works of Sigmund Freud, Vol 14. Translated and edited by Strachey J. London, Hogarth Press, 1963, pp 159–215

Friedman L: A reading of Freud's papers on technique. Psychoanal Q 60:564–595, 1991

Gold PW, Goodwin FK, Chrousos GP: Clinical and biochemical manifestations of depression: relation to the neurobiology of stress, part I. N Engl J Med 319:348–353, 1988a

Gold PW, Goodwin FK, Chrousos GP: Clinical and biochemical manifestations of depression: relation to the neurobiology of stress, part II. N Engl J Med 319:413–420, 1988b

Greenson RR: The Technique and Practice of Psychoanalysis. New York, International Universities Press, 1967

Gutheil TG: Psychodynamics in drug prescribing. Drug Therapy 2:35–40, 1977

Gutheil TG: The psychology of psychopharmacology. Bull Menninger Clin 46:321–330, 1982

Hamilton NG: Self and Others: Object Relations Theory in Practice. Northvale, NJ, Jason Aronson, 1988

Kagan J, Reznick JS, Snidman N: Biological bases of childhood shyness. Science 240:167–171, 1988

Kandel ER: Psychotherapy and the single synapse: the impact of psychiatric thought on neurobiologic research. N Engl J Med 301:1028–1037, 1979

Kandel ER: From metapsychology to molecular biology: explorations into the nature of anxiety. Am J Psychiatry 140:1277–1293, 1983

Karasu TB: Psychotherapy and pharmacotherapy: toward an integrative model. Am J Psychiatry 139:1102–1113, 1982

Kernberg OF: Notes on countertransference. J Am Psychoanal Assoc 13:38–56, 1965

Kraemer GW, Ebert MH, Lake CR, et al: Cerebrospinal fluid measures of neurotransmitter changes associated with pharmacological alteration of the despair response to social separation in rhesus monkeys. J Psychiatr Res 11:303–315, 1984

Langsley DG, Yager J: The definition of a psychiatrist: eight years later. Am J Psychiatry 145:469–475, 1988

Levin FM: Mapping the Mind: The Intersection of Psychoanalysis and Neuroscience. Hillsdale, NJ, Analytic Press, 1991

Lieberman J: Evidence for a biological hypothesis of obsessive-compulsive disorder. Neuropsychobiology 11:14–21, 1984

Lipowski ZJ: Psychiatry: mindless or brainless, both or neither? Can J Psychiatry 34:249–254, 1989

Luxenberg JS, Swedo SE, Flament MF, et al: Neuroanatomical abnormalities in obsessive-compulsive disorder detected with quantitative X-ray computed tomography. Am J Psychiatry 145:1089–1093, 1988

Mahler MS, Pine F, Bergman A: The Psychological Birth of the Human Infant: Symbiosis and Individuation. New York, Basic Books, 1975

Marcus E, Bradley S: Concurrence of Axis I and Axis II illness in treatment-resistant hospitalized patients. Psychiatr Clin North Am 10:177–184, 1987

Mavissakalian MR, Jones B, Olson S: Absence of placebo response in obsessive-compulsive disorder. J Nerv Ment Dis 178:268–270, 1990

Michels R: The future of psychoanalysis. Psychoanal Q 57:167–185, 1988

Nemiah JC: Foundations of Psychopathology. New York, Oxford University Press, 1961, pp 4, 9

Ostow M: Interactions of psychotherapy and pharmacotherapy (letter). Am J Psychiatry 140:370–371, 1983

Perry S, Cooper AM, Michels R: The psychodynamic formulation: its purpose, structure, and clinical application. Am J Psychiatry 144:543–550, 1987

Post RM, Ballenger JC, Uhde TW, et al: Kindling and drug sensitization: implications for the progressive development of psychopathology and treatment with carbamazepine, in Psychopharmacology of Anticonvulsants. Edited by Sandler M. Oxford, Oxford University Press, 1982, pp 27–53

Reiser MF: Converging sectors of psychoanalysis and neurobiology: mutual challenge and opportunity. J Am Psychoanal Assoc 33:11–34, 1985

Reiser MF: Are psychiatric educators "losing the mind?" Am J Psychiatry 145:148–153, 1988

Roose SP, Pardes H: Biological considerations in the middle years, in The Middle Years: New Psychoanalytic Perspectives. Edited by Oldham JM, Leibert RS. New Haven, CT, Yale University Press, 1989, pp 179–190

Sacks O: Neurology and the soul. The New York Review, November 22, 1990, pp 44–50

Sherwood M: The Logic of Explanation in Psychoanalysis. New York, Academic Press, 1969

Stern DN: The Interpersonal World of the Infant: A View From Psychoanalysis and Developmental Psychology. New York, Basic Books, 1985

Suomi SJ: The development of affect in rhesus monkeys, in The Psychobiology of Affective Development. Edited by Fox N, Davidson R. Hillsdale, NJ, Lawrence Erlbaum, 1984, pp 119–159

Suomi SJ, Seaman SF, Lewis JK, et al: Effects of imipramine treatment of separation-induced social disorders in rhesus monkeys. Arch Gen Psychiatry 35:321–325, 1978

Thomä H, Kächele H: Psychoanalytic Practice, Vol 1: Principles. Translated by Wilson M, Roseveare D. New York, Springer-Verlag, 1987

Thomas A, Chess S: Genesis and evolution of behavioral disorders: from infancy to early adult life. Am J Psychiatry 141:1–9, 1984

Thompson EM, Brodie HKH: The psychodynamics of drug therapy. Current Psychiatric Therapies 20:239–251, 1981

Timiras PS: The timing of hormone signals in the orchestration of brain development, in The Development of Attachment and Affiliative Systems. Edited by Emde RN, Harmon RJ. New York, Plenum, 1982, pp 47–63

Turner SM, Beidel DC, Nathan RS: Biological factors in obsessive-compulsive disorder. Psychol Bull 97:430–450, 1985

Vaillant GE: Natural history of male psychological health, V: the relation of choice of ego mechanisms of defense to adult adjustment. Arch Gen Psychiatry 33:535–545, 1976

van der Kolk BA: Psychological Trauma. Washington, DC, American Psychiatric Press, 1987

Waelder R: The principle of multiple function: observations on overdetermination, in Psychoanalysis: Observation, Theory, Application. Edited by Gutman SA. New York, International Universities Press, 1930, pp 68–83

Watson JB: Behaviorism. New York, WW Norton, 1930 (originally published in 1924)

Winnicott DW: Hate in the counter-transference. Int J Psychoanal 30:69–74, 1949

Wylie HW Jr, Wylie ML: An effect of pharmacotherapy on the psychoanalytic process: case report of a modified analysis. Am J Psychiatry 144:489–492, 1987

Chapter 2

The Theoretical Basis of Dynamic Psychiatry

Nothing is as practical as a good theory.

Kurt Lewin

Like a sailor without a sextant, a psychiatrist who sets out to navigate the dark waters of the unconscious without a theory will soon be lost at sea. Psychoanalytic theory is the foundation of dynamic psychiatry. It brings order to the seemingly chaotic inner world of the patient. It allows the psychiatrist to supplement and transcend the descriptive level of cataloging symptoms and applying diagnostic labels. It provides a means of entering and understanding the cavernous interior of the mind. Theory not only guides clinicians toward diagnostic understanding, it also informs the choice of treatment for each patient. Theoretical understanding helps the dynamic psychiatrist decide what to say, when to say it, how to say it, and what is better left unsaid.

Contemporary dynamic psychiatry subsumes three broad psychoanalytic theoretical frameworks: 1) ego psychology, derived from the classic psychoanalytic theory of Freud; 2) object relations theory, derived from the work of Melanie Klein and members of the "British School," including Fairbairn, Winnicott, and Balint; and 3) self psychology, derived from the Sullivanian interpersonal tradition but formulated and elaborated in contemporary terms by Heinz Kohut. Although volumes have been written on each of these schools of thought, here we will merely examine the salient features of the three theories. In subsequent chapters the theories will be "fleshed out" to illustrate their application to clinical situations.

Ego Psychology

Freud's early years as a psychoanalytic investigator were heavily influenced by his topographic model (described in Chapter 1). Hysterical symptoms were seen as the result of repressed memories of events or ideas. Freud hypothesized that psychotherapeutic intervention could lift repression, leading to the recall of memories. In turn, a detailed verbal description of the remembered pathogenic idea or event, accompanied by intense affect, would lead to the symptom's disappearance. For example, a young man's paralyzed arm might be the result of a repressed wish to hit his father. According to this model, the young man might regain the use of his arm by retrieving the wish from his unconscious, verbalizing it, and expressing the anger toward his father. This cathartic method, also known as abreaction, makes conscious the unconscious pathogenic memory.

But the topographic model soon began to fail Freud. He repeatedly encountered resistances in his patients to his therapeutic maneuvers. Some memories could not be brought back into consciousness. The defense mechanisms responsible for this resistance were themselves unconscious and therefore inaccessible. These observations led Freud to conclude that the ego has both conscious and unconscious components.

With the publication of *The Ego and the Id,* Freud (1923/1961) introduced his tripartite structural theory of ego, id, and superego. In the structural model, which superseded the topographic model, the ego was viewed as distinct from the instinctual drives. The conscious aspect of the ego was the executive organ of the psyche, responsible for decision making and integration of perceptual data. The unconscious aspect of the ego contained defense mechanisms, such as repression, which were necessary to counteract the powerful instinctual drives harbored in the id—specifically, sexuality (libido) and aggression.

The id is a completely unconscious intrapsychic agency that is only interested in discharging tension. The id is controlled both by the unconscious aspects of the ego and by the third agency of the structural model—the superego. For the most part, the superego is unconscious, but aspects of it are certainly conscious. This agency incorporates the moral conscience and the ego ideal. The former *proscribes* (i.e., dictates what one should *not* do based on the internalization of parental and societal values), while the latter *prescribes* (i.e., dictates what one ought to do or be). The superego tends to be more sensitive to the strivings of the id and is therefore more immersed in the unconscious than is the ego (see Figure 2–1).

Ego psychology conceptualizes the intrapsychic world as one of interagency conflict. The superego, the ego, and the id battle among themselves as sexuality and aggression strive for expression and discharge. Conflict between the agencies produces anxiety. This signal anxiety (S. Freud 1926/1959) alerts the ego that a defense mechanism is required. The mechanism of neurotic symptom formation may be understood in this manner. Conflict produces anxiety, which results in defense, which leads to a compromise between the id and the ego. A symptom, then, is a compromise formation that both defends against the wish arising from the id and gratifies the wish in disguised form.

An accountant with an obsessive-compulsive disorder was terribly concerned that he would explode in anger at his boss. He believed that he could control his anger by swallowing a hundred times in a row. This symptom defended against the eruption of anger from the id, but it also

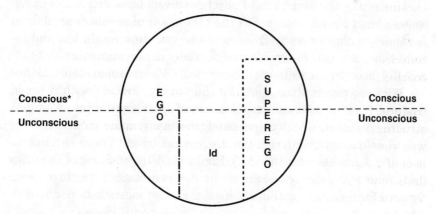

* The preconscious has been deleted for the sake of simplicity.

Figure 2–1. The structural model.

contained an attenuated form of gratification of his aggressive wish toward his boss—the process of counting and swallowing prevented him from getting his work done and therefore defied his boss and expressed his independence. Such compromise formations are a normal mental process (Brenner 1982). Neurotic symptoms represent only the pathological variety. Character traits themselves can be compromise formations and may represent adaptive and creative solutions to intrapsychic conflict.

Defense Mechanisms

Freud acknowledged the existence of other defense mechanisms, but he devoted most of his attention to repression. Freud's daughter Anna, in her landmark work, *The Ego and the Mechanisms of Defense* (A. Freud 1936/1946), expanded his work by describing in detail nine individual defense mechanisms: regression, reaction formation, undoing, introjection, identification, projection, turning against the self, reversal, and sublimation. Even more important, she acknowledged the implications that this increased scrutiny of the defensive operation of the ego had for treatment. No longer could the psychoanalyst simply attend to the uncovering of unacceptable wishes from the id. Equal attention would need to be paid to the vicissitudes of defensive efforts put forth by the ego, which would manifest themselves as resistances in treatment.

In shifting the emphasis of psychoanalysis from drives to ego defenses, Anna Freud anticipated the movement of psychoanalysis and dynamic psychiatry away from neurotic symptom formation and toward character pathology. We now partially define many forms of personality disorder according to their typical defensive operations. Hence the dynamic psychiatrist must be thoroughly familiar with a broad range of defense mechanisms because of their usefulness in understanding both neurotic problems and personality disorders.

All defenses have in common the protection of the ego against instinctual demands from the id (S. Freud 1926/1959). Some of the principal neurotic defense mechanisms are repression, displacement, reaction formation, isolation of affect, undoing, somatization, and conversion.

1. *Repression.* Freud viewed this mechanism as the queen of all defenses. It operates unconsciously by expelling unacceptable

wishes, feelings, or fantasies from conscious awareness. Although repression is used by virtually all neurotics, it is a hallmark of the hysterical neurotic and the higher-level hysterical personality (see Chapter 18).

2. *Displacement.* This defense is an unconscious process by which feelings attached to one source are redirected toward another. Transference is an obvious example of displacement, since feelings for a person in the past are transferred to a figure in the present. Phobias are the classic example of this defense, because the anxiety associated with an unconscious source is redirected to a conscious substitute, often harmless in and of itself. Displacement is also one of the chief mechanisms of disguise in dreams, where anxiety is reduced and sleep is preserved by substituting a neutral figure for a more emotionally charged one.

3. *Reaction formation.* This common defense is characterized by warding off an unacceptable wish or impulse by adopting a character trait that is diametrically opposed to it. Reaction formation is commonly found in obsessive-compulsive disorder and in those with obsessive-compulsive personality disorder.

4. *Isolation of affect.* This mechanism, also commonly found in obsessive-compulsive patients, divorces affect from ideation. A traumatic memory, for example, may be easily retrieved but will be stripped of any concomitant intense feelings. Isolation often operates hand in hand with intellectualization, which performs a similar function of avoiding affect.

5. *Undoing.* Sometimes referred to as doing and undoing, this mechanism is also characteristic of obsessive-compulsive patients. It involves magical thinking, with a symbolic action performed to reverse or cancel out a completed and unacceptable thought or action. One patient took literally the aphorism, "If you step on a crack, you'll break your mother's back." Whenever he inadvertently stepped on a crack in the sidewalk, he would return to retrace his steps so he could repeat them without hitting the crack.

6. *Somatization.* This defense, typical of hypochondriacal patients, involves the transfer of painful feelings to body parts. Psychotherapy with somatizing patients is often frustrating because feelings are unacceptable, and their emotional concerns can be communicated only through physical complaints.

7. *Conversion.* Most commonly, though not exclusively, associated with hysteria, this mechanism is characterized by the symbolic

representation of an intrapyschic conflict in physical terms. As in the case of the young man with hysterical paralysis of his arm (referred to at the beginning of this chapter), the motor or sensory symbolization frequently involves a defense against an unacceptable wish.

Defense mechanisms have been classified according to a hierarchy from the most immature or pathological to the most mature or healthy (Vaillant 1977). The primarily neurotic defenses enumerated above are only a partial list. None of us is without defense mechanisms, once again illustrating the dynamic principle that psychological health and illness are on a continuum. In fact, a profile of your typical defense mechanisms is a good barometer of your psychological health. Vaillant (1977) emphasized four mature defenses in particular: 1) *suppression*—the *conscious* (as distinct from repression, which is unconscious) banishing of unacceptable thoughts or feelings from your mind; 2) *altruism*—the subordination of your own needs and interests to those of others; 3) *sublimation*—an unconscious process by which consciously unacceptable drives or wishes are channeled into socially acceptable alternatives (e.g., a wish to stab a sibling rival is converted into a surgical career); 4) *humor*—the ability to playfully poke fun at yourself and the situation you're in—an invaluable part of mental health. Examples of the more primitive defenses will be considered along with a discussion of object relations theory later in the chapter.

Adaptive Aspects of the Ego

The ego's importance to the psyche is not limited to its defensive operations. Heinz Hartmann established himself as one of the foremost contributors to contemporary ego psychology by focusing on the nondefensive aspects of the ego. He turned the ego away from the id and refocused it on the outside world. Hartmann (1939/1958) insisted that there was a "conflict-free sphere of the ego" that develops independently of id forces and conflicts. Given an "average expectable environment," certain autonomous ego functions present at birth are allowed to flourish without being impeded by conflict. These include thinking, learning, perception, motor control, and language, to name a few. Hartmann's *adaptive* point of view, then, is an outgrowth of his concept of the existence of an autonomous, conflict-free area of the ego. Through neutralization of sexual and aggressive energies, Hartmann believed, even certain defenses could lose their connection with the instinctual forces of the id and become secondarily autonomous or adaptive.

David Rapaport (1951) and Edith Jacobson (1964) picked up where Hartmann left off and further refined his seminal contributions to ego psychology. It is commonplace today for clinicians to consider ego functions, ego strengths, and ego weaknesses as part of their routine psychodynamic evaluation of a patient. Bellak et al. (1973) systematized ego functions into scales used both for research and for clinical evaluation. The most important of these ego functions include reality testing, impulse control, thought processes, judgment, synthetic-integrative functioning, mastery-competence, and primary and secondary autonomy (after Hartmann).

Developmental Considerations

As with all psychoanalytic theories, ego psychology emphasizes developmental issues. The classical scheme associated with libidinal zones, that is, the oral, anal, and genital phases of Freud (see Chapter 1), has been elaborated as ego psychology has expanded. Erik Erikson (1959), following the lead of Hartmann, made an effort to weave interagency conflict into a broader fabric of ego psychology. He focused on psychosocial issues from the environment, which allowed him to evolve an epigenetic developmental scheme characterized by a psychosocial crisis at each phase. For example, during the oral phase of development, the infant must struggle with basic trust versus basic mistrust. The crisis of the anal phase involves autonomy versus shame and doubt. During the phallic-oedipal phase, the child grapples with initiative versus guilt.

The oedipal phase of development occupies a central place in the pathogenesis of neuroses (anxiety disorders), as well as in the dynamics of higher-level personality disorders (also called character neuroses) such as obsessive-compulsive personality and hysterical personality. Beginning at age three, children become more intensely focused on their genitals as a source of pleasure. Accompanying this interest is an intensified longing to be the exclusive love object of the parent of the opposite sex. However, at the same time, the child's dyadic or mother-and-child frame of reference changes to a triadic one with the child being aware of a rival for the affections of the parent of the opposite sex.

In the case of the male child, his first love object is his mother, which does not require a shift of affection. He desires to sleep with her, caress her, and be the center of her world. Since the father interferes with these plans, the child develops murderous wishes toward his rival. These wishes result in guilt, fear of retaliation by the father, and a sense of anxiety about that impending retaliation. Freud repeatedly observed that the leading source of the male child's anxiety during this phase of development is that the father's retaliation will come in the form of castration. To avoid this punishment, the boy renounces his sexual strivings for his mother and identifies with his father. This identification with the aggressor carries with it the decision to look for a woman *like* the mother so the boy can be *like* his father. As part of this oedipal resolution, the retaliatory father is internalized around the end of the fifth or sixth year, forming the superego, which Freud viewed as heir to the Oedipus complex.

Freud had more difficulty explaining the little girl's oedipal development. In a series of papers (1925/1961, 1931/1961, 1933/1964), he frankly acknowledged his bewilderment at female psychology, yet struggled to chart female development. One way he dealt with this difficulty was to assume that female development was basically analogous to that of males. As Freud saw it, whereas in boys the Oedipus complex is resolved by the castration complex, in girls it is *promulgated* by an awareness of "castration." In the preoedipal phases of development, in Freud's view, the little girl feels essentially like a little boy until she discovers the existence of the penis. At that point, she begins to feel inferior and falls victim to penis envy. She tends to blame her mother for her inferiority so she turns to her father as her love object, and the wish for a child from her father replaces her wish for a penis. Freud believed that one of three paths was available to the female child after discovery of her "genital inferiority": 1) cessation of all sexuality, that is, neurosis; 2) a defiant hypermasculinity; or 3) definitive femininity, which entailed renunciation of clitoral sexuality. In the normal oedipal resolution, loss of the mother's love, rather than fear of castration from the father, was postulated as the key factor.

More contemporary psychoanalytic authors have raised serious questions about Freud's formulations of female development. Stoller (1968) pointed out that the first phase of development in girls is clearly feminine, not masculine. Through extensive investigation of individuals with ambiguous genitalia and chromosomal anomalies, he clearly demonstrated that definitive femininity is established *before* the phallic-oedipal phase of development. Moreover, he persuasively argued that neither chromosomes nor genitalia are the primary source of femaleness—rather, it results from the parents' unswerving conviction of the child's gender. He shared the view of others, such as Lerner (1980) and Torok (1970), that penis envy is only one aspect of the development of femaleness, not the origin of it. All three authors pointed out the adverse therapeutic implications of viewing penis envy as a "bedrock" phenomenon (S. Freud 1937/1964) that defies further analysis and understanding. One implication of such an approach is that it may lead therapists to help female patients accept a view of themselves as an inferior form of male. It might also strengthen a patient's defensive focus on anatomical or genital deficiency and prevent exploration of underlying wishes, conflicts, and anxieties. As Lerner (1980) pointed out, a more prominent source of concern for the little girl may be the anxiety-provoking nature of her own genitals, not the supposed superiority of the penis.

Although the Oedipus complex is central to understanding neuroses and character neurosis, regressions from the oedipal phase to anal and oral issues are also common. Finally, development does not cease with the resolution of the Oedipus complex. Defensive constellations change with each succeeding phase—latency, adolescence, young adulthood, midlife, and old age. In fact, Vaillant (1976) has documented an orderly shift during adult life from immature defenses such as hypochondriasis and acting out to more mature defenses such as altruism and sublimation, suggesting that personality is truly dynamic and malleable over the entire life cycle.

Object Relations Theory

The view of ego psychology is that drives (i.e., sexuality and aggression) are primary, while object relations are secondary. (It is a well-established, though perhaps unfortunate, tradition in psychoanalytic writing to use the term *object* to mean *person.* Despite the somewhat pejorative connotations of *object,* I will retain the usage here for the sake of consistency and clarity.) In other words, the infant's most compelling agenda is tension discharge under the pressure of drives. Object relations theory, on the other hand, holds that drives emerge in the context of a relationship (e.g., the infant-mother dyad) and therefore can never be divorced from one another. Some object relations theorists

(Fairbairn 1952) would even suggest that the drives are primarily geared to object seeking rather than tension reduction.

Stated in its simplest terms, object relations theory encompasses the transformation of interpersonal relationships into internalized representations of relationships. As children develop, they do not simply internalize an object or person; rather, they internalize an entire *relationship* (Fairbairn 1940/1952, 1944/1952). A prototype of loving, positive experience is formed during periods when the infant is nursing (S. Freud 1905/1953). This prototype includes a positive experience of the self (the nursing infant), a positive experience of the object (the attentive, caretaking mother), and a positive affective experience (pleasure, satiation). When hunger returns and the infant's mother is not immediately available, a prototype of negative experience occurs, including a negative experience of the self (the frustrated, demanding infant), an inattentive, frustrating object (the unavailable mother), and a negative affective experience of anger and perhaps terror. Ultimately, these two experiences are internalized as two opposing sets of object relationships consisting of a self-representation, an object-representation, and an affect linking the two (Ogden 1983).

The internalization of the infant's mother, usually referred to as introjection (Schafer 1968), begins with the physical sensations associated with the presence of the mother during nursing but does not become meaningful until a boundary between inner and outer has developed. Around the sixteenth month of life, isolated images of the mother gradually coalesce into an enduring mental representation (Sandler and Rosenblatt 1962). At the same time an enduring self-representation forms, first as a body-representation and later as a compilation of sensations and experiences perceived as belonging to the infant.

The positively colored or "good" object-representation begins as a hallucinatory wish fulfillment growing out of the hungry infant's longing for its mother (Schafer 1968) and is later transformed into an internal presence as the infant's cognitive/perceptual apparatus develops. A major motivating force in the introjection of the positive, loving aspects of the mother seems to be the infant's fear of losing the mother (Schafer 1968). The reasons for the introjection or "taking in" of the negative, "bad" aspects of the mother are more complex. Possible motivating factors include the fantasy of controlling the object by containing it within oneself (Segal 1964), gaining a sense of mastery through repeated traumatic experiences with the object (Schafer

1968), and a preference for a "bad" object over no object at all (Schafer 1968). Clinical experience suggests that intense attachment to an internalized hostile object may also be connected with the yearning for a more positive relationship with the object (Meissner 1981). Furthermore, the object that has been introjected does not necessarily correlate with the real external object. For example, a mother who is unavailable to feed her infant on demand may simply be occupied with an older sibling, but is *experienced* and *introjected* by the infant as hostile, rejecting, and unavailable. Object relations theory acknowledges that there is *not* a one-to-one correlation between the real object and the internalized object-representation.

Object relations theory also views conflict differently than it is viewed by ego psychology. Unconscious conflict is not merely the struggle between an impulse and a defense; it is also a clash between opposing pairs of internal object relations units (Kernberg 1983; Ogden 1983; Rinsley 1977). In other words, at any one time different constellations of self-representations, object-representations, and affects vie with one another for center stage in the intrapsychic theater of internal object relations.

Internalization of object relations always involves a splitting of the ego into unconscious suborganizations (Ogden 1983). These fall into two groups:

> (1) self-suborganizations of ego, i.e., aspects of the ego in which the person more fully experiences his ideas and feelings as his own, and (2) object suborganizations of ego through which meanings are generated in a mode based upon an identification of an aspect of the ego with the object. This identification with the object is so thorough that one's original sense of self is almost entirely lost. (Ogden 1983, p. 227)

This model clearly shows the influence of Freud's notion of the superego, which is commonly experienced as though it is a "foreign body" (i.e., an object-suborganization of the ego that monitors what a self-suborganization of the ego is doing). Ogden's model also provides a pathway back from the intrapsychic to the interpersonal. In this framework, transference can be viewed as taking one of two forms—either the role of the self-subdivision of the ego or that of the object-subdivision of the ego may be externalized onto the treater, a process that will be discussed in detail later in this chapter.

A Historical Perspective

Originating in the United Kingdom, object relations theory has flourished there and in South America. Only recently has it taken hold in the United States. Melanie Klein is usually seen as the founder of the object relations movement. She emigrated from Budapest, and later from Berlin, to England in 1926, where her theory of early infantile development became highly controversial. She was influenced by Freud, but also broke new ground in her focus on internal objects. Through psychoanalytic work with children, she evolved a theory that relied heavily on unconscious intrapsychic fantasy and that compressed the developmental timetable of classical theory into the first year of life. The Oedipus complex, for example, was viewed by Klein as coinciding approximately with weaning in the latter half of the first year.

In the first few months of life, according to Klein, the infant experiences a primal terror of annihilation connected with Freud's death instinct. As a way of defending against this terror, the ego undergoes splitting, in which all "badness" or aggression deriving from the death instinct is disavowed and projected into the mother. The infant then lives in fear of the mother's persecution—which may be concretized as a fear that the mother will get inside the infant and destroy any goodness (deriving from libido) that has also been split off and is protected inside the infant. This latter fear is the primary anxiety of what Klein (1946/1975) termed the *paranoid-schizoid position*. This early mode of organizing experience gains its name from the prominent defense mechanisms of splitting of the ego ("schizoid") and projection ("paranoid"). Indeed, projection and introjection are crucial to understanding the paranoid-schizoid position. These mechanisms are used to separate "good" and "bad" as much as possible (Segal 1964). After persecuting, or bad, objects have been projected into the mother to separate them from good, or idealized objects, they may be reintrojected (i.e., taken back inside) to gain control and mastery over them. Concomitantly, the good objects may be projected to keep them safe from the "bad," which is now inside.

These oscillating cycles of projection and introjection continue until the infant begins to realize that the "bad" mother and the "good" mother are not in fact different, but are rather the same person. As children integrate the two part-objects into one whole object, they become disturbed that their sadistic, destructive fantasies toward the mother may have destroyed her. This newfound concern for the mother as a whole object is termed *depressive anxiety* by Klein and heralds the arrival of the *depressive position*. This mode of experience involves concern that one may harm others, in contrast to the paranoid-schizoid position, where the concern is that one will be harmed by others. Guilt becomes a prominent part of the affective life of the infant, who attempts to resolve it through *reparation*. This process may involve acts toward the mother that are designed to repair the "damage" inflicted on her in actuality or in fantasy. Klein recast the Oedipus complex as an effort to resolve depressive anxieties and guilt through reparation.

Klein's formulations have been criticized for relying exclusively on fantasy and thereby minimizing the influence of real persons in the environment, for overemphasizing the death instinct—a concept that is largely discounted by contemporary psychoanalytic theorists—and for attributing sophisticated adult forms of cognition to infants in their first year of life. Nevertheless, her brilliant development of the paranoid-schizoid and depressive positions is of extraordinary clinical value, especially if we view these positions as two modes of generating experience that are lifelong and that create a dialectical interplay in the mind rather than viewing them as developmental phases that are passed through or outgrown (Ogden 1986). This conceptualization of lifelong modes of experience decreases the significance of Klein's developmental timetable.

For Klein, the drives were really complex psychological phenomena intimately tied to specific object relations. Rather than originating in the body, drives are seen as merely using the body as a vehicle for expression (Greenberg and Mitchell 1983). Similarly, the drives were not viewed as simply seeking tension reduction but as being directed toward specific objects for specific reasons. This perspective and others held by Klein led to acrimonious debate in the British Psychoanalytic Society. Anna Freud was Klein's principal nemesis, and when a schism finally ruptured the society, one segment, known as the "B" group, followed Anna Freud's leadership, while the "A" group remained loyal to Klein. A third segment, the "Independent" group, refused to take sides. These factions still exist today. The Independent group, all influenced to some degree by Klein's thinking, created the theory of object relations as we know it today (Kohon 1986). This group, often referred to collectively as constituting the "British School" of object relations (Sutherland 1980), includes such luminaries as D. W. Winnicott, Michael Balint, W. R. D. Fairbairn, Paula Heimann, Margaret Little, and

Harry Guntrip. Although in fact there were significant differences in the writings of these thinkers, they are grouped together because they shared common themes. All were concerned about early development prior to the Oedipus complex, and all focused on the vicissitudes of internal object relations rather than on drive theory. Moreover, like Klein and unlike the classical analysts, they tended to treat sicker patients with psychoanalytic methods, perhaps thereby obtaining a more intimate glimpse of primitive mental states.

The British School served to counterbalance Klein's overemphasis on fantasy by stressing the influence of the infant's early environment. Winnicott (1965), for example, coined the term *the good-enough mother* to characterize the minimum environmental requirements needed by the infant in order to proceed with normal development. Balint (1979) described the feeling in many patients that something was missing, which he termed *the basic fault*. He viewed this lack as caused by the mother's failure to respond to the child's basic needs. Fairbairn (1963), perhaps the most divorced from drive theory, saw the etiology of his schizoid patients' difficulties not in drive frustration but in their mothers' failure to provide experiences that reassured them they were truly loved for themselves. He believed that the instincts or drives were not pleasure seeking but rather object seeking.

These thinkers were all impressed with the fact that a theory of *deficit,* as well as a theory of conflict, was necessary for a complete psychoanalytic understanding of the human being. Analysts have another task in addition to the analysis of conflict. They also serve as a new object to be internalized by their patients so as to bolster deficient intrapsychic structures. This point is critical for a clinical theory of object relations—the patient's internal object relations are not etched in granite; they are open to modification through new experiences. This point of view is even acknowledged to some extent by proponents of classical ego psychology, such as Blum, who credited Stone (1967) in noting: "Even in adult analysis the role of the analyst as a real new object rather than the object of transference must be considered along with identification with the analyst and analytic attitudes" (Blum 1971, p. 51).

Self and Ego

While ego psychologists tend to minimize the significance of the self in their pursuit of a thoroughgoing understanding of the ego, the object relations theorists, because of their focus on the self as it relates to objects, have sought to clarify further the place of the self in the psychic apparatus. Certain American theorists, including Kernberg, Mahler, and Edith Jacobson, have worked to integrate object relations theory with ego psychology, considering the relationship of the ego and the self.

Few concepts in modern psychoanalytic discourse are more controversial than the self. The controversy has its historical roots in Freud's ambiguous usage of *Ich*. Literally translated from the German as "I," the term was used by Freud with two different connotations. At times *Ich* referred to an impersonal intrapsychic structure, while at other times it clearly connoted the individual's personal self-experience (Kernberg 1982; Meissner 1986). Strachey's subsequent translation of *Ich* as "ego" in the Standard Edition of Freud's works profoundly influenced this controversy. Ego became definitively associated with the tripartite structural theory as one of three impersonal intrapsychic agencies. Freud's other use of the term to mean self-experience became lost in the standardization of the impersonal meaning.

Hartmann (1950/1964) further divorced the two meanings of *Ich* by differentiating ego and self according to their interactional contexts. In this view, the ego interacted with the other intrapsychic agencies, the id and superego, while the self interacted with objects. Although critics believe that this historical development blurs the distinction between psychoanalytic and sociological concepts (Kernberg 1982), other theorists find that this clarification establishes a framework for development of the theory of object relations. In other words, the self evolves as the result of interactions with significant objects in the environment and with corresponding internal objects (Meissner 1986).

Another major controversy surrounding the self is whether it refers to an intrapsychic representation of the individual or a source of action and agency in its own right. The tendency among ego psychological thinkers has been to view the self as representational rather than as a source of subjective autonomous activity (Meissner 1986). However, numerous authors (Guntrip 1968, 1971; Meissner 1986; Schafer 1976; Sutherland 1983) have expressed concern that the structural theory and the model of the self as an intrapsychic representation provide little basis for a concept of the self that includes subjective experience or personal agency. Structural theory, by its nature, is oriented to specific functions that are impersonal in nature. Sutherland (1983), for example, asserted that a basic feature of the self is its active initiating role with the environment—striving toward relatedness and unity.

There is room for both the self-as-representation and the self-as-agency. In fact, the self may be viewed as embedded in the ego and may be defined as the end product of the integration of the many self-representations (Kernberg 1982). This integrated end product, however, should not be regarded as a continuous, unvarying entity (Bollas 1987; Mitchell 1991; Ogden 1989; Schafer 1989). Although we often wish to maintain an illusion of a continuous self, the reality is that we all are composed of multiple discontinuous selves that are constantly being shaped and defined by real and fantasized relationships with others. Schafer (1989) has understood this phenomenon as a set of narrative selves or story lines that we develop to provide an emotionally coherent account of our lives. Mitchell (1991) has observed that a paradox of psychoanalytic work is that as patients learn to tolerate these multiple facets of themselves, they begin to experience themselves as more durable and more coherent.

Defense Mechanisms

In the preceding section on ego psychology, we considered several neurotic defense mechanisms. In keeping with the historical trend associating object relations theory with more profoundly disturbed patients, in this section we will discuss a number of more primitive defenses characteristic of personality disorders and psychoses: splitting, projective identification, introjection, and denial.

Splitting. This mechanism is an unconscious process that actively separates contradictory feelings, self-representations, or object-representations from one another. Although Freud (1927/1961, 1940/1964) made scattered references to splitting, it was Klein (1946/1975) who exalted it to the position of the cornerstone of emotional survival during the first few months of life. Splitting allows the infant to separate good from bad, pleasure from unpleasure, love from hate so as to preserve positively colored experiences, affects, self-representations, and object-representations in safely isolated mental compartments, free from contamination by negative counterparts. Splitting may be viewed as a basic biological mode of ordering experience, by which the endangering is separated from the endangered; it is secondarily elaborated into a psychological defense (Ogden 1986). It is also a fundamental cause of ego weakness (Kernberg 1967, 1975). The integration of libidinal and aggressive drive derivatives associated with "good" and "bad" introjects serves to neutralize aggression. Splitting prevents this neutralization and thus deprives the ego of an essential source of energy for growth.

In Kernberg's view, splitting is characterized by certain clinical manifestations: 1) alternating expression of contradictory behaviors and attitudes, which the patient regards with lack of concern and bland denial; 2) selective lack of impulse control; 3) the compartmentalization of everyone in the environment into "all good" and "all bad" camps, which is often referred to as idealization and devaluation; and 4) the coexistence of contradictory self-representations that alternate with one another. Although Kernberg viewed splitting as the key defensive operation in patients with borderline personality disorder, splitting may be observed in all patients at times (Rangell 1982), and it does not clearly differentiate borderline patients from those with other personality disorders (Allen et al. 1988). Kernberg distinguished between neurotic and borderline characters partly on the basis of the latter's preference for splitting over repression, but empirical research suggests that these two defenses operate independently and may coexist in the same individual (Perry and Cooper 1986).

Projective identification.   A second defense mechanism, projective identification, is an unconscious three-step process by which aspects of oneself are disavowed and attributed to someone else (see Figures 2–2, 2–3, and 2–4). The three steps (Ogden 1979) include: 1) The patient projects a self- or object-representation onto the treater. 2) The treater unconsciously identifies with what is projected and begins to feel or behave like the projected self- or object-representation in response to interpersonal pressure exerted by the patient (this aspect of the phenomenon is sometimes referred to as *projective counteridentification* [Grinberg 1979]). 3) The projected material is "psychologically processed" and modified by the treater, who returns it to the patient via reintrojection. The modification of the projected material, in turn, modifies the corresponding self- or object-representation and the pattern of interpersonal relatedness.

Transference and countertransference can be correlated with steps 1 and 2, respectively. As just described, projective identification has an interpersonal dimension in addition to its role as an intrapsychic defense mechanism. Splitting and projective identification, then, clearly

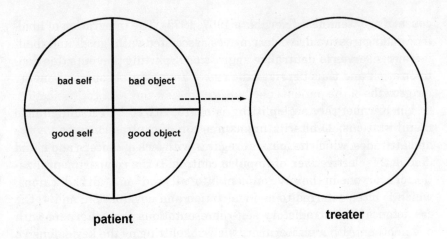

Patient disavows and projects bad internal object onto treater.

Figure 2–2. Projective identification—Step 1.

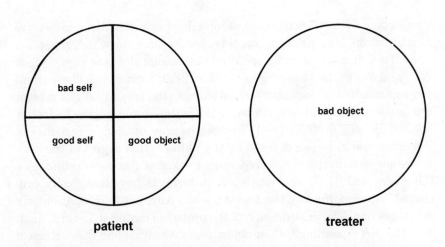

Treater unconsciously begins to feel and/or behave like the projected bad object in response to interpersonal pressure exerted by the patient (projective counteridentification).

Figure 2–3. Projective identification—Step 2.

are highly interrelated mechanisms that work together to keep "good" and "bad" separated (Grotstein 1981). The interpersonal element inherent in Ogden's definition of projective identification derives from Bion's (1962) conceptualization of the therapist as a container for the projections of the patient, much as the mother contains the projections of her infant. Other authors (Grotstein 1981; Hamilton 1988; Sandler 1987) have disagreed with broadening the definition to include a particular response of the treater to the projected aspects of the patient. They prefer a narrower view of projective identification, one that categorizes it as a purely intrapsychic defense that may or may not result in a reciprocal response from the clinician. Grotstein (1981), for example, shared Kernberg's (1987b) view that the identification occurs *within the projector* rather than within the target of the projection. By maintaining this empathic bond or identification with that which has been projected, the projector has the fantasy of control over the projected material. Most authors would agree that this element of control is central to the concept of projective identification. Sandler (1987) noted: "What one wants to get rid of in oneself can be disposed of by projective identification, and through controlling the object one can then gain the unconscious illusion that one is controlling the unwanted

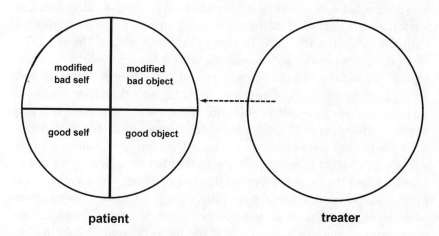

Treater contains and modifies the projected bad object, which is then reintrojected by the patient and assimilated (introjective identification).

Figure 2–4. Projective identification—Step 3.

and projected aspect of the self" (p. 20). Ogden's three-step formulation is completely in keeping with this notion except that he views the identification as occurring in both the treater and the projector rather than in the projector alone.

To confine the concept of projective identification to a defense mechanism is unduly limiting. Because of the interpersonal component, it may also be regarded as 1) a means of communication, in which patients coerce the treater into experiencing a set of feelings similar to their own; 2) a mode of object relatedness; and 3) a pathway for psychological change, in the sense that the reintrojection of the projected contents after they have been modified by the treater results in a modification of the patient. The material that the patient projects may or may not represent a "good fit." The degree to which projective identification is actualized depends, in part, on the clinician's own propensity to respond in an identificatory manner with what the patient projects (Scharff 1992). Although this model of projective identification emphasizes what takes place in a clinical setting, projective identification regularly occurs in nontherapeutic situations as well. In these nonclinical settings, the projections may be returned in completely distorted forms, or "crammed back down the patient's throat," instead of being modified or contained.

The distinction between projection and projective identification is also somewhat controversial. Grotstein (1981) conceptualized all projection as projective identification since an empathic identification with the projected material is always retained within the projector. The projection outward of something within the self would be meaningless unless the individual maintained some connection with that which is projected, in Grotstein's view. By Ogden's definition, however, all projection is not projective identification. Paranoid individuals may project malevolent intentions onto many figures in their environment with whom they never come in contact. They simply avoid those individuals and keep to themselves. Projection becomes projective identification when the target of a projection begins to be transformed by the projection. When paranoid individuals begin to have direct contact with the objects of their projections and begin to accuse those persons of malevolent motives, the targets of the projections are likely to identify unconsciously with the "bad object" projections and begin to become defensive and angry about the unfair accusations. A third view is suggested by Kernberg (1987b), who disagreed with the traditional view of projection as a primitive mechanism. He sees projection as typical of higher-level neurotic patients. He described it as involving no empathy with the material projected, no evocation in the treater of behavior typical of the projected aspects of the patient, and no process of reintrojection. Projective identification is a more primitive process, in Kernberg's view, because it involves more permeable self-other boundaries in the sense that the material returns to the patient more easily than it does in projection, where the self-other boundary is firm.

Introjection.   This third defense is an unconscious process by which an external object is symbolically taken in and assimilated as part of oneself. This mechanism may exist as a part of projective identification, where what is taken in was originally projected, or it may exist independently as the converse of projection. Classically, Freud (1917/1963) formulated depression as a result of the introjection of an ambivalently viewed object. Anger focused on this introject within the depressed patient resulted in self-depreciation and other symptoms of depression. In contemporary object relations parlance, introjection is distinguished from identification as one of the two principal modes of internalization. If a parent, for example, is *introjected,* then the parent is internalized as part of the object subdivision of the ego and is experienced as an internal presence that does not substantially alter the self-representation. On the other hand, in identification, the parent is internalized as part of the self subdivision of the ego and materially modifies the self-representation (Sandler 1990).

Denial.   The fourth defense mechanism, denial, is a direct disavowal of traumatic sensory data. Whereas repression is generally used as a defense against *internal* wishes or impulses, denial is ordinarily a defense against the external world of reality when that reality is overwhelmingly disturbing. Although associated primarily with psychoses and severe personality disorders, this mechanism may also be used by normal people, especially in the face of catastrophic events.

Developmental Considerations

The object relations formulations derived from clinical observations have been bolstered and elaborated by the infant observation studies of Margaret Mahler and her colleagues (1975). Again, in keeping with the historical thrust of object relations theory, the focus of this research has been on *preoedipal* development, specifically, from birth to around three years of age. Through observation of normal and abnormal mother-infant pairs, Mahler et al. have been able to identify three broad phases of the development of object relations.

In the first 2 months of life, an *autistic* phase occurs in which the infant appears self-absorbed and concerned with survival rather than relatedness. The period between 2 and 6 months, denoted as *symbiosis,* begins with the smile response of the infant and the visual ability to follow the mother's face. Although the infant is vaguely aware of the mother as a separate object, the infant's primary experience of the mother-infant dyad is one of a dual unity rather than of two separate people.

The third phase, *separation-individuation,* is characterized by four subphases. Between 6 and 10 months, in the subphase of *differentiation,* the child becomes aware that the mother is a separate person. This awareness may lead to the child's need for a transitional object (Winnicott 1953/1971), such as a blanket or pacifier, to help deal with the fact that the mother is not always available. *Practicing* is the next subphase; it occurs between 10 and 16 months. With the newfound locomotor skills of this age, toddlers love to explore the world on their own, although they frequently return to their mothers for "refueling." The third subphase, *rapprochement,* is characterized by a sharper awareness of the separateness of the mother and occurs between 16 and 24 months of age. This awareness brings with it a heightened sense of vulnerability to separations from mother. This separation anxiety punctures the narcissistic inflation of the practicing subphase and leads the child to check frequently on the mother's whereabouts during play periods.

The fourth and final subphase of separation-individuation is marked by the consolidation of individuality and the beginnings of object constancy. The achievement of this period, which roughly corresponds to the third year of life, is the integration of split views of the mother into a unified whole object that can be internalized as an emotionally soothing inner presence that sustains the child during the mother's absence. This achievement corresponds with Klein's depressive position and sets the stage for the child to enter the oedipal phase.

Mahler's empirical observations have been extraordinarily influential in our evolving understanding of the developmental pathogenesis of borderline personality disorder (see Chapter 15). Object relations theory is particularly relevant to those disorders whose etiology appears to relate to preoedipal problems in the mother-infant dyad prior to the introduction of triangular relationships typical of the Oedipus complex. Mahler's studies also lend empirical support to the paramount importance of object seeking in development and the impossibility of divorcing drives from object relations.

Self Psychology

While object relations theory emphasizes the *internalized* relationships between *representations* of self and object, self psychology stresses how *external* relationships help maintain self-esteem and self-cohesion. Derived from the seminal writings of Heinz Kohut (1971, 1977, 1984), this theoretical approach views the patient as in desperate need of certain responses from other persons to maintain a sense of well-being. Indeed, some observers have suggested that self psychology is fundamentally a two-person psychology (Jaenicke 1987) or a self-object psychology (Gedo 1986).

Self psychology evolved from Kohut's study of narcissistically disturbed outpatients he was treating in psychoanalysis. He noted that they seemed different from the classic neurotic patients who presented for treatment with hysterical or obsessive-compulsive symptoms. Instead, they complained of nondescript feelings of depression or dissatisfaction in relationships (Kohut 1971). They were also characterized by a vulnerable self-esteem that was highly sensitive to slights from friends, family, lovers, colleagues, and others. Kohut observed that the structural model of ego psychology did not seem adequate to explain the pathogenesis and cure of these patients' problems.

Kohut noted that these patients formed two kinds of transferences: the mirror transference and the idealizing transference. In the mirror transference the patient looks to the analyst for a confirming, validating response that Kohut linked to the "gleam in the mother's eye" in response to phase-appropriate displays of exhibitionism on the part of her small child, what Kohut called the *grandiose-exhibitionistic self*. These approving responses, according to Kohut, are essential for normal development in that they provide the child with a sense of self-worth. When a mother fails to empathize with her child's need for such a mirroring response, the latter has great difficulty in maintaining a sense of wholeness and self-regard. In response to this failure of empathy, the child's sense of self fragments, and the child desperately attempts to be perfect and to "perform" for the parent to gain the hungered-for approbation. This form of "showing off" is another manifestation of the grandiose-exhibitionistic self (Baker and Baker 1987). The same phenomena constitute the mirror transference in adults who seek treatment. The adult patient who "performs" for his or her therapist in a desperate attempt to gain approval and admiration may be developing a mirror transference.

The idealizing transference, as implied in the name, refers to a situation in which the patient perceives the therapist as an all-powerful parent whose presence soothes and heals. The wish to bask in the reflected glory of the idealized therapist is a manifestation of this transference. Just as the child may be traumatized by the empathic failures of a mother who does not provide mirroring responses to her child's grandiose-exhibitionistic self, so can that same child be traumatized by a mother who does not empathize with the child's need to idealize her or who does not provide a model worthy of idealization.

In either case, the adult patient who suffers from such early disturbances of parenting and who presents these kinds of transference dispositions is struggling with a defective or deficient self—one that is developmentally frozen at a point where it is highly prone to fragmentation. Kohut's view is that the structural model of conflict associated with ego psychology is not sufficient to explain these narcissistic needs for mirroring and idealization. Moreover, he noted a moralizing, pejorative tone in the attitudes of analysts who approached narcissism from a classical point of view. He believed that much harm was done by following Freud's (1914/1963) model, which proposed a transition from a state of primary narcissism to object love as part of the normal maturational process. The offshoot of Freud's thinking was that one should "outgrow" narcissistic strivings and be more concerned about the needs of others.

Kohut thought that this point of view was hypocritical. He asserted that narcissistic needs persist throughout life and that they parallel development in the realm of object love. He postulated a *double-axis* theory (see Figure 2–5) that allowed for ongoing development in *both* narcissistic and object love realms (Ornstein 1974). As infants mature, they attempt to capture the lost perfection of the early maternal-infant bond by resorting to one of two strategies—the grandiose self, where the perfection is captured within, and the idealized parent imago, where it is assigned to the parent. These two poles constitute the *bipolar self*. In his last book (1984), Kohut expanded this conceptualization to a *tripolar* self by adding a third pole of selfobject needs, the twinship or alter ego. This aspect of the self appears in the transference as a need to be just like the therapist. It has its developmental origins in a wish for merger that is gradually transformed into imitative behavior. For example, a young boy might play at lawn mowing while his father cuts the grass. This third pole of the self has limited clinical usefulness compared to the other two and is often excluded from discussions of selfobject transferences. If failures of empathy were typical of the parental responses to these strategies, a developmental arrest occurs. With adequate parenting, on the other hand, the grandiose self is transformed into healthy ambitions, and the idealized parent imago becomes internalized as ideals and values (Kohut 1971). Hence therapists could empathize with the narcissistic needs of their patients as developmentally normal rather than regarding them with contempt for being self-centered and immature. While classical ego psychological theory conceptualizes the patient as having infantile wishes that need to be renounced, Kohut regarded patients as having *needs* that must be understood and partially met in the treatment (Eagle 1990). Kohut's first book proposed this theoretical formulation as applicable primarily to narcissistic character pathology. By the time his last (1984, posthumously published) book appeared, he had greatly expanded the scope of self psychology:

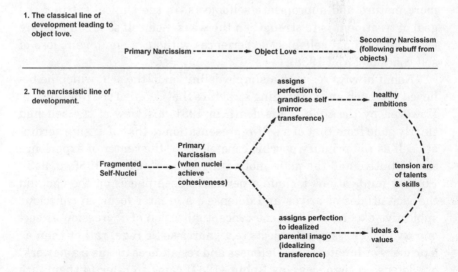

Figure 2–5. Kohut's double-axis theory (1971).

> Self psychology is now attempting to demonstrate . . . that all forms
> of psychopathology are based either on defects in the structure of the
> self, on distortions of the self, or on weakness of the self. It is trying
> to show, furthermore, that all these flaws in the self are due to distur-
> bances of self-selfobject relationships in childhood. (Kohut 1984, p. 53)

The term *selfobject* came to be a generic term to describe the role
that other persons perform for the self in regard to mirroring, idealizing, and twinship needs. From the standpoint of the growth and development of the self, others are not regarded as separate persons but as
objects to gratify these needs of the self. In a sense, then, selfobjects
may be viewed more as functions (i.e., soothing, validating) than as
people. The need for selfobjects is never outgrown, according to Kohut,
but rather persists throughout life—we need selfobjects in our environment for emotional survival much as we need oxygen in the atmosphere for physical survival (Kohut 1984).

One implication of Kohut's final theoretical statement is that separation is a myth. His view differs dramatically from Mahler's object
relations view, which pivots around intrapsychic separation, in that
self psychology views the separation of the self from the selfobject as
impossible. We all need affirming, empathic responses from others
throughout life to maintain our self-esteem. Maturation and growth
move away from a need for archaic selfobjects toward an ability to use
more mature and appropriate selfobjects. In the clinical setting, the
goal of treatment is to strengthen the weakened self so it can tolerate
less than optimal selfobject experiences without a significant loss of
self-cohesion (Wolf 1988).

Kohut always resisted a simple definition of the self, which he believed was such an overarching structure that it defied crisp definition.
However, by the time of his death in 1981, his view of the self had
clearly gone from that of a self-representation to that of a "supraordin-
ate self as the primary psychic constellation, the center of experience
and initiative and the main motivating agency" (Curtis 1985, p. 343).
Further implications include a pervasive deemphasis on the ego and
the vicissitudes of drives and defenses, a greater focus on conscious
subjective experience, and the conceptualization of aggression as secondary to failures of selfobjects (e.g., narcissistic rage) rather than as
a primary or innate drive. Defenses and resistances in this framework,
or "defense-resistances," as Kohut (1984) came to refer to them, are
viewed entirely differently: "My personal preference is to speak of the

'defensiveness' of patients—and to think of their defensive attitudes as adaptive and psychologically valuable—and not of their 'resistances' " (p. 114). Clearly, they are valuable and adaptive because they preserve the integrity of the self.

In contrast to the ego psychologists, Kohut viewed the Oedipus complex as of secondary importance. The oedipal conflicts involving sexuality and aggression are mere "breakdown products" of developmentally earlier failures in the self-selfobject matrix. If a mother adequately fulfills the selfobject needs of her child, the Oedipus complex can be weathered without the child's becoming symptomatic. The fundamental anxiety, according to self psychology, is "disintegration anxiety," which involves the fear that one's self will fragment in response to inadequate selfobject responses, resulting in an experiencing of a nonhuman state of psychological death (Baker and Baker 1987). From the standpoint of self psychology, most forms of symptomatic behavior (e.g., drug abuse, sexual promiscuity, perversions, self-mutilation, binge eating, and purging) do *not* grow out of neurotic conflict related to castration anxiety. Rather, they reflect "an emergency attempt to maintain and/or restore internal cohesion and harmony to a vulnerable, unhealthy self" (Baker and Baker 1987, p. 51). These fragmentations of the self occur along a continuum that ranges from mild worry or anxiety to severe panic over the perception that one is completely falling apart (Wolf 1988).

The emphasis of self psychology on the failures of parenting figures and the resulting deficiencies of the self resonate with the British object relations theories. Echoes of Winnicott's good-enough mothering and Balint's basic fault can be heard in the themes of self psychological writings. Although Kohut does not acknowledge the contributions of these forerunners, their influence is unmistakable. However, the object relations theorists did not develop the notion of the self to the extent that Kohut did, perhaps because of their adherence to a model of maturation that retains the moralizing potential eschewed by Kohut (Bacal 1987). Kohut also has made a significant contribution in recognizing the significance of self-esteem in the pathogenesis of psychiatric disturbances.

Developmental Considerations

Kohut formulated his concept of developmental pathogenesis by reconstructing childhood experience from the analytic data he heard from adult patients. Therefore, he did not provide a specific developmental timetable in the manner of Mahler and her colleagues. However, the infant observation research of Daniel Stern (1985, 1989) has provided considerable support for the developmental premises of self psychology, much as Mahler's work has done for object relations theory. Stern's observations of infants convinced him that they did not emerge from the womb into a state of autistic self-absorption. The infant seems to be aware of the mother or caretaker from the first days of life. Affirming and validating responses from the mothering figure are crucial for the developing infant's evolving sense of self. Stern stressed that the infant develops a sense of self-with-other in response to the caretaker's attunement. He differed with Klein in that he regarded fantasy as having only minimal significance. By contrast, he viewed the infant as primarily experiencing reality. Stern concluded that infants are adept observers of reality and only older toddlers begin to make significant use of fantasy and distortion in an effort to alter their perceptions. He even went so far as to argue that secondary process thought precedes primary process thought and is the bedrock of normal development.

Stern described five discrete senses of self. Rather than viewing these as phases that are superseded by subsequent and more mature developmental periods, he regarded them as different domains of self-experience (emergent or "body" self, core self, subjective self, verbal or categorical self, and narrative self), each of which remains for the entire life span and operates in concert with the other coexisting senses of self. From birth to 2 months of age, an emergent self appears that is predominantly a physiologically based body self. From 2 to 6 months, a core sense of self emerges that is linked with greater interpersonal relatedness. A sense of subjective self appears between 7 and 9 months and is a major event because it involves the matching of intrapsychic states between infant and mother. Between 15 and 18 months of age, coinciding with the ability to think symbolically and to communicate verbally, the verbal or categorical sense of self emerges. The narrative sense of self arrives between 3 and 5 years of age. This historical view of oneself is what Stern believed is encountered when patients tell their life stories in the analytic setting.

Stern delineated four essential features of a sense of self: coherence, affectivity, agency, and continuity (or historicity). He believed that attachment, trust, and security are not phase specific but continue to be vital issues throughout the entire life span. One of Stern's central tenets is that the infant develops as a result of sensitive affective attunement by the mother or caretaker. Kohut and subsequent self psychologists have argued that a similar form of empathic resonance is necessary in the analytic situation to strengthen the patient's self.

The Role of Theory in Clinical Practice

Faced with a bewildering array of psychoanalytic theories, one may choose to deny the value of theory altogether. Who needs it? Why not just begin *de novo* with each patient and stick to the clinical material? To advocate this approach is simply to advocate the formation of new theories. As Kernberg (1987a) noted, "All observations of clinical phenomena depend upon theories, and when we think that we are forgetting about theory, it only means that we have a theory of which we are not aware" (pp. 181–182).

A more sensible solution is to become familiar with the phenomena described by all the major theories and to focus on each perspective as it is clinically appropriate with a given patient. Psychoanalysis and psychodynamic psychiatry are tragically beset with needless polarities—is it oedipal or preoedipal, conflict or deficit, classical theory or self psychology, tension reduction or object seeking? Such questions tend to be cast in terms of right or wrong. But is it possible that all models are valid in certain clinical situations? Is it not possible for both oedipal and preoedipal, conflict and deficit, to be relevant in the understanding of an individual patient? Of course it is. Wallerstein (1983) made this point eloquently in a critique of self psychology:

> For in the flow and flux of analytic clinical material we are always in the world of "both/and." We deal constantly, and in turn, both with the oedipal, where there is a coherent self, and the preoedipal, where there may not yet be; with defensive regressions and with developmental arrests; with defensive transferences and defensive resistances and with recreations of earlier traumatic and traumatized states. (p. 31)

Wallerstein reminds us of the fundamental psychoanalytic principles of overdetermination and multiple function.

Some aspects of all three theories examined in this chapter will most likely prove useful in the treatment of the majority of patients. From a developmental perspective, certain aspects of early childhood experience are better explained by one theory than another, and with certain patients, the emphasis will be more in one direction than another, depending on the clinical data (Pine 1988). In most patients, however, we will find both deficit and conflict. As Eagle (1984) noted in his appraisal of the role of theory in psychoanalysis: "We are most conflicted in the areas in which we are deprived. . . . It is precisely the person deprived of love who is most conflicted about giving and receiving love" (p. 130). In practice, clinicians find themselves serving both as selfobjects and as real, separate objects for their patients.

For some clinicians, however, shifting from one theoretical perspective to another, depending on the patient's needs, is too cumbersome and unwieldy. Wallerstein (1988) has pointed out that it is possible for clinicians to pay attention to the *clinical phenomena* described by each theoretical perspective without embracing the entire metapsychological model. For example, one can address self- and object-representations, mirror and idealizing transferences, and impulse-defense configurations as they appear in the clinical setting without having to resort to invoking the entire theoretical edifice on which such observations are based. He believes that selfobject transferences described by self psychologists can be explained within the framework of conflict theory. Cooper (1977), on the other hand, has advocated greater theoretical flexibility. Different diagnostic categories and different patients, in his view, suggest different theoretical models. For example, to be effectively treated, certain narcissistic patients may require a self psychological approach, while individuals with neurotic conflicts may respond better to a therapeutic approach based on the principles of ego psychology.

Each of these approaches to the theoretical pluralism of modern dynamic psychiatry is workable for some clinicians. Regardless of which approach is found more suitable, all clinicians should be wary of rigidly imposing theory onto clinical material. The patient must be allowed to lead the clinician into whatever theoretical realm is the best match for the clinical material. While familiarity with all three theoretical models of dynamic psychiatry requires greater breadth of knowledge, it allows for a richer understanding of patients and their psychopathology. Finding the theoretical framework that best fits a particular patient entails a good deal of exploratory trial and error, but as we stumble through the cave, we may eventually find the path and may be far better off than other travelers with a map of an altogether different cave.

References

Allen JG, Deering CD, Buskirk JR, et al: Assessment of therapeutic alliances in the psychiatric hospital milieu. Psychiatry 51:291–299, 1988

Bacal HA: British object-relations theorists and self psychology: some critical reflections. Int J Psychoanal 68:81–98, 1987

Baker HS, Baker MN: Heinz Kohut's self psychology: an overview. Am J Psychiatry 144:1–9, 1987

Balint M: The Basic Fault: Therapeutic Aspects of Regression. New York, Brunner/Mazel, 1979

Bellak L, Hurvich M, Gedimen HK: Ego Functions in Schizophrenics, Neurotics, and Normals: A Systematic Study of Conceptual, Diagnostic, and Therapeutic Aspects. New York, Wiley, 1973

Bion WR: Learning From Experience. New York, Basic Books, 1962

Blum HP: On the conception and development of the transference neurosis. J Am Psychoanal Assoc 19:41–53, 1971

Bollas C: The Shadow of the Object: Psychoanalysis of the Unthought Known. New York, Columbia University Press, 1987

Brenner C: The Mind in Conflict. New York, International Universities Press, 1982

Cooper AM: Clinical psychoanalysis: one method or more—the relation of diagnosis to psychoanalytic treatment. Paper presented at the fall meeting of the American Psychoanalytic Association, New York, NY, December 1977

Curtis HC: Clinical perspectives on self psychology. Psychoanal Q 54:339–378, 1985

Eagle MN: Recent Developments in Psychoanalysis: A Critical Evaluation. New York, McGraw-Hill, 1984

Eagle M: The concepts of need and wish in self psychology. Psychoanalytic Psychology 7 (suppl):71–88, 1990

Erikson EH: Identity and the life cycle: selected papers. Psychol Issues 1:1–171, 1959

Fairbairn WRD: Schizoid factors in the personality (1940), in Psychoanalytic Studies of the Personality. London, Routledge & Kegan Paul, 1952, pp 3–27

Fairbairn WRD: Endopsychic structure considered in terms of object-relationships (1944), in Psychoanalytic Studies of the Personality. London, Routledge & Kegan Paul, 1952, pp 82–136

Fairbairn WRD: Psychoanalytic Studies of the Personality. London, Routledge & Kegan Paul, 1952

Fairbairn WRD: Synopsis of an object-relations theory of the personality. Int J Psychoanal 44:224–225, 1963

Freud A: The Ego and the Mechanisms of Defense (1936). Translated by Baines C. New York, International Universities Press, 1946

Freud S: Three essays on the theory of sexuality (1905), in The Standard Edition of the Complete Psychological Works of Sigmund Freud, Vol 7. Translated and edited by Strachey J. London, Hogarth Press, 1953, pp 123–245

Freud S: On narcissism: an introduction (1914), in The Standard Edition of the Complete Psychological Works of Sigmund Freud, Vol 14. Translated and edited by Strachey J. London, Hogarth Press, 1963, pp 67–102

Freud S: Mourning and melancholia (1917), in The Standard Edition of the Complete Psychological Works of Sigmund Freud, Vol 14. Translated and edited by Strachey J. London, Hogarth Press, 1963, pp 237–260

Freud S: The ego and the id (1923), in The Standard Edition of the Complete Psychological Works of Sigmund Freud, Vol 19. Translated and edited by Strachey J. London, Hogarth Press, 1961, pp 1–66

Freud S: Some psychical consequences of the anatomical distinction between the sexes (1925), in The Standard Edition of the Complete Psychological Works of Sigmund Freud, Vol 19. Translated and edited by Strachey J. London, Hogarth Press, 1961, pp 241–258

Freud S: Inhibitions, symptoms and anxiety (1926), in The Standard Edition of the Complete Psychological Works of Sigmund Freud, Vol 20. Translated and edited by Strachey J. London, Hogarth Press, 1959, pp 75–175

Freud S: Fetishism (1927), in The Standard Edition of the Complete Psychological Works of Sigmund Freud, Vol 21. Translated and edited by Strachey J. London, Hogarth Press, 1961, pp 147–157

Freud S: Female sexuality (1931), in The Standard Edition of the Complete Psychological Works of Sigmund Freud, Vol 21. Translated and edited by Strachey J. London, Hogarth Press, 1961, pp 223–243

Freud S: Femininity (1933), in The Standard Edition of the Complete Psychological Works of Sigmund Freud, Vol 22. Translated and edited by Strachey J. London, Hogarth Press, 1964, pp 112–135

Freud S: Analysis terminable and interminable (1937), in The Standard Edition of the Complete Psychological Works of Sigmund Freud, Vol 23. Translated and edited by Strachey J. London, Hogarth Press, 1964, pp 209–253

Freud S: Splitting of the ego in the process of defence (1940), in The Standard Edition of the Complete Psychological Works of Sigmund Freud, Vol 23. Translated and edited by Strachey J. London, Hogarth Press, 1964, pp 271–278

Gedo JE: Conceptual Issues in Psychoanalysis: Essays in History and Method. Hillsdale, NJ, Analytic Press, 1986

Greenberg J, Mitchell SA: Object Relations in Psychoanalytic Theory. Cambridge, MA, Harvard University Press, 1983

Grinberg L: Countertransference and projective counteridentification, in Countertransference. Edited by Epstein L, Feiner A. New York, Jason Aronson, 1979, pp 169–191

Grotstein JS: Splitting and Projective Identification. New York, Jason Aronson, 1981

Guntrip H: Schizoid Phenomena, Object-Relations, and the Self. New York, International Universities Press, 1968

Guntrip H: Psychoanalytic Theory, Therapy, and the Self. New York, Basic Books, 1971

Hamilton NG: Self and Others: Object Relations Theory in Practice. Northvale, NJ, Jason Aronson, 1988

Hartmann H: Ego Psychology and the Problem of Adaptation (1939). Translated by Rapaport D. New York, International Universities Press, 1958

Hartmann H: Comments on the psychoanalytic theory of the ego (1950), in Essays on Ego Psychology: Selected Problems in Psychoanalytic Theory. New York, International Universities Press, 1964, pp 113–141

Jacobson E: The Self and the Object World. New York, International Universities Press, 1964

Jaenicke C: Kohut's concept of cure. Psychoanal Rev 74:537–548, 1987

Kernberg OF: Borderline personality organization. J Am Psychoanal Assoc 15:641–685, 1967

Kernberg OF: Borderline Conditions and Pathological Narcissism. New York, Jason Aronson, 1975

Kernberg OF: Self, ego, affects, and drives. J Am Psychoanal Assoc 30:893–917, 1982

Kernberg OF: Object relations theory and character analysis. J Am Psychoanal Assoc 31 (suppl):247–272, 1983

Kernberg OF: Concluding discussion, in Projection, Identification, Projective Identification. Edited by Sandler J. Madison, CT, International Universities Press, 1987a, pp 179–196

Kernberg OF: Projection and projective identification: developmental and clinical aspects, in Projection, Identification, Projective Identification. Edited by Sandler J. Madison, CT, International Universities Press, 1987b, pp 93–115

Klein M: Notes on some schizoid mechanisms (1946), in Envy and Gratitude and Other Works, 1946–1963. New York, Free Press, 1975, pp 1–24

Kohon G: The British School of Psychoanalysis: The Independent Tradition. New Haven, CT, Yale University Press, 1986

Kohut H: The Analysis of the Self: A Systematic Approach to the Psychoanalytic Treatment of Narcissistic Personality Disorders. New York, International Universities Press, 1971

Kohut H: The Restoration of the Self. New York, International Universities Press, 1977

Kohut H: How Does Analysis Cure? Edited by Goldberg A. Chicago, IL, University of Chicago Press, 1984

Lerner HE: Penis envy: alternatives in conceptualization. Bull Menninger Clinic 44:39–48, 1980

Mahler MS, Pine F, Bergman A: The Psychological Birth of the Human Infant: Symbiosis and Individuation. New York, Basic Books, 1975

Meissner WW: Internalization in Psychoanalysis. New York, International Universities Press, 1981

Meissner WW: Can psychoanalysis find its self? J Am Psychoanal Assoc 34:379–400, 1986

Mitchell SA: Contemporary perspectives on self: toward an integration. Psychoanalytic Dialogues 1:121–147, 1991

Ogden TH: On projective identification. Int J Psychoanal 60:357–373, 1979

Ogden TH: The concept of internal object relations. Int J Psychoanal 64:227–241, 1983

Ogden TH: The Matrix of the Mind: Object Relations and the Psychoanalytic Dialogue. Northvale, NJ, Jason Aronson, 1986

Ogden TH: The Primitive Edge of Experience. Northvale, NJ, Jason Aronson, 1989

Ornstein PH: On narcissism: beyond the introduction, highlights of Heinz Kohut's contributions to the psychoanalytic treatment of narcissistic personality disorders. Annual of Psychoanalysis 2:127–149, 1974

Perry JC, Cooper SH: A preliminary report on defenses and conflicts associated with borderline personality disorder. J Am Psychoanal Assoc 34:863–893, 1986

Pine F: The four psychologies of psychoanalysis and their place in clinical work. J Am Psychoanal Assoc 36:571–596, 1988

Rangell L: The self in psychoanalytic theory. J Am Psychoanal Assoc 30:863–891, 1982

Rapaport D: Organization and Pathology of Thought: Selected Sources. New York, Columbia University Press, 1951

Rinsley DB: An object relations view of borderline personality, in Borderline Personality Disorders. Edited by Hartocollis P. New York, International Universities Press, 1977, pp 47–70

Sandler J (ed): Projection, Identification, Projective Identification. Madison, CT, International Universities Press, 1987

Sandler J: On internal object relations. J Am Psychoanal Assoc 38:859–880, 1990

Sandler J, Rosenblatt B: The concept of the representational world. Psychoanal Study Child 17:128–145, 1962

Schafer R: Aspects of Internalization. New York, International Universities Press, 1968

Schafer R: A New Language for Psychoanalysis. New Haven, CT, Yale University Press, 1976

Schafer R: Narratives of the self, in Psychoanalysis: Toward the Second Century. Edited by Cooper AM, Kernberg OF, Person ES. New Haven, CT, Yale University Press, 1989, pp 153–167

Scharff JS: Projective and Introjective Identification and the Use of the Therapist's Self. Northvale, NJ, Jason Aronson, 1992

Segal H: An Introduction to the Work of Melanie Klein. New York, Basic Books, 1964

Stern DN: The Interpersonal World of the Infant: A View from Psychoanalysis and Developmental Psychology. New York, Basic Books, 1985

Stern DN: Developmental prerequisites for the sense of a narrated self, in Psychoanalysis: Toward the Second Century. Edited by Cooper AM, Kernberg OF, Person ES. New Haven, CT, Yale University Press, 1989, pp 168–178

Stoller RJ: The sense of femaleness. Psychoanal Q 37:42–55, 1968

Stone L: The psychoanalytic situation and transference. J Am Psychoanal Assoc 15:3–58, 1967

Sutherland JD: The British object relations theorists: Balint, Winnicott, Fairbairn, Guntrip. J Am Psychoanal Assoc 28:829–860, 1980

Sutherland JD: The self and object relations: a challenge to psychoanalysis. Bull Menninger Clin 47:525–541, 1983

Torok M: The significance of penis envy in women, in Female Sexuality: New Psychoanalytic Views. Edited by Chasseguet-Smirgel J. Ann Arbor, MI, University of Michigan Press, 1970, pp 135–170

Vaillant GE: Natural history of male psychological health, V: the relation of choice of ego mechanisms of defense to adult adjustment. Arch Gen Psychiatry 33:535–545, 1976

Vaillant GE: Adaptation to Life. Boston, MA, Little, Brown, 1977

Wallerstein RS: Self psychology and "classical" psychoanalytic psychology: the nature of their relationship (1983), in The Future of Psychoanalysis: Essays in Honor of Heinz Kohut. Edited by Goldberg A. New York, International Universities Press, 1983, pp 19–63

Wallerstein RS: One psychoanalysis or many? Int J Psychoanal 69:5–21, 1988

Winnicott DW: Transitional objects and transitional phenomena: a study of the first not-me possession. (Int J Psychoanal 34:89–97, 1953), reprinted in Playing and Reality. New York, Basic Books, 1971, pp 1–25

Winnicott DW: The Maturational Processes and the Facilitating Environment: Studies in the Theory of Emotional Development. London, Hogarth Press, 1965

Wolf E: Treating the Self. New York, Guilford, 1988

Chapter 3

Psychodynamic Assessment of the Patient

Whenever two people meet there are really six people present. There is each man as he sees himself, each man as the other person sees him, and each man as he really is.

William James

The psychodynamic assessment of a patient does not stand apart from the thorough evaluation of history, signs, and symptoms growing out of the medical-psychiatric tradition. Dynamic psychiatrists value such information as a crucial component of the diagnostic assessment. However, their approach to gathering that information differs from the purely descriptive approach to diagnosis. Moreover, other information is of interest to the dynamic psychiatrist, so the psychodynamic assessment may be viewed as a significant extension of the descriptive medical-psychiatric evaluation.

The Clinical Interview

Any description of the psychodynamic approach to clinical interviewing must begin with the fundamental importance of the doctor-patient relationship. When psychiatrist and patient meet for the first time, two strangers are coming into contact, each with a variety of expectations concerning the other. Establishing rapport and a shared understanding must always be the first agenda in a psychodynamic interview (MacKinnon and Michels 1971; Menninger et al. 1962; Thomä and Kächele 1987). The first task of the interviewer, then, is to convey that the patient is accepted, valued, and validated as a unique person with unique problems.

Interviewers who attempt to immerse themselves empathically in their patients' experience will promote a bond between them based on the interviewer's obvious attempt to understand the patient's point of view. Such an approach does not require reassuring comments such as, "Don't worry, everything will be all right." Rather than allaying the patient's anxiety, these hollow reassurances are usually doomed to failure because they resemble similar past comments of friends and family members. They will only lead the patient to believe that the interviewer does not appreciate true suffering. Interviewers may instead build better rapport with comments such as, "I can understand how you feel, considering what you've been through." Challenging a patient's statements early in the interview will simply confirm any preexisting fears that psychiatrists are judgmental parental figures.

Differences Between Psychodynamic and Medical Interviewing

In medical interviewing, physicians pursue a direct course from the chief complaint to its etiology and pathogenesis. Patients generally cooperate with this process because they are eager to eliminate the pain or symptoms associated with their illness. Psychiatrists who attempt to steer a similarly linear course in the clinical interview will encounter potholes and detours at every turn. Moreover, psychiatrists often find that patients rarely are capable of coming quickly to the point because of their inability to pinpoint what is really bothering them (Menninger et al. 1962). They may also be highly ambivalent about giving up their symptoms because psychiatric illness is somehow always a workable adaptation. Finally, psychiatric patients are often embarrassed about their symptoms and may conceal information to make a good impression (MacKinnon and Michels 1971).

Another major difference between medical history taking and psychodynamic interviewing is the interrelationship of diagnosis and treatment. A physician evaluating a patient for appendicitis approaches the interview with a clear mind-set—diagnosis precedes treatment. In the psychodynamic interview, however, any distinction between diagnosis and treatment would be artificial (MacKinnon and Michels 1971). The dynamic psychiatrist approaches the interview with the understanding that the manner in which the history is taken may in and of itself be therapeutic. The dynamic view, which intimately links diagnosis and treatment, is empathic in the sense that it takes into account the patient's perspective. As Menninger et al. (1962) noted: "The patient comes to be *treated* and everything that is done for him, so far as he is concerned, is treatment, whatever the doctor may call it. In a sense, therefore, treatment always *precedes* diagnosis" (p. 3).

A third distinction between medical and psychodynamic interviewing lies in the dimensions of activity and passivity. To a large extent patients are passive participants in the medical diagnostic process. The patient complies with the physician's evaluation by cooperatively answering questions. The physician, however, must fit together the pieces of the diagnostic puzzle to arrive at a definitive diagnosis. The dynamic psychiatrist tries to avoid this division of roles. Instead, the dynamic approach involves actively engaging the patient as a *collaborator* in an exploratory process (Shevrin and Shectman 1973). The patient is viewed as someone with a great deal to contribute to the ultimate diagnostic understanding. If a patient begins an interview with anxiety, the psychiatrist does not try to eliminate it to facilitate the interview. On the contrary, the psychiatrist might attempt to engage the patient in a collaborative search for the origins of the anxiety with such questions as: "What concerns about this interview might cause you to be anxious right now?"; "Does this situation remind you of any similar anxiety-provoking situations in the past?"; or "Have you heard anything about me or about psychiatrists in general that might contribute to your anxiety?"

In a productive dynamic interview, the psychiatrist will elicit information regarding symptoms and history that allow for a descriptive diagnosis. To promote more openness on the part of the patient, however, psychiatrists must guard against an overemphasis on diagnostic labeling that precludes the unfolding of the complex relationship between doctor and patient. MacKinnon and Michels (1971) warned that "the interview that is oriented only toward establishing a diagnosis gives the patient the feeling that he is a specimen of pathology being examined, and therefore actually inhibits him from revealing his problems" (pp. 6–7).

A fourth difference between the medical and the dynamic orientation in clinical interviewing revolves around the selection of relevant data. Reiser (1988) expressed alarm at the tendency of contemporary psychiatric residents to stop the data collection after eliciting a symptom inventory that satisfies a descriptive diagnostic category and that allows for pharmacotherapeutic prescription. He warned that a DSM (American Psychiatric Association 1952) diagnosis is only one aspect of the diagnostic process and that the residents' lack of interest in understanding the patient as a person forms an obstacle to establishing a therapeutic relationship. For dynamic psychiatrists, the intrapsychic life of the patient is a crucial part of the data pool.

Another unique aspect of the psychodynamic interview is the emphasis on the doctor's feelings during the process. The surgeon or internist who notes feelings of anger, envy, lust, sadness, hatred, or admiration views these feelings as annoyances that interfere with evaluating the illness. The typical physician suppresses these feelings in the service of maintaining objectivity and proceeding with the examination. For the dynamic psychiatrist, such feelings constitute crucial diagnostic information. They tell the clinician something about what reactions the patient elicits in others. These considerations lead us directly to two of the most important aspects of the psychodynamic assessment—transference and countertransference.

Transference and Countertransference

Given the fact that transference is active in every significant relationship, you can be certain that transference elements exist from the first encounter between doctor and patient. Indeed, transference may even develop before the initial contact (Thomä and Kächele 1987). After making the first appointment, the soon-to-be patient may begin attributing qualities to the psychiatrist based on bits of factual information, previous experiences with psychiatrists, media portrayals of psychiatrists, positive or negative experiences with other physicians in the past, or general attitudes toward authority figures. One young man who first met his psychiatrist in the waiting room exclaimed, "Why, you're not at all like I expected you to be!" When the psychiatrist asked the patient to elaborate, the young man explained that the psychiatrist's name evoked images of a distinguished elderly man, and he was shocked at the youth of the actual psychiatrist.

Transference is a critical dimension of the evaluation because it profoundly affects the patient's cooperation with the doctor. Patients who view doctors as stern, disapproving parents, for example, will be much less forthcoming with embarrassing aspects of their history. Likewise, patients who view psychiatrists as intrusive busybodies may stubbornly withhold information and refuse to cooperate in the interview. Psychiatrists who address the transference distortions early in the interview may remove obstacles to effective history taking.

During the first few minutes of a consultation with a psychiatrist, one patient was struggling to overcome his inhibitions about talking. The psychiatrist asked if any of his actions or comments made it difficult for the patient to talk. The patient confided that he had harbored the notion that psychiatrists were like mind readers and that he needed to be wary of what he did or said in their presence. The psychiatrist replied humorously, "I'm afraid we're not that good." Both laughed, and the patient found it much easier to open up during the rest of the interview.

By definition, transference is a repetition. The feelings associated with a figure from the past are being repeated with the psychiatrist in the present situation. This premise implies that transference patterns in a clinical interview provide glimpses of significant relationships from the patient's past. The patient's view of the examiner and the patient's feelings toward the examiner are somehow repetitions. Furthermore, these repetitions also reveal a good deal about the patient's current significant relationships. Since transference is ubiquitous, the same patterns from the past are repeated again and again in all the patient's relationships. For example, a woman patient came to a psychiatrist, complaining that men seemed uninterested in her. In response to her psychiatrist's inquiries, she was able to link this feeling of being neglected with her childhood perception that her father ignored her. When the psychiatrist looked at his clock late in the interview, she accused him of not paying attention to her—just like all other men.

To keep from labeling all the patient's reactions to the doctor as transference, psychiatrists must keep in mind that the patient-doctor relationship is always a mixture of transference and a real relationship. The psychiatrist who glanced at his clock provided a kernel of reality to the patient's transference fear that yet another man was losing interest in her. Psychodynamic assessment requires continuous self-monitoring throughout the diagnostic process. The psychiatrist accused of being inattentive must question whether he really is feeling boredom (and conveying it to the patient) or whether the patient is distorting the situation. If boredom is the problem, then the psychiatrist needs to determine whether his interest is waning because of interference from his own issues, or because the patient is doing something to evoke inattentiveness, or both.

These considerations are, of course, countertransference concerns. The conceptual framework of the dynamic interview is that it involves two persons (dare I say two patients?). Each brings a personal past into the present and projects aspects of internal self- and object-representations onto the other (Langs 1976). It is commonplace for dynamic psychiatrists to find themselves relating to a patient as though the patient were someone else. The psychiatrist might note a striking physical resemblance between a patient and someone from the past. As a result, the psychiatrist then attributes qualities of the past figure to the patient.

An ongoing task for dynamic psychiatrists is to differentiate those feelings and reactions toward the patient that arise from countertransference in the narrow sense from those that arise from countertransference in the broad sense (see Chapter 1). The narrow sense involves instances where the psychiatrist's own past is being repeated in the present, while the broader definition of countertransference involves instances in which the psychiatrist's strong feelings are evoked by behavior in the patient that produces similar feelings in virtually everyone with whom the patient has contact (Hamilton 1988; Kernberg 1965). Often these two varieties of countertransference do not appear in pure form, and differentiating between the two may be a formidable task. Because the ability to make this distinction depends greatly on familiarity with one's own internal world, most dynamic psychiatrists find a personal treatment experience (either psychoanalysis or psychotherapy) of enormous value in monitoring and understanding countertransference.

The model of projective identification (see Chapter 2) is useful for understanding the broad form of countertransference (i.e., emotional reactions produced in everyone the patient encounters). Because of various provocative behaviors in the patient, the psychiatrist might begin to feel like a projected self- or object-representation of the patient. One child psychiatrist, for example, observed that she could always tell when she was dealing with a victim of child abuse because she would develop an irrational feeling of anger, accompanied by an impulse to abuse the child. In other words, an internal abusing object in the child would be projected onto the psychiatrist, who in turn felt like the internal object because of the child's obnoxious and provocative behavior. Indeed, psychiatrists can diagnose a projective identification process when they detect that they are feeling or behaving in an alien or atypical manner toward their patients. Awareness of such feelings can help the psychiatrist understand the nature of the patient's internal object world and the typical problems in the patient's interpersonal relationships.

Approaches to History Taking

The history-taking aspect of the interview should involve two simultaneous goals: a descriptive diagnosis and a dynamic diagnosis. To accomplish these goals, the psychiatrist must maintain a flexible interviewing style that shifts from a structured pursuit of specific facts (e.g., about symptoms, family history, stressors, duration of illness) to an unstructured posture of listening to the natural ebb and flow of the patient's thought processes. Throughout both structured and unstructured portions of the history taking, the examiner makes a fine-tuned assessment of the patient-doctor interaction. Kernberg (1984) characterized one form of the dynamic interview—the structural interview—as a systematic movement from a symptom inventory to an active focus on defensive operations in the here-and-now relationship with the interviewer.

Initially the interviewer must simply create an atmosphere in which the patient feels free to talk. Beginning psychiatric residents commonly err in aggressively interrogating patients only to elicit history and symptoms. Another common error is the assumption of a pseudoanalytic attitude of abstinence, virtual silence, and passivity. Residents who may be warm and personable individuals suddenly become stiff, overly formal, and cold when they interview a patient. The interviewer will get much further by becoming an active participant in the relationship—by warmly and empathically seeking to understand the patient's point of view. This posture, while dynamically informed, departs from the classical view of the analyst as a nongratifying, neutral observer (Viederman 1984). A dynamic interview is not a psychoanalytic therapy session.

The psychiatrist can learn a great deal by allowing the patient to ramble freely for a while. Initial comments should be designed to facilitate this rambling (e.g., "tell me more," "please go on," "I can understand your feeling that way," or "that must have been upsetting"). Besides eliciting essential historical and mental status data, interviewers can discern patterns of association that may reveal significant unconscious connections. The order in which events, memories, concerns, and other psychological issues are verbalized is never random. Mathematicians have long known that it is impossible for any individual to generate prolonged sequences of random numbers. Within a short time, the numbers will fall into meaningful patterns. The mind prefers order to chaos. So it is with the verbalizations of the patient. Deutsch and Murphy (1955) based their approach to interviewing—known as "associative anamnesis"—on this principle:

> The method . . . consists in recording not only what the patient said, but also how he gave the information. It is of consequence not only that the patient tells his complaints, but also in what phase of the interview, and in which connection he introduces his ideas, complaints, and recollections of his somatic and emotional disturbances. (p. 19)

Although patients may be consciously baffled by their symptoms, the ordering of their associations may provide clues to unconscious connections. For example, a 31-year-old man who came with his parents for a psychiatric evaluation began the morning with a psychiatrist while his parents met privately with a social worker in a different building. The young man began by explaining that he had been unable to keep a job. He suddenly became overwhelmed with anxiety because he was uncertain of his parents' whereabouts. The psychiatrist clarified that they were with the social worker in the office building next door. The patient asked if he could use the psychiatrist's phone to call them. The psychiatrist silently noted that the patient's anxiety about his parents' location followed immediately on the heels of his complaint of not being able to hold a job. He asked the patient if the two concerns were connected. After a moment's reflection, the patient acknowledged that when he was away from his parents at work, he worried that something would happen to them. This interchange led to a productive discussion about the patient's concerns that his growing up and becoming independent would be destructive to his parents.

Because of the central role of developmental theory in dynamic psychiatry, a developmental history must be part of a thorough dynamic assessment. Was the patient a product of an unwanted pregnancy? Did the patient's birth occur after an older sibling had died? Did the patient achieve developmental milestones such as talking, walking, and sitting up at the appropriate ages? Were there traumatic separations or losses during the formative years? Obtaining such invaluable information often necessitates interviews of parents and other family members—either by the psychiatrist or by a social worker associated with the psychiatrist. Obviously, patients will be unable to recall some significant events of childhood and will distort others.

Despite their imperfect memories for historical events, patients should nevertheless be engaged in a review of childhood and adolescent development. A fundamental principle of the dynamic interview is that the past is repeating itself in the present. To enlist the patient as a collaborator in the diagnostic process, the interviewer can encourage the patient's curiosity about links between historical events and present-day feelings. A variety of open-ended questions serve to establish this collaborative partnership: "Does the anxiety you're experiencing today remind you of feelings you've had at any time in your past?" "Were there any events in your childhood that may have contributed to your feeling as an adult that women cannot be trusted?" "Do your current marital problems have any similarities with problems you've had in other relationships in the past?" As the patient begins to collaborate in the search for links between past and present, the examiner should note particular historical events and periods that seem important to the patient. Similarly, conspicuous omissions from the developmental history are also noteworthy. Does the patient, for example, focus exclusively on one parent as the cause of all current problems while omitting any reference to the other parent? What about the patient's cultural and religious background? How do these factors affect family relationships and the acceptability of emotional problems?

After several minutes of open-ended questions designed to facilitate a free-flowing history of the present illness and family and developmental issues, the psychiatrist can then fill in the gaps with more specific, direct questions. These may be geared to the descriptive diagnosis (e.g., specific symptoms necessary for the DSM-IV [American

Psychiatric Association 1994] diagnosis, information about the duration of the illness, exclusions of other illnesses) or may be directed toward a more complete dynamic diagnosis (e.g., specific developmental traumas, relationship patterns, or recurrent fantasies and daydreams). As the patient fills in the gaps, the dynamic psychiatrist can begin to formulate hypotheses that link the patient's past relationships with current relationships and with emerging transference paradigms (Menninger 1958). In other words, how are repetitions of past relationship patterns creating problems in the present?

Axis IV of DSM-IV mandates that stressors be considered during the diagnostic appraisal of the patient. Events that precipitate an episode of illness are vital to both the descriptive and the dynamic diagnosis. Some researchers estimate that as many as 32% of psychiatric illness episodes are precipitated by stressful life events (Cooke and Hole 1983). However, careful history taking is essential when evaluating Axis IV because patients may distort their memory of a stressor's timing in an effort to retrospectively explain their illness or problems as directly attributable to an external event (Andrews and Tennant 1978).

Patients can nevertheless provide important dynamic information about their perception of the connections between events and symptoms. Again the examiner should think in terms of how issues from the past are evoked by stressors in the present. One female executive developed extraordinary anxiety after receiving a promotion. She identified the promotion as the stressor, but could not determine why it provoked anxiety, because she had sought the new job for several years. In the course of the interview, she frequently referred to her younger sister, who was divorced and supporting two children through a menial job. Further exploration of intense sibling rivalry that had existed between the sisters during childhood revealed that the executive's anxiety was related to guilt feelings. She was convinced that her promotion had been destructive to her sister. These feelings resonated with her childhood wish to triumph over her sister and be the only child in the eyes of their parents.

Holmes and Rahe (1967) have developed a scale that ranks the severity of stress in a number of different life events. Although such scales can help provide consensual estimates of the effects that accompany particular life events, the dynamic psychiatrist must approach each patient as a unique individual and not assume a priori that a certain life event has only one specific meaning. For example, one young man reacted to his father's death with a liberated sense that he was finally free to pursue his career without incessant criticism. Hence the stressor resulted in improved school performance and enhanced overall functioning.

In addition, the examiner should keep in mind that some stressors may operate at an unconscious level, preventing the patient from identifying any precipitating event when asked to do so. One function of the interview may be to work together to determine whether any stressors have been overlooked. Anniversary reactions, for example, are common stressors the patient may neglect. One chronically depressed patient became acutely suicidal on the anniversary of her brother's suicide. In another instance, when a happily married physician began having marital problems for no apparent reason, he called on a psychiatric colleague for advice. During the course of their phone conversation, the doctor suddenly realized that he was calling on the tenth anniversary of his divorce from his previous wife. This insight revealed that his current anger at his present wife was actually caused by his stormy relationship with his first wife.

The Mental Status Examination

Like descriptive psychiatrists, dynamic psychiatrists are interested in mental status data, but they approach the information somewhat differently. First, to the extent that it is reasonable and possible, they prefer to weave mental status questions into the fabric of the interview rather than to add them at the end in a list of formal mental status questions (MacKinnon and Michels 1971). Although some specific mental status questions should obviously be appended to the interview if they are not elicited during it, there is an advantage in minimizing the formal mental status examination. When these questions are brought into the body of the interview, the patient views distortions of perception, thought, and affect in a meaningful context. Moreover, in determining connections between such distortions and the illness, the patient becomes more involved as a collaborator rather than as merely a passive responder to questions, like a specimen under a microscope.

Orientation and perception.   A patient's orientation to time, place, and person is often clear in the course of history taking. To ask specific orientation questions of someone who is obviously well oriented is likely to disturb the rapport of the doctor-patient relationship. Hyper-alertness is a mental status finding that will also reveal itself without direct questioning. Significant perceptual symptoms such as auditory or visual hallucinations will often be evident at the beginning of the interview when the patient is asked to explain why psychiatric treatment is being sought. But the dynamic psychiatrist is interested in more than the presence or absence of hallucinations. If a patient hears voices, the psychiatrist wants to know what the voices say, under what circumstances they speak, whose voice it sounds like, and what the voices mean to the patient. One male paranoid schizophrenic patient always heard his father telling him that he would never amount to anything. His hallucinations correlated with his childhood experiences of never being able to do enough to please his father. Similarly, the multiply determined distortions of mind-body perception such as de-personalization may serve as windows onto intrapsychic conflicts and clashes between sets of internal object relations (Gabbard and Twemlow 1984).

Cognition.   The presence of a formal thought disorder will usually be clear from the history-taking portion of the interview. As alluded to earlier, even loose associations are connected idiosyncratically in the patient's mind. The examiner's task is to understand the nature of such connections. Delusions are also more likely to be elicited by open-ended historical questions than by specific questions about "false beliefs." The presence or absence of delusions is only part of the psychodynamic assessment; their meanings and functions are equally relevant. The grandiose delusions of the paranoid patient may serve to compensate for devastating feelings of low self-esteem.

Because cognition affects language and communication, the psychiatrist must also listen for parapraxes or slips of the tongue that reveal glimpses of the unconscious at work. A pregnant woman whose obstetrician referred her for a psychiatric consultation was resentful about seeing a psychiatrist, and at one point she exclaimed, "I don't want to be a psychiatric parent—I mean patient!" The examining psychiatrist could conclude from this parapraxis that the patient was highly ambivalent about becoming a mother.

The patient's manner of answering questions may reveal a good deal about his or her unconscious character style. The obsessive-compulsive patient may respond to questions with an overinclusive attention to detail, frequently asking the examiner to elaborate on specifically requested information. By contrast, the hysterical patient may be so completely uninterested in detail as to provide vague responses that frustrate the interviewer. The passive-aggressive patient may produce anger in the interviewer by asking for questions to be repeated and by generally thwarting attempts to elicit historical data. The paranoid patient may constantly read hidden meanings into the questions, thus placing the examiner on the defensive.

Determining the presence or absence of suicidal ideation is essential to any psychiatric evaluation. Suicidal patients should be asked outright if they have a suicide plan and if they have a support system of people they can talk to before acting impulsively. The psychodynamic assessment should discern the meaning of the contemplated suicide. Is there a reunion fantasy with a deceased loved one? Is suicide a vengeful act designed to devastate someone else just as that person once devastated the patient? Is suicide really designed to kill an internal object-representation that is hated and feared? Of the many possible solutions to a patient's problems, why is suicide so compelling?

Affect.   Observations about the patient's emotional states provide a gold mine of information about defense mechanisms. After all, the management of affect is perhaps the most important function of defenses. Patients who describe extraordinarily painful events in their lives without being moved in the least may be employing intellectualization. Hypomanic patients who assert that they always are in a good mood and are unusually jocular with the examiner may be using denial to defend against feelings such as grief and anger. Borderline patients who express contempt and hostility toward the key figures in their lives may be employing splitting to ward off any integration of good and bad feelings toward others. Mood, a subcategory of affect involving a sustained, internal feeling tone, should also be assessed. Exploration of moods with a patient often reveals that they are linked with significant self- and object-representations.

Action.   A wealth of information is communicated through nonverbal behavior in the clinical interview. What particularly sensitive subjects result in the patient's fidgeting? What topics evoke silence? What issues cause the patient to break off eye contact with the examiner? Despite the fact that patients attempt to conceal essential data from the examining psychiatrist, their nonverbal behaviors will consistently betray them. Freud made the following observation in 1905:

When I set myself the task of bringing to light what human beings keep hidden within them, not by the compelling power of hypnosis, but by observing what they say and what they show, I thought the task was a harder one than it really is. He that has eyes to see and ears to hear may convince himself that no mortal can keep a secret. If his lips are silent, he chatters with his finger-tips; betrayal oozes out of him at every pore. And thus the task of making conscious the most hidden recesses of the mind is one which it is quite possible to accomplish. (Freud 1905/1953, pp. 77–78)

Psychological Testing

Projective psychological tests, principally the Rorschach and the Thematic Apperception Test (TAT), may be extraordinarily useful adjuncts to the psychodynamic assessment. The Rorschach consists of 10 symmetrical inkblots that present ambiguous stimuli to the patient. In the face of this ambiguity, patients will reveal a great deal about themselves through their interpretations of the amorphous shapes within the inkblots. Highly sophisticated guides to Rorschach interpretations have systematized the responses according to a psychodynamic diagnostic understanding of the patient (Kwawer et al. 1980; Rapaport et al. 1968; Schafer 1954).

The TAT operates on a similar principle. A series of drawings or woodcuts, portraying persons and situations of varying degrees of ambiguity, allow patients a good deal of latitude in interpretation. Patients are asked to invent a story to describe each picture. In making up these stories, patients project their own fantasies, wishes, and conflicts into the pictures. Projective testing is especially useful for patients who are guarded and laconic in the psychiatric interview and therefore do not share their inner life freely with the psychiatrist. Many patients, however, will reveal so much about themselves in the course of the clinical interview that psychological testing is not necessary as an adjunct.

Physical and Neurological Examination

For obvious reasons, the patient's physical and neurological status is as important to the dynamic psychiatrist as it is to the descriptive psychiatrist. "The head bone is connected to the neck bone," so whatever goes wrong in the body will affect the brain—and vice versa. If the assessment is taking place in a hospital setting, dynamic psychiatrists may or may not perform their own physical and neurological examinations. If the assessment is of an outpatient in a private office, most dynamic psychiatrists prefer that an internist do the physical. Regardless of who does it, exploring the meaning of the physical is usually beneficial—both in terms of transference issues and in terms of patients' fantasies about their body. In any case, neither a descriptive nor a dynamic assessment can be complete without these data.

The Psychodynamic Diagnosis

At the completion of the psychodynamic assessment, the clinician should arrive at a descriptive diagnosis (based on DSM-IV criteria) and a psychodynamic diagnosis (based on an understanding of the patient and the illness). Although both diagnoses inform the treatment planning, the descriptive diagnosis is geared to the assignment of the correct label, while the psychodynamic diagnosis is viewed as a summary of understanding that goes beyond the label. Menninger et al. (1963) elegantly described the dynamic approach to diagnosis:

> This means diagnosis in a new sense, not the mere application of a label. It is not a search for a proper name by which one can refer to this affliction in this and other patients. It is diagnosis in the sense of understanding just how the patient is ill and how ill the patient is, how he became ill and how his illness serves him. From this knowledge one may draw logical conclusions regarding how changes might be brought about in or around the patient which would affect his illness. (pp. 6–7)

The descriptive diagnosis may assist clinicians in planning appropriate pharmacologic interventions. The dynamic diagnosis may facilitate the clinician's understanding of what the medication prescription means to the patient and whether compliance with the medication is likely to be a problem.

In this context, I want to emphasize that the usefulness of a dynamic diagnosis is not limited to patients whose prescribed treatment is dynamic psychotherapy. The therapeutic management of the patient's personality is an integral part of all psychiatric treatment that must always be considered in treatment planning (Perry et al. 1987).

Part of the dynamic diagnosis involves understanding how the five axes of DSM-IV interact with and influence one another. Because all illness grows out of a preexisting personality, consideration must be given to how the personality diagnosis on Axis II contributes to the Axis I syndrome. Obsessive-compulsive individuals, for example, often decompensate into a major depressive episode. Clinicians might therefore evaluate how the rigid and demanding superego of the obsessive-compulsive personality structure contributed to the self-loathing characteristic of the depression. This aspect of the diagnosis would not replace the contributions of biochemical and genetic factors to the depression but rather would work synergistically to provide a more complete understanding of the patient and the illness. Similarly, an Axis III diagnosis of carcinoma of the pancreas might contribute to an Axis I major depressive episode on a biological basis, but the patient's psychological reaction to the diagnosis of a malignancy might be another determinant of the depression. The patient who is diagnosed with narcissistic personality disorder on Axis II and panic disorder on Axis I might be unwilling to take medication for the panic disorder because the notion of having a major psychiatric disorder is too narcissistically injurious to tolerate.

As previously described in this chapter, Axis IV stressors, both obvious, conscious precipitants and hidden, unconscious ones, must also be evaluated in the dynamic diagnosis. Finally, it is helpful to assess how all the findings on the other four axes affect the Axis V level of functioning. Does the Axis I diagnosis account for the severity of the patient's functional impairment, or do characterological features on Axis II contribute to a lower level of functioning than is warranted by the Axis I diagnosis? A complete psychodynamic diagnosis also involves assessing the patient from the three major theoretical perspectives discussed in Chapter 2: ego psychology, object relations theory, and self psychology.

Characteristics of the Ego

A great deal can be learned about patients' overall ego strength from their work histories and their relationship patterns. Those who have been able to hold jobs and establish committed relationships for reasonably long periods are likely to have more resilient egos than those who have not.

The assessment of certain key ego functions (Bellak et al. 1973) can help psychiatrists understand a patient's strengths and weaknesses and thus enable them to prescribe the treatment program. How is the patient's reality testing? Is there an ability to distinguish what is internal from what is external, or is there a persistent pattern of delusional misperception? Is the patient's reality testing intact in structured situations but impaired in unstructured situations? What about the patient's impulse control? Is there sufficient ego to delay the discharge of impulses, or is the patient virtually driven by impulses to the point where there is danger to others or self? Judgment is another ego function that must be assessed. Can the patient adequately anticipate the consequences of actions?

In planning for the appropriate form of psychotherapy, psychiatrists should also determine the psychological mindedness of the patient. Does the patient see problems as having an internal origin, or are all difficulties externalized and blamed on others in the environment? Can the patient synthesize and integrate various bits of data and reflect on their connections to develop meaningful explanations for symptoms and interpersonal difficulties? Does the patient think in metaphors and analogies that allow for connections between various levels of abstraction? All these considerations aid in assessing the extent of psychological mindedness.

A major portion of ego assessment focuses on the defensive functioning of the ego. In the psychoanalytic setting, Waelder (1960) developed a series of questions that addresses the defensive operations of the patient. These same questions could be adapted to the dynamic assessment: *"What are the patient's desires?* What does the patient (unconsciously) want? And *of what is he afraid? . . . And when he is afraid, what does he do?"* (pp. 182–183). Pine (1990) has added additional questions to assess the relationship between drives and the ego's responses to the drives:

What wish is being expressed? what is the relation of the wish to consciousness? what is the fantasy? and how does it reflect a compromise among wish and defense and reality? how was the wish being defended against? and how effective/adaptive is the defense? can the particular anxiety seen be traced to this or that wish, ineffectively defended against? and can the particular guilt seen be understood in terms of the operation of conscience in relation to this or that wish? (pp. 44–45)

Pine also suggested that one should assess character in a similar manner by looking at the patient's characteristic defensive styles that are expressed as ego-syntonic modes of function. One can also assess the defense mechanisms on the continuum of immaturity to maturity described in Chapter 2. The patient who is able to use suppression and humor in the midst of a difficult situation is showing much greater ego strength than the patient who resorts to splitting and projective identification in the same situation.

Determining the ego's relationship to the superego is another vital part of an ego psychological assessment. Is the superego a rigid and ruthless overseer of the ego, or is there a flexibility and harmony in the relationship of superego to ego? Does the patient espouse realistic ideals, or is the patient driven by unreachable and fantastic goals? Are there antisocial tendencies in the patient characterized by an absent or underdeveloped superego? The answers to these questions also provide clues about the patient's childhood experiences with parental figures, since the superego is an internalized representation of those figures.

Object Relations

As an end result of the psychodynamic assessment, the clinician has information about the patient's interpersonal relationships in three contexts: childhood relationships, the real and transferential aspects of the relationship between the patient and the examining clinician, and current relationships outside the doctor-patient relationship. The nature of these relationships provides the psychiatrist with a good deal of information about the patient's position in family and social systems. Still needed, though, is an assessment of how the patient's family relationships influence the development of the clinical picture that brings the patient to the psychiatrist. Does an adolescent patient's symptomatic picture reflect the parents' marital problems? In other words, is the patient serving as a "carrier" of illness for the entire family?

Information about the patient's interpersonal relationships also tells a great deal about the nature of the patient's internal object relations. Interviews of family members and significant others can help sort out the extent of distortion inherent in the patient's view of other relationships. Certain easily discernible patterns seem to cut across all relationships. For example, does the patient always seem to end up as a masochistic partner in a sadomasochistic bond? Is the patient always taking care of others who are less functional and more in need of care-taking? Pine (1990) has developed a series of questions specifically targeted at object relations that can be mulled over by the clinician during the course of an interview:

> What old object relationship is being repeated? and which of the roles in the object relationship is the subject (the patient) enacting—his own or that of the other? or both? Is the patient behaving like the person he was? he wished to be in the parents' eyes? they wanted him to be? they were? he wished they were? And what early passive experiences are being repeated actively? (p. 47)

Determining the level of maturity of object relations is an integral part of this assessment. Does the patient experience others ambivalently as whole objects having both good and bad qualities? Alternatively, does the patient view others as either idealized (all good) or devalued (all bad)? Does the patient see others as need-gratifying part-objects who serve only one function for the patient rather than as separate persons with needs and concerns of their own? Finally, what about object constancy? Can the patient tolerate being apart from significant others by summoning up a soothing internal image of the person who is missed?

The Self

A thorough dynamic assessment must evaluate several aspects of the patient's self. In the broad framework of self psychology, psychiatrists should examine the durability and cohesiveness of the self. Is it prone to fragmentation in response to the smallest slight from a friend or colleague? Does the patient need to be in the spotlight continually to receive affirming responses from selfobjects?

The maturity of the patient's selfobjects should also be assessed. Are the patient's selfobject needs satisfied by a mutually gratifying relationship in the context of a long-term commitment?

In addition to self-esteem, the psychiatrist should also assess the patient's self-continuity. Is the patient much the same over time, regardless of external circumstances, or is there a generalized identity diffusion? Evidence for identity diffusion would indicate that different self-representations, split off from one another, are constantly jockeying for dominance over the total personality. Different self-representa-

tions would obviously arise in connection with different object-representations that are highly influenced by the interpersonal context at a
given moment. The boundaries of the self are also of interest. Can the
patient clearly differentiate his or her own mental contents from those
of others, or is there a general blurring of self-object boundaries? A
related aspect would be the patient's body perception. Are the patient's
body boundaries intact, or does the patient have to engage periodically
in self-mutilation to define the skin boundary? Are mind and body
viewed as connected over time, or are there episodes of depersonalization or out-of-body experience where the mind seems independent of
the body?

Explanatory Formulation

The different elements of the psychodynamic diagnosis enumerated
above are the basis of an explanatory formulation. This tentative hypothesis or working model illustrates how the elements interact to create the clinical picture presented by the patient. This summary
statement, sometimes referred to as a psychodynamic formulation
(Perry et al. 1987), may also include comments on the biological aspects of the illness and on treatment implications. Although the formulation is intended to explain the patient's condition, it does not have to
explain everything. It should succinctly highlight the major issues, especially their relevance to treatment planning.

   With some patients, one theoretical model will appear to have more
explanatory value than the other two. With other patients, however, all
three theoretical perspectives may seem useful in conceptualizing various aspects of the patient's psychopathology. As suggested in Chapter
2, clinicians should be open-minded to all three theoretical frameworks
and should embrace a "both/and" rather than an "either/or" attitude.
The formulation should also be approached with the understanding
that it undergoes continual modification as treatment proceeds. In dynamic psychiatry, diagnosis and treatment are always evolving together. A sample explanatory formulation illustrates these points:

> Ms. B, a 33-year-old single woman employed as a librarian, came to
> the hospital in the midst of a psychotic episode with paranoid fea-
> tures. She had become convinced that her mother was plotting to kill
> her, and she had barricaded herself in the apartment she shared with
> her brother.

When Ms. B reorganized after a few doses of haloperidol, she presented herself as a cheerful, Pollyannaish person, commenting, "I have no anger in me." She said she felt fine and wanted to go home. Her mother was glad to see her "back to normal," but expressed concern because Ms. B's brother was still at the apartment. He had apparently exploited his sister by moving in, eating her food, and living rent-free for the past several weeks.

According to her mother, Ms. B lived an isolated existence and had few interpersonal contacts outside several superficial relationships at work. Moreover, the patient's mother revealed that Ms. B had had one previous psychotic episode 18 months earlier when her brother had moved in with her under the same exploitative circumstances. Ms. B's mother also reported a family history of bipolar affective disorder.

The following explanatory formulation was developed:

Ms. B inherited a diathesis toward bipolar affective disorder. Her cyclic psychotic episodes, which appeared schizophreniform, were possibly a variant of bipolar illness. After stabilizing the psychosis with haloperidol, the psychiatrist could taper off that medication, and consider replacing it with lithium prophylaxis.

When Ms. B is nonpsychotic, her adjustment comes at the expense of massive denial of all negative feelings, especially anger, and results in a schizoid existence. The stressor of having her brother living parasitically in her apartment provoked so much anger in Ms. B that she could not maintain her usual defensive posture. Under pressure of this intense affect, she regressed to the paranoid-schizoid position, where an unacceptable self-representation harboring angry, murderous feelings was split off and projected onto her mother. After remission of Ms. B's psychosis with medication, she reintrojected the self-representation, which once again became buried under her denial.

The patient lacks the psychological mindedness to see any problems to work on in an exploratory therapy process. Casework or family therapy is therefore needed to remove the stressor (i.e., the brother) and to allow Ms. B to resume her previous adjustment with a follow-up regimen of medication and supportive psychotherapy to maintain her defenses.

While dynamic in its conceptualization, this formulation is in keeping with the biopsychosocial model of psychiatry championed by Engel

(1977), Fink (1988), and others in that it takes into account genetic predisposition, social-familial influences, and intrapsychic factors.

Conclusion

Table 3–1 summarizes the steps involved in a thorough psychodynamic assessment. In the final analysis, the purpose of the assessment is to inform and guide the overall treatment planning. The case of Ms. B illustrates how a psychodynamic diagnosis, and particularly an ex-

---

Table 3–1. The psychodynamic assessment

Historical data
- Present illness with attention to associative linkages and Axis IV stressors
- Past history with emphasis on how the past is repeating itself in the present
  —Developmental history
  —Family history
  —Cultural/religious background

Mental status examination
- Orientation and perception
- Cognition
- Affect
- Action

Projective psychological testing (if necessary)

Physical and neurological examination

The psychodynamic diagnosis
- Descriptive DSM-IV diagnosis
- Interactions among Axes I–V
- Characteristics of the ego
  —Strengths and weaknesses
  —Defense mechanisms and conflicts
  —Relationship to superego
- Quality of object relations
  —Family relationships
  —Transference-countertransference patterns
  —Inferences about internal object relations
- Characteristics of the self
  —Self-esteem and self-cohesiveness
  —Self-continuity
  —Self-boundaries
  —Mind/body relationship
- Explanatory formulation using above data

---

planatory formulation, can be useful even when dynamic psychotherapy is contraindicated. The treatment is nevertheless dynamically informed. The dynamic assessment assists all aspects of treatment planning. An evaluation of ego functions can contribute to a decision regarding whether an individual should be an inpatient or an outpatient. For example, the extent of impulse control may be a crucial variable in deciding whether a patient should be admitted in the first place and, if so, when the patient can be discharged. A dynamic understanding of their patients can help clinicians decide whether their patients would accept a recommendation for sex therapy, behavior modification, family therapy, or group therapy. Finally, each patient's compliance with any medication regimen will be affected by that particular patient's characterological substrate. The cases discussed in subsequent chapters will illustrate how other theoretical models can be used in developing a formulation and how the dynamic assessment of the patient guides the treatment planning.

References

American Psychiatric Association: Diagnostic and Statistical Manual: Mental Disorders. Washington, DC, American Psychiatric Association, 1952

American Psychiatric Association: Diagnostic and Statistical Manual of Mental Disorders, 4th Edition. Washington, DC, American Psychiatric Association, 1994

Andrews G, Tennant C: Editorial: life event stress and illness. Psychol Med 8:545–549, 1978

Bellak L, Hurvich M, Gedimen HK: Ego Functions in Schizophrenics, Neurotics, and Normals: A Systematic Study of Conceptual, Diagnostic, and Therapeutic Aspects. New York, Wiley, 1973

Cooke DJ, Hole DJ: The aetiological importance of stressful life events. Br J Psychiatry 143:397–400, 1983

Deutsch F, Murphy WF: The Clinical Interview, Vol I: Diagnosis: A Method of Teaching Associative Exploration. New York, International Universities Press, 1955

Engel GL: The need for a new medical model: a challenge for biomedicine. Science 196:129–136, 1977

Fink PJ: Response to the presidential address: is "biopsychosocial" the psychiatric shibboleth? Am J Psychiatry 145:1061–1067, 1988

Freud S: Fragment of an analysis of a case of hysteria (1905), in The Standard Edition of the Complete Psychological Works of Sigmund Freud, Vol 7. Translated and edited by Strachey J. London, Hogarth Press, 1953, pp 1–122

Gabbard GO, Twemlow SW: With the Eyes of the Mind: An Empirical Analysis of Out-of-Body States. New York, Praeger, 1984

Hamilton NG: Self and Others: Object Relations Theory in Practice. Northvale, NJ, Jason Aronson, 1988

Holmes TH, Rahe RH: Social Readjustment Rating Scale. J Psychosom Res 11:213–281, 1967

Kernberg OF: Notes on countertransference. J Am Psychoanal Assoc 13:38–56, 1965

Kernberg OF: Severe Personality Disorders: Psychotherapeutic Strategies. New Haven, CT, Yale University Press, 1984

Kwawer JS, Lerner HD, Lerner PM, et al (eds): Borderline Phenomena and the Rorschach Test. New York, International Universities Press, 1980

Langs RJ: The Bipersonal Field. New York, Jason Aronson, 1976

MacKinnon RA, Michels R: The Psychiatric Interview in Clinical Practice. Philadelphia, PA, WB Saunders, 1971

Menninger KA: Theory of Psychoanalytic Technique. New York, Basic Books, 1958

Menninger KA, Mayman M, Pruyser PW: A Manual for Psychiatric Case Study, 2nd Edition. New York, Grune & Stratton, 1962

Menninger KA, Mayman M, Pruyser PW: The Vital Balance: The Life Process in Mental Health and Illness. New York, Viking Press, 1963

Perry S, Cooper AM, Michels R: The psychodynamic formulation: its purpose, structure, and clinical application. Am J Psychiatry 144:543–550, 1987

Pine F: Drive, Ego, Object, and Self: A Synthesis for Clinical Work. New York, Basic Books, 1990

Rapaport D, Gill MM, Schafer R: Diagnostic Psychological Testing, Revised Edition. Edited by Holt RR. New York, International Universities Press, 1968

Reiser MF: Are psychiatric educators "losing the mind?" Am J Psychiatry 145:148–153, 1988

Schafer R: Psychoanalytic Interpretation in Rorschach Testing: Theory and Application. New York, Grune & Stratton, 1954

Shevrin H, Shectman F: The diagnostic process in psychiatric evaluations. Bull Menninger Clin 37:451–494, 1973

Thomä H, Kächele H: Psychoanalytic Practice, Vol 1: Principles. Translated by Wilson M, Roseveare D. New York, Springer-Verlag, 1987

Viederman M: The active dynamic interview and the supportive relationship. Compr Psychiatry 25:147–157, 1984

Waelder R: Basic Theory of Psychoanalysis. New York, International Universities Press, 1960

Chapter 4

Treatments in Dynamic Psychiatry I: Individual Psychotherapy

Proficiency at individual psychotherapy is perhaps the hallmark of the dynamic psychiatrist. Evolving as it does from psychoanalysis, dynamic psychiatry understandably emphasizes the nuances of the healing relationship between psychotherapist and patient. Space considerations here limit us to a brief overview of the general principles derived from the vast literature on individual psychotherapy. Specific applications of those principles will be demonstrated and explicated in Sections II and III. Readers who are interested in a more comprehensive discussion of individual psychotherapy should consult any of several outstanding texts (Basch 1980; Chessick 1974; Dewald 1964, 1971; Fromm-Reichmann 1950; Luborsky 1984; Ogden 1982; Roth 1987).

The Expressive-Supportive Continuum

Psychotherapy modeled on the technical principles of formal psychoanalysis has been designated by a number of different names: expressive, dynamic, psychoanalytically oriented, insight oriented, exploratory, uncovering, and intensive, to name a few. This form of treatment, geared to analyzing defenses and uncovering the dynamically repressed material in the unconscious, has traditionally been viewed as wholly different from another entity known as supportive psychotherapy. The latter, which is more oriented to suppressing unconscious conflict and bolstering defenses, has been widely regarded as inferior to expressive therapy. This tendency is reflected in the clinical maxim that has guided psychotherapists for years: "Be as expressive as you can be, and as supportive as you have to be" (Wallerstein 1986, p. 688).

A number of authors have recently expressed concern about this traditional dichotomy (Pine 1976, 1986; Wallerstein 1986; Werman 1984). One problem with the distinction is the implication that supportive psychotherapy is not psychoanalytically oriented. In practice, supportive psychotherapy is guided by psychoanalytic understanding every step of the way. Moreover, the dichotomy portrays expressive psychotherapy and supportive psychotherapy as highly discrete entities when, in fact, they rarely occur in pure form anywhere (Wallerstein 1986; Werman 1984). Finally, the value distinction associated with the greater prestige of expressive psychotherapy or psychoanalysis has always carried with it the assumption that change achieved as a result of insight or intrapsychic conflict resolution is somehow superior to that achieved through supportive techniques. No hard data support this assumption; the changes achieved by expressive psychotherapy have not been proven in any way superior to or more durable than those achieved by supportive psychotherapy (Wallerstein 1986).

At the conclusion of a monumental study of 42 patients treated in the Menninger Foundation Psychotherapy Research Project, Wallerstein (1986) determined that all forms of psychotherapy contain a mixture of expressive and supportive elements and that changes achieved by the supportive elements are in no way inferior to those achieved by the expressive elements. Rather than regarding expressive psychotherapy and supportive psychotherapy as two distinct modalities of treatment then, we should view psychotherapy as taking place on an expressive-supportive continuum, which is in closer keeping with the reality of clinical practice and with empirical research. With certain patients and at certain points in the therapy, the therapy will be weighted more heavily toward expressive elements, whereas with other patients and at other times, the therapy will require more attention to supportive elements. As Wallerstein (1986) noted, "All proper therapy is always both expressive and supportive (in different ways), and the question at issue at all points in every therapy should be that of expressing *how* and *when,* and supporting *how* and *when*" (p. 689).

Individual psychotherapy geared to this continuum might best be termed *expressive-supportive* or *supportive-expressive.* Even psychoanalysis, situated at the most extreme point on the expressive end of the continuum, contains supportive elements associated with the treatment structure itself and the collaboration of analyst and patient to achieve certain goals (Luborsky 1984); meanwhile, most supportive psychotherapies at the opposite end of the continuum do provide insight and understanding from time to time. Hence the effective dynamic therapist will shift flexibly back and forth along the expressive-supportive continuum, depending on the needs of the patient at a given moment in the psychotherapy process.

The concept of the expressive-supportive continuum provides a framework for considering the goals, characteristics, and indications for individual psychotherapy. Each of these elements changes accordingly as we move back and forth along the continuum.

Goals of Expressive-Supportive Psychotherapy

The ultimate goals of psychoanalysis and those treatments weighted toward the expressive end of the continuum involve the acquisition of insight, which may be defined as the capacity to understand the unconscious meanings and origins of one's symptoms and behavior. Although Freud never used the term *insight,* he did define the goal of analysis as making conscious what is unconscious, which is certainly a significant aspect of insight. In Freud's early clinical case reports, insight came through dramatic catharsis or abreaction, much the way it does in Hollywood portrayals of psychotherapeutic cures (K. Gabbard and G. O. Gabbard 1987). When Joanne Woodward in *The Three Faces of Eve,* for example, has the blazing flash of insight that her multiple personality disorder was caused by the repressed memory of having to kiss her dead grandmother, she is miraculously and dramatically cured. In real-life therapy, however, insight through catharsis is rare. Ordinarily, insight is gained gradually as resistances are methodically eroded through the therapist's interventions.

Intimately related to insight is the goal of conflict resolution. A conflict is resolved when the nature of the defense and the underlying wish are understood and the wish is renounced, or at least attenuated, making the defense no longer necessary. Classically, conflict resolution refers to oedipal conflict. Another way to view this goal is as greater ego mastery over the id or, as Freud (1933/1964) put it, "where id was, there ego shall be" (p. 80).

One distinctive aspect of psychotherapies that are highly expressive is that the therapist avoids an intense investment in curing patients of their symptoms. Instead, the therapist provides insight, with the goal of giving patients greater freedom of choice. The therapist attempts to broaden the possibilities but also to maintain a profound respect for the freedom and autonomy of the patients. Warning against excessive zeal, or *furor therapeuticus,* Khan (1987) admonished that "one must not try to cure a patient beyond his need and his psychic resources to sustain and live from that cure" (p. 18).

From an object relations standpoint, an improvement in the quality of one's relationships is a goal of psychotherapy, regardless of whether it is weighted toward the supportive or the expressive end of the continuum. As internal object relations change in the course of psychotherapy, one is able to perceive and relate to external persons differently. In contemporary practice, patients are much more likely to seek therapy because of dissatisfaction with the quality of their relationships than because of discrete symptoms, as they did in Freud's day. Hence, the importance of this goal cannot be overstated. One empirical study of analysis (Kantrowitz et al. 1987) demonstrated through projective psychological testing before and after treatment that analysis produces statistically significant improvement in the level and quality of object relations.

In self psychologically oriented psychotherapy, the goals involve strengthening the cohesiveness of the self and helping the patient choose more mature selfobjects, as alluded to in Chapter 2. In Kohut's (1984) words, "The essence of the psychoanalytic cure resides in a patient's newly acquired ability to identify and seek out appropriate selfobjects as they present themselves in his realistic surroundings and to be sustained by them" (p. 77). In other words, the goal of self psychological therapy is to help patients shift their reliance from archaic and unrealistic selfobjects to more mature and appropriate selfobjects.

The goal of psychotherapy at the supportive end of the continuum is primarily to help the patient adapt to stresses while avoiding insight into unconscious wishes and defenses (Roskin 1982). The therapist hopes to strengthen defenses to facilitate the patient's adaptive capacity to handle the stresses of daily living. This goal often involves restoring a patient to a previous level of functioning that has been compromised by a crisis. Furthermore, since supportive techniques are often used in treating patients with serious ego weaknesses, ego building is a crucial aspect of supportive psychotherapies. For example, the therapist may serve as an auxiliary ego, helping patients to test reality more accurately or to anticipate consequences of their actions and thereby improve their judgment.

Duration of Expressive-Supportive Psychotherapy

The length of expressive-supportive psychotherapy is essentially independent of the expressive-supportive continuum. Therapies that are highly supportive or highly expressive can be either brief or long. In some cases, psychoanalysis may last well over 5 years, while some supportive processes may go on even longer. On the other hand, there are instances where just one supportive or expressive therapy session (or consultation) has been highly therapeutic.

The most useful distinction is not between expressive and supportive psychotherapies but rather between open-ended psychotherapy and brief or time-limited psychotherapy. For purposes of discussion, the open-ended variety will be considered in this section and brief psychotherapy will be considered later in this chapter in recognition of its separate evolution as a special form of therapy.

Frequency of Sessions

In contrast to the duration of therapy, the frequency of sessions tends to be highly correlated with the expressive-supportive continuum. As a general rule, a greater number of weekly sessions characterizes the expressive end of the continuum. Psychoanalysis, an extremely expressive treatment, is characterized by four or five sessions a week and is usually conducted with the patient lying on a couch while the analyst sits behind the couch. Toward the middle of the continuum, however, highly expressive forms of psychotherapy usually involve one to three sessions a week with the patient sitting in a chair facing the therapist. In contrast, psychotherapy with primarily supportive goals rarely takes place more than twice a week and ordinarily occurs once a week or less often. It is not uncommon for supportive processes to have a frequency of once a month.

The issue of frequency is connected with the role of transference in the psychotherapeutic process (to be discussed later in this chapter). Clinical experience has shown that transference intensifies as the frequency of sessions increases. Since the more expressive treatments focus on the transference, these therapists usually prefer to see their patients more than once a week. In contrast, supportive processes work with transference to a lesser extent and thus do not require more than one session a week. Also, while highly expressive treatments are almost invariably administered in 45- or 50-minute sessions, supportive processes tend to use time more flexibly. Certain patients who require more frequent supportive contacts with the therapist do better with two 25-minute sessions in a week than with one 50-minute session.

The reality of psychiatric practice is that practical matters may outweigh theoretical considerations in determining the frequency of sessions. Some patients may be able to afford only one session a week even though they might do better with three. Other patients, because of inconvenient work schedules or transportation problems, may be able to get to their therapist's office only once a week. Before accepting such limitations, however, the therapist should keep in mind that resistance often finds convenient hiding places. An investigation of these practical limitations may reveal that the patient has greater flexibility in regard to time and money than can be readily acknowledged.

Free Association

In the ideal psychoanalytic situation, free association is the major mode by which the patient communicates to the analyst. This requires patients to relax their usual control over their thought processes in an effort to say whatever comes to mind without censoring their words or thoughts. In actual practice, resistances inevitably intervene when patients try to free-associate. It is often asserted, only half jokingly, that when a patient is able to free-associate without interference from resistance, that patient may be ready for termination. Patients may also use free association itself as a resistance to focusing on a particular issue in their current life situation (Greenson 1967).

Free association is also useful in highly expressive therapies, although more selectively than in analysis. The therapist, for example, may ask the patient to associate to various elements of a dream to help both patient and therapist understand unconscious connections that make interpretation of the dream possible.

Free association is far less useful further along the continuum toward the more supportively based treatments. As Greenson (1967) pointed out, the process itself requires a mature and healthy ego to maintain a split between an observing ego and an experiencing ego. Ego-deficient patients who are prone to psychosis may become increasingly regressed if allowed to free-associate in a supportive process. Moreover, such patients often lack the ego capacity to reflect on their associations and to integrate them into a meaningful and coherent understanding of unconscious issues.

Neutrality

Neutrality is perhaps the most misunderstood aspect of psychotherapeutic technique. It is frequently misinterpreted to mean coldness or aloofness (Chessick 1981). Even in the most expressive treatments, emotional warmth is a necessary part of the therapeutic relationship. Similarly, concern for the patient's unique situation is essential to establish rapport. Greenson (1967) stressed that the patient in analysis deserves explanations of new or strange procedures, such as the therapist's declining to answer direct questions. This humaneness and empathy are part of any effective doctor-patient relationship.

Therapists who remove themselves from the interpersonal field of the therapy by assuming an aloof, nonparticipatory attitude diminish their effectiveness by closing themselves off to the experience of the patient's internal object world (Hoffman and Gill 1988). On the other hand, therapists who allow themselves to be "roped into" interactions with the patient allow themselves to experience the projective identification process (i.e., countertransference in the broad sense of identification with the patient's projected self- and object-representations). The ideal model would instead involve the therapist as a participant in the therapeutic process in a spontaneous yet transitory, disciplined, and partial way (Hoffman and Gill 1988; Racker 1968). After the interaction, because of having "been there," the therapist can reflect on and analyze the exchange with an increased empathic appreciation of what others go through in their interactions with the patient. Sandler (1976) noted that the therapist may become aware of countertransference feelings only *after* responding like one of the patient's projected internal objects. This response may be an entirely silent reflection on thoughts and feelings arising within the therapist.

Neutrality, then, in no way implies detachment or emotional deadness. It is more appropriately defined as a nonjudgmental position vis-à-vis the patient's intrapsychic world (i.e., equidistant from the id, the ego, the superego, and the demands of external reality [A. Freud 1936]). In other words, the therapist does not take sides in the conflicts between the intrapsychic agencies. This position is much less applicable farther along the continuum to supportive treatments. If the superego pressure from a particular patient is so severe that it results in a suicide attempt, the therapist must take sides against the superego and restrain or hospitalize the patient. Similarly, in the supportive treatment of patients who are unable to delay the impulsive discharge of raw aggression, the therapist must side against the id.

While Anna Freud's definition is clinically useful, it is stated purely in ego-psychological terms. More recently, Greenberg (1986) has redefined neutrality as a position equidistant between an old object from the patient's past and the new object of the therapist in the present. In other words, for the patient's internal object relations to be modified, the patient must experience the therapist both as someone from the past, so that the feelings toward that person can be worked through, and as a new object, so that new forms of relatedness are internalized.

Anonymity

Freud's (1912b/1958) injunction that the analyst should strive for the opacity of a mirror has led generations of analysts to scrupulously avoid any comment or action that would reveal information about themselves to their patients. In some cases, attention to anonymity has led analysts to lead a highly restricted, even cloistered, existence. The rationale has always been that divulging too much information about oneself will interfere with the development of the transference.

Nowadays, analysts tend to be somewhat less rigid and restrictive because of a growing awareness that patients' reactions to information about their analysts' personal lives can usually be analyzed and understood (Katz 1978). Moreover, various kinds of personal information about therapists are available in their offices. Photographs of family, artwork, books, and so forth provide glimpses of the therapist's true nature. The therapist's various reactions to material the patient brings to therapy are also revealing.

Finally, even overt factual information is frequently distorted by the patient's transference. For example, in a group therapy process led by two cotherapists, one cotherapist fell sound asleep in the middle of one session. For a while the patients continued to talk as if nothing had happened. Finally, one patient observed that the sleeping cotherapist was pretending to be asleep as a way of testing the group's reactions.

Although knowledge about the therapist can be dealt with therapeutically, therapists in expressively oriented treatments should nevertheless refrain from volunteering personal information. Such material is unlikely to be of much value to the treatment and may inhibit the patient's freedom to speak about whatever comes to mind. However, anonymity is less crucial in the more supportive treatments. Therapists who reveal that they share the personal interests of their patients may encourage the development of trust and a common ground for collaboration in supportive psychotherapy.

Interventions

The interventions made by the therapist can be placed in seven categories along an expressive-supportive continuum: 1) interpretation, 2) confrontation, 3) clarification, 4) encouragement to elaborate, 5) empathic validation, 6) advice and praise, and 7) affirmation (Figure 4–1). [This expressive-supportive continuum of interventions is derived from the work of the Menninger Clinic Treatment Interventions Project, consisting of the following investigators: Jon Allen, Ph.D.; Donald Colson, Ph.D.; Lolafaye Coyne, Ph.D.; Siebolt Frieswyk, Ph.D.; Glen O. Gabbard, M.D.; Leonard Horwitz, Ph.D.; and Gavin Newsom, M.S.W.]

1. *Interpretation.* In the most expressive forms of treatment, interpretation is regarded as the therapist's ultimate decisive instrument (Greenson 1967). In its simplest form, interpretation involves making something conscious that was previously unconscious. An interpretation is an explanatory statement that links a feeling,

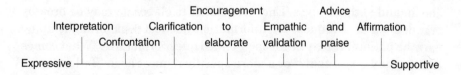

Figure 4–1. An expressive-supportive continuum of interventions.

thought, behavior, or symptom to its unconscious meaning or origin. For example, the therapist might say to a patient who is late, "Perhaps the reason you are late is that you were afraid I would react to the success you are now having the way your father reacted." Depending on the point in therapy and the patient's readiness to hear the interpretation, interpretations may focus on the transference (as in this example), on extratransference issues, on the patient's past or present situation, or on the patient's resistances or fantasies. As a general rule, the therapist does not address unconscious content via interpretation until the material is almost conscious and therefore relatively accessible to the patient's awareness.

2. *Confrontation.* The next most expressive intervention is confrontation, which addresses something the patient does not want to accept or identifies the patient's avoidance or minimization. A confrontation may be geared to clarifying how the patient's behavior affects others or to reflecting back to the patient a denied or suppressed feeling. Confrontation, which is often gentle, carries the unfortunate connotation in common parlance of being aggressive or blunt. The following example illustrates that confrontation is not necessarily forceful or hostile. In the last session of a long-term therapy process, one patient talked at great length about car problems he encountered on the way to the session. The therapist commented, "I think you'd rather talk about your car than face the sadness you're feeling about our last session."

3. *Clarification.* Farther along the continuum from expressive to supportive interventions, clarification involves a reformulation or pulling together of the patient's verbalizations to convey a more coherent view of what is being communicated. Clarification differs from confrontation because it lacks the element of denial or minimization. A clarification is aimed at helping the patient articulate something that is difficult to put into words.

4. *Encouragement to elaborate.* Closer to the middle of the continuum come interventions that are neither supportive nor expressive in and of themselves. Encouragement to elaborate may be broadly defined as a request for information about a topic brought up by the patient. It may be an open-ended question such as "What comes to mind about that?" or a more specific request as in "Tell me more about your father." Such interventions are commonly used in both the most expressive and the most supportive treatments.

5. *Empathic validation.* This intervention is a demonstration of the therapist's empathic attunement with the patient's internal state. A typically validating comment is "I can understand why you feel depressed about that" or "It hurts when you're treated that way." In the view of the self psychologists, empathic immersion in the patient's internal experience is essential, regardless of the location of the therapy on the expressive-supportive continuum (Kohut 1984; Ornstein 1986). When patients feel that the therapist understands their subjective experiences, they are more likely to accept interpretations.

6. *Advice and praise.* This category really includes two interventions that are linked by the fact that they both prescribe and reinforce certain activities. Advice involves direct suggestions to the patient regarding how to behave, while praise reinforces certain patient behaviors by expressing overt approval of them. An example of the former is "I think you should stop going out with that man immediately." An example of the latter is "I'm very pleased that you were able to tell him that you would not see him anymore." These comments are on the opposite end of the continuum from traditional psychoanalytic interventions because they are departures from neutrality and to some extent compromise the patient's autonomy in making decisions.

7. *Affirmation.* This simple intervention involves succinct comments in support of the patient's comments or behaviors, such as "Uh-huh" or "Yes, I see what you mean."

The vast majority of psychotherapeutic processes contain all these interventions at some time during the course of treatment. However, a therapy is classified as primarily expressive or primarily supportive based on which interventions predominate. These associations of interventions with the continuum are not ironclad, however. Anna Ornstein (1986) argued that empathic interpretations are the optimal therapeutic interventions for *all* classes of psychopathology, including the supportive psychotherapy of severely disturbed patients. Her empathic interpretations have three aspects: accepting patients as they are, understanding their situations, and offering explanations to help them gain insight into the origins of their difficulties. In this sense, Ornstein combined a predominantly supportive intervention (empathic validation) with a highly expressive intervention (interpretation). The essence of this self psychological approach is to convey to the patient that certain emotions or attitudes with negative connotations—such as hatred, envy, or greed—originate in completely understandable early life experiences marked by parental deprivation, neglect, or failures of empathy.

Pine (1986) advocated supportive techniques to "cushion the blow" of interpretations in the supportive therapy of fragile patients. Werman (1984, p. 83) proposed making "upward interpretations" of transference behavior or feelings to relate them to current situations rather than to early experiences, thereby preventing regression in patients with serious ego weakness. These interventions are the inverse of classical interpretations in that they provide conscious, rather than unconscious, explanations of the patient's behavior or feelings.

Transference

Freud was fond of saying that what made a therapy process psychoanalytic was a focus on transference and resistance. Certainly all forms of dynamically oriented psychotherapy pay careful attention to the state of the transference. However, the specific manner in which the transference is addressed (or left unaddressed) varies considerably, depending on the expressive-supportive dimension. In formal psychoanalysis, the highlighting and resolution of the transference is of paramount importance. Cooper (1987) noted: "Despite the diversity of analytic views that abound today, analysts seem to agree on the centrality of the transference and its interpretation in analytic process and cure, differing only in whether transference is everything or almost everything" (p. 78). Classically, the essence of the analytic process has been the development and resolution through interpretation of the transference neurosis, which may be defined as the reactivation in analysis of the patient's infantile oedipal situation with the analyst in the role of one or both parents.

Psychotherapy of a predominantly expressive nature also deals with strong transferences via interpretation, but in a more limited way (Roskin 1982). There is no attempt to be as pervasive or ambitious as in psychoanalysis. Those transference dispositions most closely related to the presenting problems are the focus of the interpretive effort. Also, the curative factors stem from forces other than interpretation alone (Chessick 1981). Wallerstein (1986) stressed, however, that on the basis of his research, the distinctions between psychoanalysis and expressive psychotherapy are blurred in actual practice.

The therapist must be careful to avoid a "blaming" approach to transference interpretation. *All* of a patient's observations about the therapist are not distortions. The patient may be responding to the therapist's real behaviors or attitudes, so the therapist must engage in ongoing self-scrutiny to sort out what is transference and what is the real contribution of the therapist to the interaction (Cooper 1987; Hoffman and Gill 1988). Attention to countertransference is the cornerstone of all treatment in dynamic psychiatry.

In therapies designed primarily to be supportive, the therapist is involved in the same process of monitoring transference developments and countertransference responses. The transference is noted inwardly but is usually not addressed or interpreted to the patient. The treatment goal in refraining from interpretation is to evoke a positive dependent transference without analyzing it (Wallerstein 1986). This transference attachment is the mechanism of the "transference cure," whereby the patient gets better to please the therapist. Although changes derived from this model have traditionally been disparaged as inferior to those stemming from conflict resolution, research (Horwitz 1974; Wallerstein 1986) suggests that they are, in actuality, stable and lasting.

Resistance

As noted in Chapter 1, resistance involves the emergence of the patient's characterological defenses within the therapeutic situation. In the more expressive therapies, analyzing and understanding resistance is part of the daily bread-and-butter work of the therapist. If, for example, the patient is consistently late to sessions or consistently silent during them, therapists may regard these resistances with interest and curiosity rather than devalue them as defiant and willful behavior. Resistances are not met with proscriptions or censure. Instead, the therapist enlists the patient's help in understanding the origins of the resistance and then addresses the resistance with interpretation.

Resistance related to transference issues is referred to as transference resistance. This involves interferences with the therapeutic work deriving from transference feelings or misperceptions. For example, a patient may feel unable to talk about masturbatory fantasies because he is convinced that his therapist disapproves of masturbation. To prevent receiving a negative judgment from the therapist, the patient therefore chooses to remain silent. In the parlance of object relations theory, a transference resistance may be understood as the patient's unconscious tendency to cling tenaciously to a particular internal object relationship. This may manifest itself as a therapeutic stalemate in which the therapist is repeatedly related to as someone else.

In Chapter 2, I noted the different perspective on resistance that is held by the self psychologists. They regard resistances as healthy psychic activities that safeguard the growth of the self (Kohut 1984). Rather than interpret them, they empathize with the patient's need for them. This view is in keeping with their concern that the classical approach of pursuing the content beneath resistance has moralistic overtones. However, this empathic approach has led some analysts to regard the self psychological technique as fundamentally supportive. It should also be noted that classical analytic technique does not include insensitive "attacks" on resistance, but rather patient understanding and examination.

As implied by the previous comments about self psychology, resistance is viewed as essential and adaptive in the context of predominantly supportive psychotherapy. Resistances are often manifestations of defensive structures that need to be bolstered as part of therapy. The therapist might even encourage resistance by pointing out to the patient that certain matters are too upsetting to discuss and should be postponed until a more auspicious moment. Similarly, delay mechanisms may be reinforced in the interest of supporting a weakened ego beset by impulses. When a patient's actions usurp verbalization of painful feelings, as in acting out, the therapist may be forced to set limits on self-destructive behavior rather than to interpret the resistance to talking, as in expressive treatment. This limit setting may involve hospitalization or insistence that the patient turn over illegal drugs to the therapist.

Working Through

Interpretations delivered by the expressive therapist rarely result in "Aha!" responses and dramatic cures. Typically, they are warded off by the forces of resistance and require frequent repetition by the therapist in different contexts. This repetitive interpretation of transference and resistance until the insight has become fully integrated into the patient's conscious awareness is known as "working through." Although the therapist's efforts are necessary, the patient does part of the work of accepting and integrating the therapist's insights between the actual therapy sessions (Karasu 1977). The triangle of insight (Menninger 1958) is a useful conceptual model for the process of working through (see Figure 4–2). Over the course of therapy, the therapist notes a certain pattern 1) in the patient's outside relationships and then links it to 2) transference patterns and to 3) antecedent relationships with family members. Eventually, the patient makes these unconscious linkages conscious. This model is related to what Luborsky (1984) referred to as the core conflictual relationship theme (CCRT). This theme usually involves a wish or a need (e.g., "I want to be spontaneous with others") that is in conflict with the control function of the ego or superego (e.g., "If I try, though, I may lose control, and therefore it's better to not even try"). This theme can be tracked throughout the course of therapy as it relates to the three sides of the triangle, and it can be pointed out to the patient each time it appears. As the patient sees the pattern come up again and again in new contexts, it becomes less alien, and the patient gains greater ego mastery over it.

This same model can be restated in terms of object relations theory. A recurrent self-object-affect constellation appears in the transference, in current extratransference relationships, and in memories of past relationships. In self psychological terms, the pattern may be the expectation of mirroring or the need to idealize others. Regardless of

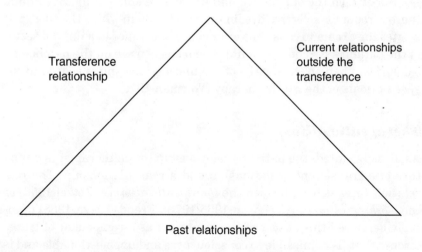

Figure 4–2. Triangle of insight (modeled after Menninger 1958).

which theoretical model is employed, however, all schools of thought view the reexperiencing of this central relationship pattern in the transference as critically important to a positive outcome. This working-through process is applied almost exclusively to treatments with a significant expressive component—it is rarely used to characterize primarily supportive processes.

Use of Dreams

In psychoanalysis and highly expressive forms of therapy, the interpretation of dreams is valued as "the royal road" to an understanding of the unconscious (S. Freud 1900/1953, p. 608). The patient's associations to the dream elements are used to understand the latent or hidden content of the dream that lies behind the manifest or overt content. The symbols of the dream can then be interpreted to help the patient further understand the unconscious issues in the dream.

In psychotherapies on the supportive end of the continuum, the therapist listens carefully to the patient's dream and thinks about it in the same way as would an expressive therapist. However, the therapist limits interpretive efforts to "upward interpretations" (Werman 1984, p. 83) that help the patient associate the dream with conscious feelings and attitudes toward the therapist as a real person and to other reality situations in waking life. Free association to the dream is not encouraged because it might lead to further regression.

In between the supportive and expressive ends of the continuum, there is room for selective dream interpretation in which the therapist relates the dream to conscious or unconscious issues in a limited sector of the patient's psychological life. The focus is more on the psychological surface than on the depths of the unconscious and is geared to the specific goals of the psychotherapy (Werman 1978).

Therapeutic Alliance

As already stated, the patient's relationship to the therapist is a mixture of a transference relationship and a real relationship. The real relationship has been termed the *therapeutic alliance* (Zetzel 1956) or the *working alliance* (Greenson 1965/1978). Freud (1912a/1958) originally described this aspect of the treatment as a component of transference that "is admissible to consciousness and unobjectionable and is the vehicle of success in psychoanalysis exactly as it is in other methods of treatment" (p. 105). He was aware that patients were unlikely to be able to use interpretations unless a proper rapport had been established (S. Freud 1913/1958). Greenson (1965/1978) later noted that a number of analytic stalemates were produced by the analyst's failure to address the development of the working alliance, which he defined as "the relatively nonneurotic, rational rapport which the patient has with his analyst" (p. 202).

After intensively studying Freud's notes from his work with the "Rat Man," Lipton (1977) was impressed by the real, cordial relationship that Freud maintained with patients. This warm and genuine relationship formed an envelope outside psychoanalytic technique within which the treatment process unfolded. Lipton argued that the silent, constricted model of the analyst, which has come to be termed classical, is a serious distortion of the way Freud actually practiced.

Major research efforts on the therapeutic alliance have confirmed its influence on the process and outcome of psychotherapy (Frieswyk et al. 1986; Hartley and Strupp 1983; Horwitz 1974; Luborsky et al. 1980; Marziali et al. 1981). Much of this research points to the strength of the therapeutic alliance as a dominant factor in the outcome of a broad range of therapies (Bordin 1979; Hartley and Strupp 1983; Luborsky et al. 1980). These studies also suggest that the nature of the therapeutic alliance in the opening phase of psychotherapy is perhaps the best predictor of the outcome of that therapy.

One application of this extensive research is that in all psychotherapies, regardless of their point on the expressive-supportive continuum, therapists must attend early on to the establishment and maintenance of the therapeutic alliance. This focus does not require the formation of a positive transference that will not allow the expression of negative feelings. Rather, therapists must help their patients quickly identify their treatment goals and then must ally themselves with the healthy aspects of their patients' egos that are striving to reach those goals. Patients will then experience their therapists as collaborators who are working *with* them rather than *against* them. When negative transference feelings enter the process, they can be examined in the context of the therapeutic alliance rather than be allowed to disrupt treatment. When working more supportively with patients with fragile egos, therapists find that the alliance is more difficult to develop and maintain (G. O. Gabbard et al. 1988; Horwitz 1974). The borderline patient's chaotic transference reactions, for example, interfere with the formation of an alliance, and it is a major therapeutic accomplishment for the patient to eventually be able to perceive the therapist as a helpful person collaborating on common goals (Adler 1979).

Mechanisms of Change

The mechanism of change in the more expressive forms of psychotherapy is one of the most controversial issues in the field. Much of the debate revolves around whether change results from the judicious use of explanatory interpretations or from the therapeutic relationship itself (Hamilton 1988). The classical view is that change depends on intrapsychic conflict resolution in response to accurate interpretations, specifically transference interpretations (Strachey 1934). In this model, the therapist interprets the patient's id impulses and wishes toward the therapist and the defenses against them. Ultimately, the patient realizes that these feelings are really directed toward figures from childhood, not the analyst. Hostile feelings toward the analyst are tamed by modification of the superego and expansion of the ego.

The last two decades have seen a gradual but profound shift in thinking away from the classical model toward an object relations/interpersonal model emphasizing the internalization of the relationship with the therapist (Cooper 1988). This shift was anticipated by the seminal work of Loewald (1956–57/1980), who compared analysis to a re-parenting process in which the child internalizes aspects of the parent. Much of this trend is also related to the renewed interest in the work of the British School on this side of the Atlantic. Ogden's (1979) conceptualization of projective identification (discussed in Chapter 2) is influenced by Bion's (1962) notion that the therapist serves as a container for the projections of the patient in the same way as the mother serves that function for her infant. This container model involves a "holding" function (Winnicott 1965) for the therapist that again has a correlate in the mother-infant relationship. By allowing the infant to be irritable, demanding, or fussy, or by letting the infant coo, sleep, feed, and so forth, the mother affords her child an opportunity to work through instinctual experience and to sort out diametrically opposed feelings (Winnicott 1986). Similarly, this holding function allows the therapist to process the projected material and return it in modified form to the patient, who then reintrojects slightly different self- and object-representations. Ogden (1988) has clarified that this process actually results in a change in the interactional mode between therapist and patient, such that patient and treater generate a new way of experiencing old psychological contents.

More recent contributions on the mechanisms of change eschew the either-or polarization of insight through interpretation versus alterations in the patient through a new relationship (Cooper 1992; Jacobs 1990; Pulver 1992). Insight and "corrective" relational experiences, while once thought to be mutually exclusive, are now regarded as compatible processes that work synergistically for therapeutic change (Jacobs 1990). Pulver (1992) has argued that "an understanding relationship cannot be maintained without insight into the dynamics of the relationship itself" (p. 204). Cooper (1992) has pointed out that the new interpersonal relationship produces insight in and of itself. It creates sufficient cognitive and affective dissonance that insight—in the form of an alteration of one's internal self- and object-representations and their affective interaction—is necessary to accommodate the internal pressures. Interpretation of content is less important than how the patient and therapist are relating to one another.

Although the internalization of the therapist and the therapeutic relationship is widely recognized as a mechanism of change in psychoanalysis and expressive forms of psychotherapy (Epstein 1979; Khan 1987; Modell 1976; Winnicott 1965), Adler (1982) pointed out that the same process is a principal mechanism of change in supportive psychotherapies. Pine (1976) has suggested that the auxiliary ego function performed by the therapist is ultimately internalized and assumed by the patient. In the vast majority of therapies, as Luborsky (1984) has suggested, change occurs partly from expressive or interpretive mechanisms and partly from supportive mechanisms deriving from the relationship.

Wallerstein's (1986) research has shed a good deal of light on the underlying mechanisms of cure in noninterpretive supportive approaches. The transference cure connected with the unanalyzed positive dependent transference has already been mentioned. One variant is the "therapeutic lifer" (pp. 690–691) who loses the gains if termination is attempted but who can be sustained at a high level of functioning as long as contact with the therapist continues indefinitely. Many patients are able to reduce the contacts to once a month or less but are prone to decompensate if there is any talk of termination. Another supportive mechanism of cure is "transfer of the transference" (p. 692), in which the positive dependency in the therapeutic relationship is transferred to another person, usually a spouse. Yet another mechanism is termed "the antitransference cure" (p. 693) and involves change through defiance and acting out against the therapist. Still other patients in Wallerstein's sample changed via a narrowly defined variant of the corrective emotional experience in which the patient's transference behavior was met by the therapist with steady concern and neutrality. This mechanism, of course, is related to the re-parenting model or the internalization of the relationship model. Finally, some patients appear to benefit from a supportive treatment geared to giving direct nonjudgmental advice. Wallerstein termed this process "reality testing and re-education" (p. 694).

Termination

Psychotherapists must resign themselves to living a professional life of continued loss. Patients come into their lives, share their most intimate thoughts and feelings, and then may never be heard from again. Because loss is an unpleasant experience for all of us, the ending of a psychotherapy process brings with it the vulnerability to transference and countertransference acting out. Although an orderly, mutually agreed upon termination is the ideal, half or more of outpatients discontinue treatment prematurely (Baekeland and Lundwall 1975), and less than 20% of patients in community mental health center populations undergo a mutually negotiated termination process (Beck et al. 1987).

In actual practice, termination may occur for a variety of reasons. It may be forced by external circumstances in the life of the therapist or the patient. Insurance companies or managed care firms may dictate the ending. The patient's own financial resources may run out. The patient may abruptly leave and refuse to return because of dissatisfaction with the therapist or anxiety over highly charged subject matter. The therapist may feel that maximum benefit has been reached and recommend termination, or the therapist and the patient may mutually agree upon a termination date.

Indications for termination are not absolute, but a good rule of thumb is that the patient is ready to stop when the goals of psychotherapy are reached. Presenting symptoms may have been eliminated or improved, the superego may have been modified, the patient's interpersonal relationships may have changed, and the patient may feel a new sense of independence. Another useful indicator is that patients are able to recognize and examine conflicts on their own and thus carry out a continuing self-analytic process without the therapist (Dewald 1971). In cases of predominantly supportive psychotherapy, indications include a stability in the patient's functioning, a reversal of any regressive processes, and an overall quiescence of symptoms. Clinicians must always recognize, however, that a certain subset of highly disturbed patients may require ongoing, infrequent therapy indefinitely (G. O. Gabbard and Wilkinson 1994; Wallerstein 1986).

Once the therapist and patient have mutually agreed upon a date for termination, a number of transference manifestations may emerge. Some of the original symptoms may reappear (Dewald 1971; Roth 1987). Negative transference may surface for the first time when the patient realizes that the therapist will not be there forever. Therapists may need to assist their patients in mourning the fantasy of ultimate gratification in the transference. In supportive treatments, the therapist must stress continuing positive rapport and avoid the mobilization of unmanageable negative transferences (Dewald 1971). Because of the formidable challenges faced by the therapist during the termination process, many therapists prefer to continue the same frequency of sessions right up to the end. Others "wean" the patient by gradually decreasing the frequency of sessions.

One of the primary countertransference risks during termination is for the therapist to become more "real" and more self-disclosing to the patient. There is little doubt that a movement toward greater therapist-patient equality occurs as termination nears, but the therapist must be mindful that too much egalitarianism or sharing of personal thoughts may reflect a countertransference wish to avoid facing the loss by creating the illusion of *beginning* a new relationship. After withholding gratification for an extended period, the therapist may be tempted to behave in a much more indulgent way toward the patient. It is significant that many cases of therapist-patient sexual involvement occur around the time of termination (G. O. Gabbard 1994).

When a patient terminates therapy unilaterally, therapists must deal with the feeling that they have somehow failed the patient. In such situations, therapists might remind themselves that the patient always has the privilege of ending the treatment and that such terminations may ultimately result in good outcomes. On the other hand, therapists can only help those patients who wish to be helped and who wish to collaborate in a process. Each therapist will have failures, and the limits of the craft must be recognized and accepted.

In instances when the termination is the therapist's unilateral decision, a different set of problems arise. When the termination is forced because of training requirements to rotate to a new clinical assignment, the therapist-in-training may wish to avoid discussing the termination process because of guilt feelings. Some therapists will even avoid letting their patients know of their departure until the last minute. In general, whenever external constraints are placed on the duration of the process, patients should be informed as early as possible so that their reactions can be accommodated as part of the treatment. When a therapist must leave the treatment for external reasons, patients often feel that the arbitrary nature of certain parental relationships has been re-created (Dewald 1971). Whatever the impact may be on the patient, the essential point is that the patient's reactions must be thoroughly explored even though the therapist may find it disconcerting to hear about the patient's anger and resentment.

Indications

Before considering the indications for weighting a psychotherapy process toward the expressive or supportive end of the continuum, therapists must understand that predicting who will respond to what form of psychotherapy is an uncertain business at best. There is some indication in the literature that healthier patients tend to do better in psychotherapy than more severely ill patients (i.e., the rich get richer [Luborsky et al. 1980]). A study of who will benefit from psychotherapy (Luborsky et al. 1988) concluded that both a positive relationship at the outset and a congruence between the core conflictual relationship theme and the content of interpretations were predictors of good outcome. The strength of the therapeutic or helping alliance in the first session or two may be the best predictor of eventual outcome, according to empirical research on the subject (Morgan et al. 1982). However, this variable is greatly affected by the nature of the patient-therapist match, which is almost impossible to quantify. Kantrowitz (1987), in a study of 22 patients in analysis, concluded that even with sophisticated psychological testing, one cannot reliably predict suitability for psychoanalysis.

Despite these caveats, it is nevertheless possible to outline patient characteristics that can help clinicians decide whether a predominantly expressive or predominantly supportive focus is indicated (see Table 4–1). Indications for a highly expressive modality, such as psychoanalysis, include 1) a strong motivation to understand oneself, 2) suffering that interferes with life to such an extent that it becomes an incentive for the patient to endure the rigors of treatment, 3) the ability not only to regress and give up control of feelings and thoughts but also to quickly regain control and reflect on that regression (regression in the service of the ego) (Greenson 1967), 4) tolerance for frustration, 5) a capacity for insight or psychological mindedness, 6) intact reality testing, 7) meaningful and enduring object relations, 8) reasonably good impulse control, and 9) ability to sustain a job (Bachrach and Leaff 1978). The ability to think in terms of metaphor and analogy, where one set of circumstances can be grasped as parallel to another, also augurs well for expressive treatment. Finally, reflective responses to trial interpretations during the evaluation period may suggest a suitability for expressive therapy.

Two general indications for supportive psychotherapy are chronic ego weaknesses or defects and regression in a healthy person who is

Table 4–1. Indications for expressive or supportive emphasis in psychotherapy

Expressive	Supportive
Strong motivation to understand	Significant ego defects of a chronic nature
Significant suffering	Severe life crisis
Ability to regress in the service of the ego	Low anxiety tolerance
Tolerance for frustration	Poor frustration tolerance
Capacity for insight (psychological mindedness)	Lack of psychological mindedness
Intact reality testing	Poor reality testing
Meaningful object relations	Severely impaired object relations
Good impulse control	Poor impulse control
Ability to sustain work	Low intelligence
Capacity to think in terms of analogy and metaphor	Little capacity for self-observation
Reflective responses to trial interpretations	Organically based cognitive dysfunction
	Tenuous ability to form a therapeutic alliance

undergoing a severe life crisis (Wallerstein 1986; Werman 1984). The former might include problems such as impaired reality testing, poor impulse control, and poor anxiety tolerance. Organically based cognitive dysfunction and lack of psychological mindedness are other indications for weighting the psychotherapy in a supportive direction. Patients with severe personality disorders who are prone to a great deal of acting out may also require supportive measures (Adler 1979; Luborsky 1984). Other patients who frequently do better with a predominantly supportive approach are those with seriously impaired object relations and a tenuous ability to form a therapeutic alliance (Adler 1982). Individuals who are in the midst of a serious life crisis, such as divorce or death of a spouse or child, or who are affected by a catastrophe such as a flood or tornado, are rarely suitable for expressive or exploratory approaches because their ego may be overwhelmed by the recent trauma. After beginning a supportive process, however, these patients will sometimes shift in an expressive direction.

Although these indications are focused on the two ends of the expressive-supportive continuum, most patients will present with a mixture of indications, some pointing in the expressive direction while others point toward the supportive end. The therapist must continually assess how—and when—to be supportive or expressive as the process proceeds.

Brief Psychotherapy

In the past 20 years, there has been a burgeoning interest and literature on forms of brief psychotherapy derived from psychoanalytic principles. Methodologically sophisticated comparisons with other treatment modalities have demonstrated that brief dynamic psychotherapy is just as helpful as other psychotherapies (Crits-Christoph 1992). A number of superb texts outline detailed guidelines for clinicians (Budman 1981; Davanloo 1980; Gustafson 1986; Horowitz et al. 1984a; Malan 1976, 1980; Mann 1973; Sifneos 1972). Also available are several comprehensive review articles that compare and contrast the approaches and attempt to integrate them (Gustafson 1984; MacKenzie 1988; Ursano and Hales 1986). Despite the variations and approaches, there are striking areas of consensus regarding the practice of brief psychotherapy. This brief discussion will emphasize those points of agreement.

Indications and Contraindications

In many ways, the indications for brief dynamic psychotherapy of an expressive nature parallel those associated with open-ended expressive psychotherapy. Important selection criteria include 1) the capacity for insight or psychological mindedness, 2) high levels of ego functioning, 3) strong motivation to understand oneself beyond mere symptom relief, 4) the capacity to form in-depth relationships (particularly an initial alliance with the therapist), and 5) the ability to tolerate anxiety. An additional point is central to selecting patients for brief psychotherapy—namely, the issue of focus. By virtue of its brevity, time-limited psychotherapy must be focal in nature in contrast to the pervasive breadth of psychoanalysis and highly expressive open-ended psychotherapy. Therefore, to proceed with brief therapy, the therapist and patient must identify the dynamic focus for the problem within the first or second evaluation session. Finally, brief therapy may be particularly helpful for relatively healthy individuals going through a developmental transition, such as moving from home, changing jobs, or having a first child.

Contraindications include the same factors that contraindicate open-ended psychotherapy of an expressive nature, but also encompass other features that might not contraindicate longer-term treatment. If a patient cannot circumscribe the problem to a focal dynamic issue, brief psychotherapy is contraindicated. Personality disorders that are amenable to longer-term expressive approaches cannot be expected to respond to short-term therapy, unless the patient presents with a situational complaint, such as grief, and unless the goals are limited to this temporary complaint (Horowitz et al. 1984a). Although some authors exclude chronically phobic or obsessional patients, Davanloo (1980) views patients with such symptoms as highly amenable to his style of brief psychotherapy.

Empirical research has confirmed that good outcomes in brief dynamic psychotherapy depend on careful selection of patients. Piper et al. (1990) have shown that the quality of object relations is one of the best predictors of outcome. Simply put, those with a capacity for more mature object relatedness tend to do better in treatment. Another study (Vaslamatzis et al. 1989) demonstrated higher dropout rates in patients who were not truly suitable for brief psychotherapy. A third project determined that bereaved patients who were highly motivated and better organized were more suitable for expressive brief therapy, whereas those with less motivation and lower organizations of the self-concept did better with supportive approaches (Horowitz et al. 1984b).

Number of Sessions

Different authors recommend different ways of handling the actual time limit of brief therapy. Mann (1973), who saw an acceptance of limits and a renunciation of magical expectations as central to the therapy process, insisted on a limit of 12 sessions. Davanloo (1980), on the other hand, averaged 15–25 sessions and does not set a specific termination at the beginning of treatment. Although Sifneos (1972) also refused to stipulate a specific number of sessions, his treatments tend to last only 12–16 sessions. As a general rule, then, brief therapy lasts as little as 2–3 months or as long as 5–6 months, and involves a range of 10–20 sessions.

Process of Therapy

Although the techniques associated with open-ended therapy are by and large applicable to brief treatments, their most striking difference is that they are markedly accelerated. Therapists must formulate their central hypothesis more quickly and must proceed to interpret resistances to insight earlier and more aggressively. Authors differ in terms of their degree of confrontation in dealing with resistances, but all acknowledge that the intensity of the process stirs up anxiety. Gustafson (1984) has stressed that confronting resistances requires an *empathic* frame of reference or else the patient will feel attacked. There is also considerable consensus among authors about the critical role played by transference interpretations in producing change. Malan (1976), appropriating Karl Menninger's triangle of insight, suggested that the therapist's primary task is to link the focused complaint to patterns in past relationships, in present relationships, and in the transference. A brief example will illustrate this process.

> Mr. C, a 35-year-old military man, came to therapy with a chief complaint of "I'm too domineering." He had been married for 8 months to his second wife, who he said was already complaining about this character trait as his first wife had. In the second session Mr. C came in and began talking about the softball game he had just left. He disagreed with the umpire's decision to call him out at home plate, but noted, "You don't argue with the umpire. What he says goes. You're

asking for trouble if you do." Later in the session he spoke of his father, who was a lieutenant colonel in the army. He described his father as an arbitrary man with whom you could not negotiate. The patient had always believed that his own opinions were not valued by his father. Still later in the session, Mr. C said, "I don't think 12 sessions are enough. But I guess we have to limit it to that. You said so."

At this point the therapist made an intervention that joined together the three sides of the triangle: "It sounds like your experiences with the umpire, your father, and me are all similar—you feel we make arbitrary decisions in which you have no say." The therapist was then able to formulate an interpretation regarding the way the patient treated both his first and second wife. He was turning the passively experienced trauma of being completely dominated by his father into an experience of active mastery with his wife. He dominated her the way his father had dominated him.

Brief Supportive Psychotherapy

There is much less literature on brief psychotherapies of a supportive nature. The primary indication for brief supportive psychotherapy is a relatively healthy person who is undergoing a specific life crisis. The techniques involved are similar to those of long-term supportive psychotherapy, namely, ego building, facilitating the development of a positive transference without interpreting it, and restoring previously adaptive defenses, as illustrated in this example:

Ms. D, a 52-year-old woman, came for consultation complaining about feelings of guilt and anxiety related to her 23-year-old daughter's out-of-wedlock pregnancy. The psychiatrist listened and empathized with the patient about the difficulty parents have seeing their children turn out differently than expected. The patient explained that she was so distracted by her guilt and anxiety over the situation that she was unable to function as usual at work or at home. The consultant attempted to restore Ms. D's usual obsessive-compulsive defenses by suggesting that she establish a structured routine at home so that she could accomplish all her usual household duties. He pointed out that staying busy would help Ms. D take her mind off her daughter. Ms. D complied with this suggestion and seemed somewhat improved at the next session. During this meeting the psychiatrist pointed out that Ms. D talked as though her daughter's pregnancy was her own responsibility. The patient responded, "You mean I didn't spread her legs?" The doctor affirmed, "That's right. You didn't spread her legs."

The patient experienced a flood of relief with the doctor's words and thanked him for relieving her guilt. She called the following week and said that she need not return since she felt "100% better."

In this example the psychiatrist first helped the patient restore adaptive defenses by encouraging a return to her usual schedule. He then utilized the patient's positive transference to absolve her of guilt. This absolution from an authority figure whom she regarded with respect, if not idealization, had much greater impact on her than it would have if she had merely told herself the same message.

Determining whether to prescribe open-ended or brief psychotherapy is a complex decision. Clearly, the presence or absence of a focal issue is of considerable relevance (Ursano and Dressler 1974). If the patient's complaint is sufficiently circumscribed, a recommendation for brief psychotherapy can put the patient to less expense and less inconvenience. Also, in one study of dropout rate in a public mental health clinic, the assignment of a specified length of therapy at the outset of treatment resulted in one-half the dropout rate compared with patients without such a clear end point (Sledge et al. 1990). However, complicated characterological problems may interfere with a patient's effective implementation of any "quick-fix" approach. In an era in which length of therapy is often determined by third- or fourth-party payers based on cost considerations, therapists must be mindful that less is not necessarily better. In a rigorous analysis of the dose-effect relationship with psychotherapy, there was clearly a positive relationship between the amount of treatment and the amount of patient benefit (Howard et al. 1986).

Finally, there is always a danger of therapists prescribing what they think the patient needs rather than what the patient wants. Is the patient asking for a fundamental examination and restructuring of personality, or is the request limited to assistance with one specific problem or complaint? The patient must clearly be a collaborator in determining the kind of treatment. We would be well advised to remember the dictum—attributed to Freud—that in some way, the patient is always right.

The Application of Theory to Technique

In Chapter 3, the role of theory in the development of an explanatory formulation was discussed. As the clinician moves from a psychodynamic assessment to psychodynamic psychotherapy, the process of tentative hypothesis formation continues. The application of theory to clinical material and to technique becomes increasingly complex, however, as more and more data enter the picture. The greatest danger is that the therapist, faced with a plethora of contradictory bits of information, will begin to organize the data by rigidly applying stereotyped theoretical formulations. All schools of thought are guilty of this tendency from time to time, as are all clinicians. To avoid this stereotyped approach, Peterfreund (1983) advocated a *heuristic* approach to the patient's verbalizations, which he defined as initiating and fostering "a process whereby patient and therapist work together to learn, discover, and understand as much as possible about the individual patient" (p. 2). The heuristic therapist does not pose as the bearer of truth who will impart it to the patient at the appropriate time. Heuristic therapists conceptualize themselves instead as barely a step ahead of the patient—a collaborator with the patient in a joint discovery of truth.

Therapists who listen carefully, without pretending to know a priori the appropriate theoretical formulation to explain the patient's psychopathology, must tolerate long periods of ambiguity wherein the etiology and pathogenesis of the patient's problems may seem puzzling. As therapists get to know their patients better, the clinical picture may or may not fit neatly into the model of self psychology, object relations theory, or ego psychology. To understand and help their patients, therapists may have to borrow bits and pieces from various theoretical models or may have to shift flexibly between models.

Wallerstein (1988) has stressed that the clinician must first and foremost address the clinical interaction with the patient in the here and now. The patient's repetition of the past in the present transference relationship does not necessarily require an extensive metapsychological model for purposes of explanation and understanding. All our theories are essentially *metaphors* that help us master the daily chaos of countertransference and ambiguity. Theory must never become our master.

Implicit in the heuristic approach to psychotherapy is acknowledgment of one's own fallibility in the therapeutic role and a special sensitivity to the patient's resistance. Whether or not we appreciate it, the patient is always "supervising" us. If a particular patient is consistently unable to make use of a particular line of interpretation, the therapist should examine the "goodness of fit" between the theoretical model and the patient's clinical picture. Rather than labeling the patient's responses to interpretations as resistance and subtly blaming the patient by repeatedly pointing out the resistance, the therapist might do far better to reconsider the theoretical model. The therapist who carefully follows the patient's lead will be able to shift approaches on a trial-and-error basis as more is learned about the patient.

> Mr. E, a young professional man in expressive-supportive psychotherapy, was reacting negatively to having to change his session from Wednesday to Thursday. He told his therapist that he felt devalued by the change in appointment times, as though he were not as important as other people on the therapist's schedule. The therapist, postulating that the patient was reexperiencing the sibling rivalry of childhood, wondered aloud if the patient might be reexperiencing a childhood feeling that his siblings got preferential treatment. The patient responded matter-of-factly that he could not relate to what the therapist had said. Mr. E reported that as a child he had been highly valued. He said that his parents had tended to treat him as if he were another parent managing the younger siblings. In fact, he often thought of himself as "the king." The therapist filed this piece of "supervision" away, until the next session, when the patient reported problems at work with his boss. This time, the therapist stayed closer to the patient's experience and offered a comment from an empathic self psychological framework, "It must hurt when your boss does not treat you like 'the king,' as your parents did." Mr. E wept in response to this comment and then opened up further about his childhood experiences, particularly the terrible burden he felt on being expected to be a parent to his siblings. He ended the session by saying that he felt understood by his therapist.

No therapy is completely free from theoretical bias. The best we can hope for is to be alert to these biases and to allow our patients to lead us into whatever theoretical domain provides the best explanation for each patient. Hypotheses are proved and disproved repeatedly as the process goes on, and the wise therapist is always eager to learn more about the human condition.

The Efficacy of Psychotherapy

The efficacy of individual psychotherapy is no longer in question. There is now overwhelming evidence that psychotherapy is an effective treatment (Luborsky et al. 1975; Smith et al. 1980). In a recent review of psychotherapy studies (Lambert et al. 1986), the authors demonstrated that the typical person seeking psychotherapy will be better off at the end of the treatment than will 80% of all the persons with the same problems who go untreated; this figure is in the same range as that found in comparable studies of antidepressant medications. Studies have also suggested that the changes produced by psychotherapeutic measures are lasting. Husby (1985), for example, replicated Malan's work on brief therapy and found that dynamic changes produced by treatment were still present at 5-year follow-up.

Despite this abundant evidence regarding efficacy, vexing questions remain. Studies that have compared one form of psychotherapy to another have yet to show any major advantages of one technique over another. Whether nonspecific factors involving the therapeutic relationship or the match between patient and therapist are more important than specific factors of technique is still unknown. Much of the difficulty is related to the extraordinary complexity of psychotherapy research. Between-group experimental designs analogous to those used in psychopharmacology studies run the risk of overlooking the trees because of the forest. In other words, the need for large-group comparisons to gain sufficient statistical power blurs the individual factors in a given patient-therapist dyad that may be compellingly significant in determining what specific kind of patient will benefit from what specific kind of intervention (Barlow and Beck 1984).

When one adds the question of the relative benefits of pharmacotherapy versus psychotherapy, the complexity increases exponentially. Elkin et al. (1988) outlined some of the major problems in such comparisons: 1) the length of psychotherapy and drug treatment are often quite different; 2) although it is relatively simple to construct a placebo design in pharmacotherapy research, to do so in psychotherapy research presents a formidable problem; 3) relationship issues inherent in the prescribing of medication are difficult to standardize—one could argue that effective medication prescription requires supportive psychotherapeutic interventions; and 4) the patient's expectation of receiving a certain form of treatment may influence that patient's ability to benefit from treatment.

Another problem in comparing pharmacotherapy and psychotherapy is the conceptualization of them as "either/or" choices. The two forms of treatment actually complement each other by working at different levels on different aspects of the illness (Karasu 1984). This synergism will be discussed at greater length in Chapter 5.

Because the between-group comparison method of psychotherapy research is fraught with problems, there has been increasing interest in recent years in intensively studying the psychotherapy process within an individual case (G. O. Gabbard et al. 1988; Rice and Greenberg 1984). This approach emphasizes the measurable changes in the patient and their connection with the therapist's interventions. Process research begins from the premise that psychotherapy is effective. What it seeks to learn is how psychotherapy is effective within the limited framework of a single patient-therapist dyad.

References

Adler G: The myth of the alliance with borderline patients. Am J Psychiatry 47:642–645, 1979

Adler G: Supportive psychotherapy revisited. Hillside Journal of Clinical Psychiatry 4:3–13, 1982

Bachrach HM, Leaff LA: "Analyzability": a systematic review of the clinical and quantitative literature. J Am Psychoanal Assoc 26:881–920, 1978

Baekeland F, Lundwall L: Dropping out of treatment: a critical review. Psychol Bull 82:738–783, 1975

Barlow DH, Beck JG: The psychosocial treatment of anxiety disorders: current status, future directions, in Psychotherapy Research: Where Are We and Where Should We Go? Edited by Williams JBW, Spitzer RL. New York, Guilford, 1984, pp 29–69

Basch MF: Doing Psychotherapy. New York, Basic Books, 1980

Beck NC, Lambert J, Gamachei M, et al: Situational factors and behavioral self-predictions in the identification of clients at high risk to drop out of psychotherapy. J Clin Psychol 43:511–520, 1987

Bion WR: Learning From Experience. New York, Basic Books, 1962

Bordin ES: The generalizability of the psychoanalytic concept of the working alliance. Psychotherapy: Theory, Research, and Practice 16:252–260, 1979

Budman SH (ed): Forms of Brief Therapy. New York, Guilford, 1981

Chessick RD: The Technique and Practice of Intensive Psychotherapy. New York, Jason Aronson, 1974

Chessick RD: What is intensive psychotherapy? Am J Psychother 35:489–501, 1981

Cooper AM: Changes in psychoanalytic ideas: transference interpretation. J Am Psychoanal Assoc 35:77–98, 1987

Cooper AM: Our changing views of the therapeutic action of psychoanalysis: comparing Strachey and Loewald. Psychoanal Q 57:15–27, 1988

Cooper AM: Psychic change: development in the theory of psychoanalytic techniques. Int J Psychoanal 73:245–250, 1992

Crits-Christoph P: The efficacy of brief dynamic psychotherapy: a meta-analysis. Am J Psychiatry 149:151–158, 1992

Davanloo H (ed): Short-Term Dynamic Psychotherapy. New York, Jason Aronson, 1980

Dewald PA: Psychotherapy: A Dynamic Approach. New York, Basic Books, 1964

Dewald PA: Psychotherapy: A Dynamic Approach, 2nd Edition. New York, Basic Books, 1971

Elkin I, Pilkonis PA, Docherty JP, et al: Conceptual and methodological issues in comparative studies of psychotherapy and pharmacotherapy, I: active ingredients and mechanisms of change. Am J Psychiatry 145:909–917, 1988

Epstein L: Countertransference with borderline patients, in Countertransference. Edited by Epstein L, Feiner AH. New York, Jason Aronson, 1979, pp 375–405

Freud A: The ego and the mechanisms of defense (1936), in The Writings of Anna Freud, Vol 2 (Revised Edition). New York, International Universities Press, 1966

Freud S: The interpretation of dreams (1900), in The Standard Edition of the Complete Psychological Works of Sigmund Freud, Vols 4, 5. Translated and edited by Strachey J. London, Hogarth Press, 1953, pp 1–627

Freud S: The dynamics of transference (1912a), in The Standard Edition of the Complete Psychological Works of Sigmund Freud, Vol 12. Translated and edited by Strachey J. London, Hogarth Press, 1958, pp 97–108

Freud S: Recommendations to physicians practising psycho-analysis (1912b), in The Standard Edition of the Complete Psychological Works of Sigmund Freud, Vol 12. Translated and edited by Strachey J. London, Hogarth Press, 1958, pp 109–120

Freud S: On beginning the treatment (1913), in The Standard Edition of the Complete Psychological Works of Sigmund Freud, Vol 12. Translated and edited by Strachey J. London, Hogarth Press, 1958, pp 121–144

Freud S: New introductory lectures on psycho-analysis (1933), in The Standard Edition of the Complete Psychological Works of Sigmund Freud, Vol 22. Translated and edited by Strachey J. London, Hogarth Press, 1964, pp 3–182

Frieswyk SH, Allen JG, Colson DB, et al: Therapeutic alliance: its place as a process and outcome variable in dynamic psychotherapy research. J Consult Clin Psychol 54:32–38, 1986

Fromm-Reichmann F: Principles of Intensive Psychotherapy. Chicago, IL, University of Chicago Press, 1950

Gabbard K, Gabbard GO: Psychiatry and the Cinema. Chicago, IL, University of Chicago Press, 1987

Gabbard GO: Psychotherapists who transgress sexual boundaries. Bull Menninger Clin 58(1), 1994

Gabbard GO, Wilkinson SM: Management of Countertransference With Borderline Patients. Washington, DC, American Psychiatric Press, 1994

Gabbard GO, Horwitz L, Frieswyk S, et al: The effect of therapist interventions on the therapeutic alliance with borderline patients. J Am Psychoanal Assoc 36:697–727, 1988

Greenberg JR: Theoretical models and the analyst's neutrality. Contemp Psychoanal 22:87–106, 1986

Greenson RR: The working alliance and the transference neurosis (1965), in Explorations in Psychoanalysis. New York, International Universities Press, 1978, pp 119–224

Greenson RR: The Technique and Practice of Psychoanalysis. New York, International Universities Press, 1967

Gustafson JP: An integration of brief dynamic psychotherapy. Am J Psychiatry 141:935–944, 1984

Gustafson JP: The Complex Secret of Brief Psychotherapy. New York, WW Norton, 1986

Hamilton NG: Self and Others: Object Relations Theory in Practice. Northvale, NJ, Jason Aronson, 1988

Hartley DE, Strupp HH: The therapeutic alliance: its relationship to outcome in brief psychotherapy, in Empirical Studies of Psychoanalytic Theories, Vol 1. Edited by Masling J. Hillside, NJ, Analytic Press, 1983, pp 1–37

Hoffman IZ, Gill MM: Critical reflections on a coding scheme. Int J Psychoanal 69:55–64, 1988

Horowitz MJ, Marmar C, Krupnick J, et al: Personality Styles and Brief Psychotherapy. New York, Basic Books, 1984a

Horowitz MJ, Marmar C, Weiss DS, et al: Brief psychotherapy of bereavement reactions: the relationship of process to outcome. Arch Gen Psychiatry 41:438–448, 1984b

Horwitz L: Clinical Prediction in Psychotherapy. New York, Jason Aronson, 1974

Howard KI, Kopta SM, Krause MS, et al: The dose-effect relationship in psychotherapy. Am Psychol 41:159–164, 1986

Husby R: Short-term dynamic psychotherapy, IV: comparison of recorded changes in 33 neurotic patients 2 and 5 years after end of treatment. Psychother Psychosom 43:23–27, 1985

Jacobs TJ: The corrective emotional experience—its place in current technique. Psychoanalytic Inquiry 10:433–454, 1990

Kantrowitz JL: Suitability for psychoanalysis. Yearbook of Psychoanalysis and Psychotherapy 2:403–415, 1987

Kantrowitz JL, Katz AL, Paolitto F, et al: Changes in the level and quality of object relations in psychoanalysis: followup of a longitudinal, prospective study. J Am Psychoanal Assoc 35:23–46, 1987

Karasu TB: Psychotherapies: an overview. Am J Psychiatry 134:851–863, 1977

Karasu TB: Politics, practice, and p value in psychotherapy, in Psychotherapy Research: Where Are We and Where Should We Go? Edited by Williams JBW, Spitzer RL. New York, Guilford, 1984, pp 372–383

Katz JB: A psychoanalyst's anonymity: fiddler behind the couch. Bull Menninger Clin 42:520–524, 1978

Khan MMR: Introduction, in Holding and Interpretation: Fragment of an Analysis, by Winnicott DW. New York, Grove Press, 1987, pp 1–18

Kohut H: How Does Analysis Cure? Edited by Goldberg A. Chicago, IL, University of Chicago Press, 1984

Lambert MJ, Shapiro DA, Bergin AE: The effectiveness of psychotherapy, in Handbook of Psychotherapy and Behavior Change, 3rd Edition. Edited by Garfield SL, Bergin AE. New York, Wiley, 1986, pp 157–211

Lipton SD: The advantages of Freud's technique as shown in his analysis of the Rat Man. Int J Psychoanal 58:255–273, 1977

Loewald HW: On the therapeutic action of psychoanalysis (1956–57), in Papers on Psychoanalysis. New Haven, CT, Yale University Press, 1980, pp 221–256

Luborsky L: Principles of Psychoanalytic Psychotherapy: A Manual for Supportive-Expressive Treatment. New York, Basic Books, 1984

Luborsky L, Singer B, Luborsky L: Comparative studies of psychotherapies: is it true that "everyone has won and all must have prizes?" Arch Gen Psychiatry 32:995–1008, 1975

Luborsky L, Mintz J, Auerbach A, et al: Predicting the outcome of psychotherapy: findings of the Penn Psychotherapy Project. Arch Gen Psychiatry 37:471–481, 1980

Luborsky L, Crits-Christoph P, Mitz J, et al: Who Will Benefit From Psychotherapy? Predicting Therapeutic Outcomes. New York, Basic Books, 1988

MacKenzie KR: Recent developments in brief psychotherapy. Hosp Community Psychiatry 39:742–752, 1988

Malan DH: The Frontier of Brief Psychotherapy: An Example of the Convergence of Research and Clinical Practice. New York, Plenum, 1976

Malan DH: Toward the Validation of Dynamic Psychotherapy: A Replication. New York, Plenum, 1980

Mann J: Time-Limited Psychotherapy. Cambridge, MA, Harvard University Press, 1973

Marziali E, Marmar C, Krupnick J: Therapeutic alliance scales: development and relationship to psychotherapy outcome. Am J Psychiatry 138:361–364, 1981

Menninger KA: Theory of Psychoanalytic Technique. New York, Basic Books, 1958

Modell AH: The "holding environment" and the therapeutic action of psychoanalysis. J Am Psychoanal Assoc 24:285–307, 1976

Morgan R, Luborsky L, Crits-Christoph P, et al: Predicting the outcomes of psychotherapy by the Penn Helping Alliance Rating Method. Arch Gen Psychiatry 39:397–402, 1982

Ogden TH: On projective identification. Int J Psychoanal 60:357–373, 1979

Ogden TH: Projective Identification and Psychotherapeutic Technique. New York, Jason Aronson, 1982

Ogden TH: On the dialectical structure of experience: some clinical and theoretical implications. Contemporary Psychoanalysis 24:17–45, 1988

Ornstein A: "Supportive" psychotherapy: a contemporary view. Clinical Social Work Journal 14:14–30, 1986

Peterfreund E: The Process of Psychoanalytic Therapy: Models and Strategies. Hillsdale, NJ, Analytic Press, 1983

Pine F: On therapeutic change: perspectives from a parent-child model. Psychoanalysis and Contemporary Science 5:537–569, 1976

Pine F: Supportive psychotherapy: a psychoanalytic perspective. Psychiatric Annals 16:526–529, 1986

Piper WE, Azim HFA, McCallum M, et al: Patient suitability and outcome in short-term individual psychotherapy. J Consult Clin Psychol 58:475–481, 1990

Pulver SE: Psychic change: insight or relationship? Int J Psychoanal 73:199–208, 1992

Racker H: Transference and Counter-transference. New York, International Universities Press, 1968

Rice LN, Greenberg LS: Patterns of Change: Intensive Analysis of Psychotherapy Process. New York, Guilford, 1984

Roskin G: Changing modes of psychotherapy. Journal of Psychiatric Treatment and Evaluation 4:483–487, 1982

Roth S: Psychotherapy: The Art of Wooing Nature. Northvale, NJ, Jason Aronson, 1987

Sandler J: Countertransference and role-responsiveness. International Review of Psychoanalysis 3:43–47, 1976

Sifneos PE: Short-Term Psychotherapy and Emotional Crisis. Cambridge, MA, Harvard University Press, 1972

Sledge WH, Moras K, Hartley D, et al: Effect of time-limited psychotherapy on patient dropout rates. Am J Psychiatry 147:1341–1347, 1990

Smith ML, Glass GV, Miller TI: The Benefits of Psychotherapy. Baltimore, MD, Johns Hopkins University Press, 1980

Strachey J: The nature of the therapeutic action of psycho-analysis. Int J Psychoanal 15:127–159, 1934

Ursano RJ, Dressler DM: Brief versus long-term psychotherapy: a treatment decision. J Nerv Ment Dis 159:164–171, 1974

Ursano RJ, Hales RE: A review of brief individual psychotherapies. Am J Psychiatry 143:1507–1517, 1986

Vaslamatzis G, Markidis M, Katsouyanni K: Study of the patients' difficulties in ending brief psychoanalytic psychotherapy. Psychother Psychosom 52:173–178, 1989

Wallerstein RS: Forty-Two Lives in Treatment: A Study of Psychoanalysis and Psychotherapy. New York, Guilford, 1986

Wallerstein RS: One psychoanalysis or many? Int J Psychoanal 69:5–21, 1988

Werman DS: The use of dreams in psychotherapy: practical guidelines. Canadian Psychiatric Association Journal 23:153–158, 1978

Werman DS: The Practice of Supportive Psychotherapy. New York, Brunner/Mazel, 1984

Winnicott DW: The Maturational Processes and the Facilitating Environment: Studies in the Theory of Emotional Development. London, Hogarth Press, 1965

Winnicott DW: Holding and Interpretation: Fragment of an Analysis. New York, Grove Press, 1986

Zetzel ER: Current concepts of transference. Int J Psychoanal 37:369–378, 1956

Chapter 5

Treatments in Dynamic Psychiatry II: Group Therapy, Family/Marital Therapy, and Pharmacotherapy

Dynamic Group Psychotherapy

We all live and work in the context of groups. Group psychotherapy provides patients an opportunity to learn how they function in groups—the roles they play, the expectations and unconscious fantasies they harbor about groups, and the obstacles they encounter in getting along with others at work and at home. Unique dimensions of group experience can be only partially explored in individual psychotherapy.

Unique Aspects of Group Experience

Much of our knowledge of the forces operating in groups is derived from the work of Wilfred Bion (1961). After World War II, Bion began conducting small group experiences at the Tavistock Clinic. His understanding of groups revolved around his observation that two groups are present in every group: 1) the "work group" and 2) the "basic assumption group." The former is involved with the actual work task of a group and is geared toward completion of the task. Few groups, however, work rationally toward attaining their goals without interference from basic assumptions (Rioch 1970).

Basic assumptions refer to the unconscious fantasies that lead groups to behave in an "as-if manner" (Rioch 1970). In other words, the group members begin to act on an assumption about the group that is different from the reality of the task at hand. Basic assumptions fall into three categories: dependency, fight/flight, and pairing. These discrete emotional states are unconscious in origin but are easily deducible from the behavior of the group. These assumptions derail the work group and prevent completion of its task. In a psychotherapy group, the task of understanding one another's problems may be steered off course by the development of basic assumptions. However, just as Freud discovered that transference in psychoanalysis is more of a therapeutic tool than an obstacle, Bion discovered that the basic assumptions themselves can be of enormous value in helping individual members of groups understand themselves in the context of the group.

Bion's initial observations of basic assumptions were at a descriptive level, but as he gained more and more experience with group dynamics, he realized that the basic assumptions were clusters of defenses against psychotic anxieties present in everyone. Groups are powerfully regressive, and they provide patients with a window into their most primitive fears. Bion realized that the mechanisms associated with the paranoid-schizoid and depressive positions identified by Melanie Klein (see Chapter 2) were also present in the basic assumptions.

The dependency basic assumption, for example, can be viewed as a cluster of defenses against depressive anxieties (Ganzarain 1980). In this basic assumption, patients behave as though they are weak, ignorant, and incapable of helping each other and as if they are totally dependent on the therapist, whom they view as godlike. The underlying fear is that their greed (i.e., their oral neediness) will engulf the therapist and result in their being abandoned. To defend against the anxiety and guilt connected with their potential destruction of the therapist (i.e., their mother at an unconscious level), the patients believe that the therapist is an inexhaustible, omniscient, and omnipotent figure who will always be there for them and who will always have the answers.

In the fight/flight basic assumption, the group has regressed to a frank paranoid-schizoid position. All "badness" is split off and projected. The wish to fight or take flight is a cluster of defenses against paranoid anxiety. To avoid an externally perceived persecutor who will destroy them, the group can either fight or run from the persecutor. The group becomes nonreflective and views action as the only solution to the perceived threat.

The pairing basic assumption is a cluster of defenses against depressive anxieties. The assumption in this instance frequently revolves around two group members who will reproduce and bring forth a messiah to rescue the group (Rioch 1970). There is a pervasive atmosphere of optimism and hopefulness, a belief that love will prevail. This Pollyannaish attitude may be viewed as a manic defense against the group's concern that destructiveness, hate, and hostility also exist within the group. Hence, in this view pairing can be viewed as a manic reparative effort (Ganzarain 1980).

Group psychotherapists must be continually vigilant for the development of basic assumptions in their groups, so that they can interpret and examine them before they become too destructive to the task of the group. Unexamined transference may lead an individual to quit psychotherapy; unexamined basic assumptions may lead to the dissolution of group therapy.

Beyond the basic assumptions, there are other unique forces operating in groups. One of the most powerful is the phenomenon of "role suction" (Redl 1963). A common observation is that an individual's behavior in a one-to-one situation may change dramatically upon entry to a group. We frequently hear, for example, about a "good boy" who "got in with the wrong crowd." Individuals who find themselves behaving differently in groups often describe themselves as being drawn or "sucked" into playing a role that seemed outside their control. An individual patient in group psychotherapy, for example, may serve as a spokesperson for the entire group, while everyone else remains silent. Another individual may serve in the role of scapegoat, behaving in such a way as to become the target for everyone's anger. Both the spokesperson and the scapegoat phenomena can be understood as group versions of projective identification (Horwitz 1983; Ogden 1982). In scapegoating, for example, the unacceptable parts of all the group members are projected onto one individual who then feels coerced into responding like the projected parts of the other patients. If the therapist supports the scapegoat and interprets the group process, the projected parts may be reintrojected.

Characteristics of
Psychotherapeutic Groups

Most group therapists meet with their groups once a week (Sadock 1983), although some who model group psychotherapy after classical psychoanalysis (Wolf 1983) may conduct as many as five group sessions a week. The sessions, which adhere to a strict time limit as in individual psychotherapy, usually last from $1\frac{1}{4}$–$1\frac{1}{2}$ hours. Although groups vary in size, the average dynamic psychotherapy group contains 8–10 members (Sadock 1983). Smaller groups may be quite useful, provided that the members actively participate and are reasonably verbal.

The composition of a dynamic therapy group may vary considerably, although heterogeneous groups are thought to have advantages over homogeneous groups (Yalom 1985). The consensus of clinicians is that groups in which everyone is similar rarely get beyond superficial levels of interaction. On the other hand, if a group is too heterogeneous, it may be dysfunctional because of the lack of common ground among the patients. Moreover, certain individuals may feel isolated if they believe that they are vastly different from everyone else in the group by virtue of their age, cultural background, or socioeconomic status. Finally, if members of the group have highly variable levels of ego strength, the group may not gel because of the difficulty in exploring psychological issues.

The consensus of the literature is that dynamic therapy groups should be heterogeneous in terms of the conflicts of the members but homogeneous in terms of a reasonably similar level of ego strength (Whitaker and Lieberman 1964; Yalom 1985). Most of the dynamic group psychotherapy literature is weighted toward the expressive end of the expressive-supportive continuum. Groups that are more supportive in nature may be more homogeneous as well. A good example of such a group is the supportive group approach often used in the treatment of schizophrenic patients (see Chapter 7). Dynamic therapy groups are typically open-ended, and new members may be added as old members terminate. However, some homogeneous groups with a focal issue to discuss, such as victims of therapist-patient sexual abuse (Sonne 1989), may meet for a time-limited therapy process.

Dynamic group psychotherapists vary in the extent to which they use a group-centered versus an individual-centered approach. In the individual-centered form of group therapy (Wolf 1983), the process is conceptualized as similar to individual psychoanalysis in a group set-

ting. The group process itself is relatively less important than interpretation of the individual's difficulties in dealing with the other group
members and with the therapist. The more extreme advocates of the
group-centered approach (Ezriel 1950) have viewed the interpretation
of group forces as much more important than the interpretation of the
individual's conflicts. In fact, Ezriel (1950) suggested that the therapist
should refrain from interpretation until a common group tension or
theme has developed. A less extreme approach was advocated by
Horwitz (1977), who proposed that individual interpretations may be
used in the service of building up the group's awareness of a common
group issue, which is then also interpreted. There are common group
experiences that everyone shares and that deserve interpretation,
such as not having all one's needs met by the leader, competition for
support, and anxiety about being ignored. However, if there is no focus
on individual issues as well, patients may feel that their individual
reasons for seeking treatment have been overlooked by the therapist.
Most group therapists today subscribe to a combined model involving
both individual- and group-centered interventions (Slipp 1988).

Transference, Countertransference, and Resistance

Transference, countertransference, and resistance are cornerstones of
dynamic group psychotherapy, just as they are in individual work.
However, the group modality itself significantly alters the transference. First, the intensity of the patients' transferences may be diluted
by their redirection to fellow patients. This displacement of the transference from therapist to peer may be beneficial, however, as it allows
a "practice ground" for working through a parental transference prior
to its development in the relationship with the therapist (Wolf 1983).
Group psychotherapy also allows for the formation of multiple transferences. The therapist then is provided with a laboratory where the
patients' internal object relations are displayed for all to see through
externalization in relationships with individual group members. Although different transferences develop in individual therapy as well,
they tend to appear over a longer period. The group setting may allow
the therapist to gain a greater familiarity with the patients' internal
object relations in a much shorter time.

Although transference may be diluted in group therapy, the converse is also true. Transference may be intensified when the entire

group is swept up with powerful feelings of either positive or negative valence. Therapists who serve as containers for all the bad object projections in the group members rapidly realize that countertransference may also be intensified in a group setting. The countertransferential demands on the group therapist may be formidable. Fortunately, there is built-in protection against untoward countertransference acting out because group patients will readily spot inappropriate behavior or misperceptions on the part of the therapist and insist on an explanation (Wolf 1983). To diffuse transference and countertransference, some therapists prefer to work with a co-therapist in group psychotherapy. Having a partner helps the therapist to process the intense feelings stirred up by the group.

Sibling rivalry and a transference wish to be the therapist's only or favorite child is a common development in all dynamic therapies. However, these issues may have a more compelling quality in group therapy, and the therapist must diligently avoid showing any favoritism for specific group members (Yalom 1985).

In addition to the patients' transference to the therapist and to other group members, there is a third form of transference that is truly unique to groups—transference to the group as a whole. This form of transference affords patients an opportunity to examine their expectations of other groups with which they live and work. The group as a total entity is often viewed as an idealized, completely gratifying "mother" that will satisfy the patient's yearning for a reunion with an unconditionally loving figure. In recognition of this tendency, Scheidlinger (1974) dubbed this phenomenon the "mother-group." When this form of transference is in full flower, the therapist may be viewed as a terrifying maternal figure in contrast to the all-giving benevolence of the group as a whole. Other authors (Gibbard and Hartman 1973) have viewed the idealized transference to the group as a whole as a defensive posture that avoids seeing the group (mother) as sadistic.

The working through of transference and resistance constitutes the bulk of the dynamic therapist's task, much as it does in individual psychotherapy. Indeed, Ganzarain (1983) suggested that working through is the key characteristic that distinguishes psychoanalytic group therapy from other forms of group treatment. He particularly emphasized the working through of primitive psychotic-like anxieties and their associated defense mechanisms. The regressive forces activated by group experience bring the patient in touch with anxiety stemming from the paranoid-schizoid and depressive positions much more rapidly and more profoundly than in individual treatment. The working through of transference is also facilitated by the input of other group members. An individual patient may attempt to validate a personal impression of the therapist by "checking it out" with other group patients. When peers confront the distortions inherent in the transference perception, the patient may be much more willing to listen and accept feedback than when it is provided by the therapist.

Indications and Contraindications

A number of indications for dynamic group psychotherapy are the same as those for expressive-supportive individual therapy. These include 1) strong motivation, 2) psychological mindedness, 3) a reasonably high level of ego strength, 4) sufficient discomfort that the patient is willing to endure the frustrations inherent in the process, and 5) problems in interpersonal relationships (Yalom 1985). However, the question that the clinician must address is: What specific criteria suggest that a patient is particularly suited for group psychotherapy rather than individual psychotherapy?

There are several kinds of problems that may be dealt with more effectively in a group setting than in individual treatment (Sadock 1983). The patient who is extraordinarily anxious around authority figures may find it easier to talk and relate in the company of peers. A patient whose primary problem seems to have originated in sibling conflicts may find that a group setting reactivates the problem in a way that makes it easier to examine and resolve. Conversely, sometimes an only child who missed out on a sibling experience and who has difficulty learning to share in adult life may find that a group is the best place to address those issues. Nonpsychotic patients who rely heavily on projection may benefit from the confrontations of other group members, who repeatedly dispute the distortions brought to the group. Borderline patients who form an intensely negative transference in individual therapy may benefit from the dilution of transference inherent in group work. However, these patients almost always require individual therapy as well (see Chapter 15).

Group therapy is generally effective for patients with higher-level personality disorders, including hysterical, obsessive-compulsive, some narcissistic, passive-aggressive, and dependent types, because a group setting may be the only place in which these patients receive feedback about how their character patterns affect others. Much of the psychopathology found in patients with personality disorders involves ego-syntonic character traits (i.e., behaviors that distress others but not the patient). The feedback from peers in group therapy often helps these patients reflect on their behavior patterns so that these traits eventually become ego-dystonic (i.e., uncomfortable to the patients themselves), which is the first step toward gaining sufficient motivation to change. The effect of group psychotherapy on particular personality disorders and the indications for combined individual and group therapy will be further addressed in Section III.

One obvious difference between individual and group psychotherapy in assessing indications is that the group therapist must constantly evaluate the fit between a prospective patient and the group as it is currently composed. One borderline patient may be quite tolerable in a group of patients with a high level of ego strength, but two may overwhelm the group with disproportionate demands for attention and disruptive acting out. Similarly, issues such as age and gender must be balanced when deciding on indications for a particular group.

Certain clinical symptomatology is consensually viewed as contraindicating dynamic group psychotherapy. These features include 1) low motivation, 2) psychotic disorganization, 3) addiction to substances, 4) antisocial personality disorder, 5) severe somatization, 6) organically based cognitive dysfunction, and 7) serious suicide risk (Yalom 1985). Addicts and patients with antisocial features may, however, be effectively treated in homogeneous groups of a confrontational nature (see Chapters 12 and 17). As is the case with indications, some patients may be contraindicated for a particular group because of the composition of that group, but might instead be suitable for a different group.

Family and Marital Therapy

Although many family and marital therapists practicing today are not dynamically oriented, the field had its origins in the work of a number of early psychoanalytically oriented clinicians, including Theodore Lidz, Lyman Wynne, Nathan Ackerman, Murray Bowen, and Virginia Satir. The focus of these early family therapists on the psychology of the individual was dramatically altered in the decades of the 1950s and 1960s by a group of Palo Alto researchers, including Gregory Bateson, Don Jackson, and Jay Haley (1956). Systemic family therapy grew out of the work of this group, and with it the emphasis shifted from the individual to the family system. Individual psychopathology and personal history both became secondary to the family as a whole, which was viewed as a system with a life of its own. Until recently, this systemic approach to family therapy, along with its subsequent elaborations by Minuchin (1974) and Selvini Palazzoli et al. (1978), has largely dominated the field of family therapy.

Bowen family therapy has grown increasingly popular in recent years. This approach is rooted in psychoanalytic theory, but the technique that has evolved from the ideas of Bowen (1978) is largely nondynamic. In this form of treatment, one individual family member meets with the therapist on an infrequent basis (often once a month) to carefully study the intergenerational patterns in the patient's family. The patient is helped to understand how the current patterns in family relationships are repetitions of patterns from past generations. The approach is strictly cognitive, and the patient is not encouraged to express feelings. Transference issues are not viewed as important and are not interpreted. On the contrary, once patients have gained an intellectual understanding of their family patterns, they are encouraged to address the unresolved issues directly with the appropriate family members.

In the last decade or so, object relations family therapy has also grown in popularity and now stands as the most prominent present-day example of psychodynamic family therapy. Since the discussion in this chapter is restricted to dynamic approaches, we will examine object relations family therapy in some detail while omitting consideration of the nondynamic schools of family therapy.

Theoretical Understanding

Working with married couples at the Tavistock Clinic in the 1950s and 1960s, Henry Dicks (1963) began to notice that relatively healthy couples—who appeared to have satisfying marriages—were often working out primitive object relationships in their marriages. He observed that each spouse tended to perceive the other as though he or she were someone else. Typically, the husband would perceive the wife as though she were an internal object-representation from his own psyche, often his own mother. Similarly, the wife would relate to the husband as though he were simply a projection from her internal world. Dicks concluded that a major source of marital discord was the failure of each partner to confirm the other's true nature or identity. Instead, the partners tended to coerce each other into behaving in highly stereotyped and constricting ways. Couples tended to deteriorate into polarized units, such as sadistic-masochistic, domineering-submissive, healthy-sick, and independent-dependent. Dicks recognized that each of these polarized halves formed a whole personality in the marital dyad, but that each individual alone was incomplete. Just as his colleague Bion was noting that groups exert a regressive force on individuals, Dicks was discovering that marriage has a similar regressive effect. Even in people with considerable ego strength, marriage seemed to regress them rapidly into parent-child relationships.

What Dicks observed, of course, was a form of transference. The marital partners were reenacting a past relationship in the present. In the language of object relations theory, the spouses were using splitting and projective identification to make an *internal* conflict an *external,* or marital, conflict, with an internal object-representation, usually a parent, split off and projected into the spouse. The projector then behaved in such a way as to coerce the spouse into behaving like the projected internal object. A husband, for example, who is used to being babied by his mother, may unconsciously recreate the situation with his mother in his marriage by acting childish and evoking a motherly response from his wife. Alternatively, the marital partner may project a self-representation into the spouse and coerce the spouse into behaving like that self-representation while the projector behaves like a complementary object-representation. The case of Mr. C in Chapter 4 was such a situation. He projected a victimized, submissive self-representation onto both his first and second wife while behaving like his domineering, aggressive father.

Marital conflict may be viewed as the re-creation of conflicts with one's parents, via splitting and projective identification. The selection of a mate is obviously much influenced by such processes. Dicks (1963) believed that such selections are "largely based on unconscious signals or cues by which the partners recognize in a more-or-less central ego-syntonic person the other's 'fitness' for joint working-through or repeating of still unresolved splits or conflicts inside each other's personalities, while at the same time, paradoxically, also sensing a guarantee that with that person they will not be worked-through" (p. 128). Hence, couples are thrown together by conflicting desires to work through unresolved object relations, on the one hand, and to simply repeat them, on the other.

Several authors have expanded this object relations understanding of marital conflict to the entire family (Scharff and Scharff 1987; Shapiro et al. 1975; Slipp 1984, 1988; Stewart et al. 1975; Zinner and Shapiro 1972, 1974). These authors noted that the identified patient in a family is frequently a carrier or container of the split-off, unacceptable parts of other family members. In that sense, the family equilibrium is maintained by this arrangement of splitting and projective identification. An adolescent boy, for example, may act on antisocial impulses that represent aspects of an unacceptable self-representation of his father that has been projectively disavowed by the father and contained by the son. A child may be idealized in the same way via projective identification of positive aspects of self- or object-representations. Object relations theory lends itself well to family therapy because its constructs (e.g., splitting and projective identification) provide a bridge from the intrapsychic to the interpersonal and from the individual to the family (Slipp 1984; Zinner 1976).

Technique

The technique of object relations therapy for couples and families grows out of the theoretical understanding. The overall goal is to help members of the family or couple reinternalize the conflicts that have been externalized via projective identification (Zinner 1976). The focus, then, must be on helping each individual to reown projected parts (Stewart et al. 1975). To accomplish this goal, the object relations family therapist will typically meet with the family for a 50-minute session every week or every other week (Slipp 1988).

The therapy process begins with a careful diagnosis of how internal self- and object-representations have been distributed throughout the family via splitting and projective identification. When this pattern becomes apparent, the therapist attempts to explain how an unconscious, collusive system is formed among family members to perpetuate pathological behavior in the identified patient. The stability of the family depends on the ability of one or more individual members to contain various projected parts of other family members. As with other forms of dynamic psychotherapy, these explanatory interpretations are usually met with resistance early on. This antitherapeutic force may take the form of attempting to get the therapist "sucked into" the family system. In other words, family members unconsciously repeat the family's pathological patterns instead of verbalizing and exploring them. In marital therapy, for example, a husband may use projective identification with the therapist in the same way he does with his spouse.

Because of these powerful resistances, object relations family therapists must be especially attuned to their countertransference reactions in the broad or objective sense. In other words, it is critically important that therapists allow themselves to be containers for the projected parts of the family members so that they can more adequately diagnose and interpret what happens within the family (Slipp 1988). Therapists are then in a position to point out the pathological collusive patterns in the here and now of the therapy process and to connect them with what goes on outside that process.

The most common form of resistance at the beginning of marital therapy is for both partners to expect the therapist to "fix" their spouse (Jones and G. O. Gabbard 1988). Because the externalization of the conflict onto the partner is so well established, both spouses are more interested in persuading the therapist that they are "right" than they are in repairing the marriage (Berkowitz 1984). Therapists must consistently avoid taking sides in such conflicts. Instead, they must help couples expand their perspective to encompass an appreciation of their own contributions to the conflict in the marriage.

The transition from seeing the problem as a marital conflict to perceiving it as an internal conflict that is played out within the couple is a difficult task for each partner. Projective identification in the marital dyad requires a continued state of conflict—the polarization inherent in the splitting process maintains the stable balance (Zinner 1976). Any effort to destabilize this arrangement is likely to be highly threatening to both marital partners. The need for the spouse to be the "bad object" may be so compelling that all therapeutic efforts are for naught (Dicks 1963). Despite their understanding of the pathological interactions between them, some couples will choose to live in a state of turmoil rather than face the anxiety associated with change.

In the final analysis, of course, change in marital therapy is not the therapist's responsibility—only the marital partners themselves can decide if they wish to change their marriage. As is true in all dynamic psychotherapies, the therapist must scrupulously avoid feeling driven by a need to change the couple. The therapist's task is to provide insight and understanding and to help the couple decide whether—and how—they wish to change their marriage (Jones and G. O. Gabbard 1988). When therapists find themselves highly invested in a particular outcome, they are frequently involved in a collusive interaction in which they have become identified with projected parts of the family members. Moreover, the more the therapist pushes for change, the more the couple is likely to resist. When the therapy becomes stalemated because of such resistance, it is sometimes useful for the therapist to lay out various options to the couple and to convey to them that they are free to choose how to proceed with their lives. Divorce or no change at all must be among those options and must be considered acceptable outcomes by the therapist. Only then will the couple realize that it is ultimately up to them how they choose to live their lives.

Brief Marital Therapy

Greenspan and Mannino (1974) have developed a model for brief marital therapy based on projective identification. This model is designed for couples with considerable ego strength and with no signs of any severe pathology. The goal of this form of treatment is limited: to confront each partner with those aspects of the spouse's personality that are not being perceived because of projective identification. After listening to the wife's version of the conflict, the therapist might ask the husband to repeat the essence of his wife's concern. If he omits a particular aspect of her feelings, the therapist will point out the omission.

The therapeutic process in this model of brief intervention helps both partners listen better and develop a fuller empathic appreciation for their spouse's internal experience. As marital partners come to acknowledge that they are distorting their perceptions of one another, they begin to realize that they do not know the person they married very well. When this approach is successful, it sets in motion a process of "checking out" each other's feelings rather than assuming that the partner feels a certain way.

Self Psychological Marital Therapy

In recent years the concepts of self psychology have also been applied to marital conflict. Kohut himself, in a footnote from his last book (1984), noted that "a good marriage is one in which one or the other partner rises to the challenge of providing the selfobject functions that the other's temporarily impaired self needs at a particular moment" (p. 220). He also noted that when selfobject needs are not supplied by a spouse, the result may be divorce and unending bitterness—a form of all-too-common chronic narcissistic rage.

Berkowitz (1985) has expanded Kohut's notions by examining the tendency for marital partners to develop selfobject transferences to their spouses. In this form of marital disharmony, one partner regulates self-esteem through a mirroring or idealizing relationship with the spouse. This arrangement creates problems because of the implicit demand for unconditional love and acceptance that no one can fulfill. When one spouse fails to validate or serve as an appropriate figure for idealization, the result may be self-fragmentation for the other spouse. Narcissistic rage and a wish for revenge may also appear at such times. Lansky (1982) has described such couples as having "narcissistically vulnerable" marriages, in which the dread of being shamed or humiliated is a key feature. One significant limitation to the self psychological approach to marital therapy, however, is that Kohut's theory does not adequately account for the motivation of one spouse to assume the role of selfobject for the other (Finkelstein 1988).

Indications and Contraindications

The "consumer" model is a commonsense approach clinicians can use in deciding whether a patient needs individual or family/marital therapy. What is the patient asking for? Does one "patient" come to the office or do two? Does the discussion focus on "my problem" or "our problem"? Is the problem viewed as having an internal origin or an external one? If parents come with their adolescent child, the problem of determining the therapy of choice may be more complex. Frequently, the adolescent is not convinced of the need for treatment and may remain silent throughout most of the first appointment. Meanwhile, the parents may go on and on about their son's or daughter's problems. The evaluating clinician needs to make a rapid determination regarding the next appointment. Will seeing only one "patient" be a collusion with the splitting and projective identification processes in the family (Stewart et al. 1975)? When in doubt, of course, the clinician may simply continue an exploratory evaluation process until the dynamics of the family are clearer. At times when one member of a couple or certain family members simply refuse to attend a therapy process, the therapist may be forced to work with only one family member or to do no treatment at all.

Slipp (1988) stressed the identified patient's level of differentiation from the family as a good rule of thumb in determining the therapy of choice. Individual psychotherapy is probably the treatment of choice with late adolescents or young adults who have managed to separate, psychologically and geographically, from their families and to live their own lives with reasonably mature defensive operations. But family therapy or a combination of family and individual therapy is likely to be most helpful with individuals in the same age group who are still living at home, or who are living separately but still find themselves emotionally involved with their families in an intense and conflictual manner.

A frequent problem that arises in individual psychotherapy is the patient's request to bring the spouse to an appointment to work on marital issues. If the individual process is well established, trying to convert it into a marital therapy process as well is rarely successful. The spouse who is brought in usually feels that the therapist's primary loyalty is to the other partner and is rarely able to form an alliance with the therapist. A better solution is to refer the couple to a marital therapist while continuing the original individual process.

Dynamic Pharmacotherapy

Several decades ago the phrase "dynamic pharmacotherapy" would have been considered a contradiction in terms. The legacy of mind/body dualism polarized dynamic and pharmacologic approaches to psychiatric disorders for many years. Fortunately, recent integrative trends have brought contemporary psychiatry to the point where combined use of medication and psychotherapy is now almost universal practice for both nonpsychotic and psychotic conditions (Thompson and Brodie 1981). An extensive study of the combined practice of pharmacotherapy and psychotherapy by the Group for the Advancement of Psychiatry (1975) found no significant problems with combining the two approaches and suggested further efforts toward integrating the two.

Even when formal psychotherapy is not part of the treatment regimen, dynamic principles are extraordinarily useful in prescribing psychotropic agents. Indeed, the effectiveness of pharmacotherapy can be significantly enhanced by a dynamic understanding of the treatment process. In the practice of psychopharmacotherapy, noncompliance remains a serious problem. Research suggests that as many as 50% of patients will refuse medication at some point during treatment (Jamison et al. 1979; Van Putten 1975). Among schizophrenic patients, 48% are estimated to be noncompliant within the first year of treatment, and the figure soars to 74% within the first 2 years (Corrigan et al. 1990). Other studies indicate that between 25% and 94% of patients who are registered at outpatient medication clinics do not actually take their medications as prescribed (Baekeland and Lundwall 1975; Eisenthal et al. 1979). Noncompliance can usually be understood with the aid of dynamic principles such as transference, countertransference, and resistance.

Transference

The psychiatrist prescribing medication is no less a transference figure than the psychotherapist. For patients, the decision to comply or not to comply with the doctor's recommendations activates unconscious issues of parental expectations. When patients refuse to take medication as prescribed, psychiatrists often react by becoming more authoritarian, insisting that their orders be followed without question. This approach usually backfires because it merely exacerbates the transference disposition to see the doctor as a demanding parental figure. A far more productive approach is to enlist patients' collaboration in exploring their concerns. A series of questions such as the following may be helpful: "Do you have any concerns about taking medications other than side effects?" "Do you remember problems with taking medication in the past?" "Have you heard anything on television or read anything in the newspaper about this medication?" "Does your family have any special feelings about taking medications?" "What do you think has caused your illness?" "Does this medication have any particular meaning to you?" "What feelings do you have toward the prescribing doctor?"

One patient experienced the prescription of an antidepressant as an empathic failure on the part of the psychiatrist. When the patient's noncompliance was explored with him, he told his doctor, "I was looking for someone to validate my feelings. Instead, you tried to medicate them away. I felt like the pill was a way of telling me to shut up." When the psychiatrist encouraged him to elaborate further, the patient was able to connect this feeling with earlier experiences with his father, whom he experienced as inattentive and uncaring about his concerns.

Other patients, especially those who have characterological tendencies to be controlling or dominating, will see medication as a threat to their counterdependent stance. Taking a pill means submitting to the domination of a powerful parental figure. These patients must be given some control over whether to take the medication (Thompson and Brodie 1981). With overly submissive patients, one often encounters the opposite situation. Pills make these patients feel "fed" and taken care of to such an extent that they may decide that they no longer need to take responsibility for any aspect of their illness.

Transference struggles may be particularly intense with whining, "manipulative *help-rejecters*" (Groves 1978). These patients systematically defeat every treatment intervention, pharmacologic or otherwise. They frequently have gone through a lengthy list of psychotropic agents without feeling any benefit. Exploring the transference dynamics may lead to the uncovering of a great deal of resentment and bitterness toward parental figures who the patient believes did not give enough nurturance. By rejecting help offered to them, these patients may be unconsciously seeking revenge against their parents (G. O. Gabbard 1988). When such patients sense that they are making their doctor miserable, they often feel a secret triumph.

A unique aspect of transference in dynamic pharmacotherapy is transference to the medication itself (Gutheil 1982). Placebo responses to medications often have this same transference quality. A manic patient, for example, became markedly subdued after one 300-mg dose of lithium carbonate, a response that could not be explained pharmacologically. Placebo side effects are also common. Another manifestation of transference to medications is the response to changing the drug rituals of chronic patients (Appelbaum and Gutheil 1980). Such patients may decompensate into psychosis with the slightest alteration of their usual medication regimen.

The transference relationship to a medication may be most obvious in situations where the pill takes the place of the absent doctor. Pills may function as transitional objects for some patients, allowing them to maintain some sense of connectedness with their psychiatrists even when seeing them quite infrequently (Book 1987). Touching or looking at the pill may have a soothing effect on the patient. In training programs, where residents rotate through services on an annual basis, patients may deal with the loss of their doctor by becoming intensely attached to the medication prescribed by the departing doctor (Gutheil 1977).

Transferences of this type are powerful and may lead to another form of noncompliance—refusal to discontinue medications because of the unconscious meaning of the medication to the patient. Transference issues must always be taken into account when prescribing psychotropic agents to paranoid patients. In more subtle cases, the patient may discontinue a medication for the ostensible reason of unpleasant side effects, when in actuality the patient is afraid of being poisoned. Insistence on compliance will greatly increase the paranoia, while empathic exploration of the nature of the fears may help the patient to realize that they are unfounded and to view the therapist as less threatening (Book 1987).

Countertransference

The prescribing of medication is just as likely as any other treatment intervention to be contaminated by countertransference. One common manifestation of countertransference is overprescription. It is not uncommon for a patient to arrive at a hospital or an emergency room with a brown paper bag full of psychoactive agents. One such patient was taking three antipsychotics, two antidepressants, lithium carbonate, and two benzodiazepines. After a few days in the hospital, it was apparent that this patient evoked intense feelings of impotence and anger in treaters. The excessive amounts of medication reflected the countertransference despair of the attending psychiatrist.

Narcissistic injury may also be a factor in countertransference. Some psychotherapists may fail to prescribe a much-needed medication because they believe that doing so would be tantamount to conceding that their psychotherapeutic skills have been ineffective. Others may induce guilt feelings in noncompliers so that they will feel obligated to comply with the prescription out of a wish not to hurt their doctor.

Some psychiatrists become anxious about intense feelings of any kind in the transference. Medication may be viewed as a way to deal with this countertransference anxiety. The discussion of side effects may also be influenced by this anxiety. Gutheil (1982), for example, noted that psychiatrists seldom discuss the sexual side effects of phenothiazines with their patients because of their own discomfort with overt sexual discussions.

Countertransference anger, which is a common response to noncompliance in patients, may take many forms. Some psychiatrists may collude with the noncompliance to demonstrate how ill their patients will get if they do not follow the "doctor's orders" (Book 1987). Others may bully patients into taking their medications or threaten to discharge them from treatment if they do not comply. Those psychiatrists who have difficulty controlling their anger may refuse to set limits on patients who demand increasing amounts of medication. In these cases the psychiatrist hopes that gratifying the demands of the patient will keep aggression and hostility out of the therapeutic relationship. Unfortunately, the patient's demandingness and anger usually escalate.

Resistance

Resistance to treatment is as powerful a force in pharmacotherapy as it is in psychotherapy. Illness may be preferable to health for numerous reasons. It is well known, for example, that patients with bipolar affective disorder may enjoy their manic episodes so much that they will stop taking their lithium. In one study of schizophrenic patients (Van Putten et al. 1976), a similar cause of resistance was uncovered. In this investigation, side effects and secondary gain had little to do with noncompliance. An ego-syntonic grandiose psychosis was the most powerful discriminating factor that distinguished schizophrenic patients who did not comply from those who did. Clearly, the noncompliers preferred their experience of psychotic grandiosity.

Denial of illness is also a prominent cause of resistance to pharmacotherapy. For some patients, any psychotropic agent carries with it the stigma of mental illness. When an acute psychotic episode goes into remission, a patient may stop the antipsychotic medication responsible for the remission because maintenance treatment connotes a chronic mental illness. Nonpsychotic patients who are quite willing to submit to psychotherapeutic treatment will balk at the suggestion of medication because they are convinced it means that they are more seriously disturbed than they like to think. Likewise, patients who have had a relative in psychopharmacologic treatment may unconsciously identify with that relative when offered the same medication (Book 1987). This identification may serve as a resistance to accepting treatment, particularly if the relative had an especially unfavorable outcome, such as suicide.

Finally, another form of resistance not related to compliance with the prescribed medication represents the flip side of the wish to deny illness. It is not at all uncommon for some patients who willingly take their medication to nevertheless resist the therapeutic effects of pharmacologic agents. These patients are so powerfully invested in their illness that they tenaciously cling to their symptoms even when these are challenged by potent psychotropic agents. For such patients, a psychotherapeutic approach is the treatment of choice.

Therapeutic Alliance

The foregoing discussion about noncompliance should make it clear that the therapeutic alliance plays a crucial role in dynamic pharmacotherapy. Numerous authors have stressed that attending to the therapeutic alliance is part of the prescribing process (Docherty and Fiester 1985; Elkin et al. 1988; Gutheil 1982; Howard et al. 1970). Although much contemporary psychopharmacological research does not quantify the doctor-patient relationship, many investigators have noted its influence on compliance. One study (Howard et al. 1970) discovered that subtle aspects of the therapist's behavior, including vocal enthusiasm, body language, and use of the patient's name, differentiated psychiatrists with low dropout rates from those with high attrition rates. This study also indicated that attention to the therapeutic alliance in the first session prevented noncompliance with drug treatment.

Studies of the dropout rate in both psychotherapeutic and psychopharmacologic treatment settings have emphasized that patient expectations can influence attrition (Freedman et al. 1958; Overall and Aronson 1963). Different patients come to a psychiatrist with different expectations of the kind of treatments available. American moviegoers might well get the impression that all psychiatrists are psychotherapists, because the effective prescription of psychotropic medication is virtually absent from cinematic depictions of psychiatrists and psychiatric treatment (K. Gabbard and G. O. Gabbard 1987). At some point in the first interview, psychiatrists should explore their patients' expectations so that the treatment prescribed is in some way consistent with them. If the treatment of choice is counter to a patient's preconceived notions, an educational effort may be necessary to convince the patient of its usefulness.

In Chapter 4, the concept of collaboration was emphasized in the discussion of the therapeutic alliance in psychotherapy. An analogous concept of "participant prescribing" (Gutheil 1982) is relevant for pharmacotherapy. The unconscious tendency of some psychiatrists to switch to a more authoritarian mode when prescribing medications is liable to backfire in the form of noncompliance. Even in the practice of internal medicine, sensitive internists are aware that they will evoke better compliance if they discuss with their patients the reasons for antibiotics, thus enlisting the patients' cooperation in the process of treatment. The variable of patient education positively influences the development of a therapeutic alliance in pharmacotherapy. All patients should be thoroughly informed about the therapeutic and side effects of any pharmacologic agent they receive. With acutely psychotic patients, however, this discussion sometimes must wait until the acute episode is under pharmacologic control.

Special types of compliance problems are often encountered when medication is added to an ongoing psychotherapy process, as in the following example:

Ms. F, a 39-year-old married professional woman, came to psychiatric treatment because of feelings of depression, low energy, lack of satisfaction in her job, difficulty sleeping, and decreased sex drive. She seemed extremely grateful for the opportunity to have someone listen to her. After a few weeks and several sessions of psychotherapy, Ms. F began to feel a great deal of trust in her therapist. She poured out her heart in a poignant and moving manner during the sessions. With a great many tears, she told of the extraordinary difficulties in her life and the problems she encountered at home and at work.

After about 6 weeks of these sessions, her therapist told her that her symptoms were of sufficient severity that he was going to prescribe a tricyclic antidepressant for her. The therapist wrote out the prescription, explained the side effects she might encounter, and sent her on her way with instructions to begin taking the medication immediately.

The following week Ms. F came for her appointment and began talking once again about her problems but made no mention of the medication. When her therapist asked her how she was doing with the agent he had prescribed, she said that she had not had time to go to the pharmacy to fill the prescription but that she would do so in the next few days. The therapist again emphasized the importance of starting on the medication as soon as possible. Ms. F minimized her failure to fill the prescription and reassured her therapist that she would do so before the next appointment.

A week passed and Ms. F returned for her therapy session. Once again she reported that she had failed to go to the pharmacy. Knowing that this lack of compliance was reflecting some dynamic that was not readily apparent, her therapist explored with her what reasons she might have for not wanting to take the medication. With some reluctance Ms. F admitted that she was very much afraid that she was receiving medication because her therapist did not want to hear all the complaints she brought to each session. Ms. F experienced the prescription as though she was being told to "shut up." Her therapist asked her if she had had any similar experiences in her life. She went on to say that her father was not a verbal person and that he had chastised her throughout her childhood and adolescence for complaining all the time. Ms. F also noted that her husband was much the same way and had urged her to go to a psychiatrist so he wouldn't have to listen to her complaints. She feared that her therapist would no longer see her for psychotherapy if she responded well to the medication.

The therapist told her that medication and psychotherapy were not mutually exclusive and that he would continue to work psychotherapeutically with her while she was taking medication. Ms. F seemed relieved to have that reassurance, and she complied with the prescription on a regular basis after that session.

Combined Treatment

Despite the history of polarization between psychotherapists and pharmacotherapists, the combination of psychotherapy and medication is a time-honored clinical practice in psychiatry. In three different analytic cases involving severe depression, Anna Freud enlisted a colleague to prescribe medication—with highly beneficial results (Lipton 1983). She was convinced that the addition of pharmacologic agents was crucial in allowing the analysis to continue. Luborsky et al. (1976) surveyed 26 research studies evaluating combined treatment and found that, in 69% of the comparisons, the combined approach was more effective than either psychotherapy or pharmacotherapy alone. Much of the professional resistance to developing an integrative model of combined treatment stems from the traditional view of the approaches as competitive rather than synergistic. Karasu (1984), however, noted:

> Psychotherapy and pharmacotherapy are not competitive or inhibitive, but each has differential effects or loci of outcome (drugs have their major manifestations upon symptom formation and affective distress, whereas psychotherapy more directly influences interpersonal relations and social adjustment); each is activated and sustained on a different time schedule (drugs may take effect sooner and be of short-term duration, while psychotherapy results may not reveal themselves until a later point in time, but last longer); and each may best relate to different disorders or their subtypes (drugs for time-limited and autonomous "state" disorders, psychotherapy for long-lasting "trait" disorders). (p. 380)

The "state/trait" distinction of Karasu is generally valid, but there are notable exceptions. Anxiety is a "state" disorder that may respond well to either modality. The same can be said of depression. On the other hand, attention-deficit disorder is a "trait" disorder that may respond well to tricyclic antidepressants (Ostow 1983). It is certainly true that the effects of psychotherapy generally take lonker to show up than the effects of pharmacotherapy. This observation has led some to propose a "two-stage treatment strategy" (Karasu 1982; Klerman 1978). In this approach, the psychopharmacologic agent is the first step, designed to relieve symptoms and set the stage for a later psychotherapy process. The goal of psychotherapy, the second step, would then be geared to interpersonal relationships, social adjustment, and improvement at work.

Despite the lack of evidence to suggest any deleterious effect of combining pharmacotherapy with psychotherapy, concern continues in some quarters about the potential for medications to obstruct or even destroy psychotherapy. Some clinicians worry, for example, that reducing anxiety will eradicate a patient's motivation for continuing the painful work of psychotherapy. Others speculate that the transference will be irreparably confounded by the introduction of medication. A comprehensive review of studies designed to investigate these concerns reveals them to be unfounded (Karasu 1982). What *is* required of clinicians who combine the approaches, however, is an awareness of the "bimodal relatedness" inherent in the dual role (Docherty et al. 1977). The patient must be viewed simultaneously as a disturbed person and as a diseased central nervous system. The former view requires an empathic subjective approach, while the latter demands an objective medical model approach. The clinician must be able to shift between these two modes gracefully yet also stay attuned to the impact of the shift on the patient.

Extensive case reports in the literature provide persuasive examples of the efficacy of combined treatment. Wylie and Wylie (1987) reported the case of a female analytic patient who could not work within the transference in the analysis until monoamine oxidase inhibitors were prescribed for her depression. The medication reduced her affective vulnerability sufficiently to enable her to risk dealing with transference feelings. Loeb and Loeb (1987) treated seven manic patients who were taking lithium carbonate while in either psychoanalysis or psychoanalytic psychotherapy. Through analysis or therapy, these patients became aware of a marked increase in their unconscious sexual impulses and their defenses against them. The patients were then able to learn that these impulses heralded the onset of a manic episode. By making these impulses conscious, they were able to prevent future manic episodes by increasing their lithium dosage.

The fundamental compatibility of biology and psychodynamics was emphasized in Chapter 1. One instance of this marriage is the increasing practice of combining pharmacotherapy and psychotherapy. Because conceptual bridges are still being built between the two approaches, much of the practice remains empirical at this point. As in all psychiatry, the guiding principle must be to help the patient rather than to remain true to one's theoretical biases.

References

Appelbaum PS, Gutheil TG: Drug refusal: a study of psychiatric inpatients. Am J Psychiatry 137:340–346, 1980

Baekeland F, Lundwall L: Dropping out of treatment: a critical review. Psychol Bull 82:738–783, 1975

Bateson G, Jackson DD, Haley J, et al: Toward a theory of schizophrenia. Behav Sci 1:251–264, 1956

Berkowitz DA: An overview of the psychodynamics of couples: bridging concepts, in Marriage and Divorce: A Contemporary Perspective. Edited by Nadelson CC, Polonsky DC. New York, Guilford, 1984, pp 117–126

Berkowitz DA: Selfobject needs and marital disharmony. Psychoanal Rev 72:229–237, 1985

Bion WR: Experiences in Groups and Other Papers. New York, Basic Books, 1961

Book HE: Some psychodynamics of non-compliance. Can J Psychiatry 32:115–117, 1987

Bowen M: Family Therapy in Clinical Practice. New York, Jason Aronson, 1978

Corrigan PW, Liberman RP, Engel JD: From noncompliance to collaboration in the treatment of schizophrenia. Hosp Community Psychiatry 41:1203–1211, 1990

Dicks HV: Object relations theory and marital studies. Br J Med Psychol 36:125–129, 1963

Docherty JP, Fiester SJ: The therapeutic alliance and compliance with psychopharmacology, in Psychiatry Update: The American Psychiatric Association Annual Review, Vol 4. Edited by Hales RE, Frances AJ. Washington, DC, American Psychiatric Press, 1985, pp 607–632

Docherty JP, Marder SR, Van Kammen DP, et al: Psychotherapy and pharmacotherapy: conceptual issues. Am J Psychiatry 134:529–533, 1977

Eisenthal S, Emery R, Lazare A, et al: "Adherence" and the negotiated approach to patienthood. Arch Gen Psychiatry 36:393–398, 1979

Elkin I, Pilkonis PA, Docherty JP, et al: Conceptual and methodological issues in comparative studies of psychotherapy and pharmacotherapy, I: active ingredients and mechanisms of change. Am J Psychiatry 145:909–917, 1988

Ezriel H: A psycho-analytic approach to group treatment. Br J Med Psychol 23:59–74, 1950

Finkelstein L: Psychoanalysis, marital therapy, and object-relations theory. J Am Psychoanal Assoc 36:905–931, 1988

Freedman N, Engelhardt DM, Hankoff LD, et al: Drop-out from outpatient psychiatric treatment. Archives of Neurology and Psychiatry 80:657–666, 1958

Gabbard GO: A contemporary perspective on psychoanalytically informed hospital treatment. Hosp Community Psychiatry 39:1291–1295, 1988

Gabbard K, Gabbard GO: Psychiatry and the Cinema. Chicago, IL, University of Chicago Press, 1987

Ganzarain RC: Psychotic-like anxieties and primitive defenses in group analytic psychotherapy. Issues in Ego Psychology 3:42–48, 1980

Ganzarain RC: Working through in analytic group psychotherapy. Int J Group Psychother 33:281–296, 1983

Gibbard GR, Hartman JJ: The significance of utopian fantasies in small groups. Int J Group Psychother 23:125–147, 1973

Greenspan SI, Mannino FV: A model for brief intervention with couples based on projective identification. Am J Psychiatry 131:1103–1106, 1974

Group for the Advancement of Psychiatry: Report No. 93: Pharmacotherapy and psychotherapy: paradoxes, problems, and progress. 9:261–434, 1975

Groves J: Taking care of the hateful patient. N Engl J Med 298:883–887, 1978

Gutheil TG: Psychodynamics in drug prescribing. Drug Therapy 2:35–40, 1977

Gutheil TG: The psychology of psychopharmacology. Bull Menninger Clin 46:321–330, 1982

Horwitz L: A group-centered approach to group psychotherapy. Int J Group Psychother 27:423–439, 1977

Horwitz L: Projective identification in dyads and groups. Int J Group Psychother 33:259–279, 1983

Howard K, Rickels K, Mock JE, et al: Therapeutic style and attrition rate from psychiatric drug treatment. J Nerv Ment Dis 150:102–110, 1970

Jamison KR, Gerner RH, Goodwin FK: Patient and physician attitudes toward lithium. Arch Gen Psychiatry 36:866–869, 1979

Jones SA, Gabbard GO: Marital therapy of physician couples, in Medical Marriages. Edited by Gabbard GO, Menninger RW. Washington, DC, American Psychiatric Press, 1988, pp 137–151

Karasu TB: Psychotherapy and pharmacotherapy: toward an integrative model. Am J Psychiatry 139:1102–1113, 1982

Karasu TB: Politics, practice, and p value in psychotherapy, in Psychotherapy Research: Where Are We and Where Should We Go? Edited by Williams JBW, Spitzer RL. New York, Guilford, 1984, pp 372–383

Klerman GL: Combining drugs and psychotherapy in the treatment of depression, in Depression: Biology, Psychodynamics, and Treatment. Edited by Cole JO, Schatzberg AF, Frazier SH. New York, Plenum, 1978, pp 213–227

Kohut H: How Does Analysis Cure? Edited by Goldberg A. Chicago, IL, University of Chicago Press, 1984

Lansky MR: Masks of the narcissistically vulnerable marriage. International Journal of Family Psychiatry 3:439–449, 1982

Lipton MA: A letter from Anna Freud. Am J Psychiatry 140:1583–1584, 1983

Loeb FF, Loeb LR: Psychoanalytic observations on the effect of lithium on manic attacks. J Am Psychoanal Assoc 35:877–902, 1987

Luborsky L, Singer B, Luborsky L: Comparative studies of psychotherapies: is it true that "everybody has won and all must have prizes?" in Evaluation of Psychological Therapies: Psychotherapies, Behavior Therapies, Drug Therapies, and Their Interaction. Edited by Spitzer RL, Klein DF. Baltimore, MD, Johns Hopkins University Press, 1976, pp 3–22

Minuchin S: Families and Family Therapy. Cambridge, MA, Harvard University Press, 1974

Ogden TH: Projective Identification and Psychotherapeutic Technique. New York, Jason Aronson, 1982

Ostow M: Interactions of psychotherapy and pharmacotherapy (letter). Am J Psychiatry 140:370–371, 1983

Overall B, Aronson H: Expectations of psychotherapy in patients of lower socioeconomic class. Am J Orthopsychiatry 33:421–430, 1963

Redl F: Psychoanalysis and group therapy: a developmental point of view. Am J Orthopsychiatry 33:135–147, 1963

Rioch MJ: The work of Wilfred Bion on groups. Psychiatry 33:56–66, 1970

Sadock BJ: Preparation, selection of patients, and organization of the group, in Comprehensive Group Psychotherapy, 2nd Edition. Edited by Kaplan HI, Sadock BJ. Baltimore, MD, Williams & Wilkins, 1983, pp 23–32

Scharff DE, Scharff JS: Object Relations Family Therapy. Northvale, NJ, Jason Aronson, 1987

Scheidlinger S: On the concept of the "mother-group." Int J Group Psychother 24:417–428, 1974

Selvini Palazzoli M, Boscolo L, Cecchin G, et al: Paradox and Counterparadox: A New Model in the Therapy of the Family in Schizophrenic Transaction. New York, Jason Aronson, 1978

Shapiro ER, Zinner J, Shapiro RL, et al: The influence of family experience on borderline personality development. International Review of Psychoanalysis 2:399–411, 1975

Slipp S: Object Relations: A Dynamic Bridge Between Individual and Family Treatment. New York, Jason Aronson, 1984

Slipp S: The Technique and Practice of Object Relations Family Therapy. Northvale, NJ, Jason Aronson, 1988

Sonne JL: An example of group therapy for victims of therapist-client sexual intimacy, in Sexual Exploitation in Professional Relationships. Edited by Gabbard GO. Washington, DC, American Psychiatric Press, 1989, pp 101–113

Stewart RH, Peters TC, Marsh S, et al: An object-relations approach to psychotherapy with marital couples, families, and children. Fam Process 14:161–178, 1975

Thompson EM, Brodie HKH: The psychodynamics of drug therapy. Current Psychiatric Therapies 20:239–251, 1981

Van Putten T: Why do patients with manic-depressive illness stop their lithium? Compr Psychiatry 16:179–183, 1975

Van Putten T, Crumpton E, Yale C: Drug refusal in schizophrenia and the wish to be crazy. Arch Gen Psychiatry 33:1443–1446, 1976

Whitaker DS, Lieberman MA: Psychotherapy Through the Group Process. New York, Atherton Press, 1964

Wolf A: Psychoanalysis in groups, in Comprehensive Group Psychotherapy, 2nd Edition. Edited by Kaplan HI, Sadock BJ. Baltimore, MD, Williams & Wilkins, 1983, pp 113–131

Wylie HW Jr, Wylie ML: An effect of pharmacotherapy on the psychoanalytic process: case report of a modified analysis. Am J Psychiatry 144:489–492, 1987

Yalom ID: The Theory and Practice of Group Psychotherapy, 3rd Edition. New York, Basic Books, 1985

Zinner J: The implications of projective identification for marital interaction, in Contemporary Marriage: Structure, Dynamics, and Therapy. Edited by Grunebaum H, Christ J. Boston, MA, Little, Brown, 1976, pp 293–308

Zinner J, Shapiro R: Projective identification as a mode of perception and behavior in families of adolescents. Int J Psychoanal 53:523–530, 1972

Zinner J, Shapiro R: The family as a single psychic entity: implications for acting out in adolescence. International Review of Psychoanalysis 1:179–186, 1974

Chapter 6

Treatments in Dynamic Psychiatry III: Dynamically Informed Hospital Treatment

The shape of psychiatric hospitalization in the 1990s has been determined for the most part by economic forces. Third and fourth parties (managed care companies) dictate that inpatient treatment must be used sparingly—only for life-threatening clinical situations that constitute "acute medical necessity." The average length of stay in many areas of the country is less than 2 weeks. The rich tradition of psychodynamically informed hospital treatment has gradually been eroded by a philosophical perspective characterized by rapid assessment and aggressive pharmacotherapy.

Hospital psychiatry is now at a historical juncture in which the healing power of human relationships is in grave jeopardy of getting lost in a flurry of rapid patient turnover, diagnosis by symptom check-lists, and biological reductionism. Empirical research (Pi et al. 1983) has demonstrated that the majority of acutely symptomatic patients will show significant improvement or even full remission after as little as a week of medication-free hospitalization.

How can we account for these improvements? Surely the hospital building itself provides little balm for the psychiatrically disturbed individual. Is it the removal from noxious environmental influences? The reduction of stimuli? Sanctuary from the world? Often, patients themselves are at a loss to identify the crucial elements that contributed to their inpatient recovery. Such was the case with William Styron's searing account of his own depression in *Darkness Visible* (1990). In an otherwise articulate narrative of his encounters with clinicians, Styron seemed unable to pinpoint exactly what helped him find his way out of his depression during his inpatient experience. He was clear on one count, however—nothing short of hospitalization worked.

Could it be that the mutative ingredient of hospital treatment amounts to a network of therapeutic relationships? Psychodynamically informed hospital treatment (Gabbard 1988) operates on the assumption that in a manner analogous to psychodynamic psychotherapy, therapeutic responses from the clinical staff are central healing factors in the milieu.

Because psychodynamic principles evolved largely from the practice of psychoanalysis, these precepts are sometimes narrowly construed to be relevant only to outpatient treatment. One psychiatric resident asked his supervisor for help in understanding a hospitalized patient, only to be told, "Dynamics apply only to outpatients, not inpatients." Nothing could be further from the truth, of course. However, the supervisor's comment reflects an unfortunate trend in modern hospital psychiatry to use the psychiatric unit as a mere holding tank where patients wait for their medication to take effect. The treatment of many patients is greatly enhanced by approaching hospital treatment with a dynamic perspective.

A Historical Review

The practitioner can draw on a long tradition of the application of psychoanalytic principles to hospital treatment. The history of the notion of the psychoanalytic hospital began with Simmel's work at Schloss Tegel (1929), where he noted that certain patients could not be analyzed outside a hospital because of various symptomatic behaviors, such as alcoholism or phobias. He had the idea that a hospital could extend the patient's hour on the couch by training hospital staff members to conduct quasi-analytic treatment in the milieu as issues of transference and resistance arose. In his creative and brilliant *Guide to the Order Sheet,* Will Menninger (1939/1982) deemphasized the model of individual psychoanalysis and attempted to apply the principles of psychoanalysis directly within the hospital by manipulation of the milieu. Working from the assumption that all symptoms and disturbed behaviors derive from disturbances in the proper fusion and expression of the two major instinctual drives—libido and aggression—he evolved a system of milieu treatment based largely on sublimation and not requiring insight. Rather than frustrating or interpreting unconscious wishes and conflicts, this approach focused on rechanneling energies into less harmful paths. For example, Menninger encouraged the direct expression of hostilities toward substitute objects; prescriptions for a patient might range from demolishing a building to punching a punching bag. Unfortunately, this second model could not take into account those patients with ego weaknesses involving impulse control problems who required a treatment designed to help them gain more control over drive expression rather than to redirect it. Moreover, this conceptualization was limited by confining itself to the dual instinct theory of the times, which tended to neglect the object relations context in which disturbed drives occur, nor did it allow for systematic examination of transference and countertransference in the milieu.

The third model grew out of an awareness that patients were recreating with various staff members in the hospital setting their conflicts with their own family members (Hilles 1968). Interpretation of maladaptive behavior patterns in terms of their roots in the past was common within this model, which relied less and less on providing substitute outlets for unconscious needs. The milieu was not seen as a therapeutic community in which real, constructive experiences with peers are stressed, but rather as a screen upon which archaic patterns are projected and then examined. Schlesinger and Holzman (1970), in describing the therapeutic aspects of the milieu of a psychiatric hospital, noted that the milieu could supplement the therapist-patient relationship by providing opportunities for patients to work out in a real context what had been talked about in therapy. It also served as a kind of training ground or laboratory where patients could practice trying to change in various ways as they progressed in psychotherapy. Schlesinger and Holzman asserted that prescribing milieu therapy for hospital patients was a complex process requiring a sensitivity to the multiple functions of a patient's involvement in the hospital milieu.

They proposed a schema based on the five points of view of psychoanalytic metapsychology: the structural, the economic, the dynamic, the adaptive, and the genetic.

A number of authors (Gabbard 1986, 1988, 1989c, 1992a; Harty 1979; Stamm 1985b; Wesselius 1968; Zee 1977) have pinpointed countertransference as an integral part of the treatment process. They offer the caveat that treatment effectiveness is impaired when staff members respond in a countertransferential manner as though they are one of the patient's parents. These countertransference influences occur regularly, rather than occasionally, and the systematic examination of the countertransference should be part of the routine work of the treatment team. A recurring theme throughout the various formulations of psychoanalytically informed hospital treatment is that patients recreate in the milieu environment their own internal object relations. This point of view is reflected in Kernberg's (1973) integrative attempt to synthesize psychoanalytic object relations theory, systems theory, and the use of group process in an overall approach to hospital treatment. One basic tenet of his approach is that there exists in all of us a potential for both higher-level object relationships—typical of the transference neurosis in individual psychoanalytic treatment—and more primitive levels of object relationships, leading to psychotic regression in group situations. He theorized that whereas the higher level of object relationship is activated in individual therapeutic relationships, the more primitive version is much more likely to be activated in group treatment modalities. A combination of individual and group treatment in hospitalization provides for intervention at both levels. Kernberg (1973) insisted that such a two-pronged treatment approach requires "a 'neutral' hospital milieu, that is, an attitude of staff basically equidistant from the different intrapsychic and external agencies involved in the patient's conflicts, and reflected in an overall friendly and generally tolerant, an interested and intellectually alert hospital atmosphere" (p. 372). In the context of this neutral atmosphere, Kernberg saw the therapeutic community and individual hospital therapy operating simultaneously to examine internal object relationships as well as to perform the ego or control function. He formulated hospital treatment "as the simultaneous diagnosis and treatment of the patient's control function and his internal world of object-relationships" (Kernberg 1973, p. 379).

In summary, the application of psychoanalytic/psychodynamic principles to hospital treatment has undergone a gradual shift during the past 60 years. The notion of containment of patients undergoing psychoanalysis gradually gave way to a second model involving prescribed interactions with milieu staff. The third and current model, because it shifts the emphasis to the systematic examination of transference and countertransference, views patients as re-creating their internal object relations in the milieu.

Dynamic Principles in Temporary Hospital Treatment

A dynamic approach provides for a diagnostic understanding that pays careful attention to patients' ego weaknesses and strengths, their intrapsychic object relations as manifested in family and social relationships, their capacity for psychological work, and the childhood origins of their current problems. A psychodynamic assessment may lead a clinician to conclude that interpretive interventions and uncovering of unconscious material are ill-advised. With patients who have significant ego weakness and/or organically based cognitive impairment, ego-supportive approaches and those geared to building self-esteem may be recommended. Because of the reality of daily hospital practice, the terms *dynamically informed* or *psychoanalytically informed* hospital treatment are preferable to *dynamic* or *psychoanalytic* hospital treatment (Gabbard 1986).

Psychoanalytic theories of development are useful in designing inpatient treatment plans. A psychoanalytically informed hospital team realizes that the majority of its patients are developmentally arrested. Knowledge of psychoanalytic theory allows the team to respond at an appropriate developmental level, accepting the notion that the patient is a child in an adult's body. This perspective helps the staff avoid the perils of depersonification (Rinsley 1982), whereby the patient is expected to behave as a mature and polite adult in spite of severe psychopathology. Such depersonification has often been the life story of the severely disturbed patient in terms of interactions with family members.

Psychoanalytic theory provides models of interventions geared to the patient's phase-appropriate developmental needs, such as empathic mirroring (Kohut 1971) and the provision of a holding environment (Stamm 1985a; Winnicott 1965). Within this context, the limits associated with hospital structure are not viewed as punishments for immature and irritating behavior but rather as external substitutes for missing intrapsychic structures. In a similar vein, staff members must perform auxiliary ego functions, such as reality testing, impulse control, anticipation of consequences (judgment), and sharpening of self–object differentiation.

These observations lead to a consideration of two facts that are immediately apparent when applying psychodynamic principles to hospital treatment: 1) The patient population of a psychiatric hospital is generally far more disturbed than the typical outpatient in dynamic therapy, and 2) expressive interventions must be leavened with a good deal of support in light of this different patient population. For example, technique in the classical psychoanalytic situation is geared to superego modification (Strachey 1934) designed to remove neurotic inhibitions that deprive the patient of pleasure from drive expression (e.g., sexual fulfillment). The majority of psychiatric patients referred to a hospital, however, are there because of unbridled and unrestrained drive expression rather than neurotic inhibitions that restrict free drive expression. Since superego lacunae are also present in many hospitalized patients, their superego development must be fostered rather than modified. Hence, as a general rule, whereas neurotic patients in expressive therapy or analysis are approached with the aim of analyzing defensive configurations and freeing the drive derivatives inhibited by these defenses, borderline or psychotic hospitalized patients are approached with the aim of taming direct expressions of impulses and drive derivatives by strengthening the ego (or the superego) and encouraging more mature defensive configurations.

Neutrality is another principle of technique that must be modified in its application to hospital treatment. If we accept Anna Freud's (1936/1966) definition of neutrality as the ability to remain equidistant from the id, the ego, and the superego, and from external reality factors, then we must acknowledge that in a majority of hospital cases the approach of the staff and of the hospital structure itself unquestionably sides with one intrapsychic agency or another. For example, when a hospital patient becomes violently aggressive toward a staff member or another patient, physical and structural measures such as restraints, seclusion, and antipsychotic medication are frequently used to control the direct drive expression. Likewise, a sexually promiscuous patient may be restricted to his or her room because the behavior is viewed as destructive to the patient. In both cases the hospital staff departs from neutrality to make a judgment that the patient's sexual and aggressive forces must be controlled. Alternatively, with severely depressed and self-destructive patients who are victimized by a relentlessly tormenting superego, the staff may actively side against the superego forces in the patient.

Technical neutrality also implies a certain objectivity that tempers untoward emotional involvement with the patient. This mental attitude may be achievable within the confines of a 50-minute period in the consulting room with a neurotic patient. Achieving this form of objectivity is much more difficult for the psychiatric nurse who faces an 8-hour shift of repeated encounters with the unmitigated rage of the borderline patient and the catastrophic terror of the psychotically regressed patient. Only an automaton could avoid being swept up at times by the powerful emotions engendered in such a setting, a point to which we shall return later.

Interpretation is another cornerstone of expressive technique. Interpretations *are* used and should be used in the treatment of many hospitalized patients, but usually in the context of considerable relationship building and preparatory comments, including confrontations, clarifications, ego-supportive measures, and reality-based advice and instructions regarding daily living on the unit. For an interpretation to be effective, it requires a patient whose psychological-mindedness, abstraction ability, and intelligence are sufficient to understand the interpretation and assimilate it into conscious awareness. Clearly, the expectation of understanding and assimilating an interpretation is a tall order for patients who suffer from cognitive dysfunctions of an organic nature or patients who are floridly psychotic and unable to organize their thinking. There may also be other patients in a psychiatric hospital whose egos would be overwhelmed and fragmented by the introduction of unconscious material via an interpretation.

A Transference-Countertransference Model

Patients who enter the hospital tend to repeat their family situations in the milieu. To be more precise, they externalize their internal object relations. The recapitulation of the patient's internal object relations in the interpersonal field of the milieu can best be understood by an examination of the defense mechanisms of splitting and projective identification. Although these mechanisms are operative in some neurotic patients, they are most prevalent in patients with borderline and psychotic levels of ego organization, features that also happen to characterize the group of patients most commonly found in inpatient settings. Moreover, these mechanisms are undoubtedly activated in part by the group dynamics inherent in inpatient team work. Splitting and projective identification work in tandem to disavow and externalize self- or object-representations often associated with specific affective states. This projective disavowal is a means of coercing persons in the environment to participate in an externalized version of an internal object relationship.

Projective identification operates unconsciously, automatically, and with compelling force. Clinicians feel "bullied" or coerced into complying with the role that has been projectively attributed to them. A basic axiom of psychodynamically informed hospital treatment acknowledges that staff members are more similar to patients than different from them. The feelings, fantasies, identifications, and introjects within patients have their counterparts in treaters. Because those counterparts may be more strongly repressed in staff, when they are activated by a patient, they often are experienced as alien forces sweeping over the treater. Symington (1990) characterized this projective identification process as a bully/victim paradigm in which one is deprived of the freedom to think one's own thoughts. Indeed, hospital clinicians who are the targets of the projected material often feel that they are in a form of bondage to the patient in that they cannot think, feel, or function in their usual therapeutic role.

Defining projective identification in this manner suggests that much of the intense countertransference experienced by staff members involved in inpatient treatment can be understood as stemming from unconscious identifications with projected aspects of the patient's internal world. However, it would be naive and oversimplistic to assume that all the emotional reactions arising in treaters can be attributed to the patient's behavior. Inpatient clinicians will also manifest emotional reactions in keeping with the classical, or narrow, form of countertransference, in which treaters react to patients as though they are people from the treaters' past. One of the advantages of working in the context of an inpatient treatment team is that staff members can help one another distinguish characteristic countertransference patterns based on the staff members' own psychological issues from those that are coerced identifications with aspects of the patient's projected internal world. It would be ideal if each staff member could make such distinctions individually, but such expectations are not realistic in hospital treatment.

To describe the mechanisms of splitting and projective identification provides only a partial explanation of the tendency for patients to externalize their internal object relations within the milieu relationships. To point out that this repetition occurs unconsciously, automatically, and with a coercive force does not adequately account for the unconscious motivational forces behind the repetition. At least four different forces can be identified that contribute to the repetition of internal object relations (Gabbard 1992b).

Active mastery of passively experienced trauma. In re-creating internalized patterns of relating in the inpatient setting, patients may be attempting to actively master passively experienced trauma (Pine 1990). By reactivating problematic relationships, patients may gain a feeling of mastery and control over past traumatic relationships because this time *they* are in charge.

Maintenance of attachments. Object relations units are also reestablished with treaters because the new relationship serves as a way of maintaining attachments to key persons from childhood, most notably parents. Even if childhood relationships with parents are abusive and conflictual, the child will nevertheless view them as a source of pleasure (Pine 1990). A sadomasochistic relationship is better than no relationship at all (Gabbard 1989b). The validity of this axiom was poignantly illustrated in a chilling news story many years ago: As a child was being beaten to death by her father, she managed to repeat over and over again, "I love you, Daddy." Hence, past relationships are repeated as a way of keeping those relationships alive. The alternative is a profound sense of abandonment and the associated separation anxiety.

A cry for help. To view projective identification only as a mechanism of defense is reductionistic (see Chapter 2). As the targeted person of the projected material powerfully experiences, it is also a form of communication (Casement 1990; Gabbard 1989a; Ogden 1982). Primitive anxieties operate in a way that make patients feel extraordinary pressure to get rid of unmanageable affects, including the self- and object-representations associated with those affects. Some relief is provided when a treater is forced to experience projected material that is overwhelming to a patient. The patient may be unconsciously communicating to the clinician, "I cannot articulate my internal experience, but by creating similar feelings in you, maybe you can empathize with my inner struggles and somehow help me." Hence, while projective identification may be designed to rid oneself of overwhelming feelings and externalize them in an interpersonal context, it is also a means of seeking help with those feelings through a rudimentary form of empathy (Casement 1990).

A wish for transformation.   Abusive internal object relations may also be externalized in the hope that they can be transformed. Sandler and Sandler (1978) have observed that patients internalize a wished-for interaction, a fantasy of themselves relating to a parent who is responding to them in a manner that is wish fulfilling. In this sense, one can infer that old relationships are repeated in the hospital with the unconscious hope that this time they will be different (i.e., both the object and the self will be transformed into the fantasy relationship for which the patient longs).

The hospital can provide a new and different form of interpersonal relatedness that facilitates the internalization of less pathological object relatedness. In the optimal milieu, the goal of hospital staff members is to relate to patients so as to avoid being provoked into responding as their internal object-representations would. By not behaving like everyone else in the patient's world, they can offer new objects and new models of relatedness for the patient.

Initial responses to a patient may be similar to those of others in the patient's environment, but as staff members familiarize themselves with the internal object world of the patient, they strive to *contain* the projections rather than identify with them. In so doing, a vicious cycle is broken. The patient is confronted with a group of persons who respond differently from everyone else. These people attempt to understand the interpersonal process instead of automatically joining the "dance."

Weiss et al. (1986), who have studied audiotaped transcripts of analyses with neurotics, have concluded that one curative factor of analysis is the analyst's failure to respond as the analysand expects. According to these investigators, a patient develops pathological beliefs based on early interactions with parental figures and then seeks unconsciously to disconfirm these beliefs in analysis so that development can proceed. Their research is very much applicable to the hospital setting, where patients continually but unconsciously test staff members to see whether they will be different from previous figures in the prehospital environment. The success of many hospital treatments depends on the ability of the hospital staff to process what is happening and to avoid identification with the projected self- and object-representations of the patient.

Within this formulation of internal object relations, the therapeutic task is to diagnose carefully the patient's self- and object-representations and to maintain a diligent vigilance regarding the nature of the projected internal selves and objects at any given time. Implied in this task is the assumption that treaters have sufficient familiarity with their own internal self- and object-configurations so that they can sort out the two varieties of countertransference.

In this transference-countertransference-based model of hospital treatment, the treatment staff must maintain an openness to the powerful feelings engendered by these patients. Examining the countertransference must be an integral part of the treatment process. The staff should freely allow themselves to serve as containers for the patient's self- and object-projections and for the affects connected with the object relations. On an individual basis, this approach means avoiding the "dedicated physician" stance described by Searles (1967), in which the treater attempts to be loving at all times as a defense against vulnerability to directing sadism and hatred toward the patient. If the treater is overcontrolled or overdefended against emotional reactions to the patient, the diagnostic process of delineating these internal object relations will be flawed. Even more importantly, the treatment process will be a charade; the patient will be unable to view the treater as a genuine person involved in a fleshed-out whole-object relationship.

Openness to countertransference reactions must similarly exist at the group level. The persons in leadership positions on the unit must foster a noncritical, accepting attitude toward the various emotional reactions of staff members to patients. If the leaders communicate that the staff is expected to keep a lid on personal feelings in the service of delivering good treatment to patients, such exhortations will resonate with the already hypertrophied superego structures of most mental health workers and further activate their internal defenses geared to repressing, suppressing, or splitting off unacceptable feelings and identifications.

Despite increasing pressure in recent years to use staff meetings for documentation of behaviorally oriented treatment plans, the staff members' emotional reactions to patients must be discussed openly and with understanding. If staff meetings become merely task-oriented administrative sessions without time for processing transference/countertransference paradigms, subsequent staff dysfunction will cause the clinical work to suffer. Furthermore, the hospital will no longer be involved in dynamically informed treatment, but simply in "case management."

The attitude of the unit or team leader is crucial in setting the tone for countertransference-based discussions. The leader must model for the other staff members by openly examining his or her own feelings and relating them to the internal object relations of the patient. The leader must also value and accept the expressions of feelings on the part of other staff members and avoid interpreting them as a manifestation of unresolved and unanalyzed conflicts within the individual staff member. When a staff member shares a disturbing feeling involved in treating a patient, the leader needs to ask questions, such as "Why does the patient need to evoke that reaction in you? What is he repeating? What figure in the patient's past are you identifying with? How can we use the feelings the patient evokes in you to understand how his spouse or friends must react to him?" The leader of the treatment team should also become familiar with each staff member's usual style of relating to patients. This awareness must include a knowledge of typical countertransference reactions to certain kinds of patients as well as functioning that is more adaptive and conflict-free. This familiarity will help the team leader pinpoint deviations from the characteristic patterns of relationships with patients. Obviously, in some instances the leader of a treatment team may need to approach individual staff members privately about their need for personal treatment or a change in career.

As the treatment of a patient evolves, a sense of objectivity is an important ideal toward which staff members should strive. It may be seen as an unreachable expectation early in treatment because so many patients evoke powerful feelings in treaters. As alluded to previously, such objectivity is particularly difficult for nursing staff members who must be with patients for an 8-hour shift. Although objectivity may be an ultimate ideal, members of the nursing staff as well as other members of the treatment team should be given the expectation that they will experience powerful feelings toward the patient that can be used as a diagnostic and therapeutic tool. A distinction can be made between having feelings and acting on them. Obviously, staff should be advised to note and discuss with other staff but to not act on feelings of a destructive or erotic nature. They should be encouraged to process their feelings in staff meetings and to use those feelings to diagnose and understand the internal object relations of the patient. As the treatment progresses, the staff members will be armed with a greater understanding of the patient's internal object relations so that they are much less prone to countertransference identification and can instead clarify patients' distortions and the nature of their internal object worlds. Hence, if the staff members are given permission to experience powerful countertransference feelings and to discuss them early in the treatment of a given patient, they will be able to approach the patient more objectively as the treatment progresses.

If treaters are inclined to deny their countertransference hatred, anger, and contempt out of guilt, they will nevertheless communicate their intense negative feelings nonverbally (Poggi and Ganzarain 1983). Patients are extraordinarily adept at detecting these communications and may, as a result, become increasingly paranoid. As staff members acknowledge their own ambivalence and deal with it more openly, patients will be able to acknowledge their ambivalence and to be less afraid of their hatred. But as long as staff members deny their hatred, they only confirm the patient's fear that such feelings are unspeakable and must be avoided at all cost.

The model of staff-patient interaction suggested here is directly analogous to the one advocated for the psychotherapist in Chapter 4. Hospital staff members must avoid aloofness and must participate in the patient's interpersonal field in a spontaneous but controlled manner. This capacity to allow oneself to be "sucked in," but only partially, is an extraordinary asset that enables treaters to gain an empathic understanding of the patient's relationship problems (Hoffman and Gill 1988).

Splitting in Hospital Treatment

One advantage of hospital treatment over individual therapy is that the patient's self- and object-representations are externalized onto various staff members all at once rather than onto the psychotherapist alone gradually over time. The hospital milieu, then, serves as a superb diagnostic and therapeutic tool for understanding the process of splitting (see Chapter 2).

Splitting in hospital treatment has been well described in a number of papers on the intense countertransference evoked by treatment-resistant borderline patients (Burnham 1966; Gabbard 1986, 1989c, 1992b; Main 1957). Empirical research suggests that splitting is not unique to borderline patients, however, but rather is characteristic of a wide variety of personality disorders (Allen et al. 1988; Perry and Cooper 1986). Staff members find themselves assuming and defending highly polarized positions against one another with a vehemence out of proportion to the importance of the issue. The patient has presented one self-representation to one group of treaters and another self-representation to another group of treaters (Burnham 1966; Cohen 1957; Gabbard 1986, 1989c, 1992b; Searles 1965). Via projective identification, each self-representation evokes a corresponding reaction in the treater that can be understood as an unconscious identification with the projected internal object of the patient. The transference/countertransference paradigm produced by one self–object constellation may differ dramatically from that produced by another. This discrepancy may first manifest itself in a staff meeting where the patient is being discussed. Staff members may become puzzled by the disparate descriptions being voiced and may ask each other, "Are we talking about the same patient?"

Full-blown splitting of this variety boldly illustrates the time-honored notion that patients recapitulate their internal object world in the hospital milieu (Gabbard 1989c). Various treaters become unconsciously identified with the patient's internal objects and play out roles in a script that is written by the patient's unconscious. Moreover, because of the element of control inherent in projective identification, there is often an obligatory quality to the treaters' responses. They feel compelled to behave "like someone else." If projective identification were not involved, the purely intrapsychic splitting that would result would cause little disturbance in the staff group. Nor would the staff group view the process as an instance of splitting, since they would probably not feel polarized and angry toward one another.

The splitting that occurs in hospital treatment represents a special instance where both intrapsychic and interpersonal splitting develop simultaneously (Hamilton 1988). The interpersonal aspects of splitting that occur in staff groups clearly parallel the intrapsychic splitting in the patient. Projective identification is the vehicle that converts intrapsychic splitting into interpersonal splitting.

Staff members who are singled out as recipients of projected internal objects of the patient are not randomly selected. More often than not, borderline patients have an uncanny ability to detect preexisting latent conflict among various staff members, and their projections may be guided accordingly. A vignette from an actual case (Gabbard 1989c) illustrates this pattern.

> Ms. G, a 26-year-old borderline patient, was admitted to the hospital in a suicidal crisis by her psychotherapist, Dr. H. Ten days after her admission, while she was still voicing suicidal ideation, Dr. H approached Mr. I, the head nurse of the unit, and said he would like to drive Ms. G to the local college campus so she could register for the semester. Mr. I replied that, according to hospital policy, patients who are on suicide precautions may not leave the unit. He suggested that Dr. H might wish to attend a unit staff meeting to further discuss the management of the patient. When Mr. I explained to Ms. G that she could not leave the unit to register, she was enraged with Mr. I and accused him of being a "tyrant" who had no regard for the individual needs of patients. She contrasted him with Dr. H, whom she idealized by saying that among all the staff members associated with her treatment, he was "the only one who understands me." At the ensuing staff meeting, a heated argument developed between Dr. H and Mr. I, who acted as a spokesperson for the unit staff. In the midst of this clash, Mr. I told Dr. H that the latter was well known for his contempt toward hospital policies and for his propensity to treat patients as "special." As a rebuttal to that accusation, Dr. H informed Mr. I that of all the nurses in the hospital, he was known as the most rigid and punitive.

This example demonstrates how splitting and projective identification do not occur in a vacuum. Ms. G clearly selected individuals who conveniently fit the internal object-relationship paradigms assigned to them. As several authors (Adler 1985; Burnham 1966; Shapiro et al. 1977) have noted, there is often a kernel of reality in the assignment of internal object projections to staff members. This vignette also reflects an observation by Burnham (1966), namely, that the cleavage is usually between those treaters who emphasize the administrative frame of reference (i.e., what is good for the group), versus those who emphasize an individualistic frame of reference based on what is good for an individual patient. Finally, while all treaters are at risk for involvement in splits, the pattern described in this vignette is perhaps most common in the treatment of borderline patients: the psychotherapist is viewed as an idealized figure, while the unit staff are devalued as insensitive and punitive. Another typical feature of this arrangement is that, in psychotherapy sessions, the patient may omit information deriving from day-to-day unit activities and instead focus exclusively on childhood memories and transference material (Adler 1985; Kernberg 1984). The psychotherapist then has no awareness of the problematic interactions on the unit and is caught by surprise when nursing staff focus attention on them.

As a result of this form of splitting, Adler (1985) noted that the hospital treatment staff may actually exclude the psychotherapist from the process of treatment planning. In this manner the unit staff members may consolidate their alliance by projecting "badness" and incompetence outside the hospital unit group onto the psychotherapist. If this process continues unchecked, it becomes impossible for the unit staff and the psychotherapist to reconcile their differences and meet halfway. Just like the patient's internal objects, they cannot be integrated. The regressive power of groups is well known and may result in the use of splitting and projective identification in otherwise well-integrated professionals (Bion 1961; Kernberg 1984; Oldham and Russakoff 1987).

When a staff group reaches this point of fragmentation, all too often the patient is blamed for attempting to divide and conquer (Rinsley 1980). What is often forgotten under these circumstances is that splitting is an *unconscious* process patients employ automatically to maintain their emotional survival. We do not generally blame patients for other defense mechanisms. The unique issue in splitting seems to be the treaters' perception that the patient is being consciously and maliciously destructive. An empathic frame of reference is useful for reminding staff members that splitting is the patient's attempt to *ward off* destructiveness for personal protection.

To summarize, splitting in hospital treatment involves four primary features: 1) the process occurs at an unconscious level; 2) the patient perceives individual staff members in dramatically different ways, based on projections of the patient's internal object-representations, and treats each staff member differentially according to those projections; 3) staff members react to the patient, via projective identification, as though they actually are the projected aspects of the patient; and 4) as a result, treaters assume highly polarized positions in staff discussions about the patient and defend those positions with extraordinary vehemence (Gabbard 1989c).

The Management of Splitting
in the Hospital

The management of splitting in a hospital setting nicely illustrates how psychodynamic principles can be practical and useful, even essential, in inpatient treatment. Any discussion of how to manage splitting in hospital treatment must begin with Burnham's (1966) caveat that the complete prevention of splitting is neither possible nor desirable. As with other defense mechanisms, splitting provides a safety valve that protects patients from what they perceive as overwhelming danger. It is a process that will develop regardless of preventive measures implemented by treaters. The essential point is that treatment staff must continuously monitor splitting to prevent it from destroying the treatment, devastating the morale of the staff, and irreparably damaging certain interstaff relationships. Instances of serious psychiatric morbidity and staff resignations have resulted from such situations (Burnham 1966; Main 1957).

Education is one important way to help staff manage splitting. All mental health professionals working with hospitalized patients should be thoroughly conversant with the concept of splitting and its variants. If unit staff members cannot recognize splitting when it develops, managing the situation may be hopeless. In discussions of countertransference, staff members can be encouraged to work toward containing projected aspects of the patient rather than acting on them. Intense feelings toward patients should be viewed as useful material for discussion and supervision rather than as forbidden reactions that must be concealed from supervisors. By developing an understanding of the mechanism of splitting, unit staff members can learn to avoid exploiting it by refusing to accept idealization that would collude with the devaluation of other staff members (Adler 1973; Shapiro et al. 1977). Staff members must also learn to monitor their countertransference tendencies to project aspects of themselves onto the patient.

Education is only a beginning, however. Regular and frequent staff meetings that include the patient's psychotherapist should be part of the weekly routine of the psychiatric unit. A spirit of open communication about differences should be established and monitored by the staff. Forty years ago, Stanton and Schwartz (1954) persuasively demonstrated the prophylactic value of ferreting out and discussing covert staff disagreements. Psychotherapists must view themselves as part of the treatment team and ally themselves with the administrative decisions of the unit team (Adler 1985). Rigid adherence to concerns about confidentiality may feed right into the patient's splitting tendencies.

One primary goal in the treatment of patients with major character pathology is the integration of split self- and object-representations. Although interpretation of the splitting mechanism can help patients achieve more moderated and realistic views of themselves and others, it is rarely sufficient to mend the cleavage that occurs at the group level in the hospital. Interpretations to the patient are best viewed as adjuncts to other interventions at the level of staff interactions. Corresponding to the psychotherapist's approach to the internal world of the patient is the staff's goal of integrating and moderating the *external* objects.

To this end, it is often useful to have the staff member identified with the bad object and the treater identified with the good object meet jointly with the patient to frankly discuss the patient's perception of what is going on. This arrangement makes it more difficult for the patient to maintain polarized views because both treaters are acting human and reasonable. Moreover, treaters who are faced with this situation ordinarily become less polarized and move toward middle ground. The very separateness demanded by the splitting mechanism is undermined. Although this confrontation may temporarily increase the patient's anxiety, it also conveys the message that negative feelings can be contained within interpersonal relationships without disastrous consequences.

When the situation is so emotionally charged that the participants are not willing to meet, an objective consultant can be brought in to mediate the discussion (Gabbard 1986). The consultant can fulfill the role of an observing ego for the group and thereby encourage those individuals involved with the splitting to identify with that function, much as Shapiro et al. (1977) described the function of the psychotherapist when meeting with borderline adolescents and their families.

These meetings presuppose a recognition by all parties of an ongoing splitting process. Such acknowledgment constitutes a major step toward successful management of the splitting. Ordinarily, staff members will be considerably reluctant to see themselves as involved in splitting. When a special meeting is called to discuss the staff dynamics around a particular patient, there may be strong resistance on the part of treaters because such a meeting might make the patient seem too special (Burnham 1966). If the patient's psychotherapist is involved in the split, and willingly attends the staff meeting, it may be with a different agenda. Especially when idealized by the patient, the therapist is likely to assume a condescending attitude as educator so the staff will understand their countertransference reactions and the dynamics of the patient as well as the psychotherapist does. The psychotherapist's implicit message in this situation is that understanding the patient will lead the unit staff to stop blaming the patient. Rather than viewing the staff meeting as a productive way to discuss a splitting process, the psychotherapist is convinced that he or she is right while everyone else is wrong. Being idealized can be so gratifying that the therapist may not wish to examine the idealization as part of a defensive process in the patient (Finell 1985). This approach will, of course, infuriate the unit staff even further and widen the split.

When a staff meeting is called to discuss potential splitting, all parties should certainly approach one another with the assumption that they are all reasonable and competent clinicians who care about the patient's welfare. When this approach works, the group feels that each staff member has brought a piece of the puzzle so that the whole becomes more clear (Burnham 1966). However, some splits seem irreparable; and just as the internal objects of the patient cannot be integrated, neither can the external objects reconcile with one another. If the therapist is in the role of the devalued object, such stalemates occasionally end with the unit staff recommending a new therapist (Adler 1985).

The earlier that splitting is discovered, the less entrenched and the more amenable to change it will be. Certain warning signals should be continually monitored in staff meetings: 1) when a treater is uncharacteristically punitive toward a patient, 2) when a treater is unusually indulgent, 3) when one treater repeatedly defends a patient against critical comments from other staff members, and 4) when one staff member believes that no one else can understand the patient (Gabbard 1989c).

When staff members can swallow their pride and accept that they may be involved in an unconscious identification with projected aspects of the patient, they can begin to empathize with their fellow staff members' feelings and perspectives. This willingness to consider someone else's point of view can lead to collaborative work on behalf of the patient that results in marked improvement in the splitting process. The patient's internal split often begins to mend at the same time the staff's external cleavage heals (Gabbard 1986). These parallel developments may be understood as the third step of projective identification—the previously split-off and projected object-representations of the patient have been contained and modified by the treaters and have then been reintrojected (in modified form) by the patient in a meaningful interpersonal context. By approaching their own differences in good faith, staff members can provide an atmosphere in the milieu where good experiences predominate over bad ones—an essential condition for facilitating the integration of love and hate in the patient.

The Multidisciplinary Treatment Team

The typical treatment team in a psychiatric hospital is made up of representatives from several mental health disciplines—a psychiatrist, a psychologist, a social worker, an activities therapist, nurses, and mental health technicians. Latent interdisciplinary rivalries are fertile soil for the development of splits within the team. Individual team members must conceptualize their job as subsuming two different tasks: one involves the specific treatment assignment that goes with the discipline, and the other involves serving as a transference object or a container of projections (Kernberg 1984). Observations from both aspects of one's job must be continually brought into staff meetings and shared with the treatment team. All patients should understand that whatever they say will be passed on to other members of the treatment team, to gain a complete picture of the patient and to map out a more effective treatment plan. In this manner, splitting can be identified before it becomes destructive.

The social worker brings data to the treatment team from family members and other significant persons who inhabit the environment in which the patient lives. These real individuals may be compared and contrasted with the objects that inhabit the patient's internal world. As social workers perform their usual tasks of gathering data and communicating back and forth between family and patient, they soon find that they are "sucked into" the family matrix. As they allow themselves to contain the projected aspects of the family members and significant others, they gain a greater appreciation of the forces that shape the patient's behavior. Similarly, the social worker's direct contacts with the patient can produce a greater appreciation of the patient's impact on the family. Finally, social workers may contribute a special perspective regarding the manner in which family conflicts are re-created in the milieu.

Members of other disciplines find that the completion of their treatment tasks is similarly affected by the patient's style of relatedness with them. The activities therapist, for example, sets out to assist the patient in completing a task. The patient's performance of that task provides a window into similar problems that the patient may encounter in vocational or educational settings. As the patient attempts to complete the task, characteristic object relations patterns are played out with the activities therapist. Nurses will encounter similar obstacles as they attempt to assist the patient with basic matters of hygiene, and psychologists will confront the same patterns as they encourage the patient to participate in psychological testing. This transference-countertransference model based on object relations theory cuts across all disciplines and forms the basis for a common language among the disciplines.

The Role of Group Treatment in the Milieu

The foregoing descriptions of the introjection and projection of self- and object-representations illustrate the need for careful monitoring of group process on every psychiatric unit. Frequent staff meetings are essential for integrating the split-off fragments circulating among staff members and patients. Similarly, regular group meetings with patients promote a careful processing of interactions between the staff and patients, and among patients themselves; they also serve to prevent acting out of conflicts that develop in these relationships. Object relations theory provides a good conceptual framework for understanding group process on the unit (Kernberg 1973, 1984; Oldham and Russakoff 1987). Stanton and Schwartz (1954) illustrated how dynamics in the patient group may directly reflect similar dynamics in the staff group. Specifically, it is commonplace for individual patients to act out covert staff conflicts. Systematic processing of interpersonal conflicts both in staff meetings and in meetings of patients and staff can be valuable in identifying parallel processes in the two groups.

The actual focus of small patient groups in the hospital varies, depending on the ego strengths and the diagnostic categories of the patients on a particular unit. In general, however, psychotherapeutic group meetings serve as an interface between the patients' intrapsychic difficulties and their conflicts in the hospital environment.

Kibel (1987) suggested that the focus of such groups should be on the interpersonal difficulties that emerge in daily life on the hospital unit. These difficulties can be linked to the patients' intrapsychic conflicts or deficiencies. He suggested deemphasizing transference in such groups because the anxiety generated by transference work might overwhelm both the individual and collective egos of the group. Horwitz (1987), on the other hand, believed that transference focus may be of value in inpatient groups by serving to strengthen the therapeutic alliance within the group. When small group meetings are properly conducted, they may also become havens or sanctuaries in which patients can ventilate their feelings about the experience of being a psychiatric inpatient and staff members can, in turn, validate those feelings and experiences (Kibel 1987). More specific use of inpatient groups will be discussed in Sections II and III in the context of distinct diagnostic entities.

Indications

One might argue that this model of treatment based on transference and countertransference is more applicable to borderline and affectively disturbed patients than it is to schizophrenic patients. The withdrawn schizophrenic patient may not appear to form a transference relationship with treaters. In fact, the schizophrenic patient's internal object relations are re-created in the hospital milieu every bit as much as those of a borderline patient. They are simply less dramatic. Rangell (1982) noted that Freud's assertion that patients suffering from narcissistic neuroses do not form transferences is the only clinical observation he made that has not been validated by subsequent analytic experience. As Brenner (1982) pointed out, the apparent absence of transference is the transference. The schizophrenic patient has re-created his or her internal object world just as the borderline patient has. This relationship vis-à-vis the hospital treaters, which must be understood, clarified, and empathized with, is similar to the process of working with a nonpsychotic patient. Even schizophrenic patients have their own unique set of characterological defenses. Although many schizophrenic patients do not require the use of this model during a brief hospitalization, this form of treatment is certainly useful for those whose defenses thwart compliance (see Chapter 7).

Another potential objection is that a conceptual framework based on the modification of object relations is not applicable to brief treatment in the same way that it is to extended hospital treatment. The fallacy in this argument is the conceptualization of the hospital treatment as occurring in a vacuum rather than as existing as one segment of a continuous effort over many months or years. There is a cumulative effect of many different disconfirmations of the unconscious expectations of the patient over time. Only with repeated failure to provoke the same pattern of responses in treaters do patients ultimately begin to assimilate and internalize the new object relations presented to them. Long-term follow-up studies of borderline patients (McGlashan 1986; Stone et al. 1987), for example, have indicated that maximal improvement does not occur until the second or third decade after discharge. Staff members of an inpatient unit or a partial hospitalization service, the psychotherapist, and friends and family may ultimately provide enough new experiences and responses to strengthen the patient's ego and improve his or her object relations to a level of increased functioning in society.

While the vast majority of psychiatric patients can be treated effectively with brief hospitalization, a subgroup of psychiatrically disturbed individuals require extended, intensive hospital treatment with a primary focus on psychodynamic issues. Indications for this form of treatment include the following: failure of less intensive treatments; absent or chaotic family/support system; impulsive or psychotic symptomatology that is extraordinarily severe and unremitting; pervasive and continued suicidal, self-destructive, or violent behavior; Axis I disorders complicated by severe Axis II pathology; treatment-defeating borderline patients; and chronic schizophrenic patients who cannot function outside a hospital without extensive vocational and social rehabilitation efforts (Gabbard 1992a). Patients who require extended hospital treatment generally evoke transference-countertransference enactments that are overwhelming to an individual but potentially workable in an inpatient setting. Marcus (1987) noted that "the problem with the sickest patients is that the affects are uncontainable by a single individual. The affects are more easily containable by the group, because at any one moment some members are not under direct threat and therefore can maintain observing ego" (p. 251). Ideally, however, psychiatric inpatient units should be used to address acute crises in the course of an illness. When the ego of the patient has been restored to its prior level of functioning, treatment can continue on an outpatient basis.

While greater lengths of stay allow for greater modification of the patient's internal object relations, equating psychodynamically informed inpatient treatment only with extended hospitalizations would be erroneous. Serious treatment errors can be inflicted on the patient just as easily in a short-term setting as in a long-term setting. A sophisticated psychodynamic understanding of the patient assists the treaters in their efforts to avoid errors of technique. For example, if they understand the nature of the object relationship that is being repeated in the milieu, they may be able to resist the temptation to gratify the transference wish. Instead, they will seek to clarify and understand it. Similarly, they may avoid the pitfall of colluding with the patient's passive stance vis-à-vis treatment. A fundamental dynamic notion is that the patient is a collaborator in the treatment process. Psychodynamically informed hospital treatment encourages patients to reflect on connections between their present situation and childhood antecedents so that they can begin to understand how they are perpetuating patterns that were scripted long ago. Intimately connected with this notion is the idea that patients are capable of taking active steps to change their situation.

In Sigmund Freud's (1914/1958) original usage of the term *acting out,* he was noting the transference tendency of patients to repeat in action something from the past rather than to remember and verbalize it. The same phenomenon occurs in hospital treatment, where patients repeat their characteristic mode of engaging others in an attempt to gratify their needs and wishes. Another basic psychodynamic notion is that patients must move in the direction of reflecting and talking about their internal experience rather than automatically allowing it to thrust them into action. This same goal is embraced by the staff members of a psychodynamically informed hospital unit. They continually remind patients that they will not engage in the "dance" that is being repeated. Instead, they will ask patients to reflect and verbalize the origins of their need for the dance. Those patients who, for reasons of cognitive dysfunction, low intelligence, or psychotic withdrawal, cannot enter into a productive verbal interchange with staff members can nevertheless benefit from the nonverbal experiential aspects of new forms of object relatedness. As Ogden (1986) has stressed, a treatment does not have to be verbal to be psychoanalytic in nature.

In the contemporary psychiatric unit, psychodynamic theory and technique must take its place alongside psychopharmacologic interventions, family work, systems theory, and sociocultural considerations. Some Axis I patients and most patients with Axis II diagnoses will benefit from this model. Other Axis I patients make symptomatic improvements without the help of a psychoanalytically based understanding. In today's smorgasbord of psychiatric interventions, resistance to conventional treatment modalities may be the primary indication for psychodynamically informed hospital treatment for patients who have Axis I diagnoses. Even with nonresistant patients, however, the great advantage of the object relations approach is that it provides staff members with a sense of mastery over intense countertransference reactions. Working with difficult hospital patients is often an unrewarding line of work. The education and understanding provided for the staff by a psychodynamically informed clinician makes the job more bearable and more meaningful in the face of the continual emotional onslaughts of highly disturbed patients.

References

Adler G: Hospital treatment of borderline patients. Am J Psychiatry 130:32–36, 1973

Adler G: Borderline Psychopathology and Its Treatment. New York, Jason Aronson, 1985

Allen JG, Deering CD, Buskirk JR, et al: Assessment of therapeutic alliances in the psychiatric hospital milieu. Psychiatry 51:291–299, 1988

Bion WR: Experiences in Groups and Other Papers. New York, Basic Books, 1961

Brenner C: The Mind in Conflict. New York, International Universities Press, 1982

Burnham DL: The special-problem patient: victim or agent of splitting? Psychiatry 29:105–122, 1966

Casement PJ: The meeting of needs in psychoanalysis. Psychoanalytic Inquiry 10:325–346, 1990

Cohen RA: Some relations between staff tensions and the psychotherapeutic process, in The Patient and the Mental Hospital: Contributions of Research in the Science of Social Behavior. Edited by Greenblatt M, Levinson DJ, Williams RH. Glencoe, IL, Free Press, 1957, pp 301–308

Finell JS: Narcissistic problems in analysts. Int J Psychoanal 66:433–445, 1985

Freud A: The ego and the mechanisms of defense (1936), in The Writings of Anna Freud, Vol 2 (Revised Edition). New York, International Universities Press, 1966

Freud S: Remembering, repeating and working-through (further recommendations on the technique of psycho-analysis II) (1914), in The Standard Edition of the Complete Psychological Works of Sigmund Freud, Vol 12. Translated and edited by Strachey J. London, Hogarth Press, 1958, pp 145–156

Gabbard GO: The treatment of the "special" patient in a psychoanalytic hospital. International Review of Psychoanalysis 13:333–347, 1986

Gabbard GO: A contemporary perspective on psychoanalytically informed hospital treatment. Hosp Community Psychiatry 39:1291–1295, 1988

Gabbard GO: On "doing nothing" in the psychoanalytic treatment of the refractory borderline patient. Int J Psychoanal 70:527–534, 1989a

Gabbard GO: Patients who hate. Psychiatry 52:96–106, 1989b

Gabbard GO: Splitting in hospital treatment. Am J Psychiatry 146:444–451, 1989c

Gabbard GO: Comparative indications for brief and extended hospitalization, in American Psychiatric Press Review of Psychiatry, Vol 11. Edited by Tasman A, Riba MB. Washington, DC, 1992a, pp 503–517

Gabbard GO: The therapeutic relationship in psychiatric hospitalization. Bull Menninger Clin 56:4–19, 1992b

Hamilton NG: Self and Others: Object Relations Theory in Practice. Northvale, NJ, Jason Aronson, 1988

Harty MK: Countertransference patterns in the psychiatric treatment team. Bull Menninger Clin 43:105–122, 1979

Hilles L: Changing trends in the application of psychoanalytic principles to a psychiatric hospital. Bull Menninger Clin 32:203–218, 1968

Hoffman IZ, Gill MM: Critical reflections on a coding scheme. Int J Psychoanal 69:55–64, 1988

Horwitz L: Transference issues in hospital groups. Yearbook of Psychoanalysis and Psychotherapy 2:117–122, 1987

Kernberg OF: Psychoanalytic object-relations theory, group processes and administration: toward an integrative theory of hospital treatment. Annual of Psychoanalysis 1:363–388, 1973

Kernberg OF: Severe Personality Disorders: Psychotherapeutic Strategies. New Haven, CT, Yale University Press, 1984

Kibel HD: Inpatient group psychotherapy–where treatment philosophies converge. Yearbook of Psychoanalysis and Psychotherapy 2:94–116, 1987

Kohut H: The Analysis of the Self: A Systematic Approach to the Psychoanalytic Treatment of Narcissistic Personality Disorders. New York, International Universities Press, 1971

Main TF: The ailment. Br J Med Psychol 30:129–145, 1957

Marcus E: Relationship of illness and intensive hospital treatment to length of stay. Psychiatr Clin North Am 10:247–255, 1987

McGlashan TH: The Chestnut Lodge follow-up study, III: long-term outcome of borderline personalities. Arch Gen Psychiatry 43:20–30, 1986

Menninger WC: The Menninger Hospital's Guide to the Order Sheet (1939). Bull Menninger Clin 46:1–112, 1982

Ogden TH: Projective Identification and Psychotherapeutic Technique. New York, Jason Aronson, 1982

Ogden TH: The Matrix of the Mind: Object Relations and the Psychoanalytic Dialogue. Northvale, NJ, Jason Aronson, 1986

Oldham JM, Russakoff LM: Dynamic Therapy in Brief Hospitalization. Northvale, NJ, Jason Aronson, 1987

Perry JC, Cooper SH: A preliminary report on defenses and conflicts associated with borderline personality disorder. J Am Psychoanal Assoc 34:863–893, 1986

Pi EH, Miller A, Rosenberg MR, et al: Therapeutic effects of psychiatric hospitalization. Journal of Psychiatric Treatment and Evaluation 5:135–142, 1983

Pine F: Drive, Ego, Object, and Self: A Synthesis for Clinical Work. New York, Basic Books, 1990

Poggi RG, Ganzarain R: Countertransference hate. Bull Menninger Clin 47:15–35, 1983

Rangell L: The self in psychoanalytic theory. J Am Psychoanal Assoc 30:863–891, 1982

Rinsley DB: Treatment of the Severely Disturbed Adolescent. New York, Jason Aronson, 1980

Rinsley DB: Borderline and Other Self Disorders: A Developmental and Object-Relations Perspective. New York, Jason Aronson, 1982

Sandler J, Sandler AM: On the development of object relations and affects. Int J Psychoanal 59:285–296, 1978

Schlesinger HJ, Holzman PS: The therapeutic aspects of the hospital milieu. Bull Menninger Clin 34:1–11, 1970

Searles HF: Collected Papers on Schizophrenia and Related Subjects. New York, International Universities Press, 1965

Searles HF: The "dedicated physician" in psychotherapy and psychoanalysis, in Crosscurrents in Psychiatry and Psychoanalysis. Edited by Gibson RW. Philadelphia, PA, JB Lippincott, 1967, pp 128–143

Shapiro ER, Shapiro RL, Zinner J, et al: The borderline ego and the working alliance: indications for family and individual treatment in adolescence. Int J Psychoanal 58:77–87, 1977

Simmel E: Psycho-analytic treatment in a sanatorium. Int J Psychoanal 10:70–89, 1929

Stamm I: Countertransference in hospital treatment: basic concepts and paradigms. Bull Menninger Clin 49:432–450, 1985a

Stamm I: The hospital as a "holding environment." International Journal of Therapeutic Communities 6:219–229, 1985b

Stanton AH, Schwartz MS: The Mental Hospital: A Study of Institutional Participation in Psychiatric Illness and Treatment. New York, Basic Books, 1954

Stone MH, Stone DK, Hurt SW: Natural history of borderline patients treated by intensive hospitalization. Psychiatr Clin North Am 10:185–206, 1987

Strachey J: The nature of the therapeutic action of psycho-analysis. Int J Psychoanal 15:127–159, 1934

Styron W: Darkness Visible: A Memoir of Madness. New York, Random House, 1990

Symington N: The possibility of human freedom and its transmission (with particular reference to the thought of Bion). Int J Psychoanal 71:95–106, 1990

Weiss J, Sampson H, the Mount Zion Psychotherapy Research Group: The Psychoanalytic Process: Theory, Clinical Observations, and Empirical Research. New York, Guilford, 1986

Wesselius LF: Countertransference in milieu treatment. Arch Gen Psychiatry 18:47–52, 1968

Winnicott DW: The Maturational Processes in the Facilitating Environment: Studies in the Theory of Emotional Development. London, Hogarth Press, 1965

Zee HJ: Purpose and structure of a psychoanalytic hospital. Journal of the National Association of Private Psychiatric Hospitals 84:20–26, 1977

Section II

Dynamic Approaches to Axis I Disorders

Chapter 7

Schizophrenia

There is no developmental period when the human exists outside of the realm of interpersonal relatedness.

Harry Stack Sullivan (1947)

Genetic studies have amply demonstrated that schizophrenia is a disease with a biological substrate (Kendler 1987; Schulsinger et al. 1988). Research efforts in the neurosciences have resulted in a quantum leap in our understanding of the etiology and pathogenesis of schizophrenia. The introduction of neuroleptic medication revolutionized the treatment of chronic patients who might otherwise have been consigned to a lifetime of institutionalization. The unfortunate downside of this progress in some quarters has been a biological reductionism in the clinical management of schizophrenic patients. The preponderance of the evidence suggests that schizophrenia is a disease involving a genetic predisposition that requires intrapsychic and interpersonal activation (Robbins 1992). Twin studies indicate a monozygotic concordance ranging from 15% to 42%, with an average of 30% (Gottesman and Shields 1982; Kringlen 1987). In view of the finding that a minority of monozygotic twins are concordant for schizophrenia, and considering the fact that approximately 90% of schizophrenic patients do not have an afflicted parent (Robbins 1992), one cannot escape the conclusion that environmental and psychological factors are of considerable importance in the development of schizophrenia. A variety of individual environmental stressors that interact with genetic vulnerability to schizophrenia have been identified and studied in monozygotic twins discordant for schizophrenia (Pollin and Stabeneau 1968).

None of the findings of biological research attenuates the impact of one irreducible fact—schizophrenia is an illness that happens to a person with a unique psychological makeup. Even if genetic factors accounted for 100% of the etiology of schizophrenia, clinicians would still be faced with a dynamically complex individual reacting to a profoundly disturbing illness. Sophisticated psychodynamic approaches to the management of the schizophrenic patient will always be vital components of the clinician's treatment armamentarium. Probably no more than 10% of schizophrenic patients are able to function successfully with a treatment approach consisting only of antipsychotic medication and brief hospitalization (McGlashan and Keats 1989). The remaining 90% require dynamically informed treatment approaches, including dynamic pharmacotherapy, individual therapy, group therapy, family approaches, and dynamically informed hospital treatment, as the crucial ingredients in the successful management of their schizophrenia.

There is no such thing as *the* treatment of schizophrenia. All therapeutic interventions must be tailored to the unique needs of the individual patient. Schizophrenia is a heterogeneous illness with protean clinical manifestations. One helpful organization of the descriptive symptomatology of the disorder is a division into three clusters: 1) positive symptoms, 2) negative symptoms, and 3) disordered personal relationships (Andreasen et al. 1982; Keith and Matthews 1984; Munich et al. 1985; Strauss et al. 1974). First proposed by Strauss et al. (1974), this model distinguishes three discrete psychopathological processes found in schizophrenic patients. Positive symptoms include disturbances of thought content (such as delusions), disturbances of perception (such as hallucinations), and behavioral manifestations (such as catatonia and agitation) that develop over a short time and often accompany an acute psychotic episode.

Whereas the florid positive symptoms constitute an undeniable "presence," the negative symptoms of schizophrenia are better categorized as an "absence" of function. These negative symptoms include restricted affect, poverty of thought, apathy, and anhedonia. Patients

in which a negative symptom picture predominates can be characterized by a number of features that suggest structural brain abnormality,
including poor premorbid adjustment, poor school performance,
greater difficulty holding jobs, poor performance on cognitive testing,
poor treatment response, early age of onset, and premorbid difficulties
in social and instrumental functioning (Andreasen et al. 1990;
McGlashan and Fenton 1992). These findings suggest that negative
symptomatology may be more closely linked to a genetic-biological substrate. This hypothesis has been substantiated by a review of twin
studies (Dworkin et al. 1988). When twins from pairs who were concordant for schizophrenia were compared with those who were discordant,
the concordant pairs had poorer premorbid adjustment, more negative
symptoms, earlier age of onset, and fewer paranoid symptoms than the
discordant pairs, suggesting that both poor premorbid social adjustment and negative symptomatology are linked with either familial or
genetic vulnerability to schizophrenia. An adoption study (Kendler et
al. 1982) found that this vulnerability is most likely related to genetic
influences rather than environmental familial factors. By contrast,
schizophrenia with predominantly positive symptoms has been correlated with severe disruption of the early family environment (Cannon
et al. 1990).

In summary, then, considerable evidence points to a stronger genetic basis for negative symptoms, with a correspondingly weaker genetic link to paranoid and other positive symptoms. Carpenter et al.
(1988) suggested a further distinction among negative symptoms. They
pointed out that certain forms of social withdrawal, blunted affect, and
apparent impoverishment of thought may actually be secondary to
anxiety, depression, environmental deprivation, or drug effects. These
manifestations should therefore not be labeled *negative symptoms* because they are short-lived and secondary. Carpenter et al. (1988) proposed the term *deficit syndrome* to refer to clearly primary negative
symptoms that endure over time. Duration of negative symptoms is
also prognostically significant. Whereas negative symptoms were once
thought to imply a bleaker prognosis, recent research suggests that
only when negative symptoms persist beyond the early phase of illness
are they likely to predict a poorer outcome (Kay 1990; McGlashan and
Fenton 1992).

Like negative symptoms, disordered personal relationships tend to
develop over a long period. These problems grow out of a characterological substrate, and include a myriad of interpersonal difficulties as var-

ied as the range of human personality. Prominent manifestations of disordered interpersonal relationships include withdrawal, inappropriate expressions of aggression and sexuality, lack of awareness of the needs of others, excessive demandingness, and inability to make meaningful contact with other people. This third category is less rigorously defined than the other two because essentially every schizophrenic patient struggles with problems in interpersonal relationships. Indeed, all three categories overlap extensively, and one schizophrenic patient may move from one group to another during the course of the illness. The most useful aspect of these three models is that they facilitate categorizing the predominant manifestations of the illness at any one time so that treatment can be adjusted accordingly. These distinctions are of heuristic and practical value not only at the level of descriptive symptoms but also in weighing dynamic considerations.

Psychodynamic Understanding of Schizophrenia

Many psychodynamic models have been proposed to assist clinicians in understanding the schizophrenic process. The conflict-versus-deficit controversy (described in Chapter 2) is a prominent feature in discussions of theories of schizophrenia. Freud himself vacillated between a conflict model and a deficit model of schizophrenia as his own conceptualization evolved (Arlow and Brenner 1969; Grotstein 1977a, 1977b; London 1973a, 1973b; Pao 1973). Much of Freud's conceptualization (1911/1958, 1914/1963, 1915/1963, 1924a/1961, 1924b/1961) developed out of his notion of *cathexis,* by which he referred to the quantity of energy attached to any intrapsychic structure or object-representation. He was convinced that schizophrenia was characterized by a decathexis of objects. At times he used this concept of decathexis to describe a detachment of emotional or libidinal investment from intrapsychic object-representations, while at other times he used the term to describe social withdrawal from real persons in the environment (London 1973a). Freud defined schizophrenia as a regression in response to intense frustration and conflict with others. This regression from object-relatedness to an autoerotic stage of development was accompanied by a withdrawal of emotional investment from object-representations and from external figures, which explained the appearance of autistic withdrawal in schizophrenic patients. Freud postulated that the patient's cathexis was then reinvested in the self or ego (1914/1963).

Some authors (London 1973a, 1973b; Wexler 1971) have viewed Freud's decathexis theory as an acknowledgment of a deficit model of schizophrenia, although Freud clearly attempted to take conflict into account as well. After developing the structural model, he revised his view of psychosis accordingly (1924a/1961, 1924b/1961). While he viewed neurosis as a conflict between the ego and the id, he regarded psychosis as a conflict between the ego and the external world. Psychosis involved a disavowal and subsequent remodeling of reality. Despite this revision, Freud continued to speak of the withdrawal of cathexis and its reinvestment in the ego. He used the withdrawal of object cathexis to explain his observation that, compared with neurotic patients, schizophrenic patients were incapable of forming transferences.

Freud's notion that schizophrenic patients do not form transference attachments was undoubtedly related to the fact that he did not attempt intensive therapeutic efforts with such patients. Harry Stack Sullivan, on the other hand, devoted his life to the treatment of schizophrenia and arrived at very different conclusions. He believed that the etiology of the disorder resulted from early interpersonal difficulties (particularly in the child-parent relationship), and he conceptualized the treatment as a long-term interpersonal process that attempted to address those early problems. Faulty mothering, according to Sullivan (1962), produced an anxiety-laden self in the infant and prevented the child from having its needs satisfied. This aspect of the self-experience was then dissociated, but the damage to self-esteem was profound. The onset of the schizophrenic illness, in Sullivan's view, was a resurgence of the dissociated self that led to a panic state and then psychotic disorganization. Sullivan always considered the capacity for interpersonal relatedness to be present in even the most withdrawn schizophrenic. His pioneering work with schizophrenic patients was carried on by his disciple, Frieda Fromm-Reichmann (1950), who stressed that schizophrenic persons are not happy with their withdrawn state. They are fundamentally lonely people who cannot overcome their fear and distrust of others because of adverse experiences early in life.

While Sullivan and his followers were developing their interpersonal theories, early ego psychologists were observing that a faulty ego boundary is one of the chief deficits in schizophrenic patients. Federn (1952) did not agree with Freud's assertion that object cathexis was withdrawn in schizophrenia. Instead, Federn emphasized the withdrawal of ego boundary cathexis. He noted that schizophrenic patients characteristically have no barrier between what is inside and what is outside, because their ego boundary is no longer psychologically invested (as it is in neurotic patients). Mahler (1952) believed that the ego boundary developed out of rhythmic cuddling, fondling, and other forms of bodily contact between infant and mother. She also believed that the absence of this normal stimulation in the mother-infant dyad led to the schizophrenic patient's difficulty with differentiating self from other. Moreover, the tendency of adult schizophrenic patients to merge or fuse psychologically with those around them can be understood as an attempt to reestablish the symbiotic bliss of early infancy. Unfortunately, this merger also creates catastrophic fears of annihilation, leading the schizophrenic patient to feel trapped between a wish for merger and a dread of disintegration. More recent authors (Blatt and Wild 1976; Grand 1982) have supported Mahler's earlier formulations by noting that the schizophrenic patients whose disturbances in body boundaries are the most severe also appear to be those with the most extensive chaos in their earliest relationships.

One question raised by the deficit-versus-conflict controversy is whether one theory can explain both neurosis and schizophrenia, or whether a separate, specific theory is needed to explain schizophrenia, which is fundamentally different from the neuroses. Arlow and Brenner (1969), for example, argued that the model of conflict, defense, and compromise formation applicable to neuroses requires no revision when applied to psychosis. The two conditions are *quantitatively* distinct but *qualitatively* similar. Psychosis, like neurosis, is a compromise formation, but it differs from neurosis in three ways: 1) regression is more severe, 2) conflicts related to aggression are more intense, and 3) disturbances of ego and superego functioning are more acute. What Freud described as decathexis, Arlow and Brenner viewed as a defensive retreat from conflict. They supported their theoretical framework with the observation that, contrary to Freud's assertion, schizophrenic patients do indeed form intense transferences. Some of these transference manifestations may be diametrically opposed to withdrawal, in that they involve a clinging, demanding wish to be taken care of. As noted in Chapter 6, the apparent absence of transference *is* the transference of some schizophrenic patients (Brenner 1982). In other words, the schizophrenic patient's withdrawal from the clinician is a repetition of a past relationship. In this model, delusions and hallucinations can be understood as symptomatic compromise formations analogous to neurotic symptoms.

Deficiency models draw some support from biological research on schizophrenia. Grotstein (1977a, 1977b), for example, in his psychoanalytic formulation of schizophrenia, viewed a constitutionally based hypersensitivity to perceptual stimuli as its central defect. This notion is supported by psychopharmacological research identifying information processing and attention dysfunction as prime target areas of antipsychotic medication (Spohn et al. 1977). The inability to screen out various stimuli and to focus on one piece of data at a time is a central difficulty for most schizophrenic patients. Grotstein (1977a, 1977b) postulated that because of this defective stimulus barrier, the unmodulated release of primitive destructive impulses resulted in a state of psychological emergency. To deal with these impulses, a schizophrenic person resorts early in life to massive defensive operations, such as splitting and projective identification, in a desperate effort to expel them onto the mothering figure. Grotstein thus accommodated both the conflict model, which involves impulses and defenses against those impulses, and the deficit model, which emphasizes fundamental neurophysiological problems related to genetic-constitutional factors.

Ogden (1980, 1982) proposed a conflict model that differs sharply from the impulse-defense model of conflict used to explain neurosis. He believed that the key conflict in schizophrenia is "between wishes to maintain a psychological state in which meaning can exist, and wishes to destroy meaning and thought and the capacity to create experience and to think" (p. 531, 1980). In this conceptualization, schizophrenic patients unconsciously attack their own mental contents, including their perceptions, feelings, and thoughts, because they threaten the patient with overwhelming pain and unmanageable conflict. These patients can thus prevent themselves from paying attention to sources of internal misery, resulting in an extreme state of "shutdown" or psychological limitation that approximates nonexperience. The schizophrenic patient experiences persistent conflict over maintaining this state versus allowing some absorption of thoughts, feelings, and perceptions of the outside world that might lead to psychological growth. The autistic inaccessibility of the schizophrenic patient may be understood from this perspective. As this core schizophrenic conflict is resolved, the patient progresses, in three broad phases, out of this severe prohibition against experience: 1) ejecting thoughts onto others through projective identification, 2) fragmenting and distorting thought content (manifested as a formal thought disorder), and 3) divesting all symbolic thought of its meaning (manifested by concreteness of thought).

Robbins (1992) has constructed a hierarchical etiological model that takes into account both neurobiological findings and psychoanalytic thinking. In his view, neurobiological factors are necessary but not sufficient to account for schizophrenia. Building on the concept of a constitutional diathesis interacting with psychological and environmental stressors, he has suggested that the developmental tasks of the child predisposed to schizophrenia take on different meanings and different modes of resolution and are shaped by the nature of the early object relations with caretakers. Moreover, caretakers may be responding to the stress of raising a vulnerable child or may have their own difficulties independent of the childrearing situation, or both.

Several psychological configurations reflect the interface between the neurobiological and the psychological. Children who ultimately develop schizophrenia have an aversion to object relations that make bonding with them difficult. Hypersensitivity to stimulation and difficulties with attention and concentration also are common pre-schizophrenia personality traits. Recent research has suggested that regionally diffuse losses of normal sensory gating in the central nervous system may be characteristic of schizophrenia (Judd et al. 1992), so that patients find it difficult to screen out irrelevant stimuli and feel a chronic sense of sensory overload. Robbins (1992) has also suggested a correlation between emotional states of mental oblivion and findings of cortical atrophy and decreased activity in the frontal lobes of schizophrenic patients. This cluster of features taken together leads to pathological forms of symbiosis with caretakers who are unable to adapt to the demands of such children. The notion of a diathesis in childhood that is present long before the onset of schizophrenic symptoms has been supported by creative research involving study of the home movies of adult-onset schizophrenia patients and their healthy siblings (Walker and Lewine 1990). Judges who viewed the films and who were blind to the psychiatric outcomes of the subjects were able to identify the preschizophrenic children reliably and distinguish them from their healthy siblings.

Pollack (1989) has applied self psychological concepts to the understanding of the schizophrenic patient's subjective experience. In keeping with Kohut's double-axis theory (see Chapter 2), he has proposed that the narcissistic injury to the self may be a more influential factor in precipitating psychotic phenomena than interpersonal loss or various aspects of object love. The primary disturbance in schizophrenic psychosis can be understood as a protracted enfeeblement or fragmentation of the self. Selfobjects in the environment, such as psychotherapists, family members, staff of psychosocial rehabilitation teams, and other support systems, must be present to provide "glue" to the fragmented self of the schizophrenic patient.

The psychodynamic notion of conflict versus deficit can be integrated with the descriptive categorization of schizophrenia in terms of the three symptom clusters (London 1973a; Munich et al. 1985). Negative symptoms, which are closely linked to biological factors and characterized by the absence of function, can clearly be viewed as deficits. Positive symptoms, however, are often associated with acute onset in response to precipitating events and are closely allied with conflict. The disorders of interpersonal relationships may arise from intrapsychic conflicts, but may also be related to basic ego defects.

Regardless of whether a conflict, deficit, or combined conflict-deficit model is invoked to explain schizophrenia, certain common threads run through all these frameworks. First, psychotic symptoms have meaning (Karon 1992). Grandiose delusions or hallucinations, for example, often immediately follow an insult to a schizophrenic patient's self-esteem (Garfield 1985; Garfield et al. 1987). The grandiose content of the thought or perception is the patient's effort to offset the narcissistic injury.

A second common thread is that human relatedness is fraught with terror for these patients. In the vast literature on the psychotherapy of schizophrenia, there is a clear consensus that a significant etiological factor is a disturbed relationship between the infant and the caretaker (McGlashan 1983). In some cases, as Sullivan observed, the mothers of schizophrenic individuals are disturbed themselves and are incapable of providing a dependable, secure holding environment for their infants. Clinicians nowadays, however, are less inclined to blame mothers for causing schizophrenia. Rather, a more balanced perspective is that a disturbed relationship results from an interaction between an infant with neurobiologically based impairments and a mother who may not be emotionally equipped to handle an unusual child. The notion of mother-infant "fit" described in Chapter 1 is certainly relevant to the etiology and pathogenesis of schizophrenia.

The model of the mother-infant fit avoids the reductionistic view that mothers or caretakers *cause* schizophrenia. This model, combined with the genetic-constitutional diathesis/environmental-psychological

stressor hypothesis, suggests that many mothers and caretakers are
exceptionally skilled at raising challenging and vulnerable children so
that the phenotypic vulnerability is not activated (Robbins 1992). In
other cases, for reasons of difficulties in the caretaker, constitutional
problems in the child, or both, the caretaker (or parent) is unable to
serve as a container for the projective identifications of the infant, and
the infant is deprived of the experience of projecting and then
reinternalizing feelings that have been modified after being processed
by the caretaker (Bion 1959/1967; Ogden 1982).

In any case, to assert that psychological and environmental variables have nothing whatsoever to do with the etiology of schizophrenia
would be naive. In a nationwide Finnish study (Tienari et al. 1985),
schizophrenic mothers' offspring who were given up for adoption were
compared blindly with a control group of adopted-away offspring of
nonschizophrenic biological parents. Of the 7 psychotic cases among
the 91 pairs, 6 were offspring of schizophrenic mothers, and only 1 was
the offspring of the matched control group. However, those offspring
who were psychotic were nearly all reared in disturbed adoptive families, while no seriously disturbed offspring were found in healthy or
mildly disturbed adoptive families

Finally, a third common thread involves the conviction of all psychodynamically oriented authors that dynamically informed therapeutic relationships with sensitive clinicians can fundamentally improve
the quality of life for schizophrenic patients. In a study of fully recovered schizophrenic patients (Rund 1990), 80% had been in long-term
psychotherapy and had attached great importance to it. Even when full
recovery is not achieved, the therapeutic relationship may still be of
extraordinary value in the patient's overall adaptation to life.

Treatment Approaches

Pharmacotherapy

Well-designed controlled studies abundantly demonstrate that antipsychotic medication is highly efficacious in managing the positive
symptoms of schizophrenia. The schizophrenic patient's accessibility
to all other forms of therapeutic intervention is greatly enhanced by
the judicious use of neuroleptics. Keith and Matthews (1984) even asserted that "freedom from positive symptoms approaches a *sine qua*

non status for psychosocial treatments" (p. 71). Negative symptoms and disordered interpersonal relationships, however, are much less affected by medication and thus require psychosocial approaches. Some of the new and atypical antipsychotic agents (such as clozapine, remoxapride, risperidone, and sulpride) appear to make a greater impact on negative symptom constellations.

Because numerous outstanding psychopharmacology texts are available, I will focus on dynamic approaches to treatment. As discussed in Chapter 5, noncompliance with prescribed medication is an ongoing problem in the treatment of many schizophrenic patients. Dynamic psychiatrists involved in the long-term management of patients suffering from schizophrenia must view medication compliance as a treatment concern. Each patient must be educated about the likelihood of relapse if medication is stopped, about signs of tardive dyskinesia, and about management of the more benign side effects. In addition, the meaning of the medication to the patient must be explored from time to time, particularly at the first sign of noncompliance. As emphasized in Chapter 5, the prescribing of antipsychotic medication must occur in the context of a therapeutic alliance that is carefully fostered through sensitivity to the patient's internal experience of all treatments.

Individual Psychotherapy

For the patient whose positive symptoms remit as a result of antipsychotic medication, treatment has just begun. Even when the hallucinations are gone, the challenge of life can be overwhelming. Relationships appear fraught with peril. Each day may bring a new wave of unspeakable terror and multiple uncertainties. The demands of a job seem out of the question. The expectations of the patient's family may appear as harsh and unrealistic. To navigate these perilous waters, such patients need a consistent, reliable, supportive human relationship.

Despite a rich clinical tradition of individual psychoanalytically oriented psychotherapy of schizophrenia, research studies have been hard pressed to demonstrate that the average schizophrenic patient is likely to reap significant benefit from such efforts (Gomez-Schwartz 1984). The Camarillo State Hospital Study (May 1968) is often cited because it was the first large-scale study that compared outcomes of schizophrenic patients according to whether they were treated with psychotherapy or with neuroleptic medication. The patient groups who received medication showed significantly greater improvement than both those who did not receive it and those who received psychotherapy alone. Moreover, no interactive effect was noted between psychotherapy and antipsychotic medication. This study has been criticized, however, because it relied on inexperienced therapists who had no particular commitment to the type of psychotherapy they were instructed to practice with their research subjects. Also, the outcome measures were not sensitive enough to pick up changes in interpersonal and general psychological functioning that might specifically respond to psychotherapy (Conte and Plutchik 1986). Two other studies that were also fraught with methodological problems (Grinspoon et al. 1972; Rogers et al. 1967) found questionable benefit from psychotherapy. Karon and VandenBos (1981) demonstrated more improvement in schizophrenic patients treated by experienced therapists, as compared with a control group of patients who received routine treatment with phenothiazines and supportive therapy, but this study has also been criticized for methodological problems such as a lack of random assignment and early transfer of patients in the drug treatment group to a chronic unit (Keith and Matthews 1984; Klein 1980).

By far the most elegantly designed study on the effects of psychotherapy with schizophrenic patients is the Boston study reported by Stanton, Gunderson, and colleagues (Gunderson et al. 1984; Stanton et al. 1984). A principal failure in previous studies had been the lack of definition in the form of psychotherapy being administered by project therapists. In the Boston study, nonchronic schizophrenic patients from diverse institutional and outpatient settings were assigned either to reality-adaptive, supportive psychotherapy (RAS) or to exploratory, insight-oriented psychotherapy (EIO). Those included in the analysis (95 of the original 164 patients) remained in their assigned treatment situation for at least 6 months. At 2-year follow-up, the investigators obtained complete data on 47 of the original sample. At this point in the data analysis, patients receiving RAS showed less recidivism and better role performance. On the other hand, patients who received EIO had greater improvements in cognition and ego functioning. The investigators concluded that overall differences between the two groups were relatively minor.

Unfortunately, despite the sophisticated methodology and design of the Boston study, generalizability of the results must be limited for several reasons. First, only 47 patients completed the 2-year course of the project; thus, many of the definitive comparisons were based on approximately 20 subjects in each treatment group (Carpenter 1984). Second, the data collection stopped after 2 years. Many experienced therapists of schizophrenic patients would consider 2 years to be merely the beginning of the middle phase of therapy. Schizophrenic patients are notoriously difficult to engage in a psychotherapeutic process. It is common for such patients to take a whole year just to be able to say "hello" to their doctor. Moreover, expecting a therapist to adhere to either a more-or-less expressive or a more-or-less supportive model in the treatment of a schizophrenic patient introduces an artificiality into the treatment being evaluated. Nowhere is flexibility more important than in the psychotherapy of schizophrenia. As stressed in Chapter 4, in a naturalistic setting, the psychotherapist will shift back and forth from expressive to supportive interventions, depending on the needs of the patient at a given moment.

The investigators themselves (Glass et al. 1989) subsequently blindly rated the actual process of therapy from audiotaped transcripts and concluded that the earlier finding of little overall differences between the two groups "concealed discrete processes within the therapies that have important and specific effects" (p. 607). Therapists who were rated as skilled in dynamic exploration produced greater improvements in global psychopathology, denial of illness, and retardation-apathy.

Finally, one other irreducible difference between the needs of research and the ambience of clinical practice should be taken into account in interpreting the data from the Boston study. The motivations, both conscious and unconscious, that lead a psychotherapist to enter into what could become a lifelong commitment to treating a schizophrenic patient are both mysterious and highly personal. Whatever forces lead a therapist and patient to "choose" each other are ignored by large-group designs that require scientifically rigorous random assignment of patient to therapist (Müller 1984). Only intensive study of individual cases can shed light on this significant contributor to psychotherapeutic success.

In a subsequent report, Gunderson (1987) acknowledged the difficulty of engaging schizophrenic patients in a long-term psychotherapy process. He noted that his study and others have suggested that about two-thirds of schizophrenic patients will drop out of psychotherapy when assigned nonspecifically as part of a research study. Gunderson carefully examined the data from the Boston study to determine the typical characteristics of those who continued in psychotherapy. His surprising finding was that they were characterized by social isolation, emotional flatness, and internal disorganization. However, they tended to have more consistent role performance than the dropout group. He also determined that dropout rate is affected by cultural norms within the hospital milieu. For example, patients from the Veterans Administration hospital used in the study were much more likely to drop out than those hospitalized at McLean Hospital, where psychotherapy is a standard part of treatment. Gunderson also concluded that longer-term hospitalization may be helpful in engaging patients. When he divided the patients according to whether they received RAS or EIO therapy, he determined that emotionally distant, thought-disordered patients with an optimistic view of their illness were most likely to continue with the former modality, while patients who were more likely to continue with the latter treatment had fairly intact reality testing, reasonably good interpersonal relatedness, and a view of their psychotic episode as an unfortunate event.

Gunderson's findings resonate with those of McGlashan's (1984, 1987) long-term follow-up study of patients treated at Chestnut Lodge. In this study, 163 schizophrenic patients previously hospitalized at Chestnut Lodge while receiving intensive psychoanalytically oriented psychotherapy were followed up an average of 15 years after discharge. About one-third of these patients had moderate-to-good outcomes (McGlashan 1984). Of the two identifiable groups whose psychosis remitted, one group attempted to integrate the psychotic experience into their life. They believed that they had gained important information from the psychotic episode, and they were curious about the meaning of their symptoms. The second group showed another pathway to stable recovery, namely, that of "sealing over" the illness. These patients tended to have a fixed, negative view of their illness and no interest in understanding their psychotic symptoms. Although both groups had achieved reasonably stable adjustments, those who integrated their experiences appear to have had somewhat superior outcomes.

These findings suggest that patients who can integrate a psychotic experience into their life may benefit from exploratory work in the context of psychotherapy, while those who seal over a psychotic episode will probably not benefit and may perhaps even be harmed by persistent exploratory attempts. Even psychotherapies that involve some insight will require significant support by the therapist. The expressive-supportive distinction is certainly less rigid in the psychotherapy of schizophrenia than in the treatment of higher-functioning patients. Regardless of whether exploratory work accompanies the supportive efforts of the therapist, certain principles of technique (Table 7–1) can guide the psychotherapy of any schizophrenic patient.

1. *The main focus should be on building a relationship.* Because most schizophrenic patients experience human relationships as risky undertakings, they often must struggle to trust a therapist enough to form a therapeutic alliance. Nonetheless, little significant therapeutic work is likely to occur without careful attention to building a solid therapeutic alliance. When Frank and Gunderson (1990) examined the role of the therapeutic alliance in the courses and outcomes of the 143 schizophrenic patients involved in the Boston Psychotherapy Study, they discovered that it was a key predictor of treatment success. Patients who formed good therapeutic alliances with their psychotherapists were more likely to remain in psychotherapy, more likely to comply with prescribed medication, and more likely to achieve better outcomes at the end of 2 years. In addition, they generally required less medication than patients who did not form good therapeutic alliances.

Much of the early work of psychotherapy must be directive and designed to repair the patient's deficits that impede development of a therapeutic alliance (Selzer 1983; Selzer and Carsky 1990;

Table 7–1. Principles of technique in the psychotherapy of schizophrenia

1. The main focus should be on building a relationship.
2. The therapist must maintain a flexible stance regarding the mode and content of therapy.
3. For psychotherapy to proceed, therapists and patients must find and maintain an optimal distance.
4. The therapist must create a holding environment.
5. The therapist must serve as a "container" for the patient.
6. The therapist must serve as an auxiliary ego for the patient.
7. The therapist must be genuine and open with the patient.
8. The therapist should postpone interpretation until the therapeutic alliance is solid.
9. The therapist must maintain respect for the patient's need to be ill.

Selzer et al 1989). Therapists must help their patients test reality, strengthen their ego boundaries (by pointing out what belongs to the patient and what belongs to others), and assist them in fostering an observing ego so that these patients can maintain some objectivity about their experiences and can therefore reflect on them. Selzer and Carsky (1990) have stressed the importance of finding an organizing object, which may be a person, an idea, or an inanimate object, that allows the patient and the therapist to talk about what is going on between them. In this stage of treatment, patients are often unable to acknowledge that they are ill and in need of treatment, and the main focus must be establishing relatedness. The treatment alliance is built largely by connecting with the nonpsychotic aspects of the patient, which exist in all persons suffering from the illness. By focusing on the interaction with the therapist, patients gradually develop a sense that two people are working together toward a common goal.

2. *The therapist must maintain a flexible stance regarding the mode and content of therapy.* Some patients may feel that simply sitting and talking in an office is not a viable situation. With such patients, the therapist may have to conduct the therapy while taking a walk or while sitting at a table over a cup of coffee. Some patients may communicate much better through an artistic medium, such as drawing or painting, and the therapist should be prepared to engage patients wherever they feel most comfortable. Playing cards or table tennis enables some patients to talk who would otherwise pass each session in anxious silence. In some ways, the model of play therapy used by child therapists is applicable to psychotherapy of schizophrenia, in that it implies an absence of rigidity in relating to the patient.

3. *For psychotherapy to proceed, therapists and patients must find and maintain an optimal distance.* Interpersonal boundaries are subject to highly idiosyncratic perceptions and distortions by the schizophrenic patient. Therapists must allow their patients to adopt a spatial and temporal distance that frees therapy from excessive anxiety. For example, patients should be informed that they can move their chair to any part of the office where they feel comfortable. Similarly, the frequency of appointments should be decided collaboratively with the patient. One hospitalized patient told her doctor, who had been seeing her four times a week, that she felt pressured by such frequent visits and simply could not talk

because of that pressure. She promised that if he would come only twice a week, she would have a great deal to say. The quality of their sessions improved markedly after the therapist acceded to her request. In addition, the therapist should not be rigidly locked into 50-minute appointments. Many patients feel much more comfortable with frequent 25- or 30-minute appointments than with less-frequent 50-minute sessions. The establishment of optimal distance also allows for silence. Some patients maintain a comfortable distance by periodically "shutting down," and the therapist must be able to accept this withdrawal as a necessary break from the intensity of their relationship.

4. *The therapist must create a holding environment.* McGlashan and Keats (1989) emphasized that, above all, psychotherapy should offer asylum. Patients must experience each psychotherapeutic session as "a safe place" where they are encircled by the caring and concern of the therapist. Feelings and thoughts that others do not understand are accepted by the psychotherapist. Similarly, withdrawal or bizarre behavior is accepted and understood without any demand that the patient must change to be acceptable. Much of this aspect of technique consists of "being-with" (McGlashan and Keats 1989), a willingness to consistently put oneself in the company of another human being without making inordinate demands.

5. *The therapist must serve as a "container" for the patient.* Powerful feelings are stirred up in the psychotherapeutic relationship, and the patient may need to project these disturbing affects onto the therapist to gain distance from them. The therapist must be able to process and detoxify these affects without acting on them (Grotstein 1976; Ogden 1980). The therapist thus contains both transference and countertransference feelings and provides a new model of relatedness to be reinternalized by the patient. Although this container function may seem routine to the psychotherapist, it presents a formidable challenge and may lead to disruptions in the therapeutic relationship. As Karon (1992) has pointed out, terror is the primary affect of the schizophrenic patient. Therapists must be able to accept feelings of terror when they are projected onto them and avoid withdrawing and being overwhelmed in the face of such powerful affects.

6. *The therapist must serve as an auxiliary ego for the patient.* The profound ego weaknesses found in the schizophrenic patient may be bolstered by the therapist's activity. If the patient's judgment is

impaired, the therapist may have to help the patient think through the consequences of actions. If the patient's reality testing is faulty, the therapist may have to point out the difference between internal and external stimuli. This auxiliary ego function may be particularly helpful in the here-and-now situation of the therapeutic relationship. One patient, for example, said to his therapist, "You're feeling hungry, aren't you?" The therapist responded by saying, "I just had lunch before we met, so I bet that you're probably feeling hungry and figured that I shared your feeling."

7. *The therapist must be genuine and open with the patient.* The opacity and anonymity characteristic of the classical analytic position are not appropriate for the treatment of patients with schizophrenia, who are in desperate need of a genuine relationship. If all negative feelings are denied and split off in the therapeutic relationship, the patient will experience the therapist as unreal. Moreover, the therapist's apparent ability to transcend all feelings of anger, boredom, hatred, and frustration will simply increase the patient's envy of the therapist (Searles 1967). This posture does not imply that the therapist should engage in extensive self-disclosure or insensitive expressions of negative affects toward the patient. Therapists may, however, share items of personal interest with the patient and may wish to validate the patient's perception of feelings such as irritation, sadness, boredom, and other unpleasant sensations.

8. *The therapist should postpone interpretation until the therapeutic alliance is solid.* McGlashan and Nayfack (1988) studied the detailed records of three different psychotherapy processes with one patient hospitalized at Chestnut Lodge. The first therapist, working from a defense-conflict model, made frequent interpretations of unconscious content, while the latter two employed a predominantly supportive strategy. The authors noted that the patient benefited far more from the latter two therapists' efforts to establish a positive, trusting relationship than from the first therapist's efforts to analyze unconscious meaning. They noted that intense demands for relatedness and in-depth exploration are likely to promote relapse in schizophrenic patients. Instead, resistance must be respected and gently eroded over a long period through gentle but persistent curiosity. Just as a surgeon must use anesthesia to operate, the therapist must carefully create an ambience of trusting relatedness to pave the way for an interpretation.

9. *The therapist must maintain respect for the patient's need to be ill.*
No matter how pathological, the illness of schizophrenia represents some form of intrapsychic solution for the patient. The omnipotent fantasy of rescuing the patient from schizophrenia is doomed to failure; it is the worst possible psychological attitude for a therapist (McGlashan 1983). Therapists must be comfortable with the possibility that patients will choose "the devil they know" rather than face the uncertainties of change and improvement. Effective psychotherapy requires an attitude in the therapist that allows the patient's wish to remain ill to be an acceptable alternative to psychotherapeutic change (Searles 1979). Why, then, should clinicians undertake psychotherapy with schizophrenic patients, given the lack of sterling research data to demonstrate its efficacy, and knowing the painstaking slowness and psychological tribulations of the process itself? Group research designs mask the shining success stories with individual patients. More significantly, small improvements in disorders of interpersonal relatedness and negative symptoms, following remission of positive symptoms through antipsychotic medication, may significantly improve the schizophrenic person's quality of life. From a practical standpoint, a solid therapeutic alliance leads to enhanced compliance with the rest of the patient's treatment. Forty-eight percent of schizophrenic patients are noncompliant with medication in the first year, and the number rises to 74% within the first 2 years (Corrigan et al. 1990). A psychotherapeutic setting provides an opportunity to explore the nature of the patient's reluctance to take medication. Therapists should also keep in mind that as many as 57% of schizophrenic patients have associated personality disorders on Axis II (Hogg et al. 1990). These characterological features may require psychotherapeutic management to prevent them from interfering with a well-established treatment plan. In the recent professional literature, schizophrenic patients have spoken eloquently about the benefits of individual psychotherapy (Anonymous 1986; Ruocchio 1989). These patients comment on the importance of having one consistent figure in their lives who is there through any adversity over many years. These patients convey how their subjective experiences of themselves and of their lives was significantly altered by a long-term psychotherapeutic relationship, even though outcome measures may not be sensitive enough to record such alterations. In the words of one patient (Anonymous 1986), "A

fragile ego left alone remains fragile. Medication or superficial support alone is not a substitute for the feeling that one is understood
by another human being" (p. 70).

Group Psychotherapy

Studies of group psychotherapy with schizophrenic patients suggest
that this modality may be useful, but emphasize the timing of its implementation. The optimal time appears to be after positive symptoms
are stabilized through pharmacologic intervention (Kanas et al. 1980;
Keith and Matthews 1984). The acutely disorganized patient is unable
to screen out environmental stimuli, and the multiple inputs from a
group setting may overwhelm the patient's already beleaguered ego
just when it is attempting to reestablish itself. One review of controlled
studies of group therapy for schizophrenia (Kanas 1986) found considerable evidence for the efficacy of inpatient group psychotherapy but a
clear trend for greater success on long-term chronic units than on acute
wards. After positive symptomatology is controlled, inpatient groups
can be highly supportive for schizophrenic patients as they are reorganizing and as they see others preparing for discharge. Efficacy studies suggest that, as an outpatient modality, group therapy may be as
effective as individual therapy (O'Brien 1983). For the patient who is
stabilized on medication, weekly sessions of 60–90 minutes can serve
to build trust and can provide a support group where patients can
freely discuss concerns such as how to manage auditory hallucinations
and how to deal with the stigma of mental illness.

Family Intervention

In the empirical research literature on the efficacy of psychosocial interventions with schizophrenia, no modality has been more substantiated than family interventions. Numerous studies (Falloon et al. 1982;
Goldstein et al. 1978; Hogarty 1984; Leff et al. 1982) have demonstrated that family treatment plus antipsychotic medication is three
times as effective as medication alone in preventing relapse. These investigations used a factor known as expressed emotion (EE), first identified by Brown et al. (1972). This term was coined to describe a style
of interaction between family members and the patient that is characterized by intense overinvolvement and excessive criticism. Although
this concept does not blame parents for causing schizophrenia in their

children, it does acknowledge that families are affected by schizophrenia and that they may become secondary contributors to relapse through an intensification of their interactions with the schizophrenic patient. In brief, high-EE families produce a greater frequency of relapse in a schizophrenic member than low-EE families.

The extensive research on EE has led to development of a sophisticated psychoeducational approach with families of schizophrenic persons. The families are trained to recognize prodromal signs and symptoms that presage relapse, are taught to reduce criticism and overinvolvement, and are helped to see that a consistent medication program can preserve optimal functioning. Other areas of education include instruction about the side effects of medications and their management, the long-term course and prognosis of schizophrenia, and the genetic and biological basis of schizophrenia. Clinicians using this approach can effectively enlist the family's help as collaborators in the prevention of relapse.

The impressive results obtained with this conceptual model of family intervention have recently been challenged, however. Some investigators have questioned whether controlling EE is the exclusive factor involved in relapse prevention. One study (MacMillan et al. 1986) found that the regular ingestion of neuroleptic medication and the preadmission duration of illness were factors that, when taken into account, canceled out the effect of EE in predicting relapse. A more recent study (Parker et al. 1988) examined 57 schizophrenic patients from the standpoint of the EE level of the household. Relapse was predicted by a one-parent household and by a poor course of prior illness, but the level of EE was not predictive. The investigators speculated that those patients with a poor course may evoke responses in relatives that are high in EE, particularly if the patient lives in a one-parent household. Falloon (1988) has pointed out that the research on EE has not included serial measures of EE that would help determine whether behavior disturbances in schizophrenic patients *provoke* high-EE responses in parents or *result from* the stress of high-EE relatedness.

Additional questions have been raised about the high-EE construct and the family interventions that it informs. Many families of schizophrenic patients feel that they are being blamed for relapse when they are merely responding to a difficult situation in the best way they can (Lefley 1992). As Kanter et al. (1987a) have noted, if families are strongly urged to remain nonintrusive, they may fail to respond appropriately when provocative behavior and lack of control are exhibited by the schizophrenic family member. Moreover, in some cases it may be assumed that a switch from high to low EE has caused patient improvement when in fact the family has simply lowered its EE as a *result* of the improvement in the patient (Hogarty et al. 1986). Researchers also question whether EE is a construct that is stable over time (Lefley 1992). Other concerns include the observation that high EE is related to other illnesses besides schizophrenia, the fact that only a certain proportion of people with schizophrenia are influenced at all by high EE, and the realization that the entire construct is essentially cultural (Jenkins and Karno 1992).

Given the controversy surrounding the relationship between relapse and EE, clinicians may be puzzled about the most useful interventions to make with families. Kanter et al. (1987a) have stressed that psychoeducational efforts involving information about the illness, support, and advice may produce results that are just as impressive as the data from the EE studies. Hatfield (1990) stressed that education is probably more helpful than treatment in working with families and that specific interventions are not necessary. Nevertheless, because highly stimulating environments tend to be difficult for schizophrenic patients to deal with, there is sound wisdom in reducing the intensity of environmental stimuli. In an attempt to synthesize the literature, Kanter et al. (1987b) concluded that most researchers now agree that "expressed emotion of families does not cause relapse, but rather is a barometer of family distress in response to disturbing symptoms, behaviors, or lifestyles of their schizophrenic relatives" (p. 1119).

Hospital Treatment

Short-term hospitalization. For the schizophrenic patient who has an acute psychotic break, brief hospitalization provides "time out"—a chance to regroup and gain new direction for the future. Antipsychotic medication relieves most of the positive symptoms. The structure of the hospital unit provides a safe haven to prevent patients from hurting themselves or others. Nursing staff members in the milieu perform auxiliary ego functions for the patient. The treatment team can also identify stressors from Axis IV of DSM-IV (American Psychiatric Association 1994) that might contribute to a psychotic episode at this particular time in the patient's life. A psychoeducational effort can begin with the patient and family to establish an optimal posthospital environment. They should be prepared for the fact that they are dealing with a lifelong disease, and that the goal is to minimize disability, not effect a lasting cure. The importance of staying on medication is emphasized, and the concept of EE may be explained as well. At the same time, the treatment team needs to convey a sense of hope. It is often useful to point out that although the disease is chronic, considerable research suggests that schizophrenic patients become more and more functional as they age (Harding et al. 1987).

The thrust of brief hospitalization is counterregressive. Defenses are restored, and the patient should be returned to functioning as expeditiously as possible. If the patient is not established in psychotherapy, the hospital may be used as a preparatory phase to get the patient ready for an outpatient psychotherapy process (Selzer 1983). The patient's omnipotence is challenged by the necessity of accommodating to the needs of others. By enforcing a routine schedule in patients' lives, some frustration of their needs and wishes is unavoidable. This optimal level of frustration helps patients improve reality testing and other ego functions (Selzer 1983). If psychotherapy can be started during the hospitalization, the patient can then maintain a sense of continuity by seeing the therapist outside the hospital. After the patient's positive symptomatology is relieved to some extent, group treatment may be instituted and may also be continued on an outpatient basis, depending on the patient's amenability to the group format. For some isolated outpatients, group meetings may be their only significant social contact.

If psychosocial rehabilitation has not been a part of the patient's treatment, the hospital team must try to help the patient find such a program prior to discharge. Psychosocial rehabilitation, which is usually defined as a therapeutic approach that encourages patients to develop their fullest capacities through environmental supports and learning procedures (Bachrach 1992), should be a major part of contemporary treatment for any person suffering from schizophrenia. This individually tailored approach involves capitalizing on the patient's strengths and competencies, restoring hope to the patient, maximizing the patient's vocational potential, encouraging the patient's active involvement in his or her own treatment, and developing social skills.

Extended hospitalization. Although brief hospitalization with rapid restoration of function and return to posthospital life is the optimal scenario, a significant percentage of schizophrenic patients are simply too impaired to work within this model. This subgroup requires extended hospitalization. These patients include those who adamantly refuse medication, do not respond to medication, are relentlessly self-destructive or suicidal, are aggressive toward others, and have no family or other support systems to help them manage the vicissitudes of daily existence. These patients require a sophisticated milieu approach that combines dynamically informed hospital treatment; psychotherapy; and repair of vocational, social, and cognitive deficits (Munich et al. 1985).

For those patients with predominantly negative symptoms, diagnosis and medication can be reassessed. Are there secondary reasons, such as depression, anxiety, and medication side effects, that might account for the negative symptoms? Similarly, the psychotherapy process, if ongoing, can be reevaluated with the collaboration of the therapist to determine whether to make a shift in strategy. Family work can proceed in a psychoeducational fashion, and family members can be enlisted in the search for ongoing stressors that prevent the patient from responding to conventional treatment. Most of all, the negative-symptom group requires social and vocational rehabilitation. Social skills groups that focus on behavioral improvement in such simple daily behaviors as eating, conversation, walking, and manners can be extraordinarily valuable for the negative-symptom group. Similarly, a careful vocational evaluation in a supervised setting in which concrete job skills are taught and developed is an essential component of extended hospitalization. As Munich et al. (1985) noted, "extended treatment designed to bring about symptom reduction and 'insight' into intrapsychic conflict alone is insufficient to return chronically schizophrenic patients to the community and sustain them there" (p. 161).

Research on posthospital adjustment and rehospitalization rates demonstrates that patients are more likely to stay out of the hospital when they have been taught adaptive behaviors and skills and have learned to control symptomatic and maladaptive behaviors during their inpatient stay (Mosher and Keith 1979). Although the behavioral focus of such milieu programs may seem antithetical to dynamic psychiatrists, this focus actually may work synergistically with dynamic approaches. Patients who improve their interpersonal relations as a result of behaviorally oriented social skills training will begin to experience changes in their object relations, which then produce material for discussion in psychotherapy.

Schizophrenic patients who are treatment resistant and therefore require extended hospitalization may also display a predominant picture of disordered interpersonal relatedness. These patients frequently have serious characterological difficulties that coexist with schizophrenia. Clinicians are sometimes prone to forget that every schizophrenic patient also has a personality. These characterological problems may therefore result in noncompliance with medication, alienation of family members and other supportive persons in the environment, denial of illness, and inability to function in a vocational setting. Extended hospitalization may be the ideal setting in which to address the characterological dimension accompanying the schizophrenia and to examine the underpinnings of the patient's noncompliance.

To a large extent, the hospital treatment of such patients follows the model outlined in Chapter 6. Via projective identification, patients attempt to reestablish their internal object world in the hospital. Hospital staff members contain those projections and provide new models of relatedness for reinternalization. In addition, patients are informed about maladaptive interactional patterns as they occur in the here and now of the hospital setting.

Many of the treatment principles described in this chapter are illustrated in the following detailed case example:

Mr. J, a 22-year-old single man from the southeastern United States, had a 3-year history of schizophrenia that had not responded either to outpatient treatment with medication or to brief hospitalization. Referred for extended psychiatric hospitalization, he came for admission accompanied by his parents. When asked to describe his problems, he recited a litany of physical complaints involving virtually every anatomical area of his body, but steadfastly denied any psychiatric problems. When he learned that he was being admitted to a psychiatric facility, he was reluctant to sign himself into the hospital. Only with repeated reassurances that a complete physical and neurological workup was part of the psychiatric evaluation would he consent to hospitalization.

The patient's somatic preoccupations precluded any history taking of his psychiatric disorder. Fortunately, his parents were able to fill in the gaps. Mr. J was the third of three children born to highly successful parents. The patient's father was a respected business executive, and his mother had a prominent administrative position in the school system. His older brother was a graduate of a prestigious medical school, and his older sister was an honors student in her MBA program. The patient himself had briefly attended college, but was forced to drop out after the onset of his illness. He complained of hypersensitivity to noise in his dormitory, and he expressed concern that others were talking about him. He finally demanded to be taken home so that he would not be humiliated by the other young men in the dormitory, who he claimed were calling him "loser," "fag," and "crazy" in the middle of the night.

After leaving college, Mr. J returned to live with his parents, where he became increasingly demanding of their time. When his father attempted to leave for work in the morning, the patient would run out the door after him and sometimes jump on the hood of his car to prevent him from leaving. He would also wake his father in the middle of the night to demand that he listen to a recital of his physical complaints. He repeatedly accused his father of neglect by saying, "What are you going to do about my pain?" Mr. J had been seen by numerous specialists, and often several specialists in one field, without any diagnosis of physical disease. He insisted that he needed continual "monitoring" from his parents so that they would be aware of the waxing and waning of his physical symptoms. Mr. J was blessed with loving and concerned parents, who attempted to accommodate his pleas for attention by spending long periods with him. On one occasion, the patient's father sat and listened to the patient's somatic preoccupations for 10 hours without a break.

Mr. J also continued to hear voices condemning him, and in one instance he assaulted a stranger on the street because he was convinced that the stranger was saying unpleasant things about him. Mr. J had been hospitalized for a few weeks each on two different occasions and had been prescribed four different antipsychotic medications at various times. Each time, the patient discontinued the medication because of his denial that he had a psychiatric condition that warranted psychotropic medication and because of anticholinergic side effects that bothered him.

Shortly after admission, a mental status examination revealed that the patient continued to suffer from auditory hallucinations, although he did not complain of "hearing voices." Rather, he was convinced that people were actually talking about him. On several occasions during the first few days of his hospitalization, he angrily confronted other patients because he thought that they were ridiculing him. All of them vehemently denied talking about him. In addition, Mr. J found it difficult to complete a thought because of a formal thought disorder that consisted of blocking and derailment. He would stop in midsentence, change the subject, then begin another sentence.

Mr. J displayed much anxiety in the hospital because none of the staff members would "monitor" his physical symptoms as his parents had. As expected, the patient attempted to re-create his family situation in the milieu. He developed intense transference attachments to his doctor and his primary nurse, whom he expected to be with him at all times. When his doctor left the unit after a meeting with him, Mr. J attempted to run out the door after him just as he had tried to stop his father from going to work.

Physical and neurological examinations revealed no significant findings. After a careful psychiatric evaluation, the treatment team developed an explanatory formulation. The patient's paranoid concerns and somatic preoccupations masked an extraordinarily low sense of self-esteem. Mr. J had grown up feeling like the "black sheep" of the family, because his limitations had precluded competition with the high achievers surrounding him. To preserve some degree of self-esteem, he formed an identity as a "victim" of disabling physical problems that kept him from performing at an acceptable level. Mr. J was then able to attribute his failures in school and in various jobs to physical illnesses.

The somatic concerns also provided an organizing focus for the patient's thoughts, thereby preventing a more profound state of psychotic fragmentation or self-dissolution. This severe somatic preoccupation was linked to his paranoid perception of ridicule from others through the mechanisms of introjection and projection. Early in life, Mr. J had internalized (as persecuting objects) the expectations and demands of his parents. Thus, strangers on the street or in the hallway who were perceived as talking about him had become these persecuting objects that he had projected onto the environment. When the persecutors were reintrojected, they became internal persecutors in the form of various aches and pains requiring immediate attention. Hence the patient felt constantly under siege by a host of tormentors, both in his environment and within his body.

On a neurophysiological level, Mr. J's inability to screen out various stimuli may have compounded his feeling of numerous sources of pain and torment. Finally, the somatizing performed yet another function: it was the only way the patient knew to maintain object relatedness and therefore defend against severe separation anxiety. This patient clearly had little interest in any diagnostic evaluations or treatment suggestions from consultants. Such findings and recommendations were far less significant to him than his concern that he needed to be continuously "monitored." The patient's litany of physical complaints was not truly designed to elicit an ameliorating response from those around him; rather, its purpose was to maintain a continual external presence so that he would not have to face his anxieties about abandonment. Paradoxically, his barrage of complaints tended to evoke the opposite response, namely, to alienate and drive away others. Initially, the treatment team attempted to control Mr. J's positive symptoms through medication. However, the patient adamantly refused the medication because he associated it with previous doctors who had told him that his pain was "all in your head."

Respecting Mr. J's need to preserve self-esteem and organize his thinking through intense investment in physical symptoms, his hospital doctor assured him that no one was questioning the severity of Mr. J's pain. The doctor explained that the patient's illness had both psychological and physical aspects. The doctor further explained that one physical manifestation of the illness was difficulty filtering out various stimuli in the environment and within the body. Through this educational approach, Mr. J's doctor thus convinced the patient that the antipsychotic medication might be worth a trial because it often had a beneficial effect on the "filtering" system. After the patient agreed to take the medication, his thought disorder greatly improved, allowing him to talk more coherently with staff members and other patients. His auditory hallucinations continued despite the medication, but abated somewhat in frequency and severity.

The treatment team then attempted to repair some of the patient's ego deficits by functioning as auxiliary egos. On one occasion, for example, a nurse was meeting with Mr. J in a closed room on the hospital unit when he began to claim that people were talking about him outside in the hallway. To demonstrate that no one was there, the nurse opened the door and walked with Mr. J into the hallway. She then explained to the patient that his illness involved voices that originated on the inside, which were then perceived as though coming from outside sources. This approach was reinforced by feedback from fellow patients in group meetings.

This patient had initially been held out of group meetings on the unit because of the overstimulating nature of that treatment modality. After being stabilized on medication, however, Mr. J began to attend the groups and frequently brought up his concern that others were talking about him. The other patients steadfastly denied these accusations, and they all encouraged him to "check it out" whenever he heard the voice. The patient's hostile accusations toward other patients and toward staff members gradually shifted to gentle inquiries as he realized that the voices did indeed emanate from within.

As Mr. J gained greater control over his positive symptoms, the treatment focus shifted to his disordered interpersonal relatedness. Via projective identification, the patient attempted to establish the same relationship with his hospital doctor that he had with his father. The hospital doctor found himself spending more time in interaction with Mr. J than with any of his other patients. The urgency with which Mr. J presented his complaints of diarrhea, stomachaches, joint pain, and so on, made his hospital doctor reluctant to disengage from Mr. J and leave the unit. One day when Mr. J frantically followed him out of the unit and continued to walk down the sidewalk with him, the doctor realized the extent to which the patient had replicated his family situation in the hospital. Mr. J felt as though he deserved the complete attention of his doctor and was oblivious to the needs of other patients who shared the same physician. The doctor then told Mr. J that he should lower his expectations of how much time the doctor would spend with him. The doctor explained to Mr. J that he would set up specific 30-minute appointments with him and would not meet with him at other times. This limit-setting approach addressed the patient's sense of entitlement.

This approach also presented a new form of object relatedness for the patient to internalize. The object relationship paradigm of a complaining, demanding self linked to an indulgent object was modified by Mr. J's experience of a new object that was caring but also limit setting. The experience with this new object correspondingly brought about changes in the patient's self-representation. Although initially frustrated, the patient became more tolerant of the doctor's absences and more accepting of limitations on his expectations of others. Moreover, the limitations Mr. J encountered in this relationship led him to discuss his separation anxiety with his doctor. Mr. J began to express concern that in the absence of a caretaking figure, his basic needs would go unmet.

When the patient was able to address these and other psychological concerns, he was referred to an individual psychotherapist not connected with the unit. The early phase of this psychotherapy was characterized by the patient's extensive reports about his physical symptoms. The patient's therapist listened to these reports with interest and concern, empathizing with his need to focus on the somatic rather than the psychological. Periodically, however, the therapist would comment that he was really unable to help the patient with any physical ailments because he had nothing to add to the extensive work of the treatment team and the consultants. As trust developed, the patient began to discuss his profound feelings of inferiority within his family context. Although his brother and sister had distinguished themselves academically, his only distinction was that he suffered from a variety of bizarre ailments that prevented him from similar success. The patient's denial of psychiatric illness, his lack of psychological-mindedness, and his lack of curiosity about his symptoms all led the therapist to take a predominantly supportive approach. Within that context, then, the patient was finally able to explore a surprisingly broad range of feelings about himself and his place in his family.

As part of the overall treatment plan, the patient became involved in a social skills group with a small number of his peers. In this setting, he received gentle confrontation about his hygiene problems, his failure to answer conversational questions, his self-absorption, and his obliviousness to the needs of others. He began to improve in all these areas in addition to generally improving his interpersonal functioning. For example, he began to say "good morning" to others who spoke to him, and he would even inquire as to their well-being. The patient also entered a vocational assessment and training program where he had to perform simple tasks under supervision. The activities therapist in charge of the program was careful to gear the level of complexity of the tasks to the patient's ability so that his self-esteem was not seriously threatened. Finally, a psychoeducational approach was employed with the patient's parents to help them accept their son's limitations. They were told that overinvolvement and excessive expectations would be counterproductive because the patient would experience them as pressure to succeed beyond his capacities.

This fragment of dynamically informed treatment illustrates how all three theoretical frameworks discussed in Chapter 2 may be useful in the treatment of one patient. Self psychological principles led the treatment team to an empathic awareness of this patient's need to maintain self-esteem, and his treaters therefore chose not to challenge his somatization. An object relations theoretical framework facilitated the doctor's understanding of this patient's problematic relationship with the doctor. Finally, the ego psychological perspective was helpful in two ways: 1) an ego-deficit model was applied in the form of the nursing staff's ego-building techniques, and 2) a conflict model was used to understand the auditory hallucinations. The persecutory voices this patient heard calling him a "loser" or "crazy" grew out of a painful conflict between the internalized expectations of his parents (in the form of his ego ideal and superego) and the reality of his limitations (realistic ego functioning). These voices always seemed more evident after the patient experienced any failure in his vocational program.

In summary, patients with schizophrenia need therapeutic figures in their lives. They need help navigating through the complicated realities of the mental health system. They also need someone to facilitate their understanding of the fears and fantasies that prevent them from complying with the various components of their overall treatment plan. Indeed, a central role of the psychotherapist is to explore compliance problems that arise in other areas of treatment. In contemporary practice, this role is often assigned to a clinical case manager, usually because the patient is not interested in therapy or because community resources cannot provide psychotherapy. Case managers serve as patient advocates, guides to mental health resources, and coordinators of the total treatment plan. Even though case management is oriented to reality and to adaptation, transference and countertransference issues arise; case managers must thus be capable of providing effective psychotherapeutic interventions (Kanter 1989). What schizophrenic patients most need, whether they are called case managers or psychotherapists, are concerned individuals who can offer compassionate human relationships for sanctuary from a confusing and threatening world.

References

American Psychiatric Association: Diagnostic and Statistical Manual of Mental Disorders, 4th Edition. Washington, DC, American Psychiatric Association, 1994

Andreasen NC, Olsen SA, Dennert JW, et al: Ventricular enlargement in schizophrenia: relationship to positive and negative symptoms. Am J Psychiatry 139:297–302, 1982

Andreasen NC, Flaum M, Swayze VW, et al: Positive and negative symptoms in schizophrenia: a critical reappraisal. Arch Gen Psychiatry 47:615–621, 1990

Anonymous: Can we talk? The schizophrenic patient in psychotherapy. Am J Psychiatry 143:68–70, 1986

Arlow JA, Brenner C: The psychopathology of the psychoses: a proposed revision. Int J Psychoanal 50:5–14, 1969

Bachrach LL: Psychosocial rehabilitation and psychiatry in the care of long-term patients. Am J Psychiatry 149:1455–1463, 1992

Bion WR: Attacks on linking (1959), in Second Thoughts: Selected Papers on Psycho-Analysis. New York, Jason Aronson, 1967, pp 93–109

Blatt SJ, Wild CM: Schizophrenia: A Developmental Analysis. New York, Academic Press, 1976

Brenner C: The Mind in Conflict. New York, International Universities Press, 1982

Brown GW, Birley JLT, Wing JK: Influence of family life on the course of schizophrenic disorders: a replication. Br J Psychiatry 121:241–258, 1972

Cannon TD, Sarnoff A, Mednick SA, et al: Antecedents of predominantly negative- and predominantly positive-symptom schizophrenia in a high-risk population. Arch Gen Psychiatry 47:622–632, 1990

Carpenter WT Jr: A perspective on the psychotherapy of schizophrenia project. Schizophr Bull 10:599–602, 1984

Carpenter WT Jr, Henrichs DW, Wagman AMI: Deficit and nondeficit forms of schizophrenia: the concept. Am J Psychiatry 145:578–583, 1988

Conte HR, Plutchik R: Controlled research and supportive psychotherapy. Psychiatric Annals 16:530–533, 1986

Corrigan PW, Liberman RP, Engel JD: From noncompliance to collaboration in the treatment of schizophrenia. Hosp Community Psychiatry 41:1203–1211, 1990

Dworkin RH, Lenzenweger MF, Moldin SO, et al: A multidimensional approach to the genetics of schizophrenia. Am J Psychiatry 145:1077–1083, 1988

Falloon IRH: Expressed emotion: current status. Psychol Med 18:269–274, 1988

Falloon IRH, Boyd JL, McGill CW, et al: Family management in the prevention of exacerbations of schizophrenia: a controlled study. N Engl J Med 306:1437–1440, 1982

Federn P: Ego Psychology and the Psychoses. New York, Basic Books, 1952

Frank AF, Gunderson JG: The role of the therapeutic alliance in the treatment of schizophrenia: relationship to course and outcome. Arch Gen Psychiatry 47:228–236, 1990

Freud S: Psycho-analytic notes on an autobiographical account of a case of paranoia (dementia paranoides) (1911), in The Standard Edition of the Complete Psychological Works of Sigmund Freud, Vol 12. Translated and edited by Strachey J. London, Hogarth Press, 1958, pp 1–82

Freud S: On narcissism: an introduction (1914), in The Standard Edition of the Complete Psychological Works of Sigmund Freud, Vol 14. Translated and edited by Strachey J. London, Hogarth Press, 1963, pp 67–102

Freud S: The unconscious (1915), in The Standard Edition of the Complete Psychological Works of Sigmund Freud, Vol 14. Translated and edited by Strachey J. London, Hogarth Press, 1963, pp 159–215

Freud S: Neurosis and psychosis (1924a), in The Standard Edition of the Complete Psychological Works of Sigmund Freud, Vol 19. Translated and edited by Strachey J. London, Hogarth Press, 1961, pp 147–153

Freud S: The loss of reality in neurosis and psychosis (1924b), in The Standard Edition of the Complete Psychological Works of Sigmund Freud, Vol 19. Translated and edited by Strachey J. London, Hogarth Press, 1961, pp 181–187

Fromm-Reichmann F: Principles of Intensive Psychotherapy. Chicago, IL, University of Chicago Press, 1950

Garfield D: Self-criticism in psychosis: enabling statements in psychotherapy. Dynamic Psychotherapy 3:129–137, 1985

Garfield D, Rogoff M, Steinberg S: Affect-recognition and self-esteem in schizophrenia. Psychopathology 20:225–233, 1987

Glass LL, Katz HM, Schnitzer RD, et al: Psychotherapy of schizophrenia: an empirical investigation of the relationship of process to outcome. Am J Psychiatry 146:603–608, 1989

Goldstein MJ, Rodnick EH, Evans JR, et al: Drug and family in the aftercare of acute schizophrenics. Arch Gen Psychiatry 35:1169–1177, 1978

Gomez-Schwartz B: Individual psychotherapy of schizophrenia, in Schizophrenia: Treatment, Management, and Rehabilitation. Edited by Bellack AS. Orlando, FL, Grune & Stratton, 1984, pp 307–335

Gottesman II, Shields J: Schizophrenia: The Epigenetic Puzzle. London, Cambridge University Press, 1982

Grand S: The body and its boundaries: a psychoanalytic view of cognitive process disturbances in schizophrenia. International Review of Psychoanalysis 9:327–342, 1982

Grinspoon L, Ewalt JR, Shader RI: Schizophrenia: Pharmacotherapy and Psychotherapy. Baltimore, MD, Williams & Wilkins, 1972

Grotstein JS: Psychoanalytic therapy of schizophrenia, in Treatment of Schizophrenia: Progress and Prospects. Edited by West LJ, Flinn DE. New York, Grune & Stratton, 1976, pp 131–145

Grotstein JS: The psychoanalytic concept of schizophrenia, I: the dilemma. Int J Psychoanal 58:403–425, 1977a

Grotstein JS: The psychoanalytic concept of schizophrenia, II: reconciliation. Int J Psychoanal 58:427–452, 1977b

Gunderson JG: Engagement of schizophrenic patients in psychotherapy, in Attachment and the Therapeutic Process: Essays in Honor of Otto Allen Will, Jr. Edited by Sacksteder JL, Schwartz DP, Akabane Y. Madison, CT, International Universities Press, 1987, pp 139–153

Gunderson JG, Frank AF, Katz HM, et al: Effects of psychotherapy in schizophrenia, II: comparative outcome of two forms of treatment. Schizophr Bull 10:564–598, 1984

Harding CM, Zubin J, Strauss JS: Chronicity in schizophrenia: fact, partial fact, or artifact? Hosp Community Psychiatry 38:477–486, 1987

Hatfield AB: Family Education in Mental Illness. New York, Guilford, 1990

Hogarty GE: Depot neuroleptics: the relevance of psychosocial factors—a United States perspective. J Clin Psychiatry 45(5,2):36–42, 1984

Hogarty GE, Anderson CM, Reiss DJ, et al: Family psychoeducation, social skills training, and maintenance chemotherapy in the aftercare treatment of schizophrenia, I: one-year effects of a controlled study on relapse and expressed emotion. Arch Gen Psychiatry 43:633–642, 1986

Hogg B, Jackson HJ, Rudd RP, et al: Diagnosing personality disorders in recent-onset schizophrenia. J Nerv Ment Dis 178:194–199, 1990

Jenkins JH, Karno M: The meaning of expressed emotion: theoretical issues raised by cross-cultural research. Am J Psychiatry 149:9–21, 1992

Judd LL, McAdams LA, Budnick B, et al: Sensory gating deficits in schizophrenia: new results. Am J Psychiatry 149:488–493, 1992

Kanas N: Group therapy with schizophrenics: a review of controlled studies. Int J Group Psychother 36:339–351, 1986

Kanas N, Rogers M, Kreth E, et al: The effectiveness of group psychotherapy during the first three weeks of hospitalization: a controlled study. J Nerv Ment Dis 168:487–492, 1980

Kanter J: Clinical case management: definition, principles, components. Hosp Community Psychiatry 40:361–368, 1989

Kanter J, Lamb HR, Loeper C: Expressed emotion in families: a critical review. Hosp Community Psychiatry 38:374–380, 1987a

Kanter J, Lamb HR, Loeper C: Expressed emotion: in reply. Hosp Community Psychiatry 38:1118–1119, 1987b

Karon BP: The fear of understanding schizophrenia. Psychoanal Psychol 9:191–211, 1992

Karon BP, VandenBos G: Psychotherapy of Schizophrenia. New York, Jason Aronson, 1981

Kay SR: Significance of the positive-negative distinction in schizophrenia. Schizophr Bull 16:635–652, 1990

Keith SJ, Matthews SM: Schizophrenia: a review of psychosocial treatment strategies, in Psychotherapy Research: Where Are We and Where Should We Go? Edited by Williams JBW, Spitzer RL. New York, Guilford, 1984, pp 70–88

Kendler KS: The genetics of schizophrenia: a current perspective, in Psychopharmacology: The Third Generation of Progress. Edited by Meltzer HY. New York, Raven, 1987, pp 705–713

Kendler KS, Gruenberg AM, Strauss JS: An independent analysis of the Copenhagen sample of the Danish adoption study of schizophrenia, V: the relationship between childhood social withdrawal and adult schizophrenia. Arch Gen Psychiatry 39:1257–1261, 1982

Klein DF: Psychosocial treatment of schizophrenia, or psychosocial help for people with schizophrenia? Schizophr Bull 6:122–130, 1980

Kringlen E: Contributions of genetic studies on schizophrenia, in Search for the Causes of Schizophrenia. Edited by Häfner H, Gattaz WF, Janzarik W. Berlin, Springer-Verlag, 1987, pp 123–142

Leff J, Kuipers L, Berkowitz R, et al: A controlled trial of social intervention in the families of schizophrenic patients. Br J Psychiatry 141:121–134, 1982

Lefley HP: Expressed emotion: conceptual, clinical, and social policy issues. Hosp Community Psychiatry 43:591–598, 1992

London NJ: An essay on psychoanalytic theory: two theories of schizophrenia, part I: review and critical assessment of the development of the two theories. Int J Psychoanal 54:169–178, 1973a

London NJ: An essay on psychoanalytic theory: two theories of schizophrenia, part II: discussion and restatement of the specific theory of schizophrenia. Int J Psychoanal 54:179–193, 1973b

MacMillan JF, Gold A, Crow TJ, et al: IV. Expressed emotion and relapse. Br J Psychiatry 148:133–143, 1986

Mahler M: On child psychosis and schizophrenia: autistic and symbiotic infantile psychoses. Psychoanal Study Child 7:286–305, 1952

May PRA: Treatment of Schizophrenia: A Comparative Study of Five Treatment Methods. New York, Science House, 1968

McGlashan TH: Intensive individual psychotherapy of schizophrenia: a review of techniques. Arch Gen Psychiatry 40:909–920, 1983

McGlashan TH: The Chestnut Lodge follow-up study, II: long-term outcome of schizophrenia and the affective disorders. Arch Gen Psychiatry 41:586–601, 1984

McGlashan TH: Recovery style from mental illness and long-term outcome. J Nerv Ment Dis 175:681–685, 1987

McGlashan TH, Fenton WS: The positive-negative distinction in schizophrenia: review of natural history validators. Arch Gen Psychiatry 49:63–72, 1992

McGlashan TH, Keats CJ: Schizophrenia: Treatment Process and Outcome. Washington, DC, American Psychiatric Press, 1989

McGlashan TH, Nayfack B: Psychotherapeutic models and the treatment of schizophrenia: the records of three successive psychotherapists with one patient at Chestnut Lodge for 18 years. Psychiatry 51:340–362, 1988

Mosher LR, Keith SJ: Research on the psychosocial treatment of schizophrenia: a summary report. Am J Psychiatry 136:623–631, 1979

Müller C: Psychotherapy and schizophrenia: the end of the pioneers' period. Schizophr Bull 10:618–620, 1984

Munich RL, Carsky M, Appelbaum A: The role and structure of long-term hospitalization: chronic schizophrenia. Psychiatric Hospital 16:161–169, 1985

O'Brien C: Group psychotherapy with schizophrenia and affective disorders, in Comprehensive Group Psychotherapy, 2nd Edition. Edited by Kaplan HI, Sadock BJ. Baltimore, MD, Williams & Wilkins, 1983, pp 242–249

Ogden TH: On the nature of schizophrenic conflict. Int J Psychoanal 61:513–533, 1980

Ogden TH: The schizophrenic state of nonexperience, in Technical Factors in the Treatment of the Severely Disturbed Patient. Edited by Giovacchini PL, Boyer LB. New York, Jason Aronson, 1982, pp 217–260

Pao P-N: Notes on Freud's theory of schizophrenia. Int J Psychoanal 54:469–476, 1973

Parker G, Johnston P, Hayward L: Parental "expressed emotion" as a predictor of schizophrenic relapse. Arch Gen Psychiatry 45:806–813, 1988

Pollack WS: Schizophrenia and the self: contributions of psychoanalytic self-psychology. Schizophr Bull 15:311–322, 1989

Pollin W, Stabeneau JR: Biological, psychological and historical differences in a series of monozygotic twins discordant for schizophrenia, in The Transmission of Schizophrenia. Edited by Rosenthal D, Kety SS. New York, Pergamon, 1968, pp 317–332

Robbins M: Psychoanalytic and biological approaches to mental illness: schizophrenia. J Am Psychoanal Assoc 40:425–454, 1992

Rogers CR, Gendlin ET, Kiesler DJ, et al (eds): The Therapeutic Relationship and Its Impact: A Study of Psychotherapy with Schizophrenics. Madison, WI, University of Wisconsin Press, 1967

Rund BR: Fully recovered schizophrenics: a retrospective study of some premorbid and treatment factors. Psychiatry 53:127–139, 1990

Ruocchio PJ: How psychotherapy can help the schizophrenic patient. Hosp Community Psychiatry 40:188–190, 1989

Schulsinger F, Parnas J, Schulsinger H, et al: Recent trends from nature-nurture research in schizophrenia, in Schizophrenia: Recent Biosocial Developments. Edited by Stefanis CN, Rabavilas AD. New York, Human Sciences Press, 1988, pp 39–53

Searles HF: The "dedicated physician" in psychotherapy and psychoanalysis, in Crosscurrents in Psychiatry and Psychoanalysis. Edited by Gibson RW. Philadelphia, PA, JB Lippincott, 1967, pp 128–143

Searles HF: Psychoanalytic therapy with schizophrenic patients in a private-practice context, in Countertransference and Related Subjects: Selected Papers. New York, International Universities Press, 1979, pp 582–602

Selzer MA: Preparing the chronic schizophrenic for exploratory psychotherapy: the role of hospitalization. Psychiatry 46:303–311, 1983

Selzer MA, Carsky M: Treatment alliance and the chronic schizophrenic. Am J Psychother 44:506–515, 1990

Selzer MA, Sullivan TB, Carsky M, et al: Working With the Person With Schizophrenia: The Treatment Alliance. New York, New York University Press, 1989

Spohn HE, Lacoursiere RB, Thompson K, et al: Phenothiazine effects on psychological and psychophysiological dysfunction in chronic schizophrenics. Arch Gen Psychiatry 34:633–644, 1977

Stanton AH, Gunderson JG, Knapp PH, et al: Effects of psychotherapy on schizophrenic patients, I: design and implementation of a controlled study. Schizophr Bull 10:520–563, 1984

Strauss JS, Carpenter WT, Bartko JJ: The diagnosis and understanding of schizophrenia, part III: speculations on the process that underlie schizophrenic symptoms and signs. Schizophr Bull 11:61–69, 1974

Sullivan HS: Schizophrenia as a Human Process. New York, WW Norton, 1962

Tienari P, Sorri A, Lahti I, et al: The Finnish adoptive family study of schizophrenia. Yale J Biol Med 58:227–237, 1985

Walker E, Lewine RJ: Prediction of adult-onset schizophrenia from childhood home movies of the patients. Am J Psychiatry 147:1052–1056, 1990

Wexler M: Schizophrenia: conflict and deficiency. Psychoanal Q 40:83–99, 1971

Chapter 8

Affective Disorders

Affective disorders, like schizophrenia, are illnesses with a strong biological component. Familial transmission of mania and depression clearly suggests that genetic factors may be crucial to their etiology. Disturbances of neurochemistry are also present. Bipolar illnesses may be effectively controlled with lithium carbonate and carbamazepine, while unipolar depression often lifts when treated with antidepressants or electroconvulsive therapy. The impressive research efforts of neuroscientists in the area of affective disorders raise the question of whether there is indeed a role for the dynamic psychiatrist in these conditions.

The answer is an unqualified yes. This affirmative response is supported by the results of the National Institute of Mental Health (NIMH) Treatment of Depression Collaborative Research Program (Elkin et al. 1989). This project examined the impact of four different treatment conditions on 239 nonbipolar, nonpsychotically depressed outpatients. One group of patients received a 16-week course of cognitive-behavior therapy (CBT), a second group received 16 weeks of interpersonal psychotherapy (IPT), a third group was placed on imipramine plus clinical management, and a fourth received a placebo plus clinical management, both administered in double-blind fashion. Sixty-eight percent of the patients completed at least 15 weeks and 12 sessions of treatment.

When the investigators examined overall functioning and reduction of depressive symptoms at 16 weeks, none of the three active treatments demonstrated any specific effectiveness over the placebo and clinical management in the mildly depressed subgroup (Elkin et al. 1989). However, when the more severely depressed and functionally impaired patients were studied, there were clear differences in outcome among the various treatment groups. The imipramine and clinical management condition produced the best outcomes, while the two psychotherapies also produced significant improvement, with IPT doing better than CBT. Those patients in the placebo with clinical management condition did poorly. Examination of recovery data indicated that both IPT and imipramine with clinical management were far superior to placebo with clinical management.

These findings reflect the fundamental interconnectedness of mind and brain, as described in Chapter 1. A condition involving aberrant neurochemical functioning in the brain can apparently be altered by psychotherapeutic intervention. Conversely, psychological dimensions of the same condition apparently respond to psychopharmacologic measures. Whereas some might assume that milder forms of depression are associated with psychological causation and that severe melancholic forms of depression are caused by purely biological factors, the situation is actually far more complex. Even in the case of severe endogenous or melancholic depressions, environmental and psychological factors may play a key role. Indeed, in one study of 100 such patients (van Praag 1989), 73% of the patients with severe melancholic depression and their significant others were able to identify a stressful event in the 6 months prior to the onset of the illness that was etiologically relevant. Findings such as these suggest that the etiology of severe depression involves a composite of forces, including psychological, interpersonal, biological, and environmental stressors, that act on the brain. The pathogenesis, on the other hand, involves actual brain dysfunction in response to the etiological forces.

Studies of the link between affective disorders and environmental stressors suggest that early life events may create a heightened vulnerability to subsequent stressors. Based on the observation that both depression and panic disorder respond to monoamine oxidase inhibitors and tricyclic antidepressants, D. F. Klein (1980) postulated that early separation experiences in childhood create a neurobiological sensitivity to abandonment that is an underlying factor in both disorders. In a study involving 1,018 pairs of female twins, Kendler et al. (1992)

documented an increased risk for major depression (as well as generalized anxiety disorder) in those women who had experienced maternal or paternal separation in childhood or adolescence. The kindling response model derived from studies of seizure thresholds has been suggested as a useful paradigm to understand the mechanisms involved in this increased vulnerability (Gold et al. 1988a, 1988b; Post et al. 1982). Painful events such as separations or losses early in life may sensitize receptor sites such that ideas and images associated with depressive states could ultimately act as conditioned stimuli capable of eliciting a major depressive episode, even without a concrete loss or external stressor in the environment. This model is consistent with psychoanalytic observations that an imagined loss or a perceived discrepancy between idealized expectations and reality may precipitate depression. The kindling phenomenon also would help explain why studies suggest a much greater role for psychosocial stressors in the first episode of major affective disorder than in subsequent episodes (Post 1992).

Gold et al. (1988a, 1988b) concluded that the kindling model argues for a combination of medication and psychotherapy in the treatment of major affective disorder. The inner conflicts brought on by prior life events may increase the burden of stress unless they are addressed psychotherapeutically. In one study of depression, DiMascio et al. (1979) found that patients receiving a combination of a tricyclic antidepressant and psychotherapy gained more symptom reduction than those who received either treatment alone. In another study (van Praag 1989), the combination of antidepressants and psychotherapy produced significantly better outcomes than antidepressants alone. In contrast with patients who received combined treatment, many of those treated only with medication claimed that they had not returned to their premorbid sense of well-being.

In addition to the benefits of combining psychotherapy and pharmacotherapy, there are several other reasons that psychodynamic interventions may be required in the treatment of depression. As noted in Chapter 5, some depressed patients will not comply with their prescribed medication for a variety of reasons, including that they feel they do not deserve to get better or they feel that taking medication stigmatizes them as mentally ill. In addition to being indicated for patients with noncompliance problems, psychotherapy must be used for those who cannot take antidepressants because of preexisting medical conditions, those who cannot tolerate side effects, and those who are partially or completely refractory to any somatic treatment.

One must also keep in mind that depression spans the entire spectrum of pathology and health and can be present in milder forms at certain times of stress even in basically healthy people. Individuals with minor depression that does not meet the DSM-IV criteria (American Psychiatric Association 1994) for a major depressive episode or dysthymia account for more disability days in the community than do persons with major depression (Broadhead et al. 1990). Physicians provide more services to persons with depressive *symptoms* than to those with formally defined depressive disorders (Johnson et al. 1992). Hence, even when these milder forms of depression lack DSM-IV criteria to be classified as major disorders, they are not necessarily benign. Medication is often ineffective in minor depression, and these patients may need psychotherapy to be restored to normal functioning.

Psychodynamic understanding and treatment are also essential in dealing with the interface of personality and depression. This interface can be subdivided into three discrete categories: 1) Axis I major depressive disorder complicated by the coexistence of personality disorders on Axis II, 2) depressive personality, and 3) characterological depression in the context of Axis II personality disorders.

A review of the literature provides ample evidence that personality disorders complicate the treatment of Axis I depressive disorders (Reich and Green 1991). In the NIMH Collaborative Study, patients with personality disorders had significantly worse outcomes in social functioning and were more likely to have residual symptoms of depression than patients without personality disorders (Shea et al. 1990). In a British study involving an 18-year follow-up of 89 depressed patients, an interactive effect of melancholia and the personality measure of neuroticism led to poor outcomes in those with both features (Duggan et al. 1991). These studies suggest that certain personality disorders may contribute to a tendency to maintain depression once it has already occurred, and characterological factors may also be responsible for poor medication compliance. Psychotherapy may be necessary in combination with medication to treat these patients effectively.

The second category, depressive personality, may have considerable overlap with the Axis I diagnosis of dysthymia. Persons in this category have chronic feelings of guilt; helplessness; persistently low self-esteem; a tendency to be self-punitive, hypercritical, and self-denying; a pattern of dependent relationships; and feelings of hopelessness about things ever changing. Among this subgroup, perhaps

40%–45% may respond to tricyclic antidepressants (Akiskal et al. 1980; Kocsis et al. 1988). In addition, many also suffer from "double-depression" (Keller and Shapiro 1982; Kocsis et al. 1988), whereby major depressive episodes are superimposed on a chronic dysthymia or depressive personality. These patients require antidepressants for the depressive episodes and psychotherapy for the chronic personality features. Despite the long-standing psychoanalytic tradition associated with the diagnosis of depressive personality (Phillips et al. 1990), the lack of empirical data kept it from replacing dysthymia in DSM-IV.

The third category subsumes those patients with severe personality disorders, especially borderline, who present with complaints of "depression" yet lack DSM-IV criteria for an Axis I disorder. Many of these patients describe a feeling of pervasive loneliness or emptiness associated with the perception that their emotional needs are not being met by others. They may also have a conscious sense of rage and frustration that separates them from the typical Axis I patient. Because this form of characterological depression is primarily associated with borderline personality disorder, it will be discussed at greater length in Chapter 15.

For all the foregoing reasons, psychodynamic understanding and treatment still play a major role in the treatment of mood disorders, despite impressive advances in the biological understanding of mania and depression. The psychiatrist who combines psychodynamic approaches with psychopharmacologic measures will be better equipped to treat the broad range of affectively disturbed patients seen in clinical practice.

Psychodynamic Understanding of Depression and Mania

In Freud's classic 1917 paper, "Mourning and Melancholia," he differentiated between grief and melancholic depression. In the former, the precipitating event is the real loss of a significant figure. In melancholia, by contrast, the lost object is *emotional* rather than real. Moreover, the melancholic patient feels a profound loss of self-esteem, accompanied by self-reproach and guilt, while the mourner maintains a reasonably stable sense of self-esteem. Freud explained the marked self-depreciation common in depressed patients as the result of anger turned inward. More specifically, the rage is directed internally because the self of the patient has identified with the lost object. In 1923, Freud noted that such introjection may be the only way for the ego to give up an object. That same year, in "The Ego and the Id," he postulated that melancholic patients have a severe superego, which he related to their guilt over having shown aggression toward loved ones.

Melanie Klein (1940/1975) linked depression to the depressive position (see Chapter 2). She understood manic-depressive states as a reflection of childhood failure to establish good internal objects. Depressed people, in other words, have never overcome the depressive position common to childhood. She contrasted this state with normal mourning, in which the depressive position is reactivated as a result of losing a loved one, but is then overcome and worked through by reestablishing the lost figure as an internal object, as well as by reinstating the good parents in the process. In Klein's view, then, depressed patients are desperately concerned that they have destroyed the loved good objects within themselves as a result of their own greed and destructiveness. As a consequence of that destruction, they feel persecuted by the hated bad objects that remain. This feeling of being persecuted by bad objects while "pining" for the lost good objects is what constitutes the essence of the depressive position, which is reactivated in melancholic states. In other words, patients may feel worthless because they sense that they have changed their good internal parents into persecutors as a result of their own destructive impulses and fantasies.

Melanie Klein noted that manic defenses, such as omnipotence, denial, contempt, and idealization, develop in response to the painful affects produced by "pining" for the lost love objects. These defenses are used in the service of 1) rescuing and restoring the lost love objects, 2) disavowing the bad internal objects, and 3) denying slavish dependency on love objects. Clinically, patients may express these manic operations through a denial of any aggression or destructiveness toward others, a euphoric disposition that is contrary to their actual life situation, an idealization of others, or a scornful, contemptuous attitude toward other people that serves to disavow the need for relationships. An integral aspect of the manic defensive posture is often a wish to triumph over parents and thus reverse the child-parent relationship. This desire for triumph may in turn give rise to guilt and depression. In Klein's view, this mechanism is partly responsible for the depression that frequently develops after success or promotion.

Melanie Klein's formulation is useful because it helps clinicians to understand how the psychological function of a manic episode can coexist with biological determinants. The defensive function of mania is most clearly evident in dysphoric manic patients (Post et al. 1989), whose anxiety and depression "break through" a manic episode, necessitating a resurgence of manic denial. Moreover, in a much more attenuated form, hypomanic defenses are typically enlisted to defend against the threat of depressive affects or grief. One patient, for example, described feeling "high" after learning of his mother's death. He felt powerful, expansive, and liberated from dependency. Despite these feelings, he was able to note how odd it was that he was not grief stricken.

Although both Freud and Klein saw aggression as pivotal to the understanding of depression, Bibring (1953) believed that depression was a primary affective state unrelated to aggression turned inward. He viewed depression as arising from the tension between ideals and reality. Three highly invested narcissistic aspirations—to be worthy and loved, to be strong or superior, and to be good and loving—are held up as standards of conduct. However, the ego's awareness of its actual or imagined inability to measure up to these standards produces depression. As a result, the depressed person feels helpless and powerless. Bibring thought that, in certain cases, the ego's awareness of its helplessness may lead to aggression turned inward, but only as a secondary phenomenon. He believed that any narcissistic frustration or injury that lowers self-esteem might precipitate a clinical depression. Alone among all authors writing on the psychodynamics of depression, Bibring (1953) did not postulate that the superego played a key role. Rather, he postulated that tension arises within the ego itself, not between the ego and another intrapsychic agency. He succinctly described this depression as "a partial or complete collapse of the self-esteem of the ego, since it feels unable to live up to its aspirations (ego ideal, superego) while they are strongly maintained" (p. 26). He understood manic elation either as a compensating secondary reaction to depression or as an expression of the fantasy fulfillment of the individual's narcissistic aspirations.

Revising Freud's formulation, Jacobson (1971a) suggested that melancholic patients actually act as if they were the worthless, lost love object, even though they do not assume all the characteristics of that object. The self, then, is experienced as the bad object, and eventually this bad internal object or the lost external love object is transformed into the sadistic superego. The ego then becomes "a victim of the superego, as helpless and powerless as a small child who is tortured by his cruel, powerful mother" (p. 252).

> Ms. K was a 49-year-old homemaker who became psychotically depressed. She became convinced that she was thoroughly worthless, and she was preoccupied with how her father had beaten her as a child because she was such a "bad little girl." At times the bad introject of the abusive, hated father was absorbed into the patient's self-view, and she would cut herself both as self-punishment and as a way of attacking the internal object. At other times, the father would be experienced as a separate internal object, or a harsh superego, who would rebuke her for being bad. In these instances, Ms. K would hear a hallucinated voice, saying, "You are bad" and "You deserve to die."

The internal object world of Ms. K indicates how, in psychotic depression, there may be a fusion of the self with the object, on the one hand, or a reactivation of an internal object relationship in which a tormenting bad object, or primitive superego, persecutes a bad self, on the other. Jacobson believed that mania could be understood as a magical reunion of the self with the harsh superego figure, thus changing that figure from a punitive tormenter into a loving, all-good, forgiving figure. This idealized object may then be projected into the external world to establish highly idealized relationships with others whereby all aggression and destructiveness are denied.

Based on extensive experience in the psychotherapy of severely depressed patients, Arieti (1977) postulated a preexisting ideology in persons who become severely depressed—namely, living not for oneself, but for another person—what Arieti termed the *dominant other*. Most commonly, the spouse is the dominant other, but an organization or an ideal may also serve that function. When a transcendent purpose or aim occupies this place in the individual's psychological world, it is referred to as the dominant goal or dominant ideology. Arieti's concept is somewhat reminiscent of Bibring's, because of its emphasis on the patient's helplessness upon realizing that the goal is unattainable. These patients generally cannot imagine or accept any alternate frameworks that might allow them to give up the dominant goal. They realize that living for someone or something else is not working out for them, but they feel unable to change. They believe that life is worthless if they cannot elicit the response they wish from the dominant other or if they cannot achieve their impossible goal. They adhere rigidly to an unrealistic life plan that they cannot give up.

We can summarize the various theoretical formulations of depression by concluding that whatever biochemical contributions there may be, patients experience depression psychologically as a disturbance of self-esteem in the context of failed interpersonal relationships. These childhood relationships are internalized and reactivated in adulthood with the onset of major affective disorders. The tormenting internal world of object relationships is then also externalized into current relationships in the patient's world. Depression illustrates the close relationship between an individual's intimate interpersonal interactions and the maintenance of self-esteem (Strupp et al. 1982). In self psychological terms, depression may be viewed as the despair resulting from the failure of selfobjects to gratify the self's needs for mirroring, twinship, or idealization.

Psychodynamics of Suicide

Many different psychiatric disorders can culminate in the tragic outcome of suicide. Suicide is most prominently associated with major affective disorders, however, so it is therefore considered in detail in the context of this chapter. Before examining the psychodynamic perspective on suicide, a caveat is in order. Determinants of suicidal behavior may be biological as well as psychological. The psychodynamics revealed by psychotherapeutic work with suicidal patients may in some respects be *secondary* to neurochemical changes, so all available somatic treatment modalities must be used aggressively along with the psychotherapeutic approach. In many cases, psychotherapy alone is insufficient with seriously suicidal patients. In one comparison study (Lesse 1978), only 16% of the severely depressed psychotherapy patients had a positive outcome, while 83% of the patients who received both psychotherapy and pharmacotherapy and 86% of those who received electroconvulsive therapy had good results. Saving the patient's life is far more important than theoretical purity.

Suicidal behavior and ideation, like all other acts and thoughts, are the end products of the principles of overdetermination and multiple function (see Chapter 1). Motivations for suicide are highly varied and often obscure (Meissner 1986). The clinician must therefore listen carefully to each patient, noting the particular transference-countertransference developments before reaching any closure on the dynamic underpinnings of suicide.

In keeping with his understanding of the dynamics of depression, Freud (1917/1963) assumed that the ego could kill itself only by treating itself as an object, so he postulated that suicide results from displaced murderous impulses—that is, destructive wishes toward an internalized object are directed instead against the self. After the development of the structural model (1923/1961), Freud redefined suicide as the victimization of the ego by a sadistic superego. Karl Menninger's (1933) view of suicide was a bit more complex. He believed that at least three wishes might contribute to a suicidal act—the wish to kill, the wish to be killed, and the wish to die. The wish to kill may be directed not only toward an *internal* object. Clinical experience confirms again and again that suicide is often designed to destroy the lives of the survivors. Depressed patients often feel, for example, that suicide is the only satisfactory revenge against their parents. The patient's spouse may similarly be the "target" of a suicide.

A recurring theme in the object relations of suicidal patients is the drama between a sadistic tormentor and a tormented victim. As in the case of Ms. K, there is often a persecuting internal object that makes the patient miserable. Alternatively, the patient who identifies with the persecutor may torment everyone in his or her environment. In some cases, the patient may believe that the only possible outcome of the drama is to submit to the tormentor through suicide (Meissner 1986). This internal persecuting figure has been referred to as the "hidden executioner" (Asch 1980).

In other cases, aggression plays a far less prominent role in the motivation for suicide. Fenichel (1945) noted that suicide may be the fulfillment of a reunion wish, that is, a joyous and magical rejoining with a lost loved one, or a narcissistic union with a loving superego figure. Object loss frequently lies behind suicidal behavior, and many suicidal patients reveal strong dependency yearnings toward a lost object (Dorpat 1973). In this regard, suicide may be a regressive wish for reunion with a lost maternal figure. The last words of the Reverend Jim Jones in the 1978 mass homicide and suicide in Guyana were "Mother . . . Mother," spoken just before he shot himself in the head. A pathological grief process is often involved in suicides, particularly those that occur on the anniversary of the death of a loved one. Research has demonstrated, for example, that there is a statistically significant correlation between suicide and the anniversary of a parent's death (Bunch and Barraclough 1971). When an individual's self-esteem and self-integrity depend on attachment to a lost object, suicide may seem to be the only way to restore self-cohesion.

> Ms. L was a 24-year-old psychotically depressed woman who, 2 years earlier, had lost her twin brother to suicide. Following his death, she had withdrawn from life, intent on killing herself. Moreover, she had become psychotically identified with her brother to the point that she identified herself as male and as having his first name. She had been refractory to antidepressant medication, lithium carbonate, and electroconvulsive therapy. She felt that she could not continue living in the absence of her brother. Ms. L ultimately committed suicide on the anniversary of her brother's death.

To assess suicide risk with any given patient, these psychodynamic themes must be put in the context of a set of predictors of suicide risk. A prospective examination of 954 patients (Clark and Fawcett 1992) revealed that it was useful to differentiate short-term from long-term risk factors in attempting to predict suicide. Seven factors predicted suicide within 1 year of entry into the study: panic attacks, psychic anxiety, severe loss of pleasure and interests, depressive turmoil involving a rapid switching of mood from anxiety to depression to anger or vice versa, alcohol abuse, diminished concentration, and global insomnia. Long-term risk factors included hopelessness, suicidal ideation, suicidal intent, and a history of previous suicide attempts. Hopelessness, which has repeatedly been shown to be a better predictor of suicide risk than depression, may be linked to a rigidly held view of the self that cannot be shifted despite repeated disappointments. If one cannot live up to rigidly held expectations of what the self should be, hopelessness may result, and suicide may seem the only way out. In similar vein, Arieti (1977) has noted that certain patients who cannot shift their dominant ideology or their expectation of the dominant other may also be at high risk for suicide. In assessing suicidal ideation, a higher risk exists when the ideation is *ego-syntonic*—these patients find suicidal ideation acceptable and appear to have given up the fight against the urge to kill themselves.

To put suicide in a psychodynamic context, clinicians must understand the nature of the precipitating event, the conscious and unconscious motivations, and the preexisting psychological variables that increase the likelihood of acting on suicidal thoughts. Through the use of projective psychological testing, researchers (Smith 1983; Smith and Eyman 1988) have studied and identified four patterns of ego functioning and internal object relations paradigms that differentiate individuals who made serious attempts from those who merely made gestures to control significant others. The serious attempters exhibited 1) an inability to give up infantile wishes for nurturance, associated with conflict about being openly dependent; 2) a sober but ambivalent view toward death; 3) excessively high self-expectations; and 4) overcontrol of affect, particularly aggression. Although this pattern applies more to men than to women (Smith and Eyman 1988), an inhibitory attitude toward aggression distinguishes serious female attempters from those who make mild gestures. These test findings imply that the preexisting psychological structures that favor suicide are more consistent across individual patients than are the various motivations behind a particular suicidal act.

Treatment Considerations

Research Findings

Highly expressive psychotherapy specifically aimed at relieving depression has not been rigorously tested. After reviewing the literature on short-term dynamic psychotherapy of depression, Strupp et al. (1982) concluded that although some reports indicated improvement of depressive symptomatology, "no definitive statement can be made regarding the unique effectiveness of short-term dynamic treatment approaches for the amelioration of depression" (p. 238). They further concluded that because the patients had not been selected on the basis of depression and because most of the studies had not isolated changes in depression, the research simply had not specifically addressed the issue. Moreover, the tradition in psychoanalytic psychotherapy is not to develop specific technical approaches for specific diagnostic entities, but rather to strengthen the patient's adaptive capacities by improving self-esteem, by modifying the superego, by strengthening and expanding the ego, and by altering the patient's internal object relations. Finally, studies of brief dynamic psychotherapy are more concerned with the strengths and weaknesses of the patient's personality than with a specific intervention or a specific symptom.

Although more expressive forms of psychotherapy have not been rigorously tested, a modified version of dynamic psychotherapy—interpersonal therapy (IPT)—*has* been subjected to such tests. IPT is not always identified as dynamically informed supportive psychotherapy, but it can be regarded as such. This treatment was developed with the assumption that depression occurs in an interpersonal context and will improve as relationships improve (Elkin et al. 1985). It derives explicitly from a psychodynamic model, even though its focus is interpersonal rather than intrapsychic. Interventions, which tend to be noninterpretive, are focused more on the here and now than on childhood experiences. Four basic problem areas are identified in the course of IPT: 1) role transitions, 2) interpersonal deficits, 3) role disputes, and 4) pathological grief (Rounsaville et al. 1984). The therapist actively helps the patient develop strategies to manage problems in each area, providing reassurance and some education about problem-solving skills as well. From a relatively neutral position, the therapist allows the patient to identify the topic to be discussed in each session and then offers advice rather sparingly. The therapist is more active and practical than in expressive psychotherapy, and the major technical approach is not guided by any attempt to bring about a major personality change through the achievement of insight into underlying conflicts. Instead, change is sought through education, combating demoralization, social manipulation, or problem solving, and the IPT therapist addresses underlying psychological conflict only if work at these levels stalls or the patient shows strong resistance to the treatment (Rounsaville et al. 1984).

The NIMH Collaborative Study clearly demonstrated that 16 weeks of this treatment was much more effective than placebo in alleviating depression, particularly the more severe forms of depression. Moreover, IPT has been shown to be of considerable value in preventing recurrent episodes in patients with unipolar depression. In a study of 74 patients with recurrent unipolar depression (Frank et al. 1989), those who received once-monthly sessions of IPT were significantly less likely to experience a subsequent episode of depression when compared at the end of an 18-month follow-up with those who received imipramine. In a later report on 120 patients in a randomized 3-year maintenance trial (Frank et al. 1990), 84% of those patients who received a combination of imipramine and IPT had no recurrence in the first year, while only 60% of those on imipramine alone avoided relapse. Moreover, the degree of prophylaxis associated with IPT was directly related to the specificity of the interpersonal focus within the sessions (Frank et al. 1991).

The efficacy of combined pharmacotherapy and psychotherapy in *prevention* is mirrored in studies that suggest its superiority to either modality alone in the *treatment* of depressive episodes (DiMascio et al. 1979; van Praag 1989). As Karasu (1990) has suggested, medication and psychotherapy address different sets of target symptoms. Symptoms of depression that preferentially respond to pharmacotherapy include vegetative signs, anhedonia, psychomotor retardation, delusions, and auditory hallucinations. Symptoms that are more likely to respond to psychotherapy include low self-esteem, inappropriate guilt feelings, lack of motivation, interpersonal problems, chronic feelings of hopelessness, and social withdrawal. Therapy is also useful for understanding and preventing psychosocial stressors. Either modality alone will only address a subgroup of depressive symptoms.

The other form of psychotherapy found to be effective with depression in the NIMH Treatment of Depression Collaborative Research Program was cognitive-behavior therapy. Although derived from a different tradition than psychoanalytic thinking, many areas overlap between cognitive-behavior therapy and psychodynamic therapy in both theory and technique (Altshuler and Rush 1984; Blatt and Maroudas 1992). Cognitive theory proposes that underlying schemata regarding self-worth and self-expectations lead to highly negative views of the self, the world, and the future. These perfectionistic demands on the self and the associated feelings of failure relate very closely to the psychodynamic idea that depression represents a discrepancy between the ideal self and the reality of the actual self. Cognitive-behavior therapy deals more in direct teaching, explaining, offering of support and admiration for progress, and assigning of homework than does psychodynamic therapy. However, both techniques focus on the patient's unrealistic expectations and seek to relieve pressures for unrealistically high performance. Both therapies also view positive transference as a vehicle to assist in the change process.

In an investigation of patient characteristics predictive of treatment response in the NIMH Treatment of Depression Collaborative Study (Sotsky et al. 1991), the investigators were able to identify predictors of differential treatment outcome that might assist clinicians in assigning patients with specific characteristics to specific modalities. Low social dysfunction predicted superior response to interpersonal psychotherapy. Low cognitive dysfunction predicted superior response to cognitive-behavior therapy and to imipramine. High work dysfunction predicted superior response to imipramine. High depres-

sion severity and impairment predicted superior response to imipramine and to interpersonal psychotherapy.

Treatment Principles

Despite the limited research literature on specific treatment techniques for depression, there is certainly compelling evidence that psychodynamically derived psychotherapy is effective. The abundant
clinical literature on the treatment of affective disorders fleshes out
the research data with rich descriptions of case material that capture
a feeling of "being there" with the patient. Because the general principles to be gleaned from this literature apply equally to hospital treatment and to psychotherapy, the two forms of treatment will be
considered together in this discussion.

Mania. The treatment of the bipolar patient is somewhat more
straightforward than that of the unipolar patient. By and large, manic
patients will not benefit from psychotherapeutic interventions until
they are first pharmacologically controlled. The very nature of the
manic defensive position mandates denial of all psychological problems. It is rarely possible to penetrate this denial when the patient is
in a full-blown manic episode. After pharmacological stabilization, psychotherapy of an expressive-supportive nature may play a key role in
several different respects. First, problems with medication compliance
may require psychotherapeutic exploration before they can be resolved. In addition, psychotherapeutic or psychoanalytic work while
patients are in the euthymic phase of the illness may help prevent
manic or depressive episodes. A 10-year follow-up study (Feinstein and
Wolpert 1973; Wolpert 1981) identified two types of therapeutic failures. One, a pharmacotherapeutic failure, involved a reluctance to increase the lithium dose when the patient became more physiologically
activated just prior to a manic episode. The other, a psychotherapeutic
failure, stemmed from lack of attention to psychological issues that
precipitated episodes. These two types of failures are similar to the two
precipitants of manic or depressive episodes: biological factors in some
cases, and psychological factors in others.

As briefly noted in Chapter 5, Loeb and Loeb (1987) found the combination of lithium carbonate and psychoanalysis or psychoanalytically oriented psychotherapy useful with a series of bipolar patients,
because the psychoanalytic techniques allowed the patients to become

consciously aware of a resurgence of sexual fantasies and wishes prior to the onset of a manic episode. These previously unconscious thoughts served as a signal to these patients that they needed to increase their lithium dose. Pollock (1977) advocated the psychoanalysis of manic-depressive patients medicated on lithium during the euthymic phase because of the frequent presence of obsessive-compulsive character pathology during this phase. Finally, patients settling down after a manic episode in which they were floridly out of control must frequently deal with feelings of intense guilt and shame about their behavior during the episode. Psychotherapeutic assistance may help these patients come to terms with such feelings.

In recent years there has been a growing awareness of the limitations of lithium carbonate prophylaxis of bipolar disorder. When 73 manic patients were followed up 1.7 years after hospitalization, more than 40% had experienced a recurrence of the mania during the follow-up period (Harrow et al. 1990). Of particular note was that manic patients taking lithium carbonate did not show better outcomes than those who were not taking the medication. In a 2-year prospective study of relapse in 61 outpatients with bipolar illness (Ellicott et al. 1990), relapse could not be explained by changes in lithium levels or medication compliance. However, there was a significant association between stressful life events and relapse. The investigators concluded that psychological interventions at times of high stress are crucial in preventing recurrences. By recognizing the limitations of lithium carbonate prophylaxis, clinicians now have a greater appreciation for the role of psychotherapeutic interventions with bipolar patients.

From a Kleinian perspective, the fundamental psychotherapeutic task with the bipolar patient is to facilitate the work of mourning, that is, to work through the depressive position more successfully. The threat of aggressive, persecutory feelings leads to the need for manic defenses to deny them. Following a manic episode, patients may be acutely aware of their own destructiveness and may feel remorseful about the harm they have caused others during the manic phase. The psychotherapist may then be presented with an optimal moment to help the patient integrate the loving and aggressive sides of the internal self- and object-representations. If the therapist can maintain a supportive, holding environment while exploring the patient's concerns about aggression, the patient will become more capable of internalizing a relationship in which good predominates over bad and love predominates over hate. Melanie Klein (1940/1975) noted that as feelings of persecution and aggression decrease, manic defenses become necessary to the patient. Finally, the internalization of the therapist reinstates the lost "good objects" from childhood.

Depression. Contrary to conventional wisdom, the usefulness of psychodynamic approaches to depression are not limited to the milder, more neurotic forms of the condition. Psychotherapeutic intervention may, in fact, be essential to the treatment of more severe, psychotic forms of depression, especially in those cases where somatic treatments have been ineffective or refused by the patient. Arieti (1977) reported on the intensive psychotherapy of 12 severely depressed patients for whom he had follow-up data for 3 years or more. Seven had shown full recovery and an additional 4 were markedly improved. Regarding the severity of the depression, however, certain fundamental technical principles should guide the clinician.

The first step in treatment, regardless of whether the patient is in a hospital or is an outpatient, is the establishment of a therapeutic alliance. To build the necessary rapport, the clinician must simply listen and empathize with the patient's point of view. Perhaps the most common error both of family members and of beginning mental health professionals is to try to cheer up the patient by focusing on the positive. Comments, such as "You have no reason to be depressed—you have so many good qualities" or "Why should you be suicidal? There's so much to live for," are likely to backfire. These "cheerleading" comments are experienced by depressed patients as profound failures of empathy, which may lead patients to feel more misunderstood and alone and therefore more suicidal.

On the contrary, clinicians who work with these patients must convey their understanding that there is indeed a reason to be depressed. They can empathize with the painfulness of the depression, while also enlisting the patient's help in a collaborative search for its underlying causes. The initial approach must be supportive but firm (Arieti 1977; Lesse 1978). Premature interpretations, such as "You're not really depressed—you're angry," will also be experienced as unempathic and as off the mark. The clinician will be most helpful simply by listening and attempting to comprehend the patient's understanding of the illness.

During the early phases of information gathering, the clinician develops an explanatory formulation of the patient's depression. What events apparently precipitated the depression? What narcissistically valued aspiration has the patient failed to achieve? What is the patient's dominant ideology? Who is the dominant other for whom the patient is living and from whom the patient is not receiving the desired responses? Is there guilt connected with aggression or anger, and if so, toward whom is the patient angry? Is there frustration of the self's strivings for selfobject responses?

While the clinician listens to the patient's story and develops hypotheses about the psychodynamic basis of the depression, the patient forms a transference attachment to the therapist. In Arieti's (1977) terms, the therapist becomes a "dominant third," in addition to the dominant other in the patient's life. Many of the same concerns that are problematic in the patient's primary relationships will also surface in the transference. Arieti pointed out that building a therapeutic alliance may require therapists to conform to certain of the patient's expectations during the initial stages of psychotherapy, thus facilitating the repetition of the patient's pathology in the therapeutic relationship. When enough information has been gathered, the therapist may have to shift to a more expressive approach and interpret to the patient the dominant-other pattern that has caused so much difficulty. Arieti observed that "the patient must come to the conscious realization that he did not know how to live for himself. He never listened to himself; in situations of great affective significance he was never able to assert himself. He cared only about obtaining the approval, affection, love, admiration, or care of the dominant other" (p. 866). After this realization, a good deal of anger toward the dominant other may surface.

After the dominant ideology has been laid bare, the therapist's task is then to help the patient conceive of new ways of living. In Bibring's (1953) terms, either the idealized aspirations must be modified sufficiently to be realized, or they must be relinquished and replaced with other goals and objectives. At the prospect of developing new life patterns and purposes, these patients may depend on their therapist for answers. If therapists collude by telling their patients what to do, they will simply reinforce any feelings of low self-esteem and ineffectiveness (Betcher 1983; Maxmen 1978). Pleas from patients to solve their dilemmas can simply be turned back to them with the explanation that they are in the best position to make alternative life plans.

Central to the psychodynamic approach with depressed patients is the establishment of the interpersonal meaning and context of their depression. Unfortunately, patients often tenaciously resist these interpersonal implications (Betcher 1983). They frequently prefer to view their depression and their suicidal wishes as occurring in a vacuum, fervently insisting that no one is to blame but themselves. Careful attention to transference-countertransference developments may lead to breakthroughs with this form of resistance. In both psychotherapy and hospital treatment, patients recapitulate their internal object relationships as well as their patterns of relatedness with external figures. Depressed patients, in particular, engender strong feelings. In the course of such treatment, the therapist may experience despair, anger, wishes to be rid of the patient, powerful rescue fantasies, and a myriad of other feelings. All these emotional responses may reflect how others in the patient's life feel as well. These interpersonal dimensions of the depression may be involved in causing or perpetuating the condition. To examine the impact of the patient's condition on others, the therapist must enlist the patient's collaboration by using these feelings constructively in the therapeutic relationship. Many refractory cases of depression have become deadlocked in the repetition of a characteristic pattern of object relatedness that has strong characterological underpinnings and is therefore difficult to alter.

Mr. M was a respected chemist who required hospitalization when he became suicidally depressed at the age of 41. While Mr. M had been an outpatient, every known antidepressant medication had been tried in therapeutic doses with monitored serum levels, and electroconvulsive therapy had been used during the first weeks of his hospital stay. None of these somatic interventions had alleviated his depression in the least. Nevertheless, the patient continued to maintain that he was a victim of a "chemical imbalance" which was the doctor's responsibility to restore. Mr. M complained of self-doubt, feelings of worthlessness, inability to sleep, inability to work or concentrate, and hopelessness about the future. He felt that all his accomplishments were meaningless and that he had driven his wife to distraction by his repeated demands to comfort him. Mrs. M despaired because everything she offered her husband seemed to be of no help whatsoever. Whenever she attempted to point out positive aspects of her husband's life, he would respond with a "yes, but" comeback, dismissing her points as irrelevant.

The resident in charge of Mr. M's treatment and the other unit staff members on the treatment team shared Mrs. M's frustration. Mr. M demanded that they attend to his needs, but then dismissed all their suggestions and insights as useless. The entire treatment staff felt de-skilled, impotent, and exhausted in the face of Mr. M's depression. Whenever the various residents on call during the evening hours made rounds on the hospital unit, Mr. M engaged them in long discussions about his depression. He would list the medications that had been tried and would expound on the role of neurotransmitters in depression. He would then ask for advice on his condition. Inevitably, the resident making rounds would be drawn into this discussion in an attempt to alleviate the suffering of this obviously intelligent and well-informed individual. Every suggestion made by any resident, however, would be discounted by Mr. M as "not helpful." By the end of these discussions, the on-call residents would feel that all the time spent with Mr. M was for naught, and they would leave feeling drained and devalued.

The resident in charge of Mr. M's treatment and the staff of the hospital team presented their dilemma with Mr. M to the resident's supervisor, who pointed out how the patient's internal world was being re-created in the milieu. By assuming the role of the "help-rejecting complainer," Mr. M was reestablishing an internal object relationship characterized by a long-suffering and victimized self-representation connected to an impotent and useless object-representation. Mr. M used the reactivation of this internal object relationship to torment everyone around him. He was thus able to discharge an enormous reservoir of rage stemming from his childhood interactions with his mother, who he felt had failed to provide for his needs.

As a result of this consultation, a dramatic shift took place in the treatment approach. The resident and the nursing staff primarily involved with Mr. M were able to disengage from their heroic therapeutic efforts and began to enlist the patient's collaboration in figuring out what was happening. No longer a passive recipient of "medical" treatment, the patient was now involved as an active collaborator in a psychological process of reflection and understanding.

The object relations paradigm that was being acted out in the milieu was clarified and described for the patient. At the same time, the case social worker explained the psychoanalytically based understanding to Mrs. M to facilitate alleviation of her extraordinary guilt and to help her understand that the present situation was a recapitulation of an unresolved childhood experience. When the treatment team stopped responding like Mr. M's internal object-representation, Mr. M began presenting himself differently. He was initially enraged at their suggestion that he should accept any responsibility for his condition. The resident explained to him, however, that everything possible in terms of pharmacologic interventions had been tried and that now Mr. M would have to consider his own contributions to the feeling that he was "stuck" in the depths of despair. This change in approach presented Mr. M with a new object relationship to contend with. After his initial stubbornness, he did a good deal of psychological work. He got in touch with his rage at his mother for not giving him the validation and love that he felt he required, as well as his delight in tormenting his wife to get back at his mother.

The case of Mr. M illustrates how a severe depression that is refractory to conventional somatic treatments may be related to formidable characterological resistances that cause the patient to become "stuck" in an unresolved self–object relationship. As described in Chapter 6, a breakthrough in such treatment can occur when the treatment staff begins to disconfirm the patient's expectation that they will respond like the projected object-representation; instead, the staff members provided a new model of understanding as well as a new series of objects and interactions for internalization by the patient.

Another aspect of the breakthrough with Mr. M was that staff members realized that he was not only a victim of an illness but also a victimizer of those around him. In discussing the secondary gain frequently associated with depression, Bibring (1953) noted that some depressed patients exploit their illnesses to justify their veiled expressions of destructive and sadistic impulses toward others. Mr. M had forced his wife into a maternal role with him, only to deem her maternal treatment of him worthless. In commenting on the hidden sadism frequently found in the depressed patient, Jacobson (1971b) noted: "The depressive never fails to make his partner, often his whole environment, and especially his children feel terribly guilty, pulling them down into a more and more depressed state as well" (p. 295). Indeed, the entire treatment staff had begun to feel like Mrs. M. They felt increasingly guilty because they could not find any way to intervene therapeutically with Mr. M, and they became more depressed and drained as a result of each successive failure. Jacobson also pointed out that some depressed patients (such as Mr. M) may establish a vicious cycle that drives their partners away just when their love is most needed. Spouses of such patients rapidly get fed up and may begin to act cruelly or neglectfully as a result of their feelings of inadequacy, thus hurting these patients when they are most needy and vulnerable. Treaters may fall into a similar pattern by becoming sarcastic or cold because their patients repeatedly reject their help.

The clinical vignette regarding Mr. M also underscores the importance of involving the family when treating a severely depressed patient. The literature on families of depressed patients clearly indicates that relapse rates, the course of depression, and suicidal behavior are all affected by family functioning (Keitner and Miller 1990). In one study (Hooley and Teasdale 1989), the single best predictor of relapse was the depressed patient's perception that his or her spouse was highly critical. Paralleling the research on families of schizophrenic patients, studies have also shown that high expressed emotion in family members of depressed patients may be influential in contributing to relapse (Hooley et al. 1986; Vaughn and Leff 1976). Depressed patients provoke a good deal of hostility and sadism in their family members, and clinicians must help relatives overcome their guilt feelings about such reactions so that they can appreciate them as understandable responses to a depressed family member.

Treatment of the Suicidal Patient

Few events in a psychiatrist's professional life are more disturbing than a patient's suicide. In one study (Chemtob et al. 1988), approximately half of those psychiatrists who had lost a patient to suicide experienced stress levels comparable to persons recovering from a parent's death. A completed suicide is a reminder of the limitations inherent in our craft. The natural tendency, whether in hospital practice or in psychotherapy, is for clinicians to go to great lengths to prevent suicide. To implement reasonable measures to prevent patients from taking their life is certainly good judgment from a clinical standpoint, responsible behavior from an ethical standpoint, and sound defensive medicine from a medicolegal standpoint. However, when the role of savior becomes all-consuming, the results may be countertherapeutic.

First, clinicians must always keep in mind one unassailable fact—patients who are truly intent on killing themselves will ultimately do so. No amount of physical restraint, careful observation, and clinical skill can stop the truly determined suicidal patient. One such patient was placed in a seclusion room with nothing but a mattress. All his clothing and possessions were taken away, and he was checked at regular 15-minute intervals around the clock. Between the 15-minute rounds, the patient began jumping on the mattress so hard that he was able to repeatedly bang his head against the ceiling until he finally broke his neck. Such incidents illustrate that hospital staff members must acknowledge to themselves that they cannot prevent all suicides from occurring on an inpatient unit. Olin (1976) has even suggested that if suicides never occur in a particular hospital, the staff members in the milieu may be taking too much responsibility for the behavior of the patients. Instead, clinicians should repeatedly stress that it is ultimately each patient's responsibility to learn to verbalize suicidal impulses rather than act on them.

After completed suicides, clinicians often feel guilty for not having detected warning signs that would have allowed them to predict an imminent suicide attempt. Despite an accumulating body of literature on short-term and long-range risk factors for suicide, our ability to predict the suicide of an individual patient is still severely limited. Goldstein et al. (1991) studied a group of 1,906 inpatients with affective disorders. Using data on risk factors, the researchers applied stepwise multiple logistic regression to develop a statistical model that would successfully predict suicide. This model failed to identify a single patient who committed suicide. The investigators reluctantly concluded that even among a high-risk group of inpatients, predicting suicide based on our current understanding of the phenomenon is not possible. The primary means of assessing imminent suicide risk in a clinical setting is the verbal communication of intent by a patient or an action that is clearly suicidal in intent. Clinicians cannot read minds and must not berate themselves for their perceived failures when no clear verbal or nonverbal indications of suicidality were present.

Psychodynamic clinicians tend to agree that treaters who fall prey to the illusion that they can save their patients from suicide are actually decreasing their chances of doing so (Hendin 1982; Meissner 1986; Richman and Eyman 1990; Searles 1967/1979; Zee 1972). One salient psychological concern in the seriously suicidal patient is the desire to be taken care of by an unconditionally loving mother (Richman and Eyman 1990; Smith and Eyman 1988). Some therapists err in attempting to gratify this fantasy by meeting the patient's every need. They may accept phone calls from the patient any time of the day or night and throughout their vacations. They may see the patient 7 days a week in their office. Some have even become sexually involved with their patients in a desperate effort to gratify the unending demands associated with the depression (Twemlow and Gabbard 1989). This kind of behavior exacerbates what Hendin (1982) has described as one of the most lethal features of suicidal patients—namely, their tendency to assign others the responsibility for their staying alive. By attempting to gratify these ever-escalating demands, the therapist colludes with the patient's fantasy that there really is an unconditionally loving mother out there somewhere who is different from everyone else. Therapists cannot possibly sustain that illusion indefinitely; those who attempt to do so are setting up the patient for a crushing disappointment that may increase the risk of suicide.

Clinicians who are drawn into the role of savior with suicidal patients often operate on the conscious or unconscious assumption that they can provide the love and concern that others have not, thus magically transforming the patient's wish to die into a desire to live. This fantasy is a trap, however, because, as Hendin (1982) has noted, "The patient's hidden agenda is an attempt to prove that nothing the therapist can do will be enough. The therapist's wish to see himself as the suicidal patient's savior may blind the therapist to the fact that the patient has cast him in the role of executioner" (pp. 171–172). Therapists are more useful to suicidal patients when they diligently try to understand and analyze the origin of the suicidal wishes instead of placing themselves in bondage to the patient.

Therapists should be on the lookout for idealizing transferences, which often form rapidly when patients are looking for a rescuer. Predicting and interpreting transference disappointments early in the process may be helpful. Some therapists openly acknowledge that they cannot stop the patient from committing suicide and offer instead the opportunity to understand why the patient thinks that suicide is the only option (Henseler 1991). Often this admission has a calming effect and may produce greater collaboration in the psychotherapeutic task.

It is useful to distinguish between *treatment* and *management* of the suicidal patient. The latter includes measures such as continuous observation, physical restraints, and removal of sharp objects from the environment. Although these interventions are useful in preventing the patient from acting on suicidal urges, management techniques do not necessarily decrease a patient's future vulnerability to resorting to suicidal behavior. *Treatment* of suicidal patients—consisting of a psychotherapeutic approach to understanding the internal factors and external stressors that make the patient suicidal—is needed to alter the fundamental wish to die.

The countertransference elicited by the suicidal patient presents a formidable obstacle to treatment. Some clinicians simply avoid any responsibility for seriously depressed patients who are at risk for killing themselves. Those who do attempt to treat such patients often believe that their *raison d'être* is negated by the patient's wish to die. A patient's suicide is also the ultimate narcissistic injury for the treater.

Clinicians' anxiety about the suicide of the patient may stem more from the fear that others will blame them for the death than from concern for the individual patient's welfare (Hendin 1982). It is commonplace for therapists to set one standard for others and another for themselves—the therapist who assures others that they are not responsible for their patient's suicide may feel an exaggerated sense of responsibility for keeping his or her own patients alive, often with the assumption that others will be critical if the patient dies.

Therapists who treat seriously suicidal patients will eventually begin to feel tormented by the repeated negation of their efforts. Countertransference hate is likely to develop at such times, and treaters will often harbor an unconscious wish for the patient to die so that the torment will end. Maltsberger and Buie (1974) have noted that feelings of malice and aversion are among the most common countertransference reactions connected with the treatment of severely suicidal patients. The inability to tolerate their own sadistic wishes toward such patients may lead treaters to act out countertransference feelings. The authors caution that while malice may be more unacceptable and uncomfortable, aversion is potentially more lethal because it can lead clinicians to neglect their patients and provide an opportunity for a suicide attempt. On an inpatient unit, this form of countertransference may be manifested by simply "forgetting" to check on the patient as dictated by the suicidal observation ordered.

Countertransference hatred must be accepted as part of the experience of treating suicidal patients. It often arises in direct response to the patient's aggression. Suicide threats may be held over the therapist's head like the mythical sword of Damocles, tormenting and controlling the therapist night and day. Similarly, the family members of patients may be plagued with the concerns that if they make one false move or one unempathic comment, they will be responsible for a suicide. If countertransference hate is split off and disavowed by the therapist, it may be projected onto the patient, who then must deal with the therapist's murderous wishes in addition to the preexisting suicidal impulses. Clinicians may also deal with their feelings of aggression by reaction formation, which may lead to rescue fantasies and exaggerated efforts to prevent suicide. Searles (1967/1979) has warned therapists of the perils of this defensive style:

> And the suicidal patient, who finds us so unable to be aware of the murderous feelings he fosters in us through his guilt- and anxiety-

producing threats of suicide, feels increasingly constricted, perhaps indeed to the point of suicide, by the therapist who, in reaction formation against his intensifying, unconscious wishes to kill the patient, hovers increasingly "protectively" about the latter, for whom he feels an omnipotence-based physicianly concern. Hence it is, paradoxically, the very physician most anxiously concerned to *keep the patient alive* who tends most vigorously, at an unconscious level, to drive him to what has come to seem the only autonomous act left to him—namely, suicide. (p. 74)

Psychotherapists who treat suicidal patients must help them come to terms with their dominant ideology (Arieti 1977) and their rigidly held life fantasies (Richman and Eyman 1990; Smith and Eyman 1988). When there is a disparity between reality and the patient's constricted view of what life should be like, the therapist can help the patient mourn the loss of the life fantasy. This technique may paradoxically require the therapist to acknowledge the patient's hopelessness so that the lost dreams can be mourned and replaced by new ones that are more realistic. For example, one 23-year-old man became suicidal when he realized that he would never be accepted to Harvard, a dream he had cherished since early childhood. The therapist acknowledged that admission to Harvard was highly unlikely and then helped the patient accept the loss of that dream. At the same time, he helped the patient consider alternative pathways to an education that would build the patient's self-esteem. Thus the therapist helped the patient see how much misery is caused by unrealistically high expectations (Richman and Eyman 1990).

To treat suicidal patients effectively, clinicians must distinguish the patient's responsibility from the treater's responsibility. Physicians in general and psychiatrists in particular are characterologically prone to an exaggerated sense of responsibility (Gabbard 1985). We tend to blame ourselves for adverse outcomes beyond our control. Ultimately, we must reconcile ourselves to the fact that there are terminal psychiatric illnesses. Patients must bear the responsibility for deciding whether they will commit suicide or work collaboratively with their therapist to understand the wish to die. Fortunately, the vast majority of patients contemplate suicide with some ambivalence. The part of the suicidal individual that questions the suicidal solution may lead these patients to choose life over death.

References

Akiskal HS, Rosenthal TL, Haykal RF, et al: Characterological depressions: clinical and sleep EEG findings separating "subaffective dysthymias" from "character spectrum disorders." Arch Gen Psychiatry 37:777–783, 1980

Altshuler KZ, Rush AJ: Psychoanalytic and cognitive therapies: a comparison of theory and tactics. Am J Psychother 38:4–17, 1984

American Psychiatric Association: Diagnostic and Statistical Manual of Mental Disorders, 4th Edition. Washington, DC, American Psychiatric Association 1994

Arieti S: Psychotherapy of severe depression. Am J Psychiatry 134:864–868, 1977

Asch SS: Suicide and the hidden executioner. International Review of Psychoanalysis 7:51–60, 1980

Betcher RW: The treatment of depression in brief inpatient group psychotherapy. Int J Group Psychother 33:365–385, 1983

Bibring E: The mechanism of depression, in Affective Disorders: Psychoanalytic Contributions to Their Study. Edited by Greenacre P. New York, International Universities Press, 1953, pp 13–48

Blatt SJ, Maroudas C: Convergences among psychoanalytic and cognitive-behavioral theories of depression. Psychoanalytic Psychology 9:157–190, 1992

Broadhead WE, Blazer DG, George LK, et al: Depression, disability days, and days lost from work in a prospective epidemiological survey. JAMA 264:2524–2528, 1990

Bunch J, Barraclough B: The influence of parental death and anniversaries upon suicide dates. Br J Psychiatry 118:621–626, 1971

Chemtob CM, Hamada RS, Bauer G, et al: Patients' suicides: frequency and impact on psychiatrists. Am J Psychiatry 145:224–228, 1988

Clark DC, Fawcett J: An empirically based model of suicide risk assessment for patients with affective disorder, in Suicide and Clinical Practice. Edited by Jacobs D. Washington, DC, American Psychiatric Press, 1992, pp 55–73

DiMascio A, Weissman MA, Prusoff BA, et al: Differential symptom reduction by drugs and psychotherapy in acute depression. Arch Gen Psychiatry 36:1450–1456, 1979

Dorpat TL: Suicide, loss, and mourning. Suicide Life Threat Behav 3:213–224, 1973

Duggan CF, Lee AS, Murray RM: Do different subtypes of hospitalized depressives have different long-term outcomes? Arch Gen Psychiatry 48:308–312, 1991

Elkin I, Parloff MB, Hadley SW, et al: NIMH Treatment of Depression Collaborative Research Program. Arch Gen Psychiatry 42:305–316, 1985

Elkin I, Shea T, Watkins J, et al: NIMH Treatment of Depression Collaborative Research Program: general effectiveness of treatments. Arch Gen Psychiatry 46:971–982, 1989

Ellicott A, Hammen C, Gitlin M, et al: Life events and the course of bipolar disorder. Am J Psychiatry 147:1194–1198, 1990

Feinstein SC, Wolpert EA: Juvenile manic-depressive illness: clinical and therapeutic considerations. Journal of the American Academy of Child Psychiatry 12:123–136, 1973

Fenichel O: The Psychoanalytic Theory of Neurosis. New York, WW Norton, 1945

Frank E, Kupfer DJ, Perel JM: Early recurrence in unipolar depression. Arch Gen Psychiatry 46:397–400, 1989

Frank E, Kupfer DJ, Perel JM, et al: Three-year outcomes for maintenance therapies in recurrent depression: contributing factors. Arch Gen Psychiatry 47:1093–1099, 1990

Frank E, Kupfer DJ, Wagner EF, et al: Efficacy of interpersonal psychotherapy as a maintenance treatment of recurrent depression. Arch Gen Psychiatry 48:1053–1059, 1991

Freud S: Mourning and melancholia (1917), in The Standard Edition of the Complete Psychological Works of Sigmund Freud, Vol 14. Translated and edited by Strachey J. London, Hogarth Press, 1963, pp 237–260

Freud S: The ego and the id (1923), in The Standard Edition of the Complete Psychological Works of Sigmund Freud, Vol 19. Translated and edited by Strachey J. London, Hogarth Press, 1961, pp 1–66

Gabbard GO: The role of compulsiveness in the normal physician. JAMA 254:2926–2929, 1985

Gold PW, Goodwin FK, Chrousos GP: Clinical and biochemical manifestations of depression: relation to the neurobiology of stress, part I. N Eng J Med 319:348–353, 1988a

Gold PW, Goodwin FK, Chrousos GP: Clinical and biochemical manifestations of depression: relation to the neurobiology of stress, part II. N Eng J Med 319:413–420, 1988b

Goldstein RB, Black DW, Nasrallah A, et al: The prediction of suicide: sensitivity, specificity, and predictive value of a multimyriad model applied to suicide among 1,906 patients with affective disorders. Arch Gen Psychiatry 48:418–422, 1991

Harrow M, Goldberg JF, Grossman LS, et al: Outcome in manic disorders: a naturalistic follow-up study. Arch Gen Psychiatry 47:665–671, 1990

Hendin H: Psychotherapy and suicide, in Suicide in America. New York, WW Norton, 1982, pp 160–174

Henseler H: Narcissism as a form of relationship, in Freud's *On Narcissism*: An Introduction. Edited by Sandler J, Person ES, Fonagy P. New Haven, CT, Yale University Press, 1991, pp 195–215

Hooley JM, Teasdale JD: Predictors of relapse in unipolar depressives: expressed emotion, marital distress, and perceived criticism. J Abnorm Psychol 98:229–235, 1989

Hooley JM, Orley J, Teasdale JD: Levels of expressed emotion and relapse in depressed patients. Br J Psychiatry 148:642–647, 1986

Jacobson E: Psychotic identifications, in Depression: Comparative Studies of Normal, Neurotic, and Psychotic Conditions. Edited by Jacobson E. New York, International Universities Press, 1971a, pp 242–263

Jacobson E: Transference problems in depressives, in Depression: Comparative Studies of Normal, Neurotic, and Psychotic Conditions. Edited by Jacobson E. New York, International Universities Press, 1971b, pp 284–301

Johnson J, Weissman MM, Klerman GL: Service utilization and social morbidity associated with depressive symptoms in the community. JAMA 267:1478–1483, 1992

Karasu TB: Toward a clinical model of psychotherapy for depression, II: an integrative and selective treatment approach. Arch Gen Psychiatry 147: 269–278, 1990

Keitner GI, Miller IW: Family functioning and major depression: an overview. Am J Psychiatry 147:1128–1137, 1990

Keller MB, Shapiro RW: "Double-depression": superimposition of acute depressive episodes on chronic depressive disorders. Am J Psychiatry 139: 438–442, 1982

Kendler KS, Neale MC, Kessler RC, et al: Childhood parental loss and adult psychopathology in women: a twin study perspective. Arch Gen Psychiatry 49:109–116, 1992

Klein DF: Anxiety reconceptualized. Compr Psychiatry 6:411–427, 1980

Klein M: Mourning and its relation to manic-depressive states (1940), in Love, Guilt and Reparation and Other Works 1921–1945. New York, Free Press, 1975, pp 344–369

Kocsis JH, Frances AJ, Voss C, et al: Imipramine treatment for chronic depression. Arch Gen Psychiatry 45:253–257, 1988

Lesse S: Psychotherapy in combination with antidepressant drugs in severely depressed outpatients—20-year evaluation. Am J Psychother 32:48–73, 1978

Loeb FF, Loeb LR: Psychoanalytic observations on the effect of lithium on manic attacks. J Am Psychoanal Assoc 35:877–902, 1987

Maltsberger JT, Buie DH: Countertransference hate in the treatment of suicidal patients. Arch Gen Psychiatry 30:625–633, 1974

Maxmen JS: An educative model for inpatient group therapy. Int J Group Psychother 28:321–338, 1978

Meissner WW: Psychotherapy and the Paranoid Process. Northvale, NJ, Jason Aronson, 1986

Menninger KA: Psychoanalytic aspects of suicide. Int J Psychoanal 14:376–390, 1933

Olin HS: Psychotherapy of the chronically suicidal patient. Am J Psychother 30:570–575, 1976

Phillips KA, Gunderson JG, Hirschfeld RMA, et al: A review of the depressive personality. Am J Psychiatry 147:830–837, 1990

Pollock GH: Foreword, in Manic-Depressive Illness: History of a Syndrome. Edited by Wolpert EA. New York, International Universities Press, 1977, pp 1–2

Post RM: Transduction of psychosocial stress into the neurobiology of recurrent affective disorder. Am J Psychiatry 149:999–1010, 1992

Post RM, Ballenger JC, Uhde TW, et al: Kindling and drug sensitization: implications for the progressive development of psychopathology and treatment with carbamazepine, in Psychopharmacology of Anticonvulsants. Edited by Sandler M. Oxford, Oxford University Press, 1982, pp 27–53

Post RM, Rubinow ER, Uhde TW, et al: Dysphoric mania: clinical and biological correlates. Arch Gen Psychiatry 46:353–358, 1989

Reich JH, Green AI: Effect of personality disorders on outcome of treatment. J Nerv Ment Dis 179:74–82, 1991

Richman J, Eyman JR: Psychotherapy of suicide: individual, group, and family approaches, in Understanding Suicide: The State of the Art. Edited by Lester D. Philadelphia, PA, Charles C Thomas, 1990, pp 139–158

Rounsaville BJ, Chevron ES, Weissman MM: Specification of techniques in interpersonal psychotherapy, in Psychotherapy Research: Where Are We and Where Should We Go? Edited by Williams JBW, Spitzer RL. New York, Guilford, 1984, pp 160–172

Searles HF: The "dedicated physician" in the field of psychotherapy and psychoanalysis (1967), in Countertransference and Related Subjects. Madison, CT, International Universities Press, 1979, pp 71–88

Shea MT, Pilkonis PA, Beckham E, et al: Personality disorders and treatment outcome in the NIMH Treatment of Depression Collaborative Research Program. Am J Psychiatry 147:711–718, 1990

Smith K: Using a battery of tests to predict suicide in a long term hospital: a clinical analysis. Omega 13:261–275, 1983

Smith K, Eyman J: Ego structure and object differentiation in suicidal patients, in Primitive Mental States of the Rorschach. Edited by Lerner HD, Lerner PM. Madison, CT, International Universities Press, 1988, pp 175–202

Sotsky SM, Glass DR, Shea MT, et al: Patient predictors of response to psychotherapy and pharmacotherapy: findings in the NIMH Treatment of Depression Collaborative Research Program. Am J Psychiatry 148:997–1008, 1991

Strupp HH, Sandell JA, Waterhouse GJ, et al: Psychodynamic therapy: theory and research, in Short-Term Psychotherapies for Depression. Edited by Rush AJ. New York, Guilford, 1982, pp 215–250

Twemlow SW, Gabbard GO: The lovesick therapist, in Sexual Exploitation in Professional Relationships. Edited by Gabbard GO. Washington, DC, American Psychiatric Press, 1989, pp 71–87

van Praag H: Moving ahead yet falling behind: a critical appraisal of some trends in contemporary depression research. Neuropsychobiology 22:181–193, 1989

Vaughn CE, Leff JP: The influence of family and social factors on the course of psychiatric illness: a comparison of schizophrenic patients and neurotic patients. Br J Psychiatry 129:125–137, 1976

Wolpert EA: On the nature of manic-depressive illness, in The Course of Life: Psychoanalytic Contributions Toward Understanding Personality Development, Vol III: Adulthood and the Aging Process. Edited by Greenspan SI, Pollock GH. Adelphi, MD, National Institute of Mental Health (DHHS Publ No [ADM] 81–1000), 1981, pp 443–452

Zee HJ: Blindspots in recognizing serious suicidal intentions. Bull Menninger Clin 36:551–555, 1972

Chapter 9

Anxiety Disorders

As a rule, what is out of sight disturbs men's minds more seriously than what they see.

Julius Caesar

Anxiety is an affect that was instrumental in the birth of psychoanalysis and psychodynamic psychiatry. Nearly 100 years ago, Freud (1895/1962) coined the term *anxiety neurosis* and identified two forms of anxiety. One form was the diffuse sense of worry or dread that originated in a repressed thought or wish and was curable through psychotherapeutic intervention. The second form of anxiety was characterized by an overwhelming sense of panic, accompanied by manifestations of autonomic discharge, including profuse sweating, increased respiratory and heart rates, diarrhea, and a subjective sense of terror. This latter form, in Freud's view, did not result from psychological factors. Rather, it was conceptualized as the result of the physiological build-up of libido related to a lack of sexual activity. He referred to this form as *actual neurosis*.

By 1926 Freud had further refined his understanding of anxiety as a result of his recent creation, the structural model. Anxiety was now viewed as the result of psychic conflict between unconscious sexual or aggressive wishes stemming from the id and corresponding threats of punishment from the superego. Anxiety was understood as a *signal* of the presence of danger in the unconscious. In response to this signal, the ego mobilized defense mechanisms to prevent unacceptable thoughts and feelings from emerging into conscious awareness. If signal anxiety failed to adequately activate the ego's defensive resources, then intense, more persistent anxiety or other neurotic symptoms would result. In this sense, anxiety was conceptualized by Freud as both a symptomatic manifestation of neurotic conflict and an adaptive signal to ward off awareness of neurotic conflict.

In Freud's model, anxiety is an ego affect. The ego controls access to consciousness and, through repression, divorces itself from any association with instinctual impulses from the id. It censors both the impulse itself and the corresponding intrapsychic representation. A repressed instinctual wish or impulse may still find expression as a symptom, although it is likely to be displaced and disguised by the time it reaches symptomatic expression. Depending on the defensive operations and symptomatic manifestations, the resulting neurosis might take the form of an obsessional thought, a compulsive ritual, a hysterical paralysis, or a phobia.

One unfortunate consequence of the deliberate effort to be atheoretical in the development of the DSM-III (American Psychiatric Association 1980), DSM-III-R (American Psychiatric Association 1987), and DSM-IV (American Psychiatric Association 1994) nosology is the sacrifice of classical neurotic entities and the psychodynamic model of symptom formation associated with them. These have been replaced by three separate categories: anxiety disorders, somatoform disorders, and dissociative disorders. The first of these categories, anxiety disorders, has been further subdivided into panic disorder, phobias, obsessive-compulsive disorder, posttraumatic stress disorder, and generalized anxiety disorder. Although this classification accommodates the recent biological research delineating different kinds of anxiety, it also encourages clinicians to think about anxiety as an *illness* rather than as an overdetermined *symptom* of unconscious conflict. In many cases, patients presenting with anxiety have no idea what they are anxious about.

In other cases, the anxiety may be attached to a conscious, acceptable fear that masks a deeper, less acceptable concern. The task of the psychodynamic clinician is to understand the unconscious origins of such anxiety. Freud originated the idea that each successive developmental period in a child's life produces a characteristic fear associated with that phase. Based on Freud's discoveries and those of subsequent psychoanalytic investigators, a developmental hierarchy of anxiety (see Table 9–1) can be constructed to assist the psychodynamic clinician in determining the unconscious sources of a patient's symptomatic anxiety.

At the most mature level, anxiety originating in the superego can be understood as guilt feelings or pangs of conscience about not living up to an internal standard of moral behavior. During the oedipal phase, anxiety focuses on potential damage to or loss of the genitals at the hands of a retaliatory parental figure. This fear may be expressed metaphorically as loss of another body part or any other form of physical injury. Moving back in the developmental hierarchy to a somewhat earlier anxiety, we find the fear of losing the love or approval of a significant other (originally a parent). A developmentally more primitive source of anxiety is the possibility of losing not just the object's love but also the object itself—what is usually referred to as separation anxiety. The most primitive forms of anxiety are persecutory anxiety and disintegration anxiety. The former derives from the Kleinian paranoid-schizoid position, in which the primary anxiety is that persecuting objects from outside will invade and annihilate the patient from within. Disintegration anxiety may derive either from the fear of losing one's sense of self or boundedness through merger with an object or from concern that one's self will fragment and lose its integrity in the absence of mirroring or idealizing responses from others in the environment.

Whenever anxiety forms part of the clinical picture, the psychodynamic psychiatrist must enlist the patient's collaboration in identifying the developmental origins of the anxiety. This information may be ascertained within a 1-hour interview, or it may take an extensive evaluation. Anxiety, like most symptoms, is often multiply determined by issues deriving from a variety of developmental levels, as illustrated in the following case example (an earlier version of this case was pub-

Table 9–1. A developmental hierarchy of anxiety

Superego anxiety	Fear of loss of the object (separation anxiety)
Castration anxiety	
Fear of loss of love	Persecutory anxiety
	Disintegration anxiety

lished in the *Bulletin of the Menninger Clinic* [Gabbard and Nemiah 1985]):

> Mr. N was a never-married, unemployed 20-year-old who was hospitalized with free-floating anxiety and hypochondriacal concerns. Although he had experienced these difficulties for several years, they had been exacerbated several months before admission when his parents separated and indicated that they were intent on divorce. His anxiety and hypochondria became so overwhelming that he was unable to function in school or to hold a job. He deteriorated until he began to spend most of each day in bed, arising in the late afternoon to go to a local video arcade for the evening with younger adolescents. Several times a week his absorption in the video games was interrupted by an anxious conviction that he was suffering from a serious illness and might die at any moment. Seeking reassurance, he would abruptly rush to the office of his family internist or to the local hospital's emergency room. This behavior pattern resulted in several thousand dollars of medical bills that were charged to the patient's father.
>
> Mr. N indicated that his problems had begun in the 10th grade, when he felt as if his life was falling apart. He had found the sexual awakening that accompanied puberty highly disturbing, and he still longed to return to an earlier time when gender distinction seemed irrelevant. In describing his developmental years, the patient portrayed both his father and his mother as intrusive and voyeuristic parents who violated generational boundaries and failed to respect his privacy. Mr. N recalled that when he was 7, his father had once forced him to pose nude in the backyard of his grandmother's house for a photograph. He also reported that his father had often watched him dress for hockey practice and had even suggested that underpants were not necessary. As he reached puberty, he began to leave his shirttails untucked to avoid his father's "ogling." Mr. N said that his mother would sometimes playfully try to remove his towel when he left the shower. His mother also complained to him about his father's sexual inadequacy, even speculating that her husband might be worried about the patient growing up and taking his place. Thus, Mr. N thought that both his parents viewed him as a "sex object."
>
> Physical and neurological examinations were entirely normal. Routine laboratory examinations were also within normal limits. The only significant medical history was that the patient had had a congenital residual appendage of the left testicle surgically removed when he was 10.
>
> Mr. N described himself as "asexual" but reported homosexual

fantasies regarding young men in their late adolescence, whom he admired and idolized from a distance. He had, however, refused sexual interaction with those young men who had offered it. He reported limited experience with heterosexual necking and petting that had always stopped short of genital involvement. Voyeuristic tendencies were reflected in his view of himself as a person content with watching others. He indicated that he enjoyed seeing healthy, virile young men and happy young women together. The role of sex partner was clearly too anxiety-provoking for him.

Mr. N had considerable difficulty with self-other differentiation. Whenever he interacted with other patients on the unit, he began to assume their characteristics. For example, when a young female patient became psychotic, Mr. N was convinced that he, too, was disorganizing. When another patient needed bladder surgery, Mr. N reported urinary symptoms to his doctor and suggested that he might need such surgery as well. This tendency to overidentify with his peers and to take on their attributes led him to distance himself from other patients. Similarly, he would not work closely with staff members. However, this self-imposed distance made him feel anxious about being alone. As a compromise between too much distance or too much closeness, he would provoke staff members and other patients into negative interactions with him. He repeatedly broke the structure established for him in order to evoke persecutory attacks from staff members or peers. He would then feel victimized and would lash out with contempt and outrage at those he perceived as persecuting him. This pattern of interactions seemed repetitive of behavior that had occurred with his father. At times during the patient's hospitalization, his father would scream at him over the phone about his lack of motivation and his irresponsibility, occasionally reducing him to tears. As a result, Mr. N often complained about his father's tyrannical tendencies: "I'm angry at him. I feel smothered and exploited by my father. He controls my life, but if he doesn't, my life falls apart."

This patient met the criteria for the Axis I diagnoses of generalized anxiety disorder and hypochondriasis. He also met the Axis II criteria for borderline personality disorder because of his multiple "neurotic" symptoms (including free-floating anxiety and hypochondriacal concerns), his profound identity disturbance, his inappropriate and intense anger, his pattern of unstable and intense interpersonal relationships, his affective instability, and his intense separation anxiety.

As a result of a thorough evaluation of the patient's anxiety, an explanatory formulation was derived that illustrated the multiple determinants of that symptom. At the phallic-oedipal level, his anxiety was related to castration concerns. His perception of his mother as seductive and exhibitionistic led him to flee her house and live with his father after his parents had separated. Projective psychological testing with the Thematic Apperception Test (TAT) was highly revealing, as in the following story the patient told:

> This woman is the mother of a male child who is masturbating. She opens the door, and with a look of disgust, yet happiness, she sees her young son masturbating. He is confused and doesn't understand what he is doing. It was just instinctual. She gets a vicarious thrill over seeing her child do this, but they also both feel guilty—a perverse pleasure. She takes an intense interest in her son's sex life.

In addition to illustrating the threat of a possible incestuous relationship, this story also reflects the presence of inadequately repressed polymorphous perverse sexual impulses, particularly along the exhibitionistic-scopophilic axis. This perceived availability of his mother made Mr. N particularly fearful of retaliation by his father. In the patient's own words, "Virility is linked to an explosive instinct. It must be controlled." His homosexual preoccupations may also have been an effort to defend against his castration anxiety by avoiding the competitive heterosexual arena with its risks of retaliation. The castration threat may similarly come from the opposite sex, as revealed in his comment, "I'm afraid of intercourse. I'm afraid my penis will be slashed if I were to have intercourse." The surgery on Mr. N's testicular appendage at age 10 may have further reinforced his castration anxiety.

Mr. N's anxiety, however, cannot be explained by relying solely on phallic-oedipal determinants. The origins of his problems with self-other differentiation may have been partially linked with the history of sexual intrusiveness of both parents and their failure to establish firm generational boundaries between the patient and themselves. During a visit from Mr. N's father, the patient and his father spent almost 2 hours in the patient's room, lying opposite each other (on the couch and on the bed), simply staring at one another, and talking only briefly. Nursing staff who observed them noted that they seemed like mirror images of one another.

Another determinant of Mr. N's anxiety was his sense that others could violate his boundaries to take him over from within. He felt as if this takeover happened whenever he became close to other patients on the unit because he began to assume their symptoms. He experienced this invasion as a threat to the integrity of his tenuously organized sense of self, and he was terrified of disintegrating and disappearing as he was engulfed by the object with which he fused. Thus his reaction to this combination of persecutory anxiety and disintegration anxiety led him to maintain more distance from others to avoid fusing with them. However, this defensive maneuver in turn created intense separation anxiety. Of note is that Mr. N linked his first attack of anxiety to leaving home for college. To deal with his separation concerns, the patient provoked others into relating to him as though they were persecutors. Via projective identification, the patient would externalize an internal object relationship of persecutor-victim and attempt to enact it with staff members. In an effort to obtain reassurance that he was loved, he pressured staff members to act like his angry and controlling father. He could gain this form of reassurance only through a struggle or argument, since a loving and more positive interaction threatened him with fusion. He would frequently leave a particular hospital activity because of unbearable anxiety. When questioned about this pattern, he confided that he was attracted to another young man who also participated in that activity and often had homosexual fantasies about him. Whenever he felt threatened by becoming physically close to the other man, Mr. N would return to the unit. However, upon arriving there, he would then become anxious about being separated from this fantasy object, and to feel less alone and abandoned, he would provoke struggles with the staff members.

Mr. N's dilemma of needing to attach and merge himself with someone else in order to survive, yet fearing engulfment and loss of identity, was a prominent resistance to treatment. He saw any movement from the primitive persecutor-victim stance to a more mature object relationship as abandonment of the only familiar form of relatedness. He repeatedly expressed a wish to leave the hospital but indicated that his father would fall apart if he improved—a projective description of what he perceived would happen to *him* upon improvement. The primitive nature of Mr. N's anxiety was vividly evident in a parapraxis he had made once while complaining about his psychotherapy and expressing a wish to leave the hospital. Changing the subject to a physical complaint about some insect bites on his legs, he complained, "I am being completely eaten up by all these insights—I mean, insects."

The principle of multiple function is particularly well illustrated by exploring the patient's hypochondriacal anxiety about becoming seriously or fatally ill. Like Mr. J in Chapter 7, Mr. N had anxiety that can be viewed as an introjection of the persecutory object. In other words, Mr. N's anxiety that an outside persecutor would invade him and take over was transformed into a fear that he was being destroyed from within by an internal persecutor in the form of an illness. His constant attention to his body was an extraordinary effort to shore up his weakly cathected body boundaries and to distinguish the external from the internal.

The case of Mr. N illustrates how anxiety may serve as a window into the relevant developmental issues with which the patient struggles. Analogous to a stream of light passing through a prism, his anxiety breaks into at least four components: castration anxiety, separation anxiety, persecutory anxiety, and disintegration anxiety.

Biological Dimensions of Anxiety

Recent neurobiological research has confirmed Freud's original observation that there are essentially two forms of anxiety: one largely determined by psychological issues and another driven by autonomous biological factors outside the realm of psychological content. It is now well established that panic attacks respond to imipramine and monoamine oxidase inhibitors, whereas anticipatory anxiety does not (Cooper 1985; Kandel 1983; Nemiah 1981). Panic attacks may also be experimentally induced by an infusion of lactate. Further evidence of a biological basis for panic disorder includes a higher incidence of panic disorder in panic patients' families than in control subjects' families (Crowe et al. 1983) and a 31% concordance for panic disorder in monozygotic twins compared to 0% for dizygotic twins (Torgersen 1983).

As noted in Chapter 1, research on the locus coeruleus has been productive in defining the biological dimensions of anxiety. As the source of nearly three-quarters of the brain's norepinephrine supply, the locus coeruleus is the largest noradrenergic nucleus in the brain (Redmond 1987). Whereas Freud viewed the ego as the *psychological* seat of anxiety, modern neurobiological researchers have identified the locus coeruleus as the *biological* seat of anxiety. Neural pathways enter this nucleus from every level of the central nervous system, and efferent pathways lead to all the major physiological systems involved in panic attacks. The locus coeruleus appears to regulate the anxiety level of the organism through the activation or deactivation of inhibitory neurons, which are activated by gamma-aminobutyric acid (GABA).

Benzodiazepines appear to work similarly by activating the inhibitory neurons in the locus coeruleus. Conversely, a feeling of panic can be created in human subjects by deactivating the GABA-controlled neurons with piperoxane and yohimbine (Redmond 1987). Hence, dysregulation of the GABA system in the locus coeruleus may serve as a biologically based etiology of panic disorder, irrespective of psychological concerns (Cooper 1985).

Although Freud appeared to grow more interested in the notion of signal anxiety later in his career, he always maintained that physiological anxiety was instrumental to the development of panic states. More recently, Nemiah (1981) has linked Freud's early formulations with the biological differences between panic attacks and anticipatory anxiety. To produce classical panic disorder, an underlying neural structure must be triggered by psychological or physiological factors. Without this neural structure, the end result will be a milder form of anticipatory anxiety. Nemiah (1981) noted that "in patients with a diathesis for panic attacks resulting from specific, predisposing neural structures, the anxiety aroused by the psychological conflicts, when these are present, will take the form of panic; whereas in individuals without this neural predisposition, it will appear in the less intense form of anticipatory, signal anxiety" (p. 119). The existence of a neural mechanism for anxiety does not, however, preclude the usefulness of psychotherapeutic techniques. Effective psychotherapy most likely results in long-term structural and functional changes in the brain that are related to changes in the expression of specific genes (Kandel 1983). Moreover, as noted in Chapter 1, with certain patients who have intense separation anxiety, just hearing the therapist's voice over the telephone can quiet a panic attack as rapidly as the most potent pharmacologic agent.

Panic Disorder

Although panic attacks generally last only a matter of minutes, they produce considerable distress within the patient. In addition to alarming physiological symptoms, such as choking, dizziness, sweating, shaking, and tachycardia, patients with panic disorder often sense imminent doom. Most patients with panic disorder also have agoraphobia (i.e., a fear of being in a location or situation from which escape would be difficult or extremely embarrassing). Because panic attacks are recurrent, patients often develop a secondary form of anticipatory anxiety, worrying constantly about when and where the next attack will occur. Panic disorder patients with agoraphobia often restrict their travel to try to control the dreaded situation of having a panic attack in a place they cannot leave easily.

Panic disorder, as discussed in the previous section, may appear psychologically contentless. The attacks may come "out of the blue," without apparent environmental or intrapsychic precipitants. As a result, the psychodynamic psychiatrist's role is often—and unfortunately—deemed irrelevant in treating these patients. A significant percentage of patients with panic disorder have such attacks because of psychodynamic factors and thus may respond to psychological interventions (Nemiah 1981, 1984). Psychodynamic clinicians should thoroughly investigate the circumstances of the attacks and the history of each panic disorder patient to determine whether psychological factors are relevant.

Although the evidence for neurophysiological factors in panic disorder is impressive, these observations are more persuasive regarding pathogenesis than regarding etiology. None of the neurobiological data explains what triggers the onset of a panic attack. In a pilot study involving psychodynamic interviews with nine consecutive patients with panic disorder, an objective research psychiatrist was able to identify meaningful stressors preceding the onset of the panic attacks in every case (Busch et al. 1991).

Indeed, several lines of evidence suggest that psychological factors may be relevant to panic attacks (Gabbard 1992a). Panic disorder patients may have a higher incidence of stressful life events, particularly loss, compared with controls, in the months preceding the onset of panic disorder (Faravelli and Pallanti 1989). Also, in one study (Klein 1964), 50% of 32 patients with agoraphobia had histories of separation anxiety, and in this group, panic attacks often followed the loss of a significant person. In another control study of patients with panic disorder (Roy-Byrne et al. 1986), the experimental group not only experienced significantly more stressful life events in the year preceding the onset of panic but also felt greater distress about the events in their lives than did the control subjects.

Some of the most intriguing data regarding panic disorder concern the rate of response to placebo. Anywhere from 25% (Coryell and Noyes 1988; Mavissakalian 1988) to 43% (Ballenger et al. 1988) of patients with panic disorder show improvement with placebo. These findings are striking when compared with the almost total absence of response to placebo in patients with obsessive-compulsive disorder (Mavissakalian et al. 1990). Such a dramatic response to placebo is certainly suggestive of psychological influences. Transference factors associated with receiving a pill from a concerned physician may well work to alleviate the symptoms.

Cognitive-behavioral treatments have also proved effective in the treatment of panic disorder (Beck et al. 1992). The impressive efficacy of this psychotherapeutic approach lends further credence to the notion that psychological factors are at work. A recent study by Shear et al. (1991) has even demonstrated that lactate induction of panic can be effectively reversed through successful cognitive therapy. These findings, coupled with a variety of case reports of successful treatment of panic disorder with either psychoanalysis or psychodynamic psychotherapy (Abend 1989; Milrod and Shear 1991; Sifneos 1972), provide persuasive evidence that psychological interventions have a major role to play in the treatment of panic disorder.

The idea that psychological trauma may produce neurophysiological changes in panic disorder is supported by findings from a large study of female twins (Kendler et al. 1992a). Investigators in this project studied the relationship between parental loss prior to age 17 years and adult psychopathology in 1,018 pairs of female twins. They found that panic disorder was significantly and strongly associated with both parental death and separation. Moreover, maternal separation early in life was much more likely to result in panic disorder than was paternal separation. Contrary to conventional wisdom, the impact of parental loss was three times greater for panic disorder than it was for major depression.

All these data taken together suggest that the etiology of panic disorder may well involve the unconscious meaning of events, while the pathogenesis may involve neurophysiological factors triggered by the psychological reaction to the events. Busch et al. (1991) concluded: "Since each individual interprets the meaning of these events differently, an external stressor may or may not lead to the onset of panic in a neurophysiologically susceptible individual. This suggests that there is a crucial psychological variable that mediates between external events and panic onset" (p. 321).

These research findings are borne out by clinical experience with patients who suffer from poorly developed object constancy (see Chapter 15). Such patients cannot summon an internal image of their therapist in times of distress to help them soothe their anxiety. Over long weekends or during their therapist's vacations, these patients may develop full-blown panic attacks triggered by the thought of losing their therapist. They may fear that their therapist has died or is on the verge of rejecting or abandoning them. In such circumstances, just hearing their therapist's voice over the telephone can completely eliminate the panic within a few seconds. One psychiatrist in private practice routinely left a message on his answering machine over the weekend so that his patients would know where to reach him. Upon hiring a secretary, he relegated to her the task of recording the answering machine message. On the first Monday morning after the secretary recorded the message, three patients called him to complain. One patient angrily stated, "I need to hear *your* voice, not hers! It's either your voice or a Xanax!"

As poignantly illustrated by this comment, the *sound* of the therapist's voice was enough to reassure this patient that he was truly still available. Indeed, in this case the therapist's voice had a therapeutic effect as potent as a pharmacologic agent. Often patients suffering from a lack of object constancy are able to ultimately develop an internalized image of their therapist over the course of long-term, expressive-supportive psychotherapy. As a result of this internalization process, both the separation anxiety and the panic attacks may improve considerably. In Waldinger and Gunderson's (1987) study of successfully completed treatments of borderline patients with long-term psychodynamic psychotherapy, they found that by the end of the fifth year, none of the patients experienced panic in response to their therapist's departure, further evidence that psychotherapy may produce permanent neurophysiological alterations.

Panic disorder patients frequently require a combination of drug therapy and psychotherapy (Nemiah 1984). Even when patients with panic attacks and agoraphobia have their symptoms pharmacologically controlled, they are often reluctant to venture out into the world again and may require psychotherapeutic interventions to help them overcome this fear (Cooper 1985; Zitrin et al. 1978). Some patients present with major resistances to medication, often because they believe it stigmatizes them as being mentally ill, so psychotherapeutic intervention is required to help them understand and eliminate their reservations about pharmacotherapy. Still others discontinue medications on their own because of their inability to tolerate side effects. Another reason for adding psychotherapy to pharmacotherapy is that clinicians who rely exclusively on medication for the treatment of panic disorder may eventually have to deal with withdrawal symptoms and relapse rates as high as 71%–95% (Beck et al. 1992). Finally, characterological difficulties in patients may interfere with compliance. The presence of personality disorders, particularly those in Cluster B (e.g., antisocial, borderline, narcissistic, histrionic), has been shown to adversely affect the treatment outcomes of patients with panic disorder (Reich 1988). For a comprehensive and effective treatment plan, these patients require psychotherapeutic approaches in addition to appropriate medications. In all patients with symptoms of panic disorder or agoraphobia, a careful psychodynamic evaluation will help weigh the contributions of biological and dynamic factors.

Mr. O, a 27-year-old office worker, came to an outpatient clinic with a complaint of panic attacks that occurred whenever he attempted to leave town. He was initially unable to link the panic to any psychological content, but further exploration by the evaluating psychiatrist revealed a number of contributing factors. Mr. O had just purchased a new house, and his wife was pregnant with their first child. When the psychiatrist commented on the increased responsibility associated with these events, the patient replied that he felt more like 7 than 27. He went on to say that he was not sure that he was prepared to shoulder the responsibilities of a husband and father accountable for the mortgage on a house. The psychiatrist asked Mr. O to describe in more detail the circumstances of the panic attacks. Mr. O again explained that he had them whenever he started to leave town. The psychiatrist asked about the purpose of these trips, which Mr. O explained was to go hunting with his father. The psychiatrist asked if anything unpleasant had ever happened on these trips. After a few moments' reflection, Mr. O replied that he had accidentally shot his father in two different hunting accidents, although fortunately his father had sustained only minor wounds on each occasion.

The psychiatrist then developed a tentative explanatory formulation based on his evaluation that Mr. O's panic disorder was related to psychological conflict. Recent events in his life had placed him more squarely in competition with his father as a husband, father, and breadwinner. These events activated long-standing aggressive wishes toward his father that were based on repressed and unconscious oedipal rivalry. The impulse to destroy his father had emerged in the form of accidents on two previous hunting trips. Now whenever Mr. O planned to leave town with his father to go hunting, the threatened emergence of the aggressive impulses created signal anxiety that was transformed into a full-blown panic attack because this particular patient had the underlying neural substrate necessary to transform anxiety into panic. The result was an avoidance of situations in which the destructive wishes and the imagined retaliation (castration) would be activated.

To understand the dynamic factors involved in triggering the panic, the patient began expressive-supportive psychotherapy with an expressive emphasis. As the process proceeded, Mr. O began to talk more and more about his attachment to his mother. It soon emerged that his mother had also been terrified of separations. As a child, each time Mr. O went outside, his mother would warn him about the many dangers he might encounter. Through the psychotherapy process, Mr. O eventually realized that he shared his mother's anxiety about separations. He noted that whenever his wife was away on business, he worried the entire time because he feared that she might die and thus abandon him. The patient's oedipal anxieties were clearly compounded by more primitive anxieties about object loss, originally of his mother but now of his wife.

After approximately 2 years of psychotherapy, Mr. O was free from panic attacks and from anticipatory anxiety as well. He had received a promotion at work that he was able to handle without anxiety. His new job necessitated driving out of town almost every workday, and he was able to do so without experiencing any panic.

Several years later, Mr. O returned for further treatment when two life events reactivated the underlying neural structure that mediated his panic attacks. A private business he had started had become enormously successful, resulting in a much more affluent life-style. Moreover, his father had been diagnosed as having incurable cancer. This time a combination of medication (alprazolam) and psychotherapy was required to reduce Mr. O's panic attacks to manageable proportions.

Phobias

Anxiety disorders as a group are the most prevalent of all major groups of mental disorders (Regier et al. 1988), and among anxiety disorders, phobias are by far the most common. Phobias are divided into three categories in DSM-IV: 1) agoraphobia without history of panic disorder, 2) specific phobia, and 3) social phobia. The DSM-III-R term *simple phobia* was replaced by *specific phobia* in DSM-IV because of the ambiguous relationship of phobic symptoms to panic attacks and because a subtyping scheme involving the phobic stimulus (e.g., situational type, natural environment type) seemed to improve specificity. Similarly, a subtyping scheme has been developed in DSM-IV for social phobia because the growing literature on the condition indicates that social phobia may be either generalized or limited.

The psychodynamic understanding of phobias illustrates the neurotic mechanism of symptom formation described at the beginning of this chapter. When forbidden sexual or aggressive thoughts that might lead to retaliatory punishment threaten to emerge from the unconscious, signal anxiety is activated, which leads to the deployment of three defense mechanisms—displacement, projection, and avoidance (Nemiah 1981). These defenses eliminate the anxiety by once again repressing the forbidden wish, but the anxiety is controlled at the cost of creating a phobic neurosis. A clinical example illustrates the phobic symptom formation more concretely:

> Mr. P was a 25-year-old junior executive who had just completed an MBA and taken his first position with a corporation. He had developed a social phobia that involved an intense fear of meeting new people at work or in social situations. He also developed intense anxiety whenever he had to speak in front of a group of people at work. When forced to confront the feared situations, he would become short of breath and stumble over his words to such an extent that he could not complete sentences.
>
> Brief dynamic therapy was recommended for Mr. P because of his notable ego strengths, the focal nature of his symptom, his good overall functioning, a high level of motivation, and considerable psychological-mindedness. In the third session, Mr. P clarified for the therapist that the worst part of meeting new people was having to introduce himself. The following exchange took place:

> Therapist: What's difficult about saying your name?
> Patient: I have no idea.
> Therapist: If you reflect about your name for a minute, what comes to mind?
> Patient: (after a pause) Well, it's also my father's name.
> Therapist: How does that make you feel?
> Patient: A bit uncomfortable, I guess.
> Therapist: Why is that?
> Patient: Well, I haven't had a great relationship with him. Ever since he left my mom when I was 4 years old, I've seen very little of him.

Therapist: So you had to live alone with your mother after he left?

Patient: That's right. My mom never remarried, so I had to be the man of the house from an early age, and I didn't feel ready to take on so much responsibility. I've always resented that. When I was a kid, everybody always said that I acted like such an adult. That used to bother me because I felt like I was just pretending to be an adult when I was really a child inside. I felt like I was fooling everybody, and if they found out, they would be mad at me.

Therapist: I wonder if that's how you feel now when you introduce yourself.

Patient: I think that's exactly how I feel. To say my name is to say I'm trying to be my father.

The therapist's interpretation helped Mr. P realize that his anxiety was related to guilt and shame about prematurely filling his father's shoes. He imagined that others would see through this charade, or deceit, and disapprove of him. After 10 sessions of brief dynamic therapy, the patient overcame his social phobia and was able to function well at work and in social settings.

At the height of Mr. P's oedipal phase of development, his father left him alone with his mother. In that original anxiety-generating situation, he had feared castration or retaliatory punishment (from his father) for taking his father's place with his mother. As an adult, Mr. P dealt with anxiety by displacing the original feared situation onto an insignificant and seemingly trivial derivative of that situation, namely, saying his name during introductions. Symbolically, this simple social grace had taken on the meaning of replacing his father. The patient's second defensive maneuver was to project the feared situation outward onto the environment so that the threatened punishment or disapproval came from external rather than internal sources (i.e., the superego). The patient's third and final defense mechanism was avoidance. By avoiding all situations in which he had to introduce himself or speak in front of others, Mr. P could maintain control over his anxiety, but at the cost of restricting his social life and jeopardizing his performance at work.

Mr. P's anxiety about speaking in front of others is widely shared. In one metropolitan survey (Pollard and Henderson 1988), one-fifth of the individuals contacted in the city of St. Louis had a social phobia about public speaking or performing. When the investigators modified that figure by including the "significant distress" criteria of DSM-III, the prevalence rate fell to 2%. Exact figures on social phobia are difficult to ascertain, however, because the diagnosis is often applied to general interpersonal patterns of shyness and avoidance of the opposite sex because of fear of rejection. The continuum ranges from social phobia at one end to a generalized characterological style of relating, known as avoidant personality disorder (see Chapter 19), at the other. Thus, differentiating between discrete phobias and personality styles is not an easy task.

Phobias fit nicely into a model of genetic-constitutional diathesis in interaction with environmental stressors. Kendler et al. (1992b) studied 2,163 female twins and concluded that the best model for the disorder is an inherited phobia-proneness that requires environmental etiological factors specific to the individual to produce a full-blown phobic syndrome. In their study population, one of the clear environmental stressors associated with an increased risk for phobia was parental death before the age of 17 (Kendler et al. 1992a).

Social phobia can be used to illustrate this interaction between constitution and environment. There is now considerable evidence that the expectation that critical scrutiny by others will result in humiliation and embarrassment has some basis in temperament. Kagan and his colleagues at Harvard (1988) studied cohorts of children using a longitudinal design that compared consistently inhibited with consistently uninhibited children. Their observations suggest that most children who are behaviorally inhibited belong to a qualitatively distinct category of infants who are born with a lower threshold for limbic-hypothalamic arousal in response to unexpected changes in the environment or novel events that cannot be assimilated easily. Kagan et al. (1988) referred to this temperamental construct as "behavioral inhibition to the unfamiliar." However, they also concluded that some form of chronic environmental stress must act on the original temperamental disposition present at birth to result in shy, timid, and quiet behavior at 2 years of age. They postulated such stressors as humiliation and criticism from an older sibling, parental arguments, and death or separation from a parent. Finally, Kagan and colleagues emphasized the importance of differentiating children who are quiet and shy in unfamiliar social situations because of temperamental factors from those who are that way because of environmental factors alone. Physiological measures may be helpful in distinguishing the two groups.

Rosenbaum et al. (1992) extended the work of Kagan et al. (1988) by evaluating parents of behaviorally inhibited children from a nonclinical cohort studied by Kagan. Parents of these children were at greater risk for anxiety disorders, mainly social phobia. Parents of those children with behavioral inhibition and anxiety had significantly higher rates of two or more anxiety disorders as compared with two different sets of parents in control groups. One possible interpretation of their findings is that those children with behavioral inhibition who go on to develop manifest anxiety disorders are exposed to parents with greater anxiety who may convey to the children that the world is a dangerous place.

Social phobia is a condition with a high rate of comorbidity. In a study of 13,000 adults (Schneier et al. 1992), lifetime major comorbid disorders were present in 69% of subjects with social phobia. These investigators made the point that in the absence of comorbidity, social phobia is rarely treated by mental health professionals. One can postulate that the genetic-constitutional diathesis described by Kagan et al. (1988), Rosenbaum et al. (1992), and others may predispose to a number of anxiety disorders.

Clinical work with socially phobic patients reveals that certain characteristic internal object relationships are present. Specifically, these patients have internalized representations of parents, caretakers, or siblings who shame, criticize, ridicule, humiliate, abandon, and embarrass (Gabbard 1992b). These introjects are established early in life and then repeatedly projected onto persons in the environment who are then avoided. While these patients may have a genetic predisposition to experience others as hurtful, positive experiences can mitigate those effects to some extent. It is as though a genetically programmed template is present at birth. To the extent that caretakers behave like the programmed template, the individual will become increasingly fearful of others and develop social phobia. To the extent that caretakers are sensitive to the child's fearfulness and compensate, the introjects will be more benign, less threatening, and less likely to produce the adult syndrome of social phobia.

Because of considerable success in treating phobias with behavioral desensitization and, to a lesser extent, tricyclic antidepressants such as imipramine, psychodynamic approaches have fallen somewhat out of favor in the treatment of phobias. In patients with characteristics similar to those of Mr. P, expressive psychotherapy is often effective. Other patients may benefit from a more supportive approach with or without medication. A controlled study of 111 patients with simple phobia, agoraphobia, or mixed phobia confirmed the effectiveness of supportive psychotherapy plus medication (Zitrin et al. 1978). One group of patients received behavioral therapy plus a placebo, a second group received behavioral therapy plus imipramine, and a third group received supportive therapy plus imipramine. No differences were found between the supportive and behavioral therapy groups that received imipramine; both improved considerably in 70%–86% of the cases. At 1-year follow-up, 83% of the patients in all three groups who had shown improvement had not relapsed. The investigators concluded that psychotherapy's greatest influence was in those patients whose core phobic disorder had been brought under pharmacological control with imipramine.

The interpersonal ramifications of phobias often benefit from a dynamic approach as well. By virtue of being housebound, severely agoraphobic individuals often require caretaking from another significant person, such as a spouse or parent. It is common, for example, for an agoraphobic woman and her husband to have accommodated to her condition over a period of many years. The husband may actually feel more secure knowing that his wife is always in the house. If the agoraphobia is treated, the couple's equilibrium may destabilize. The husband may become more anxious because of a fear that his wife will begin to seek out other men now that she is leaving the house. Adequate assessment and treatment of phobias must include a careful assessment of how the phobia fits into the patient's network of relationships. A psychodynamic understanding of the interpersonal context of a phobia may thus be crucial to dealing with resistances to conventional treatments such as behavioral desensitization and medication.

Obsessive-Compulsive Disorder

Obsessions are defined as recurrent ego-dystonic thoughts, whereas compulsions are ritualized actions that *must* be performed to relieve anxiety. The complaints of these patients fit into five primary categories: 1) rituals involving checking, 2) rituals involving cleaning, 3) obsessive thoughts unaccompanied by compulsions, 4) obsessional slowness, and 5) mixed rituals (Baer and Jenike 1986). Those patients who are involved in cleaning rituals or obsessive thoughts about germs and contamination bear considerable resemblance to phobic patients. Recent research has suggested that obsessive-compulsive disorder (OCD) is much more common than had been previously thought (Karno et al. 1988). The lifetime prevalence is between 1.2% and 2.4%, a figure many times greater than all previous estimates. OCD is often complicated by depression and by serious impairment in occupational and social functioning so that family members and co-workers of OCD patients may be significantly affected by the illness as well.

Despite the long-established tradition of the diagnosis of obsessive-compulsive neurosis, DSM-III reclassified OCD as an anxiety disorder because the primary function of an obsession or ritual seems to be regulation of anxiety. The classical formulation of the defensive regression inherent in obsessive-compulsive neurosis has been succinctly summarized by Nemiah (1988):

> In the face of stimuli that arouse anxiety-provoking oedipal libido, instead of repressing the drive and converting the energy into somatic symptoms as in hysteria or displacing and projecting it as in the phobic neurosis, the patient with an obsessive-compulsive neurosis retreats from the oedipal position and regresses along the path of psychosexual development to the anal phase, a regression often aided by the presence of anal fixations resulting from disturbances in the patient's initial passage through that developmental stage during early childhood. (p. 243)

Another product of the regression is the unraveling of the smooth fusion between aggressive and sexual drives that is characteristic of the oedipal phase. Feelings of love and hatred are no longer fused, so the obsessive-compulsive neurotic individual is typically plagued with intense ambivalence. The simultaneous presence of loving and hateful feelings leaves the patient consumed with doubt about the appropriate course of action and, like Hamlet, paralyzed with indecision. As noted in Chapter 2, the person with an obsessive-compulsive neurosis characteristically uses the defenses of isolation, reaction formation, intellectualization, and undoing to cope with the primitive sexual and aggressive drives that must be contained and controlled.

The psychodynamic explanation of OCD has been challenged by recent biological research. A number of investigators have suggested that is a biological basis exists for the disorder because of several observations, including a higher rate of concordance for OCD in monozygotic than dizygotic twins, an increased prevalence in patients with Tourette's syndrome and in their families, and a dramatic response in some patients to psychosurgery (Elkins et al. 1980; Lieberman 1984;

Turner et al. 1985). Moreover, a quantitative study using computed tomography revealed that the caudate nucleus volume is significantly less in OCD patients than in healthy controls (Luxenberg et al. 1988). Preliminary investigations suggest that the head of the caudate nucleus plays a central role in OCD symptom mediation (Baxter et al. 1992). Another study compared 41 medication-free OCD patients with 29 normal controls on tasks involving fine motor coordination, involuntary movement, and sensory and visio-spatial function (Hollander et al. 1990). The OCD group showed significantly more signs of central nervous system dysfunction than did the controls, providing further evidence for a neurological deficit in some patients with OCD. Finally, in contrast to conditions such as panic disorder, in which one-fourth to one-third of the patients respond to placebo, empirical investigations suggest that OCD has virtually no placebo response (Mavissakalian et al. 1990). The consensus of current thinking is that OCD involves a biological predisposition that interacts with psychological and environmental factors (Rachman and Hodgson 1980).

The literature on treatment outcomes also suggests a biological component. Medications such as clomipramine and fluvoxamine have been found to be effective with some OCD patients (Jenike et al. 1986; Perse 1988; White and Cole 1988). Also, the symptoms of OCD patients are notoriously refractory to psychoanalysis and insight-oriented psychotherapy (Jenike et al. 1986; Nemiah 1988; Perse 1988; Zetzel 1970). (Obsessive-compulsive personality disorder responds well to these treatments, as discussed in Chapter 19.) Pharmacologic response, however, does not provide definitive answers to questions of etiology or pathogenesis (Zetin and Kramer 1992). Neurotransmitter changes associated with medications may relate either directly or indirectly to the primary cause of the condition. Moreover, as with panic disorder, OCD may be precipitated by environmental stressors. In one investigation (Buttolph and Holland 1990), 69% of patients with OCD were able to relate the onset or exacerbation of their symptoms to pregnancy, childbirth, or parental care of their children. In another study of 106 female OCD patients (Neziroglu et al. 1992), pregnancy—more than any other life event—was associated with the onset of OCD. Thirty-nine percent of the patients in the sample who had children experienced symptom onset during pregnancy. In addition, four of the five women who had had an abortion or a miscarriage had experienced the onset or exacerbation of OCD symptoms during pregnancy. That the symptoms wax and wane according to the presence or absence of stress in the patient's life is also well known. Improvement may occur when tension is reduced, while increased stress or recurrence of the original precipitating situation will worsen symptoms (Black 1974).

Although most clinicians would agree that pharmacotherapy is a crucial part of a comprehensive treatment plan for patients with OCD, medication such as clomipramine should not be regarded as the sole treatment. The Clomipramine Collaborative Study Group (1991) studied 520 OCD patients in 21 centers and found that the mean reduction in symptoms at the end of 10 weeks of treatment with clomipramine was only 38%–44%. Also, without associated behavior therapy, relapse on clomipramine is high (Zetin and Kramer 1992). The best response rates reported in the literature have been to behavioral techniques involving in vivo exposure combined with response prevention (Barlow and Beck 1984). However, behavior modification also results in a high relapse rate, and Marks (1981) has pointed out that such treatment requires extensive cooperation from the patient. Because time-consuming and anxiety-provoking homework is required for behavioral treatment, many patients simply refuse to cooperate. Even without treatment, an estimated 40% of OCD patients will experience either total remission or considerable improvement in their symptoms (Baer and Jenike 1986).

Many OCD patients seem to hang onto their symptoms, tenaciously resisting treatment efforts. The symptoms themselves may fend off psychotic disintegration in some patients, thereby performing a highly useful function in terms of psychological homeostasis. Because the symptoms of OCD may accompany any level of underlying personality or ego organization (Cornfield and Malen 1978), a careful psychodynamic evaluation should also focus on the function of the symptoms in the patient's overall intrapsychic structure. Despite the refractory nature of many obsessive-compulsive symptoms, psychodynamic therapy may considerably improve the interpersonal functioning of OCD patients. Dynamic approaches may also be crucial in helping patients overcome resistances to taking medication, as described in the case of Mr. A in Chapter 1. Symptoms of OCD often lead to extraordinary relationship problems for these patients, and the diagnosis of OCD is associated with a high risk of divorce or separation (Zetin and Kramer 1992). Psychodynamic therapy therefore may be the only effective modality for addressing the relationship problems secondary to the symptoms. Dynamic group psychotherapy, in particular, may be useful in this realm, as illustrated in the following clinical example:

Mr. Q was a 33-year-old law clerk who had suffered from OCD since childhood. He had been in individual psychotherapy for 1 year with no improvement, so his individual therapist, thinking that group psychotherapy might more adequately address his interpersonal problems, referred him to an expressive therapy group with a male and female cotherapist. During the first few months of his participation in the group, Mr. Q tended to monopolize the discussion with long, rambling, self-absorbed discourses that effectively shut out other group members. When they attempted to comment or react to what he was saying, he would raise his voice and speak more rapidly to drown them out. Much of what he said seemed designed to convince the group that he harbored no sexual or aggressive feelings. Paradoxically, Mr. Q's manner seemed quite aggressive to the other group members. They gradually but forcefully began to confront him about his monopolistic tendencies. As is frequently the case with OCD patients, Mr. Q was much better able to hear and accept confrontation from other patients in the group than from the two cotherapists.

Over several years, gradual changes emerged in Mr. Q. He began to listen to others in response to being repeatedly confronted. For the first time, he became aware that his obsessionalism had an impact on others. As he listened more, he also became more empathic and sensitive to other people's concerns. As he developed more trust in the group, he was able to confide in them about his compulsive rituals. When a group session went badly, he would drive from the therapist's office back to his office along the same route he used in coming to therapy. Sometimes he would even drive back and forth several times before going home, having fantasies that he could erase whatever had happened in the therapy session (an example of the defense mechanism of undoing). To his surprise, the other patients in the group were able to accept the fact that he had symptoms without condemning him for them.

Similarly, Mr. Q was gradually able to share his sexual conflicts with the group. He had originally stated that he never looked at a woman "below the neck," as a way of reassuring the group that his sexual feelings were under control. As he felt more comfortable, however, he was able to say that he struggled daily with erotic feelings toward a variety of people in his life. He was even able to express erotic transference feelings toward the female cotherapist. To his amazement, no retaliation or censure was forthcoming from either the male cotherapist or the other patients. With the help of such benign and accepting responses from the group, Mr. Q began to learn that his expectation of criticism from others was a projection of his own harsh superego. After many years of group therapy, he was finally able to experience greatly improved interpersonal functioning, which paid off both in his personal life and in his work relationships. Moreover, with the superego modification achieved through group therapy, Mr. Q's anxiety decreased considerably. As his anxiety level fell, his need for compulsive rituals and obsessional thoughts also decreased accordingly.

The case of Mr. Q demonstrates how interpersonal relatedness can be intimately linked to the need for obsessive-compulsive symptoms. Throughout the course of his group psychotherapy, he was able to repeatedly express his forbidden thoughts, feelings, and fantasies, with no disastrous consequences from either the cotherapists or his peers in the group. From an object relations standpoint, Mr. Q internalized new forms of object relatedness that led to decreased anxiety and therefore to less need for the symptoms.

Like agoraphobic patients, those with OCD may derive considerable secondary gain from their symptoms. Whatever the reasons for their initial appearance, the symptoms may be perpetuated and solidified by their role in family relationships. Just as Mr. Q controlled the group with his obsessional rambling, other patients with OCD may control their entire families, so effective treatment must often include attention to the family dynamics.

Ms. R was a 45-year-old married mother of two children who was consumed with obsessive-compulsive cleaning rituals in her home. She was convinced that germs and vomit had contaminated various items in her household, and as a result, she spent most of each day scrubbing things and washing her family's clothing. Whenever her husband and two children returned from work or school, she insisted that they immediately shower and hand over all the clothes they had worn that day so that she could place them in the washing machine. Ms. R would also go through her daughter's purse, compulsively cleaning every item that might be contaminated and checking for new contents brought in from outside the home. Her husband and children felt so controlled that they felt guilty about leaving the house. Finally their exasperation led them to take her to a psychiatrist, seeking hospitalization. Immediately after she was admitted, her cleaning rituals completely disappeared. Because her symptoms were no longer useful in controlling the family, Ms. R lost psychological investment in them. However, as soon as she arrived home after being discharged, the symptoms returned.

One useful contribution the psychodynamic clinician can make in treating OCD is to investigate the precipitants that initiate or exacerbate symptoms. By helping patients and their families to understand the nature of these stressors, the symptoms can be managed more effectively.

Posttraumatic Stress Disorder

Until recently, posttraumatic stress disorder (PTSD) went largely unrecognized by the majority of American psychiatrists. Because of its longtime exclusion from the official diagnostic nomenclature, many clinicians did not include PTSD in their differential diagnosis of syndromes associated with anxiety. Years of diligent lobbying by veterans' groups spurred the American Psychiatric Association to officially recognize PTSD as a diagnostic entity worthy of inclusion in the 1980 version of DSM-III. Even today, some psychiatrists believe that PTSD is not a discrete diagnostic category, but rather a mixture of depression and anxiety. The delay in recognizing PTSD is ironic in light of the extensive reports of "shell shock" from World War I, "traumatic war neuroses" from World War II, and other long-term psychological reactions of holocaust survivors and victims of various civilian disasters.

This long-overdue realization of the high prevalence of stress-related disorders resulted from a confluence of several factors. First of all, the severe and disabling effects of the trauma of the Vietnam War simply would not go away. We now know, as a result of a painstaking survey by the Centers for Disease Control (1988) in Atlanta, that 15% of all Vietnam veterans have suffered PTSD at some time since their service discharge. Second, the devastating effects of incest, sexual abuse, and rape have finally been fully recognized by the psychiatric profession. We now know that somewhere between 38% and 45% of all women have had experiences of childhood sexual abuse (Russell 1986; Wyatt 1985). An investigation of 1,007 randomly selected young adults in Detroit studied exposure to traumatic events of any kind and found a lifetime prevalence of 39.1% (Breslau et al. 1991). The rate of PTSD in those who were exposed was 23.6%, yielding a lifetime prevalence of 9.2%.

In concert with the increasing awareness that PTSD is common, studies have documented the effects of trauma on the individual. In 1976, Horowitz published his landmark work on the impact of trauma on personality. He observed that trauma victims alternate between denying the event and compulsively repeating it through flashbacks or nightmares. Thus the mind attempts to process and organize overwhelming stimuli. Horowitz identified eight common psychological themes that follow severe trauma: 1) grief or sadness, 2) guilt about one's angry or destructive impulses, 3) fear that one will become destructive, 4) guilt about surviving, 5) fear that one will identify with the victims, 6) shame about feeling helpless and empty, 7) fear that one will repeat the trauma, and 8) intense anger directed toward the source of the trauma.

The inclusion of PTSD in the DSM-III category of anxiety disorders has been somewhat controversial, because anxiety is merely one of a whole constellation of symptoms. Indeed, the DSM-IV Advisory Subcommittee voted unanimously to classify PTSD in a new stress-response category (Brett 1993).

Another major controversy in the transition from DSM-III-R to DSM-IV was the nature of the stressor criterion. The DSM-III-R statement that the event needed to be outside the range of usual human experience was so narrow that it excluded patients who had unequivocal posttraumatic symptoms. The data reported by Breslau et al. (1991) document that exposure to traumatic events and PTSD itself are so prevalent that insisting that stressors be outside the range of normal human experience makes little sense. The other aspect of controversy around the stressor criterion involves the individual's subjective response to trauma. Whereas the severity of the posttraumatic symptoms was once thought to be directly proportional to the severity of the stressor, empirical studies suggest otherwise. In a prospective investigation of 51 burn patients (Perry et al. 1992), PTSD was predicted by *smaller* burns, by less perceived emotional support, and by greater emotional distress. More severe or extensive injury did *not* predict posttraumatic symptoms. The findings of this study are in keeping with the growing consensus that PTSD is perhaps more dependent on subjective factors than on the severity of the stressor. Hence, a majority of the DSM-IV Advisory Committee supported a revision of the stressor criterion that would emphasize the individual's subjective response to the event (Kilpatrick and Resnick 1993).

Despite the DSM-IV Advisory Subcommittee's recommendation to create a new stress response category, PTSD was retained in the anxiety disorder section. However, the stressor criterion was significantly changed so that both of the following criteria are required: "1) the person has experienced, witnessed, or been confronted with an event or events that involve actual or threatened death or serious injury, or a threat to the physical integrity of oneself or others; 2) the person's response involved intense fear, helplessness, or horror. Note: In children, it may be expressed instead by disorganized or agitated behavior." These changes address both the subjective factors and the greater prevalence of traumatic events in the general population.

This revision in DSM-IV reflects the importance of careful psychodynamic evaluation of both the meanings the patient assigns to the event and the patient's specific psychological vulnerabilities when assessing various environmental triggers (Ursano 1987; West and Coburn 1984). In the Detroit study (Breslau et al. 1991), it was determined that the risk for developing PTSD could be linked to early separation from parents, neuroticism, family history of anxiety, and preexisting anxiety or depression. The authors concluded that a personal predisposition to develop PTSD was necessary for the symptoms to emerge. The aspects of subjective perception that have been most widely documented involve the experience of extreme fear, the attribution of personal helplessness, the perception of life threat, and the perception of potential for physical violence (March 1993). These specific aspects of the stressor criterion have been incorporated in the DSM-IV revision.

Most people do not develop PTSD even when faced with horrifying trauma. Moreover, events that seem to be relatively low in severity may trigger PTSD in certain individuals because of the subjective meaning assigned to the event. Old traumas may be reawakened by present-day circumstances. Davidson and Foa (1993) suggest that the following predisposing vulnerability factors influence whether or not PTSD develops: 1) genetic-constitutional vulnerability to psychiatric illness; 2) adverse or traumatic experiences in childhood; 3) certain personality characteristics (such as those found in antisocial, dependent, paranoid, and borderline patients); 4) recent life stresses or changes; 5) a compromised or inadequate support system; 6) recent heavy alcohol use; and 7) a perception that the locus of control is external rather than internal.

The DSM-IV criteria focus primarily on circumscribed traumatic events. They do not capture the more complex form of PTSD in which the victim is subjected to prolonged and repeated trauma while in captivity under total control of the perpetrator (Herman 1992). Whereas this syndrome may coexist with the more simple forms of PTSD, a variety of symptoms extend beyond the DSM-IV definition: somatization, dissociation, protracted depression, pathological changes in identity and in relationships, repetition of harm through self-mutilation, and revictimization. Personality disorders are frequently misdiagnosed in this group because the pleomorphic symptom picture may be misunderstood as the survivor's underlying character.

The modern psychodynamic view of PTSD has been greatly influenced by the work of Krystal (1968, 1984, 1988). Through extensive investigations of survivors of Nazi persecution, Krystal has connected impairment in the expression and tolerance of affects to psychic trauma. He noted a high prevalence of psychosomatic diseases both in concentration camp survivors and in veterans of war. Like most psychosomatic patients, these individuals also suffer from alexithymia—the inability to identify or verbalize feeling states. In Krystal's view, psychic trauma in childhood results in an *arrest* of affective development, while trauma in adulthood leads to a *regression* in affective development. The end result in both cases is that survivors of trauma cannot use affects as signals. Because any powerful emotion is viewed as a threat that the original trauma will return, these patients somatize affects or medicate them by abusing prescription drugs. Krystal also observed that in posttraumatic states, these individuals may suffer impairment in their ability to perform self-caring and self-soothing functions. They can no longer relax and calm themselves sufficiently to fall asleep naturally.

The treatment of choice is still unclear at this point. One implication of Krystal's observations about PTSD is that exploratory psychotherapy designed to help "reenact" the trauma may be harmful to these patients. Those with alexithymia will experience only the physiological correlates of the emotional states without registering feelings in the psychological realm, resulting in further deterioration in their psychosomatic condition (Sifneos 1973). Even getting patients to talk about the trauma may be a formidable task. Krystal has pointed out that in situations of incest or child abuse, the victimized children have usually been threatened with disaster if they break their silence. He also has observed characteristic countertransference reactions to victims of disasters. Psychiatrists and other mental health professionals may avoid such patients or regard them with scorn, resulting in less-than-adequate treatment. This countertransference may be exacerbated by a certain subgroup of trauma survivors who feign the syndrome of PTSD or who fiercely hold on to their symptoms with no wish to change. For those patients with preexisting personality disorders, a stressor may represent a convenient nidus for externalizing their problems and disavowing any responsibility for their situation. If PTSD is associated with reimbursement or restitution by the government or other agency, the resistance may intensify. The devastating effects of psychic trauma may well be so unpleasant to confront that treaters will conveniently lump together genuine victims and assorted malingerers.

No treatment is wholly satisfactory for PTSD. Long-term neurobiological alterations in noradrenergic and serotonergic functioning, the hypothalamic-pituitary-adrenocorticol axis, the endogenous opioid system, and the diurnal sleep cycle have led researchers to try to identify a specific medication that could address these changes. Although almost every medication has been tried, double-blind controlled studies indicate that no medication has been successful in completely eradicating the symptoms (Solomon et al. 1992). Both phenelzine and imipramine are superior to placebo in reducing intrusive symptoms (such as nightmares, flashbacks, and intrusive memories), but they do not affect avoidance symptoms. Other antidepressants such as amitriptyline and desipramine seem to affect depressive symptoms but not those of PTSD. Similarly, alprazolam reduces anxiety but not PTSD. Moreover, clinicians should be wary of alprazolam because its short half-life makes the risk of rebound anxiety and serious withdrawal symptoms much greater (Friedman 1991).

Most investigators agree that medication is most useful as an adjunct to psychotherapy (Friedman 1991; Solomon et al. 1992). Different forms of psychotherapy may have differential effects. Brom et al. (1989) compared patients receiving dynamic therapy, hypnotherapy, and systematic desensitization. All three treatment groups showed more improvement in symptom scores than a control group. Dynamic therapy achieved greater reduction in avoidance symptoms but had less impact on intrusive symptoms. The desensitization and hypnotherapy groups showed the reverse pattern. Behavioral techniques have proven to be effective, but the relaxation necessary for behavioral modalities may be difficult for PTSD patients to achieve because of their impaired self-soothing abilities (Krystal 1984).

Individual psychotherapy must be highly personalized for patients suffering from PTSD. Reconstructions of traumatic experiences with accompanying emotional catharsis may be helpful (West and Coburn 1984), but a careful assessment of the patient's ego capacities must precede such therapeutic work. Certain patients will be overwhelmed by such reconstruction and will react with clinical deterioration. The integration of split-off traumatic experiences must be titrated in keeping with a particular patient's capacity for such integration. The therapist may have to contain projected aspects of the traumatized self until the patient is ready to reintegrate them (Peebles 1989). Clinicians must be aware that suicide attempts and suicidal preoccupation may occur with PTSD. In one study of Vietnam veterans suffering from PTSD, Hendin and Haas (1991) found that combat-related guilt was the most significant predictor of the wish to kill oneself. Many of these patients felt that they deserved to be punished because they had been transformed into murderers. Goals of psychotherapy with these patients should be modest in most cases—cure or complete removal of symptoms may be too ambitious. A more reasonable ambition is to halt any further decline, support areas of adequate functioning, and reestablish the patient's personal integrity (Lindy et al. 1984). Some reason for optimism may be construed in the finding that natural remission occurs within 3 months in more than half of all acute PTSD cases following rape (Davidson and Foa 1993), and provision of support may be all that is necessary.

Acute Stress Disorder

A new diagnostic entity, acute stress disorder, was added to DSM-IV after considerable debate about whether it belonged with the dissociative disorders or the anxiety disorders. Although the final decision was to include it with the anxiety disorders, the diagnosis is clearly a hybrid that has elements of both PTSD and dissociative disorders. Acute stress disorder has the same stressor criteria as PTSD—the person must have experienced an event that involves threat of death or serious injury and must have responded to it with intense feelings of helplessness, horror, or fear. However, the symptoms resulting from the stressor must have emerged within 4 weeks of the traumatic event and must have lasted for a minimum of 2 days and a maximum of 4 weeks. In other words, this category allows for PTSD-like syndromes that may appear sooner than PTSD, last for a briefer time, or serve as a prodrome to a more typical case of PTSD.

In addition to criteria that reflect PTSD symptoms (such as re-experiencing the event, avoiding stimuli that arouse memories of the trauma, and displaying hyperarousal), the diagnosis of acute stress disorder also requires at least three of the following dissociative symptoms: amnesia for important aspects of the trauma; depersonalization; derealization; a decreased awareness of one's surroundings; or a subjective sense of detachment, numbing, or lack of emotional responsiveness. The treatment for this condition is fundamentally the same as that for other forms of dissociative disorder and is therefore covered in Chapter 10 under "General Considerations."

Generalized Anxiety Disorder

The DSM-IV criteria for generalized anxiety disorder (GAD) have sought to clarify the boundary between this disorder and normal worry. The anxiety must be excessive, difficult to control, and frequent enough that it occurs more days than not for at least a 6-month period. It must also cause clinically significant distress or impair occupational, social, or other important areas of functioning. The diagnosis requires that the focus of the anxiety not be confined to features of other Axis I disorders, such as worry about having a panic attack, concern about contamination, fear of being embarrassed in public, and so forth. The anxiety must be pervasive enough that the patient focuses on a number of activities or events as targets of the anxiety. The quality of life for GAD patients is materially affected by their continual apprehensions about their future, their current life circumstances, their financial situation, the possibility of harm coming to their family members, and assorted other aspects of life. They may experience physical tension and mild symptoms of sympathetic discharge, but nothing approaching the level of panic disorder.

When psychodynamic clinicians evaluate patients whose chief complaint is anxiety, they must make a critical decision about which treatment to prescribe—a decision that is likely to be influenced by theoretical bias, by political forces in contemporary psychiatry, and by concerns about cost-effectiveness. Shectman et al. (1989) have nicely captured the nature of this dilemma:

> Are we growth facilitators, or are we removers and suppressors of circumscribed psychological distress? Just what is the object of our efforts? In its most extreme form, do we address the problem (i.e., the symptom) in a patient or deal with a patient who has a problem? And who is to make the determination about such matters: the patient?

us? both of us together? But what if there is a difference of opinion about what ought or should be done? (p. 494)

Turning to the literature can, of course, provide essential information to help with such decisions. Numerous studies demonstrate the efficacy of behavioral techniques, pharmacotherapeutic techniques—and even brief dynamic psychotherapy—in treating patients with anxiety. However, large-scale group designs tell clinicians nothing about how to determine which individual is likely to benefit from which treatment (Barlow and Beck 1984).

One of the unfortunate consequences of the revised nomenclature in DSM-III, DSM-III-R, and DSM-IV is that the clinical community now treats anxiety as a disorder in its own right instead of recognizing that in certain cases it is a signal of unconscious turmoil that deserves investigation. In writing about anxiety from a psychoanalytic viewpoint, Appelbaum (1977) referred to it as

a universal, and in that respect normal, phenomenon which may be at any given moment, for any given person, adaptive or maladaptive, too intense or too mild, centered around substitute objects rather than the originally feared ones, an aspect of existential uncertainty or "neurotic" conviction. (p. 164)

The quantitative view of anxiety implies that "less is better." In assessing subjects in the Menninger Foundation Psychotherapy Research Project, 18 of 35 patients showed increased anxiety at termination of psychoanalysis or psychotherapy (Appelbaum 1977). However, 13 of these 18 cases were judged by independent raters to have changed for the better. In evaluating these results, the investigators (Appelbaum 1977; Siegal and Rosen 1962) differentiated between primary anxiety, which is disorganizing to the patient (analogous to panic disorder), and anxiety used as a signal. The researchers noted that an increase in anxiety tolerance—defined as the capacity to experience anxiety without having to discharge it—often occurs as a result of dynamic psychotherapy and reflects expansion of the ego. Many of the improved patients showed a striking capacity to use ideational activity more efficiently in the service of binding anxiety. The investigators concluded that the mere presence or absence of anxiety after treatment was not sufficient to understand or evaluate change. It may well be that greater ego mastery over anxiety allows one to confront certain existential concerns inherent in life in a more forthright manner.

Anxiety appears in response to numerous situations over the course of the life cycle. Whether patients should resort to medication each time they are anxious should be a question of considerable concern to psychiatrists. One can eliminate physiological components of anxiety with medication without addressing the cognitive aspects of the worry that remain. The following clinical vignette is illustrative:

Ms. S. was a 23-year-old graduate student who came for consultation because of periodic episodes of intense anxiety. About three times a month she would begin worrying about death while lying in bed. Typically, she would start ruminating in the following manner: "I am 23 now; in only 7 years, I'll be 30. Then I'll be 40, and my kids will be grown. Then I'll be a grandparent and retire, and then I'll die." These thoughts led to concerns that her parents, both of whom were alive and well, would soon die. As these thoughts escalated, the anxiety she experienced increased to the point where her heart was racing and she could not fall asleep.

After a diagnostic evaluation, several possible interventions were discussed with her: prescription of antianxiety medication, psychotherapeutic exploration of the causes of anxiety, or a combination of the two. She replied pointedly that she had no interest in medication. "How can a pill make my fear of death go away?" she inquired. She made it clear that she wanted to understand the origins of her anxiety so she could master her fears.

She embarked on a course of psychotherapy that led to increasing ideational mastery over the disturbing affect. Her therapist empathized with Ms. S regarding the frightening nature of death but also noted that concerns about living often contributed to fears about death. He asked her what was going on in her life that might contribute to her anxiety. She immediately replied that it had nothing to do with her husband's being stationed overseas. Her eyes started to tear up, and her therapist handed her a box of tissues.

Ms. S ignored the box of tissues and continued talking about how young people were dying of AIDS and cancer. Her therapist asked her why she had not taken a tissue when it was offered to her. She said she thought it would have been a sign of weakness. Her therapist inquired if it had always been difficult for her to acknowledge that she needed the help of other people. She responded that all her life everyone had told her their problems, and she could never acknowledge that she had problems and needed help from others. Her therapist suggested to her that she might need to present a pseudoindependent facade as a way of denying her neediness. She readily acknowledged that she dreaded the feeling of weakness associated with being vulnerable and needy. Her therapist pointed out to her that death was the ultimate situation of vulnerability and neediness. She then responded that the worst thing about death, in her mind, would be having to go through it alone.

As Ms. S continued to explore sources of her anxiety, she revealed a history of having significant difficulties with the expression of anger. She feared that her anger would come out in an explosion that would drive others away from her. Her nighttime anxiety often arose after seeing violent movies. She said it bothered her a great deal that others expressed their anger in such a violent, forthright manner while she worked so diligently to control hers. Further psychotherapeutic exploration led to the uncovering of a good deal of anger at her father that she had been unable to express. Her unconscious concern was that her anger would be so explosive that it would destroy him.

After 2 months of psychotherapy, the episodes of intense anxiety disappeared. Ms. S still worried about death to some extent, but she had developed greater mastery over the fear as she understood the underlying concerns about the impact of her anger and her fears of being abandoned and alone. In other words, a broadened ideational mastery of the affect enabled her to control her symptoms.

The case of Ms. S illustrates the time-honored principle that in clinical psychiatry we must adapt the treatment to the patient. Contrary to the point of view of some third-party payers, the most appropriate treatment for a patient is not necessarily the most cost-effective. While some clinicians would argue that an antianxiety agent might have more quickly and more cheaply eliminated the patient's symptom, Ms. S was asking for something other than symptom relief. As Barber and Luborsky (1991) have argued, specific anxiety disorder diagnoses require different treatments in different circumstances with different patients. Psychodynamic psychotherapy may be the treatment of choice for the patient who is psychologically minded, motivated to understand the matrix from which the symptom arises, and willing to invest the time, money, and effort in a therapy process. Ms. S did not ask for medication and would probably not have taken it if it had been prescribed.

Antianxiety agents may decrease or remove anxiety, but they may ultimately prove to be a dead-end solution. The most obvious problem is that medication is likely to be effective only as long as the patient continues to take it. The frequency of relapse after patients stop taking benzodiazepines, for example, is estimated at 63%–81% (Rickels et al. 1980, 1986). Pharmacotherapeutic measures also fail to address the underlying factors that create the anxiety. Another compelling reason to question the regular use of benzodiazepines for generalized anxiety disorder is that they produce dependence and withdrawal syndromes in nearly half the patients who use them for more than 1 year (Noyes et al. 1988). Even when used in low doses for short-term treatment, benzodiazepines can cause significant withdrawal symptoms in patients with generalized anxiety disorders (Fontaine et al. 1984; Lapierre et al. 1982; Pecknold et al. 1982; Preskorn and Denner 1977). Alprazolam, a benzodiazepine that has enjoyed considerable popularity in recent years, has come to be recognized as causing a particularly thorny set of problems. Besides creating dependence and withdrawal symptoms, this drug's period of effectiveness becomes shorter and shorter over time. Patients find themselves anxiously watching the clock as they await their next dose, and they often report early-morning "rebound," in which they wake up filled with anxiety because the medication's calming effect has worn off (Herman et al. 1987). Although clonazepam seems to alleviate some of these problems, patients may still encounter dependence and withdrawal symptoms (Lydiard et al. 1988).

Alternative nonbenzodiazepine antianxiety agents have been developed to deal with these difficulties, but results with them have also been less than satisfactory. Beta blockers such as propranolol are no more effective in generalized anxiety disorder than placebo (Noyes 1985). Although buspirone eliminates the danger of dependence, it has rather limited efficacy in patients with chronic anxiety. In one study (Rickels et al. 1988), nearly half the subjects discontinued treatment during the first month, while another 26% stopped taking the medication over the next 5 months. The main complaint of these subjects was that their anxiety was not relieved. Moreover, patients who have already tried benzodiazepines derive even less anxiolytic effect from buspirone (Schweizer et al. 1986).

Medication may at times be a crucial short-term adjunct to psychotherapeutic interventions for generalized anxiety disorder. However, it must not be oversold to patients as a definitive treatment for anxiety. Patients need to learn to tolerate anxiety as a meaningful signal in the course of psychotherapy. Those with reasonably good ego strength come to view anxiety as a window into the unconscious.

The treatment of anxiety must begin with a thoughtful and thorough psychodynamic evaluation, with anxiety conceptualized as a multidetermined "tip of the iceberg." The clinician must diagnose the nature of the patient's underlying fear (see Table 9–1). In addition, the role of anxiety in the patient's personality organization must be assessed. What is the ego's capacity to tolerate anxiety and to endure an exploration of the anxiety's origins? Do particular constellations of internal object relations seem to evoke anxiety? Is the anxiety connected with concerns about dissolution of the self? Prescribing the appropriate psychodynamic intervention depends partly on the patient's clinical situation and interests. Some patients may quickly respond well to brief educational and clarifying comments and then require no further treatment. Others, such as Mr. P, who have highly focal symptoms and certain notable ego strengths, may have their anxiety ameliorated with brief dynamic therapy. Neurotic patients with fewer focal complaints and a more thoroughgoing interest in fundamental personality change may require psychoanalysis. Finally, patients with serious character pathology who complain of anxiety, such as Mr. N, will need long-term expressive-supportive psychotherapy before they are likely to experience symptom relief.

References

Abend SM: Psychoanalytic psychotherapy, in Handbook of Phobia Therapy: Rapid Symptom Relief in Anxiety Disorders. Edited by Lindemann C. Northvale, NJ, Jason Aronson, 1989

American Psychiatric Association: Diagnostic and Statistical Manual of Mental Disorders, 3rd Edition. Washington, DC, American Psychiatric Association, 1980

American Psychiatric Association: Diagnostic and Statistical Manual of Mental Disorders, 3rd Edition, Revised. Washington, DC, American Psychiatric Association, 1987

American Psychiatric Association: Diagnostic and Statistical Manual of Mental Disorders, 4th Edition. Washington, DC, American Psychiatric Association 1994

Appelbaum SA: The Anatomy of Change: A Menninger Report on Testing the Effects of Psychotherapy. New York, Plenum, 1977

Baer L, Jenike MA: Introduction, in Obsessive-Compulsive Disorders: Theory and Management. Edited by Jenike MA, Baer L, Minichiello WE. Littleton, MA, PSG Pub Co, 1986, pp 1–9

Ballenger JC, Burrows GD, DuPont RL Jr, et al: Alprazolam in panic disorder and agoraphobia: results from a multicenter trial, I: efficacy in short-term treatment. Arch Gen Psychiatry 45:413–422, 1988

Barber JP, Luborsky L: A psychodynamic view of simple phobia and prescriptive matching: a commentary. Psychotherapy 28:469–472, 1991

Barlow DH, Beck JG: The psychosocial treatment of anxiety disorders: current status, future directions, in Psychotherapy Research: Where Are We and Where Should We Go? Edited by Williams JBW, Spitzer RL. New York, Guilford, 1984, pp 29–69

Baxter LR, Schwartz JM, Bergman KS, et al: Caudate glucose metabolic rate changes with both drug and behavior therapy for obsessive-compulsive disorder. Arch Gen Psychiatry 49:681–689, 1992

Beck AT, Sokol L, Clark DA, et al: A crossover study of focused cognitive therapy for panic disorder. Am J Psychiatry 149:778–783, 1992

Black A: The natural history of obsessional neurosis, in Obsessional States. Edited by Beech HR. London, Methuen, 1974, pp 19–54

Breslau N, Davis GC, Andreski P, et al: Traumatic events and posttraumatic stress disorder in an urban population of young adults. Arch Gen Psychiatry 48:216–222, 1991

Brett EA: Classifications of posttraumatic stress disorder in DSM-IV: anxiety disorder, dissociative disorder, or stress disorder? in Posttraumatic Stress Disorder: DSM-IV and Beyond. Edited by Davidson JRT, Foa EB. Washington, DC, American Psychiatric Press, 1993, pp 191–204

Brom D, Kleber RJ, Defares PB: Brief psychotherapy for posttraumatic stress disorders. J Consult Clin Psychol 57:607–612, 1989

Busch FN, Cooper AM, Klerman GL, et al: Neurophysiological, cognitive-behavioral, and psychoanalytic approaches to panic disorder: toward an integration. Psychoanalytic Inquiry 11:316–332, 1991

Buttolph ML, Holland AD: Obsessive-compulsive disorders in pregnancy and childbirth, in Obsessive-Compulsive Disorders: Theory and Management. Edited by Jenike MA, Baer L, Minichiello WE. Chicago, IL, Year Book Medical, 1990, pp 89–95

Centers for Disease Control Vietnam Experience Study: Health status of Vietnam veterans, I: psychosocial characteristics. JAMA 259:2701–2707, 1988

Clomipramine Collaborative Study Group: Clomipramine in the treatment of patients with obsessive-compulsive disorder. Arch Gen Psychiatry 48:730–738, 1991

Cooper AM: Will neurobiology influence psychoanalysis? Am J Psychiatry 142:1395–1402, 1985

Cornfield RB, Malen RL: A multidimensional view of the obsessive character. Compr Psychiatry 19:73–78, 1978

Coryell W, Noyes R: Placebo response of panic disorder. Am J Psychiatry 145:1138–1140, 1988

Crowe RR, Noyes R, Pauls DL, et al: A family study of panic disorder. Arch Gen Psychiatry 40:1065–1069, 1983

Davidson JRT, Foa EB (eds): Epilogue, in Posttraumatic Stress Disorder: DSM-IV and Beyond. Washington, DC, American Psychiatric Press, 1993, pp 229–235

Elkins R, Rapoport JL, Lipsky A: Obsessive-compulsive disorder of childhood and adolescence: a neurobiological viewpoint. Journal of the American Academy of Child Psychiatry 19:511–524, 1980

Faravelli C, Pallanti S: Recent life events and panic disorder. Am J Psychiatry 146:622–626, 1989

Fontaine R, Chouinard G, Annable L: Rebound anxiety in anxious patients after abrupt withdrawal of benzodiazepine treatment. Am J Psychiatry 141:848–852, 1984

Freud S: On the grounds for detaching a particular syndrome from neurasthenia under the description "anxiety neurosis" (1895), in The Standard Edition of the Complete Psychological Works of Sigmund Freud, Vol 3. Translated and edited by Strachey J. London, Hogarth Press, 1962, pp 85–117

Freud S: Inhibitions, symptoms and anxiety (1926), in The Standard Edition of the Complete Psychological Works of Sigmund Freud, Vol 20. Translated and edited by Strachey J. London, Hogarth Press, 1959, pp 75–175

Friedman MJ: Biological approaches to the diagnosis and treatment of posttraumatic stress disorder. Journal of Traumatic Stress 4(1):67–91, 1991

Gabbard GO, Nemiah JC: Multiple determinants of anxiety in a patient with borderline personality disorder. Bull Menninger Clin 49:161–172, 1985

Gabbard GO: Psychodynamic psychiatry in the decade of the brain. Am J Psychiatry 149:991–998, 1992a

Gabbard GO: Psychodynamics of panic disorder and social phobia. Bull Menninger Clin 56(2) (suppl A):A3–A13, 1992b

Hendin H, Haas AP: Suicide and guilt as manifestations of PTSD in Vietnam combat veterans. Am J Psychiatry 148:586–591, 1991

Herman JL: Complex PTSD: a syndrome in survivors of prolonged and repeated trauma. Journal of Traumatic Stress 5:377–391, 1992

Herman JB, Rosenbaum JF, Brotman AW: The alprazolam to clonazepam switch for the treatment of panic disorder. J Clin Psychopharmacol 7:175–178, 1987

Hollander E, Schiffman E, Cohen B, et al: Signs of central nervous system dysfunction in obsessive-compulsive disorder. Arch Gen Psychiatry 47:27–32, 1990

Horowitz MJ: Stress Response Syndromes. New York, Jason Aronson, 1976

Jenike MA, Baer L, Minichiello WE (eds): Obsessive-Compulsive Disorders: Theory and Management. Littleton, MA, PSG Pub Co, 1986

Kagan J, Reznick JS, Snidman N: Biological bases of childhood shyness. Science 240:167–171, 1988

Kandel ER: From metapsychology to molecular biology: explorations into the nature of anxiety. Am J Psychiatry 140:1277–1293, 1983

Karno M, Golding JM, Sorenson SB: The epidemiology of obsessive-compulsive disorder in five U.S. communities. Arch Gen Psychiatry 45:1094–1099, 1988

Kendler KS, Neale MC, Kessler RC, et al: Childhood parental loss and adult psychopathology in women: a twin study perspective. Arch Gen Psychiatry 49:109–116, 1992a

Kendler KS, Neale MC, Kessler RC, et al: The genetic epidemiology of phobias in women: the interrelationship of agoraphobia, social phobia, situational phobia, and simple phobia. Arch Gen Psychiatry 49:273–281, 1992b

Kilpatrick DG, Resnick HS: Appendix III: a description of the posttraumatic stress disorder field trial, in Posttraumatic Stress Disorder: DSM-IV and Beyond. Edited by Davidson JRT, Foa EB. Washington, DC, American Psychiatric Press, 1993, pp 243–250

Klein DF: Delineation of two drug-responsive anxiety syndromes. Psychopharmacologia 5:397–408, 1964

Krystal H (ed): Massive Psychic Trauma. New York, International Universities Press, 1968

Krystal H: Psychoanalytic views on human emotional damages, in Post-Traumatic Stress Disorder: Psychological and Biological Sequelae. Edited by van der Kolk BA. Washington, DC, American Psychiatric Press, 1984, pp 1–28

Krystal H: Integration and Self-Healing: Affect, Trauma, Alexithymia. Hillsdale, NJ, Analytic Press, 1988

Lapierre YD, Tremblay A, Gagnon A, et al: A therapeutic and discontinuation study of clobazam and diazepam in anxiety neurosis. J Clin Psychiatry 43:372–374, 1982

Lieberman J: Evidence for a biological hypothesis of obsessive-compulsive disorder. Neuropsychobiology 11:14–21, 1984

Lindy JD, Grace MC, Green BL: Building a conceptual bridge between civilian trauma and war trauma: preliminary psychological findings from a clinical sample of Vietnam veterans, in Post-Traumatic Stress Disorder: Psychological and Biological Sequelae. Edited by van der Kolk BA. Washington, DC, American Psychiatric Press, 1984, pp 43–57

Luxenberg JS, Swedo SE, Flament MF, et al: Neuroanatomical abnormalities in obsessive-compulsive disorder detected with quantitative X-ray computed tomography. Am J Psychiatry 145:1089–1093, 1988

Lydiard RB, Roy-Byrne PP, Ballenger JC: Recent advances in the psychopharmacological treatment of anxiety disorders. Hosp Community Psychiatry 39:1157–1165, 1988

March JS: What constitutes a stressor? the "criterion A" issue, in Posttraumatic Stress Disorder: DSM-IV and Beyond. Edited by Davidson JRT, Foa EB. Washington, DC, American Psychiatric Press, 1993, pp 37–54

Marks IM: Review of behavioral psychotherapy, I: obsessive-compulsive disorders. Am J Psychiatry 138:584–592, 1981

Mavissakalian MR: The placebo effect in agoraphobia, II. J Nerv Ment Dis 176:446–448, 1988

Mavissakalian MR, Jones B, Olson S: Absence of placebo response in obsessive-compulsive disorder. J Nerv Ment Dis 178:268–270, 1990

Milrod B, Shear MK: Psychodynamic treatment of panic: three case histories. Hosp Community Psychiatry 42:311–312, 1991

Nemiah JC: A psychoanalytic view of phobias. Am J Psychoanal 41:115–120, 1981

Nemiah JC: The psychodynamic view of anxiety, in Diagnosis and Treatment of Anxiety Disorders. Edited by Pasnau RO. Washington, DC, American Psychiatric Press, 1984, pp 115–137

Nemiah JC: Psychoneurotic disorders, in The New Harvard Guide to Psychiatry. Edited by Nicholi AM Jr. Cambridge, MA, Belknap Press of Harvard University Press, 1988, pp 234–258

Neziroglu F, Anemone R, Yaryura-Tobias JA: Onset of obsessive-compulsive disorder in pregnancy. Am J Psychiatry 149:947–950, 1992

Noyes R Jr: Beta-adrenergic blocking drugs in anxiety and stress. Psychiatr Clin North Am 8:119–132, 1985

Noyes R Jr, Garvey MJ, Cook BL, et al: Benzodiazepine withdrawal: a review of the evidence. J Clin Psychiatry 49:382–389, 1988

Pecknold JC, McClure DJ, Fleuri D, et al: Benzodiazepine withdrawal effects. Prog Neuropsychopharmacol Biol Psychiatry 6:517–522, 1982

Peebles MJ: Posttraumatic stress disorder: a historical perspective on diagnosis and treatment. Bull Menninger Clin 53:274–286, 1989

Perry S, Difede J, Musngi G, et al: Predictors of posttraumatic stress disorder after burn injury. Am J Psychiatry 149:931–935, 1992

Perse T: Obsessive-compulsive disorder: a treatment review. J Clin Psychiatry 49:48–55, 1988

Pollard CA, Henderson JG: Four types of social phobia in a community sample. J Nerv Ment Dis 176:440–445, 1988

Preskorn SH, Denner LJ: Benzodiazepines and withdrawal psychosis: report of three cases. JAMA 237:36–38, 1977

Rachman S, Hodgson R: Obsessions and Compulsions. Englewood Cliffs, NJ, Prentice-Hall, 1980

Redmond DE Jr: Studies of the nucleus locus coeruleus in monkeys and hypotheses for neuropsychopharmacology, in Psychopharmacology: The Third Generation of Progress. Edited by Meltzer HY. New York, Raven, 1987, pp 967–983

Regier DA, Boyd JH, Burke JD, et al: One-month prevalence of mental disorders in the United States. Arch Gen Psychiatry 45:977–986, 1988

Reich JH: DSM-III personality disorders and the outcome of treated panic disorder. Am J Psychiatry 145:1149–1152, 1988

Rickels K, Case WG, Diamond L: Relapse after short-term drug therapy in neurotic outpatients. International Pharmacopsychiatry 15:186–192, 1980

Rickels K, Case WG, Downing RW, et al: One-year follow-up of anxious patients treated with diazepam. J Clin Psychopharmacol 6:32–36, 1986

Rickels K, Schweizer E, Csanalosi I, et al: Long-term treatment of anxiety and risk of withdrawal: prospective comparison of clorazepate and buspirone. Arch Gen Psychiatry 45:444–450, 1988

Rosenbaum JF, Biederman J, Bolduc EA, et al: Comorbidity of parental anxiety disorders as risk for childhood-onset anxiety in inhibited children. Am J Psychiatry 149:475–481, 1992

Roy-Byrne PP, Geraci M, Uhde TW: Life events of the onset of panic disorder. Am J Psychiatry 143:1424–1427, 1986

Russell DEH: The Secret Trauma: Incest in the Lives of Girls and Women. New York, Basic Books, 1986

Schneier FR, Johnson J, Hornig CD, et al: Social phobia: comorbidity and morbidity in an epidemiological sample. Arch Gen Psychiatry 49:282–288, 1992

Schweizer E, Rickels K, Lucki I: Resistance to anti-anxiety effect of buspirone in patients with a history of benzodiazepine use (letter). N Engl J Med 314:719–720, 1986

Shear MK, Fyer AJ, Ball G, et al: Vulnerability to sodium lactate in panic disorder patients given cognitive-behavioral therapy. Am J Psychiatry 148:795–797, 1991

Shectman F, Ross JL, Simpson W: Controversial issues in psychodynamic and symptom-focused treatment. Bull Menninger Clin 53:493–500, 1989

Siegal RS, Rosen IC: Character style and anxiety tolerance: a study of intrapsychic change, in Research in Psychotherapy, Vol II. Edited by Strupp H, Luborsky L. Baltimore, MD, French-Bray Printing Co, 1962, pp 206–217

Sifneos PE: Short-Term Psychotherapy and Emotional Crisis. Cambridge, MA, Harvard University Press, 1972

Sifneos PE: The prevalence of "alexithymic" characteristics in psychosomatic patients. Psychother Psychosom 22:257–262, 1973

Solomon SD, Gerrity ET, Muff AM: Efficacy of treatment of posttraumatic stress disorder: an empirical review. JAMA 268:633–638, 1992

Torgersen S: Genetic factors in anxiety disorders. Arch Gen Psychiatry 40: 1085–1089, 1983

Turner SM, Beidel DC, Nathan RS: Biological factors in obsessive-compulsive disorder. Psychol Bull 97:430–450, 1985

Ursano RJ: Posttraumatic stress disorder: the stressor criterion (commentary). J Nerv Ment Dis 175:273–275, 1987

Waldinger RJ, Gunderson JG: Effective Psychotherapy with Borderline Patients: Case Studies. New York, Macmillan, 1987

West LJ, Coburn K: Posttraumatic anxiety, in Diagnosis and Treatment of Anxiety Disorders. Edited by Pasnau RO. Washington, DC, American Psychiatric Press, 1984, pp 79–133

White K, Cole JO: Is there a drug treatment for obsessive-compulsive disorder? (forum). Harvard Medical School Mental Health Letter 5(3):8, 1988

Wyatt GE: The sexual abuse of Afro-American and White-American women in childhood. Child Abuse Negl 9:507–519, 1985

Zetin M, Kramer MA: Obsessive-compulsive disorder. Hosp Community Psychiatry 43:689–699, 1992

Zetzel ER: The Capacity for Emotional Growth. New York, International Universities Press, 1970

Zitrin CM, Klein DF, Woerner MG: Behavior therapy, supportive psychotherapy, imipramine, and phobias. Arch Gen Psychiatry 35:307–316, 1978

Chapter 10

Dissociative Disorders

At the dawn of dynamic psychiatry, two men, Janet and Freud, were perplexed by a variety of hysterical phenomena they were observing. To explain altered states of consciousness such as amnesia and fugue, Janet postulated that memories of trauma persist as relatively unassimilated fixed ideas that serve as foci for the development of such states. He suggested that under specific circumstances, nervous energies holding mental functions together could be lowered sufficiently that certain functions would escape central control, a process he referred to as dissociation.

Freud, on the other hand, postulated the concept of repression, an active banishment of certain mental contents from conscious awareness into the domain of the dynamic unconscious. While these unacceptable feelings remained out of awareness, they continued to be active in the unconscious mind and might reemerge in the form of symptoms. Freud and Janet parted ways on this point, in that Freud postulated that hysterical phenomena resulted from active mental processes, while Janet argued for the role of passive mental processes (Nemiah 1989).

Psychiatric interest in dissociation waned for many years, but now, a century later, dissociative disorders have recaptured center stage in the field of psychiatry. The growth of psychiatric attention to these phenomena parallels the rise in awareness of the centrality of trauma

in the etiology and pathogenesis of many disorders. Indeed, the literature on posttraumatic stress disorder has burgeoned in the last decade
along with the exponential increase in writings on dissociative disorders. Dissociation is, above all, a response to trauma, and some would
argue that most dissociative syndromes are posttraumatic disorders
(Putnam 1985; Spiegel 1991b).

The prevalence of dissociative psychopathology within the general
public may be as high as 5%–10% (Ross et al. 1990; Ross 1991). Minor
instances of dissociation, such as "highway hypnosis," transient feelings of strangeness, or "spacing out," are even more common. If one
regards the unity of consciousness as an achievement rather than a
given (Spiegel 1991b), the ubiquity of dissociative phenomena comes
as no surprise. The most comprehensively studied dissociative disorder, multiple personality disorder (MPD), occurs at a rate of approximately 3.3% of all inpatient admissions to psychiatric units (Ross et al.
1991).

The primary function of dissociation is to serve as a protective response to overwhelming trauma. Ludwig (1983) has noted its similarity to the freezing and sham-death reflexes in lower species when
confronted with predators, suggesting that there may be Darwinian
survival value in the defense. Dissociation is certainly adaptive for a
child faced with trauma in that it allows an escape from a horrific reality situation, provides a way to isolate catastrophic experience, au-
tomatizes behaviors, and suggests a means of resolving irreconcilable
conflicts. To a large degree, dissociative phenomena constitute a new
paradigm for psychoanalysis and dynamic psychiatry (Loewenstein
and Ross 1992). Psychoanalytic thinking traditionally has focused on
unconscious wishes, needs, and drives in concert with the defenses
against them. From an etiological perspective, intrapsychic fantasy
has played a greater role than external trauma. Dissociative disorders
have leveled the playing field so that psychodynamic clinicians must
now give equal (or greater) weight to the pathogenetic influences of
real events.

Pathological forms of dissociation are identified by disturbances or
alterations in the normally integrative functions of memory, identity,
or consciousness (Putnam 1991). DSM-IV (American Psychiatric Association 1994) includes the following diagnostic entities within the category of dissociative disorders: dissociative identity disorder (multiple
personality disorder), depersonalization disorder, dissociative disorder
not otherwise specified, dissociative amnesia, and dissociative fugue

(these last two disorders have been changed from psychogenic amnesia and psychogenic fugue in DSM-III-R [American Psychiatric Association 1987] to make them compatible with the International Classification of Diseases [ICD]).

General Considerations

Before delving into the specific dissociative disorders, some general considerations about the phenomenon of dissociation are necessary to provide a background context for understanding the individual dissociative disorders. The link between hypnotizability and dissociation has been observed for many years, and it has been well documented that hysterical patients who manifest dissociative symptoms are also highly hypnotizable (Bliss 1980; Spiegel 1984; Spiegel and Fink 1979; Steingard and Frankel 1985). Dissociation and hypnotizability are closely related but different phenomena that are difficult to distinguish in groups high in both capacities (Frankel 1990). Many symptoms typical of dissociative disorders can be elicited with hypnosis in certain subjects who are highly hypnotizable (Putnam 1991). Spiegel (1990) has referred to hypnosis as "controlled dissociation elicited in a structured setting" (p. 247). Hypnosis and severe states of dissociation have in common the characteristic of complete absorption in certain aspects of experience while keeping other aspects out of awareness.

As just noted, dissociation arises as a defense against trauma. Spiegel (1990) has observed that most of the principal symptoms of posttraumatic stress disorder (PTSD) have a dissociative quality about them. Empirical research has also established that combat veterans with PTSD have higher rates of dissociation than do comparable veterans without PTSD (Bremner et al. 1992). Similar observations have been made about the relationship between childhood physical or sexual abuse and dissociative symptoms. Chu and Dill (1990) found that 63% of a sample of 98 female psychiatric inpatients had a history of childhood sexual or physical abuse. Of this group, 83% had dissociative symptom scores above the median. Their data confirm that significantly higher levels of dissociative symptoms are found in patients with a history of childhood abuse as compared with those without such a history. Hence among those who have the capacity, dissociation can be considered an integral part of the short-range and long-range way that some people adapt to trauma. Dissociative defenses perform the dual function of helping victims remove themselves from the trauma at the time it occurs while also delaying the necessary working-through that places it in perspective with the rest of their lives. Approximately 25%–50% of trauma victims experience some kind of detachment from the trauma, while others have partial to total amnesia for the event (Spiegel 1991a). These mental mechanisms allow victims to compartmentalize the experience so that it is no longer accessible to consciousness—it is as though the trauma did not happen to them.

Both repression and dissociation are defense mechanisms, and in both, the contents of the mind are banished from awareness. They differ, however, in the way the dismissed mental contents are handled. In the case of repression, a *horizontal split* is created by the repression barrier, and the material is transferred to the dynamic unconscious. By contrast, a *vertical split* is created in dissociation so that mental contents exist in a series of parallel consciousnesses (Kluft 1991a). Moreover, the repression model has usually been invoked as a response to forbidden wishes, such as oedipal desires for the opposite-sex parent, rather than to external events. Hence, dissociation may be mobilized by trauma, while repression is activated by highly conflictual wishes (Spiegel 1990). Once mobilized, however, dissociation can be reactivated by wishes and desires.

In most cases of dissociation, disparate self-schemas, or representations of the self, must be maintained in separate mental compartments because they are in conflict with one another (Horowitz 1986). Memories of the traumatized self must be dissociated because they are inconsistent with the everyday self that appears to be in full control. One manager of a convenience store, for example, had dissociated a trauma involving anal rape during a holdup of the store because the image of himself as subjugated and humiliated in that situation was completely in conflict with his usual sense of himself as a manager who could "take charge" of all situations.

The treatment of acute traumatic dissociative reactions must take into account this difficulty in integrating the traumatized self with the established self-concept and move cautiously in the direction of integrating traumatic memories so that the established view of the self can slowly assimilate the traumatized self without being overwhelmed by it. Similarly, patients must be allowed to maintain control of their memories to avoid feeling the profound sense of helplessness they experienced during the trauma. Spiegel (1991a) suggested that hypnosis may be useful in this regard because the on-off quality of the hypnotic state reassures the patients that they have control of turning off memories that are too unbearable to face. Also, guilt and shame connected with the humiliation of the trauma must be faced because these feelings often get in the way of confronting the helplessness the patients feel by contributing to a fantasy that they actually could have controlled the situation if they had only done something differently. The trauma must ultimately be confronted if the dissociation is to resolve, and the therapist can play a crucial role in titrating the patient's exposure to the trauma in manageable doses.

The foregoing description of dissociation, the psychodynamic understanding of the phenomenon, and the treatment principles outlined are useful in many of the dissociative disorders not otherwise specified, as well as in acute stress disorder (classified with the anxiety disorders [see Chapter 9]), dissociative amnesia, and dissociative fugue. Dissociative amnesia and dissociative fugue are focal forms of dissociative disorder. Dissociative amnesia involves one or more episodes of inability to recall important personal trauma, while dissociative fugue involves sudden, unexpected travel away from home associated with the inability to recall one's past and confusion about one's personal identity. While other symptoms (such as depression, anxiety, and hyperarousal) are secondary to trauma and often accompany dissociative disorders, these additional symptoms are generally refractory to treatment unless the dissociative process is directly addressed (Putnam 1991).

Dissociative Identity Disorder (Multiple Personality Disorder)

Few disorders in psychiatry have been as controversial as dissociative identity disorder, or what has traditionally been called multiple personality disorder (MPD) (the two names for this disorder will be used interchangeably in this chapter). Much like the patients who suffer from it, the disorder itself has had to struggle for survival. Once thought to be either a fabrication or a one-in-a-million rarity, MPD was accorded attention primarily in the popular media and in books marketed to the lay public. Over the last two decades, however, a remarkably comprehensive scientific literature has appeared that now allows us to characterize the disorder with considerable precision. One can speculate that society's willingness to acknowledge the alarming prevalence of sexual and physical abuse of children has persuaded the scientific community to take dissociative disorders such as MPD much more seriously.

Kluft (1991a) has defined MPD as "a complex, chronic, dissociative psychopathology characterized by disturbances of memory and identity. It is distinguished from other mental disorders by the ongoing coexistence of relatively consistent but alternating subjectively separate identities and recurrent episodes of memory distortion, frank amnesia, or both" (p. 161). The condition is found in females nine times as often as in males and can be difficult to diagnose. In contrast to the dramatic and florid cases occasionally showcased in the media, most MPD patients are highly secretive and prefer to conceal their symptoms. In a typical case, an average of 7 years of treatment (during which numerous diagnostic labels have been applied) have elapsed before the MPD diagnosis is established (Loewenstein and Ross 1992; Putnam et al. 1986). Diagnosis is particularly problematic because 80% of MPD patients have only certain "windows of diagnosability" during which their condition is clearly discernible to clinicians (Kluft 1991a). Diagnostic rigor has been improved by a screening instrument known as the Dissociative Experiences Scale (DES), a 28-item self-report questionnaire that is both reliable and valid (Putnam 1991). Although the DES can be used effectively to identify high-risk patients, a definitive diagnosis must be established by structured interviews such as the Dissociative Disorders Interview Schedule (Ross 1989) or the Structured Clinical Interview for DSM-III-R Dissociative Disorders (SCID-D) (Steinberg et al. 1991).

When clinicians are diagnosing a disorder known as *multiple personality,* they must at all times remain cognizant that the appellation is something of a misnomer. DSM-IV recognizes this problem by changing the official nomenclature to dissociative identity disorder (DID). The patient's personality actually consists of the sum total of all the "personalities" (generally referred to as *alters*) and their interactions with one another (Coons 1984; Kluft 1984a; Putnam 1989). Putnam (1989) clarified that alters are "highly discrete states of consciousness organized around a prevailing affect, sense of self (including body image), with a limited repertoire of behaviors and a set of state-dependent memories" (p. 103). If the alters present themselves in the course of a clinical interview, the diagnosis is not much of a challenge. However, since the majority of patients attempt to keep their symptoms hidden, most DID patients present rather formidable diagnostic problems. Consequently, the clinician must maintain a high index of suspicion when taking a history and interviewing new patients.

Kluft (1991a) provided a checklist of items that should cause an interviewer to consider the diagnosis of MPD. Because well over 95% of patients with MPD have a history of childhood physical and/or sexual abuse, inquiries about such matters should be a routine part of a psychiatric diagnostic evaluation. Patients with a variety of diagnoses and a history of previous treatment failures also may raise suspicions about the diagnosis. A pleomorphic symptom picture, with fluctuating levels of function, severe headaches, or other pain syndromes may be part of the picture. Clinicians should be particularly active in asking patients about episodes of amnesia, distortions or lapses in time, instances in which others have told them they did things that they themselves cannot remember, and inability to recall childhood events during the latency years from ages 6 to 11. Patients may also give a history of discovering objects in their possession that they cannot remember acquiring or handwriting that they cannot recognize. Particular types of visual and auditory hallucinations also suggest MPD. Distinct voices experienced as "in the head" and with specific attributes, often urging the patient to action, are common in patients suffering from MPD (Kluft 1991a; Putnam 1991). Visual hallucinations may be vivid and involve complex scenes that represent flashbacks of trauma (Putnam 1991). When patients make passing reference to themselves as "we" or comment on themselves in the third person, the possibility of multiplicity should be considered.

Experienced clinicians can be more direct in their pursuit of alters. Some will attempt to elicit other entities through a drug-facilitated interview or through hypnosis. Alternatively, clinicians can focus on particularly perplexing events, amnestic periods, or sexual experiences and attempt to probe for further information. In some cases this form of inquiry will precipitate the spontaneous emergence of alters (Kluft 1991b). When one female patient with MPD hesitated while talking about her experiences with a former boyfriend, the interviewer asked her to elaborate on that relationship. His focused inquiries caused her to shift into a child alter who was 7 years old. Another technique that is sometimes fruitful is to ask, "Is there anyone else there that I should talk to?"

While the average number of alters is approximately 13 to 15, Kluft (1988) has pointed out that usually 6 or fewer of the alters spend significant amounts of time in executive control of the patient. Moreover, the mean is inflated by complex cases in which 26 or more alters are present. Realizing that the mode is 3 and the median is 8 to 10 places the numbers in clearer perspective.

The separate "personalities" begin adaptively as a way in which patients convince themselves that childhood trauma is occurring to "someone else." They soon gain secondary forms of autonomy and may hold a quasi-delusional belief in their separateness, even to the point that they believe they can mutilate their bodies or otherwise behave self-destructively without really hurting themselves (Kluft 1991a). Alters are well known to present differences in handedness, handwriting, voice, and dialect, and may be named or nameless. Significant differences in brain electrical activity across alters has been demonstrated by spontaneous EEG and visually evoked potentials (Putnam 1991), and optical differences have also been documented (Miller 1989).

The diagnostic criteria for DID (or MPD) have been revised slightly in DSM-IV. First, while DSM-III-R required that more than one personality have *full* control at recurrent times, the new criteria have modified that stipulation in acknowledgment of the fact that in many cases of DID, one alter may impinge on another or may order another to do something. The second and more controversial change has been to reintroduce the amnesia criterion (see Table 10–1). While in most cases the primary personality is indeed amnestic for the alters, some

---

Table 10–1. DSM-IV criteria for dissociative identity disorder (multiple personality disorder)

A. The presence of two or more distinct identities or personality states (each with its own relatively enduring pattern of perceiving, relating to, and thinking about the environment and self).

B. At least two of these identities or personality states recurrently take control of the person's behavior.

C. Inability to recall important personal information that is too extensive to be explained by ordinary forgetfulness.

D. Not due to the direct effects of a substance (e.g., blackouts or chaotic behavior during alcohol intoxication) or a general medical condition (e.g., complex partial seizures). Note: In children, the symptoms are not attributable to imaginary playmates or other fantasy play.

Source. DSM-IV. Because the criteria sets were not final at press time, the reader should consult DSM-IV for final criteria.

experts have pointed out that this situation is variable (Kluft 1991a) and that many DID patients go through periods during which the amnesia barrier is more permeable than usual. They may also experience amnesia for their amnesia.

Psychodynamic Understanding

An attempt to understand this most perplexing disorder must begin with an examination of its origins. The current thinking about the etiology of MPD is succinctly summarized in the four-factor theory proposed by Kluft (1984b), which includes the following criteria: 1) the capacity to dissociate defensively in the face of trauma must be present; 2) traumatically overwhelming life experiences, such as physical and sexual abuse, exceed the child's adaptational capacities and usual defensive operations; 3) the precise form taken by the dissociative defenses in the process of alter formation are determined by shaping influences and available substrates; and 4) soothing and restorative experiences by caretakers or significant others are unavailable so that the child experiences a profound inadequacy of stimulus barriers.

One clear implication of the four-factor etiological model is that trauma is necessary but not sufficient to cause MPD. At the risk of stating the obvious, not everyone who is abused as a child develops MPD. Psychodynamic thinking has a significant contribution to make in understanding the factors that lead to the full-blown syndrome. The concepts of intrapsychic conflict and deficit are relevant in MPD just as they are in other conditions (Marmer 1991). Traumatic experience may lead to a variety of conflicts around such issues as guilt over sexual arousal or guilt over collusion with the abusers. Kluft's fourth factor, the lack of soothing caretakers to whom the child can turn, is a major contributor to deficit in MPD. In van der Kolk's (1987) extensive study of trauma in primates and human beings, he concluded that the availability of a soothing caretaker who can be unconditionally trusted when self-soothing capacities are inadequate is by far the most important factor in overcoming the impact of psychological trauma. Marmer (1991) has suggested that in the absence of nurturing adults, children who ultimately develop MPD must use themselves (or their alters) as transitional objects.

Ganaway (1989) has expanded on Kluft's third factor, regarding the formation of dissociative defenses, by focusing on how characterological features and specific characteristics of memory and cognition converge in highly hypnotizable individuals. Moreover, he has examined the authenticity of trauma memories in the context of the role that fantasy plays in memory. A more detailed discussion of these issues will be undertaken in the section on treatment considerations.

Self-destructive behaviors in MPD patients cry out for psychodynamic explanation. Revictimization is a pattern of behavior that MPD patients share with other victims of incest and childhood abuse (Browne and Finkelhor 1986; van der Kolk 1989). Rape, prostitution, and sexual exploitation by therapists all occur at higher rates with incest victims than with others. Some gender differences exist in this pattern of re-creation of victimization. Abused men and boys tend to identify with their aggressors and later victimize others as adults, whereas women who were abused become attached to abusive men and allow themselves and their offspring to be victimized further (Carmen et al. 1984).

Often, children who grow up in families in which parents abuse them do not have soothing caretakers to whom they can turn to mitigate the trauma. In the absence of such persons, the victims turn to their tormentors (van der Kolk 1989), and this pattern of object relationships persists into adulthood when they look for partners who will continue the "dance" they established as children. Abused children come to believe that an abusive parent is better than no parent at all. The predictability of such relationships helps them defend against the threat of abandonment: the devil one knows is often better than the devil one does not know. The repetition of traumatic relationships is also an example of an attempt to actively master passively experienced trauma. The victims seek to have more control over what was completely outside their control as children.

The intergenerational dimensions of sexual abuse are well known (Carmen et al. 1984; Gelinas 1986; van der Kolk 1989). Parents who abuse their children tend to be abuse victims themselves. In many cases these parents are outraged that their innocence was taken away from them at such a tender age. They may experience profound envy of their own children's innocence, so through the abuse of their children, they enviously attack and spoil what was similarly taken from them (Grotstein 1992).

When MPD patients recall their childhood sexual abuse, they often blame themselves for the events that occurred to them. It is commonplace to hear them refer to themselves as "sluts" or "whores" who deserve what they got. As children they frequently held on to the belief that they received such punishment because they were bad children who had misbehaved. Although to some extent this shame and guilt can be explained by introjective identifications with "bad" parents, the self-blame can also be understood as a desperate attempt to make sense out of a horrific situation. For small children to believe that the world is a malevolent place in which they are subject to random acts of violence is profoundly chilling. Alternatively, if they can believe that their parents are basically good people who have their own interests at heart, their experience makes more sense. The fact that their parents treat them the way they do must reflect that they are bad and deserve it. When clinicians try to persuade these patients that what happened was not their fault, the patients often feel that they are misunderstood. There may be an adaptive aspect to this posture in abuse victims. Women who have been raped have a better prognosis if they blame themselves, because the locus of control is perceived as internal rather than external, and as a result, there is a diminished sense of helplessness (van der Kolk 1989).

One of the most controversial psychodynamic issues involves the relationship between dissociation and splitting. This debate is usually cast in terms of whether MPD patients are similar to or different from patients with borderline personality disorder (BPD). Empirical research has presented a mixed picture regarding this controversy. In one sample of MPD patients, 70% also qualified for a diagnosis of BPD (Horevitz and Braun 1984). In another study in which Minnesota Multiphasic Personality Inventory (MMPI) scores of 10 MPD patients were compared with those of 10 BPD patients, no significant differences were found (Kemp et al. 1988). To complicate matters further, the role of childhood trauma in the etiology of BPD has now been extensively documented (Herman et al. 1989; Nigg et al. 1991; Ogata et al. 1990; Westen et al. 1990; Zanarini et al. 1989).

On the other hand, one study of MPD patients that used psychological testing found that these patients have higher levels of ego organization than do typical borderline patients (Armstrong and Loewenstein 1990). They were able to experience others as "whole objects" rather than split part objects, and they lacked the typical ego weaknesses seen in borderline patients. In Kluft's (1991a) study of MPD patients, he noted that one-third rapidly ceased to show borderline features after they had settled into treatment, one-third lost their apparent BPD as their MPD resolved, and one-third retained BPD features even after their personalities had been integrated. He concluded that MPD may generate a "phenocopy" of BPD and that only a small minority of MPD patients actually have true BPD. Kluft has also suggested that clinicians should not make the diagnosis of BPD in an MPD patient unless the borderline criteria are present across several different personalities.

There is a general tendency within the MPD literature to stress the ways in which dissociation is different from splitting. Young (1988) noted that alters tend not to be polarized around contradictory ego states, but rather have many overlapping characteristics. Marmer (1991) argued that whereas in MPD the self is split more than the objects, the reverse is true in BPD. Kluft (1991b) has pointed out that dissociation differs from splitting in three ways: first, it is associated with a psychobiological switching process; second, the different states that result have significantly different psychophysiological characteristics; and finally, in contrast to splitting, amnestic barriers are often constructed between alters. Davies and Frawley (1992) distinguish dissociation from splitting on the basis that the former involves a cleavage of ego states, while the latter involves a division between a good object and a bad object—a point also made by Kluft (1991c).

A careful examination of the mechanisms of dissociation and splitting suggests that they have both similarities and differences (P. Lerner, "Some Thoughts on Dissociation" [unpublished manuscript], 1992). Both are characterized by active separation and compartmentalization of mental contents. Both are used defensively to ward off unpleasant experiences and affects. Both are disruptive to the formation of a smooth and continuous sense of self. On the other hand, they differ in terms of which ego functions are disrupted. Kernberg (1975) made it clear that impulse control and tolerance for anxiety and frustration are specifically impaired in splitting. By contrast, in dissociation, memory and consciousness are affected. Finally, dissociation is a broader mechanism than splitting—a variety of divisions occur in dissociation, not simply separations into polarized extremes of affective valence.

The literature on dissociation in MPD has focused almost exclusively on the divisions in the self while taking little notice of the corresponding division of objects linked to the self-representations. Fairbairn (1940/1952, 1944/1952) was the first to stress that the child internalizes not an object but an *object relationship.* Davies and Frawley (1992) made note of this dimension when they commented that dissociation is not only a defense but also a process that protects and preserves the entire internal object world of the abused child in split-off form. Citing Fairbairn's thinking, Grotstein (1992) has reached similar conclusions: "All mental cleavages are based ultimately on the divisions of perceptions and experiences in regard to objects—and the selves related to each of them. Thus, the dissociation that typifies the multiple personality disorder constitutes, from this point of view, a division of the ego into vertical splits based upon corresponding vertical splits in one's incompatible experiences of the object" (p. 68).

One of the practical implications of this conceptualization is that each alter presents a self in relationship to a fantasied internal object. Ganaway (1989) has recognized this linkage in his observation that two common transference-countertransference scenarios based on internal object relationships are 1) a safe and loved child self in relation to an unconditionally loving, good parent, and 2) a victimized, disbelieved, and betrayed child self in relation to an abusive or abuse-enabling parent. In some cases an alter may also represent an internal object rather than a self. This state of affairs is most prominent when one of the alters clearly plays the role of the abusive internalized parent. In this case the alter exists with a corresponding fantasy of a self to which it relates. While this view of the MPD patient's internal world is highly complex, it is of crucial importance in effective psychotherapy.

Treatment Considerations

The treatment of choice for multiple personality disorder is individual dynamically oriented expressive-supportive psychotherapy, augmented with hypnosis when necessary (Kluft 1991a). Despite the bleak and traumatic nature of these patients' early experiences, the prognosis for patients who are motivated to work in psychotherapy is positive. However, the treatment must address the multiplicity directly, because the syndrome will not remit spontaneously without psychotherapy specifically tailored to resolve it (Kluft 1985). The psychotherapeutic process proceeds most favorably if two sessions are allotted per week.

Loewenstein and Ross (1992) conceptualized the psychotherapy as occurring at two different levels of abstraction. At one level, the alters are worked with as more or less concrete entities whose barriers must be broken down. At a more abstract level, the whole system of "personalities" is regarded as the "real" person, and psychotherapy proceeds along classical ego-psychological lines, in which dissociative defenses are relinquished and replaced by more mature defenses.

The psychotherapy of patients with MPD is generally long and arduous. There is no definitive brief psychotherapy for this condition. Kluft (1991a, 1991b) has outlined a set of guidelines for the successful psychotherapy of MPD. It must begin with the establishment of a firm and secure treatment frame. Because of the history of boundary violations in these patients, such details as length of session, payment of fees, appointment times, and use of words rather than touch must all be established from the beginning. A strong therapeutic alliance is crucial for the treatment to proceed, and this may be facilitated by a self psychological approach of empathizing with the patient's subjective experience during the opening phase of the therapy. Alliances will need to be made with alters as well as with the host personality—in particular, agreements not to hurt the patient, not to sabotage the treatment, and not to take flight. The therapist must take an active role in emphasizing cooperation, identification, empathy, and collaboration among the alters, so that their conflicts are minimized and their separateness ultimately becomes redundant. To accomplish this integration, therapists must be fair-minded and not play favorites with any of the alters, nor should they significantly change their behavior when relating to the different personalities.

After cooperation among the alters has been established and the patient-therapist alliance is solid, efforts must be made to uncover traumas from the past and help the patient abreact. The therapist's job is to titrate and process the material in a way that the patient can tolerate. Kluft's "rule of thirds" is helpful in this regard—the therapist and patient must get into the difficult traumatic material within the first third of the session, work on it during the second third, and process and metabolize it during the final third of the session. If the material cannot be accessed by the end of the first third of the session, the patient will probably not have sufficient time to recover from the intensity of the abreaction.

A detached position of classical abstinence and anonymity is likely to be viewed by the MPD patient as rejecting or even abusive, so it is imperative that the therapist create an atmosphere of warmth and acceptance. The therapist must also inculcate a sense of hope and correct any cognitive errors that the patient brings to the sessions.

After the traumatic memories have been sufficiently worked through across the alters, the patient reaches the stage of *resolution,* consisting of smooth collaboration among alters. As the patient develops a new and secure stance about both the self and the external world, the alters blend into a unity, referred to as *integration*. Following integration, traditional psychodynamic psychotherapy is possible, in which gains can be solidified, losses can be mourned, and interpretive resolution of conflict is addressed. Many MPD patients have suffered from a poorly developed sense of self because of extended periods of amnesia for childhood and adolescence. Effective psychotherapy recovers much of what has been lost and helps the patient piece together a chronological narrative or autobiography that provides the basis for a newly formed self (Putnam 1990).

Hypnosis may or may not be used as an adjunct to psychotherapy. In some cases, an alter can be summoned simply by asking to speak with that alter by name. In other cases, the therapist must initiate a trance to gain access to a particular alter. Kluft (1991a) has stressed that because of the inherent hypnotic nature of the dissociative process, all MPD treatments involve hypnosis whether the therapist introduces it or not. He has suggested that therapists who do not wish to use deliberate hypnotic techniques may wish to call on the services of one who does.

There is a broad consensus among clinicians who write about the treatment of MPD that a solid grounding in the principles of psychodynamic psychotherapy is essential for successful treatment (Ganaway 1989; Kluft 1991a; Loewenstein and Ross 1992; Marmer 1991). Simple catharsis and abreaction will result in neither integration nor recovery. In fact, repeating the trauma over and over again in psychotherapy may even reinforce the preoccupation and fixation of the patient with the trauma (van der Kolk 1989). The increasing popularity of dissociative disorders among mental health professionals in recent years has led to a bandwagon phenomenon in which poorly trained psychotherapists have enthusiastically undertaken abreactive techniques. Without proper understanding of psychodynamic principles, these therapies frequently become stalemated in a state of "status abreacticus" (Ganaway 1992).

Attention to psychodynamic concepts such as transference, resistance, countertransference, and working through is required to achieve satisfactory recovery. A common finding in the treatment of patients with MPD is that they are intensely loyal to the abusive internal object and reluctant to give up the attachment through the processes of integration and mourning. A great deal of working through is necessary to undo the adhesiveness of the libido to this powerful introject. Marmer (1991) also has emphasized the need to help patients rewrite their autobiographies to revise the meaning of the trauma. For example, even though the fact of incest cannot be altered, a patient may come to understand that her only way of surviving was to submit to her father's advances.

While the emphasis in this discussion has been on intensive integrative psychotherapy with a goal of recovery, not all MPD patients are suitable for such an approach. Some patients do not have the means to fund an extended psychotherapy process. Others refuse to undergo integration because they feel that the psychic pain would be unbearable. Still others have egos so fragile that reexperiencing past traumas would overwhelm them. In such cases, prolonged suicidal crises or psychotic decompensations may result if the therapist nevertheless pushes on.

A better strategy in such cases is to take a more supportive approach in which the goals are maximizing the function of and encouraging harmonious collaboration among the alters. If the therapist can simply enlist the cooperation of problematic alters and persuade them that cooperation is in their best interests, the result may be a better adaptation to the stresses of living. In some cases a pharmacotherapeutic adjunct such as fluoxetine or another serotonin selective reuptake inhibitor may also serve a supportive function by decreasing the hyperarousal of the patient (van der Kolk 1989). The serotonergic axis appears to be involved in the high arousal states found in traumatized patients, and increasing the available serotonin at the synapses appears to decrease the likelihood that current stressors will be experienced as the recurrence of past trauma. Those patients who are treated with supportive psychotherapy and who do not attempt integration will, however, continue to be at high risk for relapse (Kluft 1991a).

Countertransference dimensions. Few disorders create countertransference reactions of the intensity witnessed with MPD patients. Ganzarain and Buchele (1988) have pointed out that at home, incest victims are often treated as either favorites or objects of violence and sadism. Similarly intense reactions, polarized in the same directions, occur in the treatment of adult MPD patients. Much of the emotional reaction to these patients is linked to a dialectic involving belief versus skepticism. At one extreme, many mental health professionals still do not believe that MPD is a bona fide psychiatric disorder. Some clinicians view the disorder as iatrogenically created by gullible therapists who misuse hypnosis, even though there is no evidence to sustain that etiological view (Braun 1984; Gruenewald 1984; Ross 1989). In one survey of clinicians who treat MPD patients (Dell 1988), over half had encountered such severe skepticism in colleagues that malicious harassment of the therapist and interference with the treatment of the patient had occurred. Skeptical directors of inpatient units forbade therapists to admit their MPD patients. When such patients were hospitalized, unit chiefs would forbid nursing staff to treat the patient as MPD or to see videos of dissociated alters. Inpatient unit staff would frequently tell MPD patients that therapists had misdiagnosed them.

At the other extreme, some therapists uncritically believe everything their MPD patients tell them, no matter how outlandish. They become fascinated by the condition and completely lose track of professional boundaries. They attempt to love the patient back to health and to be a better parent than the original parents. They may treat the patients with a "chimney sweeping" mentality of endlessly forcing abreaction of traumatic memories with the naive expectation that all will be well once the patient is "cleaned out." The following vignette illustrates this pattern:

Ms. T was a 26-year-old MPD patient who was referred to a tertiary care dissociative disorders unit after having been in psychotherapy for 1 year with a male therapist who reported no improvement in the patient's suicidality and self-mutilation despite treatment. He had seen the patient 5 to 6 hours per week throughout the year of therapy. When the patient required hospitalization, he spent hours with the patient in the security of a seclusion room abreacting memories of past trauma. He had allowed the patient's bill to accumulate to several thousand dollars because he had not asked Ms. T to pay for several months. He also indicated that Ms. T and he were writing a book together about the treatment.

After Ms. T's hospitalization on the dissociative disorders unit to which she had been referred, she began to reveal horrific stories about satanic cult abuse in her past. She would provide grisly details of human sacrifice and react with an affective display that was compelling to watch. She "recalled" that she had been a "breeder" for the cult so they would have babies to sacrifice. She reported that after giving birth to the babies, the cult members would grind them up in a meat grinder and then mix them in with the soil used in their garden so corroborating evidence of the murders could not be found. When Ms. T was sent for a routine gynecologic exam, it was discovered that she had in fact never delivered a child.

The doctor in charge of Ms. T's treatment called her previous therapist to explain these findings. He discounted the gynecologic evidence and said it was of paramount importance for the staff to believe Ms. T. He said if the staff did not believe her reports, they were simply repeating the past trauma when adults did not believe her tales of abuse.

This seemingly preposterous account is not at all uncommon in centers that treat patients with MPD. Descriptions such as these have resulted in some degree of polarization within the MPD field. Some clinicians argue that satanic cult abuse is a widespread phenomenon, while others have expressed concern that certain therapists are iatrogenically creating "false memories" about such activity. Clinicians must strive to maintain a middle-of-the-road position that acknowledges the reality of child abuse, some of which may occur in cult circumstances, but also encompasses a healthy skepticism about implausible events. Ganaway (1989) has pointed out that satanic cult abuse offers a clear distinction between good and evil that can help incest victims make sense out of the confusing experience of being betrayed by their parents. Fantasies and pseudomemories can play a crucial role in the development of a network of dissociated alters, and these patients, because of their high suggestibility, are also likely to produce material they think their therapist expects. As children, MPD victims often vainly try to please and win the approval of the abusive parent, and this internalized object relationship can be enacted in the transference-countertransference paradigm of the psychotherapy by dutifully reenacting one detailed abuse scene after another for a therapist who is fascinated by such data.

Empirical research indicates that memories for personally experienced traumatic events can be altered by new experiences and that entire events that never happened can be injected into memory (Loftus 1993). The veridicality of the accounts, however, becomes secondary to the enactment of an internal object relationship through projective identification. In the case of Ms. T, a self-representation that demanded to be believed had coerced an object response from the therapist that involved an unconditionally loving, accepting, and believing idealized parent. The therapist had become involved in a *folie à deux* situation in which he was incapable of stepping back from the interaction and looking at its transference-countertransference dimensions.

Psychotherapists of MPD patients will inevitably enter into the dissociative states of their patients (Davies and Frawley 1992; Gabbard 1992). As Marmer (1991) has described it:

> It is useful to conceptualize the treatment setting as a dramatic transferential reenactment in which the therapist sometimes plays the part of a figure in the patient's past, sometimes plays the patient while the patient plays the part of a past figure, sometimes plays the patient while the patient plays the therapist, and sometimes experiences dissociation and confusional states as the patient evokes in the therapist what the patient has experienced. (p. 681)

The task of the therapist is to observe the countertransference pressures without losing the perspective that a significant object relationship is being enacted. By noting what is taking place between patient and therapist, the therapist not only avoids countertransference acting out but also acquires valuable information about the patient's internal world that can be usefully brought forth into the therapy.

The therapist must avoid the role of "arbiter of historical truth." What people remember is always a complex mixture of fantasy and reality (Arlow 1969; Gediman 1991; Grotstein 1992). Therapists must listen to the material with a nonjudgmental attitude of curiosity without being coerced into declaring that what they have heard is 100% accurate or totally false. Kluft (1988) cautioned that clinicians must avoid "the expression of fascination, surprise, excitement, dismay, belief, disbelief, or the voicing of any opinion that could cause the alters to feel the need to demonstrate their authenticity" (p. 53). Therapists can certainly acknowledge that, given the diagnosis of MPD, traumatic childhood experiences undoubtedly occurred. They do not, however, need to confirm or deny precise details. It is often useful to explore with certain patients why they have such a fervent need for the therapist to adopt the role of the ultimate arbiter of truth.

A useful way to look at the transference-countertransference developments in the psychotherapy of MPD patients is to conceptualize them as episodes in an unfolding drama involving four principal characters: a victim, an abuser, an idealized omnipotent rescuer, and an uninvolved mother (Davies and Frawley 1992; Gabbard 1992). These characters oscillate in various complementary pairings between patient and therapist through the transference-countertransference enactments that develop in the psychotherapy. The first three characters in the cast—the victim, the abuser, and the idealized omnipotent rescuer—interact in a predictable pattern that represents a convergence of countertransference in the narrow sense and countertransference in the broad sense via projective identification. When a history of victimization emerges in a patient, something powerful tugs on the heartstrings of therapists that urges them to somehow try to repair the damage by becoming the good parents that the patient never had.

This rescuer-victim paradigm with which the psychotherapy begins, however, is fraught with problems. The patient is not likely to see the therapist's motives in the same way the therapist sees them. Patients who have been abused as children often assume that everyone will abuse them because they have no reason to think otherwise. Given this perspective, these patients are inherently mistrustful of reassurances from therapists who assert that they will not abuse the patient. Reassurances may make therapists feel better, but they rarely make patients feel better. Professions of caring are intrinsically suspect to patients who have been exploited under the guise of being loved.

Most MPD patients have not had the benefit of growing up with generational boundaries and limits enforced by effective, caring parents. They often experience the professional boundaries of the therapeutic situation as a cruel form of withholding. They may demand demonstrations of caring that involve extended sessions, physical contact, self-disclosure from the therapist, and round-the-clock availability. If therapists begin to "go the extra mile" to gratify these requests, their efforts are doomed to failure. The attempt to become a parental substitute bypasses the patient's need to mourn and raises false hopes that a parental relationship is available if only the patient can find the right person.

When a therapist attempts to gratify a patient's escalating demands for evidence that the therapist cares, the patient's sense of entitlement is activated. Treatment of most MPD patients sooner or later reveals their underlying conviction that they are entitled to compensation in the present for the abuse they experienced in the past (Davies and Frawley 1992). As the demands further escalate, the therapist may quickly develop a feeling of being tormented. Through processes of introjective and projective identification, the cast of characters has changed in such a way that the therapist has become the victim and the patient has become an abuser. Abusive or malevolent introjects residing within the patient have taken hold, while the victim-self of the patient is projected onto the therapist. Moreover, therapists may create a fertile field for this identification with the patient's/victim's self-representation as a result of guilt feelings related to their growing resentment and hatred of the patient. Patients may sense this development and accuse the therapist of not really caring. In an effort to deny their feelings of resentment at being asked to do too much and to go too far, therapists try even harder to prove that their motives are pure. At such moments therapists may secretly feel that they have been "found out" and react by trying to mask their irritation. An acknowledgement of one's limits may be the most therapeutic way to manage one's countertransference feelings when things reach this point (Gabbard 1986; Gabbard and Wilkinson 1994).

The third act of the drama unfolds in certain instances when the escalating pattern of increasing demands by the patient is accompanied by increasing efforts by the therapist to gratify those demands. At the height of their exasperation with the failure of all therapeutic efforts, therapists may resort to drastic boundary crossings with the patient that in effect repeat the childhood abuse. The therapist then has become the abuser with the patient once again in the role of victim. The most tragic—and, unfortunately, all-too-frequent—manifestation of this third paradigm is overt sexual contact between therapist and patient. Other common examples include sadistic verbal abuse of the patient, attempts to provide nurturance by sitting the patient on the therapist's lap and "reparenting" the patient, taking the patient on family outings with the therapist's family, and so forth. In such situations the therapist's rage at being thwarted is often completely disavowed. What began as a rescue effort has ended up as a reenactment of exploitation and abuse.

Many MPD patients suffer from a form of learned helplessness in which they believe that no effort on their part can change their fate. They assume that when trapped, they have no recourse. These patients have no sense of agency or efficacy to call upon. In this sense they are what Kluft (1990) has termed "sitting ducks" for all forms of abuse and boundary violations by therapists who use their patients to gratify their own needs.

The three roles of victim, abuser, and idealized omnipotent rescuer are the most dramatic and obvious manifestations of the introjective-projective processes at work in the psychotherapy of MPD patients. The fourth role, the uninvolved mother, shows itself in a somewhat more subtle way (Gabbard 1992). Patients will often perceive this persona in the therapist's silence, which is interpreted as indifference and rejection. In response to this perception of indifference, the patient may feel a sense of nonbeing—described by Bigras and Biggs (1990) as "negative incest"—a deadness or emptiness related to the absent mother who made no attempt to intervene in the incestuous relationship between her husband and her daughter.

The deadness or emptiness experienced by the patient may foster complementary feelings of helplessness and despair in the psychotherapist. There may be long periods in the psychotherapy when the patient remains aloof and distant from the therapist and evokes feelings of deadness or nonbeing in the countertransference (Levine 1990; Lisman-Pieczanski 1990).

The following excerpt from a psychotherapy session with an MPD patient depicts this countertransference identification with the uninvolved mother:

Ms. U: If I could just leave this damn hospital, everything would be fine. My only problem is I hate to be confined like this, and it makes me want to mutilate.

Therapist: But I wonder if confinement is really your only problem. You certainly mutilated a great deal before you were admitted to the hospital.

Ms. U: But I need to see my children and my husband. Don't you understand? They won't let them visit me here.

Therapist: The last time they visited you here, you ended up making a serious suicide attempt.

Ms. U: (blandly) I wanted to cut the artery in my wrist and end everything.

Therapist: Well, then, I can imagine that the staff would be reluctant to have you leave the structure and protection of the hospital.

Ms. U: I need to give it a try out of here for a while. I think if I could just be with my family outside the hospital, then I'd be fine.

Therapist: What would you do if anxiety came over you and you felt like mutilating?

Ms. U: (with utter seriousness) I could have a beer or two to settle myself down.

Therapist: It's very important that you see that your problems are not external. You carry your problems within you wherever you go, and no matter whether you're confined to a hospital or home with your family, you'll still have them. Until you make some effort to integrate and face the painful experiences from the past, you'll continue to mutilate yourself and wish to commit suicide.

Ms. U: I don't want to face the pain of integrating the personalities. It would be unbearable.

Therapist: But you're in considerable pain now. Can it be that much worse?

Ms. U: (blandly) I don't know, but I don't want to find out.

As the therapist continued to get nowhere with this line of reasoning, he found himself getting increasingly drowsy. Associated with the sleepy feeling, he felt as though he were withdrawing further and further away from the patient. He began looking at the clock and wishing the time was up. He found himself thinking about what he would do later in the day. He even felt that he no longer really cared if the patient got better or not. The patient also seemed to be drifting further and further away from him. As he observed this remarkable lapse in empathic attunement, it dawned on the therapist that he was becoming the absent, uninvolved mother of her childhood. His efforts to help had been thwarted, and he had a deep sense of despair and hopelessness about anything ever changing. He wondered if the patient's mother, too, had felt that way when she realized that she was forever excluded from the bond between her daughter and her husband and felt powerless or helpless to change anything about it.

Countertransference responses such as the one described by Ms. U's therapist may also reflect an empathic identification with a sense of nonbeing at the core of the patient's self in response to the distant maternal identification in the patient (Gabbard 1992). There comes a time in the psychotherapy of MPD patients when the demandingness of the patient is so overwhelming that therapists find themselves wishing the patient would disappear or go elsewhere for treatment. In such reactions an identification with the uninvolved mother is easily detected, and therapists must be mindful that such unconscious collusions may lead unwittingly to suicide attempts on the part of the patient.

The primitive states of psychological deadness depicted in this transference-countertransference paradigm may relate to profound maternal deprivation that severely compromised the infant's developing sense of self. In the absence of the maternal provision of soothing sensory experience, the infant may not establish a secure feeling of sensory boundedness. The self-mutilation so common in MPD patients can be understood as a way of reestablishing boundedness at the skin border to deal with anxiety about losing intactness of the ego boundary.

Ogden (1989) has characterized this mode of generating experience as the autistic-contiguous position. In this primitive state the process of attributing meaning to experience ceases. Therapists may experience MPD patients as imprisoned in such a primitive state that they are completely unreachable. Therapists may then be imbued with a sense of hopelessness in dealing with the patient's anxiety about lack of body integrity secondary to deprivation of close sensory experiences with mother.

Hospital treatment. Depending on their level of ego organization and the degree of comorbidity, many MPD patients will require hospitalization at some point in the course of psychotherapy. The duration of the inpatient stay may be as short as several days to deal with a readily resolvable crisis or many months to prevent the severely decompensated patient from committing suicide (Kluft 1991d).

MPD patients who enter general psychiatry units often find themselves in the role of the classic "special" patient (Burnham 1966; Gabbard 1986). They are regarded both by staff members and by other patients as having special relationships with their psychotherapists and often become scapegoated as a result. Skeptical staff members will begin arguments about what name to use with the patient, the validity of the abuse history, whether or not the patient is responsible for her actions, and a myriad of other issues. Although on the surface the reactions of unit staff may appear to be a typical case of splitting, this situation actually is an example of preexisting philosophical and scientific disagreement among the professional staff that is often blamed on the patient (Gabbard 1989). Matters may be made worse when other patients in milieu groups react with disbelief and contempt when an MPD patient denies behavior that others have witnessed.

Because of these considerations, many patients with MPD do better on specialized inpatient units for dissociative disorders. Although behavior is usually more manageable on such units because staff members accept the illness as real, splitting problems may occur when certain staff members are exposed to one aspect of the patient while other staff members are confronted with a totally different dimension of the patient (Gabbard 1989). Kluft (1991d) has provided several helpful guidelines. A contractual agreement must be made with the patient at the beginning of the stay that stipulates her consenting to respond to her legal name when addressed by it in the milieu. The patient should be told that staff cannot be expected to respond to different alters in different ways when they emerge on the unit. Only the individual therapist will address the separate alters. A patient who cannot make a contract on behalf of all alters must be structured at the level of the most dangerous or self-destructive alter. This agreement avoids the inevitable confusion in staff members about privileges and responsibilities given the variability of functioning of the different alters. Kluft (1991d) also suggested that nursing staff must continually explain rules and policies to patients, as some alters will not be familiar with them.

Group psychotherapy. Kluft (1991d) has cautioned that MPD patients may have considerable difficulty with unstructured verbal group psychotherapy on hospital inpatient units. If a patient cannot contract to attend as an alter that will conform to the rules of the group, Kluft suggests that the patient should be excluded from group work. Another problem that frequently emerges stems from the suggestibility of this patient population. When one patient hears another speak of the abuse she suffered as a child, there may be a "contagion" effect, in which the first patient believes that everything reported by the second patient also happened to her. As a result, reports of cult abuse may grow increasingly fantastic if they are discussed in inpatient groups. Clearly, the underlying competitive themes in such groups need to be addressed.

On the other hand, homogeneous outpatient group psychotherapy may be useful. Coons and Bradley (1985) reported on a $2\frac{1}{2}$-year program of outpatient group psychotherapy for eight MPD patients who met weekly for 75 minutes. Although the process started out slowly because of difficulties with trust, much hope was generated, and the group experience was viewed as a valuable adjunct to individual psychotherapy (all patients had to be in concomitant individual processes to be accepted into the group). The patients mistrusted the male co-therapist for some time, and approximately a year passed before the patients finally discussed their childhood abuse experiences. Themes of negative self-worth and anger at parents were prevalent. Dissociation was sometimes used avoidantly, although less often than expected. In a typical session, no more than one dissociative episode was observed. The patients in the group were able to gain considerable insight by viewing the dissociation of other group members. In this regard, witnessing the dissociative episodes of others helped some patients accept their own diagnosis.

Depersonalization

The term *depersonalization neurosis* first appeared in the DSM-II (American Psychiatric Association 1968) to characterize a syndrome involving a feeling of unreality and estrangement from one's body, self, or surroundings. In DSM-III (American Psychiatric Association 1980) and DSM-III-R, the term evolved to describe a form of dissociative disorder involving a change in the experience or perception of the self in such a way that one's own reality was temporarily changed or lost. In addition, persistence and severity were incorporated into the definition to differentiate it from the various types of depersonalization that occur in normal (i.e., nonpsychiatrically ill) people. The DSM-IV changes are only minor but continue to stress that either marked distress or impairments in social or occupational functioning are necessary for the diagnosis (see Table 10–2).

Derealization is ordinarily part of the depersonalization disorder and refers specifically to a sense of being estranged from one's environment. Depersonalization may take a multitude of forms, including a feeling that one's body is numb or dead, a feeling that certain body parts (such as the feet or hands) are not connected with the rest of the body, feelings of being detached from one's self-image so that one seems unfamiliar, and the sense of observing oneself at a distance (Gabbard and Twemlow 1984). The subjective experience of frank detachment from one's body is actually rather infrequent in depersonalization,

---

Table 10–2. DSM-IV criteria for depersonalization disorder

A. Persistent or recurrent experiences of feeling detached from, and as if one is an outside observer of, one's mental processes or body (e.g., feeling like one is in a dream).

B. During the depersonalization experience, reality testing remains intact.

C. The depersonalization causes clinically significant distress or impairment in social, occupational, or other important areas of functioning.

D. The depersonalization experience does not occur exclusively during the course of another disorder, such as schizophrenia, panic disorder, or another dissociative disorder, and is not due to the direct physiological effects of a substance (e.g., drugs of abuse, medication) or a general medical condition (e.g., temporal lobe epilepsy).

Source. DSM-IV. Because the criteria sets were not final at press time, the reader should consult DSM-IV for final criteria.

characterizing only 19% of psychiatric patients with the disorder (Noyes et al. 1977). Although *déjà vu* experiences are commonly linked with depersonalization, they are actually the obverse of depersonalization and should be maintained as distinct entities (Nemiah 1989). In other words, in *déjà vu,* what is new is experienced as being familiar, while in depersonalization what is familiar is experienced as being new or unreal.

The DSM-IV criteria stress persistence and severity, because as many as 50% of the normal population will have an occasional isolated experience of depersonalization (Nemiah 1989). Other demographic features of depersonalization include its occurrence twice as often in women as in men and predominantly in persons under the age of 40 (Nemiah 1989). Transient depersonalization may also appear as a response to life-threatening danger such as accidents, serious illnesses, and the like (Gabbard and Twemlow 1984; Noyes et al. 1977; Steinberg 1991). There may be survival value in developing a split between an observing self and a participating self in a moment of crisis so that a person has the necessary detachment to think of ways to maneuver out of a perilous situation.

Depersonalization occurring in normal persons exposed to danger has no essential differences from episodes that occur in the context of psychiatric illness (Noyes et al. 1977). Among psychiatric patients, depersonalization is the third most common complaint, following depression and anxiety (Cattell and Cattell 1974). In fact, depersonalization is relatively uncommon as a pure disorder and is more frequently a symptom connected with other illnesses such as schizophrenia, multiple personality disorder, depression, or anxiety disorders (Nemiah 1989). The experience of depersonalization, whether accompanying an illness or not, is typically unpleasant and mobilizes affects such as anxiety, panic, and emptiness. It is experienced as pathological, strange, and dreamlike and often leads people to seek medical attention (Gabbard and Twemlow 1984). Depersonalization has a chronic course in about half the cases but may be highly variable in terms of the degree of dysfunction it causes the individual (Steinberg 1991).

Psychodynamic Understanding

Although the etiology of depersonalization remains obscure in most cases, psychodynamic explanations evolving from treatment situations have been shown to be clinically useful. Rosenfeld (1947/1966) viewed depersonalization as a defense against primitive destructive impulses and persecutory anxieties stemming from the paranoid-schizoid position. Blank (1954) regarded depersonalization as a defense against primitive anxiety stemming from oral rage and oral deprivation. Stamm (1962) concurred with Rosenfeld and Blank regarding the deeply regressive aspects of depersonalization as a defense.

The most current psychodynamic view of depersonalization is that it represents the internalization of conflicting identifications. Jacobson (1959) observed that unacceptable identifications are defended against by disowning and denying the undesirable part of the ego. Sarlin (1962) shared the view of Jacobson and pointed out that depersonalization may reflect a conflict between the patient's parents that has become internalized as two conflicting aspects of the child. Arlow (1966) viewed depersonalization as a defensive means of attributing warded-off impulses in a dangerous situation to the participating self, which is then experienced as estranged by the observing self. In this manner the dangerous conflict is viewed as taking place within a stranger rather than within the self.

This wish to distance oneself from a dangerous situation that conflicts with one's predominant ego identification may be highly relevant to situations when depersonalization occurs in the context of childhood abuse.

Ms. V was a 19-year-old woman who was in psychiatric treatment for chronic suicidality and uncontrollable self-mutilating tendencies. She had been involved in incestuous sexual relations with her stepfather since the age of 8 and had only recently stopped the behavior. She frequently complained of depersonalization and was able to identify its origins at age 8 when the sexual involvement began. When her stepfather would begin to have sexual relations with her, the anxiety created by the sexual contact was so great that she would find herself in a detached position across the room observing the sexual acts as though she were a spectator. Her body would seem unreal to her, like a "rubber manikin."

Although the depersonalization began under these incestuous circumstances, it soon generalized to any situation when stress or anxiety was prominent, such as a family argument at the dinner table. By the time she was 19, it had become a chronic state in which she felt unreal and dead much of the time. She cut on her forearms to feel a sense of relief from this unpleasant depersonalized state. The pain of the cut was preferable to the estrangement that she experienced.

The defensive function of Ms. V's depersonalization could be stated in the form of an inner reassurance: "That is not me who is experiencing the sexual molestation. That is not my body, because I am over here in another part of the room watching it happen to a stranger." The sexual relations with her stepfather could then be attributed to a bad, degraded self that was split off and not part of her. She also was able to defend against her own instinctual pleasure inherent in the gratification of the oedipal wish and the triumph over her mother.

Depersonalization may not always be a defense against danger from without or drive pressures from within. From a self psychological perspective, depersonalization may also be a reflection of disturbances in the consolidation of a cohesive and stable sense of self (Gabbard 1983; Stolorow 1979). The depersonalization state in these patients may reflect their panic over the fragmenting of the self when mirroring and affirming selfobject responses are not forthcoming from others.

Treatment Considerations

Discussions of treatment must begin with the recognition that transient or normal depersonalization requires little more than reassurance. In some cases of chronic depersonalization, patients who have accommodated to the disorder will not particularly feel a need for treatment (Steinberg 1991; Torch 1981). If the depersonalization is secondary to an underlying primary disorder, the clinical improvement of the primary disorder in response to appropriate treatment may also resolve the depersonalization.

Pharmacotherapy may be useful in alleviating the symptoms of depersonalization. Ambrosino (1973) and Noyes et al. (1987) have reported that tricyclic antidepressants such as desipramine and imipramine may result in improvement. Fluoxetine has also been reported as effective in treating depersonalization (Hollander et al. 1989).

Psychodynamic psychotherapy designed to identify the underlying dynamics to help patients achieve control over depersonalization may be effective in some cases (Lehmann 1974; Steinberg 1991; Torch 1987). The approach advocated by Torch is centered on abreacting traumatic memories that may have produced depersonalization. Mastery is provided by the understanding of what led to the symptom, and the patient typically feels a greater sense of control. Dynamic therapy may also be useful to examine underlying problems of conflicting ego identifications, particularly as they reflect stresses in the family of origin. In the final analysis, however, the decision to embark on a course of dynamic therapy is often based on patient attributes that may not be directly related to the depersonalization symptom, such as motivation to understand, psychological mindedness, prominent ego strengths, and intellectual curiosity about oneself.

References

Ambrosino S: Phobic anxiety—depersonalization syndrome. New York State Journal of Medicine 73:419–425, 1973

American Psychiatric Association: Diagnostic and Statistical Manual of Mental Disorders, 2nd Edition. Washington, DC, American Psychiatric Association, 1968

American Psychiatric Association: Diagnostic and Statistical Manual of Mental Disorders, 3rd Edition. Washington, DC, American Psychiatric Association, 1980

American Psychiatric Association: Diagnostic and Statistical Manual of Mental Disorders, 3rd Edition, Revised. Washington, DC, American Psychiatric Association, 1987

American Psychiatric Association: Diagnostic and Statistical Manual of Mental Disorders, 4th Edition. Washington, DC, American Psychiatric Association, 1994

Arlow JA: Depersonalization and derealization, in Psychoanalysis—A General Psychology: Essays in Honor of Heinz Hartmann. Edited by Loewenstein RM, Newman LM, Schur M, et al. New York, International Universities Press, 1966, pp 456–478

Arlow JA: Fantasy, memory, and reality testing. Psychoanal Q 38:28–51, 1969

Armstrong JG, Loewenstein RJ: Characteristics of patients with multiple personality and dissociative disorders on psychological testing. J Nerv Ment Dis 178:448–454, 1990

Bigras J, Biggs KH: Psychoanalysis as incestuous repetition: some technical considerations, in Adult Analysis and Childhood Sexual Abuse. Edited by Levine HB. Hillsdale, NJ, Analytic Press, 1990, pp 173–196

Blank HR: Depression, hypomania, and depersonalization. Psychoanal Q 23:20–37, 1954

Bliss EL: Multiple personalities: report of 14 cases with implications for schizophrenia and hysteria. Arch Gen Psychiatry 37:1388–1397, 1980

Braun BG: Hypnosis creates multiple personality: myth or reality? Int J Clin Exp Hypn 32:191–197, 1984

Bremner JD, Southwick S, Brett E, et al: Dissociation and posttraumatic stress disorder in Vietnam combat veterans. Am J Psychiatry 149:328–332, 1992

Browne A, Finkelhor D: Impact of child sexual abuse: a review of the research. Psychol Bull 99:66–77, 1986

Burnham DL: The special-problem patient: victim or agent of splitting? Psychiatry 29:105–122, 1966

Carmen EH, Reiker PP, Mills T: Victims of violence and psychiatric illness. Am J Psychiatry 141:378–379, 1984

Cattell JP, Cattell JS: Depersonalization: psychological and social perspectives, in American Handbook of Psychiatry, 2nd Edition, Vol 3. Edited by Arieti S, Brody EB. New York, Basic Books, 1974, pp 766–799

Chu JA, Dill DL: Dissociative symptoms in relation to childhood physical and sexual abuse. Am J Psychiatry 147:887–892, 1990

Coons PM: The differential diagnosis of multiple personality: a comprehensive review. Psychiatr Clin North Am 7:51–67, 1984

Coons PM, Bradley K: Group psychotherapy with multiple personality patients. J Nerv Ment Dis 173(9):515–521, 1985

Davies JM, Frawley MG: Dissociative processes and transference-countertransference paradigms in the psychoanalytically oriented treatment of adult survivors of childhood sexual abuse. Psychoanalytic Dialogues 2:5–36, 1992

Dell PF: Professional skepticism about multiple personality. J Nerv Ment Dis 176:528–531, 1988

Fairbairn WRD: Schizoid factors in the personality (1940), in Psychoanalytic Studies of the Personality. London, Routledge & Kegan Paul, 1952, pp 3–27

Fairbairn WRD: Endopsychic structure considered in terms of object-relationships (1944), in Psychoanalytic Studies of the Personality. London, Routledge & Kegan Paul, 1952, pp 82–136

Frankel FH: Hypnotizability and dissociation. Am J Psychiatry 147:823–829, 1990

Gabbard GO: Further contribution to the understanding of stage fright: narcissistic issues. J Am Psychoanal Assoc 31:423–441, 1983

Gabbard GO: The treatment of the "special patient" in a psychoanalytic hospital. International Review of Psychoanalysis 13:333–347, 1986

Gabbard GO: Splitting in hospital treatment. Am J Psychiatry 146:444–451, 1989

Gabbard GO: Commentary on "Dissociative processes and transference-countertransference paradigms . . . " by Jody Messler Davies and Mary Gail Frawley. Psychoanalytic Dialogues 2:37–47, 1992

Gabbard GO, Twemlow SW: With the Eyes of the Mind: An Empirical Analysis of Out-of-Body States. New York, Praeger, 1984

Gabbard GO, Wilkinson SM: Management of Countertransference With Borderline Patients. Washington, DC, American Psychiatric Press, 1994

Ganaway GK: Historical versus narrative truth: clarifying the role of exogenous trauma in the etiology of MPD and its variants. Dissociation 2:205–220, 1989

Ganaway GK: Hypnosis, dissociation and multiple personality disorder: a psychodynamic clinician's perspective. Paper presented at the annual meeting of the Society of Clinical and Experimental Hypnosis, Washington, DC, October 24, 1992

Ganzarain RC, Buchele BJ: Fugitives of Incest: A Perspective From Psycho-analysis and Groups. Madison, CT, International Universities Press, 1988

Gediman HK: Seduction trauma: complemental intrapsychic and interpersonal perspectives on fantasy and reality. Psychoanalytic Psychology 8:381–401, 1991

Gelinas DJ: Unexpected resources in treating incest families, in Family Resources: The Hidden Partner in Family Therapy. Edited by Karpel MA. New York, Guilford, 1986, pp 327–358

Gruenewald D: On the nature of multiple personality: comparisons with hypnosis. Int J Clin Exp Hyp 32:170–190, 1984

Grotstein JS: Commentary on "Dissociative processes and transference-countertransference paradigms . . . " by Jody Messler Davies and Mary Gail Frawley. Psychoanalytic Dialogues 2:61–76, 1992

Herman JL, Perry JC, van der Kolk BA: Childhood trauma in borderline personality disorder. Am J Psychiatry 146:490–495, 1989

Hollander E, Fairbanks J, Decaria C, et al: Pharmacologic dissection of panic and depersonalization (letter). Am J Psychiatry 146:402, 1989

Horevitz RP, Braun BG: Are multiple personalities borderline? an analysis of 33 cases. Psychiatr Clin North Am 7:69–87, 1984

Horowitz MJ: Stress Response Syndromes, 2nd Edition. Northvale, NJ, Jason Aronson 1986

Jacobson E: Depersonalization. J Am Psychoanal Assoc 7:581–610, 1959

Kemp K, Gilbertson AD, Torem M: The differential diagnosis of multiple personality disorder from borderline personality disorder. Dissociation 1:41–46, 1988

Kernberg OF: Borderline Conditions and Pathological Narcissism. New York, Jason Aronson, 1975

Kluft RP: An introduction to multiple personality disorder. Psychiatric Annals 14:19–24, 1984a

Kluft RP: Treatment of multiple personality disorder: a study of 33 cases. Psychiatr Clin North Am 7:9–29, 1984b

Kluft RP (ed): The natural history of multiple personality disorder, in Childhood Antecedents of Multiple Personality. Washington, DC, American Psychiatric Press, 1985, pp 197–238

Kluft RP: The phenomenology and treatment of extremely complex multiple personality disorder. Dissociation 1:47–58, 1988

Kluft RP (ed): Incest-Related Syndromes of Adult Psychopathology. Washington, DC, American Psychiatric Press, 1990

Kluft RP: Multiple personality, in American Psychiatric Press Review of Psychiatry, Vol 10. Edited by Tasman A, Goldfinger SM. Washington, DC, American Psychiatric Press, 1991a, pp 161–188

Kluft RP: Thoughts on the psychodynamic psychotherapy of the dissociative disorders. The Psychodynamic Letter 1(4):1–5, 1991b

Kluft RP: Clinical presentations of multiple personality disorder. Psychiatr Clin North Am 14:605–629, 1991c

Kluft RP: Hospital treatment of multiple personality disorder: an overview. Psychiatr Clin North Am 14:695–719, 1991d

Lehmann LS: Depersonalization. Am J Psychiatry 131:1221–1224, 1974

Levine HB: Clinical issues in the analysis of adults who were sexually abused as children, in Adult Analysis and Childhood Sexual Abuse. Edited by Levine HB. Hillsdale, NJ, Analytic Press, 1990, pp 197–218

Lisman-Pieczanski N: Countertransference in the analysis of an adult who was sexually abused as a child, in Adult Analysis and Childhood Sexual Abuse. Edited by Levine HB. Hillsdale, NJ, Analytic Press, 1990, pp 137–147

Loewenstein RJ, Ross DR: Multiple personality and psychoanalysis: an introduction. Psychoanalytic Inquiry 12(1):3–48, 1992

Loftus EF: The reality of repressed memories. Am Psychol 48:518–537, 1993

Ludwig AM: The psychobiological functions of dissociation. Am J Clin Hypn 26:93–99, 1983

Marmer SS: Multiple personality disorder: a psychoanalytic perspective. Psychiatr Clin North Am 14:677–693, 1991

Miller SD: Optical differences in cases of multiple personality disorder. J Nerv Ment Dis 177:480–486, 1989

Nemiah JC: Dissociative disorders (hysterical neuroses, dissociative type), in Comprehensive Textbook of Psychiatry, 5th Edition. Edited by Kaplan H, Saddock B. Baltimore, MD, Williams & Wilkins, 1989, pp 1028–1044

Nigg JT, Silk KR, Westen D, et al: Object representations in the early memories of sexually abused borderline patients. Am J Psychiatry 148:864–869, 1991

Noyes R Jr, Hoenk PR, Kuperman S, et al: Depersonalization in accident victims and psychiatric patients. J Nerv Ment Dis 164:401–407, 1977

Noyes R Jr, Kuperman S, Olson SB: Desipramine: a possible treatment for depersonalization disorder. Can J Psychiatry 32:782–784, 1987

Ogata SN, Silk KR, Goodrich S, et al: Childhood sexual and physical abuse in adult patients with borderline personality disorder. Am J Psychiatry 147:1008–1013, 1990

Ogden TH: The Primitive Edge of Experience. Northvale, NJ, Jason Aronson, 1989

Putnam FW: Dissociation as a response to extreme trauma, in Childhood Antecedents of Multiple Personality Disorder. Edited by Kluft R. Washington, DC, American Psychiatric Press, 1985, pp 65–97

Putnam FW: Diagnosis and Treatment of Multiple Personality Disorder. New York, Guilford, 1989

Putnam FW: Disturbances of "self" in victims of childhood sexual abuse, in Incest-Related Syndromes of Adult Psychopathology. Edited by Kluft RP. Washington, DC, American Psychiatric Press, 1990, pp 113–131

Putnam FW: Dissociative phenomena, in American Psychiatric Press Review of Psychiatry, Vol 10. Edited by Tasman A, Goldfinger SM. Washington, DC, American Psychiatric Press, 1991, pp 145–160

Putnam FW, Guroff JJ, Silberman EK, et al: The clinical phenomenology of multiple personality disorder: review of 100 recent cases. J Clin Psychiatry 47:285–293, 1986

Rosenfeld H: Analysis of a schizophrenic state with depersonalization (1947), in Psychotic States: A Psycho-Analytic Approach. New York, International Universities Press, 1966, pp 13–33

Ross CA: Multiple Personality Disorder: Diagnosis, Clinical Features, and Treatment. New York, Wiley, 1989

Ross CA: Epidemiology of multiple personality disorder and dissociation. Psychiatr Clin North Am 14:503–517, 1991

Ross CA, Joshi S, Currie R: Dissociative experiences in the general population. Am J Psychiatry 147:1547–1552, 1990

Ross CA, Anderson G, Fleisher WP, et al: The frequency of multiple personality disorder among psychiatric inpatients. Am J Psychiatry 148:1717–1720, 1991

Sarlin CN: Depersonalization and derealization. J Am Psychoanal Assoc 10:784–804, 1962

Spiegel D: Multiple personality as a post-traumatic stress disorder. Psychiatr Clin North Am 7:101–110, 1984

Spiegel D: Trauma, dissociation, and hypnosis, in Incest-Related Syndromes of Adult Psychopathology. Edited by Kluft RP. Washington, DC, American Psychiatric Press, 1990, pp 247–261

Spiegel D: Dissociation and trauma, in American Psychiatric Press Review of Psychiatry, Vol 10. Edited by Tasman A, Goldfinger SM. Washington, DC, American Psychiatric Press, 1991a, pp 261–275

Spiegel D: Foreword to Dissociative disorders (Section II), in American Psychiatric Press Review of Psychiatry, Vol 10. Edited by Tasman A, Goldfinger SM. Washington, DC, American Psychiatric Press, 1991b, pp 143–144

Spiegel D, Fink R: Hysterical psychosis and hypnotizability. Am J Psychiatry 136:777–781, 1979

Stamm J: Altered ego states allied to depersonalization. J Am Psychoanal Assoc 10:762–783, 1962

Steinberg M: The spectrum of depersonalization: assessment and treatment, in American Psychiatric Press Review of Psychiatry, Vol 10. Edited by Tasman A, Goldfinger SM. Washington, DC, American Psychiatric Press, 1991, pp 223–247

Steinberg M, Rousaville B, Cicchetti D: Detection of dissociative disorders in psychiatric patients by a screening instrument and a structured diagnostic interview. Am J Psychiatry 148:1050–1054, 1991

Steingard S, Frankel FH: Dissociation and psychotic symptoms. Am J Psychiatry 142:953–955, 1985

Stolorow RD: Defensive and arrested developmental aspects of death anxiety, hypochondriasis and depersonalization. Int J Psychoanal 60:201–213, 1979

Torch EM: Depersonalization syndrome: an overview. Psychiatr Q 53:249–258, 1981

Torch EM: The psychotherapeutic treatment of depersonalization disorder. Hillside Journal of Clinical Psychiatry 9:133–143, 1987

van der Kolk BA: Psychological Trauma. Washington, DC, American Psychiatric Press, 1987 van der Kolk BA: The compulsion to repeat the trauma: re-enactment, re-victimization, and masochism. Psychiatr Clin North Am 12:389–411, 1989

Westen D, Ludolph P, Misle B, et al: Physical and sexual abuse in adolescent girls with borderline personality disorder. Am J Orthopsychiatry 60:55–66, 1990

Young WC: Psychodynamics and dissociation: all that switches is not split. Dissociation 1:33–38, 1988

Zanarini MC, Gunderson JG, Marino MF, et al: Childhood experiences of borderline patients. Compr Psychiatry 30:18–25, 1989

Chapter 11

Paraphilias and Sexual Dysfunctions

Paraphilias

Few psychiatric disorders are fraught with as many moralistic overtones as the paraphilias. To determine that an individual is deviant in
the area of sexuality implies the establishment of a clear norm for sexual behavior. Who will establish such norms? Shall psychiatry be the
moral guardian of sexual behavior? Can we use terms such as *sexual
deviation, perversion,* or even *paraphilia* without sounding pejorative?

The evolution of the definition of perverse activity reveals the extent to which psychiatric nosology mirrors the society from which it
emanates. In the context of a culture that viewed normal sexuality in
relatively narrow terms, Freud (1905/1953) defined sexual activity as
perverse according to several criteria: 1) it focused on nongenital regions of the body; 2) rather than coexisting with the standard practice
of genital intercourse with an opposite-sex partner, it superseded and
replaced such practice; and 3) it tended to be the exclusive sexual practice of the individual. Freud noted that traces of perversion could be
found in virtually anyone whose unconscious was subject to psychoanalytic exploration.

Since Freud's early paper, cultural attitudes about sexuality have
undergone dramatic changes. As sexuality became a legitimate area

for scientific study, it became apparent that "normal" couples engage in a variety of sexual behaviors. Oral-genital relations, for example, became widely accepted as healthy sexual behavior. Homosexuality and anal intercourse similarly were removed from the list of perverse activities. Most recently, concern about AIDS has increased the public's awareness of the relatively high prevalence of anal sexual relations among heterosexual couples.

Psychoanalytic writers have repeatedly confirmed Freud's observation that there is a latent perverse core in all of us (Chasseguet-Smirgel 1983; McDougall 1980, 1986; Stoller 1975, 1985). Thus a more accepting attitude about perverse sexuality has accompanied psychoanalytic advances. McDougall (1986) pointed out that perverse fantasies are regularly found in all adult sexual behavior, but tend to cause few problems because they are not experienced as compulsive. She suggested using the term _neosexuality,_ to reflect the innovative nature of the practice and the individual's intense investment in its pursuit. She has stressed that clinicians must be empathic with their patients, who experience these sexual demands as necessary for emotional survival.

Stoller (1975, 1985) has advocated a narrowed definition of perverse activity. Referring to perversion as "the erotic form of hatred" (1975, p. 4), he asserted that cruelty and the wish to humiliate and degrade one's sexual partner as well as oneself are the crucial determinants of whether a behavior is perverse. From this perspective, the individual's intent is a critical variable in defining perversion. As his view evolved (1985), Stoller added another dimension to this definition. Recognizing that in normal sexual arousal there is a touch of hostility and a desire to humiliate, he concluded that intimacy was a critical differentiating factor. An individual is perverse only when the erotic act is used to avoid a long-term, emotionally intimate relationship with another person. Conversely, sexual behavior is not perverse when it is in the service of establishing a stable intimate relationship.

In an effort to be nonjudgmental in its definition of paraphilias, the DSM-IV (American Psychiatric Association 1994) has suggested restricting the term to situations in which nonhuman objects are used, in which actual humiliation or pain is inflicted on oneself or one's partner, or in which children or nonconsenting adults are involved. To deal with the continuum between fantasy and action, DSM-IV has developed a spectrum of severity. In "mild" forms, patients are quite distressed about their paraphilic sexual urges but do not act on them. In "moderate" degrees of severity, patients translate their urges into action, but only occasionally. In "severe" cases, patients repeatedly act on their paraphilic urges. Finally, in an effort to be more scientific and less pejorative, DSM-IV uses the term *paraphilia* rather than *perversion* or *deviation.*

Although the intent of DSM-IV is admirable, Stoller (1985) argued that the change of the official term from *perversion* to *paraphilia* (which occurred originally in DSM-III-R) is a misguided attempt to "sanitize" perversions. *Perversion,* in his view, is useful precisely because it has nasty and sinful connotations:

> *Perversion* is so pejorative. It reeks of sin, accusation, vindictiveness, and righteousness. It has its absoluteness. In it thunder God and his agents on earth. (p. 4)

Stoller has argued for retaining the term *perversion* because a sense of sinning is a prerequisite for a perverse activity to create erotic excitement. Since both points of view have merit, the two terms will be used interchangeably in this chapter.

Psychodynamic Understanding of Paraphilias

To a large extent, the etiology of paraphilias remains shrouded in mystery. Although certain studies have suggested that biological factors contribute to the pathogenesis of perversions (Berlin and Meinecke 1981), the data are far from definitive. Even if biological factors are present, psychological issues obviously play a crucial role in determining the choice of paraphilia and the underlying meaning of the sexual acts. Psychoanalytic understanding has greatly illuminated the dark recesses of the perverse psyche. However, we must appropriately and modestly note that psychodynamic models can shed light on the meaning of a perversion without necessarily establishing a definitive etiology (Person 1986).

The classical view of perversions is deeply embedded in drive theory. Freud (1905/1953) believed that these disorders illustrated how instinct and object are divorced from one another: "It seems probable that the sexual instinct is in the first instance independent of its object" (p. 148). Moreover, he defined perversions in part by contrasting them with neuroses. In the latter condition, neurotic symptoms represent a transformation of repressed perverse fantasies. In perversions, however, the fantasies become conscious and are directly expressed as ego-syntonic, pleasurable activities. Hence, Freud described neuroses as the negative of perversions: neurotic symptoms were desexualized perverse fantasies. In the classical view, perversions may be fixations or regressions to infantile forms of sexuality persisting into adult life (Fenichel 1945; Sachs 1986). Some remnant of infantile experience is preserved in consciousness and is the carrier of all infantile sexuality through the process of displacement. A perverse act becomes a fixated and ritualized procedure that is the only route to genital orgasm. In the classical formulation (Fenichel 1945), the decisive factor that prevents orgasm through conventional genital intercourse is castration anxiety. Perversions thus serve the function of denying castration. (Because the overwhelming majority of patients suffering from paraphilias are male, the formulations presented here will presume male gender.)

Freud (1905/1953) appreciated the complexity of perversions, which are multilayered. He noted, for example, the myriad unconscious determinants of voyeurism and exhibitionism, which are opposite sides of the same coin. In his clinical work, he observed that any "active" perversion was always accompanied by a "passive" counterpart. In this formulation, the sadist would have a masochistic core, whereas the voyeur would suffer from unconscious exhibitionistic desires.

More recent psychoanalytic investigators have concluded that drive theory alone is insufficient to explain much of the perverse fantasies and behavior seen clinically and that the relational aspects of perversions are crucial for a comprehensive understanding (McDougall 1980, 1986; Mitchell 1988). According to Stoller (1975, 1985), the essence of perversion is a conversion of "childhood trauma to adult triumph" (1975, p. 4). Patients are driven by their fantasies of avenging humiliating childhood traumas caused by their parents. Their method of revenge is to dehumanize and humiliate their partner during the perverse act or fantasy.

Perverse sexual activity may also be a flight from object relatedness (Mitchell 1988). Many persons suffering from paraphilias have incompletely separated and individuated from their intrapsychic representations of their mothers. As a result, they feel that their identity as a separate person is constantly being threatened by fusion or engulfment from internal or external objects. Sexual expression may be the one domain in which they can assert their independence. Whereas

Stoller (1975, 1985) viewed perversions as expressions of the desire to humiliate, Mitchell (1988) understood them as a defiance of the over-bearing influence of the internal mothering figure. One aspect of the relief experienced by paraphilic patients after they have acted on their sexual desires is their feeling of triumph over the controlling mother within.

McDougall (1986) has noted other object relational meanings of the *neosexualities*. She has suggested that sexual behavior evolves from a complicated matrix of identifications and counteridentifications with our parents. Each child is involved in an unconscious psychological drama that stems from the parents' unconscious erotic desires and conflicts. Hence, the obligatory nature of any neosexuality is programmed by parental scripts internalized by the child. In McDougall's view, deviant sexual behavior may function partly to protect the introjected objects from the patient's aggression by acting out the unconscious drama "written" by the parents.

Kohut (1971, 1977) has offered a self psychological perspective on the function of perversions. In his view, perverse activity involves a desperate attempt to restore the integrity and cohesiveness of the self in the absence of empathic selfobject responses from others. The sexual activity or fantasy may help the patient feel alive and intact when threatened by abandonment or separation. Perverse behavior in the course of psychotherapy or analysis may thus be a reaction to failures of empathy by the therapist, leading to a temporary disruption of the self-selfobject matrix established between patient and therapist (Miller 1985). In Kohut's (1977) view, the behavioral manifestations of perversions are secondary phenomena: "After the breakup of the primary psychological unit (assertively demanded empathy-merger with the selfobject), the drive appears as a disintegration product; the drive is then enlisted in the attempt to bring about the lost merger (and thus the repair of the self) by pathological means, i.e., as enacted in the fantasies and actions of the pervert" (p. 128).

Although not a self psychologist, McDougall (1986) has also noted a profound fear of loss of identity or sense of self at the core of much perverse activity. Certain sexual practices or sexual objects become like a drug that the patient uses to "medicate" a sense of inner deadness and a fear of self-disintegration. In these patients, McDougall has observed a faulty internalization process that impeded their use of transitional objects in childhood during their efforts to separate from maternal figures.

Traditional clinical wisdom has suggested that perversions are rare in women. This point of view has been changing in recent years as the result of empirical research and clinical observation demonstrating that perverse fantasies are actually common in women. In a comprehensive study of female perversions, Kaplan (1991) pointed out that clinicians have failed to identify perversions in women because they involve more subtle dynamics than the more obvious sexuality of men's perversions. Sexual acts stemming from female paraphilias involve unconscious themes of separation, abandonment, and loss. For example, some women who have been sexually abused as children adopt an exaggerated stereotype of female sexiness in an effort to wreak vengeance on men and reassure themselves about their femaleness.

Before considering the dynamics of each individual paraphilia, we should note that the reasons remain obscure for individual preference of one perverse fantasy or act over another. Also, different paraphilias often coexist in the same person. Finally, a wide range of psychiatric diagnoses and levels of personality organization may be present in a paraphilic individual. Perversions have been observed, for example, in psychotic patients, in those with personality disorders, and in relatively intact or neurotic patients. Polymorphous perverse sexuality is commonly found in patients with borderline personality organization (Kernberg 1975). Paraphilias that involve overt cruelty to others are often present in patients with antisocial personality disorder. Thus, the psychodynamic understanding of any individual patient involved in perverse sexual activity implies a thoroughgoing comprehension of how the perversion interacts with the patient's underlying character structure. For example, patients with neurotic organization may use a paraphilic activity to facilitate genital potency, whereas patients near the psychotic border may use the same activity to fend off a sense of dissolution of the self (Person 1986).

Exhibitionism and Voyeurism

By publicly exposing his genitals to strange women or girls, the exhibitionist reassures himself that he is not castrated (Fenichel 1945; Freud 1905/1953). The reaction of shock that his actions produce helps him deal with castration anxiety and gives him a feeling of power over the opposite sex. Stoller (1985) has pointed out that exhibitionistic acts typically follow a situation in which the offender felt humiliated, often at the hands of a woman. In turn, the exhibitionist avenges this humiliation by shocking strange women. Moreover, displaying his genitals enables the man to regain some sense of worth and positive masculine identity. Frequently these men reveal a profound insecurity about their sense of maleness. Stoller (1985) noted that castration anxiety does not completely capture the motivation for the exhibitionistic act. In his view, the threat "is best put in identity terms; for humiliation is about 'existence anxiety,' threat to core gender identity" (p. 20). Exhibitionists often feel that they made no impact on anyone in their family, and thus they have had to resort to extraordinary measures to be noticed (Mitchell 1988). Each exhibitionistic act may therefore be an attempt to reverse a childhood traumatic situation.

The flip side of exhibitionism—voyeurism—also involves a violation of a strange woman's privacy, an aggressive but secretive triumph over the female sex. Fenichel (1945) linked voyeuristic tendencies to a fixation on the primal scene of childhood, in which the child either witnesses or overhears parental intercourse. This early traumatic experience could arouse the child's castration anxiety and then lead him to reenact the scene again and again as an adult in an attempt to actively master a passively experienced trauma. Fenichel also identified an aggressive component in looking, conceptualizing it as a guilt-avoiding displacement of the wish to be directly destructive to women. Even patients who are not prone to overtly voyeuristic activities may exhibit common derivatives such as curiosity and anxiety about looking. Some patients are even reluctant to glance around their therapist's office for fear that their curiosity will be construed as destructive or that they will see something forbidden. Mitchell (1988) has observed that exhibitionism and voyeurism capture an essential quality typical of all perversions: "a dialectic between surface and depth, between the visible and the secret, between the available and the withheld" (p. 111).

Sadism and Masochism

Persons who require sadistic fantasies or actions to achieve sexual gratification are often unconsciously attempting to reverse childhood scenarios in which they were the victim of physical or sexual abuse. By inflicting on others what happened to them as children, they gain revenge and a sense of mastery over the childhood trauma at the same time. Masochistic patients who require humiliation and even pain to achieve sexual pleasure may also be repeating childhood experiences of abuse. Fenichel (1945) believed that masochistic patients are making a sacrifice—accepting a "lesser evil" in place of castration. They may also be firmly convinced that they deserve punishment for their conflictual sadistic wishes. In some cases, these patients defend against separation anxiety by submitting to abuse. They are frequently convinced that a sadomasochistic relationship is the only available form of object relatedness: an abusive relationship is better than no relationship.

Sadism and masochism are unique in that they are the only classical perversions that are acknowledged to occur regularly in both sexes (Person 1986). Although masochism has been stereotypically linked to women, muted forms of sadistic and masochistic fantasies are regularly found in almost everyone. The practices of male homosexuals and the reports of female prostitutes even suggest that masochistic sexual activities may be more common in men. Sacher-Masoch, the 19th century Austrian writer from whom the term derives, was, in fact, a poet of male masochism. All sexual arousal may indeed be linked to aggressive wishes (Stoller 1985). Patients who come to psychotherapy or psychoanalysis with sexual inhibitions often reveal highly sadistic fantasies that prevent them from becoming sexually involved with other people.

In relational terms, sadism often develops from a particular internal object relationship in which the withholding and distant object requires a forceful effort to overcome its resistance to the corresponding self-representation (Mitchell 1988). Similarly, masochistic surrender may be an enactment of an internal object relationship in which the object will respond to the self only when humiliated.

From a self psychological perspective, masochistic behavior is a frantic effort to restore a sense of aliveness or self-cohesion. Although apparently self-destructive, masochism may be experienced by the patient as self-restorative. Stolorow et al. (1988) reported the treatment of a highly disturbed 19-year-old patient who repeatedly asked the therapist to hit her. In response to the therapist's persistent inquiries about why she would want him to strike her, she wrote: "Physical pain is better than spiritual death" (p. 506). In the absence of physical pain and abuse at the hands of others, this patient felt that she did not exist and was not connected with anyone else. These authors noted that masochistic patients often organize their entire lives to meet their parents' needs. As a result, their own internal affective experience becomes remote and unavailable because it has been sacrificed in the service of their parents.

Fetishism

To achieve sexual arousal, fetishists require the use of an inanimate object, often an article of women's underwear, or a shoe, or a nongenital body part. Freud originally explained fetishism as stemming from castration anxiety. The object chosen as a fetish symbolically represented the "female penis," a displacement that helped the fetishist overcome castration anxiety. Following the premise that male awareness of the female genitals increased a man's fear of losing his own genitals and becoming like a woman, Freud thought that this unconscious symbolization explained the relatively common occurrence of fetishism. He also used this formulation to develop his concept of the splitting of the ego (1940/1964)—coexisting in the fetishist's mind are two contradictory ideas: denial of castration and affirmation of castration. The fetish represents both.

Although Greenacre (1970, 1979) also viewed castration anxiety as central to the understanding of fetishism, she noted that it has its origins in earlier pregenital disturbances. Chronic traumatic interactions in the first few months of life may thus be instrumental in producing fetishism. Because of severe problems in the mother-infant relationship, the infant is unable to be soothed by the mother or by transitional objects. To experience bodily integrity, the child thus requires a fetish, something "reassuringly hard, unyielding, unchanging in shape, and reliably durable" (1979, p. 102). These early pregenital disturbances are reactivated later when the male child or adult is concerned about genital integrity. In essence, Greenacre saw the fetish as functioning like a transitional object.

Kohut (1977) held a somewhat similar view about fetishism, although couched in self psychological terms. He described a male patient whose childhood was characterized by the traumatic unavailability of his mother. The patient made a fetish of underpants, which served as a substitute for the unavailable selfobject. In contrast to this patient's feelings of helplessness about his mother, he could maintain total control over this nonhuman version of a selfobject. Thus what appears to be an intense sexual need for a fetishistic object may actually reflect severe anxiety about the loss of one's sense of self (Mitchell 1988).

Pedophilia

Of all the perversions, pedophilia is the most likely to create feelings of disgust and contempt in treaters. In fulfilling his sexual desires, the

pedophile may irreparably damage innocent children. Some conceptual framework or psychodynamic formulation can enable clinicians to
maintain a degree of empathy and understanding when attempting to
treat these patients. According to the classical view (Fenichel 1945;
Freud 1905/1953), pedophilia represents a narcissistic object choice—
that is, the pedophile sees a child as a mirror image of himself as a
child. Pedophiles were also regarded as impotent and weak individuals
who sought children as sexual objects because they would offer less
resistance or create less anxiety than adult partners, thus enabling
pedophiles to avoid castration anxiety.

In clinical practice, many pedophiles are found to suffer from narcissistic character pathology, including psychopathic variants of narcissistic personality disorder (see Chapter 17 for a detailed discussion
of the interface between narcissistic and antisocial personality disorders). Sexual activity with prepubescent children may shore up the
pedophile's fragile self-esteem. Similarly, many individuals with this
perversion choose professions in which they can interact with children
because the idealizing responses of children help them maintain their
positive self-regard. In return, the pedophile often idealizes these children; thus, sexual activity with them involves the unconscious fantasy
of fusion with an ideal object or restoration of a youthful, idealized self.
Anxiety about aging and death may be warded off through sexual activity with children. Socarides (1988) described a pedophilic patient
who fended off engulfment from his mother through his pedophilic activities. This patient sought to escape his unconscious feminine identification by incorporating masculinity from a prepubescent male child.
Sexual relations with a boy made this patient feel as if he were part of
the boy. At a deeper level, merger with the boy represented a wish to
incorporate the breast of the mother and thus compensate for an absence of effective mothering early in life.

When pedophilic activity occurs in conjunction with a narcissistic
personality disorder with severe antisocial features, or as part of an
outright psychopathic character structure (see Chapter 17), the unconscious determinants of the behavior may be closely linked to the
dynamics of sadism. Sexual conquest of the child is the tool of vengeance. Pedophiles were frequently victims of childhood sexual abuse
themselves, and a sense of triumph and power may accompany their
transformation of a passive trauma into an actively perpetrated victimization.

Power and aggression are also prominent concerns of pedophiles whose sexual activity is limited to incestuous relationships with their own children or stepchildren. These men often feel unloved by their wives, and they elicit caretaking responses from their children by portraying themselves as victims (Ganzarain and Buchele 1990). The flip side of their martyred self-presentation, however, is a sense of control and power over their sexual partners. These incestuous fathers harbor extraordinary hostility toward women, and they often think of the penis as a weapon to be used in acts of vengeance against women. Some have even acknowledged that feelings of intense anger produce erections (Ganzarain and Buchele 1990).

Transvestism

In this common paraphilia, the male patient dresses as a woman to create sexual arousal in himself that leads to heterosexual intercourse or masturbation. The patient may behave in a traditionally masculine manner while dressed as a man but then become effeminate when dressed as a woman. The classic psychoanalytic understanding of cross-dressing involves the notion of the phallic mother. By imagining that his mother possesses a penis, even if it is not clearly visible, the male child overcomes his castration anxiety. The act of cross-dressing may thus be an identification with the phallic mother (Fenichel 1945).

At a more primitive level, the little boy may identify with his mother to avoid anxiety about separation. His awareness of genital differences between him and his mother may activate anxiety that he will lose her because they are separate individuals. Clinical work with transvestites reveals that when they cross-dress, they commonly experience some degree of fusion with an intrapsychic maternal object. This reassures them that they are not in danger of losing the soothing maternal presence within. These men are always heterosexual, but their sexuality is often inhibited (Person 1986).

Treatment Approaches

Patients with paraphilias are notoriously difficult to treat. Over many years, they have developed a carefully crafted erotic solution to their problems, and they are rarely interested in giving it up (McDougall 1986). Why would someone wish to halt a practice that produces great pleasure? Most perversions are ego-syntonic; only exceptional patients who are distressed by their symptoms willingly seek treatment. Per-

sons with fetishes generally view their fetishism as nothing more than
a personal idiosyncrasy—certainly not a psychiatric symptom
(Greenacre 1979). They typically seek treatment for other reasons, and
the fetishism emerges in the course of therapy or analysis.

The vast majority of paraphilic patients come to treatment under
pressure. A marital crisis may bring a transvestite to clinical attention
under threat of divorce. In instances of voyeurism, exhibitionism, and
particularly pedophilia, legal pressures often mandate treatment as a
condition of probation or as an alternative to incarceration. A court
date may be pending, so the patient will go through the motions of
treatment to "look good" in court and to influence the judge to drop any
charges. In every case of paraphilia, the first order of business is to
clarify the legal situation. The clinician may decide to defer a decision
on long-term treatment until after the disposition of the case in court.
Those patients who continue to seek treatment after all legalities have
been resolved may have better prognoses (Reid 1989).

Another major impediment to the treatment of patients with perversions is the countertransference responses they evoke. If indeed we
all struggle with unconscious perverse wishes, as Freud and countless
others since his time have repeatedly suggested, then it is reasonable
to assume that we may react to the perverse patient as we would to our
own perverse impulses. We are filled with disgust, anxiety, and contempt. Our natural impulse is to respond punitively—to moralize, to
chide, to lecture, and to do what we can to "stamp out" the perversity.
We also recoil in horror at the prospect of anyone allowing full rein to
such impulses when we ourselves carefully control them. Another
countertransference tendency is to collude with the patient's avoidance
of the perversion by talking about other aspects of his life. Clinicians
can avoid their own feelings of disgust and contempt by avoiding the
whole area of sexual pathology. With some patients—pedophiles, in
particular—certain therapists may feel that they simply cannot be effective because of their intense countertransference hatred. In these
instances, it is best to refer the patient elsewhere.

One final reason for treatment difficulty with persons suffering
from perversions is the associated psychopathology. Perverse fantasy
and behavior are difficult enough to alter, but when the patient's condition is complicated by borderline, narcissistic, or antisocial character
pathology, the prognosis becomes even more guarded.

In spite of—or perhaps because of—all these difficulties in the
treatment of paraphilias, psychodynamic approaches are generally re-

garded as a major component of any treatment plan or even the *preferred* form of treatment (Fogel 1991; Kaplan 1991; McDougall 1980, 1986; Person 1986; Rosen 1964, 1979; Stoller 1985). One must have modest goals, however, because outcome studies have yet to demonstrate that any treatment is highly effective with this group of patients. Although behavioral techniques are widely used and have had some limited success on a short-term basis, long-term results are disappointing (Person 1986), and recidivism rates are unaltered in criminal populations of pedophiles (Rice et al. 1991).

Antiandrogen medications, such as cyproterone acetate (CPA) and medroxyprogesterone acetate (MPA, Depo-Provera), are also popular treatment modalities. Their usefulness is limited, however, by a number of significant drawbacks. First, they have serious side effects, including pulmonary embolism and thrombophlebitis. Second, the problem of noncompliance is formidable—one study (Berlin and Meinecke 1981) had a dropout rate of greater than 50%. The same study also revealed that 15% of the subjects had recurrent perverse behavior even while taking the medication. Testosterone injections can be illegally purchased on the street without much difficulty. A final disadvantage of antiandrogen agents is that they lower the sexual drive by reducing plasma testosterone levels, but do nothing to alter the deviation itself. If the medication is discontinued, within a week or so the patient's deviant behavior recurs (Travin et al. 1985). However, dynamically oriented psychotherapy in combination with antiandrogen medications might increase compliance and lower the dropout rate (Reid 1989). Marshall et al. (1991) made the following observation: "Whether we can reasonably expect MPA to produce treatment benefits seems debatable, but if it serves to lower risk while changes induced by psychotherapy gradually take hold, then it will be an effective component in treatment" (p. 472).

The growing consensus seems to be that no single treatment is effective for all paraphilias and that individually tailored approaches are required (Adson 1992; Schwartz 1992). Integrative models include such modalities as individual psychotherapy, dynamic group psychotherapy, cognitive reframing, behavioral reconditioning, and relapse prevention (Schwartz 1992). Most clinicians agree that before treatment can be effective, patients must accept full responsibility for their actions and for the damage they have caused. Treatment goals generally include assisting patients in overcoming their denial, helping them develop empathy for their victims, identifying and treating deviant sexual arousal, identifying social deficits and inadequate coping skills, challenging cognitive distortions, and developing a comprehensive relapse-prevention plan that includes avoidance of situations in which they are likely to be tempted.

Psychotherapeutic treatments. Individual expressive-supportive psychotherapy with an expressive emphasis is often the preferred method of treatment, but a therapist's expectations must nevertheless be modest. Although many patients will make considerable gains in object relatedness and ego functioning, their underlying perverse tendencies may be modified to a lesser degree. In general, those patients with higher-level character organizations have a better outcome than those with borderline levels of organization (Person 1986). More specifically, when the perversion primarily functions to increase and facilitate sexual potency secondary to phallic-oedipal conflict, psychotherapeutic intervention is likely to be more effective than in those cases where the paraphilia functions to prevent disintegration of the self.

Similarly, those patients who are psychologically minded, who possess some degree of motivation, who have some distress about their symptoms, and who are curious about the origins of their symptoms are likely to do better than those who lack such qualities. Socarides (1988) has reported that pedophiles fixated at a phallic-oedipal level with considerable ego strength may do quite well in psychoanalysis. Other clinicians have also reported positive results with highly expressive therapy and psychoanalysis (McDougall 1980; Rosen 1964, 1979).

Certain problems typically arise when paraphilic persons are treated with dynamic psychotherapy. These patients rarely wish to focus on the perversion itself and often actively assert that it is no longer a problem for them. Although psychotherapists must treat disorders associated with the paraphilia, they must also vigorously confront such denial from the beginning. As Kohut (1971) has pointed out, the perverse activity and fantasy often exist in a split-off and compartmentalized area of the personality. One therapeutic task is to integrate the perverse behavior with the central sector of the patient's personality functioning so that it can be addressed along with the rest of the patient's life.

Another frequently encountered dilemma in psychotherapy centers around the avoidance of a punitive stance vis-à-vis the patient's perverse activity. Some states have reporting laws that require a therapist to break confidentiality if pedophilic activity is uncovered during psychiatric treatment. Even apart from the legal and ethical considerations, perverse behavior is likely to evoke highly disapproving responses in therapists. Sensitive patients often detect the therapist's struggle to refrain from being punitive. Clever patients may exploit this countertransference struggle by accusing their therapist of being harsh and cruel because of the therapy's focus on the perverse symptom. Patients may also avoid discussing the symptom by instead professing their feelings of shame, embarrassment, and humiliation.

If the patient can overcome his initial resistance to forming a therapeutic alliance in the service of understanding the perverse symptom, then both patient and therapist can begin to search for unconscious meanings of the symptom and its function within the patient's personality. Most paraphilias operate in an object relations context outside the patient's awareness. Many patients with paraphilias experience their fantasies and behavior as essentially nonpsychological, and they are unaware of any connections between their symptoms and feeling states—or between their symptoms and life events—that may increase their need for the symptoms. Much of the therapist's effort must therefore go into explaining these connections. The therapist can also point out the relational aspects of the perverse fantasy or behavior.

> Mr. W, a 22-year-old college student, was hospitalized following an arrest for exposing himself to female students on the campus. He would sit in his car in the parking lot of the women's dormitory with his genitals exposed. As female students walked by, some would look in the car and react with shock, which substantially excited him. During his brief hospitalization, Mr. W agreed to start psychotherapy, but he was basically a reluctant participant. He told his therapist that his embarrassment and depression upon being arrested and hospitalized would prevent him from ever resorting to exhibitionism again. He preferred to use the therapy to talk about other problems, such as his difficulties with self-esteem and with applying himself to his studies at college.
>
> The therapist confronted this denial and suggested that the problem of exhibitionism had not disappeared simply because Mr. W had been hospitalized. Following discharge from the hospital, Mr. W continued to struggle with exhibitionistic impulses, occasionally giving in to them. Each time he reported such impulses in therapy, his therapist would invite reflection on possible precipitants of the impulses or actions. Mr. W seemed genuinely perplexed as he searched his mem-

ory for antecedent events or feelings. The wish to expose himself was so integral to his identity that he did not think of it as developing out of any affective or relational context.

On one occasion after Mr. W exposed himself, his therapist pointed out that the episode of exposure had occurred immediately after a young woman in one of his classes had turned him down when he asked her out for a date. Mr. W acknowledged that he had felt rebuffed and humiliated and that he could understand the possibility that exposing himself was an expression of his anger and revenge when women failed to respond to him. He began to notice a pattern of increasing exhibitionistic impulses whenever he experienced a rebuff or rejection from any woman he pursued romantically. With help from the therapist, Mr. W was able to link his anger at women with his deep resentment of his mother for returning to full-time work outside the home when Mr. W was 2 years old.

When the therapy began to address these sensitive aspects of Mr. W's relationships with women, he abruptly terminated treatment. Several years later, however, he wrote to his therapist, indicating that he had found the key to overcoming his urge to expose himself. Although his exhibitionistic tendency still haunted him once in a while, he had managed to control it by teaching himself "to learn to love women." He had discovered, through a positive relationship with a young woman, that some women actually did care about him. He thanked the therapist for helping him see that he had been distorting the feelings women had toward him. When he realized that women did not automatically resent him because he was a man, he felt less fearful around them and less compelled to take revenge against them through exhibitionistic activity.

Marital therapy may be critical to the successful treatment of paraphilias. A marital crisis may precipitate the patient's seeking of treatment in the first place. Marital therapy can often help delineate how the perverse activity reflects sexual and emotional difficulties in the marital dyad. It may also alleviate the wife's unwarranted feelings of guilt and responsibility for the behavior and can instead facilitate a sense that she is part of its solution rather than part of its cause (Kentsmith and Eaton 1978). An exploration of marital discord may also reveal that the paraphilia is a container or "scapegoat" that deflects the focus from other more problematic areas in the marriage (Reid 1989). Clinicians must therefore be innovative in using the patient's spouse as an adjunctive therapist in refractory cases of paraphilia. For example, one man who was unresponsive to a number of treatments for his exhibitionism was able to control the symptom only when his wife agreed to drive him everywhere he went.

In cases of pedophilia that occur in the context of incest, family therapy is ordinarily an integral part of the overall treatment plan. Mothers typically collude in these incestuous arrangements by scotomizing the abundant evidence of father-daughter (or occasionally father-son) sexual relations. These mothers frequently grew up as parentified children who never received the nurturance they needed in childhood because they were too busy taking care of their own parents and siblings (Gelinas 1986). They tend to marry highly needy, dependent men as a continuation of their propensity for caretaking. Because of chronic feelings of neglect, the mother in such a family is likely to be highly ambivalent about raising children, and when they arrive, she may feel overwhelmed and neglect her husband as a result. As mother and father become more estranged, the father turns to one of the children—usually the eldest daughter—for nurturance, leading to a second generation of the parentified-child pattern. This child is likely to feel responsible for filling the mother's shoes, and when part of that responsibility entails sexually satisfying her own father, she may subordinate her own needs and rights to his. She exists to satisfy the needs of others. Indeed, family therapy in cases of incest often reveals that the victim protects the offender and maintains loyalty toward him. Effective family therapy requires careful attention to these dynamics. The victim's loyalty to the offender must be acknowledged and respected. It is also helpful to focus on the father's wish for relatedness and emotional connectedness rather than on sexuality or perversion (Gelinas 1986). Incest victims often report that the only warmth they ever received in their family of origin was from the father. The depletion of the mother's emotional resources must also be addressed empathically, and the therapist must bolster her ego capacities. The therapist who approaches the family by identifying and seeking to punish villains will be met with massive resistance—the family members will "circle the wagons" to exclude an outside attacker who does not appreciate the homeostatic balance within the family system.

Dynamic group psychotherapy is another modality that has been used effectively with patients suffering from perversions. Voyeurs and exhibitionists may respond well to group modalities. In one study (Rosen 1964), 21 of 24 patients were recovered or improved at follow-up 6–36 months later. Legally enforced group therapy with sex offenders, such as pedophiles, has also obtained satisfactory results, even on an outpatient basis (Ganzarain and Buchele 1990; Rappeport 1974). These groups provide a mixture of support and confrontation from other offenders who are intimately familiar with the patient's problem, just as homogeneous groups of drug addicts and alcoholics bring group pressure to bear to change destructive behavior. Ganzarain and Buchele (1990) have found that excluding severely disturbed pedophiles—those with organic brain syndrome, psychosis, substance abuse, pure sociopathy, and exclusive perversions—can facilitate identification of a subgroup of pedophiles who will respond well to expressive group psychotherapy. Although patients in their group of offenders frequently denied responsibility and externalized blame, many suffered from unconscious guilt feelings and a profound sense of shame and humiliation about having been discovered. Typically, however, these feelings were fended off by considerable resistance to psychotherapeutic exploration. Because the treatment was legally mandated, many of the offenders viewed the group therapists as agents of the court and therefore assumed the posture of "doing time." Those patients with lower degrees of sociopathy and greater unconscious guilt feelings ultimately were able to use the group therapy process to understand that their hatred of women grew out of their wish to be loved. This understanding led to greater control of sexual impulses and general improvement in their capacity for object relations.

Hospital treatment. Those paraphilic patients most likely to be hospitalized are pedophiles and, to a lesser extent, exhibitionists, who are simply unable to control their behavior on an outpatient basis. Many of the same countertransference problems described for psychotherapeutic treatments also arise in hospital treatment. The patient's denial of his perversion may lead staff members to collude with him by focusing on other problems. One exhibitionist would regularly sit in the lounge of the hospital unit with an erection visible underneath his sweatpants. However, no one on the nursing staff reported noticing this behavior until the doctor pointed out that one manifestation of countertransference with this patient was a fear of looking. This same patient would also often stand nude in his room until a female nurse made rounds; he would then act surprised and indignant when she saw him. When the patient's doctor brought up this behavior in a group meeting on the unit, the patient tried to marshal support from his fellow patients by accusing the doctor of being insensitive and cruel by embarrassing him in front of his peers.

In general, patients with paraphilias will object to discussing their problems in group meetings or community meetings on an inpatient unit. However, when staff members comply with requests to avoid sexual issues in treatment meetings, they are colluding with the patient's tendency to go through an entire hospitalization without dealing with the perversity that necessitated the hospitalization. Patients must be told initially that *all* treatment issues will be discussed in group meetings. Many pedophiles are extraordinarily smooth individuals who will charm other patients into avoiding confrontations. Thus, patients with paraphilias may never benefit from feedback from other patients about the paraphilia's impact on them.

> Mr. X, a 41-year-old teacher, had been extensively involved in pedophilic sexual activities for many years. When the hospital staff insisted that he mention his child-molesting in the community meeting on the unit, Mr. X complied, but in such a manner that he received no feedback from any of the other patients. He began by saying that he loved children and was concerned about the future of America. He talked at great length about his love for his own two daughters and his concern about how his hospitalization might affect them. He admitted to sexual behavior with children, but made it sound benign. He explained that he had never forced any sexual activity on any child and he claimed that, in fact, all his victims had enjoyed their physical contact with him. He spoke of it in terms of "hugging" and "stroking," and he maintained that it had always occurred in the context of a loving friendship. By the time he finished his narrative account, the other patients were quite sympathetic. The psychiatrist in charge of the meeting asked if anyone were shocked or repulsed by Mr. X's behavior. Everyone denied any such reaction.

Pedophiles on a hospital unit may virtually paralyze the patient group from giving them the effective feedback it gives other patients. In addition, those with striking antisocial personality features may simply lie so that their perverse behavior is never dealt with during their hospitalization. One such patient maintained for all 6 weeks of his hospitalization that he had been falsely accused. On the day of his discharge, he acknowledged to his doctor with a chuckle that he actually had molested a child but had not wanted to admit it. As this patient packed his bags to leave the unit, his doctor was left feeling frustrated and impotent to do anything to improve the patient's condition.

Other pedophiles may convince staff members that they are complying with treatment by going through the motions required by it. They appear to use the insights gained in psychotherapy about the origin of their impulses and desires but secretly have no interest in changing themselves. They "play the game" of hospital treatment because it is far preferable to prison, where pedophiles are often subject to gang rape. One pedophile who was a model patient during his hospitalization reported that his pedophilic impulses were thoroughly under control at discharge. He even said that he was no longer turned on by children. Upon transfer to a halfway house after discharge, he continued to report that he was no longer troubled by his pedophilic desires. This illusion was shattered when the police issued a warrant for his arrest stemming from two instances of child molestation. This pattern of deceiving staff members while going through the motions of treatment is all too common among this patient population. Some pedophiles may therefore do far better in correctional facilities with specialized programs for sex offenders that involve group confrontational approaches.

Sexual Dysfunctions

The increased popularity of behavioral techniques in the treatment of sexual dysfunctions (Masters and Johnson 1970) may have led some clinicians to view psychodynamic approaches as less relevant to the treatment of these disorders. Over the past two decades, however, sex therapists have encountered numerous individuals and couples who, for a variety of reasons, are unsuited for brief behavioral sex therapy. As a result, the prescription of specific treatments for specific sexual dysfunctions has become increasingly sophisticated. Moreover, these disorders have served as models for the development of combined therapeutic techniques that include mixtures of behavioral and dynamic interventions (Kaplan 1974, 1979, 1986).

There is little question that certain patients can benefit from the techniques of Masters and Johnson. These researchers originally reported an 80% success rate with their 2-week intensive sex therapy program in St. Louis (1970). Data on the efficacy of psychodynamic psychotherapy in the treatment of sexual dysfunctions, however, are less available. One study that appeared shortly after the original Masters and Johnson report suggested less-impressive results (O'Connor and Stern 1972). Ninety-six patients who were treated 2–4 times a week for at least 2 years with psychoanalysis or psychoanalytically oriented psychotherapy for functional disorders had a success rate of 25% for the female subgroup and 57% for the males. Kaplan (1986) has pointed out that comparisons such as these are inappropriate since the patients in the O'Connor and Stern study probably had a much greater degree of associated psychopathology. Much of the effectiveness of the Masters and Johnson approach can be attributed to the select group of patients who sought their treatment. By and large, they were highly motivated, financially secure professional couples who could take 2 weeks out of their lives to devote themselves intensively to a sex therapy program. Kaplan also noted that specific diagnoses greatly influenced the success of sex therapy. Problems intrinsic to the desire phase are often resistant to sex therapy, and most results for this disorder would be comparable to those reported in the O'Connor and Stern (1972) study. Discrepancy of sexual desire between partners is the most commonly treated sexual dysfunction, and one survey of sex therapists revealed that only half such couples were cured with sex therapy (Kilmann et al. 1986).

The fact that the most common sexual dysfunction is effectively treated by sex therapy only half the time reflects the need for dynamic approaches in addition to behavioral treatments. Clinicians have long known that when a sexual problem is the chief complaint in an initial interview, it is often only the tip of the iceberg. In some cases, the sexual problem may be a "red herring" to distract the clinician from far more serious and urgent problems. In other cases, it may serve to "contain" a variety of intimately related intrapsychic, marital, and family problems. Patients most likely to respond to brief sex therapy are usually suffering from mild performance anxiety in the context of a reasonably healthy personality structure and a reasonably gratifying marital relationship. Patients whose sexual problems are associated with severe character pathology (e.g., borderline and narcissistic personality disorders) or serious Axis I syndromes (e.g., panic disorder, schizophrenia, and major affective disorder) will not benefit from brief behavioral sex therapy and should therefore not be assigned that form of treatment (Kaplan 1986). Similarly, couples with entrenched patterns of pathological relatedness and chronic feelings of resentment and bitterness are not suitable candidates for brief sex therapy. Typically, these couples will not practice the assigned sex therapy exercises but will instead become more openly conflictual (Lansky and Davenport 1975). Even couples with greater psychological health may resist practicing the sensate focus exercises that are often part of behavioral sex therapy treatment because the exercises activate unconscious anxiety (Kaplan 1986). The treatment of sexual symptoms must therefore be highly individualized and must be based on a careful psychiatric and psychodynamic evaluation. Organic causes, especially for erectile disorders, must be ruled out, thereby facilitating an accurate psychiatric diagnosis.

Psychodynamic Understanding of Sexual Dysfunctions

Most sexual dysfunctions catalogued in DSM-IV may be categorized as disorders of desire, arousal, or orgasm. Problems related to orgasm are generally improved with brief behaviorally oriented sex therapy, which illustrates that symptoms produced by unconscious determinants can be alleviated by behavioral techniques without recourse to dynamic understanding. Indeed, brief sex therapy may be the most cost-effective treatment for individuals and couples who have difficulty attaining orgasm but who have no serious associated psychopathology. Disorders associated with desire and arousal tend to be more refractory to brief sex therapy because they are anchored in more deep-seated psychopathological factors (Kaplan 1986; Reid 1989). This discussion will focus on problems in these areas.

The psychodynamic understanding of the male or female patient who has no desire for sex, or of the male patient who has desire but is unable to achieve an erection, begins with a careful understanding of the symptom's situational context. If the patient is involved in an intimate relationship, the clinician must determine whether the problem of desire or arousal is specific to the partner or is generalized to all potential sexual partners. Sexual difficulties that are specific to the couple must be understood in the context of the interpersonal dynamics of the dyad, while other, primarily intrapsychic difficulties would occur with any partner. Clinicians must remember, though, that desire problems, like all other psychological symptoms, are multiply determined.

Levine (1988) has delineated three discrete elements of sexual desire that must function in synchrony for adequate desire and arousal: drive, wish, and motive. Drive is rooted in biology and may be affected by physical factors, such as hormonal levels, medical illnesses, and medications. The wish element is more intimately connected to conscious cognitive or ideational factors. For example, in the presence of a normal drive component, an individual may wish to not have sex because of religious prohibitions or because of a fear of contracting AIDS. The third element, motive, is intimately related to unconscious object relational needs and is the component most likely to be the focus of therapeutic intervention.

The clinician must assess all three elements, according to Levine, and must attempt to understand why these are not integrated into a functional whole. Numerous factors may interfere with an individual's motivation. One partner in the marriage may be having an extramarital affair and may simply have no interest in the spouse. Or one spouse may feel so chronically resentful and angry toward the other that sexual relations are out of the question. Problems in the couple's nonsexual relationship probably account for most instances of inhibited sexual desire (ISD). A sexual partner's distortions can also play a key role in disturbing motivation. In many couples who enter sex or marital therapy, the spouses are unconsciously relating to one another as if to the opposite-sex parent. When this occurs, sexual relations may unconsciously be experienced as incestuous, so the partners manage the anxiety associated with this taboo by avoiding sex altogether. Simpson (1985) has reported a case of sex therapy in which the wife was highly resistant to carrying out the prescribed exercises. When this resistance was explored dynamically, the wife was able to acknowledge to the therapist that part of her wanted her husband to fail in sex therapy. She revealed her fear that her husband would become a "womanizer" like her father if he regained adequate sexual functioning. This transference distortion of her husband threatened to undermine the success of the sex therapy. Even single individuals in therapy or analysis may experience transference-like attachments to a potential sex partner that result in disorders of motivation.

Mr. Y was a 25-year-old, single professional man who entered psychoanalysis because of various problems in his capacity to work and love. The drive component of Mr. Y's sexual desire was entirely adequate—he masturbated several times a day to relieve intense sexual tension. The wish component of desire was also intact. He aspired to sexual relations with an appropriate female and fantasized about doing so. However, the motivational element seemed lacking, as evidenced by his characteristic behavior pattern each time he became attracted to a woman. As he talked about the woman in analysis, he would become tearfully convinced that he would ultimately lose the current object of his longings. His anticipation of the loss aroused such intense feelings of grief and so overwhelmed him that he would decide not to pursue a relationship at all but instead to simply retreat into solitary masturbation.

Each time Mr. Y experienced these feelings of anticipatory loss, his analyst would try to elicit any associations to previous events or life experiences that might bring up analogous feelings. After a considerable period of analytic work, the patient finally began to make sense of his feelings. When the patient was 5 years old, his father had been away at war for a year. During this time, Mr. Y had been "the man of the house," occupying a special position with his mother in the absence of his chief rival for her affections. At times he had even slept in bed with her. When Mr. Y's father returned, however, the patient suffered a devastating loss of this special, intimate relationship with his mother.

The patient's memory of this period in his life helped him understand his motives not to pursue sexual relations. As soon as he became infatuated with a woman, he began to form a maternal transference attachment. Reexperiencing her (at an unconscious level) as his mother, he became convinced that she, too, would "dump" him for another man, just as his mother had turned him aside for his father. Mr. Y feared confronting that grief again, which led him to avoid sexual relations. This insight also put Mr. Y in touch with considerable castration anxiety. He realized that he was deeply worried that his penis might be injured during sex, a concern that he eventually associated with his fear of retaliation for having taken his father's place in his mother's bed.

Our capacity for sexual arousal and desire is clearly connected intimately with our internal object relations. Scharff (1988) has developed an object relations model of inhibited sexual desire based on Fairbairn's (1952) theories of development (see Chapter 2). Fairbairn postulated two "bad object" systems, the libidinal ego and object, in which the ego longs for a tantalizing object, and the antilibidinal ego and object, in which the ego feels hatred and anger toward an attacking, abandoning, or negligent object. The rejecting or antilibidinal object attempts to eliminate the exciting or libidinal object. In Scharff's model, then, this antilibidinal system interferes with sexual excitement, which derives from the libidinal system.

These metapsychological abstractions can be more easily understood by examining the development of a typical relationship. Individuals are attracted to one another as a result of activation of the

libidinal or need-exciting object system. Via mutual projective identification, each regards the other as the exciting object. To maintain the
idealized "in love" state, each must repress the antilibidinal or rejecting object. However, as the luster and freshness of the relationship
wear off, the repressed object relations unit begins to surface, particularly when needs are inevitably frustrated. At this point, the rejecting
object of the antilibidinal system is projected into the partner, and sexual excitement is contaminated by the perception of the partner as
persecuting or abandoning.

In Scharff's model, clinicians must evaluate disturbances of desire
according to three different areas of internal and external object relations: 1) the external realities of the couple's current marital relationship; 2) the internal object world of each individual and how it affects
the capacity for sexual intimacy; and 3) the current family constellation (including children, elderly parents, and other factors) and how it
affects sexual desire. Scharff has noted that sexual desire is greatly
affected by the developmental stage of the marriage itself.

A psychodynamic assessment of inhibited sexual desire must acknowledge the possibility that the "designated patient" may not be the
one who needs the treatment. Kaplan (1988) has studied couples in
which one partner is so exquisitely sensitive to rejection that the other
partner will lose interest in having sexual relations. In many of these
cases, the female partner suffers from panic disorder in which the
man's absorption in pleasure is perceived as an abandonment of her.
No amount of reassurance from the male partner will convince the
woman of his commitment to her. Kaplan recommended that the apparently "asymptomatic" partner may need to realize that her efforts
at control instead lead her partner to withdraw from sexual intimacy.

Primitively disturbed patients, especially those with schizophrenia
and severe borderline features, may find the prospect of genital fusion
overwhelming to their fragile ego. Motivational factors in these patients
that lead to inhibited sexual desire are related to the primitive anxiety
states described in Chapter 9, including disintegration anxiety, persecutory anxiety, and a fear of fusing with one's partner. Abstaining from
sexual relations may thus appear to safeguard the integrity of the self.

Treatment Considerations

The clinician who assesses functional sexual disorders must decide
whether to prescribe brief behavioral sex therapy, couples therapy, psy-

choanalysis or expressive-supportive psychotherapy, pharmacotherapy, or any combination of these. Lief (1981) estimated that 30%–40% of all sexual dysfunctions will improve symptomatically with brief behavioral techniques. Of those who do not benefit from behavioral therapy, 20% will require marital therapy, 10% will need long-term individual expressive-supportive psychotherapy, and about 30% will need some combination of marital and sex therapy. Kaplan's (1986) estimates are similar, but she has also advocated pharmacotherapy. Approximately one-fourth of the patients at her sex clinic whose problems involved sexual aversion or phobic sex avoidance also met the diagnostic criteria for panic disorder. However, she found that prescribing sensate focus techniques for those patients only increased their anxiety, and thus defeated the treatment. Antipanic medication, such as desipramine, imipramine, monoamine oxidase inhibitors, and clonazepam, may all be helpful for these patients. But Kaplan (1988) also concluded that these medications do not cure the patient and stressed that attention to dynamic issues should accompany pharmacotherapeutic intervention.

Indications for the various modalities may not always be clear during the initial evaluation. Brief behavioral sex therapy is likely to be successful if a couple is highly motivated, if neither partner suffers from serious psychopathology, if each partner is reasonably satisfied with the relationship, and if the dysfunction is based on performance anxiety and related to the orgasm phase. Couples who have inhibited sexual desire and are generally disillusioned with the relationship may require marital therapy for a time to address basic problems in their relationship. If the couple decides to stay together after marital therapy, then sex therapy techniques can be more appropriately recommended.

Couples who seem appropriate candidates for brief sex therapy techniques but who undermine the process by not practicing the exercises may require a hybrid treatment that Kaplan (1979) has labeled *psychosexual therapy*. In this treatment, the therapist prescribes behavioral exercises and then addresses any resistances to practicing the exercises with dynamic psychotherapy. Kaplan has found this combination of techniques to be critical to successful treatment with certain patients. The dynamic portion of the treatment allows exploration of themes such as the patient's intense guilt feelings about sexual pleasure. Parental transferences to the partner can also be uncovered and explored. In addition, many patients have unconscious conflicts about being successful in any endeavor—including sexual performance, which may have to be examined. Kaplan (1986) has also found that some patients unconsciously act out the role of "loser" or "failure" that they have been assigned in their family of origin.

A strong consensus in the literature indicates that patients suffering from severe character pathology or deeply ingrained neurotic conflicts about sexuality should be treated in psychoanalysis or expressive-supportive psychotherapy (Kaplan 1986; Levine 1988; Reid 1989; Scharff 1988). Sometimes these problems surface only during an extended evaluation with sex therapy (Scharff 1988). Certain patients may remain unconvinced of the need for long-term intensive individual psychotherapy until they have tried brief methods and found them ineffective. Extended sex therapy also allows the therapist to gain a greater grasp of the internal object relations of each member of the couple. As described in the section on object relations family and marital therapy in Chapter 5, the therapist "contains" the various projective identifications from both spouses. Therapists who are open to this process can diagnose problematic patterns of object relatedness in the couple through "firsthand experience." When there is deep-seated neurotic conflict about sexuality or when there is severe character pathology, however, sex therapy will often exacerbate these problems (Lansky and Davenport 1975). The prescribed sensate focus exercises will force the couple to confront issues that are habitually avoided because of the way their relationship has been organized.

Mrs. Z was a 46-year-old homemaker who entered sex therapy with her husband because of her total lack of interest in sexual relations. After several unproductive sessions, the sex therapist referred Mrs. Z for individual expressive-supportive psychotherapy. She felt relieved when she first saw her individual psychotherapist because she realized that she would not be "forced into sexual relations" with her husband.

She described her marital relationship as involving a caretaking role for herself that produced no gratitude from her husband. He had retired 4 years earlier and now spent his days lying around the house watching television. She was not happy with their relationship, but she seemed to have little interest in changing it. She repeatedly berated herself, saying that she did not deserve a better life than what she had. When this pattern of being unable to enjoy success was pointed out to her by the therapist, Mrs. Z confided that every time she had felt good in her life, she had been "zapped." She then recounted numerous examples, including the death of one of her children, to illustrate how she had always been punished for any positive feelings she had about events in her life.

Although Mrs. Z talked about a wide range of topics in her psychotherapy, she steadfastly refused to mention anything about her sexuality or the sexual problems that brought her to treatment in the first place. Her therapist began to feel as though he were coercing her into dealing with her sexual problems. When he gently asked her about them, she responded as though to a rapist, feeling violated and withdrawing into silence. The therapist used his countertransference feelings to diagnose an internal object relation that had been externalized in the psychotherapy. He said to Mrs. Z, "You seem to react as though I am traumatizing you with my questions about sexuality. Is this repeating any sexually related trauma from your past?" Mrs. Z broke down and tearfully acknowledged a history of early sexual trauma at the hands of an uncle. She also opened up further about her first marriage, explaining that she had had a number of extramarital affairs that led to two illegal abortions. She had always been a "daddy's girl," and she wondered if she had been looking for her father in all those affairs. This insight was coupled with an awareness that she had stopped having affairs when her father died about 18 years earlier. Her father had been involved in some of her marital problems that had resulted from her promiscuity, and he had seemed highly distressed by her unfaithfulness to her husband. She even speculated that her promiscuous behavior in her first marriage might have caused her father's death. With interpretations from the therapist, Mrs. Z began to understand that her self-sacrifice and selfless devotion to caring for her husband was a form of psychological reparation for the damage she believed she had inflicted on her father. She also began to understand that she denied herself sexual pleasure to punish herself for her promiscuity and the two abortions.

The case of Mrs. Z illustrates how deeply ingrained sexual problems may be ego-syntonic because they fulfill certain psychological needs. Many patients with sexual dysfunctions are actually convinced that they should *not* experience sexual pleasure, so they are therefore invested in maintaining their symptomatology. The treatment of sexual dysfunctions is a highly value-laden area of psychiatry. Clinicians must temper their countertransference need to cure with a respect for the patient's right to choose a particular pattern of sexual adjustment. Kaplan (1986) has noted that some women who fail to reach orgasm nevertheless report satisfying sexual relations; such women usually do not seek treatment for sexual dysfunction. In addition, many voluntary celibates in religious orders lead happy and productive lives. Finally, clinicians must keep in mind that, for some patients, a sexual symptom is nothing more than an admission ticket to psychotherapy. Once inside the door, these patients become more interested in other areas of their life and the sexual symptoms lose significance.

References

Adson PR: Treatment of paraphilias and related disorders. Psychiatric Annals 22:299–300, 1992

American Psychiatric Association: Diagnostic and Statistical Manual of Mental Disorders, 4th Edition. Washington, DC, American Psychiatric Association, 1994

Berlin FS, Meinecke CF: Treatment of sex offenders with antiandrogenic medication: conceptualization, review of treatment modalities, and preliminary findings. Am J Psychiatry 138:601–607, 1981

Chasseguet-Smirgel J: Perversion and the universal law. International Review of Psychoanalysis 10:293–301, 1983

Fairbairn WRD: Psychoanalytic Studies of the Personality. London, Routledge & Kegan Paul, 1952

Fenichel O: The Psychoanalytic Theory of Neurosis. New York, WW Norton, 1945

Fogel GI, Myers WA (eds): Perversions and Near-Perversions in Clinical Practice: New Psychoanalytic Perspectives. New Haven, CT, Yale University Press, 1991

Freud S: Three essays on the theory of sexuality (1905), in The Standard Edition of the Complete Psychological Works of Sigmund Freud, Vol 7. Translated and edited by Strachey J. London, Hogarth Press, 1953, pp 123–245

Freud S: Splitting of the ego in the process of defence (1940), in The Standard Edition of the Complete Psychological Works of Sigmund Freud, Vol 23. Translated and edited by Strachey J. London, Hogarth Press, 1964, pp 271–278

Ganzarain RC, Buchele BJ: Incest perpetrators in group therapy: a psychodynamic perspective. Bull Menninger Clin 54:295–310, 1990

Gelinas DJ: Unexpected resources in treating incest families, in Family Resources: The Hidden Partner in Family Therapy. Edited by Karpel MA. New York, Guilford, 1986, pp 327–358

Greenacre P: The transitional object and the fetish: with special reference to the role of illusion. Int J Psychoanal 51:447–456, 1970

Greenacre P: Fetishism, in Sexual Deviation, 2nd Edition. Edited by Rosen I. Oxford, Oxford University Press, 1979, pp 79–108

Kaplan HS: The New Sex Therapy: Active Treatment of Sexual Dysfunctions. New York, Brunner/Mazel, 1974

Kaplan HS: Disorders of Sexual Desire and Other New Concepts and Techniques in Sex Therapy. New York, Simon & Schuster, 1979

Kaplan HS: The psychosexual dysfunctions, in Psychiatry, Revised Edition. Edited by Cavenar JO Jr. Vol 1: The Personality Disorders and Neuroses. Edited by Cooper AM, Frances AJ, Sacks MH. Philadelphia, PA, JB Lippincott, 1986, pp 467–479

Kaplan HS: Intimacy disorders and sexual panic states. J Sex Marital Ther 14:3–12, 1988

Kaplan LJ: Female Perversions: The Temptations of Emma Bovary. New York, Doubleday, 1991

Kentsmith DK, Eaton MT: Treating Sexual Problems in Medical Practice. New York, Arco, 1978

Kernberg OF: Borderline Conditions and Pathological Narcissism. New York, Jason Aronson, 1975

Kilmann PR, Boland JP, Norton SP, et al: Perspectives of sex therapy outcome: a survey of AASECT providers. J Sex Marital Ther 12:116–138, 1986

Kohut H: The Analysis of the Self: A Systematic Approach to the Psychoanalytic Treatment of Narcissistic Personality Disorders. New York, International Universities Press, 1971

Kohut H: The Restoration of the Self. New York, International Universities Press, 1977

Lansky MR, Davenport AE: Difficulties of brief conjoint treatment of sexual dysfunction. Am J Psychiatry 132:177–179, 1975

Levine SB: Intrapsychic and individual aspects of sexual desire, in Sexual Desire Disorders. Edited by Leiblum SR, Rosen R. New York, Guilford, 1988, pp 21–44

Lief HI (ed): Sexual Problems in Medical Practice. Monroe, WI, American Medical Association, 1981

Marshall WL, Jones R, Ward T, et al: Treatment outcome with sex offenders. Clinical Psychology Review 11:465–485, 1991

Masters WH, Johnson V: Human Sexual Inadequacy. Boston, MA, Little, Brown, 1970

McDougall J: Plea for a Measure of Abnormality. New York, International Universities Press, 1980

McDougall J: Identifications, neoneeds and neosexualities. Int J Psychoanal 67:19–31, 1986

Miller JP: How Kohut actually worked. Progress in Self Psychology 1:13–30, 1985

Mitchell SA: Relational Concepts in Psychoanalysis: An Integration. Cambridge, MA, Harvard University Press, 1988

O'Connor JF, Stern LO: Results of treatment in functional sexual disorders. NY State J Med 72:1927–1934, 1972

Person ES: Paraphilias and gender identity disorders, in Psychiatry, Revised Edition. Edited by Cavenar JO Jr. Vol 1: The Personality Disorders and Neuroses. Edited by Cooper AM, Frances AJ, Sacks MH. Philadelphia, PA, JB Lippincott, 1986, pp 447–465

Rappeport JR: Enforced treatment—is it treatment? Bull Am Acad Psychiatry Law 2:148–158, 1974

Reid WH: The treatment of psychiatric disorders: revised for the DSM-III-R. New York, Brunner/Mazel, 1989

Rice ME, Quinsey VL, Harris GT: Sexual recidivism among child molesters released from a maximum security psychiatric institution. J Consult Clin Psychol 59:318–386, 1991

Rosen I (ed): Pathology and Treatment of Sexual Deviation: A Methodological Approach. London, Oxford University Press, 1964

Rosen I (ed): Sexual Deviation, 2nd Edition. London, Oxford University Press, 1979

Sachs H: On the genesis of perversions. Translated by Goldberg RB. Psychoanal Q 55:477–488, 1986

Scharff DE: An object relations approach to inhibited sexual desire, in Sexual Desire Disorders. Edited by Leiblum SR, Rosen R. New York, Guilford, 1988, pp 45–74

Schwartz BK: Effective treatment techniques for sex offenders. Psychiatric Annals 22:315–319, 1992

Simpson WS: Psychoanalysis and sex therapy: a case report. Bull Menninger Clin 49:565–582, 1985

Socarides CW: The Preoedipal Origin and Psychoanalytic Therapy of Sexual Perversions. Madison, CT, International Universities Press, 1988

Stoller RJ: Perversion: The Erotic Form of Hatred. New York, Pantheon, 1975

Stoller RJ: Observing the Erotic Imagination. New Haven, CT, Yale University Press, 1985

Stolorow RD, Atwood GE, Brandchaft B: Masochism and its treatment. Bull Menninger Clin 52:504–509, 1988

Travin S, Bluestone H, Coleman E, et al: Pedophilia: an update on theory and practice. Psychiatr Q 57:89–103, 1985

Chapter 12

Substance-Related Disorders and Eating Disorders

In this chapter I consider two diagnostic categories that involve discrete self-destructive symptoms. Substance abuse is defined by the ingestion of chemicals that may lead to addiction, life-threatening physical problems, and a host of emotional problems. Eating disorders are defined by overeating, voluntary purging, and starvation. Both groups of disorders present a complex problem for psychodynamic clinicians: What is the role of dynamic approaches in disorders that require symptom control as a major thrust of the therapeutic effort? In some quarters, psychodynamic understanding is considered irrelevant to the management of addiction and eating disorders. However, a considerable body of clinical and research literature suggests otherwise.

Substance-Related Disorders

Because psychodynamic psychiatrists often become frustrated in their efforts to treat alcoholic patients, they may abandon or avoid such efforts. Relapse is common, and interpretations of unconscious motivations often seem to have little impact on the drinking behavior itself.

Psychodynamic models of alcoholism are regarded with skepticism both by mental health professionals and by society at large.

Two other models—the moral model and the disease model— receive much greater support (Cooper 1987). The moral model views alcoholic individuals as bearing complete responsibility for their alcoholism. From this point of view, alcoholic persons are hedonistic individuals interested only in their own pursuit of pleasure, with no regard for the feelings of others. This model has its roots in the fundamentalist religious belief that alcoholism is a sign of moral turpitude. Failings of willpower are closely linked to notions of sin, and punishment through the legal system is often regarded as the appropriate way to deal with alcoholic individuals. Eliminating drinking behavior is a matter of overcoming weak willpower to "pull oneself up by the bootstraps."

The phenomenal success of Alcoholics Anonymous (AA) has led to the increasing popularity of the disease model of alcoholism. In contrast to the moral model, this paradigm relieves the alcoholic person of responsibility for his or her illness. Just as a diabetic person is not held responsible for diabetes, the alcoholic individual is not held responsible for alcoholism. Alcoholic persons are viewed as having an inherent predisposition to addiction to exogenous substances; psychological factors are irrelevant. Although this model originated as a backlash to moralizing reactions to—and inhumane treatment of—alcoholic persons, it has recently gained support from genetic studies of the offspring of alcoholic individuals. Even when raised apart from their alcoholic parents, these children have an increased risk of developing alcoholism as adults (Goodwin 1979; Schuckit 1985). A study of 1,030 female twin pairs (Kendler et al. 1992) suggested that the heritability of the liability to develop alcoholism is in the range of 50%–60%.

Further support for the disease model has come from Vaillant's (1983) prospective study of male alcoholic patients throughout the course of their adult lives. He found that the eventual development of alcoholism could not be predicted from adverse childhood experiences or even from psychological profiles of these subjects as young adults. The only reliable predictor of adult alcoholism was antisocial behavior. Vaillant concluded that depression, anxiety, and other psychological characteristics often associated with alcoholic persons were *consequences,* rather than causes, of the disorder. Furthermore, psychotherapy and psychological conceptualizations of alcoholism play a minor role in clinical understanding and treatment planning. Vaillant thus decided that enforced abstinence through AA has the greatest likelihood of success.

A shift in focus from alcoholic patients to those who abuse drugs reveals wide usage of the same two models. The moral model is more widely applied to drug abusers than to alcoholic persons, however, largely because of the extensive overlap between crime and drug abuse. Much of the controversy over the appropriate response to the national drug problem involves whether addicted persons are more effectively handled through legalistically oriented punitive approaches or medically oriented therapeutic approaches. Drug abusers have sought to replicate the success of AA by developing organizations such as Narcotics Anonymous (NA). But the disease model and its associated self-help groups have been less successful with drug abusers, as Vaillant himself (1988) has pointed out, because of apparent fundamental differences between alcoholic persons and polydrug abusers that require differential approaches. In view of these essential differences, the following section will examine the psychodynamic understanding of alcoholic persons and drug abusers in turn.

Psychodynamic Approaches to Alcoholism

The AA approach to the problem of alcoholism has been highly effective in the treatment of many individuals. Although the AA organization itself promotes the disease model, its methods address psychological needs and facilitate lasting structural personality changes (Mack 1981). Abstinence is achieved in an interpersonal context where alcoholic individuals can experience a caring and concerned community of fellow sufferers. These caring figures can be internalized in the same manner that a psychotherapist is internalized, and they can assist the alcoholic individual with affect management, impulse control, and other ego functions, also as a psychotherapist would. Hence the psychodynamic model can facilitate an understanding of some of the changes rendered by the AA approach (Mack 1981).

For many alcoholic persons, the psychological changes encouraged by AA and the abstinence associated with commitment to its ideals and regular attendance at the meetings are sufficient treatment. The psychodynamically sensitive clinician, understanding the value of this approach, must have the good judgment to leave well enough alone. Clinical experience has repeatedly demonstrated, however, that AA is not suitable for all patients who suffer from alcoholism. It apparently works best for those who can accept the idea that they have no control over their drinking and thus need to surrender to a "higher power," and for those who are essentially free of other psychiatric disorders.

Most alcoholism experts would agree that alcoholism is a heterogeneous disorder with a multifactorial etiology (Donovan 1986). What works for one patient may not work for another, and all the treatments are surrounded with controversy. Clinicians should keep in mind that a myriad of evaluation studies on the effectiveness of various treatments for alcoholism suggest that only 26% of treated alcoholic patients are still abstinent 1 year later (Parloff et al. 1986), in contrast to the "spontaneous remission" rate of 19%. Clearly, no treatment is definitive, and clinicians must consider each patient individually, making a careful psychiatric evaluation before developing an individually tailored treatment plan.

Unfortunately, the disease model has promulgated the "de-psychologizing" of alcoholism. The conclusions drawn by Vaillant (1983) are in conflict with those based on other longitudinal studies, which suggest that personality factors may be important to an understanding of vulnerability to alcoholism (Sutker and Allain 1988). Moreover, Vaillant's conclusions are only as valid as his instruments of measurement. Dodes (1988) has observed that Vaillant's methods are not capable of identifying a critical feature in alcoholic patients—namely, their disturbance in self-esteem as revealed by an inability to care for themselves. Also, those people predisposed to alcoholism may be vulnerable to regression, despite the presence of overtly positive childhood relationships (Mack 1981).

Perhaps the major difficulty with the treatment approach suggested by Vaillant and other strict adherents to the disease model is that it ignores the heterogeneity of the disorder. Alcoholism is not a monolithic entity. In fact, one might more accurately refer to the "alcoholisms" (Donovan 1986). Numerous studies attest that there is no single "alcoholic personality" that predisposes to alcoholism (Donovan 1986; Nathan 1988; Sutker and Allain 1988). Nonetheless, personality variables and psychological issues are highly relevant in the treatment of many alcoholic patients. A narrow interpretation of the disease model might lead clinicians to ignore how these factors contribute to relapse in the course of the illness.

Although no specific personality traits are connected with alcoholism, psychoanalytic observers have repeatedly noted structural defects, such as ego weakness and difficulty in maintaining self-esteem

(Donovan 1986). Both Kohut (1971) and Balint (1979) noted that alcohol serves the function of replacing missing psychological structures and thereby restores some sense of self-regard and inner harmony. Unfortunately, these effects last only as long as the intoxication. Khantzian (1982) also observed that alcoholic patients had problems with self-esteem, the modulation of affect, and the capacity for self-care. Investigators of borderline personality disorder have consistently noted parallels between alcoholic patients and patients with borderline personality disorder (Hartocollis 1982; Kernberg 1975; Knight 1953; Rinsley 1988); in particular, they share such traits as poor anxiety tolerance, poor affective control, and the use of splitting as a predominant defense (see Chapter 14). This linkage of alcoholism with borderline personality disorder has been further substantiated by empirical studies (Nace et al. 1983; Vaglum and Vaglum 1985) that suggest that 30%–39% of alcoholic persons have coexisting borderline pathology. Other common diagnoses accompanying alcoholism are depression (Weissman and Myers 1980) and sociopathy (Schuckit et al. 1970).

These studies are cited not to convince readers that all alcoholic persons suffer from coexisting psychiatric disorders or preexisting intrapsychic deficits, but rather to highlight the obvious fact that addiction to alcohol occurs in a *person*. An individual may develop alcoholism as the final common pathway of a complex interaction between structural deficits, genetic predisposition, familial influences, cultural contributions, and other assorted environmental variables. A thorough psychodynamic evaluation of the patient will consider the alcoholism and all its contributing factors in the context of the total person. Whether depression, for example, is a cause or a consequence of alcoholism, or a completely separate disease state, is of more interest to researchers than to clinicians. When alcoholic individuals sober up and look back at the wreckage caused by their alcoholic existence, they are commonly faced with a good deal of depression. This depression stems from the painful recognition that they have hurt others (frequently those most important to them). They must also mourn the things (e.g., relationships, possessions) that they have lost or destroyed as the result of their addictive behavior. Although antidepressant medication may alleviate the depression, psychotherapy can assist in the process of working through these painful issues. Also, assessment and treatment of suicide risk must be part of the overall planning in the treatment of alcoholic patients. Twenty-five percent of all suicides occur in alcoholic individuals, and an alcoholic person's likelihood of suicide is between 60 and 120 times higher than that of a person who is not psychiatrically ill (Murphy and Wetzel 1990).

Another implication of the observation that alcoholism occurs in an individual is that each person will prefer and accept different treatment options. Dodes (1988) has noted: "Some patients are able to use only psychotherapy, others can use only AA, and there are those who will best be treated with a combination of the two. Accurate prescription of treatment requires individual clinical judgment" (pp. 283–284). Many alcoholic individuals find AA unworkable either because of their embarrassment at having to speak in front of a group or because of their philosophical opposition to the notion of a "higher power." Although Vaillant (1981) has declared psychotherapy to be wasteful in the treatment of alcoholism, some patients are able to maintain sobriety with psychotherapy alone (Dodes 1984; Khantzian 1985a). An unfortunate "straw man" stereotype often applied to the dynamic psychotherapy of alcoholic patients is that the therapist uncovers unconscious motivations for drinking while ignoring the patient's actual drinking behavior. The fact that psychotherapy can be misused by some patients and by some therapists does not mean, however, that it should be written off as a treatment (Dodes 1988).

Patients involved in AA are often in psychotherapy as well. In one study, more than 90% of the abstinent alcoholic patients in AA who sought psychotherapy found it helpful (Brown 1985). Psychotherapy and AA often work synergistically. Dodes (1988) has observed that alcoholic patients may develop, in self psychological terms, an idealizing or mirror transference to the AA organization. They view it as a caring, idealized figure in their life that sustains and supports them. This transference may be split off from the psychotherapeutic transference, and the psychotherapist is wise to delay analyzing it. Eventually, the selfobject functions of AA can be internalized enough to improve self-care and heighten self-esteem. After some degree of internalization, psychotherapists can shift the therapy from a supportive to a more expressive emphasis.

Rosen (1981), who has identified separation-individuation problems in alcoholic persons, believed that psychotherapy is helpful in weaning patients from a symbiotic attachment to AA, but only after they have established sobriety through the help of the organization. Other researchers have argued that abstinence is not an absolute requirement for effective psychotherapy (Dodes 1984; Pattison 1976). If a therapist demands abstinence, some patients will refuse treatment altogether. In fact, it is naive to expect total abstinence in the course of long-term psychotherapy. Very few alcoholic individuals are unambivalent about giving up their symptomatic drinking; any lack of motivation should be viewed as a symptom rather than as a contraindication for psychotherapy (Cooper 1987). However, if patients continue to drink heavily, with no capacity for or interest in exploring their reasons for drinking, they may be unable to use the psychotherapeutic process and may instead require hospitalization to be effectively treated. In any case, abstinence should not be an absolute requirement for proceeding with therapy.

Group psychotherapy is also commonly used in both inpatient and outpatient treatment of alcoholism. As with all other treatment modalities, this modality is rarely used in isolation, so it is difficult to determine its effectiveness. More commonly, it is part of a comprehensive treatment plan that also involves many other interventions. A recent review of studies involving group psychotherapy of alcoholic patients suggested the empirical validity of using group psychotherapy as an adjunctive treatment (Brandsma and Pattison 1985). Group psychotherapeutic approaches often involve intense confrontation of the self-destructive nature of the addiction as a way of cutting through the denial so prominent in alcoholic persons (Bratter 1981).

Other therapists (e.g., Khantzian 1986) have cautioned against a confrontational approach. Because of the difficulty that many alcoholic patients have in regulating affects such as anxiety, depression, and anger, confrontation in a group setting can be counterproductive or even harmful. Cooper (1987) shared Khantzian's view that confrontation should be used judiciously. He believed that the therapist should empathize with the alcoholic individual's defensive need to avoid painful affect. Cooper advocated inpatient groups that focus on the here and now but are less confrontational. He reported a 55% abstinence rate with patients in such groups, compared with 16% for patients in an inpatient group program without group psychotherapy. Those patients who remained in group therapy for at least 25 hours also demonstrated greater compliance with other aspects of the program.

Psychodynamic Approaches to Drug Abusers

Although the disease model is popular in many drug rehabilitation programs, psychodynamic approaches are more widely accepted and valued in the treatment of drug abusers than in the treatment of alcoholic persons. Vaillant (1988), for example, noted that polydrug abusers, in contrast to alcoholic individuals, are more likely to have had unstable childhoods, more likely to use drugs as "self-medication" for psychiatric symptoms, and more likely to benefit from psychotherapeutic efforts to address their underlying symptomatology and character pathology.

A considerable body of research literature supports the association of personality disorder and depression with the development of drug addiction (Blatt et al. 1984a; Kandel et al. 1978; Paton et al. 1977; Treece 1984; Treece and Khantzian 1986). These studies suggested that whereas initiation to marijuana use may be related to peer pressure in adolescence, use of and eventual addiction to hard drugs are not. One study found impaired relationships with parents and depression to be highly significant predictors of eventual abuse of illicit drugs, whereas sociodemographic variables were not (Kandel et al. 1978). Another study of high school students who became involved in heavy drug use identified depression as the most potent predictor of all personality variables (Paton et al. 1977). Treece (1984) concluded that the key factor differentiating the chronic drug-addicted person from the controlled or casual abuser is the presence in the former of a severe personality disorder.

Compared with alcoholic persons, drug abusers are much more likely to have significant coexisting psychiatric disorders. In a large epidemiological study involving interviews with 20,291 persons (Regier et al. 1990), drug abusers had a 53% rate of comorbidity as compared to only 37% for alcoholic individuals. Studies of narcotic-addicted individuals have found other psychiatric diagnoses in as many as 80%–93% (Khantzian and Treece 1985; Rounsaville et al. 1982). The comorbidity rate is also high among cocaine abusers. As many as 73% of those seeking treatment meet lifetime criteria for another psychiatric disorder, with anxiety disorders, antisocial personality disorder, and attention deficit disorder ordinarily preceding the onset of the cocaine abuse, and affective disorders and alcohol abuse usually following the onset of the cocaine abuse (Rounsaville et al. 1991). In a sample of 100 substance abusers (Nace et al. 1991), 57 had personality disorders. The investigators pointed out that a uniform approach to the treatment of substance abusers is inadequate because those with personality disorders require different treatment approaches. Substance abusers with personality disorders are more depressed, more impulsive, more isolated, and generally less satisfied with their lives than are substance abusers without such disorders.

These research findings have played a key role in the development of sophisticated psychodynamic formulations of substance abuse problems. The early psychoanalytic interpretation of all substance abuse as a regression to the oral stage of psychosexual development has been replaced by an understanding of most drug abuse as *defensive* and *adaptive* rather than regressive (Khantzian 1985b, 1986; Wurmser 1974). Drug use may actually reverse regressive states by reinforcing defective ego defenses against powerful affects such as rage, shame, and depression. The early psychoanalytic formulations often depicted persons with drug addictions as pleasure-seeking hedonists bent on self-destruction. Contemporary psychoanalytic investigators understand addictive behavior more as a reflection of a deficit in self-care than as a self-destructive impulse (Khantzian 1986). This impairment in self-care results from early developmental disturbances that lead to an inadequate internalization of parental figures, leaving the addicted person without the capacity for self-protection. Hence the majority of chronic drug-addicted individuals exhibit a fundamental impairment in judgment about the dangers of drug abuse.

Equally important in the pathogenesis of drug addiction is the impaired regulatory function in affect and impulse control and in maintenance of self-esteem (Treece and Khantzian 1986). These deficits create corresponding problems in object relations. Heavy polydrug use has been related directly to the addicted person's incapacity for tolerating and regulating interpersonal closeness (Nicholson and Treece 1981; Treece 1984). Contributing to these relationship problems are the narcissistic vulnerability inherent in interpersonal risks and the inability to modulate the affects associated with closeness. Dodes (1990) noted that addicted individuals tend to feel powerless as a reflection of a specific narcissistic impairment. Their addictive behavior wards off a sense of powerlessness or helplessness by controlling and regulating their affective states. Narcissistic rage and humiliation impels them to use drugs as a way of reestablishing a sense of power. The ingestion of a drug can thus be viewed as a desperate attempt to compensate for deficits in ego functioning, low self-esteem, and related interpersonal problems. Treece and Khantzian (1986) succinctly noted: "The critical factor in both severe and mild disturbances is that a given substance or substances be experienced as meeting a peremptory adaptive need, thus providing not only relief, but the experience, at least temporarily, of increased capacity to cope and to function" (p. 405). In this sense, most drug use that is severe enough to lead to dependency may be a form of self-medication (Khantzian 1985b).

The notion that drug-addicted individuals are medicating them-selves to obtain relief from painful affect states leads directly to another observation of contemporary psychodynamic investigators— namely, that specific substances are chosen for specific psychological and pharmacologic effects according to each abuser's needs. The most painful affect is likely to be what determines the choice of drug. Khantzian (1985a) has noted that cocaine appears to relieve distress associated with depression, hyperactivity, and hypomania, while nar-cotics apparently tone down feelings of rage.

An in-depth study of narcotic-addicted individuals led Blatt et al. (1984a, 1984b) to conclude that heroin addiction is multiply deter-mined by 1) the need to contain aggression, 2) a yearning for gratifica-tion of longings for a symbiotic relationship with a maternal figure, and 3) a desire to alleviate depressive affects. Although the research data indicate that a small subgroup of individuals with narcotic addic-tions also suffers from antisocial personality disorder (Rounsaville et al. 1982), Blatt et al. have identified a larger group of severely neurotic opiate-addicted persons, which may represent the majority. These in-dividuals struggle with feelings of worthlessness, guilt, self-criticism, and shame. Their depression appears to intensify when they attempt to become close to others, so they withdraw into isolated "bliss" brought on by heroin or other narcotics, which has both regressive and defen-sive dimensions. The depressive core of the opiate-addicted individual was further substantiated by a comparison study (Blatt et al. 1984a, 1984b), which found persons with opiate addictions to be significantly more depressed than polydrug abusers. This study also identified self-criticism as a main component of their depression.

The finding of Blatt and his colleagues of a high correlation be-tween superego-ridden, self-critical, depression-prone personality fea-tures and opiate addiction has received support from Wurmser's (1974, 1987a, 1987b) psychoanalytic work with addicted patients. He has ar-gued that those addicted individuals amenable to psychoanalytic ther-apy do not suffer from underdeveloped superegos, like antisocial persons with addictions, but rather from an excessively harsh con-science. The intoxicating substance is sought as an escape from a tor-menting superego. Many drug abusers employ the defense of splitting to disavow a drug-abusing self-representation that alternates with a non-drug-abusing self-representation. These individuals often feel as if someone else has taken over for a brief period. Wurmser has identified success as a prominent trigger for an episode of drug abuse. Positive feelings associated with successful achievement seem to produce an altered state of consciousness characterized by feelings of guilt and shame. Impulsive drug use is seen as the solution to these painful affects. Recurring crises of this kind are characterized by an overbearing conscience that becomes so intolerable that temporary defiance seems the only means of relief.

Although early studies with narcotic-addicted patients suggested that psychotherapy materially contributes to the recovery of addicted persons, much of this research was subsequently discounted because of methodological problems. More recently, a number of reports from the Veterans Administration–Penn Study (Woody et al. 1983, 1984, 1985, 1986, 1987) have persuasively demonstrated with rigorous methodology that adding psychotherapy to the overall treatment plan of opiate-addicted patients produces clear benefits. Narcotic-addicted patients in a methadone maintenance program were randomly assigned to one of three treatment conditions: 1) drug counseling alone with paraprofessionals, 2) expressive-supportive psychotherapy plus drug counseling, or 3) cognitive-behavioral psychotherapy plus counseling. Of 110 patients who completed the full treatment program, those receiving psychotherapy improved considerably more than those who received counseling alone. Expressive-supportive psychotherapy based on dynamic principles resulted in greater improvement in psychiatric symptoms and more success in finding and holding a job than did cognitive-behavioral psychotherapy (Woody et al. 1983). Those patients who were depressed showed the most improvement, followed by patients who had opiate dependency but no other psychiatric disorder. Those with antisocial personality disorder alone did not benefit from psychotherapy (Woody et al. 1985). Antisocial patients improved only when depression was also a symptom.

When the researchers divided the 110 psychotherapy patients into groups according to the severity of their psychiatric symptoms, they noted that patients in the low-severity group made equal progress with counseling or with psychotherapy, while patients with a medium degree of severity had better outcomes with treatment plans combining both of these approaches (although some improved just with counseling). However, the group with extremely severe psychiatric symptoms achieved little progress with counseling alone, but made considerable progress when psychotherapy was added: at 7-month follow-up, those patients in the group who received psychotherapy used both illicit and prescribed drugs far less often than did those who did not receive psychotherapy. These changes were sustained at 12-month follow-up (Woody et al. 1987), even though the subjects were no longer in psychotherapy (the duration of psychotherapeutic treatment was 6 months).

The investigators (Woody et al. 1986) drew several conclusions about the psychotherapy of patients with opiate addictions: 1) Both expressive-supportive and cognitive-behavioral psychotherapy can help those narcotic-addicted persons who can become engaged in and will regularly attend such a treatment program. 2) Patients with significant psychiatric disturbances are the best candidates for psychotherapy and will benefit from it the most. 3) The psychotherapist must be integrated into the overall treatment program and must collaborate with other staff members in the treatment. The researchers believed that there were clear benefits to locating the psychotherapy sessions in the same facility as the rest of the methadone maintenance program. Psychotherapy that is fragmented from the rest of the treatment is unlikely to succeed.

Psychotherapy with drug abusers is a treatment approach that indirectly addresses the addiction by focusing on the associated psychopathology. Most clinicians believe that abstinence from the abused substance is a prerequisite to adequate treatment through psychotherapeutic technique of the underlying disturbances—anxiety, depression, personality disorder, self-esteem problems, or ego deficits. The exception would be a drug substitution program such as methadone maintenance. Once abstinence is achieved, the addicted person often feels despair at having given up something more than a drug—a valued part of the self (Treece and Khantzian 1986). Both therapist and patient realize that abstinence alone does not automatically lead to changes in other areas of life. As abstinent persons with addictions struggle with their longing for the drug and their grief over its loss, the therapist must address their tenaciously defended belief that drug use is an adaptive solution to life's problems. The therapist must identify the underlying problems of modulating affects, of regulating self-esteem, and of relating to others, so as to help the addicted person discover alternative answers to those problems.

One difficulty that psychotherapists will most likely encounter is the alexithymia common in many addicted patients (Krystal 1982–83). In other words, most of these patients are unable to recognize and identify their internal feeling states. A good deal of education may have to occur during the early phases of therapy, with the therapist explaining how the experience of unpleasant feelings initially leads to drug abuse. These patients must be helped to contain and tolerate their affects so that they can substitute words describing their inner states for actions such as the ingestion of a drug. The therapist can assist patients in this regard by identifying feelings that occur during the therapy hour.

An individual psychotherapy process is much more likely to be successful in the context of a comprehensive program. Khantzian (1986) suggested the concept of the primary care therapist—an individual who facilitates the addicted patient's involvement with all treatment modalities. The therapist analyzes the patient's resistance to accepting other forms of treatment, such as NA or group therapy, but also provides a holding environment for dealing with the strong affects mobilized in the treatment process. The primary care therapist must also participate in treatment decisions involving other modalities. In this model, the emphasis is more supportive than expressive at the beginning of treatment, and the therapist's role is similar to that of a hospital doctor working with an inpatient.

Treece and Khantzian (1986) have identified four essential components of a treatment program for mastery of drug dependence: 1) a substitute for the dependency on chemicals (e.g., NA, an alternative system of beliefs, or a benign dependency on a person or religious institution); 2) adequate treatment for other psychiatric disorders, including appropriate psychotropic medication and psychotherapy; 3) enforced abstinence (e.g., drug antagonists, urine surveillance, probation, drug substitutes such as methadone, external support systems) during a psychological maturational process; and 4) promotion of growth and structural personality change through psychotherapy.

Wurmser (1987b) also advocated a multi-pronged approach, but with more expressive psychotherapy. Because he conceptualized an overbearing superego as central to the pathogenesis of compulsive drug use, he cautioned therapists to avoid being punitive or critical with their patients and to refrain from "preaching" to them about drug abuse. A more appropriate role for therapists, in Wurmser's view, is to attempt to understand the superego pressures on the patient, much as in working with a severely neurotic patient. He also believed that therapists should devote their time to looking at underlying issues rather than just focusing on the drug abuse, which can be taken up by other members of the treatment team.

Although no major controlled studies of dynamic group psychotherapy with addicted patients share the methodological sophistication of

the Veterans Administration–Penn Study on individual psychotherapy, group psychotherapy has become a component of many programs
because of the clinical impression that it is helpful to many patients.
Because group psychotherapy is rarely the only treatment modality
used in these programs, it is difficult to determine whether any specific
therapeutic aspects of group therapy are not also present in other modalities. However, practically speaking, many addicted persons are
helped by talking with others who have had the same problem. Also,
because denial is a prominent defense in all substance abusers, a group
setting of peers facilitates a powerful confrontation of denial and com-
pels addicted individuals to accept the seriousness of their substance
abuse. The same caveats about the negative effects of overly aggressive
confrontation that were mentioned in the section on group psychotherapy of alcoholic patients also apply to group psychotherapy of addicted
persons. Effective groups provide as much support as they do confrontation. Inpatient programs often rely more on groups for the practical
reason that enforcing attendance is easier with inpatients than with
outpatients (Woody et al. 1986). A commonly encountered resistance to
groups in both inpatient and outpatient facilities is that many members may have committed crimes and are therefore reluctant to open
up in groups for fear that confidentiality will be breached.

In summary, the indications for expressive-supportive psychotherapy can be conceptualized as the following: 1) serious psychopathology
other than drug abuse; 2) engagement in an overall treatment program
that includes NA or another support group, enforced abstinence, possibly a drug substitute such as methadone, and appropriate psychotropic medication; 3) no diagnosis of antisocial personality disorder
(unless depression is also present) (treatment considerations with antisocial personality disorder are discussed in detail in Chapter 16); and
4) sufficient motivation to keep session appointments and become engaged in the process. The indications for an expressive or supportive
emphasis after the process is well launched are largely determined by
the same factors that determine the emphasis in any other psychotherapeutic process (see Table 4–2 in Chapter 4).

Eating Disorders

Anorexia nervosa and bulimia nervosa appear to be disorders of our
time. The electronic media bombard the public with images of slender
women who "have it all." In many areas of Western culture, food is in

abundance, a precondition for binge eating behavior. Individuals affected by these disorders tend to be Caucasian, educated, female, economically advantaged, and ensconced in Western cultures (Johnson et al. 1989). Anorexia nervosa is virtually unknown in countries where thinness is not considered a virtue (Powers 1984). Media images of females, moreover, suggest that external appearance is far more important than internal identity. Although intrapsychic and biological factors should not be minimized in the etiology and pathogenesis of eating disorders, those factors clearly interface with a particular sociocultural period in Western civilization to produce a syndrome that reflects the culture. Anorexia nervosa has more than doubled in incidence since the 1960s, while the prevalence of bulimia nervosa has been found to be approximately 1% in adolescent and young adult females (Fairburn and Beglin 1990). These disturbing figures indicate that the disorder may be an increasingly common solution to a variety of intrapsychic, familial, and environmental stressors.

Anorexia Nervosa

The label *anorexia nervosa* can be misleading, since the first word of the phrase implies that loss of appetite is the central problem. The diagnostic hallmark of anorexia nervosa is actually a fanatical pursuit of thinness related to an overwhelming fear of becoming fat. An arbitrary cutoff of less than 85% of minimal normal body weight for age and height is often used to make the diagnosis. Amenorrhea is a prominent feature of anorexia nervosa in females. Although 5%–10% of cases are male, their clinical features and psychodynamics are remarkably similar to those of females.

Psychodynamic understanding. For the last two decades, the seminal contributions of Hilde Bruch (1973, 1978, 1982, 1987) have served as a beacon in the darkness for clinicians treating anorexic patients. She observed that the preoccupation with food and weight is a relatively late occurrence emblematic of a more fundamental disturbance in self-concept. Most patients with anorexia nervosa have a thoroughgoing conviction that they are utterly powerless and ineffective. The illness often occurs in "good girls" who have spent their life trying to please their parents, only to suddenly become stubborn and negativistic in adolescence. The body is often experienced as separate from the self, as though it belongs to the parents. These patients lack any sense of autonomy to the point that they do not even feel in control of their bodily functions. The premorbid defensive posture of being a perfect little girl ordinarily defends against a profound underlying feeling of worthlessness. Anorexia nervosa develops, in Bruch's (1987) own words, as "an attempt at self-cure, to develop through discipline over the body a sense of selfhood and interpersonal effectiveness. Anorexics transform their anxiety and psychological problems through manipulation of food intake and size" (p. 211).

Bruch traced the developmental origins of anorexia nervosa back to a disturbed relationship between the infant and its mother. Specifically, the mother appears to parent the child according to her own needs rather than those of the child. When the child-initiated cues do not receive confirming and validating responses, the child cannot develop a healthy sense of self. Instead, the child experiences herself simply as an extension of her mother, not as a center of autonomy in her own right. This understanding is in keeping with early psychoanalytic formulations about the pathogenesis of psychosomatic disorders in children in which an "appersonation" of the child was noted (Sperling 1944). The child is not perceived as a separate individual, but rather as the "right arm" of the mother.

Bruch, then, understood the behavior of the anorexic patient as a frantic effort to gain admiration and validation as a unique and special person with extraordinary attributes. More recently, Bruch (1987) has suggested that the clinical picture may be changing somewhat because it is more and more difficult for the anorexic patient to feel unique, given the increasing prevalence of the disorder and the media attention on eating disorders of all kinds. The illness has now become imbued with a sense of competition to be the thinnest or the most unique.

Masterson (1972, 1977) noted a similarity between the dynamics of certain anorexic patients and those of patients with borderline personality disorders (see Chapter 15). Lacking any sense of identity, the child develops a false self to please the mother. The little girl tries to be the perfect child as a way to reassure herself that her mother will not abandon her. This forced role causes resentment to build up over the years, however, and the anorexic syndrome develops as a full-scale rebellion in which the patient attempts to assert her true self, which has long lain dormant and undeveloped.

Family therapists, such as Selvini Palazzoli (1978) and Minuchin (Minuchin et al. 1978), have confirmed and elaborated some of the dynamic concepts of Bruch and Masterson. Minuchin and his colleagues described a pattern of enmeshment in the families of anorexic patients, where there is a general absence of generational and personal boundaries. Each family member is overinvolved in the life of every other family member to the extent that no one feels a sense of separate identity apart from the family matrix. Selvini Palazzoli (1978) has also noted that patients with anorexia nervosa have been unable to psychologically separate from their mothers, which results in a failure to achieve any stable sense of their own bodies. The body is thus often perceived as if it were inhabited by a bad maternal introject, and starvation may be an attempt to stop the growth of this hostile, intrusive internal object.

The extreme defensive posture of anorexia nervosa suggests that a powerful underlying impulse warrants such a strategy. Indeed, Boris (1984b) noted that intense greed forms the core of anorexia nervosa. Oral desires are so uacceptable, however, that they must be dealt with projectively. Through projective identification, the greedy, demanding self-representation is transferred to the parents. In response to the patient's refusal to eat, the parents become obsessed with whether or not the patient is eating; they become the ones who have desires. In a formulation influenced by Kleinian thinking, Boris conceptualized anorexia nervosa as an inability to receive good things from others because of an inordinate desire to possess. Any act of receiving food or love confronts these patients squarely with the fact that they cannot possess what they desire. Their solution is to not receive anything from anyone. Envy and greed are often closely linked in the unconscious. The patient envies the mother's good possessions—love, compassion, nurturance—but to receive them simply increases the envy. Renouncing them supports the unconscious fantasy of spoiling what is envied, not unlike the fox in Aesop's fable who concluded that the grapes he couldn't reach were sour. The patient conveys the following message: "There is nothing good available for me to possess, so I will simply renounce all my desires." Such renunciation makes the anorexic patient the object of the desire of others and, in her fantasy, the object of their envy and admiration, because they are "impressed" by her self-control. Food symbolizes their positive qualities that she desires in herself; being enslaved by hunger is preferable to desiring to possess the maternal figure.

Most developmental formulations of the origins of anorexia nervosa focus on the mother-daughter dyad. Bemporad and Ratey (1985), however, have observed a characteristic pattern of paternal involvement with anorexic daughters. The typical father was superficially caring and supportive but emotionally abandoning of his daughter whenever she truly needed him. In addition, many fathers of anorexic patients seek emotional nurturance from—rather than give it to—their daughters. Both parents often are experiencing serious disappointment in their marriage, leading each parent to seek emotional sustenance from the daughter. In self psychological terms, the daughter may be treated as a selfobject that provides mirroring and validating functions for each parent but is denied her own sense of self.

To summarize our psychodynamic understanding of anorexia nervosa, the overt behavior of self-starvation is a multiply determined symptom. It is 1) a desperate attempt to be special and unique, 2) an attack on the false sense of self fostered by parental expectations, 3) an assertion of a nascent true self, 4) an attack on a hostile maternal introject viewed as equivalent to the body, 5) a defense against greed and desire, and 6) an effort to make others—rather than the patient—feel greedy and helpless.

These psychodynamic factors are also accompanied by certain characteristic cognitive features. These features include misperception of one's own body image, all-or-nothing thinking, magical thinking, and obsessive-compulsive thoughts and rituals. The presence of obsessive-compulsive symptoms has led some researchers to wonder whether obsessive-compulsive personality disorder coexists with anorexia nervosa. This assumption is confounded by the notorious unreliability of personality disorder diagnoses in the presence of starvation (Kaplan and Woodside 1987; Powers 1984). Many symptoms, including obsessive-compulsive behavior, appear secondary to starvation. Also, premorbid personality characteristics are accentuated in states of nutritional deficiency. The fear of being fat has itself been shown to moderate when the patient begins to eat and gain weight (Garfinkel and Garner 1982).

Treatment approaches. Clinicians who treat patients who have anorexia nervosa are in consensus that the treatment goals must not be focused narrowly on weight gain (Boris 1984a, 1984b; Bruch 1973, 1978, 1982, 1987; Chessick 1985; Hsu 1986; Powers 1984). A "two-track" approach, advocated by Garner et al. (1986), includes a first step of restoration of eating for weight gain. Once this step is accomplished, the second step of psychotherapeutic intervention can begin. Anorexic patients show much greater improvement when provided with a mixture of family therapy and dynamic individual therapy than when they are simply managed with educational measures designed to control weight (Hall and Crisp 1983). Long-term, individual expressive-supportive psychotherapy is the cornerstone of the treatment. Unless the patient's underlying disturbance of the self and the associated distortions of internal object relations are addressed, the patient will follow a course of repeated relapse and revolving-door hospital admissions (Bruch 1982). For those patients living at home, family therapy may be a valuable adjunct to individual therapy. Although some patients appear to benefit from group psychotherapy (Lieb and Thompson 1984; Polivy 1981), the limited data suggest that those who benefit most do not have associated personality disorders (Maher 1984).

Hospitalization may also be a beneficial adjunct to individual psychotherapy. Although no indications for inpatient treatment are universally agreed on, a weight loss of 30% of normal body weight is a good rule of thumb to use in determining whether inpatient treatment is necessary (Garfinkel and Garner 1982). Approximately 80% of all anorexic patients will gain weight with hospital treatment (Hsu 1986), provided that the hospital staff can create a specific milieu. As described in Chapter 6, the hospital staff must be wary of the patient's unconscious efforts to reenact the family struggle in the hospital milieu. They must convey an interest in helping the patient restore weight without becoming excessively concerned about it and without making demands similar to those the patient's parents would make. The patient can be helped to cope with the fear of losing control by arranging an eating plan of frequent but small meals with a member of the nursing staff who is available to discuss the patient's anxiety about eating. Weight gains should be reported to the patient with concomitant positive reinforcements. Any surreptitious vomiting or purging should be confronted and controlled with structural measures such as locking the bathroom door. Members of the treatment staff may need to reassure the patient that they will not allow too much weight gain, thus helping the patient develop a sense of trust in them.

If individual and family therapy were being conducted prior to admission, these should continue during hospitalization. If the patient's hospitalization is her first treatment contact, however, these adjunctive therapies should be implemented as part of the hospital treatment. Antidepressant medication is helpful with patients who meet the criteria for major depression. (Milder forms of depression improve with weight gain.) Brief hospitalizations are rarely curative, nor are treatment programs that demand a normal average weight and then ignore the intense anxiety aroused by such a demand (Bruch 1982). At least 50% of the patients who successfully control their anorexia nervosa with inpatient treatment will relapse within a year (Hsu 1980). For the 20% who do not respond to brief hospitalization, extended hospitalization is indicated.

Individual expressive-supportive psychotherapy often takes several years of painstaking work because of the formidable resistance posed by the anorexic patient. Four guiding principles of technique are useful (see Table 12–1).

1. *Avoid excessive investment in trying to change the eating behavior.* As Boris (1984b) observed, "What we call their symptoms they call their salvation" (p. 315). The patient views anorexia nervosa as the solution to an internal problem. Psychotherapists who immediately define it as a problem that must be changed reduce their chances of forming a viable therapeutic alliance. The behavior associated with anorexia nervosa elicits demands and expectations for change from the patient's parents. Through projective identification, the therapist is likely to experience powerful pressure to identify with the patient's projected internal objects that are associated with the parents. Instead of acting on that pressure and becoming a parental figure, the therapist must try to understand the patient's internal world. One form of this reenactment is the equation of eating with talking. Just as the patient provokes her parents by refusing to eat, she will attempt to provoke the therapist by refusing to talk (Mintz 1988). At the beginning of the therapy, it may thus be helpful to clarify that the primary goal of the treatment is to understand the patient's underlying emotional disturbance rather than the problem of not eating (Bruch 1982; Chessick 1985). Although Boris (1984a) advocated complete avoidance of psychotherapeutic focus on eating, Bruch (1982) suggested that

---

Table 12–1. Technical principles in the psychotherapy of anorexic patients

1. Avoid excessive investment in trying to change the eating behavior.
2. Avoid interpretations early in the therapy.
3. Carefully monitor countertransference.
4. Examine cognitive distortions.

psychotherapy is not feasible unless the patient weighs in the neighborhood of 95 pounds. She explains to her patients that their capacity for thinking and communicating will improve if they can get their weight at least to that level.

2. *Avoid interpretations early in the therapy.* Interpretations of unconscious wishes or fears will be experienced by the anorexic patient as a repetition of her life story. *Someone else* is telling her what she really feels, while her conscious experience is minimized and invalidated. Rather, the therapist's task should be to validate and empathize with the patient's internal experience (Bruch 1987; Chessick 1985). The therapist should take an active interest in what the patient thinks and feels, conveying the message that the patient is an autonomous person entitled to her own ideas about her illness. Of major importance is helping the patient define her own feeling states. The actions and decisions stemming from these feelings must be legitimized and respected. The therapist can help the patient explore various options but should refrain from telling her what to do (Chessick 1985). This empathic, ego-building, supportive approach in the early phases of therapy will facilitate introjection of the therapist as a benign object. Bruch (1987) suggested emphasizing the positive and conceptualizing the therapy as an experience in which patients will discover their positive qualities. She acknowledged that her approach has many similarities to Kohut's (1984) self psychological approach. Chessick (1985) shared this view that insight into unconscious conflict is unlikely to be curative with these patients. Although slightly more optimistic about the use of interpretations, Boris (1984a) recommended withholding interpretations until the patient finds herself. Even then, he advocated talking "to the air" instead of directly to the patient, thereby providing some distance in the relationship and respecting her boundaries. Such interpretations should be delivered as hypotheses, as though talking to an imaginary colleague rather than as making a definitive pronouncement directly to the patient.

3. *Carefully monitor countertransference.* Anorexic patients commonly believe that their parents want them to gain weight so that other people won't view the parents as failures (Powers 1984). The therapist is likely to become anxious about similar matters. Therapists who work within the framework of a comprehensive treatment team, in particular, may begin to feel that others are negatively judging their work if their patients fail to gain weight.

This countertransference concern may lead the therapist to fall into the trap of identifying with the patient's parents. The ideal situation for individual psychotherapy is for another treater to monitor weight gain, leaving the therapist free to explore the patient's underlying psychological issues. When hospitalization is required for weight control, the admitting psychiatrist can manage food intake while the psychotherapist continues the psychotherapeutic work in the hospital. In this setting, the psychotherapist can work productively with the team.

4. *Examine cognitive distortions.* Misperceptions of body size and illogical cognitive beliefs should be explored with the patient non-judgmentally (Powers 1984). The therapist thus serves as an auxiliary ego to help the patient sharpen her powers of observation and her critical thinking (Chessick 1985). Clearly, the psychotherapist must assume an educative role with these patients, helping them understand the effects of starvation on cognition. However, the therapist must seek to educate while making no demand for change. Alternatively, the therapist can simply explore the consequences of the patient's choices.

These technical guidelines, while useful, are not to be taken as a "cookbook" formula for the psychotherapy of anorexic patients. Therapists must be flexible, persistent, and stable in the face of the patient's tendency to "wait out" the therapy process until she can once again be left alone. Body image distortions, which often approach delusional proportions, may be particularly refractory to educational and therapeutic efforts. Therapists must be wary of countertransference despair and frustration that might lead them to attempt to force the patient to "see things as they really are."

Finally, clinicians who treat anorexic patients must confront the lethality of the illness. Studies of long-term outcome suggest that approximately 14% of patients suffering from anorexia nervosa will die from suicide or complications of the illness (Hsu 1991). There is nonetheless reason for optimism: 75% of patients show significant improvement when evaluated 4 years after onset.

Bulimia Nervosa

Patients with bulimia nervosa are generally distinguished from those with anorexia nervosa on the basis of relatively normal weight and the presence of binge eating and purging. Emaciated patients who are also binge eating and purging are often classified as anorexics, bulimic subgroup (Hsu 1986). This diagnostic classification reflects how the concept of anorexia nervosa has become blurred by the cultural fascination with bulimia (Bruch 1987). In Bruch's view, the two syndromes have little in common—the rigid self-discipline and harsh conscience of the anorexic patient contrast sharply with the impulse-ridden, irresponsible, and undisciplined behavior of the bulimic person. The condensed term *bulimarexia* is thus a "semantic atrocity" (Bruch 1987), in that it mistakenly implies similarity.

Bruch's view, however, is not supported by accumulating data that suggest considerable linkage between the two disorders (Garner et al. 1986). At least 40%–50% of all anorexic patients also have bulimia (Garfinkel et al. 1980; Hall et al. 1984; Hsu et al. 1979). Long-term follow-up data suggest that over a long period of time, anorexia nervosa may give way to bulimia nervosa, but that the reverse pattern is much rarer (Hsu 1991). In light of these findings, DSM-IV (American Psychiatric Association 1994) subtypes anorexia nervosa according to the presence or absence of bulimic symptoms and precludes the diagnosis of bulimia nervosa in the presence of anorexia nervosa when the bulimia occurs only during episodes of anorexia nervosa.

Part of the reason for the blurring of diagnostic boundaries between anorexic and bulimic behavior is that the clinical picture can be so varied. Concurrent psychiatric disorders are common (Yager 1984), and over half of all bulimic patients may suffer from associated personality disorders (Johnson et al. 1989). Yager (1984) has eloquently observed:

> Bulimia is not a disease. Nor is it a simple habit. Bulimia is heterogeneous and, like pneumonia, it may result from a variety of causes. I have found it useful to conceptualize bulimia as a habit or behavioral pattern embedded in a personality, in turn embedded in a biology, and all this embedded in a culture in which bulimia seems to be developing at an increasing rate. (p. 63)

Psychodynamic understanding. When considering the psychodynamics of bulimia, therapists must keep in mind this heterogeneity. The various contributors to our dynamic understanding of bulimia are likely to be analogous to the proverbial blind men reporting their perceptions of an elephant based on their particular vantage points. As always, dynamic understanding must be individualized. A clinical picture of bulimia may be observed in patients with vastly different char-acter structures, ranging from psychotic through borderline to neurotic (Wilson 1983). Anorexia and bulimia are essentially opposite sides of the same coin (Mintz 1988). While the anorexic patient is characterized by both greater ego strength and greater superego control, the bulimic patient may suffer from a generalized inability to delay impulse dis-charge, based on a weakened ego and a lax superego. Binge eating and purging are not usually isolated impulse problems; rather, they typi-cally coexist with impulsive, self-destructive sexual relationships and with polydrug abuse.

Mintz (1988) has observed that patients may shift from anorexia to bulimia when powerful urges to binge finally overcome and erode defense mechanisms such as repression and denial. The object rela-tions of the bulimic patient can be the flip side of those of the anorexic patient as well. Bulimic patients typically use interpersonal relation-ships as a way of eliciting damage or punishment from external sources, while anorexic patients tend to withdraw from interpersonal relationships. Mintz explained the source of the bulimic patient's need for punishment as an enormous reservoir of unconscious aggression directed toward parental figures. This rage is displaced onto food, which is then cannibalistically destroyed. Neither anorexic patients nor bulimic patients can regulate their relationships satisfactorily, so they also displace conflicts in relationships onto food. The anorexic pa-tient maintains control over her aggressive feelings toward people by refusing to eat, while the bulimic patient symbolically destroys and incorporates people by gorging.

Those authors who have studied the developmental origins of bu-limia have identified extensive difficulty with separation both in the parents and in the individual patient. A common theme in the develop-mental history of bulimic patients is the absence of a transitional object, such as a pacifier or blanket, to help the child separate psycho-logically from her mother (Goodsitt 1983). This developmental struggle to separate may be played out instead by using the body itself as a transitional object (Sugarman and Kurash 1982), with the ingestion of food representing a wish for symbiotic merger with the mother and the expulsion of food an effort at separation from her. Like the mothers of anorexic patients, the parents of children who grow up to be bulimic often relate to their children as extensions of themselves (Humphrey and Stern 1988; Strober and Humphrey 1987). These children are used as selfobjects to validate the self of the parent. Each member of the family depends on all the other members to maintain a sense of cohesion. Although this pattern characterizes the families of anorexic patients, a particular mode of managing unacceptable "bad" qualities is predominant in bulimic families. The bulimic family system apparently involves a strong need for everyone to see themselves as "all good." Unacceptable qualities in the parents are often projected onto the bulimic child, who becomes the repository of all "badness." By unconsciously identifying with these projections, she becomes the carrier of all the family's greed and impulsivity. The resulting homeostatic balance keeps the focus on the "sick" child rather than on conflicts within or between the parents.

The psychodynamic observations about difficulties with separation in bulimic patients have been confirmed by empirical research (Patton 1992). A group of 40 patients with eating disorders was compared with a control group of 40 women with normal eating patterns to see how they would respond to subliminal or supraliminal stimuli. Each group was shown an abandonment or a control stimulus at exposure durations that were either subliminal or supraliminal. Following exposure to an abandonment stimulus, the group with eating disorders ate significantly more crackers than did subjects in the control group. The investigators concluded that binge eating was indeed a defense against an unconscious fear of abandonment.

In many instances, then, bulimic patients concretize the object relations mechanisms of introjection and projection. Ingestion and expulsion of food may directly reflect the introjection and projection of aggressive, or "bad," introjects. In many cases, this splitting process is further concretized by the patient. She may regard protein as "good" food, which is therefore retained rather than purged, and carbohydrates or junk food as "bad" food, which is consumed in huge quantities, only to be regurgitated. On the surface, this strategy of managing aggression may be compelling—the expulsion of badness in the form of vomit leaves the patient feeling good. However, the residual feeling of "goodness" is unstable because it is based on splitting, denial, and projection of aggression rather than on integration of the bad with the good.

Treatment considerations.   The most important single principle in the treatment of bulimia is individualization of the treatment plan. Concurrent psychiatric disorders, such as depression, personality disorders, and drug abuse, should be addressed as part of comprehensive treatment planning. "Assembly line treatment programs" (Yager 1984) that treat all bulimic patients alike will only help a fraction of them because of a failure to recognize and appreciate the inherent heterogeneity of the bulimic population. About one-third of all bulimic patients represent a relatively healthy subgroup who will respond well to a time-limited approach involving brief cognitive-behavior therapy and a psychoeducational program (Johnson and Connors 1987; Johnson et al 1989). Support groups such as Overeaters Anonymous (OA) may also sustain this subgroup of patients without further treatment. However, if bulimic patients treated with cognitive-behavior therapy and antidepressants are followed up for more than 2 years, 16%–50% are still diagnosable as having bulimia nervosa, and 9%–37% are plagued with occasional episodes of bingeing and purging (Hsu 1991).

Although dynamic approaches may not be indicated or necessary for all patients, they still may benefit the majority. Among nonresponders, as many as two-thirds may have borderline personality disorder (Johnson et al. 1989), while others may have other personality disorders or significant depression. These patients usually require long-term, expressive-supportive psychotherapy and often need psychopharmacologic intervention as well. Many patients also frankly resent a behavioral approach to their bulimic symptoms (Yager 1984). Focusing on the patient's overt behavior while neglecting her internal world may recapitulate the patient's experience of growing up with parents who are more concerned about surface than substance. Yager (1984) has suggested that as many as 50% of all bulimic patients are dissatisfied with behavior modification techniques. Some patients will even experience the task of writing a daily diary about their eating habits as demeaning, because they may view their eating problems as symptomatic of more fundamental disturbances. Treatment that does not match the patient's interests and belief system is doomed to failure (Yager 1984).

Moreover, effective behavioral approaches, whether with sexual disorders or eating disorders, require a solid therapeutic alliance. Johnson et al. (1987) found that symptomatic management of bulimia from a cognitive-behavioral perspective depends on a strong therapeutic alliance and that the analysis of transference facilitates the development and maintenance of that alliance. In their model, one therapist performs both tasks (i.e., reinforcement of symptom control and analysis of transference that interferes with the follow-through of behavioral techniques).

Bulimia nervosa can be life-threatening. Patients have been known to alter their electrolyte balance sufficiently to precipitate cardiac arrest. Blood chemistry monitoring should therefore be part of the outpatient management of these patients, with hospitalization as a backup strategy. Since many bulimic patients also suffer from borderline personality disorder or major affective disorders, hospitalization may be required in the face of a suicide attempt or severe self-mutilation. The hospital treatment must follow an individualized comprehensive treatment plan, in addition to the task of gaining symptom control through locking bathrooms, implementing a normal meal schedule, providing psychoeducational assistance from a dietitian, and encouraging the keeping of a diary. Hospitalization often provides the therapist with an opportunity to better understand the patient's internal object relations; thus, it facilitates more sophisticated diagnostic understanding and more precise treatment planning:

Ms. AA was a 19-year-old college student with a mixture of bulimic and anorexic symptoms. She was hospitalized after "firing" her psychotherapist and completely losing control of her binge eating and purging. Her parents, who were quite exasperated with her behavior, brought her to the hospital because they felt hopeless about ever getting her to eat properly. During the first week of hospitalization, Ms. AA informed her hospital doctor that she planned to remain aloof and distant because she did not want to get attached to a doctor again only to be disappointed. Regular meals and group meetings were immediately implemented, but the patient refused to go to meals or to attend the group. She insisted that she was capable of dieting only by eating when and what she wanted. She pointed out to her doctor that her weight was remaining constant, so there was no need for concern.

The nursing staff became increasingly irritated with Ms. AA for her utter lack of cooperation. The more stubborn and resistant the patient became, the more the staff insisted that she follow the structure of the hospital program. In one staff meeting, the hospital doctor observed that the patient had succeeded in recapitulating her family situation. By asserting that she should have control over her diet, she provoked others into attempting to take control of her eating. She could then feel victimized by the controlling forces around her, just as she felt victimized by her parents.

Ms. AA's doctor met with her and pointed out to Ms. AA that she was attempting to provoke the hospital staff into a reenactment of her family situation. She asked the patient to reflect on what she might gain from this reenactment. Ms. AA responded by indicating to her doctor that she was not interested in talking. Three days later, she told her doctor that she had been hoarding medications and sharp objects in a locked drawer in her hospital room so that she might attempt suicide. She said that she had decided to tell her doctor because she really did not want to die. She also indicated that it was terribly difficult for her to communicate feelings to her doctor because she believed that she would become uncontrollably dependent and would lose any sense of her own self. She was certain that dependency on her doctor would lead to her being exploited and mistreated according to the doctor's needs rather than her own treatment needs.

This information helped the hospital staff understand Ms. AA's resistance to the treatment structure. By refusing to cooperate, this patient was attempting to establish a sense of self independent of the demands and expectations of others. Cooperation with the nursing staff and collaboration with her hospital doctor carried the risk that she would become a mere extension of others, as she had in her family. Once this underlying anxiety surfaced, the staff members allowed Ms. AA to have more say in her eating program. With a member of the nursing staff, she was able to collaborate on and then follow a program that was acceptable to both of them.

Just when Ms. AA seemed to be improving, however, her hospital doctor received a call at home on Christmas morning as her family was opening presents. A hospital nurse was calling to inform her that Ms. AA had smuggled in and then taken a large number of laxatives and had been having diarrhea all morning. The nurse was worried that Ms. AA might require emergency medical treatment, so Ms. AA's doctor felt compelled to go to the hospital to see the patient. Two days later, when Ms. AA was medically stable, her doctor confronted her about the transference hostility involved in her purging, then suggested that perhaps Ms. AA had wished to spoil her doctor's Christmas morning. Although the patient blandly denied any such possibility, her doctor had to suppress intense anger at Ms. AA for the timing of her acting out. It gradually dawned on the doctor that the act of purging had enabled the patient to expel her own aggression. As a result, she could not relate to the doctor's interpretation of her act as hostile. The doctor's anger suggested projective identification, however, with the doctor unconsciously serving as a container of the patient's projected anger.

Although this case illustrates a more refractory patient with borderline personality disorder as part of the clinical picture, the transference/countertransference struggles are not atypical of what individual therapists commonly encounter with these patients. Therapists may find themselves repeatedly provoked into accepting the "badness" the patient is attempting to expel. They may also feel "vomited on" when the patient repeatedly spits back at them all their therapeutic efforts. The recapitulation of the family pattern in hospital treatment or in individual psychotherapy helps the clinician understand the patient's role within the family system. Because bulimia is so often part of a homeostatic balance in the family, family therapy or family intervention in association with individual therapy is frequently needed. By ignoring the family system, the therapist runs the risk that the patient's improvement will be terribly threatening to other family members. Defensive reactions to this threat may include an insidious undermining of the bulimic patient's treatment or the development of a serious dysfunction in another family member. The family's need for the bulimic patient's illness must be respected, and the parents must feel "held" and validated so that they will not sabotage the treatment (Humphrey and Stern 1988).

Dynamic group psychotherapy may also be a useful adjunctive treatment. A growing empirical literature testifies to the efficacy of group psychotherapy for patients with bulimia nervosa (Harper-Giuffre et al. 1992; Liedtke et al. 1991; Mitchell et al. 1990). In a review of 18 different reports of this modality with bulimic patients in an outpatient setting, Oesterheld et al. (1987) found reason for guarded optimism. The consensus was that group psychotherapy effectively reduced bulimic symptoms by an average of 70%. However, these figures appear inflated because most studies excluded dropouts from their calculations. Dropout rates tended to be high even though most groups had excluded patients with borderline personality disorder and other severe character pathology. Long-term follow-up data were also lacking. The group therapists appeared to agree, much as did the individual therapists, that a stable remission requires both insight and symptom control.

In summary, the indication for a dynamic approach to bulimia nervosa is a lack of response to time-limited psychoeducational and cognitive-behavioral methods. As with anorexia nervosa, individual psychotherapy of an expressive-supportive nature is the cornerstone of treatment. Garfinkel and Goldbloom (1993) recently reviewed the research literature on therapy for bulimia nervosa and found that, although a number of therapeutic approaches are effective, convincing evidence is still lacking to support the specificity of any one particular therapeutic modality. Family interventions in the form of support, education, and possibly family therapy are also generally necessary to validate the individual therapy. Some form of symptom control is required in conjunction with the other approaches. Brief hospitalization, support groups such as OA, and group psychotherapy can all assist the patient with symptom control. Some individual psychotherapists also consider symptom control as part of the treatment process. A substantial subset of bulimic patients with associated severe character pathology, suicidal tendencies, and propensities toward life-threatening electrolyte disturbances will require psychotherapy in the context of long-term hospitalization. These patients defy the most diligent efforts of treaters to structure their lives. They seem bent on a self-destructive course that may indeed be fatal without extended hospital treatment.

References

American Psychiatric Association: Diagnostic and Statistical Manual of Mental Disorders, 4th Edition. Washington, DC, American Psychiatric Association, 1994

Balint M: The Basic Fault: Therapeutic Aspects of Regression. New York, Brunner/Mazel, 1979

Bemporad JR, Ratey J: Intensive psychotherapy of former anorexic individuals. Am J Psychother 39:454–466, 1985

Blatt SJ, McDonald C, Sugarman A, et al: Psychodynamic theories of opiate addiction: new directions for research. Clinical Psychology Review 4:159–189, 1984a

Blatt SJ, Rounsaville B, Eyre SL, et al: The psychodynamics of opiate addiction. J Nerv Ment Dis 172:342–352, 1984b

Boris HN: On the treatment of anorexia nervosa. Int J Psychoanal 65:435–442, 1984a

Boris HN: The problem of anorexia nervosa. Int J Psychoanal 65:315–322, 1984b

Brandsma JM, Pattison EM: The outcome of group psychotherapy [with] alcoholics: an empirical review. Am J Drug Alcohol Abuse 11:151–162, 1985

Bratter TE: Some pre-treatment group psychotherapy considerations with alcoholic and drug-addicted individuals. Psychotherapy: Theory, Research and Practice 18:508–515, 1981

Brown S: Treating the Alcoholic: A Developmental Model of Recovery. New York, Wiley, 1985

Bruch H: Eating Disorders: Obesity, Anorexia Nervosa, and the Person Within. New York, Basic Books, 1973

Bruch H: The Golden Cage: The Enigma of Anorexia Nervosa. Cambridge, MA, Harvard University Press, 1978

Bruch H: Psychotherapy in anorexia nervosa. International Journal of Eating Disorders 1(4):3–14, 1982

Bruch H: The changing picture of an illness: anorexia nervosa, in Attachment and the Therapeutic Process. Edited by Sacksteder JL, Schwartz DP, Akabane Y. Madison, CT, International Universities Press, 1987, pp 205–222

Chessick RD: Clinical notes toward the understanding and intensive psychotherapy of adult eating disorders. Annual of Psychoanalysis 22/23:301–322, 1985

Cooper DE: The role of group psychotherapy in the treatment of substance abusers. Am J Psychother 41:55–67, 1987

Dodes LM: Abstinence from alcohol in long-term individual psychotherapy with alcoholics. Am J Psychother 38:248–256, 1984

Dodes LM: The psychology of combining dynamic psychotherapy and Alcoholics Anonymous. Bull Menninger Clin 52:283–293, 1988

Dodes LM: Addiction, helplessness, and narcissistic rage. Psychoanal Q 59:398–419, 1990

Donovan JM: An etiologic model of alcoholism. Am J Psychiatry 143:1–11, 1986

Fairburn CG, Beglin SJ: Studies of the epidemiology of bulimia nervosa. Am J Psychiatry 147:401–408, 1990

Garfinkel PE, Garner DM: Anorexia Nervosa: A Multidimensional Perspective. New York, Brunner/Mazel, 1982

Garfinkel PE, Goldbloom DS: Bulimia nervosa: a review of therapy research. Journal of Psychotherapy Practice and Research 2:38–50, 1993

Garfinkel PE, Moldofsky H, Garner DM: The heterogeneity of anorexia nervosa: bulimia as a distinct subgroup. Arch Gen Psychiatry 37:1036–1040, 1980

Garner DM, Garfinkel PE, Irvine MJ: Integration and sequencing of treatment approaches for eating disorders. Psychother Psychosom 46:67–75, 1986

Goodsitt A: Self-regulatory disturbances in eating disorders. International Journal of Eating Disorders 2(3):51–60, 1983

Goodwin DW: Alcoholism and heredity. Arch Gen Psychiatry 36:57–61, 1979

Hall A, Crisp AH: Brief psychotherapy in the treatment of anorexia nervosa: preliminary findings, in Anorexia Nervosa: Recent Developments in Research. Edited by Darby PL, Garfinkel PE, Garner DM, et al. New York, Alan R Liss, 1983, pp 427–439

Hall A, Slim E, Hawker F, et al: Anorexia nervosa: long-term outcome in 50 female patients. Br J Psychiatry 145:407–413, 1984

Harper-Giuffre H, MacKenzie KR, Sivitilli D: Interpersonal group psychotherapy, in Group Psychotherapy for Eating Disorders. Edited by Harper-Giuffre H, MacKenzie KR. Washington, DC, American Psychiatric Press, 1992, pp 105–145

Hartocollis P: Borderline syndrome and alcoholism, in Encyclopedic Handbook of Alcoholism. Edited by Pattison EM, Kaufman E. New York, Gardner Press, 1982, pp 628–635

Hsu LKG: Outcome of anorexia nervosa: a review of the literature (1954 to 1978). Arch Gen Psychiatry 37:1041–1046, 1980

Hsu LKG: The treatment of anorexia nervosa. Am J Psychiatry 143:573–581, 1986

Hsu LKG: Outcome studies in patients with eating disorders, in Psychiatric Treatment: Advances in Outcome Research. Edited by Mirin SM, Gossett JT, Grob MC. Washington, DC, American Psychiatric Press, 1991, pp 159–180

Hsu LKG, Crisp AH, Harding B: Outcome of anorexia nervosa. Lancet 1:61–65, 1979

Humphrey LL, Stern S: Object relations and the family system in bulimia: a theoretical integration. Journal of Marital and Family Therapy 14:337–350, 1988

Johnson C, Connors ME: The Etiology and Treatment of Bulimia Nervosa: A Biopsychosocial Perspective. New York, Basic Books, 1987

Johnson C, Connors ME, Tobin D: Symptom management of bulimia. J Consult Clin Psychol 55:668–676, 1987

Johnson C, Tobin DL, Enright A: Prevalence and clinical characteristics of borderline patients in an eating-disordered population. J Clin Psychiatry 50:9–15, 1989

Kandel DB, Kessler RC, Margulies RZ: Antecedents of adolescent initiation into stages of drug use: a developmental analysis, in Longitudinal Research on Drug Use. Edited by Kandel DB. New York, Hemisphere, 1978, pp 73–78

Kaplan AS, Woodside DB: Biological aspects of anorexia nervosa and bulimia nervosa. J Consult Clin Psychol 55:645–653, 1987

Kendler KS, Heath AC, Neale MC, et al: A population-based twin study of alcoholism in women. JAMA 268:1877–1882, 1992

Kernberg OF: Borderline Conditions and Pathological Narcissism. New York, Jason Aronson, 1975

Khantzian EJ: Psychopathology, psychodynamics, and alcoholism, in Encyclopedic Handbook of Alcoholism. Edited by Pattison EM, Kaufman E. New York, Gardner Press, 1982, pp 581–597

Khantzian EJ: Psychotherapeutic interventions with substance abusers–the clinical context. J Subst Abuse Treat 2:83–88, 1985a

Khantzian EJ: The self-medication hypothesis of addictive disorders: focus on heroin and cocaine dependence. Am J Psychiatry 142:1259–1264, 1985b

Khantzian EJ: A contemporary psychodynamic approach to drug abuse treatment. Am J Drug Alcohol Abuse 12:213–222, 1986

Khantzian EJ, Treece C: DSM-III psychiatric diagnosis of narcotic addicts: recent findings. Arch Gen Psychiatry 42:1067–1071, 1985

Knight RF: Borderline states. Bull Menninger Clin 17:1–12, 1953

Kohut H: The Analysis of the Self: A Systematic Approach to the Psychoanalytic Treatment of Narcissistic Personality Disorders. New York, International Universities Press, 1971

Kohut H: How Does Analysis Cure? Edited by Goldberg A. Chicago, IL, University of Chicago Press, 1984

Krystal H: Alexithymia and the effectiveness of psychoanalytic treatment. International Journal of Psychoanalytic Psychotherapy 9:353–378, 1982–83

Lieb RC, Thompson TL II: Group psychotherapy of four anorexia nervosa inpatients. Int J Group Psychother 34:639–642, 1984

Liedtke R, Jäger B, Lempa W, et al: Therapy outcome of two treatment models for bulimia nervosa: preliminary results of a controlled study. Psychother Psychosom 56:56–63, 1991

Mack JE: Alcoholism, AA, and the governance of the self, in Dynamic Approaches to the Understanding and Treatment of Alcoholism. Edited by Bean MH, Zinberg NE. New York, Free Press, 1981, pp 128–162

Maher MS: Group therapy for anorexia nervosa, in Current Treatment of Anorexia Nervosa and Bulimia. Edited by Powers PS, Fernandez RC. Basel, Switzerland, Karger, 1984, pp 265–276

Masterson JF: Treatment of the Borderline Adolescent: A Developmental Approach. New York, Wiley, 1972

Masterson JF: Primary anorexia nervosa in the borderline adolescent: an object-relations view, in Borderline Personality Disorders: The Concept, the Syndrome, the Patient. Edited by Hartocollis P. New York, International Universities Press, 1977, pp 475–494

Mintz IL: Self-destructive behavior in anorexia nervosa and bulimia, in Bulimia: Psychoanalytic Treatment and Theory. Edited by Schwartz HJ. Madison, CT, International Universities Press, 1988, pp 127–171

Minuchin S, Rosman BL, Baker L: Psychosomatic Families: Anorexia Nervosa in Context. Cambridge, MA, Harvard University Press, 1978

Mitchell JE, Pyle RL, Eckert ED, et al: A comparison study of antidepressants and structured intensive group psychotherapy in the treatment of bulimia nervosa. Arch Gen Psychiatry 47:149–157, 1990

Murphy GE, Wetzel RD: The lifetime risk of suicide in alcoholism. Arch Gen Psychiatry 47:383–392, 1990

Nace EP, Saxon JJ Jr, Shore N: A comparison of borderline and nonborderline alcoholic patients. Arch Gen Psychiatry 40:54–56, 1983

Nace EP, Davis CW, Gaspari JP: Axis II comorbidity in substance abusers. Am J Psychiatry 148:118–120, 1991

Nathan PE: The addictive personality is the behavior of the addict. J Consult Clin Psychol 56:183–188, 1988

Nicholson B, Treece C: Object relations and differential treatment response to methadone maintenance. J Nerv Ment Dis 169:424–429, 1981

Oesterheld JR, McKenna MS, Gould NB: Group psychotherapy of bulimia: a critical review. Int J Group Psychother 37:163–184, 1987

Parloff MB, London P, Wolfe B: Individual psychotherapy and behavior change. Ann Rev Psychol 37:321–349, 1986

Paton S, Kessler R, Kandel D: Depressive mood and adolescent illicit drug use: a longitudinal analysis. J Genet Psychol 131:267–289, 1977

Pattison EM: Nonabstinent drinking goals in the treatment of alcoholism: a clinical typology. Arch Gen Psychiatry 33:923–930, 1976

Patton CJ: Fear of abandonment and binge eating: a subliminal psychodynamic activation investigation. J Nerv Ment Dis 180:484–490, 1992

Polivy J: Group psychotherapy as an adjunctive treatment for anorexia nervosa. Journal of Psychiatric Treatment and Evaluation 3:279–283, 1981

Powers PS: Psychotherapy of anorexia nervosa, in Current Treatment of Anorexia Nervosa and Bulimia. Edited by Powers PS, Fernandez RC. Basel, Switzerland, Karger, 1984, pp 18–47

Regier DA, Farmer ME, Rae BS, et al: Comorbidity of mental disorders with alcohol and other drug abuse: results from the Epidemiologic Catchment Area (ECA) Study. JAMA 264:2511–2518, 1990

Rinsley DB: The Dipsas revisited: comments on addiction and personality. J Subst Abuse Treat 5:1–7, 1988

Rosen A: Psychotherapy and Alcoholics Anonymous: can they be coordinated? Bull Menninger Clin 45:229–246, 1981

Rounsaville BJ, Weissman MM, Kleber H, et al: Heterogeneity of psychiatric diagnosis in treated opiate addicts. Arch Gen Psychiatry 39:161–166, 1982

Rounsaville BJ, Anton SF, Carroll K, et al: Psychiatric diagnoses of treatment-seeking cocaine abusers. Arch Gen Psychiatry 48:43–51, 1991

Schuckit MA: Genetics and the risk for alcoholism. JAMA 254:2614–2617, 1985

Schuckit MA, Rimmer J, Reich T, et al: Alcoholism: antisocial traits in male alcoholics (abstract). Br J Psychiatry 117:575–576, 1970

Selvini Palazzoli M: Self-Starvation: From Individual to Family Therapy in the Treatment of Anorexia Nervosa. Translated by Pomerans A. New York, Jason Aronson, 1978

Sperling O: On appersonation. Int J Psychoanal 25:128–132, 1944

Strober M, Humphrey LL: Familial contributions to the etiology and course of anorexia nervosa and bulimia. J Consult Clin Psychol 55:654–659, 1987

Sugarman A, Kurash C: The body as a transitional object in bulimia. International Journal of Eating Disorders 1(4):57–67, 1982

Sutker PB, Allain AN: Issues in personality conceptualizations of addictive behaviors. J Consult Clin Psychol 56:172–182, 1988

Treece C: Assessment of ego functioning in studies of narcotic addiction, in The Broad Scope of Ego Function Assessment. Edited by Bellak L, Goldsmith LA. New York, Wiley, 1984, pp 268–290

Treece C, Khantzian EJ: Psychodynamic factors in the development of drug dependence. Psychiatr Clin North Am 9:399–412, 1986

Vaglum S, Vaglum P: Borderline and other mental disorders in alcoholic female psychiatric patients: a case control study. Psychopathology 18:50–60, 1985

Vaillant GE: Dangers of psychotherapy in the treatment of alcoholism, in Dynamic Approaches to the Understanding and Treatment of Alcoholism. Edited by Bean MH, Zinberg NE. New York, Free Press, 1981, pp 36–54

Vaillant GE: The Natural History of Alcoholism. Cambridge, MA, Harvard University Press, 1983

Vaillant GE: The alcohol-dependent and drug-dependent person, in The New Harvard Guide to Psychiatry. Edited by Nicholi AM Jr. Cambridge, MA, Belknap Press of Harvard University Press, 1988, pp 700–713

Weissman MM, Myers JK: Clinical depression in alcoholism. Am J Psychiatry 137:372–373, 1980

Wilson CP (ed): Fear of Being Fat: The Treatment of Anorexia Nervosa and Bulimia. New York, Jason Aronson, 1983

Woody GE, Luborsky L, McLellan AT, et al: Psychotherapy for opiate addicts: does it help? Arch Gen Psychiatry 40:639–645, 1983

Woody GE, McLellan AT, Luborsky L, et al: Severity of psychiatric symptoms as a predictor of benefits from psychotherapy: the Veterans Administration–Penn Study. Am J Psychiatry 141:1172–1177, 1984

Woody GE, McLellan AT, Luborsky L, et al: Sociopathy and psychotherapy outcome. Arch Gen Psychiatry 42:1081–1086, 1985

Woody GE, McLellan AT, Luborsky L, et al: Psychotherapy for substance abuse. Psychiatr Clin North Am 9:547–562, 1986

Woody GE, McLellan AT, Luborsky L, et al: Twelve-month follow-up of psychotherapy for opiate dependents. Am J Psychiatry 144:590–596, 1987

Wurmser L: Psychoanalytic considerations of the etiology of compulsive drug use. J Am Psychoanal Assoc 22:820–843, 1974

Wurmser L: Flight from conscience: experience with the psychoanalytic treatment of compulsive drug abusers, I: dynamic sequences, compulsive drug use. J Subst Abuse Treat 4:157–168, 1987a

Wurmser L: Flight from conscience: experience with the psychoanalytic treatment of compulsive drug abusers, II: dynamic and therapeutic conclusions from the experiences with psychoanalysis of drug users. J Subst Abuse Treat 4:169–179, 1987b

Yager J: The treatment of bulimia: an overview, in Current Treatment of Anorexia Nervosa and Bulimia. Edited by Powers PS, Fernandez RC. Basel, Switzerland, Karger, 1984, pp 63–91

Chapter 13

Dementia and Other Cognitive Disorders

It is faulty in principle to try to make a distinction between so-called organic and functional diseases, as far as symptomatology and therapy are concerned. In both conditions, one is dealing with abnormal functioning of the same psychophysical apparatus and with the attempts of the organism to come to terms with that. If the disturbances—whether they are due to damage to the brain or to psychological conflicts—do not disappear spontaneously or cannot be eliminated by therapy, the organism has to make a new adjustment to life in spite of them. Our task is to help the patients in this adjustment by physical and psychological means; the procedure and goal of the therapy in both conditions is, in principle, the same.

—Kurt Goldstein (1952)

In this classic cautionary statement against mind-brain dualism, Goldstein reminds us of the fundamental interdependence of psychology and biology. The traditional distinction between organic and functional syndromes implies that psychology is irrelevant to the former and biology irrelevant to the latter. Because the term *organic* generally denotes the presence of actual anatomical damage to neuronal and glial structures, some psychiatrists view such disorders as outside their purview and therefore refer patients with them to neurologists. Dynamic psychiatrists in particular may view patients with structural brain damage as so lacking in the capacity for abstraction that they are inaccessible to psychotherapeutic intervention. This abdication is unfortunate because dynamic clinicians have much to contribute to the cognitively impaired patient.

In DSM-III-R (American Psychiatric Association 1987), patients with structural brain impairment were referred to as having *organic mental syndromes.* This term has been replaced by *delirium, dementia, amnestic, and other cognitive disorders* in DSM-IV (American Psychiatric Association 1994) because of increasing concern that the term *organic* had outlived its usefulness (Spitzer et al. 1992; Tucker et al. 1990). With increasing knowledge of how the central nervous system functions, the notion of "organic" versus "nonorganic" psychiatric disorders has become less meaningful. Referring to major psychiatric disorders such as schizophrenia and bipolar affective disorder as "nonorganic" or "functional" fails to connote the biological substrate of both diseases. In addition, contributors to DSM-IV had some concern that the organic/nonorganic distinction might encourage continued stigmatization of people with psychiatric disorders by suggesting that no true medical or biological basis existed for their illnesses.

Psychodynamic understanding of cognitive impairment disorders dates back to the seminal work of Hollós and Ferenczi on general paresis in 1925. They noted that damage to brain tissue sets off a process of psychological regression designed to maintain self-esteem. The patient regresses, in their view, to an earlier developmental stage in which the damaged ego functions are not yet fully evolved. In this regressed state, the patient can deny the significance of the impairments since they are not necessary for intact functioning at that developmental level.

As Hollós and Ferenczi (1925) were aware, conditions that affect the brain also affect the mind. The personality is the end result of a series of complex functions occurring in cortical (and subcortical) structures. Psychodynamic factors in disorders involving brain damage can most productively be discussed by dividing the conditions into those present from birth and those involving insult to brain tissue later in the life cycle (Lewis 1986). In those conditions present from birth, the psychological issues of each developmental phase throughout the life cycle are shaped by the patient's neuroanatomical deficits. In those conditions occurring later, development has been unencumbered by neural dysfunction, so the major issue is adjustment to the loss of a previous level of functioning. The discussion in this chapter will focus on those cognitive impairment disorders for which dynamic approaches are particularly useful. Adult minimal brain dysfunction (developmental learning disabilities and residual attention-deficit disorder) is one disorder present from birth in which the dynamic psychiatrist may play a key role. Brain injury and dementia are conditions of later onset that will also be discussed.

Conditions Present From Birth: Adult Minimal Brain Dysfunction

Genetic-constitutional and perinatal sources of brain damage play a key role in each subsequent developmental phase throughout the life cycle. Although at one time children were believed to "outgrow" the syndrome of minimal brain dysfunction or attention deficit disorder, it is now clear that residual problems, although somewhat masked, may persist into adult life (Bellak 1977; Hartocollis 1968). Clinicians should therefore have a high index of suspicion when a patient presents with a history of poor response to conventional psychiatric or psychological treatments, a chronic inability to perform at the level expected by teachers and parents, a history of repeated life frustrations, problems with spatial orientation (such as getting lost or experiencing difficulty distinguishing between left and right), emotional outbursts, restlessness, a spotty job history, memory impairment, and marked discrepancies between performance and verbal IQ scores.

Patients who grow up with minimal brain dysfunction frequently have a host of subtle deficits that can be categorized according to specific ego functions (Bellak 1977). Primary autonomous functions (such as perception, memory, and motor abilities) are the most commonly affected ego capacities. Next are impairments in the ability to regulate and control impulses and affects, which will be manifested as frequent temper outbursts, assaults, and poor tolerance for frustration. The ego function involved with providing a barrier to internal and external stimuli is also easily overloaded. Although the thought processes of such patients may be formally intact, their ability to think abstractly is typically compromised. The ego function known as *sense of reality* will often show several characteristic deficits, including spatial disorientation, unclear body boundaries, and difficulty discriminating between right and left. Finally, because these patients suffer a fundamental impairment in synthetic-integrative functioning, they may struggle to bring contradictory ideas or feelings together into a unified whole.

Psychodynamic Understanding

To understand adult patients with congenital forms of brain impairment, clinicians must consider the impact of a compromised neural substrate on the achievement of normal developmental tasks. The growing infant struggles daily with an underlying tension between the pressure of drives and affects, on the one hand, and cortical control, on the other. Drive pressures resist mastery when the infant lacks the usual endowment of functioning cortex (Weil 1978). Similarly, the conflict-free or autonomous spheres of ego functioning (such as intellect, thinking, perception, motility, and language) are dependent on constitutional endowment (Hartmann 1939/1958).

Numerous authors have commented on the effects of structurally based cognitive deficits on the development of the self and on the internalization of object relations (Allen et al. 1988; Buchholz 1987; Kafka 1984; Lewis 1986; Palombo 1979; Pickar 1986; D. N. Stern 1985; Weil 1978). As Daniel Stern (1985) noted, the development of the self depends on mutual cuing between mother and infant that derives from an empathic bond formed by their sensitive attunement to the emotional reactions of one another. Infants with structurally based cognitive dysfunction will be unable to perceive accurately or to integrate effectively the affective signals from the mother. When the child fails to respond to the mother as she expects, the mother may become anxious, thus inserting tension and discord into the infant-mother interactions. Parents may experience an infant or child who responds abnormally or who is otherwise defective as a profound narcissistic injury (Buchholz 1987). The parents may recoil from the child and convey their sense of disappointment and anxiety in all their subsequent interactions, leading to a disturbance of the child's feelings of self-esteem (Abrams and Kaslow 1976). Alternatively, the parents may become overinvolved and overprotective. As these children grow and develop, they continue to fall short of parental expectations, resulting in further feelings of failure and humiliation. Such children have poorer cortical control of impulses, leading to more parental reprimands, to more interactions in which others are angry and punitive, and to experiences with parents who convey, through their excessive anxiety, that separation from a parental figure is dangerous (Pickar 1986; Weil 1978). Because these children are often unable to effectively appreciate cause-effect sequences, they do not link the rejection responses of others to their own behavior, resulting in feelings of victimization and helplessness (T. Bryan 1977).

Defects in an individual's primary autonomous ego functions of visual and auditory perception and memory will adversely affect that person's ability to achieve object constancy. Children with learning disabilities and minimal brain dysfunction often suffer from an incapacity to soothe themselves because they have never been able to internalize and maintain comforting maternal figures as affectively meaningful images. As a result, they may struggle to maintain a stable sense of self. Their inability to accurately perceive social signals from others contributes to their frequently observable ineptitude in relating to others in a socially appropriate manner (J. H. Bryan et al. 1980).

To compensate for their profound feelings of inadequacy and incompetence, individuals with minimal brain dysfunction may develop a defensive grandiosity. Kafka (1984) reported on one such patient who came to analysis. Having grown up with a host of learning disabilities and other cognitive deficits, the patient had felt like a "faker" all his life. To deal with his sense that something fundamental was missing, he assumed a defensive posture of independence and grandiosity. He was embarrassed and humiliated about his dependency on others for help with his spatial disorientation. Because he associated these disabilities with a lack of masculinity, he felt deeply ashamed.

Some individuals can compensate for their neuropsychological deficits by overdeveloping other areas of ego functioning. The inventor Thomas Edison, who suffered from learning disabilities, is one famous example. However, when compensatory efforts fail, the young person may avoid dealing with the enormous frustration of repeated failure by turning to juvenile delinquency (Pickar 1986). Instead of dealing with the shame and humiliation associated with trying but failing to meet the academic and social expectations of others, the adolescent may adopt a posture of contempt toward the values of parents, teachers, and society in general. Membership in a gang of peers may also promote the adolescent's feelings of power and acceptance.

Treatment Considerations

Therapeutic nihilism with brain-damaged patients is unwarranted. As Lewis (1986) noted: "The unqualified belief that brain damage renders a person inaccessible to meaningful psychological change through psychotherapy is erroneous and derives from the misconception that brain damage is a monolithic entity" (p. 78). The therapist cannot expect the tendency toward concrete thinking to completely disappear, but many patients achieve substantial gains in their ability to think symbolically or abstractly (Buchholz 1987). Even in a highly expressive treatment like psychoanalysis, Kafka (1984) found that no significant modifications of technique were necessary for such a patient. He did note that his patient responded with narcissistic mortification to minor slips of the tongue because such incidents seemed to expose his defects. In addition, Kafka often had to repeat interpretations patiently and tactfully in various contexts using different examples.

Adapting the treatment approach to patients who suffer from more severe cognitive deficits requires a precise understanding of how those deficits affect these patients' ability to use psychotherapy. For example, Lewis (1986) described a patient who had suffered since early childhood from memory disturbances that impaired her ability to evoke a soothing mental image of her therapist. She was unable to maintain continuity between her twice-weekly hour-long sessions because she couldn't recall the therapist's words or appearance. Simply changing the appointment time to one-half hour each weekday allowed the patient to internalize the therapeutic process more effectively because she could now remember how the therapist looked and sounded.

Repeated failures of empathy characterize the life stories of such patients. Beginning with parents, other people do not understand the nature or extent of these cognitive limitations and repeatedly expect more than these patients can deliver. Because of this life pattern, some clinicians (Buchholz 1987; Palombo 1979) have suggested using a self psychological approach. The repeated experiences of self-fragmentation and deflation connected with the lack of mirroring responses from others can be addressed as these feelings develop in the transference. The therapist can empathically reflect the patient's strivings for admiration and approbation and can give meaning to how the cognitive impairments have interfered with those strivings. Thus the therapist serves as a selfobject who helps the patient grieve, assists the patient in building a more cohesive self, and encourages self-forgiveness as well.

When behavioral dyscontrol is a major feature of the patient's clinical picture, hospitalization may be required. Conventional psychiatric treatments usually have proved ineffective for these patients. Frequently, diagnosticians have missed the brain-based dimension because of its subtlety and because of more florid symptoms of personality disorder. Clinicians who assume that all the symptomatology is related to character pathology may develop considerable countertransference frustration when patients react to interventions with wandering attention, poor memory, and failure to reflect on meanings. As the treater's irritation grows, the patient feels increasingly like a failure for not responding properly to treatment, thus recapitulating past experiences with parents, teachers, and employers.

One study of treatment-refractory inpatients drew a psychological profile of patients who suffered from severe psychiatric disorders complicated by "organic" features (Allen et al. 1988; Colson and Allen 1986). Problems with self-esteem and affect modulation are two commonalities in this group of patients. Rarely do these patients have clear-cut neurological disorders, and they are therefore difficult to diagnose. The cumulative diagnostic picture of neurological soft signs, borderline abnormalities on EEG, and spotty deficits on neuropsychological testing implicates CNS dysfunction. Subcortical involvement, manifested by episodes of behavioral dyscontrol and affective storms, appears of greater relevance than cortical impairment. These patients feel powerless in the face of overwhelming eruptions of affect. In a desperate attempt to gain some sense of mastery and control, they pretend that their episodes are volitional acts designed to intimidate others—a response similar to a grandiose delusion. Their explosions lead to increased isolation from others, great embarrassment, and decreased self-esteem. These patients live in fear of further loss of control. To deal with this threat, they develop extreme defensive postures against any affect whatsoever by becoming constricted and superficial, much like persons with alexithymia. To ward off feelings, they commonly employ the defenses of denial and externalization.

The high expectations of treaters and parents contribute to a vicious cycle with these patients. Because they are unable to live up to such high expectations, their self-esteem plummets and their frustration grows, leading to further vulnerability to affective explosions. These episodes of dyscontrol elicit additional negative feedback from parents and treaters and further erode their self-esteem. The diagnosis of the brain-based contribution often is therapeutic in and of itself, and these patients generally respond with relief to it. The diagnosis also leads to lowered expectations from both parents and clinicians. As a result, the vicious cycle is interrupted, and the patients develop better self-esteem and an increased sense of mastery as their episodes of dyscontrol decrease and their sense of chronic failure diminishes.

Mr. BB, a 20-year-old single male, was hospitalized after repeated episodes of temper outbursts leading to physical altercations with fellow employees. The patient's father, a prosperous factory owner, had given Mr. BB a job because all previous attempts at gainful employment had failed. At work, Mr. BB was viewed as "the boss's son." Minor allusions to preferential treatment of Mr. BB by his father provoked outbursts of aggression by Mr. BB. At admission, Mr. BB's father clearly indicated that he was fed up with his son. He cataloged a long list of life failures, including poor school performance, athletic failures, and "laziness" manifested by an inability to keep a job. Mr. BB hung his head in shame as this list was rattled off, and he seemed particularly wounded when his father compared him with an older brother who had recently attained a graduate professional degree.

On the hospital unit, Mr. BB related to others in a formal, constricted manner that made his occasional outbursts seem to come from out of the blue. In one typical instance, he was returning to the unit after an activities therapy session when he suddenly started shoving another male patient walking beside him. With a look of rage, he pinned the patient to the ground, snatched his wallet from his pants pocket, and threw it onto the roof of the hospital. Mr. BB was returned to the unit and confined to his room. In a subsequent group meeting, the other patient and the staff member who had accompanied them described the incident in detail, particularly noting its inexplicability because there was no apparent trigger. With much bravado, Mr. BB claimed that the other patient had provoked him by making fun of him. He maintained that the attack was justified. As a result of this and other incidents, the other patients on Mr. BB's team (and several staff members) began to feel intimidated and frightened by Mr. BB.

Of course, Mr. BB's violent outbursts led to further isolation from the patient community. He was confined to his room for much of the time to decrease stimulation and to protect the other patients. In a one-to-one session with his psychiatrist, he allowed his defensive facade to yield to other feelings. He confided that after each episode of dyscontrol, he felt "like an idiot." He said that he had no idea why he had attacked his male peer on the way back to the hospital unit. His psychiatrist asked Mr. BB what had happened in the activity period preceding the assault. He replied that he had been asked to make a wooden bowl in the wood shop. Asked how his bowl had turned out, Mr. BB responded, "As usual, I screwed up." His psychiatrist then asked if it was possible that attacking the other patient was his way of dealing with his frustration. Mr. BB acknowledged that it probably was, and then added that he would do anything to prevent future outbursts but that he was pessimistic about any treatment being helpful. He had dealt with such outbursts all his life and doubted that anything could control them.

A detailed neuropsychiatric evaluation revealed the following findings, which suggested a brain-based component to Mr. BB's problems: 1) a history of learning disabilities from early grade school through high school, 2) difficulties with right-left discrimination, 3) a childhood history of hyperactivity and other symptoms of attention deficit disorder, and 4) moderate perceptual deficits on neuropsychological testing. A 24-hour sleep-deprivation EEG with nasopharyngeal leads was entirely normal, and even an ambulatory EEG monitor failed to reveal any abnormalities in the temporal lobes. Results of a CT scan were also within normal limits.

Carbamazepine was tried on an empirical basis and seemed to reduce the frequency and intensity of Mr. BB's behavioral dyscontrol episodes. The main thrust of the treatment, however, was a careful explanation to Mr. BB and his family of the implications of these findings. Initially, Mr. BB's parents were quite resistant to the idea that their son had a subtle form of brain damage from early in life. Eventually, though, they were persuaded when the neuropsychologist discussed the testing in detail with them and explained the nature of the physical impairment. The parents' anger and frustration with their son gradually diminished as they began to understand the extent of his limitations. This diagnosis helped put the patient's history in perspective, and it led Mr. BB's parents to rethink their expectations for his vocational future. After the psychiatrist explained that Mr. BB's lowered stimulus barrier led to his overstimulation when he was around other people, the father arranged for a job for Mr. BB at a satellite facility where he could do repetitive menial tasks in isolation from other workers. This arrangement not only lowered the expectations of high job performance but also removed interpersonal triggers of the dyscontrol episodes.

Mr. BB responded favorably to the reports of the diagnostic evaluation and particularly to the lowered expectations of his parents. He said he felt like "the pressure was off." The new job arrangement worked satisfactorily for him. Although he remained socially isolated, his self-esteem increased considerably because of his improved mastery of the episodes of dyscontrol and because of his ability to perform adequately at his new job.

Conditions of Later Onset: Brain Injury and Dementia

The human brain that receives an insult later in the developmental life cycle involves a different set of therapeutic issues. In these instances, the patient has deteriorated from a previous level of functioning, and both the patient and the family must adjust to the change. These conditions fall into two broad categories: 1) acute brain injuries with a sudden alteration of functioning and 2) progressive degenerative diseases with a gradual decline. Both forms of insult will be considered in the ensuing discussion. Excluded from consideration are delirium, states of drug intoxication or withdrawal, and other acute insults that rapidly clear when the medical condition or toxic agent has been dealt with, because psychodynamic issues are less relevant to such conditions.

Psychodynamic Understanding

The self, at the most fundamental level, is a product of brain functioning. Damage to brain tissue may produce significant alterations in an individual's sense of identity, thus causing family and loved ones to feel that the patient is no longer the same person. Brain trauma typically affects the frontal and temporal lobes, dramatically influencing the patient's ability to interpret the meaning of stimuli and to connect them with relevant feelings (Prigatano 1989). Such alterations strike at the very heart of the personality.

The awareness of the self is difficult to localize to one area of the brain. Studies of patients whose cerebral hemispheres have been surgically disconnected (Sperry et al. 1979) have suggested that the sense of self is present in both halves of the brain. It appears to be a complex schema to which different brain regions make different contributions.

Patients react to their loss of identity in certain characteristic ways. Goldstein (1952), one of the first investigators of the psychological effects of brain damage, described an anxiety state that he termed the *catastrophic condition* or *reaction*. When brain-injured patients were asked to perform a simple task that had been no problem for them prior to the trauma, they became angry, agitated, and extremely anxious. Goldstein observed that they perceived their failure to complete the task as a danger to their very existence. As a reaction to this threat, patients characteristically restrict their lives so that they are not exposed to unfamiliar situations or impossible tasks. Thus they defend against catastrophic anxiety by avoiding awareness of their defects. These patients commonly become excessively orderly to the point of being obsessive-compulsive. Keeping everything in place gives them the illusion of control over their environment. It also transforms passivity into activity and provides a concrete solution to a complex, abstract problem.

When brain-injured patients can restrict their lives sufficiently, they may appear remarkably free of anxiety and oblivious to their deficits. Despite showing evidence of memory problems, childish behavior, and a short temper, they often may deny any limitations. In fact, one study (Oddy et al. 1985) found that 40% of patients studied 7 years after an insult to the brain disavowed any disability whatsoever. Clinicians may struggle to differentiate between neurogenic and psychogenic denial in such patients. Lewis (1991) has pointed out that, in contrast to psychological forms of denial, neurogenic denial remits within hours or days of the injury, appears as a pattern of overall deficits rather than as an isolated symptom, and does not produce anxiety or agitation in patients who are confronted with it.

The gradual loss of functioning typical of dementia syndromes generally presents a somewhat different picture. People with dementia preserve a sense of who they are until relatively late in the course of the illness. They may be able to perform their usual work and conduct their usual social routines reasonably well. As McHugh and Folstein (1986) noted: "It is the retention of the habitual, the concrete, and the basics of a self in the face of a progressive and severe deterioration in the skills of analysis, abstraction, comprehension, and memory that gives the demented patient his particular appearance" (p. 335). The patient may initially note some problem with recent memory. The most common alteration of personality in the early stage is a progressive indifference or apathy (Cummings 1987). As the illness progresses, the patient is likely to experience increasing difficulty with calculation, performance of complex tasks, and fluency of language. At this point in the illness, when patients realize that they cannot perform the tasks they were once able to, catastrophic reactions may emerge that are similar to those in brain-injured patients. Similarly, eruptions of anger and even combativeness may develop as the disease progresses.

From a psychodynamic perspective, the loss of mental faculties associated with progressive dementia can be understood as a regressive process in the ego, in which more mature defense mechanisms give way to more primitive modes of defense (Weiner 1991). Aspects of the personality that have been partially suppressed by a biologically intact cortex gradually emerge as defensive layers are eroded. High-level defenses such as altruism are replaced by self-absorption, for example. Denial and projection are perhaps the two most common primitive defenses used by persons with dementia. When a memory failure occurs, patients with dementia blame others rather than acknowledge responsibility for the error themselves.

In many aging patients with dementia of the Alzheimer's type, the tragedy of the illness is that self-awareness may remain intact as a number of the mental faculties deteriorate. Because recent memory tends to be sacrificed before remote memory, many patients can clearly recollect how they used to be, which makes their current dysfunctional state all the more disturbing to them. To a large extent, the continuity of the self over time depends on the capacity of memory. When remote memories begin to fade as the illness progresses, then the patient's identity begins to disappear along with the memories. Ultimately, the patient cannot recognize loved ones and family members and can no longer remember significant life events.

Internal objects—particularly, soothing introjects—may also be sacrificed as part of the dementia process. Memory involves others as much as the self. The following case example demonstrates how the loss of memory may be associated both with the loss of a soothing introject and with the recurrence of anxieties from early in life.

Mr. CC was a 75-year-old man who requested psychiatric consultation because his difficulty with memory and cognition associated with Alzheimer's disease made him feel that he was "losing his mind." Three years prior to seeing a psychiatrist, he had been told by his internist that he would need to stop trying to work part time because of difficulties with cognition. Following that conversation, Mr. CC had noted increasing problems with memory, abstraction, computation, and verbal expressive language, all of which were limiting his daily activities. He was also feeling intensely anxious at night when he went to bed.

When asked about previous episodes of anxiety, Mr. CC recounted his early history. At the age of $2\frac{1}{2}$, he was sent to live with his grandmother after the death of his parents. The first time he remembered having an anxiety attack was shortly thereafter. Mr. CC recalled listening at night to his grandmother's breathing on the other side of his bedroom wall. He heard her stop breathing and then experienced a sense of panic, which led him to assume a fetal position, rock himself, and call her name. He was filled with a sense of dread that his grandmother would die as his parents had. Mr. CC subsequently experienced anxiety when he had to leave his grandmother and enter kindergarten. Throughout his childhood and adolescence, he experienced anxiety verging on panic each time he faced any form of separation, geographic move, or role change.

Throughout his adult life, Mr. CC had maintained connections with nurturing figures in his environment to ward off any feelings of separation anxiety or panic. For example, he married a woman 20 years younger than he as a way of assuring that she would not abandon him through death and leave him alone and isolated. He had been largely free of anxiety symptoms until the age of 72, when his internist informed him that he was suffering from Alzheimer's disease. The dementia process upset an equilibrium that he had achieved through considerable struggle early in life. His feeling that he was beginning to "lose his mind" was associated with the loss of his grandmother's soothing internal presence. As he lay in bed at night, he once again experienced a terror of abandonment associated with his failing memory. As a result, he became increasingly dependent and clinging in relationship to his wife.

Treatment Considerations

Treatment planning depends on a careful assessment of several factors (Lewis 1986; Prigatano and Klonoff 1988): 1) the exact manner in which the brain insult has affected the sensory, motor, and cognitive spheres; 2) the patient's psychological reaction to the organic deficits; 3) the impact of both the brain insult and the patient's reaction on the patient's psychological and social adjustment; 4) the contribution of the patient's premorbid personality structure to the clinical picture; and 5) differentiation of those symptoms that are direct sequelae of the brain damage from those that are associated with previously defended conflicts or ego deficits, now released as a result of the trauma. This type of assessment requires a detailed history from a family member or a significant other in the patient's life.

Part of the assessment of such patients should include an evaluation of their suitability for expressive-supportive psychotherapy. Lewis
and Rosenberg (1990) have delineated five useful indicators for selecting which neurologically impaired patients can benefit from dynamic
therapy: 1) personal motivation, both to begin and to remain in a psychotherapeutic process; 2) a history of at least one meaningful interpersonal relationship; 3) a degree of success and active mastery in
some area of life; 4) absence of serious language problems of either an
expressive or receptive type; and 5) absence of frontal lobe symptoms,
such as anosognosia, severe apathy, or marked impulsiveness, that
would make psychotherapy impossible. Another factor that may be
critical in determining suitability for psychotherapy is the patient's
financial situation as a result of the brain injury. When workers' compensation substantially reimburses patients for their injuries, psychotherapy may be ineffective. If patients are rewarded financially for
remaining disabled, their conditions frequently deteriorate and their
motivation to change through psychotherapy may be severely compromised (Prigatano and Klonoff 1988).

A growing literature documents the value of dynamic psychotherapy for brain-injured patients (Ball 1988; Lewis 1986; Lewis and Rosenberg 1990; Morris and Bleiberg 1986; Prigatano and Klonoff 1988;
J. M. Stern 1985). A major goal of any psychotherapeutic process with
these patients is to help them accept the extent of their deficits and
their limitations in terms of returning to work. To accomplish this goal,
the therapist must be sensitive to the narcissistic injury inherent in
accepting the irreparable damage to one's skills, intellectual capabilities, talents, and even the very essence of one's personality. It is essential for the therapist to respect and empathize with the patient's need
to use denial (Lewis 1991). Blunt confrontations of denial are likely to
accomplish nothing and may even destroy any hope of developing a
therapeutic alliance. Promoting self-acceptance of these cognitive limitations requires therapists to gradually expose their patients to the
reality of the deficits in a way that allows the patients to briefly mourn
week by week, over an extended period. A psychoeducational model in
which the nature of the deficits and their implications are explained in
small units of information that the patient is capable of assimilating
may be useful at the beginning of therapy (Prigatano and Klonoff
1988). Drawings or diagrams may help patients with these limitations
to visualize what the therapist is describing. As patients mourn the
loss of their previous identity and their previous level of functioning,

anger at themselves and others connected with the accident is likely to surface. Therapists can then help patients forgive themselves and others so that they can get on with their life.

Both individual dynamic psychotherapy and family or marital therapy may be necessary to help patients adjust to changes in intimate relationships. Spouses may be upset or bewildered by the new behaviors of their brain-damaged partners, such as childishness, concretistic thinking, paranoid accusations, and uninhibited passion (Prigatano and Klonoff 1988). Psychoeducational approaches may help family members understand the organic contribution to these behaviors. However, explorations of themes such as guilt and anger at the patient for having the accident must also be addressed. Frequently, families will completely rearrange their life-styles to provide round-the-clock companionship and assistance to the brain-injured patient (Ball 1988). If this unnecessarily smothering behavior goes unchecked, it will lead to increasing resentment. Interpretations of reaction formation that defend against anger may help family members return to a closer approximation of their normal lives before the accident. Family members may also find it helpful to explore guilt feelings related to fantasies of causing the accident by what they did or did not say. Reasonable expectations of the spouse and other family members should be discussed individually with the patient during the psychotherapeutic process.

The dynamic therapist of a brain-injured patient must also be cognizant of the time course of the recovery and its effect on the therapeutic process. Three general phases can be identified (J. M. Stern 1985). In the first phase, the patient is unable to process what has happened. The usual ego defenses are overwhelmed, and the therapist must serve as a consistent, supportive, auxiliary ego that provides missing functions to the patient and explains what the patient is going through. In the second phase, patients start to understand what has happened to them and are prone to feel that they have been victimized by a menacing and malevolent world. All "badness" is split off and projected onto others, including the therapist. In this phase, therapists must contain the destructive impulses and the malevolent self- and object-representations projected onto them and yet continue to be an observing ego for the patient. Developing trust in others is a major task in the recovery of brain-injured patients, and a trusting alliance with a therapist can be a first step in this direction. Therapists can promote trust by explaining the meaning of the patient's experience and by sharpening the differentiation between what is happening inside the patient and what is actually going on in external reality. As cognitive functioning improves, patients enter the third phase, in which intrapsychic conflicts become more prominent. The therapist's task in this phase is to help patients form a new identity by connecting past experiences and self-representations with current experiences of themselves. The patient's idealization of the past may be questioned by the therapist to facilitate integration of the past with the present. Grief and loss are central themes during this phase.

Several authors (Lewis 1986; Lewis and Rosenberg 1990; Prigatano et al. 1984; Prigatano and Klonoff 1988) have emphasized the necessity for psychotherapy to address characterological issues that predate the injury. These premorbid personality dispositions may profoundly affect the patient's rehabilitation process. For example, Morris and Bleiberg (1986) described a patient who became oppositional to a rehabilitation therapist whom he experienced as a controlling mother. This patient's characterological tendency to see others as controlling was diagnosed through the transferential relationship to the therapist. A dynamically informed decision was then made to allow the patient more control over rehabilitation and treatment planning.

Problems with self-esteem and affect modulation almost invariably surface in the psychotherapy and rehabilitation of patients suffering from brain trauma. However, these two areas are also problematic for many persons suffering from personality disorders. Psychotherapists must avoid being seduced into thinking that all psychological symptoms are directly related to the brain injury. It is common for narcissistic, antisocial, and borderline patients to place themselves in situations that involve risk of injury, and these characterological dimensions may have to be addressed during psychotherapy. Also, characterological tendencies are often exacerbated by brain damage, causing patients to become "more like they already are." To deal with the loss of control arising from the destruction of brain tissue, an obsessive-compulsive patient may become increasingly obsessive-compulsive. Hysterical or histrionic patients may become more cognitively diffuse and affectively labile in response to brain injury. Psychotherapists must not abandon their treatment of personality disorders simply because of a patient's brain injury.

Many clinicians are guardedly optimistic about the treatment of brain-injured patients. Progressive dementia, on the other hand, often elicits profound pessimism in treaters. When treatable causes of dementia (e.g., depression, hypothyroidism, vitamin deficiencies, porphyria, neoplasm, and encephalitides) are ruled out, some clinicians reluctantly diagnose Alzheimer's disease and withdraw from a therapeutic role. This unfortunate withdrawal is associated with the view that Alzheimer's, which accounts for more than half of all dementias, is untreatable. From a psychodynamic perspective, however, there is no such thing as an untreatable dementia. Approximately one-third of these patients will require treatment for associated symptoms of depression and psychosis (Wragg and Jeste 1989). Even in the absence of such symptoms, however, much can be done to help these patients and their families deal with Alzheimer's on a daily basis. The following case example illustrates some useful principles of management:

> Mr. DD was a 59-year-old Protestant minister with a 4-year history of deterioration in his mental functioning. Members of his congregation had noticed a sense of apathy about him and a sloppiness in his administrative functioning. Church bulletins were poorly organized, and he seemed to be less conscientious about carrying out his commitments to various parishioners. Mr. DD's wife noticed that he often failed to fulfill simple requests. She would become angry at him for "selective hearing" when he indicated to her that he had forgotten what she said.
>
> Mrs. DD brought her husband for psychiatric evaluation, complaining that he was "just not the same." Mr. DD conceded that he felt as if something was happening to him, but he was unable to be more specific than to say that he could not remember as well as he used to. Mrs. DD complained that their marital relationship was deteriorating because her husband did not attend to her needs as he had in the past. Mr. DD expressed hurt at the feedback from members of his congregation, and he noted that he was starting to feel like a failure.
>
> Mental status examination revealed problems with short-term memory and calculation and minor difficulties with orientation to time. Mr. DD also showed signs of mental inertia, as he was unable to move from one subject to another or from one task to another unless given considerable time. Extensive diagnostic studies ruled out causes of dementia stemming from trauma, infection, neoplasm, and normal pressure hydrocephalus, or from autoimmune, metabolic, hematologic, vascular, and toxic factors. Also negative were findings from a CT scan, skull X rays, and electroencephalography. Neuropsychological testing was more productive, with the following results noted: 1) mild-to-moderate deficits in manual dexterity, 2) mild-to-moderate deficits in perceptual functioning, 3) mild-to-moderate def-

icits in recent memory, 4) diffuse organic dysfunction typical of progressive neurological disease, and 5) a decrease in attention span.

After the diagnosis of dementia of unknown origin was determined (Alzheimer's in a 59-year-old man is unusual but not unheard of), the diagnostic findings were explained to the patient and his wife. When Mrs. DD could accept her husband's structural brain damage, she was able to lower her expectations for his responses to her. Instead of assuming that he would always react to her verbal comments as he had in the past, she tried new ways of relating to him. At the psychiatrist's suggestion, she slowed her rate of speech and repeated comments that did not seem to register. She also tried rewording comments that Mr. DD did not seem to understand. Above all, she no longer was so easily irritated with him, leading to more positive interactions between the two of them and a corresponding increase in Mr. DD's self-esteem.

Mr. DD had always been an orderly, fastidious person with prominent obsessive-compulsive character traits. To deal with his sense that his intellectual and administrative capacities were deteriorating, he had begun to read the Bible 2 or 3 hours a day, both to encourage divine intervention and to attempt to gain mastery over the information he hoped to impart to his congregation. The evaluating psychiatrist helped Mr. DD marshal his obsessive-compulsive character traits more effectively. As a result, Mr. DD began to sit down with his wife each morning to write out a daily schedule of what he had to do between breakfast and bedtime. Moreover, he began to carry a notebook at all times so he could write down what other people told him and thereby remember what he had to do.

Mr. DD's self-esteem had depended on his role as minister, and his inability to continue in that capacity inflicted a deep narcissistic wound. Initially, he protested when the psychiatrist advised him to reduce his responsibilities. However, with Mr. DD's permission, his associate minister was enlisted as an ally in devising ways for Mr. DD to continue to serve the church without being placed in situations where he was faced with impossible tasks. For example, the associate minister began to prepare and type the weekly bulletin, but Mr. DD continued to operate the printer to produce the required number for the Sunday service. Thus Mr. DD continued to feel productive, which helped him preserve some degree of self-esteem. By avoiding tasks that were beyond his capabilities, he also avoided repeated narcissistic injuries.

The case of Mr. DD illustrates several useful principles in the dynamically informed management of dementia: 1) attend to self-esteem issues; 2) assess characteristic defense mechanisms and help the patient use them constructively; 3) find ways to replace defective ego functions and cognitive limitations, such as keeping calendars for orientation problems, taking notes for memory problems, and making schedules for problems of secondary autonomous functioning; and 4) assist family members in developing new ways of relatedness that shore up the patient's self-esteem by decreasing negative interactions.

Patients in the early stages of Alzheimer's dementia may use denial to prevent the full impact of the illness from entering conscious awareness. Clinicians treating such patients must respect their need for denial but also help them to tie up loose ends with business and family before it is too late (Martin 1989). Those who treat Alzheimer's patients are apt to face countertransference struggles that interfere with such planning. They must be alert to feelings of helplessness, guilt, failure, wishes to abandon the patient, and hopelessness.

Although these measures do not prevent the ultimate deterioration associated with dementia of the Alzheimer's type, they do result in an improved quality of life during the gradual but inevitable downhill course of the disease. Ultimately, the patient's family members are the main focus of intervention, as they struggle with anger, guilt, grief, and exhaustion in the face of the patient's inexorable decline. In fact, family therapy is probably the dynamic treatment of choice in Alzheimer's dementia (Lansky 1984). Blaming of self and others is a frequent development in family members. Also, the readjustment of family roles may require intervention. The final task, of course, involves the acceptance of death. Clinicians who struggle along with these families in such situations will often find the treatment process a trying one, but they can pride themselves on having made a significant impact on the lives of all involved.

References

Abrams JC, Kaslow FW: Learning disability and family dynamics: a mutual interaction. Journal of Clinical Child Psychology 5:35–40, 1976

Allen JG, Colson DB, Coyne L: Organic brain dysfunction and behavioral dyscontrol in difficult-to-treat psychiatric hospital patients. Integrative Psychiatry 6:120–130, 1988

American Psychiatric Association: Diagnostic and Statistical Manual of Mental Disorders, 3rd Edition, Revised. Washington, DC, American Psychiatric Association, 1987

American Psychiatric Association: Diagnostic and Statistical Manual of Mental Disorders, 4th Edition. Washington, DC, American Psychiatric Association, 1994

Ball JD: Psychotherapy with head-injured patients. Medical Psychotherapy 1:15–22, 1988

Bellak L: Psychiatric states in adults with minimal brain dysfunction. Psychiatric Annals 7:575–589, 1977

Bryan JH, Sherman RE, Fisher A: Learning disabled boys' nonverbal behaviors within a dyadic interview. Learning Disability Quarterly 3:65–72, 1980

Bryan T: Learning disabled children's comprehension of nonverbal communication. Journal of Learning Disabilities 10:501–506, 1977

Buchholz ES: The legacy from childhood: considerations for treatment of the adult with learning disabilities. Psychoanalytic Inquiry 7:431–452, 1987

Colson DB, Allen JG: Organic brain dysfunction in difficult-to-treat psychiatric hospital patients. Bull Menninger Clin 50:88–98, 1986

Cummings JL: Dementia syndromes: neurobehavioral and neuropsychiatric features. J Clin Psychiatry 48(suppl):3–8, 1987

Goldstein K: The effect of brain damage on the personality. Psychiatry 15:245–260, 1952

Hartmann H: Ego Psychology and the Problem of Adaptation (1939). Translated by Rapaport D. New York, International Universities Press, 1958

Hartocollis P: The syndrome of minimal brain dysfunction in young adult patients. Bull Menninger Clin 32:102–114, 1968

Hollós S, Ferenczi S: Psychoanalysis and the Psychic Disorder of General Paresis. Translated by Barnes GM, Keil G. New York, Normal & Mental Disease Publishing, 1925

Kafka E: Cognitive difficulties in psychoanalysis. Psychoanal Q 53:533–550, 1984

Lansky MR: Family psychotherapy of the patient with chronic organic brain syndrome. Psychiatric Annals 14:121–129, 1984

Lewis L: Individual psychotherapy with patients having combined psychological and neurological disorders. Bull Menninger Clin 50:75–87, 1986

Lewis L: The role of psychological factors in disordered awareness, in Awareness of Deficit After Brain Injury: Clinical and Theoretical Issues. Edited by Prigatano GP, Schachter DL. New York, Oxford University Press, 1991, pp 223–239

Lewis L, Rosenberg SJ: Psychoanalytic psychotherapy with brain-injured adult psychiatric patients. J Nerv Ment Dis 17:69–77, 1990

Martin RL: Update on dementia of the Alzheimer type. Hosp Community Psychiatry 40:593–604, 1989

McHugh PR, Folstein MF: Organic mental disorders, in Psychiatry, Revised Edition. Edited by Michels R, Cavenar JO Jr. Vol 2: Schizophrenia, Affective Disorders, and Dementias. Edited by Guze SB, Helzer JE. Philadelphia, PA, JB Lippincott, 1986, pp 333–353

Morris J, Bleiberg J: Neuropsychological rehabilitation and traditional psychotherapy. International Journal of Clinical Neuropsychology 8:133–135, 1986

Oddy M, Coughlan T, Tyreman A: Social adjustment after closed head injury: a further follow-up seven years after injury. J Neurol Neurosurg Psychiatry 48:564–568, 1985

Palombo J: Perceptual deficits and self-esteem in adolescence. Clinical Social Work Journal 7:34–61, 1979

Pickar DB: Psychosocial aspects of learning disabilities: a review of research. Bull Menninger Clin 50:22–32, 1986

Prigatano GP: Work, love, and play after brain injury. Bull Menninger Clin 53:414–431, 1989

Prigatano GP, Klonoff PS: Psychotherapy and neuropsychological assessment after brain injury. Journal of Head Trauma Rehabilitation 3:45–56, 1988

Prigatano GP, Fordyce DJ, Zeiner HK, et al: Neuropsychological rehabilitation after closed head injury in young adults. J Neurol Neurosurg Psychiatry 47:505–513, 1984

Sperry RW, Zaidel E, Zaidel D: Self-recognition and social awareness in the deconnected minor hemispheres. Neuropsychologia 17:153–166, 1979

Spitzer RL, First MB, Williams JBW, et al: Now is the time to retire the term "organic mental disorders." Am J Psychiatry 149:240–244, 1992

Stern DN: The Interpersonal World of the Infant: A View From Psychoanalysis and Developmental Psychology. New York, Basic Books, 1985

Stern JM: The psychotherapeutic process with brain-injured patients: a dynamic approach. Isr J Psychiatry Relat Sci 22:83–87, 1985

Tucker G, Popkin M, Caine E, et al: Reorganizing the "organic" disorders. Hosp Community Psychiatry 41:722–724, 1990

Weil AP: Maturational variations and genetic-dynamic issues. J Am Psychoanal Assoc 26:461–491, 1978

Weiner MF: Dementia as a psychodynamic process, in The Dementias: Diagnosis and Management. Edited by Weiner MF. Washington, DC, American Psychiatric Press, 1991, pp 29–46

Wragg RE, Jeste DV: Overview of depression and psychosis in Alzheimer's disease. Am J Psychiatry 146:577–587, 1989

Section III

Dynamic Approaches to Axis II Disorders

Chapter 14

Cluster A Personality Disorders: Paranoid, Schizoid, and Schizotypal

Paranoid Personality Disorder

Paranoid thinking is not in and of itself pathological. As described in Chapter 2, the paranoid-schizoid position is a basic mode of organizing experience that persists in the human psyche throughout the life cycle. In this mode, dangerous or unpleasant thoughts and feelings are split off, projected outward, and attributed to others. This mode is readily accessible in all kinds of group experiences, such as political conventions, sporting events, and institutional dynamics. At certain historical junctures, entire cultures have been pervaded by paranoid thinking, as in the "witch hunts" of the McCarthy era in this country.

The paranoid personality disorder, however, is a distinct pathological entity that is independent of cultural factors and is not a transient state growing out of the nexus of group dynamics. It involves a pervasive style of thinking, feeling, and relating to others that is extraordinarily rigid and unvarying. These individuals live within the paranoid-schizoid position. Seven common features comprise the diagnostic criteria; at least four must be present to make the diagnosis (see Table 14–1). Moreover, the patient's suspicious beliefs must stop short of being delusional and must occur independently of an Axis I psychotic

419

diagnosis such as schizophrenia or delusional disorder. Minor changes were made in the DSM-IV criteria (American Psychiatric Association 1994) to reduce overlap with other disorders. For example, Item A(6), "perceives attacks on his or her character or reputation that are not apparent to others and is quick to react with anger or to counterattack," clarifies that anger appears as a retaliation for perceived attacks, rather than as an outburst motivated purely by internal issues.

As with most personality disorders, the key features of the paranoid personality disorder are ego-syntonic. Paranoid patients are often brought to treatment by family members or co-workers who are fed up with the patient's constant allegations and accusations. A boss, for example, may insist that an employee seek treatment—or look elsewhere for a job. A spouse who is tired of accusations of infidelity may use the threat of divorce to force the paranoid individual into treatment. Even

---

Table 14–1. DSM-IV diagnostic criteria for paranoid personality disorder

A. A pervasive distrust and suspiciousness of others such that their motives are interpreted as malevolent, beginning by early adulthood, and present in a variety of contexts, as indicated by at least *four* of the following:

   1. suspects, without sufficient basis, that others are exploiting or deceiving him or her

   2. is preoccupied with unjustified doubts about the loyalty or trustworthiness of friends or associates

   3. is reluctant to confide in others because of unwarranted fear that the information will be used maliciously against him or her

   4. reads hidden demeaning or threatening meanings into benign remarks or events

   5. persistently bears grudges, i.e., is unforgiving of insults, injuries, or slights

   6. perceives attacks on his or her character or reputation that are not apparent to others and is quick to react angrily or to counterattack

   7. has recurrent suspicions, without justification, regarding fidelity of spouse or sexual partner

B. Does not occur exclusively during the course of schizophrenia, a mood disorder with psychotic features, or another psychotic disorder, and is not due to the direct physiological effects of a general medical condition. Note: If criteria are met prior to the onset of schizophrenia, add "premorbid," e.g., "paranoid personality disorder (premorbid)."

Source. DSM-IV. Because the criteria sets were not final at press time, the reader should consult DSM-IV for final criteria.

when paranoid patients enter treatment willingly, they usually remain unconvinced that they are psychiatrically disturbed. Their presenting problems revolve around how others have mistreated and betrayed them.

The diagnostic criteria reflect a way of thinking that can be conceptualized as a distinctly paranoid cognitive style (Shapiro 1965). This style of thinking is characterized by an unrelenting search for hidden meanings, for clues to uncover the "truth" behind a situation's face value. The obvious, the superficial, and the apparent merely mask the reality. This endless search involves an intense hyperalertness of attention, evidenced by a guardedness related to this continuous attentional monitoring. A paranoid individual constantly scans the environment for anything out of the ordinary—a style of thinking that takes a considerable toll in physical and emotional tension. The paranoid patient is simply unable to relax.

Paranoid thinking is also characterized by a lack of flexibility. The most persuasive argument will generally have no impact on the rigid and unswerving beliefs of the paranoid person. In fact, those persons who attempt to argue with a person who has a paranoid personality disorder will simply find themselves becoming the target of suspicion. The paranoid person's thinking differs from that of the paranoid schizophrenic person in that it is not delusional. In fact, patients with paranoid personality disorder tend to have remarkably accurate perceptions of their environment. However, their judgments about those perceptions are generally impaired. Reality itself is not distorted; rather, the *significance* of apparent reality is misconstrued (Shapiro 1965). This characteristic cognitive style may be difficult to diagnose because the paranoid individual is often closemouthed and guarded. In fact, even projective testing may only identify the paranoid individual as a more-or-less normal person who is simply inhibited.

Psychodynamics of the Paranoid Personality Disorder

An understanding of the characteristics of the paranoid-schizoid position is essential to an understanding of the paranoid patient. As noted in Chapter 2, splitting is a central defense mechanism in this mode of organizing experience. Feelings of love and hate toward the same object must be separated from one another. Any movement toward integration creates intolerable anxiety that stems from the fear that the hatred will overpower and destroy the love. From the standpoint of the paranoid patient, emotional survival requires the patient to split off all "badness" and project it onto outside figures. One manifestation of this defensive maneuver is that the normal internal world of aggressor and victim is transformed into a life experience in which the paranoid individual is constantly in the role of victim vis-à-vis external aggressors or persecutors. The view that paranoid patients have of the world thus relieves their internal tension between introjects. If a paranoid individual is forced to reinternalize what has been projected, the heightened internal tension will result in increased rigidity and defensiveness (Shapiro 1965).

Another characteristic of the paranoid-schizoid position is that the patient's experience of others is discontinuous; no relationship is perceived as enduring over time. Rather, the patient has only the perception of the moment. Patients with paranoid personality disorder approach every relationship with the belief that the other person will eventually "slip up" and confirm their suspicions. In the paranoid-schizoid mode of existence, the patient lives in a state of unremitting anxiety stemming from a conviction that the world is peopled with untrustworthy and unpredictable strangers (Ogden 1986). Even when a stable, helpful therapist has worked with a paranoid patient over a long period, one minor disappointment can lead the patient to completely disregard the therapist's previous behavior and to feel—with unswerving conviction—that the therapist is untrustworthy. The therapist has been "unmasked." Thus, good experiences with a person in the past can be totally erased by the present situation.

The self in the paranoid-schizoid mode of experience is incompletely developed. Self-experience is also equated with the current experience. There is no interpreting subject to mediate between symbol and symbolized (i.e., between perceptions and thoughts and the feelings about those perceptions) (Ogden 1986). Experience is literally taken at face value. Patients with paranoid personality disorder are unable to think, "It is *as if* this other person is trying to hurt me." Instead, they *know* that the other person harbors malevolent intentions. Similarly, in the transference relationship with the therapist, the paranoid patient is unable to say, "I feel that I am reacting to you *as if* you are as sadistic as my father was." The patient simply experiences the therapist as sadistic. Feelings are not personal creations of the patient, but rather things-in-themselves. When patients develop a mediating self that is able to interpret accurately and to think symbolically in "as if" terms, then they have achieved the depressive position (Ogden 1986).

Projection and projective identification are two key defense mechanisms of the paranoid personality disorder. Projection substitutes an external threat for an internal one; projective identification goes a step further. In addition to externalizing threats, projective identification "controls" persons in the environment by binding them to the paranoid person in highly pathological ways. The need to control others reflects the terribly low self-esteem at the core of paranoia (Meissner 1986). Deep down, the paranoid patient feels inferior, weak, and ineffectual. Thus, the grandiosity or sense of "specialness" often seen in these patients can be understood as a compensatory defense that makes up for feelings of inferiority.

The low self-esteem at the heart of the paranoid personality disorder leads these individuals to develop a keen sense of attunement to issues of rank and power. They are intensely concerned that persons in authority will humiliate them or expect them to be submissive (Shapiro 1965). They perceive threats to their autonomy as omnipresent. A recurring fear about their interpersonal relationships is that they will result in subjection to external control; they fear that anyone who tries to be close to them is secretly trying to take over. This concern may surface as a dread of passive homosexual impulses, originally described by Freud (1911/1958) in the case of the psychotically disturbed Judge Schreber. However, all paranoid individuals are not necessarily concerned about passive homosexual impulses. Overt homosexuality and paranoid personality disorder can and do exist in the same person. The main point is rather that these patients are concerned about *all* passive surrender to *all* impulses and to all persons (Shapiro 1965).

Successful treatment can provide a glimpse of what lies beneath the projective system: a good deal of depressive content (Meissner 1976) and diametrically opposing self-representations. Coexisting with the special, entitled, grandiose version of the self is a weak, worthless, inferior polar opposite. Akhtar (1990) has systematically examined these coexisting self-representations and characterized them as follows: "Outwardly, paranoid individuals are demanding, arrogant, mistrustful, driven, unromantic, moralistic, and acutely vigilant towards the external environment. Internally, however, they are frightened, timid, self-doubting, gullible, inconsiderate, vulnerable to erotomania, and cognitively unable to grasp the totality of actual events" (pp. 21–22). Therapists who are aware of this other dimension of the paranoid personality can more easily empathize with these difficult patients.

The developmental failure to achieve object constancy is a characteristic of paranoid patients that organizes much of their behavior and thinking (Blum 1981; Auchincloss and Weiss 1992). Because they cannot maintain a loving connection with an internal object-representation, they are convinced that love relationships are dangerous and unstable. To deal with the terrors associated with object inconstancy, the paranoid patient constructs fantasies of concrete and magical connectedness to objects (Auchincloss and Weiss 1992). Paranoid individuals impose an extreme either-or requirement on relationships. Either the object of their attention is thinking about them continuously or that person is emotionally indifferent to them—a thought paranoid patients find intolerable. This set of anxieties concerning indifference and connectedness is largely responsible for the willingness of paranoid patients to constrict their freedom in the service of feeling a concrete and magical connection to objects.

Treatment Approaches

Because of their suspiciousness, paranoid patients usually do poorly in group psychotherapy. Most treatment efforts must therefore be initiated in the context of individual therapy, despite the formidable challenge to the individual psychotherapist. As noted earlier, these patients often enter treatment under some external pressure, and they have the utmost difficulty trusting anyone. In light of these obstacles, the first step in psychotherapy should be to build a therapeutic alliance. This process is made more difficult by the tendency of paranoid patients to evoke defensive responses in others. The therapist is no exception, as the following vignette illustrates:

> Patient: I'm really angry with you because I've been sitting in the waiting room for half an hour. You told me to be here at 9:30 today.
> Therapist: No, that's not true. I said 10 A.M.
> Patient: You said 9:30.
> Therapist: (a little louder and more forcefully) I said 10 o'clock. I wrote it down in my book.
> Patient: You're trying to trick me! You won't admit you're wrong, so you try to make me think that I'm the one who's wrong.
> Therapist: (louder still) If I were wrong, I would admit it. On the contrary, I think you are the one who won't admit to being wrong, and you attribute that to me!

Patient: I'm not going to take this harassment. I'll find another therapist!

This slightly caricatured interaction illustrates the projective identification cycle that is extraordinarily common in paranoid patients.
The patient treats the therapist as a persecuting bad object. The therapist feels coerced into being defensive and ends up giving an interpretation that attempts to force the projection back onto the patient. The
patient responds by feeling attacked, misunderstood, and deceived. To
avoid this escalating cycle, the therapist must empathize with the
patient's need to project as a means of emotional survival. The therapist must be willing to serve as a container for feelings of hatred, badness, impotence, and despair (Epstein 1979). Attempting to return
such feelings prematurely will simply lead the patient to feel an increased internal tension and to become more rigid. The therapist must
be able to accept blame, even to the point of acknowledging a lack of
ability to help the patient (Epstein 1984). Most therapists have strong
countertransference resistances to accepting responsibility for a failing treatment; they just naturally become defensive when their patients accuse them of incompetence. However, by acknowledging the
low self-esteem that creates the need to see fault in others, therapists
can empathize with their patient's point of view and genuinely seek
suggestions for how to make the treatment more productive. Becoming
defensive is also a natural reaction to being accused of dishonesty. Defensiveness, however, may be misinterpreted as confirmation that the
therapist has something to hide. Openness is by far the best policy with
paranoid patients. If they act suspicious about the therapist's records
or process notes, then the therapist would do well to share those notes
with the patients and to thereby use them as a therapeutic intervention. Refusal to share notes will simply incite further paranoia.

Throughout the psychotherapy, particularly during the early
phases of building an alliance, the therapist must avoid responding
defensively—like everyone else in the patient's environment. The therapist should not challenge the patient's construction of events or the
patient's perception of the therapist, no matter how negative. The therapist should merely ask for more detail and should empathize with the
patient's feelings and perceptions. Above all, the therapist must resist
the frequent countertransference tendency to be rid of undesirable projections by forcing them back onto the patient via premature interpretations (Epstein 1979). As in the previous example, interpretations of

this kind will simply confirm the perception that the therapist is highly invested in attacking the patient. The same situation might be handled quite differently using these principles of technique:

> Patient: I'm really angry with you because I've been sitting in the waiting room for half an hour. You told me to be here at 9:30 today.
> Therapist: Let me see if I understand you correctly. Your understanding was that you were to see me today at 9:30 instead of 10 o'clock?
> Patient: You said 9:30.
> Therapist: I can certainly see why you might be angry at me then. Having to wait for someone for 30 minutes would make most people angry.
> Patient: You admit that you told me to come at 9:30?
> Therapist: Frankly, I don't remember saying that, but I'd like to hear more about your recall of that conversation so I can find out what I said to give you that impression.

In this scenario, the therapist accepts blame nondefensively without admitting to any fault. The therapist contains the patient's projection and seeks to find out more information about how it arose. By being willing to entertain the possibility of having indeed misled the patient, the therapist validates the patient's perception as legitimate and worthy of further discussion. Finally, the therapist does not attempt to return what has been projected in the form of an interpretation.

Therapists also need to empathize with the patient's tendency to be guarded. There is a certain adaptive quality in guardedness; paranoid patients who talk extensively about their perceptions are likely to alienate others. Therapists who allow for periods of silence and constriction instead of intrusively asking questions may help the patient to open up a bit more. Another technique for building an alliance is to focus on the patient's state of tension secondary to the extraordinary vigilance necessary to maintain the paranoid cognitive style. Comments such as, "Your nerves must be shot," or "You must be exhausted after all of this," may help the patient feel understood. When the patient is willing to talk, the therapist should encourage elaboration, which may reveal historical antecedents to the current situation of stress (Meissner 1976).

Countertransference exasperation and impatience may develop as these patients describe how others are constantly thinking about them and scrutinizing their behavior in an unrelenting manner. Therapists may have to fight off urges to confront the grandiosity and to deflate the notion that the patient is the center of the universe. An appreciation of the defensive function of this perception in terms of its role in maintaining connectedness may be helpful to the therapist struggling with countertransference. Challenging the paranoid construct of magical connectedness prematurely will rupture any semblance of a developing therapeutic alliance. Over time, however, the fear of indifference and the need to feel connected with others can be gently interpreted in the service of establishing greater object constancy (Auchincloss and Weiss 1992).

The overall goal of psychotherapeutic work with paranoid patients is to help them shift their perceptions of the origin of their problems from an external locus to an internal one. This shift can only follow an unhurried timetable that is unique to each patient. The therapist must withstand repeated barrages of accusations and suspicions without becoming exasperated or despairing. As the patient opens up more, the therapist can begin to label the patient's feelings and thereby help the patient distinguish between emotions and reality (Meissner 1976). Therapists can also help their patients define gaps in their knowledge. For example, a therapist might ask, "Did your boss say that he hates you?" When the patient responds negatively to the question, the therapist can comment matter-of-factly about the patient's limited knowledge of the boss's feelings. Such questions must be worded tactfully and neutrally so as not to inordinately challenge the patient's view of the world. The therapist need not take a pro or con position in the matter, but should only indicate that more information is necessary (Meissner 1976).

Throughout the entire psychotherapy process, the therapist must contain feelings rather than act on them. This containment will provide the patient with a new object relationship different from those previously encountered. The different experience is eventually internalized over time. This relationship model of change is complemented by gradual changes in thinking. The key is for such patients to entertain a "creative doubt" (Meissner 1986) about their perceptions of the world. As patients move from the paranoid-schizoid position to encounter the depressive elements within, they begin to experience a sense of self that can mediate and interpret experience. Things may become "as if " they are a certain way rather than as *really* a certain way. Patients may also allow longer glimpses of their feelings of worthlessness and inferiority so that depressive elements can be worked through in the transference. In the most optimal circumstances, these patients can reveal a yearning for acceptance, love, and closeness that is associated with their frustration and disappointment with early figures in their lives (Meissner 1976). As a result, they can begin the process of mourning those attachments.

Case Example

A brief report of the early stages of psychotherapy with a patient suffering from paranoid personality disorder will illustrate some of the technical principles described in the foregoing paragraphs. The bracketed comments below indicate how theory and technique relate in this case.

> Mr. EE was a 42-year-old accountant who had been on disability for a year because of his continual complaints of allergies to substances in the work environment. After receiving a promotion, he had moved into a new office where he had experienced a sudden onset of several troublesome physical symptoms, including headaches, sluggish thinking, tightening in the chest, blurred vision, generalized aching, weakness, easy fatigability, and lack of motivation. Mr. EE attributed these symptoms to the new paneling and carpeting in the office and to vibrations in the floor from the blower system. The ill effects began to dissipate whenever he left the office and were often gone by the time Mr. EE visited a doctor. He had had numerous diagnostic evaluations by various specialists, only one of whom had thought that there was any physical basis for the complaints. Mr. EE used this isolated opinion to vindicate his own view. He was pressured into psychotherapy by the management of his firm, who were concerned that his disability was becoming permanent. In the initial stages of therapy, Mr. EE denied any emotional problems other than marital tension, for which he blamed his wife. He spoke at length about his symptoms and maintained that he was convinced of their physical origin regardless of the negative findings of most of the specialists. [The patient reveals himself to be totally impervious to rational arguments from experts. He also displays grandiosity by believing that he knows more than the doctors.]
>
> When asked about his interpersonal relationships, Mr. EE said that he and his father were not on speaking terms because his father had deceived him in business deals. Moreover, he complained that his father was always harder on him than on all his brothers. He summa-

rized his description of his father by saying that he was an unfair and untrustworthy man. Mr. EE went on to describe his wife as deceitful. She had "tricked" him into having a child by failing to use birth control and becoming pregnant. He said that he had never forgiven his wife for her trickery—8 years previously—and he said that their marriage had been a disaster ever since. He said that the only way this situation could change would be for her to become more trustworthy. [The patient has projected malevolent persecuting objects onto close figures in his family and sees them as the source of all his problems. The patient himself acknowledges no contributions to these difficulties in family relationships and suggests that the only possible solutions involve change in others instead of in him.]

Throughout the first psychotherapy session, Mr. EE listened intently to the therapist, often asking for further clarification of comments. He seemed to be listening for hidden messages in the most benign communications. Mr. EE was also hyperalert to any slight body movements of the therapist, often misinterpreting them as indications of boredom or disinterest. After listening for some time, the therapist commented empathically, "You must feel awful right now. Your boss is on your back to get therapy, you feel physically miserable, and your wife and you are not speaking to each other." The patient responded to this empathic comment by opening up a little more, admitting that he had always been "thin-skinned." He acknowledged that he was often considerably disturbed by minor things that did not bother other people. [The therapist's empathic validation of Mr. EE's beleaguered self-esteem allowed him to feel understood. This beginning alliance allowed the patient to acknowledge a problem in himself for the first time, namely, that he was "thin-skinned."]

Mr. EE described his relationship with his son in cold, calculating terms by saying, "We're together more than average for the population at large." [This description reveals the inability of the paranoid personality to feel emotional warmth and tenderness in relationships because having such feelings would make him vulnerable to rejection or attack.] Mr. EE changed the subject to his concerns about the doctors who had examined him. He expressed a strong belief that all doctors are basically incompetent, and he seemed convinced that one doctor had almost caused him to have a cerebral hemorrhage with a certain medication. He described three psychiatrists who had previously examined him as all incompetent. He then asked the therapist if he knew of a particular nonpsychiatric medication. When the therapist admitted to being unfamiliar with the drug, Mr. EE quickly responded that the therapist was probably as much of a "quack" as the other doctors. [The paranoid person's fear of being controlled, allied with feelings of inferiority in "one-down" relationships, often lead to devaluation and demeaning of other people. By devaluing the therapist, Mr. EE reassures himself that he has nothing to envy and no reason to feel inferior.]

When Mr. EE continued to disparage the opinions of the many specialists he had seen, the therapist noted, "This must be very demoralizing for you." Mr. EE responded sharply, "You're trying to lead me on!" [Here the therapist's attempt to empathize by introducing a new feeling exceeded the patient's ability to admit to that feeling. The patient's reaction might have been more positive if the therapist had stayed closer to the words and feeling states that the patient himself had described.]

As Mr. EE continued to talk about his current state of affairs, he was able to acknowledge that he had found it difficult to adjust to disability and unemployment after being in an executive position. Sensing an opening regarding the self-esteem issue, the therapist noted that being unable to work must have been quite a blow. Mr. EE responded by asking the therapist, "Do you think I am weak?" [Again the therapist's ability to empathize with the patient's low self-esteem rather than becoming defensive allowed Mr. EE to reveal concern about his underlying weakness and inferiority.]

Prevention of Violence

Although patients who suffer from any of a broad variety of psychiatric disorders may become violent, paranoid patients pose a particular threat to psychiatrists. An understanding of the dynamics of paranoia may help avert assault. To prevent the escalation of aggression, psychiatrists should keep in mind several principles of management:

1. *Do everything possible to help the patient save face.* The core of paranoia is low self-esteem, so psychiatrists should empathize with the patient's experience and not challenge the truth of what the patient says. In a busy outpatient clinic, a resident who saw a paranoid patient for the first time suspected that he was not telling the truth about his current living situation. He told the patient that he was going to check up on his statement by calling the halfway house where the patient said he lived. As the resident reached in his desk drawer for the telephone book, the patient struck him in the face with his fist. This unfortunate incident leads directly into another major principle of violence prevention.

2. *Avoid arousing further suspicion.* Because of the basic distrust of these patients, all interventions must be geared to avoiding any increase in their paranoia. Each movement should be explained slowly and carefully. The movements themselves should be performed slowly and in clear view. You might say, for example, "Now I'm going to reach in my desk and get an appointment slip so that you'll know when our next meeting is." You should also avoid being overly friendly to these patients, since such behavior is in stark contrast to their usual experience and will simply further arouse their suspicions.

3. *Help the patient maintain a sense of control.* Control is of extraordinary importance to paranoid patients, who are likely to fear loss of control as much as the therapist fears it. The therapist must avoid panic at all costs. A therapist who displays fear that the patient will lose control will only heighten the patient's own fears of losing control. Much of the anxiety among paranoid individuals stems from a fear that others will try to be in control; for this reason, anything the therapist can do to indicate respect for these patients' autonomy will help reduce their anxiety about passive surrender. Interventions should acknowledge their right to view the situation as they see it. For example, the therapist might tell such a patient, "I think your feelings are legitimate about the situation, given what you've been through, and I respect your right to feel that way."

4. *Always encourage these patients to verbalize rather than to violently act out anger.* Get them to discuss their anger in as much detail as possible. Encourage a consideration of the logical consequences of becoming violent. If possible, provide constructive alternatives to violence so that these patients can begin to see that there are other options. Supporting the anger as a legitimate reaction does not mean endorsing aggressive action. The therapist who feels immediately threatened may attempt to translate this threat into words. When one psychiatry resident sensed that a new patient was about to erupt in violence, he said, "I wonder if you're feeling like you want to hit me right now." The patient nodded in assent. The resident then replied, "Maybe if we go take a walk and you tell me about the feelings you're having, you'll be able to avoid acting on those feelings." This calm, matter-of-fact approach taken helped the patient feel more in control, and the patient actually thanked the resident for his help.

5. *Always give paranoid individuals plenty of breathing room.* Their fear of passive surrender to others is heightened by physical proximity. Avoid a seating arrangement where they feel trapped in the office. Violent individuals have been shown to need greater distance from others to feel secure (Kinzel 1971). Avoid sitting too close, as well as touching them, even in the most benign manner. One paranoid woman began carrying a gun to her therapy sessions after her therapist persisted in hugging her at the end of each session.

6. *Finally, be attuned to your own countertransference in dealing with potentially violent patients* (Felthous 1984). Countertransference denial is common both in hospital staff members and in therapists who work with paranoid individuals. They may fail to ask important historical questions for fear of confirming their worst fears about their patients' potential for violence. Treaters must acknowledge their own fears and then must avoid situations of jeopardy with patients who have been assaultive in the past. Therapists may also use countertransference projection to disavow their own aggression and externalize it onto their patients. Projective identification may provoke patients to violence when therapists see destructiveness and aggression only in their patients and not in themselves. One study of psychiatrists who have been assaulted by patients (Madden et al. 1976) found that 53% of the psychiatrists had in some way been provocative toward the patient prior to being assaulted.

Schizoid and Schizotypal Personality Disorders

In addition to paranoid personality disorder, Cluster A in Axis II of DSM-IV subsumes schizoid and schizotypal personality disorders. Although these are distinct entities, they will be considered together here because both the dynamic understanding of and the therapeutic approaches to these disorders have much in common. Prior to DSM-III (American Psychiatric Association 1980), a distinction was not made between these two personality disorders. The creators of DSM-III considered the schizoid personality disorder of DSM-II (American Psychiatric Association 1968) too broad, however, so they divided that category into three subtypes—schizoid, avoidant, and schizotypal—with the publication of DSM-III in 1980. The inclusion of avoidant personality disorder was disturbing to many clinicians because it was a little-used diagnosis with no clinical tradition. The decision to distinguish between schizoid and avoidant was based on the classification system of Millon (1969, 1981), who apparently influenced final decisions concerning diagnostic categories in Axis II (Akhtar 1987; Gunderson 1983). Millon justified the distinction because of the different ways that persons in the two categories approached interpersonal relationships. The schizoid individual was viewed as incapable of and uninterested in forming relationships with others. The avoidant person was alleged to be both interested in and capable of forming interpersonal bonds but afraid of humiliation and disapproval in the context of such interactions.

Criticism of this distinction has come from many quarters (Akhtar 1987; Gunderson 1983; Kernberg 1984). Critics have pointed out that the withdrawal of interest in others that is characteristic of schizoid individuals is only an apparent retreat. These patients may secretly yearn for closeness but because of their fears instead assume a defensive posture of detachment (Kernberg 1984). Moreover, the assumption is that the schizoid personality is more closely linked to a deficit model of psychopathology, while the avoidant personality is a disorder of conflict, a distinction that implies a better prognosis for the latter without any data to support such a position (Akhtar 1987; Gunderson 1983). Empirical studies (Morey 1985; Reich and Noyes 1986) have found this distinction highly questionable as well. Finally, psychoanalysts and dynamically oriented psychiatrists were concerned that the DSM-III-R (American Psychiatric Association 1987) version of schizoid personality disorder deviated from the extensive psychoanalytic literature on schizoid phenomena by taking overt behavior at face value (Akhtar 1987). (For a superb overview of the psychoanalytic and descriptive literature on this subject, see Akhtar 1987.) The DSM-IV version of schizoid personality disorder has been modified to bring greater specificity and clarity to the diagnosis (see Table 14–2). Criterion A(4) has been revised to stress the schizoid patient's difficulty in enjoying everyday activities. Criterion A(6) has been modified to acknowledge the underlying sensitivity of schizoid individuals by emphasizing their *apparent* indifference to praise or criticism.

Although these criteria still fail to address the schizoid individual's secret longing for relationships, they do acknowledge that behind the outward appearance of detachment, the patient may experience strong emotions and may even have sexual feelings despite evincing no such interest outwardly. The DSM-III-R criteria for avoidant personality also changed to more closely resemble a "phobic character." The decision to separate schizoid and schizotypal personality disorders seems to have been largely related to genetic studies (Kendler et al. 1981; Kety et al. 1971; Rosenthal et al. 1971) that suggested a muted version of schizophrenia characterized by more or less intact reality testing, difficulties in relationships, and mild thought disturbances. The link between schizotypal personality and schizophrenia was further bolstered by McGlashan's (1983) long-term follow-up study, which demonstrated that schizotypal and schizophrenic patients had similar outcomes. The outcomes of borderline patients, on the other hand, were more typical of those associated with affective disorders. The designation of certain close relatives of schizophrenic individuals as schizotypal replaced the more problematic term *borderline schizophrenia,* which was easily confused with borderline personality disorder. Some critics (Siever and Gunderson 1979) have questioned the appropriateness of classifying a variant of a psychotic condition as a person-

---

Table 14–2. DSM-IV criteria for schizoid personality disorder

A. A pervasive pattern of detachment from social relationships and a restricted range of expression of emotions in interpersonal settings, beginning by early adulthood, and present in a variety of contexts, as indicated by at least *four* of the following:

  1. neither desires nor enjoys close relationships, including being part of a family
  2. almost always chooses solitary activities
  3. has little, if any, interest in having sexual experiences with another person
  4. takes pleasure in few, if any, activities
  5. lacks close friends or confidants other than first-degree relatives
  6. appears indifferent to the praise or criticism of others
  7. shows emotional coldness, detachment, or flattened affectivity

B. Does not occur exclusively during the course of schizophrenia, a mood disorder with psychotic features, another psychotic disorder, or a pervasive developmental disorder, and is not due to the direct physiological effects of a general medical condition. Note: If criteria are met prior to the onset of schizophrenia, add "premorbid," e.g., "schizoid personality disorder (premorbid)."

Source. DSM-IV. Because the criteria sets were not final at press time, the reader should consult DSM-IV for final criteria.

ality disorder. In their view, the diagnosis depends to a large extent on symptoms resembling schizophrenia rather than on sustained patterns of relating to others, which are used to define the other personality disorders.

Between the appearance of DSM-III-R and the publication of DSM-IV, further empirical research demonstrated the link between schizotypal personality disorder and schizophrenia. Further analysis of the data from the Chestnut Lodge Follow-Up Study (Fenton and McGlashan 1989) demonstrated that three DSM-III criteria for schizotypal personality disorder predicted schizophrenia at long-term follow-up. The predictive power of these three key characteristics—magical thinking, suspiciousness or paranoid ideation, and social isolation—suggested that schizotypal personality disorder belongs in the schizophrenia spectrum. Another study demonstrated that the morbid risk for schizophrenia-related disorders in the first-degree relatives of patients with schizotypal and paranoid personality disorders is significantly higher than in the first-degree relatives of patients with other personality disorders (Siever et al. 1990).

Because of the compelling evidence that schizotypal personality disorder is related to schizophrenia in terms of biological, genetic, phenomenological, outcome, and treatment-response characteristics, serious consideration was given to moving the diagnosis out of Axis II into Axis I as part of the "schizophrenia and other psychotic disorders" section of DSM-IV. However, because of its resemblance to other personality disorders in regard to factors such as pervasiveness, stability, and onset, schizotypal personality disorder was retained in Axis II but with some significant changes in criteria (see Table 14–3). First of all, to make the criteria more specific, the psychotic-like symptoms must be persistent and not simply confined to discrete periods of affective symptomatology such as anger, anxiety, or depression. This modification helps distinguish schizotypal from borderline personality disorder. Criterion A(8) clarifies that these patients do not simply avoid others because of problems with past relationships (Siever et al. 1991). Criterion A(9) emphasizes that the severe social anxiety does not decrease with familiarity, thereby distinguishing schizotypal from avoidant personality disorder.

As Gunderson (1983) pointed out, persons with schizotypal personality disorder are much the same as schizoid individuals except that the definition of this disorder includes a few symptoms suggestive of an attenuated form of schizophrenia. In actuality, schizoid and schizotypal patients form a continuum, so it is somewhat arbitrary to draw a dividing line between the two entities. Schizotypal patients themselves form a continuum, from those on one end who are much like schizoid patients (except for a few more oddities of behavior and communication) to those closer to schizophrenia who are prone to brief psychotic episodes. The ensuing discussion of the psychoanalytic understanding of these conditions assumes that they are inherently similar.

Psychodynamic Understanding

Schizoid and schizotypal patients often live on the fringes of society. They may be ridiculed as "weirdos," "oddballs," or "misfits," or they

---

Table 14–3. DSM-IV criteria for schizotypal personality disorder

A. A pervasive pattern of social and interpersonal deficits marked by acute discomfort with, and reduced capacity for, close relationships as well as by cognitive or perceptual distortions and eccentricities of behavior beginning by early adulthood, and present in a variety of contexts, as indicated by at least *five* of the following:

1. ideas of reference (excluding delusions of reference)
2. odd beliefs or magical thinking that influence behavior and are inconsistent with subcultural norms (e.g., superstitiousness, belief in clairvoyance, telepathy, or "sixth sense"; in children and adolescents, bizarre fantasies or preoccupations)
3. unusual perceptual experiences, including bodily illusions
4. odd thinking and speech (e.g., vague, circumstantial, metaphorical, overelaborate, or stereotyped)
5. suspiciousness or paranoid ideation
6. inappropriate or constricted affect
7. behavior or appearance that is odd, eccentric, or peculiar
8. lack of close friends or confidants other than first-degree relatives
9. excessive social anxiety that does not diminish with familiarity and tends to be associated with paranoid fears rather than negative judgments about self

B. Does not occur exclusively during the course of schizophrenia, a mood disorder with psychotic features, another psychotic disorder, or a pervasive developmental disorder. Note: If criteria are met prior to the onset of schizophrenia, add "premorbid," e.g., "schizotypal personality disorder (premorbid)."

Source. DSM-IV. Because the criteria sets were not final at press time, the reader should consult DSM-IV for final criteria.

may merely be left alone to pursue a solitary and idiosyncratic existence. Their isolation and anhedonia may lead others to feel sorry for them and reach out to them. More often than not, however, the individuals who make such gestures give up after being repeatedly rebuffed. Family members may become so exasperated that they force their schizoid relative into a treatment situation. Parents of adolescents or young adults may bring their son or daughter to a psychiatrist out of concern that their child is not getting enough out of life (Stone 1985). Other schizoid and schizotypal patients come to psychiatric treatment voluntarily because of painful loneliness.

The inner world of the schizoid patient may differ considerably from the individual's outward appearance. Indeed, these people are often a bundle of contradictions. Akhtar (1987) has grouped these contradictions into overt and covert manifestations: "The schizoid individual is 'overtly' detached, self-sufficient, absent-minded, uninteresting, asexual, and idiosyncratically moral while 'covertly' being exquisitely sensitive, emotionally needy, acutely vigilant, creative, often perverse, and vulnerable to corruption" (p. 510). These polarities do not reflect conscious and unconscious personality traits. Rather, they represent a splitting or fragmentation of the self into different self-representations that remain unintegrated. From a psychodynamic perspective, the "schizoid" designation reflects this fundamental splitting of the self. The result is a diffuse identity—schizoid patients are not sure who they are, and they feel buffeted by highly conflictual thoughts, feelings, wishes, and urges. This identity diffusion makes relating to others problematic. Indeed, perhaps the most striking feature of schizoid and schizotypal patients is their apparent nonrelatedness to others. Psychoanalytic work with these patients suggests that they definitely have feelings and strivings for others, but that the patients themselves are frozen developmentally at an early stage of relatedness (Lawner 1985). These patients seem to base their decision to be isolated on a conviction that their failure to receive what they needed from their mothers means that they can make no further attempt to receive anything else from subsequent significant figures (Nachmani 1984).

Much of our understanding of the inner world of the schizoid patient derives from the work of the British object relations theorists. Balint (1979) viewed these patients as having a fundamental deficit in their ability to relate—a "basic fault" caused by significant inadequacies in the mothering they received as infants. He believed that the schizoid patient's difficulty in relating to others stems from this basic incapacity rather than from conflict (as in neurotic patients). Fairbairn (1954), perhaps the foremost contributor to our understanding of schizoid patients, viewed the schizoid retreat as a defense against a conflict between a wish to relate to others and a fear that one's neediness would harm others. The infant who initially perceives its mother as rejecting may withdraw from the world. However, the infant's neediness grows until it is experienced as insatiable. The infant then fears that its greed will devour the mother and leave it alone again. Hence the very object that the infant most needs may be destroyed by its own incorporative strivings. Fairbairn termed this concern the "Little Red Riding Hood Fantasy," based on the fairy tale in which the little girl finds, to her horror, that her grandmother has disappeared, leaving her alone with her own projected oral greed—in the form of a devouring wolf.

Just as Little Red Riding Hood may project her greed onto the wolf, infants may project their own greed onto their mothers, whom they then view as devouring and dangerous. This infantile dilemma is frozen in time for schizoid patients, who first fear that they will devour others with their neediness, and then fear being devoured by others. This fundamental dilemma of schizoid patients mandates that they will vacillate between the fear of driving others away by their neediness, on the one hand, and the fear, on the other hand, that others will smother or consume them. As a result, all relationships are experienced as dangerous and to be avoided. Because the decision to be nonrelated leaves the schizoid individual alone and empty, there is often a "schizoid compromise" (Guntrip 1968), in which the patient simultaneously clings to and rejects others.

Schizoid patients live under the constant threat of abandonment, persecution, and disintegration (Appel 1974). To take anything in from someone else risks the triggering of intense longings for dependency and merger. Love is equated with fusing with someone else, losing one's identity, and destroying the other person. Although the writing of the British School has focused on schizoid patients, the descriptions provided by Balint, Guntrip, and others refer to schizotypal patients as well (Stone 1985).

The schizoid patient's characteristic retreat from interpersonal relations may serve an important developmental function. Winnicott (1963/1965) believed that the isolation of the schizoid patient preserves an important authenticity that is absolutely sacred to the evolving self of the patient: "There is an intermediate stage in healthy development in which the patient's most important experience in relation to the good or potentially satisfying object is the refusal of it" (p. 182). The schizoid withdrawal is a way to communicate with the "true self" within instead of sacrificing that authenticity to artificial interactions with others that would lead to a "false self." Winnicott suggested that we all have this noncommunicating core, and that we must respect the schizoid individual's right—and need—to be noncommunicative. Periods of extreme abstinence and isolation may help schizoid individuals get in touch with this sequestered self so that it can be integrated with other self-representations (Eigen 1973).

Schizoid patients who allow their therapists to have access to their inner worlds will often reveal omnipotent fantasies. These usually accompany the reclusive aspects of the self to which the patient retreats. Like other aspects of the hidden self, they serve as a "sanctuary from exposure" (Grotstein 1977) to shore up fragile self-esteem and to allay anxiety about self-disintegration. Like paranoid patients, schizoid patients have omnipotent fantasies that increase in frequency in inverse proportion to their level of self-esteem (Nachmani 1984). Lacking good internal self- and object-representations to help accomplish essential work toward success in relationships or careers, schizoid patients employ fantasies of omnipotence to bypass such work and directly achieve their grandiose fantasies. Schizoid patients often feel a great deal of shame about their fantasies and are reluctant to share them with their therapists until they feel secure in the relationship.

Individual Psychotherapy

Schizoid and schizotypal patients may be helped with individual expressive-supportive therapy, dynamic group psychotherapy, or a combination of the two. Since the thought of the interactional demands of a group setting usually produces a good deal of anxiety, most of these patients will feel more comfortable beginning with an individual process. Much of the modern literature on the psychotherapy of schizoid and schizotypal personality disorders suggests that the mechanism of therapeutic action is likely to be internalization of a therapeutic relationship rather than interpretation of conflict (Appel 1974; Gabbard 1989; Khan 1983; Nachmani 1984; Stone 1983, 1985; Winnicott 1963/1965).

The task of the therapist is to "thaw" the patient's frozen internal object relations by providing a new experience of relatedness. The schizoid style of relatedness emerges from inadequacies in the patient's earliest relationships with parental figures—what Epstein (1979) referred to as primary maturational failure. Throughout life, the patient has evoked similar reactions from those in the environment, producing secondary maturational failures. In other words, the schizoid patient may go through life distancing everyone. Therapists must figure out how to relate to the patient in a maturationally corrective way. Therapists must not allow themselves to be driven away or alienated like everyone else in the patient's life.

To say that the goal of therapy is to provide a new relationship for internalization is deceptively straightforward and simple. Yet this strategy presents formidable obstacles. First, the patient's basic mode of existence is nonrelatedness. The therapist is asking a nonrelating person to move in the direction of greater relatedness. As expected, the therapist's efforts to provide a new model of relatedness will be met with emotional distance and a good deal of silence.

Therapists who attempt to treat withdrawn schizoid patients must have extraordinary patience because of the slow, painstaking internalization process. They must also adopt a permissive, accepting attitude about silence. Specifically, silence must be viewed as more than simply resistance—it is also a specific form of nonverbal communication that may provide essential information about the patient.

During long periods of silence, the therapist must recognize that a relationship is still occurring. Through projective identification, the patient's behavior will evoke certain responses in the therapist that contain valuable diagnostic information about the patient's internal world (Gabbard 1989). One patient who, throughout childhood, had been given "the silent treatment" by his father, stopped talking in his therapy; his unconscious intent was to induce the therapist to feel what the patient had experienced as a child when his father "shut down." Thus, like a mother who holds and processes the elements projected onto her from her infant, the therapist must contain and modify the patient's projections before the patient can reintroject them.

With this model, the therapist's emotional reactions to the patient, however subtle, are the primary source of information about the patient. When the silence is prolonged, therapists must be wary of turning the tables and projecting their own self- and object-representations onto the patient. This state of affairs is beautifully depicted in Ingmar Bergman's moving film, *Persona,* in which a mute patient is treated by a nurse. After many unsuccessful attempts to get the patient to speak, the nurse becomes frustrated and begins to project aspects of herself onto the patient. Driven crazy, the nurse begins to treat the patient as an embodiment of her own internal world (Gabbard 1989).

This model of therapy requires therapists to receive their patient's projections and to monitor their own without being swept into countertransference acting out. When therapists feel like quitting or giving up on a patient, they must view those feelings like any others in the process and attempt to understand them. As mentioned in Chapter 4 in the discussion of psychotherapy, the projective identifications might be diagnosed and understood only after the therapist has been "coerced" into playing a specific role vis-à-vis the patient. Therapists must silently note the interactions taking place between them and their patients and then use that information to inform subsequent interactions. Ogden (1982) summarized the therapist's task in such situations:

> The perspective of projective identification neither requires nor excludes the use of verbal interpretation; the therapist attempts to find a way of talking with and being with the patient that will constitute a medium through which the therapist may accept unintegrable aspects of the patient's internal object world and return them to the patient in a form that the patient can accept and learn from. (p. 42)

Indeed, a decision not to interpret may be the most therapeutically potent strategy with schizoid and schizotypal patients. If silence is interpreted as resistance, these patients may feel responsible and humiliated for their incapacity to communicate (Khan 1983; Nachmani 1984). On the other hand, by refraining from interpretation and accepting silence, the therapist may legitimize the private, noncommunicative core of the self referred to by Winnicott (1963/1965). With certain patients, the therapist must respect their silent self. It may be the only viable technical approach to building a therapeutic alliance (Gabbard 1989).

Therapists greatly value interpersonal relatedness. We want to mean something to our patients. Accepting silent nonrelatedness runs counter to our training and psychological predisposition. Our natural tendency is to burden our patients with the expectation that they should be different than they are. Specifically, we want our patients to talk to us and to relate to us. However, that expectation means that we must ask patients to confront the very pain they avoid by schizoid withdrawal. Greater expectations from the therapist will paradoxically lead the patient to further detachment, as Searles (1986) observed:

> Winnicott's (1941/1958) concept of the . . . good-enough holding envi-
> ronment implies that the analyst be not merely relatively stably
> there, for the patient, but also relatively destructible (psychologically)
> by the patient, time and again, as the patient's persistent needs for
> autistic (omnipotent) functioning still require. Hence the analyst
> needs intuitively to provide his own absence, perhaps as often as his
> own presence, to the patient at timely moments. (Searles 1986, p. 351)

Certain patients will respond to this tolerant, empathic acceptance
with greater openness in the therapeutic relationship. These patients
may begin to speak about hidden aspects of the self, eventually integrating these into a more cohesive sense of self. At the beginning of a
psychotherapy process, it is difficult to know which patients are likely
to benefit from it. Stone (1983), writing about schizotypal (borderline
schizophrenic) patients, suggested that those who do a bit better in
psychotherapy have some depressive symptoms or some capacity for
emotional warmth and empathy. He warned therapists to be wary of
excessive countertransference expectations, because only limited progress can be expected. In Stone's view, therapists must be able to tolerate the disappointing possibility that their patients will progress only
in areas other than relatedness. In general, those patients with better
ego functioning (i.e., more intact reality testing, better judgment,
smaller amounts of cognitive slippage) will do better in treatment than
those patients with more profoundly disturbed ego functioning. With
patients in the latter group, therapists may need to function as an auxiliary ego, helping patients supportively with various tasks such as
reality testing, judgment, and self-object differentiation. Stone (1985)
also pointed out that, like schizophrenic patients (see Chapter 7),
schizoid patients need more than expressive-supportive psychotherapy. Lower-functioning schizotypal patients also need social skills
training, reeducation, and various social supports. Medication is rarely
useful unless the patient has a psychotic episode or affective symptoms
from a concomitant Axis I disorder.

Dynamic Group Psychotherapy

In general, schizoid patients are prime candidates for dynamic group
psychotherapy (Appel 1974; Azima 1983). Group therapy is oriented
toward helping patients with socialization, which is exactly where
schizoid patients suffer most. It is also a setting in which a good deal
of new parenting can take place. For many schizoid patients, their

peers in a group process can function as a reconstructed family, eventually being internalized by these patients to counterbalance their more negative and frightening internal objects (Appel 1974).

Such patients can benefit considerably simply by having regular exposure to others. Some schizoid patients literally have no social outlets beyond their group therapy sessions. As they begin to feel accepted and to find that their worst fears are not realized, they gradually become more comfortable with people. In a manner similar to the individual therapy process described earlier, the reactions of other group members may provide a corrective experience that runs counter to all previous relationship experiences. Some difficulties that arise in the group psychotherapy of schizoid patients include resentment from other patients who have to "spill their guts" while the schizoid patient remains silent. These feelings may lead to a kind of "ganging up" to force the schizoid patient to talk. At such moments, the therapist must support the schizoid member of the group and help the other patients accept that patient's need to be silent (Azima 1983). The other patients may also simply ignore a withdrawn schizoid patient and proceed as if that patient was not there. In these instances, the therapist's task is to bring the patient into the group by pointing out how a pattern that takes place outside the group is repeating itself inside the group. Schizotypal patients tend to benefit from group therapy much as schizoid patients do, but those whose behavior is bizarre or whose thinking is psychotic may become scapegoats because they are simply too different from other members of the group. With such patients, individual therapy alone may be the preferred modality.

A combination of group and individual psychotherapy is ideal for many schizoid patients because the social field they encounter in the group can be discussed and processed with their individual psychotherapist. A significant number of schizoid patients will feel, however, that a recommendation for group therapy is like "being thrown to the lions." They may even feel betrayed when their therapist makes the suggestion. A preliminary step to group referral is often the working through of these patients' fantasies about what will happen in group therapy.

Case Example

Mr. FF was a 23-year-old single man with schizoid personality disorder. He worked as a nurse's aide on the night shift in a nursing home and took daytime classes at a local university. He liked working at night because very few interpersonal demands were made on him. His supervisor frequently slept, so he was free to read novels. When he was not sleeping, Mr. FF would spend many hours in vigorous bodybuilding exercises. He would then pose nude in front of the mirror and flex his muscles and admire himself. Much of the posing and flexing was accompanied by omnipotent fantasies of becoming an Olympic decathlon winner. He also imagined that if he achieved a certain level of bodily perfection, he would then be attractive to a college girl in one of his classes that he could never bring himself to speak to.

Mr. FF was deeply concerned about the fact that he had been adopted. He spoke about it with great shame, as though convinced that it reflected some inherent flaw. In his view, the early rejection by his biological mother was a sign that he was so inherently undesirable that others would also certainly reject him if given the chance.

Like many schizoid patients, Mr. FF had a perverse streak that took the form of exhibitionism. He would place himself in situations where women would come upon him in the nude. He would then act surprised and immediately leave the scene so as to avoid prosecution. However, the sexual pleasure he derived from this activity led him into more and more risky adventures. He once switched the men's and women's labels on the locker room doors in a gymnasium so that women would enter the men's locker room and find him standing there nude, drying himself after showering.

Mr. FF eventually came to an outpatient clinic where he sought group psychotherapy. He was concerned that his exhibitionism was getting out of hand and might lead to legal consequences, and he was genuinely disturbed by the loneliness of his existence. He sought group psychotherapy because he had previously tried individual psychotherapy for 2 years. He reported that he had remained silent throughout practically the entire therapy. Finally, he and the therapist had mutually decided that there was no point in continuing. Mr. FF also reported that he had a strong desire to overcome his fear of other people, and he believed that group therapy might be a good way to deal with that fear.

Mr. FF began a dynamic group psychotherapy process with a reasonably high-functioning group of other patients with assorted personality disorders. He attended regularly but sat silently through much of the group's discussion. Little by little, he was able to reveal more and more about himself. Something of a breakthrough occurred when he mustered enough courage to talk about the female classmate who was the object of his fantasies. One female patient in the group responded by saying, "Why don't you ask her out? You're an attractive man." Moved by this comment, Mr. FF replied that no one had ever told him that before.

The support and positive feedback this patient received from other group members bolstered his self-esteem and allowed him to speak more frequently and more openly. When he finally was able to discuss his exhibitionism, he experienced considerable relief that no one recoiled in horror at his revelation.

After several years of group therapy, Mr. FF's anxieties about relationships and his self-regard had improved to the point that he was able to begin dating and to form some appropriate peer relationships with males. The episodes of exhibitionism gradually decreased, although they tended to recur whenever the group took a vacation and Mr. FF felt abandoned by the therapist and his fellow patients.

The case of Mr. FF illustrates how the overt absence of object relations in schizoid personality disorder may be accompanied by intense fantasies of relatedness and by covert sexual activities of a perverse nature. Long periods of exercise are also fairly common in schizoid and schizotypal individuals. Physical activity of this kind may serve to "burn off" sexual energy or, as in the case of Mr. FF, may also be a way to build self-esteem by fantasizing that others will find the individual more attractive as a result of such efforts.

Although a number of perversions are commonly found in schizoid individuals, exhibitionism seems to hold a particular significance for these patients. Fairbairn (1954) observed that schizoid individuals frequently overvalue their mental contents, perceiving them as extraordinarily precious. They fear giving anything of themselves because in so doing they would deplete their narcissistically prized contents. Fairbairn noted that schizoid patients commonly use exhibitionism as a defense against the fear of giving. To be more exact, "showing" becomes a substitute for "giving," since the latter carries the fear of losing something precious while the former does not. Although the exhibitionism was overt in the case of Mr. FF, it frequently appears in sublimated forms, such as involvement in the performing arts.

Group psychotherapy provided Mr. FF with a new series of relationships to internalize. The relatedness with his fellow patients (and with the therapist) disconfirmed his expectations of how others would respond to him. Instead of being alienated by him, the group members accepted him as he was and confirmed his desirability as a person. Thus the validation of other patients in group therapy may have a more powerful impact on a schizoid patient than similar validation by an individual therapist. The schizoid patient may write off the positive regard of the therapist as an attitude contrived for therapeutic effect; the therapist is "just doing his job." Many schizoid and schizotypal patients are much more refractory to treatment than Mr. FF. As Stone (1985) suggested, therapists must genuinely respect their patient's need to be different and must not feel compelled to transform a patient into someone else. In treating schizoid and schizotypal patients, we would all be well advised to remember the wisdom of Thoreau: "If a man does not keep pace with his companions, perhaps it is because he hears a different drummer. Let him step to the music which he hears, however measured or far away" (Thoreau 1937/1950, p. 290).

References

Akhtar S: Schizoid personality disorder: a synthesis of developmental, dynamic, and descriptive features. Am J Psychother 61:499–518, 1987

Akhtar S: Paranoid personality disorder: synthesis of developmental, dynamic, and descriptive features. Am J Psychother 44:5–25, 1990

American Psychiatric Association: Diagnostic and Statistical Manual of Mental Disorders, 2nd Edition. Washington, DC, American Psychiatric Association, 1968

American Psychiatric Association: Diagnostic and Statistical Manual of Mental Disorders, 3rd Edition. Washington, DC, American Psychiatric Association, 1980

American Psychiatric Association: Diagnostic and Statistical Manual of Mental Disorders, 3rd Edition, Revised. Washington, DC, American Psychiatric Association, 1987

American Psychiatric Association: Diagnostic and Statistical Manual of Mental Disorders, 4th Edition. Washington, DC, American Psychiatric Association 1994

Appel G: An approach to the treatment of schizoid phenomena. Psychoanal Rev 61:99–113, 1974

Auchincloss EL, Weiss RW: Paranoid character and the intolerance of indifference. J Am Psychoanal Assoc 40:1013–1037, 1992

Azima FJC: Group psychotherapy with personality disorders, in Comprehensive Group Psychotherapy, 2nd Edition. Edited by Kaplan HI, Sadock BJ. Baltimore, MD, Williams & Wilkins, 1983, pp 262–268

Balint M: The Basic Fault: Therapeutic Aspects of Regression. New York, Brunner/Mazel, 1979

Blum HP: Object inconstancy and paranoid conspiracy. J Am Psychoanal Assoc 29:789–813, 1981

Eigen M: Abstinence and the schizoid ego. Int J Psychoanal 54:493–498, 1973

Epstein L: Countertransference with borderline patients, in Countertransference. Edited by Epstein L, Feiner AH. New York, Jason Aronson, 1979, pp 375–405

Epstein L: An interpersonal-object relations perspective on working with destructive aggression. Contemporary Psychoanalysis 20:651–662, 1984

Fairbairn WRD: An Object-Relations Theory of the Personality. New York, Basic Books, 1954

Felthous AR: Preventing assaults on a psychiatric inpatient ward. Hosp Community Psychiatry 35:1223–1226, 1984

Fenton WS, McGlashan TH: Risk of schizophrenia in character disordered patients. Am J Psychiatry 146:1280–1284, 1989

Freud S: Psycho-analytic notes on an autobiographical account of a case of paranoia (dementia paranoides) (1911), in The Standard Edition of the Complete Psychological Works of Sigmund Freud, Vol 12. Translated and edited by Strachey J. London, Hogarth Press, 1958, pp 1–82

Gabbard GO: On "doing nothing" in the psychoanalytic treatment of the refractory borderline patient. Int J Psychoanal 70:527–534, 1989

Grotstein JS: The psychoanalytic concept of schizophrenia, I: the dilemma. Int J Psychoanal 58:403–425, 1977

Gunderson JG: DSM-III diagnoses of personality disorders, in Current Perspectives on Personality Disorders. Edited by Frosch JP. Washington, DC, American Psychiatric Press, 1983, pp 20–39

Guntrip HJS: Schizoid Phenomena, Object-Relations, and the Self. New York, International Universities Press, 1968

Kendler KS, Gruenberg AM, Strauss JS: An independent analysis of the Copenhagen sample of the Danish adoption study of schizophrenia, II: the relationship between schizotypal personality disorder and schizophrenia. Arch Gen Psychiatry 38:982–984, 1981

Kernberg OF: Severe Personality Disorders: Psychotherapeutic Strategies. New Haven, CT, Yale University Press, 1984

Kety SS, Rosenthal D, Wender PH, et al: Mental illness in the biological and adoptive families of adopted schizophrenics. Am J Psychiatry 128:302–306, 1971

Khan MR: Hidden Selves: Between Theory and Practice in Psychoanalysis. New York, International Universities Press, 1983

Kinzel AF: Violent behavior in prisons, in Dynamics of Violence. Edited by Fawcett J. Chicago, IL, American Medical Association, 1971

Lawner P: Character rigidity and resistance to awareness of the transference. Issues in Ego Psychology 8:36–41, 1985

Madden DJ, Lion JR, Penna MW: Assaults on psychiatrists by patients. Am J Psychiatry 133:422–425, 1976

McGlashan TG: The borderline syndrome, II: is it a variant of schizophrenia or affective disorder? Arch Gen Psychiatry 40:1319–1323, 1983

Meissner WW: Psychotherapeutic schema based on the paranoid process. International Journal of Psychoanalytic Psychotherapy 5:87–114, 1976

Meissner WW: Psychotherapy and the Paranoid Process. Northvale, NJ, Jason Aronson, 1986

Millon T: Modern Psychopathology: A Biosocial Approach to Maladaptive Learning and Functioning. Philadelphia, PA, WB Saunders, 1969

Millon T: Disorders of Personality: DSM-III, Axis II. New York, Wiley, 1981

Morey LC: An empirical comparison of interpersonal and DSM-III approaches to classification of personality disorders. Psychiatry 48:358–364, 1985

Nachmani G: Hesitation, perplexity, and annoyance at opportunity. Contemporary Psychoanalysis 20:448–457, 1984

Ogden TH: Projective Identification and Psychotherapeutic Technique. New York, Jason Aronson, 1982

Ogden TH: The Matrix of the Mind: Object Relations and the Psychoanalytic Dialogue. Northvale, NJ, Jason Aronson, 1986

Reich J, Noyes R Jr: Differentiating schizoid and avoidant personality disorders (letter). Am J Psychiatry 143:1062, 1986

Rosenthal D, Wender PH, Kety SS, et al: The adopted-away offspring of schizophrenics. Am J Psychiatry 128:307–311, 1971

Searles HF: My Work With Borderline Patients. Northvale, NJ, Jason Aronson, 1986

Shapiro D: Neurotic Styles. New York, Basic Books, 1965

Siever LJ, Gunderson JG: Genetic determinants of borderline conditions. Schizophr Bull 5:59–86, 1979

Siever LJ, Silverman JM, Horvath TB, et al: Increased morbid risk for schizophrenia-related disorders in relatives of schizotypal personality disordered patients. Arch Gen Psychiatry 47:634–640, 1990

Siever LJ, Berstein DP, Silverman JM: Schizotypal personality disorder: review of its current status. Journal of Personality Disorders 5:178–193, 1991

Stone MH: Psychotherapy with schizotypal borderline patients. J Am Acad Psychoanal 11:87–111, 1983

Stone MH: Schizotypal personality: psychotherapeutic aspects. Schizophr Bull 11:576–589, 1985

Thoreau HD: Walden, in Walden and Other Writings of Henry David Thoreau. Edited by Atkinson B. New York, The Modern Library, 1937/1957, p 290

Winnicott DW: The observation of infants in a set situation (1941), in Through Paediatrics to Psycho-Analysis. New York, Basic Books, 1958, pp 52–69

Winnicott DW: Communicating and not communicating leading to a study of certain opposites (1963), in The Maturational Processes and the Facilitating Environment. New York, International Universities Press, 1965, pp 179–192

Chapter 15

Cluster B Personality Disorders: Borderline

Our consideration of Cluster B personality disorders begins with the borderline patient, because borderline personality disorder serves as a reference point for the entire cluster. Narcissistic, antisocial, and histrionic personality disorders are often defined by how they differ from borderline personality disorder. Moreover, when *borderline* is used in the broad sense of a spectrum (Meissner 1988) or a personality organization (Kernberg 1967), all the personality disorders in Cluster B, along with those in Cluster A as well, may be subsumed under the general category of borderline conditions. Unfortunately, the increasing popularity of the borderline diagnosis in the last two decades has made it something of a psychiatric "wastebasket"—both overused and misused. Patients who are diagnostically confusing may receive the label *borderline* by default. A brief historical survey of the term *borderline* in American psychiatry may shed light on the place of borderline personality disorder (BPD) in the current nomenclature.

Evolution of the Term

In the late 1930s and throughout the 1940s, clinicians began to describe certain patients who were not sick enough to be labeled schizophrenic but who were far too disturbed for classical psychoanalytic

449

treatment. In an effort to capture the "in between" state typical of these patients, Hoch and Polatin (1949) referred to this group as having pseudoneurotic schizophrenia characterized by a symptomatic pattern of "panneurosis," "pananxiety," and "pansexuality." Robert Knight (1954) further characterized this ill-defined group by focusing on several impairments in ego functioning, including the inability to plan realistically, the incapacity to defend against primitive impulses, and the predominance of primary process thinking over secondary process thinking.

These early contributors were observing a "messy" syndrome that did not fit well into preexisting diagnostic rubrics. Grinker et al. (1968) brought some diagnostic rigor to the syndrome in the early 1960s with their statistical analysis of approximately 60 such patients who were hospitalized in Chicago. A cluster analysis of data on these patients suggested that there were four subgroups of borderline patients (see Table 15–1). These patients appeared to occupy a continuum from the "psychotic border" (Type I) all the way to the "neurotic border" (Type IV). In between the two extremes could be found a group with predominantly negative affects and difficulty maintaining stable interper-

---

Table 15–1. Grinker's four subtypes of borderline patients

Type I: The Psychotic Border:
  A. Inappropriate, nonadaptive behavior
  B. Problems with reality testing and sense of identity
  C. Negative behavior and openly expressed anger

Type II: Core Borderline Syndrome:
  A. Pervasive negative affect
  B. Vacillating involvement with others
  C. Anger acted out
  D. Inconsistent self-identity

Type III: As-If Group:
  A. Tendency to copy identity of others
  B. Affectless
  C. Behavior more adaptive
  D. Relationships lacking in genuineness and spontaneity

Type IV: Neurotic Border:
  A. Anaclitic depression
  B. Anxiety
  C. Neurotic and narcissistic features

Source. Based on Grinker et al. 1968.

sonal relationships (Type II), and another group (Type III) character-ized by a generalized lack of identity, resulting in a need to borrow identity from others.

Grinker and his associates (1968) also attempted to identify com-mon denominators in the borderline syndrome that were present re-gardless of the subtype. They came up with the following four key features: 1) anger as the main or only affect, 2) defects in interpersonal relationships, 3) absence of consistent self-identity, and 4) pervasive depression. One of the most significant contributions of this empirical study was the finding that the borderline syndrome was clearly dis-tinct from schizophrenia. Grinker et al. found that these patients do not deteriorate into frank schizophrenia over time. Rather, they are stably unstable (Schmideberg 1959) throughout the course of their ill-ness. This discovery helped refute the belief some skeptics held that borderline patients were actually schizophrenic.

Gunderson and Singer (1975) reviewed the descriptive literature and delineated six features as the basis for a rational diagnosis of bor-derline patients: 1) an intense affect of a predominantly depressed or angry nature, 2) impulsivity, 3) a superficial adaptation to social situ-ations (which helped differentiate these patients from schizophrenics), 4) transient psychotic episodes, 5) a proneness to loose thinking in pro-jective testing or other unstructured situations, and 6) a vacillating pattern of relationships that shifts from extreme dependency to tran-sient superficiality. Gunderson (1984) continued his study of the bor-derline diagnosis with the intent of identifying criteria that would clearly distinguish the borderline personality from other psychiatric diagnoses. By 1990, Gunderson and his colleagues (Zanarini et al. 1990b) were able to identify clear discriminating features based on re-search that focused on descriptive characteristics (see Table 15–2).

Table 15–2. Discriminating characteristics of borderine personality disorder

Quasi-psychotic thought	Demandingness/entitlement
Self-mutilation	Treatment regressions
Manipulative suicide efforts	Countertransference difficulties
Abandonment/engulfment/ annihilation concerns	

Source. Based on Zanarini et al. 1990b, pp. 165–166.

Many of these criteria are interrelated. Borderline patients are consumed with establishing exclusive one-to-one relationships with no risk whatsoever of abandonment. They may demand such relationships with an air of entitlement that overwhelms and alienates others. Moreover, when they do become close with another person, a set of twin anxieties are activated. On the one hand, they begin to worry that they will be engulfed by the other person and lose their own identity in this primitive merger fantasy. On the other hand, they experience anxiety verging on panic related to the conviction that they are about to be rejected or abandoned at any moment. To prevent being alone, borderline patients may resort to wrist-cutting or suicidal gestures, hoping to elicit rescue by the person to whom they are attached. Cognitive distortions, such as quasi-psychotic thought (defined as transient, circumscribed, and/or atypical strains on reality testing), also may occur in the context of interpersonal relationships. Near-delusional perceptions of abandonment by loved ones are common, and psychotic transference regressions may appear when patients become attached to their therapists. Clinicians who witness this kaleidoscopic display of shifting ego states are prone to a variety of intense countertransference reactions, including rescue fantasies, guilt feelings, transgressions of professional boundaries, rage and hatred, anxiety and terror, and profound feelings of helplessness (Gabbard 1993; Gabbard and Wilkinson 1994).

While Gunderson and Grinker et al. focused primarily on descriptive diagnostic criteria, Otto Kernberg (1967, 1975) sought to characterize borderline patients from a psychoanalytic perspective. Using a combined ego psychological–object relations approach, he coined the term *borderline personality organization* to encompass a group of patients who showed characteristic patterns of ego weakness, primitive defensive operations, and problematic object relations. He observed a variety of symptoms in these patients, including free-floating anxiety, obsessive-compulsive symptoms, multiple phobias, dissociative reactions, hypochondriacal preoccupations, conversion symptoms, paranoid trends, polymorphous-perverse sexuality, and substance abuse. Kernberg cautioned, however, that descriptive symptoms were not sufficient for a definitive diagnosis. He believed instead that the diagnosis rested on a sophisticated structural analysis that revealed four key features (Table 15–3).

1. *Nonspecific manifestations of ego weakness.* One aspect of ego functioning is the capacity to delay the discharge of impulses and to

modulate affects such as anxiety. Borderline patients, in Kernberg's view, are unable to marshal ego forces to perform those functions because of inherent nonspecific weaknesses. Similarly, they have a difficult time sublimating powerful drives and using their conscience to guide behavior.

2. *Shift toward primary-process thinking.* Like Robert Knight, Kernberg noted that these patients tend to regress into psychotic-like thinking in the absence of structure or under the pressure of strong affects. However, these shifts primarily occur in the context of generally intact reality testing.

3. *Specific defensive operations.* Foremost among these defenses was splitting, which Kernberg viewed as an active process of separating contradictory introjects and affects from one another (see Chapter 2). Splitting operations in the person with BPD manifest themselves clinically as follows: a) an alternating expression of contradictory behaviors and attitudes, which the patient regards with a lack of concern and bland denial; b) a compartmentalization of all persons in the patient's environment into "all good" and "all bad" camps, with frequent oscillations between camps for a given individual; and c) coexisting contradictory views and images of oneself (self-representations) that alternate in their dominance from day to day and from hour to hour.

Table 15–3. Kernberg's criteria for borderline personality organization

---

I. Nonspecific manifestations of ego weakness
   A. Lack of anxiety tolerance
   B. Lack of impulse control
   C. Lack of developed subliminatory channels
II. Shift toward primary-process thinking
III. Specific defensive operations characteristic of borderline personality organization
   A. Splitting
   B. Primitive idealization
   C. Early forms of projection, especially projective identification
   D. Denial
   E. Omnipotence and devaluation
IV. Pathological internalized object relations

Source. Based on Kernberg 1975.

A 41-year-old Catholic priest was admitted to a psychiatric
hospital upon discovery that he had engaged in extensive
sexual behavior with children of both sexes. Shortly after admission, his routine laboratory studies revealed a positive
test for syphilis. When confronted with the lab result, the
priest responded, "I don't know how that's possible. I'm a celibate priest." The resident treating the priest simply pointed
out that the patient had been admitted to the hospital because of his extensive sexual activity with minors. The priest
blandly responded to this confrontation by saying, "What do
you expect? I'm only human."

This clinical vignette illustrates how contradictory self-representations coexist in the borderline patient—a "celibate priest" coex-
isted with a promiscuous, bisexual pedophile. Moreover, the
priest's matter-of-fact response was typical of the bland denial that
many borderline patients display when confronted with the splitting maneuvers they employ. Other defenses, such as primitive idealization, omnipotence, and devaluation, similarly reflect splitting
tendencies (i.e., others are seen in wholly positive or wholly negative terms). Projective identification, in which self-representations
or object-representations are split off and projected onto others in
an effort to control them, is another prominent defense in borderline personality organization, according to Kernberg.

4. *Pathological internalized object relations.* As a result of splitting,
   the person with borderline personality organization does not view
   other people as having a mixture of positive and negative qualities.
   Instead, others are divided into polar extremes and are regarded,
   in the words of one patient, as "either gods or devils." These individuals cannot integrate libidinal and aggressive aspects of others,
   which inhibits their ability to truly appreciate the internal experiences of other people. Their perceptions of others may alternate
   daily between idealization and devaluation, which can be highly
   disturbing for anyone in a relationship with such a person. Similarly, their inability to integrate positive and negative representations of the self results in profound identity diffusion, as illustrated
   by the previous example of the priest.

Kernberg's concept of borderline personality organization is distinct from the actual phenomenological characteristics that identify a

specific personality disorder. In other words, his term encompasses many different personality disorders. In his view, patients with narcissistic, antisocial, schizoid, paranoid, infantile, and cyclothymic personality disorders, for example, are all characterized by an underlying borderline personality organization.

Because of the burgeoning literature on borderline conditions during the decades of the 1960s and 1970s, BPD was added to DSM-III (American Psychiatric Association 1980). (There is no precise equivalent category in DSM-II [American Psychiatric Association 1968]. Prior to the publication of DSM-III, borderline patients were usually diagnosed with the DSM-II category of schizophrenia, latent type.) In developing diagnostic criteria for BPD, an effort was made both to include the descriptive features identified by Gunderson and to reflect the structural analysis of Kernberg.

One of the major controversies revolving around the DSM-III and DSM-III-R (American Psychiatric Association 1987) criteria for BPD concerned the failure to include the empirically and clinically observed brief psychotic episodes. This situation has been rectified in DSM-IV (American Psychiatric Association 1994) by adding criterion 9—transient, stress-related paranoid ideation or severe dissociative symptoms (see Table 15–4). Empirical research has demonstrated that virtually all borderline patients experience some form of disturbed cognition, while at least 40% experienced quasi-psychotic thought (Zanarini et al. 1990a). Furthermore, as previously noted, quasi-psychotic thought has been shown to be one of the most discriminating features of BPD, and its inclusion in DSM-IV was designed to increase the clinician's capacity to distinguish the diagnosis from other Axis II disorders. Finally, the emphasis on persistent self-image distortions in criterion 3 and on dissociative symptoms in criterion 9 provides a recognition of the link between childhood trauma and BPD.

There is also considerable controversy over whether the term *borderline* should be applied to a specific personality disorder or should be used broadly, as Kernberg used it, to describe a dimension of personality (Gunderson and Zanarini 1987). Grinker and his associates (1968) clearly believed that there were several subcategories of the borderline syndrome, constituting a spectrum. Meissner (1984, 1988) categorized borderline conditions differently than Grinker et al., but he, too, believed that limiting the usage of the term *borderline* to a specific personality disorder was misleading. He noted that there were clear descriptive groupings within the spectrum, specifically, a hysterical continuum and a schizoid continuum. Adler (1981) and Rinsley (1985) also regarded borderline conditions as comprising a continuum on which the core borderline patient described by DSM-IV represents the lower end and the patient with narcissistic personality disorder represents the upper end. In a retrospective study of 180 inpatients who had been diagnosed with BPD by DSM-III criteria, Fyer et al. (1988) found that 91% had another diagnosis as well, while 42% had two or more additional diagnoses. They speculated that the diagnosis of borderline personality is often applied to a heterogeneous group of patients whose symptoms overlap extensively with those of other diagnoses. To avoid conceptual confusion (and because related personality disorders, such as paranoid, schizoid, narcissistic, antisocial, and histrionic, are discussed at length in other chapters of this volume), the discussion in this chapter will be confined to those patients with the borderline features described by DSM-IV.

Table 15–4.   DSM-IV diagnostic criteria for borderline personality disorder

---

A pervasive pattern of instability of interpersonal relationships, self-image, and affects, and marked impulsivity beginning by early adulthood and present in a variety of contexts, as indicated by at least *five* of the following:

1. frantic efforts to avoid real or imagined abandonment (Note: Do not include suicidal or self-mutilating behavior covered in criterion 5)

2. a pattern of unstable and intense interpersonal relationships characterized by alternating between extremes of idealization and devaluation

3. identity disturbance: persistent and markedly disturbed, distorted, or unstable self-image or sense of self

4. impulsivity in at least two areas that are potentially self-damaging (e.g., spending, sex, substance abuse, reckless driving, binge eating) (Note: Do not include suicidal or self-mutilating behavior covered in criterion 5)

5. recurrent suicidal behavior, gestures, or threats, or self-mutilating behavior

6. affective instability due to a marked reactivity of mood (e.g., intense episodic dysphoria, irritability, or anxiety usually lasting a few hours and only rarely more than a few days)

7. chronic feelings of emptiness

8. inappropriate, intense anger, or lack of control of anger (e.g., frequent displays of temper, constant anger, recurrent physical fights)

9. transient, stress-related paranoid ideation or severe dissociative symptoms

---

Source.   DSM-IV. Because the criteria sets were not final at press time, the reader should consult DSM-IV for final criteria.

Demographic Features and
Course of Illness

At least three-fourths of the patients who are diagnosed with BPD are female (Gunderson et al. 1991). This finding may be due largely to cultural biases stemming from sex-role stereotypes, because male patients who have the features of BPD are often diagnosed as having narcissistic or antisocial personality disorders. BPD is by far the most commonly used Axis II diagnosis, with a prevalence somewhere between 15% and 25% in clinical populations (Gunderson and Zanarini 1987). Its prevalence in the general population probably ranges between 1.8% and 4% (Baron et al. 1985; Gunderson and Zanarini 1987; Loranger et al. 1982; Swartz et al. 1990). The legitimacy of the diagnostic category of BPD has been substantiated by long-term follow-up studies demonstrating that, over time, borderline patients continue to manifest consistent clinical symptomatology; in the vast majority of cases, these patients do not shift into other major psychiatric disorders (Gunderson and Zanarini 1987).

Since all the major long-term follow-up studies (McGlashan 1986; Plakun et al. 1985; Stone et al. 1987; Werble 1970) have focused on subjects who have had rather extensive treatment experiences, the untreated course of BPD remains something of a mystery. In fact, the key follow-up studies have been undertaken with patients who have had long-term (1–2 years), psychoanalytically oriented hospital treatment. These studies suggest that BPD usually becomes apparent in late adolescence or young adulthood and that it runs a rocky course during its first decade of treatment, leading many clinicians to become discouraged with the patient's lack of progress. However, after approximately 5 or 6 years of treatment, borderline patients often begin to show substantial improvement that peaks in the second decade after their first hospitalization.

In the sample of 251 borderline patients studied by Stone and his colleagues (1987), approximately two-thirds were "recovered" or doing reasonably well after a decade or so, although many of these patients continued to receive outpatient treatment. In the Austen Riggs study (Plakun et al. 1985), borderline patients achieved a mean Global Assessment Scale score of 67, which placed them in the "good" range of functioning after a mean follow-up period of 15 years (comparable to Stone's study). In the Montreal study at the Jewish General Hospital (Paris et al. 1987), borderline patients were also reinterviewed at a mean of 15 years after hospitalization, and the investigators found that 75% of the patients no longer met the criteria for BPD as defined by Gunderson's Diagnostic Interview for Borderlines. In McGlashan's (1986) follow-up study of 81 patients originally hospitalized at Chestnut Lodge, most of the patients were able to live independently and to adjust satisfactorily to work. However, the sample revealed a bimodal distribution when it came to functioning in intimate relationships: while one group managed to maintain meaningful intimate relationships over time, the other group adjusted to life by avoiding close interpersonal contact.

All of these studies suggest that clinicians have reason for optimism in the treatment of borderline patients. The patients studied all had better outcomes than did schizophrenic patients who were used in comparison groups, and they were very similar to patients with affective disorders on most measures. This optimism is tempered, however, by the finding that between 3% and 10% of the borderline patients committed suicide.

Relationship With Affective Disorders

When the term *borderline* first appeared in the psychiatric literature in the 1950s and 1960s, it clearly denoted a clinical entity that was "on the border" of psychosis or, more specifically, schizophrenia. As time has passed and long-term follow-up data have accumulated on the course of BPD, this disorder has been more closely linked to affective disorders than to schizophrenia (McGlashan 1983; Rinsley 1981b; Stone 1980; Stone et al. 1987). Whereas the course of schizotypal personality disorder is similar to that of schizophrenia, the course of BPD is distinctly different from that of schizophrenia but quite similar to that of affective disorder (McGlashan 1983).

The interface between Axis I major depression and BPD has been the source of ongoing controversy in clinical psychiatry. In one long-term follow-up study (Stone et al. 1987), there was a 69% overlap between major affective disorder and BPD. Another study found an 80% lifetime prevalence of major depression in patients with both dysthymia and BPD (Zanarini et al. 1989a). However, newer research has suggested that the comorbidity between major affective disorder and BPD is nonspecific in light of findings that other personality disorders have equal or higher frequencies of concurrence with major depression

(Barasch et al. 1985; Fyer et al. 1988; Gunderson and Phillips 1991; Pfohl et al. 1984; Shea et al. 1987).

Similar shifts have occurred in the thinking about family history data and pharmacologic response. Whereas earlier studies had suggested a higher prevalence of affective disorder in the relatives of borderline patients, newer data have indicated that these linkages do not hold if borderline probands who also have major affective disorder on Axis I are removed from consideration (Gunderson and Phillips 1991). The unpredictable and uneven response of borderline patients to antidepressant medications also suggests that depression in borderline patients may be a different entity than Axis I major depression in nonborderline patients. Reviewing all the available evidence about the interface between BPD and major depression, Gunderson and Phillips (1991) concluded that the two disorders often coexist in one person but are otherwise unrelated.

A common problem confronting the clinician is differentiating the characterological depression typical of borderline personality from the major affective disorder that may coexist with BPD. A knowledge of the specific characteristics of each type of depression can assist clinicians in making this determination (Table 15–5). Borderline patients may use the term *depression* to describe chronic feelings of boredom, emptiness, and loneliness, but diagnostically may lack the vegetative signs of Axis I major depression (Gunderson and Zanarini 1987). Moreover, conscious feelings of rage are often intermingled with the characterological depression of the borderline patient, in contrast to the patient with a more autonomous and endogenous type of depression (Gunderson and Phillips 1991). Clinicians must keep in mind, however, that while these distinctions are helpful, both forms of depression may coexist in the same patient and may require pharmacologic intervention.

When psychopharmacologic agents are necessary to address the Axis I component of the depression in borderline patients, monoamine oxidase inhibitors such as tranylcypromine have been shown to be therapeutically effective (Cowdry and Gardner 1988). Whether tricyclic antidepressants are as useful is more controversial (Gunderson and Zanarini 1987; Soloff et al. 1986). In general, psychopharmacologic treatment approaches to borderline personality should be geared to target symptoms, such as the use of antidepressant medication for symptoms of depression. For behavioral dyscontrol, carbamazepine has been effective, while trifluoperazine has been helpful for psychotic or paranoid distortions of thinking (Cowdry and Gardner 1988). Because borderline patients frequently complain of anxiety, clinicians may be tempted to prescribe antianxiety agents such as benzodiazepines. However, these agents, particularly alprazolam, may cause disinhibition, resulting in increased problems with impulse control (Cowdry and Garner 1988; Gardner and Cowdry 1985). Since drug abuse is common in borderline patients, the potential for dependency on benzodiazepines is another reason to avoid their usage.

Evidence from three uncontrolled open trials indicates that fluoxetine may also be helpful in some borderline patients (Cornelius et al. 1990; Norden 1989; Markovitz et al. 1991). All three studies showed improvement primarily in the areas of impulsivity and self-injury, and the presence or absence of major depression did not appear to affect outcome in any of the trials. These preliminary findings, cou-

Table 15–5. Differential diagnosis of major depressive disorder and characterological depression typical of borderline personality disorder

Borderline Characterological Depression	Shared Characteristics	Major Depressive Disorder
1. Loneliness	1. Depressed mood: early onset, sustained	1. Guilt feelings, remorse
2. Emptiness	2. Worthlessness hopelessness	2. Withdrawal/agitation
3. Repeated suicidal gestures	3. Object hunger (without gestures)	3. Suicidality
4. Conscious rage	4. Dependency in relationships	4. Stable relationships
5. Demanding, hostile dependent relationships	5. Fragile self-esteem	5. Concern with defeat, failures
6. Concern with interpersonal loss, separation		6. Caregiving welcomed (with history of independence)
7. Illusory self-sufficiency (with history of dependency)		7. More severe vegetative symptoms

Source. Based on Gunderson and Phillips 1991.

pled with the unpredictable response of most borderline patients to traditional antidepressant medications, lend further credence to the notion that depression in borderline patients is qualitatively different from typical major depressive disorder. Gunderson and Phillips (1991) have postulated that impulse dysregulation rather than affective problems may be primary in BPD.

While pharmacotherapy is an important adjunct in the treatment of BPD, medications must be prescribed judiciously. These patients commonly accumulate large numbers of prescriptions from a variety of doctors, all of whom share feelings of frustration in their attempts to satisfy the unending demands for attention. Borderline patients may repeatedly test their treating clinicians to see if they "really care." Limiting prescription medication is only one way for the psychiatrist to use firm limits with the borderline patient. When a psychopharmacologic agent is used to treat a target symptom, clinicians must be careful to emphasize that the agent is not a panacea and that the main thrust of treatment must be a slow and painful examination of relationship patterns, both in the transference and in the patient's life outside the therapeutic relationship.

In one survey of dynamic psychotherapists who were highly experienced in the treatment of borderline patients (Waldinger and Frank 1989), 90% of the respondents acknowledged that they prescribed medication for the borderline patients they were seeing in therapy. They were more likely to prescribe when they were feeling pessimistic about a particular patient's ability to work psychotherapeutically. These therapists also reported that nearly half the patients misused prescribed medication. This abuse was intimately connected with transference themes, and the investigators suggested that therapists should actively explore the patient's fantasies about the medication to prevent misuse.

Psychodynamic Understanding

Kernberg

Kernberg (1975) linked the etiology and pathogenesis of BPD to the developmental scheme of Margaret Mahler (Mahler et al. 1975). Readers may wish to review this scheme, outlined in Chapter 2, before continuing with this discussion. Specifically, Kernberg viewed borderline patients as having successfully traversed Mahler's symbiotic phase so that self and object can be clearly distinguished but also as having become fixated during the separation-individuation phase. Kernberg targeted the rapprochement subphase, between approximately 16 and 30 months, as the chronological site of this developmental crisis. At this stage, the child becomes alarmed about the potential for its mother to disappear and at times displays a frantic concern about her location. From this developmental standpoint, borderline patients can be viewed as repeatedly reliving an early infantile crisis in which they feared that attempts to separate from their mother would result in her disappearance and abandonment of them. In the adult form of this childhood crisis, individuals are unable to tolerate periods of being alone and fear abandonment from significant others. Patients with BPD also may be overwhelmed with anxiety in the face of major separations from their parents or other nurturing figures. The reasons for the fixation at the rapprochement subphase are related, in Kernberg's view, to a disturbance of the mother's emotional availability during this critical period, due either to a constitutional excess of aggression in the child or to maternal problems with parenting, or even a combination of both.

An important component of this fixation is the lack of object constancy typical of the borderline patient. Like other children, throughout the period of separation-individuation, these children are unable to integrate the good and bad aspects of themselves and their mothers. These contradictory images are kept separate via splitting, so that both the mother and the self are seen as alternating between being thoroughly bad and thoroughly good. But whereas most children of nearly 3 years of age will have object constancy solidified sufficiently so that they can embrace a whole object view of the mother and the self, such is not true of borderline-prone individuals. At that point, children can generally tolerate separation somewhat better because they have internalized a whole, soothing, internal image of their mother that sustains them in times of her physical absence. Since borderline persons lack this internal image, they have little or no object constancy, which contributes significantly to their intolerance of separation and aloneness.

The end result of this developmental fixation is a condition that Kernberg (1966) characterized by its predominance of negative introjects. Although he allowed for environmental sources for these negative internalized self- and object-representations, Kernberg's theory emphasized the significance of a constitutional excess of oral aggression in borderline patients. This factor reduces the borderline patient's ability to integrate good and bad images of self and other; these patients are convinced that the overwhelming "badness" will destroy any "goodness" in themselves or in others. When the bad introjects are projected outward, borderline patients feel at the mercy of malevolent persecutors. When reintrojected, the bad introjects make them feel unworthy and despicable, occasionally leading to suicidal thoughts. This innate aggression also impedes the borderline patient's passage through the oedipal phase. Thus, oedipal conflicts in borderline patients often appear more raw and primitive, compared with those in neurotic patients.

Masterson and Rinsley

The formulation of Masterson and Rinsley (1975) also focused on the rapprochement subphase of separation-individuation. However, they stressed the behavior of the mother rather than the innate aggression of the child. They found that the mothers of borderline patients, whom Masterson and Rinsley viewed as typically borderline themselves, were highly conflicted about their children growing up. As a result, the child receives a message from the mother that growing up and becoming one's own person will result in the loss of maternal love and support. A key corollary of this message is that remaining dependent constitutes the only available means of maintaining the maternal bond. This powerful maternal communication provokes "abandonment depression" any time the prospect of separation or autonomy presents itself to the child.

According to Masterson and Rinsley, 1975, this rapprochement subphase crisis between child and mother becomes rarefied as two separate split object relations units (see Table 15–6). These units consist of three entities: a part-self-representation, a part-object-representation, and an affect that connects the two. The rewarding object relations unit (RORU) is associated with feelings of being loved and gratified. It includes a maternal part object that is affirming, loving, and supportive. In association with this positively regarded maternal introject, there is a part-self-representation of a "good child" who is obedient and passive. The withdrawing object relations unit (WORU) is associated with feelings of rage, abandonment, depression, and helplessness. The maternal part object is malevolent and critical, while the part-self-representation is a "bad child" who is guilty and undesirable.

The fixation at this fragmented level leaves the borderline patient feeling that there are only two choices—you can feel abandoned and bad, or like Peter Pan, you can feel good only by denying reality and never growing up. Rinsley (1988) subsequently found this formulation of split object relations unit to be somewhat oversimplified and limiting in its therapeutic implications. He went on to apply the constructs of Fairbairn (1954) to the borderline personality (Rinsley 1987) and to focus on the developmental differences between borderline and narcissistic personality disorders (Rinsley 1984, 1985, 1989). By so doing, Rinsley has moved away from his earlier emphasis, with Masterson, on the conflict-related origin of BPD and toward a deficit or "insufficiency" model.

In his later formulations, Rinsley (1981a, 1984, 1985, 1986, 1988, 1989), like Adler (1985), emphasized the significance of absent or seriously deficient evocative memory (object impermanency) in the pathogenesis of BPD. He conceptualized the developmental failure of borderline individuals in terms of Mahler's interrelated processes of separation and individuation, with severe impairment of both separation and individuation in the borderline personality. In contrast, in the

---

Table 15–6.   Role of the mother in the borderline syndrome (Masterson and Rinsley)

Mother-Infant Interaction in Rapprochement Subphase:
- Reward for regression, clinging
- Withdrawal for separation-individuation

Split Object Relations Units:
- Withdrawing (aggressive) part-unit

Maternal Part-Object	+	Affect	+	Part-Self-Representation
attacking, critical, hostile, withdrawing approval		*anger, frustration, feeling thwarted*		*inadequate, bad, helpless, guilty, ugly, empty*

- Rewarding (libidinally gratifying) part-unit

Maternal Part-Object	+	Affect	+	Part-Self-Representation
approval, support, and reward for regressive, clinging behavior		*feeling good, being fed, gratification of wish for reunion*		*good, passive, compliant*

Source.   Based on Masterson and Rinsley 1975.

case of the "higher-level" narcissistic personality, a failure of the separation process has occurred with apparent relative intactness of the individuation process (see Chapter 16).

Adler

Whereas the psychodynamic models of Kernberg and of Masterson and Rinsley are derived essentially from conflict models of psychopathology, Adler's (1985) understanding of BPD is based on a deficit or "insufficiency" model. Inconsistent or unreliable mothering, in Adler's view, causes the borderline patient's failure to develop a "holding-soothing" internal object. Adler, who was heavily influenced by the self psychological theories of Kohut (see Chapter 2), understood the borderline patient as being in search of selfobject functions from external figures because of the absence of nurturing introjects.

Adler emphasized the developmental framework of Selma Fraiberg (1969) in contrast to that of Mahler. He noted that at approximately 18 months of age, according to Fraiberg, the normal child is ordinarily able to summon up an internal image of a maternal figure even in the physical absence of that figure. This capacity for "evocative memory," as Fraiberg termed this cognitive achievement, is only tenuously established in the borderline patient, according to Adler. In situations of stress, or in the throes of an intense transference, borderline patients tend to regress until they can no longer recall important figures in their environment who are not physically present unless an object such as a picture is available as a reminder. Adler conceptualized this observation as a regression to a developmental age between 8 and 18 months, before evocative memory has been achieved.

The borderline patient's lack of a holding-soothing internal object accounts for several aspects of borderline psychopathology. This lack creates feelings of emptiness and depressive tendencies. It is also responsible for the clinging dependency so commonly seen in borderline patients. In the absence of selfobject responses from significant others, borderline individuals have inadequate internal resources to sustain them and are prone to fragmentations of the self. This dissolution of the self is accompanied by a profound emptiness described as "annihilation panic" by Adler. Finally, the absence of a holding-soothing introject leads to a chronic oral rage in borderline patients related to their feeling that mothering figures were not emotionally available during childhood.

Critiques of Psychodynamic Models

Although the discussion of the three psychodynamic models presented here in no way represents a comprehensive overview of the psychoanalytic discourse regarding borderline disorders, it should serve to acquaint readers with the three points of view that lie at the heart of much of the controversy around this diagnostic category. More to the point, each model has specific treatment implications that are themselves perhaps even more controversial than the diagnostic understanding. Much of the literature involves critiques of the positions set forth by these theorists. Those who localize the developmental disturbance to the rapprochement subphase have been taken to task by no less a critic than Margaret Mahler herself (Mahler and Kaplan 1977), who pointed out that focusing on one subphase of separation-individuation is somewhat reductionistic in that such a posture fails to acknowledge or appreciate the influence of other subphases, as well as oedipal influences, in the pathogenesis of BPD. She expressed doubt that a discrete linear relationship exists between disturbances in one subphase of separation-individuation and later adult manifestations of psychopathology. Gunderson (1984) also has pointed out that empirical studies of parents of borderline patients suggest that inadequate parenting is not confined to particular developmental subphases, but rather is pervasive throughout all phases of childhood. Moreover, neglect appears more common than overinvolvement. These studies also indicate that *both* parents, rather than only the mother, are typically neglectful of their parental responsibilities. Masterson and Rinsley were criticized by Esman (1980) for unfairly blaming mothers in their formulation while not sufficiently taking into account constitutional factors, such as organically based cognitive dysfunction, that may contribute to problems in the separation-individuation phase.

Whereas Masterson and Rinsley were accused of blaming mothers, Kernberg was criticized for attributing constitutionally based oral rage to borderline patients. Atwood and Stolorow (1984), for example, suggested that Kernberg's observations of excessive aggression in borderline patients may be viewed as an iatrogenic artifact stemming from Kernberg's early confrontation and interpretation of negative transference. Kernberg's model was also criticized by the Kris Study Group (Abend et al. 1983) and by Meissner (1988) for underemphasizing the developmental problems of borderline patients at the genital-oedipal phase and for focusing on the fixation at a preoedipal level rather than viewing it as a possible regression from oedipal issues to earlier conflicts. Meissner (1988) argued that some developmental defects can be found at the lower end of the borderline spectrum, even before the separation-individuation phase, while at the opposite end of the spectrum, oedipal and postoedipal disturbances contribute to the adult clinical manifestations of borderline pathology. In a comprehensive critique of the underlying assumptions about borderline object relations, Westen (1990) criticized all of the major theoretical formulations for adhering to developmental timetables that are seriously in error. He argued that borderline object relations cannot be reduced to preoedipal fixations because they more closely resemble normative social cognition stemming from the latency and early adolescent years. He persuasively pointed out that empirical developmental research does not support theories derived from clinical observations in the consulting room.

Adler was similarly criticized for his developmental weighting toward oral issues and his relative neglect of oedipal conflicts in his understanding of the borderline patient (Finell 1988; Meissner 1988). Adler was also taken to task for emphasizing cognitive deficits (i.e., problems with evocative memory) as a pivotal feature in psychodynamic understanding, given the fact that such defects are primarily found in borderline patients close to the psychotic border (Meissner 1988) but may be completely absent in higher-level borderline patients. Finally, Kernberg (1988) pointed out that Adler's emphasis on the absence of "good introjects" neglects the influence of hostile introjects in borderline pathology.

All of the psychodynamic models have more recently been criticized for understating the role played by childhood trauma and abuse in the etiology and pathogenesis of BPD. Empirical research has largely substantiated the estimation that many borderline patients have experienced real victimization in their childhood relationships with parents and other caretakers. As early as 1977, a family study of borderline patients (Walsh 1977) found that 64% of the probands reported highly conflicted relationships with their parents, characterized by frank abuse, parental hostility, and overt devaluation.

Since Walsh's original study, numerous subsequent reports have confirmed a high incidence of abuse during childhood in the history of borderline patients. Herman et al. (1989) found that 68% of a sample of 21 borderline patients had been sexually abused as children, 71% had been physically abused, and 62% had witnessed serious domestic violence. Westen et al. (1990) were able to find evidence of physical and/or sexual abuse in more than 50% of the medical records of inpatient adolescents diagnosed with BPD.

Ogata et al. (1990) compared experiences of abuse and neglect in 24 borderline adults with those of 18 depressed controls. In the borderline group, 71% had a history of childhood sexual abuse, 10% had a history of physical abuse, 17% reported a history of physical neglect, and 65% reported multiple abuses. When compared with the control group of depressed patients, the incidence of childhood sexual abuse and combined sexual and physical abuse was significantly higher for the borderline patients. No differences were found between groups for either neglect or physical abuse unaccompanied by sexual abuse.

Another comparison study (Zanarini et al. 1989b) categorized childhood abuse in one of three forms: verbal, physical, and sexual. The investigators compared 50 borderline outpatients with 26 outpatients who had dysthymia and 29 who had antisocial personality disorder. Of the borderline patients, 58% reported a history of sexual abuse, physical abuse, or both. Verbal abuse, however, was actually more common than either physical or sexual abuse. Fully 72% of the borderline patients reported verbal abuse as compared to 46% with physical abuse and 26% with sexual abuse. In the same sample, 76% reported significant neglect by parents or caretakers during childhood.

Baker et al. (1992) studied 29 borderline inpatients compared with 15 depressed patients and 14 normal individuals. Borderline patients rated their parents, especially their fathers, not only as more unfavorable on negative scales than did those in the normal control group and the depressed group but also as less favorable on positive scales than did the comparison groups. A significant portion of the variance in father scores, but not in mother scores, was related to the age of the respondent and the history of sexual abuse. The investigators concluded that these borderline patients had a greater tendency to view the world in negative, malevolent ways than did the patients in the comparison groups. Also, 77.4% of the borderline patients reported histories of sexual abuse, compared to only 33% of the depressed patients and 21.4% of the normal control group. However, only 35.5% of the borderline patients had experienced incestuous sexual abuse, with 16.1% reporting abuse by the father, 3.2% abuse by the mother, and 25.8% abuse by siblings.

The extensive histories of trauma in many borderline patients have led many investigators to look for overlap between posttraumatic stress disorder (PTSD) and BPD (Gunderson and Sabo 1993; Herman et al. 1989). Indeed, one-third of borderline patients fulfill criteria for PTSD (Swartz et al. 1990). Although perceptual symptoms occur in both diagnostic groups, they tend to be associated with traumatic memories in PTSD patients, while symptoms are more often triggered by relationships in borderline patients (Gunderson and Sabo 1993). Traumatic experiences in childhood may contribute to image-distorting defenses such as splitting, denial, and projective identification. An abusive, sadistic parent must be kept separate from the idealized fantasy parent so that the former does not destroy the latter. Similarly, abused children are more likely to develop distorted representations of themselves as bad or powerful. Gunderson and Sabo (1993) have stressed that the phenomenological overlap between PTSD and BPD can be disentangled through a careful history that distinguishes enduring patterns or personality traits from a rapid, adult-onset symptomatic picture.

Zanarini et al. (1989b) also studied the separation histories of their borderline patients and controls and found that 74% had experienced loss or prolonged separation from a caretaker during some period before the age of 18. This finding, while striking, was not too dissimilar from that found in antisocial patients and dysthymic patients. However, when the separations were examined for the period of early childhood, borderline patients had a significantly higher percentage of such experiences than did dysthymic patients.

At least five major studies (H. Frank and Paris 1981; Goldberg et al. 1985; Paris and H. Frank 1989; Paris and Zweig-Frank 1992; Soloff and Millward 1983; Zweig-Frank and Paris 1991) suggest that borderline patients experience their parents as emotionally neglectful. In the most recent of these studies (Zweig-Frank and Paris 1991), 62 borderline patients were compared with 99 nonborderline patients through the use of the Parental Bonding Instrument. As might be expected, borderline patients were significantly more likely than those in the control group to remember their fathers and mothers as having been less caring. Whereas many of the psychodynamic theories focus on maternal failures in the etiology and pathogenesis of borderline pathology, this study indicated that *both parents* are remembered as creating difficulties during the childhoods of these patients. There was a pattern of "affectionless control" in that both parents failed to provide emotional support and prevented the children from separating. Zweig-Frank and Paris (1991) pointed out that as children, borderline patients were unfortunate in that their negative experiences with one parent were unmitigated by any counterbalancing positive experiences with the other parent.

The results of all these empirical investigations taken together suggest a mixed and complex picture of the etiology and pathogenesis of BPD. Clearly, there are many pathways to the development of borderline psychopathology. Although many patients have experienced some combination of loss, neglect, physical abuse, verbal abuse, and sexual abuse, 20%–40% of borderline patients have experienced neither abuse nor neglect. No etiological factor alone appears to be sufficient or specific for the development of BPD.

In a comprehensive review of the role of childhood sexual abuse in the etiology of BDP, Paris and Zweig-Frank (1992) pointed out that one-third of *all women* in North America have been victims of childhood sexual abuse, while only approximately 2% of the population suffers from BPD. Childhood sexual abuse has varying degrees of pathogenicity, depending on a host of factors (Browne and Finkelhor 1986). The duration and frequency of the abuse are of great importance, as is the relationship between the offender and the child. By far the most pathogenic form of childhood sexual abuse is father-daughter incest, because it involves a betrayal of trust as well as a sexual act. The majority of incest reports, however, do not involve father-daughter incest. Other parameters that influence the impact of childhood sexual abuse are the age of the child at the onset of the abuse, the type of sexual act, the presence or absence of force, disclosure of the abuse, and the parents' reaction to that disclosure.

Most of the studies on the role of abuse in BPD do not differentiate between incest and extrafamilial childhood sexual abuse. Those that do suggest that approximately one-third or less of borderline patients have experienced incest. To complicate matters further, one cannot be sure which of these elements was the more pathogenic: the incest itself or other areas of family interaction. The family environment in households where incest occurs is generally characterized by high levels of dysfunctional interactions (Paris and Zweig-Frank 1992). Neglect and other forms of abuse may be equally important in BPD pathogenesis.

Some of the contradictory views expressed in the psychodynamic theories may reflect differing developmental experiences and different populations of borderline patients. For example, patients who have experienced early childhood loss or neglect may fail to develop a holding-soothing introject, as described by Adler (1985). The work of Zweig-Frank and Paris (1991) indicated that other patients were subjected to overcontrol in childhood (by both mother and father) and therefore may suffer from abandonment concerns such as those described by Masterson and Rinsley (1975) and Kernberg (1975). Controlled research has also documented a high correlation between separation-individuation issues and borderline psychopathology (Dolan et al. 1992).

Sexual, physical, and verbal abuse undoubtedly figure into the etiology in some subgroups of borderline patients. Prominent PTSD symptoms, such as dissociation, wrist-cutting or other forms of self-mutilation, hyperarousal, and flashbacks, may be particularly common in these patients (see Chapter 10). This subgroup may also have a stormier treatment course than do other borderline patients. Nigg et al. (1991) found that a history of sexual abuse in borderline patients was associated with the presence of sadistic and malevolent internal object-representations, while those without such histories had no similar introjects. Finally, in each study some borderline patients appeared to lack a history of abuse or neglect. Some members of this subgroup may fit Kernberg's (1975) model of excessive constitutional aggression. Clinicians must be wary of a knee-jerk readiness to blame parents for all of the difficulties that accompany BPD.

One final source of empirical data that may support Kernberg's notion of constitutional factors in the etiology of BPD is the neurobiological and genetic research. These studies may also support the paradigm of a biologically determined diathesis acted on by environmental stressors. Silverman et al. (1991) found some evidence of familial transmission of the affective and impulsive personality traits in families of borderline patients. Coccaro et al. (1989) reported a significantly decreased level of serotonergic activity in a male population of borderline patients. Since serotonin has been linked to behavioral inhibition (Siever and Davis 1991), the diminished availability of serotonin in the central nervous system may partially account for impulsive behavior in borderline patients. The aforementioned response to fluoxetine lends some support to this hypothesis. Grotstein (1987) has conceptualized the essence of borderline psychopathology as impaired self-regulation related, at least in part, to neurocognitive deficits. Some research has confirmed the presence of soft signs of neurological deficit, including a history of attention deficit disorder, episodic dyscontrol syndrome, learning problems, poor impulse control, and conduct disorders (Andrulonis 1991; Andrulonis et al. 1981). Other studies have confirmed the presence of subtle neuropsychological deficits (Swirsky-Sacchetti et al. 1993; vanReekum et al. 1993).

This survey of the controversy surrounding the etiology must lead us to the conclusion that no one cause can account for borderline psychopathology. A complex multifactorial etiology is more likely involved, and clinicians must carefully assess the contributions of the various factors involved to construct an informed treatment plan.

Individual Psychotherapy

The goals in individual psychotherapy of patients with BPD are ambitious. They include strengthening the ego so that patients can better tolerate anxiety and can gain greater control over impulses; integrating split self- and object-representations so that patients have a coherent, sustained, and fully rounded view of themselves and others; and firmly establishing a soothing-holding introject so that separations from significant figures can be tolerated. There is no shortcut to the accomplishment of these goals, which require intensive work with a therapist over a long period. Until the internal object world of these patients changes, they will have little relief from the unrelenting misery of their existence.

Expressive Versus Supportive Approaches

Although clinicians often disagree about whether psychotherapy should be weighted predominantly toward the expressive or the supportive end of the expressive-supportive continuum, they concur on the extraordinary difficulty in undertaking individual psychotherapy of borderline patients. These patients are likely to quit psychotherapy, to act out self-destructively, to make inordinate demands for special treatment from their therapists, to provoke therapists into ill-advised professional boundary crossing, and to torment therapists with unrelenting phone calls at all hours of the day and night. A major problem in the psychotherapy of borderline individuals is the tenuous nature of the therapeutic alliance (Adler 1979; Gabbard et al. 1988; Gorney 1979; Kernberg 1976; Masterson 1976; Modell 1976; Zetzel 1971). These patients have great difficulty viewing their therapist as a helpful figure who is working collaboratively with them toward mutually perceived goals.

In the McLean Borderline Psychotherapy Engagement Project (A. F. Frank 1992), 60% of the first 60 patients studied discontinued their therapy within 6 months. Evaluations of the reasons for this substantial dropout rate suggested that as many as 77% had difficulties in developing an alliance with their therapists. After 6 months of treatment, solid therapeutic alliances were still rather uncommon even among those patients who continued in therapy.

Much of the controversy in the literature regarding the relative value of expressive versus supportive interventions revolves around which approach is more likely to foster the development and maintenance of the therapeutic alliance. Without a rudimentary therapeutic alliance, the therapist may not have a patient. The borderline patient may rapidly develop an intense negative transference, which mobilizes primitive character defenses that interfere with the establishment of an alliance (Kernberg 1976). Some clinicians (Boyer 1977; Kernberg 1975) believe that these transference distortions should be addressed early through transference interpretations. Such interpretations pave the way for the patient to view the therapist more accurately and allow the therapeutic alliance to develop with fewer psychological obstacles. Interpretation of primitive defensive operations in the here and now of the transference relationship serves to help patients integrate their "good" and "bad" views of the therapist into a more realistic "whole object" perception.

Masterson (1976) and Modell (1976) proposed quite a different technical approach. They suggested that interpretation must be delayed until the patient has developed sufficient trust in the therapist's intentions and reliability. Modell emphasized that a "holding" environment must be established as a prerequisite to interpretive interventions. This point of view is in keeping with Adler's conceptualization of the primary goal of psychotherapy as the establishment of a soothing-holding introject to sustain the patient in times of separation and aloneness. Adler (1979) saw the therapeutic alliance as something of a "myth" in the psychotherapy of borderline patients. These patients are unable to experience psychotherapy as a working collaboration, at least in the early phases. Because borderline patients are initially incapable of appreciating the real qualities of their therapists, they are maintained in psychotherapy by the soothing, supportive experience of a stable selfobject transference. As patients increasingly internalize the relationship, Adler believed, they become capable of allying themselves with the therapist in the service of pursuing common therapeutic goals. Adler viewed as a major therapeutic accomplishment the patient's perception of the therapist as a real and separate person who is invested in helping the patient. Zetzel (1971) was perhaps the strongest advocate of a supportive approach. She believed that interpretive psychotherapy is too disruptive of the therapeutic alliance and that low-frequency supportive psychotherapy (once a week or less) is the only effective way to maintain an alliance with borderline patients.

This controversy over the relative merits of expressive and supportive interventions is reflected in the contradictory findings of the Menninger Foundation's Psychotherapy Research Project. The project's quantitative study (Kernberg et al. 1972) revealed that borderline patients treated by skilled therapists who focused intently on the transference showed a significantly better outcome than did those treated by skilled therapists who focused less on the transference. In contrast, the prediction study of the project (Horwitz 1974), using both quantitative and qualitative assessments of the treatment process, suggested that a series of patients, some of whom were borderline and were treated by predominantly supportive methods, showed greater gains in supportive treatment than anticipated. Finally, as reported in Chapter 4, Wallerstein's (1986) examination of the data from this project suggested that all treatments were characterized by a mixture of expressive and supportive interventions. These apparently contradictory findings with regard to transference focus remain unresolved, in part because the original design of the study had several shortcomings relevant to this issue: 1) the specific diagnostic category of BPD was not used; 2) a detailed process study was not undertaken, so that essential treatment developments could only be roughly approximated at the termination of treatment; and 3) the therapeutic alliance was not one of the project's variables. Retrospectively, however, the prediction study found the therapeutic alliance useful in conceptualizing results (Horwitz 1974).

Much of the current controversy surrounding the psychotherapy of borderline patients can be understood as another unfortunate example of the "either/or" approach to the application of theory to clinical practice, discussed at some length in Chapter 2. Both approaches are useful for *some* patients at *some* points in the treatment. We are dealing with a spectrum of highly heterogeneous patients who require individually tailored psychotherapeutic approaches (Meissner 1988). To a large extent, the same indications for expressive or supportive emphasis (see Table 4–2 in Chapter 4) that guide the clinician's work with other diagnostic entities apply to psychotherapy with borderline patients. Stone's (1987) follow-up study of borderline patients who were sufficiently disturbed to require extended hospitalization revealed that only about one-third of those patients who originally appeared amenable to expressive psychotherapy were truly suited for that approach. However, large aggregate studies of this nature, while useful, do not address the nuances of the therapeutic process at a more microcosmic level. Process research of individual sessions has demonstrated that, at least with some patients, transference interpretation may serve to improve the therapeutic alliance (Gabbard et al. 1988).

As a general rule, higher-level borderline patients with greater ego strengths and greater psychological mindedness will be more able to use expressively oriented psychotherapy than those closer to the psychotic border, who will need a supportive emphasis. Most will require a flexible stance by the therapist, with shifts between interpretive and noninterpretive interventions geared to the state of the patient's relatedness to the therapist at a given moment (Gunderson 1984). In a study of borderline patients who discontinued psychotherapy, Gunderson et al. (1989) found that more than half the dropouts departed in anger following early confrontation by their therapists. These findings led Gunderson and his colleagues to advocate more supportive techniques early in therapy, as described by Masterson (1976) and Adler (1985). Recognition of a history of childhood trauma may help the therapist appreciate the adaptive value of the patient's defensive strategies. This empathy with the patient may result in a more supportive, less confrontative approach, leading to fewer dropouts (Gunderson and Sabo 1993).

Even shifting between the conceptual frameworks of Kernberg and Adler is both possible and reasonable with many patients, because the common ground in these approaches serves as a basis for integration (Goldstein 1989). The result of the integration of split self- and object-representations, a goal advocated by Kernberg (1975), is the development of object constancy, a state closely related to Adler's "evocative memory" in that it enables the patient to tolerate being alone without disorganizing into a state of panic. Moreover, the patient's subjective experience of the absence of "good" soothing introjects (Adler's position) is not essentially different from the patient's experience of a predominance of "bad" hostile introjects (Kernberg's position). Adler and Rhine (1988) demonstrated with case material how containing projections from the patient may constitute a selfobject function for the therapist, thus integrating Kernberg's object relations concept of projective identification with Adler's self psychological concept of selfobject. Finally, no single theory is likely to insulate the therapist from the tumultuous emotional upheaval experienced by both partners of the therapeutic dyad. Most therapists find themselves using a trial-and-error approach until they can clearly determine which interventions are most effective with a given patient.

Kernberg himself seems to have developed a greater regard for the effects of supportive psychotherapy as his own technique has evolved. In his 1984 examination of the psychotherapy of borderline patients, he discussed exploring transference fantasies without necessarily interpreting them as one would in highly expressive treatment: "This exploration is not connected interpretively with the patient's unconscious relation to the therapist or with his unconscious past. It is, instead, used for confronting the patient with the reality of the treatment situation and with parallel distortions in his external life" (p. 163). This modification still places Kernberg's approach at a far more expressive point on the continuum than Adler's, but more clearly emphasizes the value of noninterpretive interventions.

In a review of the literature on intensive psychotherapy with borderline patients, Waldinger (1987) distilled the diverse technical approaches of a variety of clinicians into eight basic tenets that are consensually valued in the psychotherapy of borderline patients. These eight technical principles are also useful in organizing a discussion of interventions.

Establish a stable treatment framework. Because of the chaotic nature of the borderline patient's life, stability must be imposed from external sources. Although a hospital milieu would be the most extreme way to provide external structure, the psychotherapist can also introduce some stability into the patient's life by setting consistent appointment times, ending sessions on time even though the patient may insist on staying longer, establishing clear expectations about fee payment, and developing an explicit policy about the consequences of missed appointments.

Avoid a passive therapeutic stance. The silent, reflective stance of the psychoanalyst working with a neurotic patient is usually not suitable for effective psychotherapy with borderline patients. These patients will often misinterpret silence as a lack of caring or even as a malevolent withholding of support. The alliance is facilitated instead by greater verbalizations by the therapist, even simple affirming comments such as "I see" or open-ended questions such as "Do you have any other thoughts about that?" When the patient is silent, the therapist would do better to inquire about the silence rather than to let it continue for a prolonged period. The only exception to this rule of thumb is a small subset of extraordinarily oppositional patients, who may take an oath of silence as a way of defeating the therapist (Gabbard 1989a). These patients are probably treatable only in an inpatient setting.

Contain the patient's anger. Virtually all clinicians who write about the treatment of borderline patients acknowledge the extraordinary challenge of maintaining a therapeutic posture in the face of these patients' verbal barrages of contempt and hatred. The therapist will often feel provoked into becoming defensive or retaliating with hostile or sarcastic interpretations. Alternatively, the therapist may subtly withdraw from an emotional investment in the patient, consciously or unconsciously hoping that the patient will quit therapy and find someone else to torment. The optimal approach to containing the patient's projected hateful parts has already been described in Chapter 14 in a discussion of the psychotherapy of the paranoid patient. Indeed, anger is often part of a paranoid transference development that is a typical feature of the psychotherapy of borderline patients. The therapist should empathize with the patient's need to split good and bad self- and object-representations and to project the bad outside the self as a way to control it and keep it from destroying the good representations. The therapist who returns the "badness" prematurely will simply increase the patient's feeling of being attacked. As Grotstein (1982) has pointed out, the therapist functions essentially as a container, not an interpreter, until the patient is once again able to own these projected aspects. Until that time, transference interpretations are unlikely to be understood or processed.

Containing the patient's anger often requires the therapist to tolerate periods of psychotic transference. It is not uncommon for disturbances of reality testing to surface only in the context of the therapy session. After leaving the session, the patient may rapidly reorganize and return to normal functioning. One patient, for example, assumed a prone position on the analytic couch during each therapy session because she was convinced that her therapist would rape her. But after the hour, she would return to work with no apparent difficulty. Supportive inquiries and empathic understanding are much more useful in such situations than interpretations, which the borderline patient will only experience as an attack.

Confront self-destructive behaviors. Borderline patients frequently display magical thinking about their self-destructive behavior. They may be completely oblivious to the actual consequences of their actions because they fantasize that their behavior will have different results. Waldinger (1987) stressed that therapists should make their patients look at these consequences. One patient who had been hospitalized several times because she inflicted cigarette burns on her forearms insisted that this behavior relieved her internal tension. She believed that mental health workers unnecessarily made a "big deal" out of her behavior. Whenever she was hospitalized, she complained that the nursing staff did not understand how much relief the self-burning gave her. The therapist pointed out that the actual consequence of this repeated burning was that the patient had created a "revolving-door situation" at the hospital that prevented her from maintaining stable employment or meaningful relationships.

Promiscuous sexual behavior may be similarly confronted. For example, a male homosexual patient told his therapist that he felt a strong need for homosexual encounters because the swallowing of semen from a virile, masculine male made him feel more masculine. His therapist pointed out that despite this fantasy, the real consequence of swallowing other men's semen was the risk of contracting AIDS.

Establish the connection between feelings and actions. Action is often the language of the borderline patient. These patients feel so controlled by powerful affect states that action may seem the only viable way to achieve relief. However, much of this pattern is ego-syntonic so that patients are often unaware that their actions are motivated by feelings. Their conscious experience may be that impulses simply come "out of the blue." The therapists of borderline patients thus must look repeatedly for precipitating feeling states whenever they are confronted with acting-out behavior. One patient went out and bought eight candy bars, eating them all in the space of 10 minutes after a man had called her for a date. Although this patient saw no connection between the two events, the therapist helped her understand that the prospect of going out on a date filled her with anxiety, which she in turn tried to relieve through binge eating.

Set limits. This form of intervention is often implemented as part of a contractual agreement at the beginning of psychotherapy (Kernberg 1984). Therapists may wish to establish a number of "ground rules," including no phone calls between sessions, the verbalization of suicidal feelings to the therapist before acting on them, and a willingness to accept hospitalization when suicidal impulses are out of control. Some therapists are flexible on these matters; others prefer more structure. Adler (1985), for example, believed that in the early phases of treatment, the therapist's availability by phone is instrumental to the establishment of a stable, holding selfobject transference. Likewise, Adler and Buie (1979) have recommended interventions such as sending a postcard during vacation to reassure the patient of the therapist's existence, providing occasional extra sessions in a crisis, and allowing the patient to know the whereabouts of the therapist during vacations. Giovacchini (1986) has noted that many patients experience some rudimentary object constancy just by knowing their therapist's phone number and whereabouts during a vacation. Even those therapists who allow for this flexibility, however, realize the importance of setting limits when such flexibility is exploited by the patient. Therapists must develop a sense of their own limits. Specifically, they should decide how much outside contact they can tolerate and still treat the patient.

Many borderline patients experience the usual professional boundaries as cruel and punitive deprivation by the therapist. They may demand more concrete demonstrations of caring, such as hugs, extended sessions, decreases in the fee, and around-the-clock availability (Gabbard and Wilkinson 1994). Some therapists who experience guilt feelings about the setting of limits may begin to cross professional boundaries with borderline patients in the name of flexibility or suicide prevention (Gutheil 1989). One male therapist, for example, began seeing a female patient twice a week for psychotherapy, but within a year was seeing the patient seven times a week. On Sundays, he would make a special trip to his office just to see this patient. When a consultant questioned this behavior, the therapist defended it as necessary to prevent the patient from committing suicide. He also acknowledged that he allowed the patient to sit on his lap during their sessions, justifying this behavior as a way to provide the patient with the mothering that she had not received as a child. Many cases of therapist-patient sex involve borderline patients (Gabbard 1989c). One female patient insisted that nothing short of an orgasm induced by her male therapist would result in her improvement. She threatened to kill herself if her therapist would not comply. After two different therapists indulged her demands, she eventually killed herself anyway—their misguided expressions of "caring" failed either to address her basic problems or to relieve her emotional pain (Eyman and Gabbard 1991). The dynamics of erotic and erotized transference are discussed more fully in Chapter 18, but the tragic end of this particular patient underscores the futility of trying to gratify the patient's demands. The more gratification that borderline patients receive, the more insatiable they become.

In a succinct summary of the group of behaviors that require limit setting, Waldinger (1987) identified those that threaten the safety of the therapist or the patient, and those that jeopardize the psychotherapy itself. Suicide is an ever-present risk with borderline patients, and therapists must be ready to hospitalize their patients when these impulses become overwhelming. Therapists often find themselves in the untenable position of heroically attempting to treat lethal patients by having continuous contact with them. One therapist ended up talking on the phone to a borderline patient for an hour every night to prevent her from killing herself.

Maintain the focus of interventions on the here and now.   In the psychotherapy of borderline patients, the action is in the transference. The patient's view of the therapist will shift kaleidoscopically from day to day or even within a single session. When the patient attempts to integrate bad and good representations of the therapist, the depressive anxieties created by that attempt at synthesis may produce intense concern about harming the therapist. If the therapist is perceived as insufficiently empathic or understanding, that concern can shift in the twinkling of an eye to anxiety more typical of the paranoid-schizoid position, namely, a perception of the therapist as a malevolent figure intent on sadistic torment. These shifts must be addressed as they occur rather than allowing the patient to take flight from transference into emotionally distant reconstructions of childhood experiences.

> Ms. GG was a 24-year-old woman who came to psychotherapy after repeated failures with other therapists. She was unable to live outside her parents' home, despite the fact that she was intelligent and personally engaging. She had held countless jobs, none for more than 3 months. Although in the initial interview she was able to impress employers enough to convince them to hire her, as soon as she started

succeeding at the job, she would become extraordinarily anxious and would act up in a way that caused her to be fired.

As soon as she came to therapy, Ms. GG developed an immediate wish for the therapist to take care of her. She wanted to be his only patient and to be seen five times a week instead of twice a week. She told the therapist that he was "warm and wonderful," unlike the other therapists she had seen. She felt that she would greatly improve if she could just be in his presence every day of the week. This idealizing transference rapidly turned to a devaluing one when the therapist offered his opinion that twice-weekly therapy would be preferable since one of Ms. GG's difficulties was in dealing with frustration. At this point, Ms. GG exploded; she accused her therapist of being cruel and unempathic because he was simply basing the treatment on what he thought was best rather than responding to her needs. She stormed out of his office and said she was not coming back. Ten minutes later, she called her therapist from a pay phone, told him he was "a son of a bitch" and hung up. Ten minutes after that, she called again, this time to apologize and to say that she would return for her next session. The therapist simply responded that that would be fine with him.

At the next psychotherapy session, Ms. GG did not refer to the upheaval that had occurred in the previous session. She chatted amicably with the therapist as though no rift had ever occurred between them. The therapist offered an empathic interpretation: "It seems like you need to keep the hateful feelings that occurred last time out of the session today so that they won't destroy the positive feelings you're having in here today." That intervention allowed the patient to talk about how frustrating it was for her when other people would not respond to her dependency needs as she wanted them to.

This brief vignette illustrates a useful principle enunciated by Pine (1986): "Strike while the iron is cold" (p. 528). If the therapist had delivered any interpretive intervention when this patient was full of rage, she would simply have felt attacked. By waiting until Ms. GG had calmed down, however, the therapist was better able to get her to reflect on the interpretation itself. Moreover, the therapist made no effort to elaborate the interpretation by bringing in childhood antecedents. Staying in the here and now kept this patient from taking flight from the transference situation.

Monitor countertransference feelings. Implicit in this entire discussion of psychotherapy has been the centrality of attending to the countertransference. Containing the projected parts of the patient and reflecting on the nature of these projections will help the therapist understand the patient's internal world (Gabbard and Wilkinson 1994). Moreover, ongoing attention to one's own feelings prevents countertransference acting out. Each therapist has personal limits regarding how much hatred or anger is tolerable. If the therapist closely monitors countertransference feelings, this limit can be handled constructively rather than destructively. For example, a therapist might use countertransference feelings therapeutically by saying to the patient, "I'm getting the feeling that you are trying to make me angry at you instead of letting me help you. Let's see if we can understand what's happening here." Alternatively, the therapist may have to set limits on the patient's verbal barrages based on countertransference reactions, as follows: "I really don't feel I can work with you effectively if you continue to shout at me. I think it's important for you to work on controlling your anger so you can express it to me without screaming." Therapists must be real and genuine with borderline patients, or they will only increase the patient's envy of them as saintly figures that are basically nonhuman (Searles 1986).

The outcome of psychotherapy with borderline patients is always uncertain. A study of completed cases by Waldinger and Gunderson (1987) indicated that even with experienced therapists and analysts, the dropout rate is high. Approximately one-third of their sample actually completed treatment. However, this research also suggested that those patients who stay in treatment derive substantial improvement from it.

Hospital Treatment

The principles of psychoanalytically informed hospital treatment are outlined in Chapter 6. In addition, the management of splitting in hospital treatment, an essential ingredient in work with borderline patients, is also discussed in that chapter. Readers are therefore referred back to Chapter 6 for the basic principles of the hospital treatment of borderline patients. Several other points specific to patients with borderline personality will be covered here.

There are essentially two models used in the treatment of borderline patients: 1) brief hospitalization for crisis intervention in the context of outpatient psychotherapy and 2) extended, psychodynamically informed hospital treatment with the goals of ego-building and modification of the patient's internal object world. The indications for the second model, in the simplest possible terms, involve an inability to use the first model. In actual practice, this category would include several groups of patients (with some patients overlapping different categories): 1) relentlessly self-destructive or suicidal patients who are too lethal to be treated outside an inpatient setting; 2) "special" patients, who create intense countertransference problems related to splitting and projective identification (Burnham 1966; Gabbard 1986; Main 1957); 3) extraordinarily hateful patients who venomously attack those who attempt to help them (Gabbard 1989b); and 4) passively oppositional patients who refuse to talk or participate in any aspect of the treatment plan (Gabbard 1989a). All four of these groups are occasionally characterized as "negative therapeutic reactions," although some may ultimately be treatable, given the intensive approaches available in long-term hospitalization.

Short-Term Hospital Treatment

The patient who requires brief hospitalization in the course of psychotherapy is likely to be in a crisis involving a psychotic regression, self-destructive behavior, or suicidal impulses. There may be varying degrees of turmoil in the psychotherapy process as well. Since the goal of short-term hospitalization is rapid restoration of the patient's defenses and adaptive functioning, the inpatient staff must convey a counterregressive expectation. Treaters in the milieu must communicate to such patients that they can control impulses despite their disclaimers. Although external controls, such as cold, wet sheet packs, restraints, and antipsychotic medication, may be necessary at times, the emphasis is on helping these patients take responsibility for self-control. The weakened ego of the patient can be supplemented with a firm, consistent structure involving a regular schedule, clear consequences for impulsive acting out, and a predictable pattern of group and individual meetings with staff members and other patients.

The usual tendency of the newly admitted borderline patient is to expect, on demand, lengthy individual sessions with members of the nursing staff. When nurses are actually "roped into" attempting to gratify these demands, the patient typically deteriorates in direct proportion to the amount of time spent in these one-to-one "therapy" sessions. Borderline patients do much better when the nursing staff can build into the regular structure brief 5- to 10-minute meetings.

Staff members in the milieu and the unit structure itself function as auxiliary egos for borderline patients. Rather than attempting exploratory or interpretive work, the unit staff can help patients identify precipitants of their crises, delay impulse discharge by seeking alternatives, anticipate consequences of their actions, and clarify their internal object relations (as described in Chapter 6). Another function of brief hospitalization is that it affords a more accurate view of the patient's internal world. Finally, the milieu staff can often assist the psychotherapist in understanding the nature of a crisis or impasse that occurs in the patient's psychotherapy. In addition to addressing any splitting processes (as described in Chapter 6), the milieu staff can help the therapist by validating the therapist's competence and worth as a clinician (Adler 1984). From the self psychological perspective of Adler, the unit nurses and other personnel can perform selfobject functions for both the patient and the therapist (Adler 1987).

Extended Hospitalization

Extended, psychoanalytically informed hospital treatment of borderline patients essentially follows the model outlined in Chapter 6. Much of the treatment involves ego-building, because those patients who require extended hospital treatment have more profound ego weaknesses than do patients who do not require lengthy hospitalization. The hospital's emphasis must be on the patient's substitution of words for actions, despite the patient's protestations that such a shift is impossible.

There must also be a unit norm that discourages keeping secrets. Anything the patient says to one staff member must be shared with other staff members in meetings. The staff of the unit must be able to repeatedly say "no" to the patient in a matter-of-fact, caring way that conveys no malice. Otherwise, the patient may not be able to integrate the fact that "good" caring figures are the same persons who implement restrictive measures (i.e., "bad" interventions). This integration of internal self- and object-representations is another primary goal of extended inpatient treatment.

Limits applied to a patient must always be based on an empathic understanding of the patient's need for limits rather than on any sadistic attempt at control, which is how the patient usually views such restrictions.

Ms. HH became extremely angry and tearful when her mother left after a family visit during her long-term hospitalization. She screamed at the social worker and threw a book at him as she accused him of taking her mother away. The nursing staff asked Ms. HH to control herself and go to her room but were forced to put her in four-point leather restraints when she continued to be assaultive toward other staff members. Throughout the process of implementing these restrictions, the nursing staff repeatedly told Ms. HH that they understood how upset she was because she missed her mother terribly and felt that she could not survive without her. Since the patient lacked a soothing maternal introject to comfort her, the nursing staff was performing that function by attempting to soothe her and reassure her as they put her into restraints. Moreover, Ms. HH's psychiatrist suggested that a photograph of her mother should be placed where the patient could see it, thereby helping Ms. HH to deal with her problems with evocative memory and object constancy. The patient seemed relieved upon seeing the picture and commented that without it she could not even remember what her mother looked like. With these measures, the patient calmed down within 30 minutes, and the restraints were removed.

Suicidal and self-mutilative behavior is often a significant problem in extended hospitalization because borderline patients attempt to control the entire treatment staff just as they have controlled their family and loved ones outside the hospital with such behavior. The staff members must stress that each patient is ultimately responsible for controlling such behavior and that realistically no one can prevent a patient from committing suicide. Borderline patients often make superficial cuts on themselves with paperclips, beverage cans, light bulbs, and other objects that are generally available even in hospitals. While the actual damage from such superficial scratching may be minimal, the unit staff should carefully investigate the origins of the mutilation. Is it connected with depersonalization episodes or dissociation? Is there a history of childhood sexual abuse? Does the patient warrant a trial of fluoxetine? Is the behavior primarily manipulative in an effort to gain attention from the staff? When the mutilation is consistently mild, staff members may deal with it by establishing a weekly appointment for the patient with a nonpsychiatric physician, such as an internist, who works closely with the hospital unit (Gabbard 1986). In this manner, the mutilative behavior loses its control function and allows the staff and the patient to work on other more central issues. If any serious consequences occur from the mutilation, the internist can treat them appropriately.

The chronically suicidal borderline patient may engender intense countertransference feelings in staff members, who perceive the attempts and gestures as manipulative and therefore begin to react to the patient's suicidal threats with a lack of concern. The inpatient staff must keep in mind that suicide attempters are 140 times more likely to commit suicide than nonattempters (Tuckman and Youngman 1963), and that roughly 10%–20% of all suicide attempters eventually kill themselves (Dorpat and Ripley 1967).

As the result of changes in reimbursement patterns and aggressive managed care and utilization review, fewer and fewer borderline patients have access to extended dynamically informed hospital treatment. In many cases, this form of treatment is now taking place in partial hospital settings or community residence programs. Many of the same principles of milieu and group treatment apply to such settings, although the containment of lethal behavior is much more problematic with the reduced structure inherent in partial hospitalization.

Family Therapy

Therapeutic modification of the borderline patient's internal object world generally requires an intensive individual psychotherapy process. Work with the family, however, is often an essential adjunct to the overall treatment plan. The use of formal family therapy is far less common than that of one or more family interventions in the course of treatment (Brown 1987). Inpatient treatment, for example, provides clinicians with the opportunity to meet with the patient's family and to understand those interactions as compared and contrasted with a recapitulation of the patient's internal object world in the milieu via splitting and projective identification (see Chapter 6). In outpatient psychotherapy, the individual process may be undermined by the countertherapeutic efforts of family members who feel threatened by any change in the designated patient. Family interventions or, in severe cases, family therapy may therefore be required for a successful individual treatment.

The first step of family intervention is to identify the role family interactions play in the pathogenesis and maintenance of the borderline patient's symptomatology. As described in Chapter 5, splitting and projective identification are extremely common mechanisms that serve to maintain a pathological homeostasis in the family system. For example, a parent may ward off bad internal self- or object-representations and project them onto an adolescent or young adult offspring, who subsequently identifies with these projections and becomes the symptomatic member of the family.

In diagnosing family patterns, therapists should avoid imposing their own theoretical constructs on the family. For example, although certain psychodynamic models (Masterson and Rinsley 1975) might presuppose overinvolvement on the part of the mother, empirical research (Gunderson and Englund 1981; Gunderson et al. 1980) has suggested that overinvolved parents are less common than neglectful ones. Neglectful parents of borderline patients tend to be needy themselves and therefore often fail to provide their children with guidance in the form of rules or "structure." This finding in Gunderson's research underscores the necessity to "re-parent" the borderline patient in extended hospital treatment by establishing firm structure and clear consequences for structure breaks in the treatment milieu. When working during inpatient treatment with a family characterized by this pattern of neglect and neediness, a social worker or other mental health professional may have to "parent the parents" of the borderline patient. Moreover, in discharge planning, the parents may need help in learning how to serve as a constructive support system for their borderline child, which may include getting help for themselves on an ongoing basis.

In families where overinvolvement is a pervasive pattern, family intervention must respect the needs of each family member for the other members. The parents may suffer from borderline psychopathology themselves and may be terribly threatened by the prospect of "losing" their borderline offspring through treatment. Clinicians must take seriously the possibility that a significant improvement in the designated patient may result in a severe decompensation in a parent, who will be thrown into a panic because of the perceived separation (Brown 1987). In these instances, a family therapist should help the family deal with the dilemmas created by change in the patient as well as in the family system as a whole. The therapist must conscientiously avoid any attempt to "pry apart" the borderline patient and the family. Such efforts will be viewed by both the family and the patient as a highly threatening attack that will simply cause them to "circle the wagons" and increase their enmeshment. Family therapists produce better results when they assume a nonjudgmental, neutral position regarding change, empathizing with the family's need to remain together because of the stability inherent in the overinvolvement (Jones 1987). Any change in the system must come from *within* rather than being imposed by mental health professionals, who traditionally place a high value on separation and autonomy.

Group Psychotherapy

Group psychotherapy may also be a beneficial adjunct to individual psychotherapy of borderline patients. As Ganzarain (1980) and Horwitz (1977) have noted, all groups are prone to employ the borderline defenses of splitting and projective identification. Group psychotherapy affords the borderline individual an opportunity to understand these defenses as they occur in a group context. Most contributors to the literature on group psychotherapy of the borderline patient, however, suggest that the borderline patient is most effectively treated in groups of patients who suffer from neuroses or higher-level personality disorders (Day and Semrad 1971; Horwitz 1977; Hulse 1958; Slavson 1964).

Likewise, the consensus of the literature is that borderline patients in group psychotherapy need concomitant individual psychotherapy (Day and Semrad 1971; Horwitz 1977; Hulse 1958; Slavson 1964; Spotnitz 1957). The dilution of transference in group psychotherapy significantly benefits both the borderline patient and the therapist. The intense rage that is ordinarily mobilized in borderline patients when they are frustrated in treatment may thus be diluted and directed toward other figures besides the individual therapist. Similarly, the strong countertransference reactions to borderline patients may be diluted by the presence of other people.

Horwitz (1977) has pointed out that the individual psychotherapist may serve a crucial supportive function when the borderline patient's anxiety escalates in response to confrontation in the group setting. The individual therapist ideally should be someone other than the group therapist, because "it is antitherapeutic for the group therapist to see some patients individually while not seeing others privately as well" (p. 415). Horwitz also identified abrasive characterological traits as an indication for group psychotherapy in addition to individual psychotherapy. He has observed that borderline patients seem more willing to accept confrontation and interpretation about such traits from their peers in group psychotherapy than from a therapist. They may also find it easier to accept their therapist's interpretations as part of a group-centered theme than when the interpretations single them out as individuals.

Despite the advantages of working in a group context, therapists will find certain inherent difficulties in the group psychotherapy of borderline patients. Such patients may easily become scapegoated because of their more primitive psychopathology and their greater tendency to express affect in a direct manner. The therapist may be required to support the borderline patient when scapegoating emerges as a group theme. Moreover, borderline patients may also experience an increase in their feelings of deprivation because of competition with the group for the nurturance of the therapist. Finally, borderline patients tend to maintain a certain distance in group psychotherapy because of their primary attachment to the individual therapist.

References

Abend SM, Porder MS, Willick MS: Borderline Patients: Psychoanalytic Perspectives. New York, International Universities Press, 1983

Adler G: The myth of the alliance with borderline patients. Am J Psychiatry 47:642–645, 1979

Adler G: The borderline-narcissistic personality disorder continuum. Am J Psychiatry 138:46–50, 1981

Adler G: Issues in the treatment of the borderline patient, in Kohut's Legacy: Contributions to Self Psychology. Edited by Stepansky PE, Goldberg A. Hillsdale, NJ, Analytic Press, 1984, pp 117–134

Adler G: Borderline Psychopathology and Its Treatment. New York, Jason Aronson, 1985

Adler G: Discussion: milieu treatment in the psychotherapy of the borderline patient: abandonment and containment. Yearbook of Psychoanalysis and Psychotherapy 2:145–157, 1987

Adler G, Buie DH Jr: Aloneness and borderline psychopathology: the possible relevance of child development issues. Int J Psychoanal 60:83–96, 1979

Adler G, Rhine MW: The selfobject function of projective identification: curative factors in psychotherapy. Bull Menninger Clin 52:473–491, 1988

American Psychiatric Association: Diagnostic and Statistical Manual of Mental Disorders, 2nd Edition. Washington, DC, American Psychiatric Association, 1968

American Psychiatric Association: Diagnostic and Statistical Manual of Mental Disorders, 3rd Edition. Washington, DC, American Psychiatric Association, 1980

American Psychiatric Association: Diagnostic and Statistical Manual of Mental Disorders, 3rd Edition, Revised. Washington, DC, American Psychiatric Association, 1987

American Psychiatric Association: Diagnostic and Statistical Manual of Mental Disorders, 4th Edition. Washington, DC, American Psychiatric Association, 1994

Andrulonis PA: Disruptive behavior disorders in boys and the borderline personality disorder in men. Annals of Clinical Psychiatry 3:23–26, 1991

Andrulonis PA, Glueck BC, Stroebel CF, et al: Organic brain dysfunction and the borderline syndrome. Psychiatr Clin North Am 4:47–66, 1981

Atwood GE, Stolorow RD: Structures of Subjectivity: Explorations in Psychoanalytic Phenomenology. Hillsdale, NJ, Analytic Press, 1984

Baker L, Silk KR, Westen D, et al: Malevolence, splitting, and parental ratings by borderlines. J Nerv Ment Dis 180:258–264, 1992

Barasch A, Frances A, Hurt S, et al: Stability and distinctness of borderline personality disorder. Am J Psychiatry 142:1484–1486, 1985

Baron M, Gruen R, Asnis L, et al: Familial transmission of schizotypal and borderline personality disorders. Am J Psychiatry 142:927–934, 1985

Boyer LB: Working with a borderline patient. Psychoanal Q 46:386–424, 1977

Brown SL: Family therapy and the borderline patient, in The Borderline Patient: Emerging Concepts in Diagnosis, Psychodynamics, and Treatment, Vol 2. Edited by Grotstein JS, Solomon MF, Lang JA. Hillsdale, NJ, Analytic Press, 1987, pp 206–209

Browne A, Finkelhor D: Impact of child sexual abuse: a review of the research. Psychol Bull 99:66–77, 1986

Burnham DL: The special-problem patient: victim or agent of splitting? Psychiatry 29:105–122, 1966

Coccaro EF, Siever LJ, Klar HM, et al: Serotonergic studies in patients with affective and personality disorders: correlates with suicidal and impulsive aggressive behavior. Arch Gen Psychiatry 46:587–599, 1989

Cornelius JR, Soloff PH, Perel JM, et al: Fluoxetine trial in borderline personality disorder. Psychopharmacol Bull 26:151–154, 1990

Cowdry RW, Gardner DL: Pharmacotherapy of borderline personality disorder: alprazolam, carbamazepine, trifluoperazine, and tranylcypromine. Arch Gen Psychiatry 45:111–119, 1988

Day M, Semrad E: Group therapy with neurotics and psychotics, in Comprehensive Group Psychotherapy. Edited by Kaplan HI, Sadock BJ. Baltimore, MD, Williams & Wilkins, 1971, pp 566–580

Dolan BM, Evans C, Norton K: The separation-individuation inventory: association with borderline phenomena. J Nerv Ment Dis 180:529–533, 1992

Dorpat TL, Ripley HS: The relationship between attempted suicide and committed suicide. Compr Psychiatry 8:74–79, 1967

Esman AH: Adolescent psychopathology and the rapprochement process, in Rapprochement: The Critical Subphase of Separation-Individuation. Edited by Lax RF, Bach S, Burland JA. New York, Jason Aronson, 1980, pp 295–297

Eyman JR, Gabbard GO: Will therapist-patient sex prevent suicide? Psychiatric Annals 21:669–674, 1991

Fairbairn WRD: An Object-Relations Theory of the Personality. New York, Basic Books, 1954

Finell JS: Book review of Borderline Psychopathology and Its Treatment (by Gerald Adler). Psychoanal Rev 75:491–493, 1988

Fraiberg S: Libidinal object constancy and mental representation. Psychoanal Study Child 24:9–47, 1969

Frank AF: The therapeutic alliances of borderline patients, in Borderline Personality Disorder: Clinical and Empirical Perspectives. Edited by Clarkin JF, Marziali B, Munroe-Blum H. New York, Guilford, 1992, pp 220–247

Frank H, Paris J: Recollections of family experience in borderline patients. Arch Gen Psychiatry 38:1031–1034, 1981

Fyer MR, Frances AJ, Sullivan T, et al: Comorbidity of borderline personality disorder. Arch Gen Psychiatry 45:348–352, 1988

Gabbard GO: The treatment of the "special patient" in a psychoanalytic hospital. International Review of Psychoanalysis 13:333–347, 1986

Gabbard GO: On "doing nothing" in the psychoanalytic treatment of the refractory borderline patient. Int J Psychoanal 70:527–534, 1989a

Gabbard GO: Patients who hate. Psychiatry 52:96–106, 1989b

Gabbard GO (ed): Sexual Exploitation in Professional Relationships. Washington, DC, American Psychiatric Press, 1989c

Gabbard GO: An overview of countertransference with borderline patients. Journal of Psychotherapy Practice and Research 2:7–18, 1993

Gabbard GO, Wilkinson SM: Management of Countertransference With Borderline Patients. Washington, DC, American Psychiatric Press, 1994

Gabbard GO, Horwitz L, Frieswyk S, et al: The effect of therapist interventions on the therapeutic alliance with borderline patients. J Am Psychoanal Assoc 36:697–727, 1988

Ganzarain RC: Psychotic-like anxieties and primitive defenses in group analytic psychotherapy. Issues in Ego Psychology 3:42–48, 1980

Gardner DL, Cowdry RW: Alprazolam-induced dyscontrol in borderline personality disorder. Am J Psychiatry 142:98–100, 1985

Giovacchini PL: Psychic integration and object constancy, in Self and Object Constancy: Clinical and Theoretical Perspectives. Edited by Lax RF, Bach S, Burland JA. New York, Guilford, 1986, pp 208–233

Goldberg RL, Mann LS, Wise TN, et al: Parental qualities as perceived by borderline personality disorders. Hillside Journal of Clinical Psychiatry 7:134–140, 1985

Goldstein WN: An integration of the views of Kernberg and Adler on borderline pathology. Bull Menninger Clin 53:300–309, 1989

Gorney JE: The negative therapeutic interaction. Contemporary Psychoanalysis 15:288–337, 1979

Grinker Jr RR, Werble B, Drye RC: The Borderline Syndrome: A Behavioral Study of Ego-Functions. New York, Basic Books, 1968

Grotstein JS: The analysis of a borderline patient, in Technical Factors in the Treatment of the Severely Disturbed Patient. Edited by Giovacchini PL, Boyer LB. New York, Jason Aronson, 1982, pp 261–288

Grotstein JS: The borderline as a disorder of self-regulation, in The Borderline Patient: Emerging Concepts in Diagnosis, Psychodynamics, and Treatment, Vol 1. Edited by Grotstein JS, Solomon MF, Lang JA. Hillsdale, NJ, Analytic Press, 1987, pp 347–383

Gunderson JG: Borderline Personality Disorder. Washington, DC, American Psychiatric Press, 1984

Gunderson JG, Englund DW: Characterizing the families of borderlines: a review of the literature. Psychiatr Clin North Am 4:159–168, 1981

Gunderson JG, Phillips KA: A current view of the interface between borderline personality disorder and depression. Am J Psychiatry 148:967–975, 1991

Gunderson JG, Sabo AN: The phenomenological and conceptual interface between borderline personality disorder and PTSD. Am J Psychiatry 150:19–27, 1993

Gunderson JG, Singer MT: Defining borderline patients: an overview. Am J Psychiatry 132:1–10, 1975

Gunderson JG, Zanarini MC: Current overview of the borderline diagnosis. J Clin Psychiatry 48 (suppl 8):5–14, 1987

Gunderson JG, Kerr J, Englund DW: The families of borderlines: a comparative study. Arch Gen Psychiatry 37:27–33, 1980

Gunderson JG, Frank AF, Ronningstam EF, et al: Early discontinuance of borderline patients from psychotherapy. J Nerv Ment Dis 177:38–42, 1989

Gunderson JG, Zanarini MC, Kisiel CL: Borderline personality disorder: a review of data on DSM-III-R descriptions. Journal of Personality Disorders 5:340–352, 1991

Gutheil T: Borderline personality disorder, boundary violations, and patient-therapist sex: medicolegal pitfalls. Am J Psychiatry 146:597–602, 1989

Herman JL, Perry JC, van der Kolk BA: Childhood trauma in borderline personality disorder. Am J Psychiatry 146:490–495, 1989

Hoch P, Polatin P: Pseudoneurotic forms of schizophrenia. Psychiatr Q 23:248–276, 1949

Horwitz L: Clinical Prediction in Psychotherapy. New York, Jason Aronson, 1974

Horwitz L: Group psychotherapy of the borderline patient, in Borderline Personality Disorders: The Concept, the Syndrome, the Patient. Edited by Hartocollis PL. New York, International Universities Press, 1977, pp 399–422

Hulse WC: Psychotherapy with ambulatory schizophrenic patients in mixed analytic groups. Archives of Neurology and Psychiatry 79:681–687, 1958

Jones SA: Family therapy with borderline and narcissistic patients. Bull Menninger Clin 51:285–295, 1987

Kernberg OF: Structural derivatives of object relationships. Int J Psychoanal 47:236–253, 1966

Kernberg OF: Borderline personality organization. J Am Psychoanal Assoc 15:641–685, 1967

Kernberg OF: Borderline Conditions and Pathological Narcissism. New York, Jason Aronson, 1975

Kernberg OF: Technical considerations in the treatment of borderline personality organization. J Am Psychoanal Assoc 24:795–829, 1976

Kernberg OF: Severe Personality Disorders: Psychotherapeutic Strategies. New Haven, CT, Yale University Press, 1984

Kernberg OF: Book review of *Borderline Psychopathology and Its Treatment* (by Gerald Adler). Am J Psychiatry 145:264–265, 1988

Kernberg OF, Burstein ED, Coyne L, et al: Psychotherapy and psychoanalysis: final report of the Menninger Foundation's Psychotherapy Research Project. Bull Menninger Clin 36:3–275, 1972

Knight RP: Borderline states, in Psychoanalytic Psychiatry and Psychology: Clinical and Theoretical Papers (1953). Edited by Knight RP, Friedman CR. New York, International Universities Press, 1954, pp 97–109

Loranger AW, Oldham JM, Tulis EH: Familial transmission of DSM-III borderline personality disorder. Arch Gen Psychiatry 39:795–799, 1982

Mahler MS, Kaplan LJ: Developmental aspects in the assessment of narcissistic and so-called borderline personalities, in Borderline Personality Disorders: The Concept, the Syndrome, the Patient. Edited by Hartocollis PL. New York, International Universities Press, 1977, pp 71–85

Mahler MS, Pine F, Bergman A: The Psychological Birth of the Human Infant: Symbiosis and Individuation. New York, Basic Books, 1975

Main TF: The ailment. Br J Med Psychol 30:129–145, 1957

Markovitz PJ, Calabrese JR, Schulz SC, Meltzer HY: Fluoxetine in the treatment of borderline and schizotypal personality disorders. Am J Psychiatry 148:1064–1067, 1991

Masterson JF: Psychotherapy of the Borderline Adult: A Developmental Approach. New York, Brunner/Mazel, 1976

Masterson JF, Rinsley DB: The borderline syndrome: the role of the mother in the genesis and psychic structure of the borderline personality. Int J Psychoanal 56:163–177, 1975

McGlashan TH: The borderline syndrome, II: is it a variant of schizophrenia or affective disorder? Arch Gen Psychiatry 40:1319–1323, 1983

McGlashan TH: The Chestnut Lodge follow-up study, III: long-term outcome of borderline personalities. Arch Gen Psychiatry 43:20–30, 1986

Meissner WW: The Borderline Spectrum: Differential Diagnosis and Developmental Issues. New York, Jason Aronson, 1984

Meissner WW: Treatment of Patients in the Borderline Spectrum. Northvale, NJ, Jason Aronson, 1988

Modell AH: "The holding environment" and the therapeutic action of psychoanalysis. J Am Psychoanal Assoc 24:285–307, 1976

Nigg JT, Silk KR, Westen D, et al: Object representations in the early memories of sexually abused borderline patients. Am J Psychiatry 148:864–869, 1991

Norden MJ: Fluoxetine in borderline personality disorder. Prog Neuropsychopharmacol Biol Psychiatry 13:885–893, 1989

Ogata SN, Silk KR, Goodrich S, et al: Childhood sexual and physical abuse in adult patients with borderline personality disorder. Am J Psychiatry 147:1008–1013, 1990

Paris J, Frank H: Perceptions of parental bonding in borderline patients. Am J Psychiatry 146:1498–1499, 1989

Paris J, Zweig-Frank H: A critical review of the role of childhood sexual abuse in the etiology of borderline personality disorder. Can J Psychiatry 37:125–128, 1992

Paris J, Brown R, Nowlis D: Long-term follow-up of borderline patients in a general hospital. Compr Psychiatry 28:530–535, 1987

Pfohl B, Stangle D, Zimmerman M: The implications of DSM-III personality disorders for patients with major depression. J Affect Disord 7:309–318, 1984

Pine F: Supportive psychotherapy: a psychoanalytic perspective. Psychiatric Annals 16:526–529, 1986

Plakun EM, Burkhardt PE, Muller JP: 14-year follow-up of borderline and schizotypal personality disorders. Compr Psychiatry 26:448–455, 1985

Rinsley DB: Borderline psychopathology: the concepts of Masterson and Rinsley and beyond. Adolesc Psychiatry 9:259–274, 1981a

Rinsley DB: Dynamic and developmental issues in borderline and related "spectrum" disorders. Psychiatr Clin North Am 4:117–132, 1981b

Rinsley DB: A comparison of borderline and narcissistic personality disorders. Bull Menninger Clin 48:1–9, 1984

Rinsley DB: Notes on the pathogenesis and nosology of borderline and narcissistic personality disorders. J Am Acad Psychoanal 13:317–328, 1985

Rinsley DB: Object constancy, object permanency, and personality disorders, in Self and Object Constancy: Clinical and Theoretical Perspectives. Edited by Lax RF, Bach S, Burland JA. New York, Guilford, 1986, pp 193–207

Rinsley DB: A reconsideration of Fairbairn's "original object" and "original ego" in relation to borderline and other self disorders, in The Borderline Patient: Emerging Concepts in Diagnosis, Psychodynamics, and Treatment, Vol 1. Edited by Grotstein JF, Solomon MF, Lang JA. Hillsdale, NJ, Analytic Press, 1987, pp 291–231

Rinsley DB: A review of the pathogenesis of borderline and narcissistic personality disorders. Adolesc Psychiatry 15:387–406, 1988

Rinsley DB: Developmental Pathogenesis and Psychoanalytic Treatment of Borderline and Narcissistic Personalities. Northvale, NJ, Jason Aronson, 1989

Schmideberg M: The borderline patient, in American Handbook of Psychiatry, Vol 1. Edited by Arieti S. New York, Basic Books, 1959, pp 398–416

Searles HF: My Work With Borderline Patients. Northvale, NJ, Jason Aronson, 1986

Shea MT, Glass Dr, Pilkonis PA, et al: Frequency and implications of personality disorder in a sample of depressed outpatients. Journal of Personality Disorders 1:27–42, 1987

Siever LJ, Davis KL: A psychobiological perspective on the personality disorders. Am J Psychiatry 148:1647–1658, 1991

Silverman JM, Pinkham L, Horvath TB, et al. Affective and impulsive personality disorder traits in the relatives of patients with borderline personality disorder. Am J Psychiatry 148:1378–1385, 1991

Slavson SR: A Textbook in Analytic Group Psychotherapy. New York, International Universities Press, 1964

Soloff PH, Millward JW: Developmental histories of borderline patients. Compr Psychiatry 24:574–588, 1983

Soloff PH, George A, Nathan RS, et al: Progress in pharmacotherapy of borderline disorders: a double-blind study of amitriptyline, haloperidol, and placebo. Arch Gen Psychiatry 43:691–697, 1986

Spotnitz H: The borderline schizophrenic in group psychotherapy: the importance of individualization. Int J Group Psychother 7:155–174, 1957

Stone MH: The Borderline Syndromes: Constitution, Personality, and Adaptation. New York, McGraw-Hill, 1980

Stone MH: Psychotherapy of borderline patients in light of long-term follow-up. Bull Menninger Clin 51:231–247, 1987

Stone MH, Stone DK, Hurt SW: Natural history of borderline patients treated by intensive hospitalization. Psychiatr Clin North Am 10:185–206, 1987

Swartz M, Blazer D, George L, et al: Estimating the prevalence of borderline personality disorder in the community. Journal of Personality Disorders 4:257–272, 1990

Swirsky-Sacchetti T, Gorton G, Samuel S, et al: Neuropsychological function in borderline personality disorder. J Clin Psychol 49:385–396, 1993

Tuckman J, Youngman WF: Suicide risk among persons attempting suicide. Public Health Rep 78:585–587, 1963

vanReekum R, Conway CA, Gansler D, et al: Neurobehavioral study of borderline personality disorder. J Psychiatry Neurosci 18:121–129, 1993

Waldinger RJ: Intensive psychodynamic therapy with borderline patients: an overview. Am J Psychiatry 144:267–274, 1987

Waldinger RJ, Frank AF: Clinicians' experiences in combining medication and psychotherapy in the treatment of borderline patients. Hosp Community Psychiatry 40:712–718, 1989

Waldinger RJ, Gunderson JG: Effective Psychotherapy With Borderline Patients: Case Studies. New York, Macmillan, 1987

Wallerstein RS: Forty-Two Lives in Treatment: A Study of Psychoanalysis and Psychotherapy. New York, Guilford, 1986

Walsh F: The family of the borderline patient, in The Borderline Patient. Edited by Grinker RR, Werble B. New York, Jason Aronson, 1977, pp 158–177

Werble B: Second follow-up study of borderline patients. Arch Gen Psychiatry 23:3–7, 1970

Westen D: Towards a revised theory of borderline object relations: contributions of empirical research. Int J Psychoanal 71:661–693, 1990

Westen D, Ludolph P, Misle B, et al: Physical and sexual abuse in adolescent girls with borderline personality disorder. Am J Orthopsychiatry 60:55–66, 1990

Zanarini MC, Gunderson JG, Frankenburg FR: Axis I phenomenology of borderline personality disorder. Compr Psychiatry 30:149–156, 1989a

Zanarini MC, Gunderson JG, Marino MF, et al: Childhood experiences of bor-
    derline patients. Compr Psychiatry 30:18–25, 1989b
Zanarini MC, Gunderson JG, Frankenburg FR: Cognitive features of border-
    line personality disorder. Am J Psychiatry 147:57–63, 1990a
Zanarini MC, Gunderson JG, Frankenburg FR, et al: Discriminating border-
    line personality disorder from other Axis II disorders. Am J Psychiatry
    147:161–167, 1990b
Zetzel ER: A developmental approach to the borderline patient. Am J Psychi-
    atry 127:867–871, 1971
Zweig-Frank H, Paris J: Parents' emotional neglect and overprotection accord-
    ing to the recollections of patients with borderline personality disorder.
    Am J Psychiatry 148:648–651, 1991

Chapter 16

Cluster B Personality Disorders: Narcissistic

O, you are sick of self-love, Malvolio, and taste with a distemper'd appetite. To be generous, guiltless, and of free disposition, is to take those things for birdbolts that you deem cannon bullets.*

Olivia in Act I, Scene v
of Shakespeare's *Twelfth Night*

*blunt-headed arrows for shooting birds

Healthy Versus Pathological Narcissism

In Shakespeare's comedy, it is clear to both Olivia and the audience that Malvolio's love of himself and his tendency to experience mild slights as devastating attacks are indications that he is "sick." In contemporary psychiatric practice, however, the distinction between healthy and pathological degrees of narcissism is fraught with difficulty. A certain measure of self-love is not only normal but also desirable. Yet the point on the continuum of self-regard where healthy narcissism turns into pathological narcissism is not easy to identify.

Another confounding factor is that certain behaviors may be pathologically narcissistic in one individual while simply a manifestation of healthy self-regard in another. Let us imagine, for example, a 15-year-old boy who stands in front of the mirror blow-drying his hair for 45 minutes in order to get every hair perfectly in place. Most of us would chuckle to ourselves at this image and realize that vanity of this sort is entirely normal for a pubescent youngster. Now let us shift to an image of a 30-year-old man who spends the same amount of time every morning in front of the mirror with a blow dryer. This visual picture is a bit more disconcerting, because such excessive self-absorption is far from the norm for a man of this age. If we now imagine a 45-year-old man engaged in the same activity, we again become a bit more charitable in our attitude because, as was the case with the adolescent boy, we understand such behavior as part of a developmental phase in the life cycle that we often refer to as midlife crisis. Before making a definitive determination about the relative health or pathology in this individual, however, we would want to know more about his other activities.

The above examples illustrate how narcissism is judged differently depending on the phase of the life cycle through which one is passing. Even though we are aware of these developmental distinctions, the term *narcissistic* is rarely used as a compliment to refer to someone with healthy self-esteem. On the contrary, the term is much more commonly used pejoratively as a synonym for "son of a bitch," especially when referring to colleagues and acquaintances whom we find unpleasant. Also, the term is often invoked to refer to someone whose success and confidence we envy. Since we all struggle with narcissistic issues, we must always be wary of the potential for hypocrisy in labeling others as narcissistic. Some (Lasch 1979) would argue that the history of humankind suggests that we have always been selfish and that nothing is gained by applying a psychiatric label to such qualities.

To complicate things further, we live in a narcissistic culture (Lasch 1979; Rinsley 1986). We are slavishly devoted to electronic media that thrive on superficial images and ignore substance and depth. We view consumption of material goods as the road to happiness. Our fear of aging and death keeps plastic surgeons in business. We are consumed with the glamour of celebrity. Books with titles like *Looking Out for Number 1* make the best-seller list. Competitive sports, the great American pastime, teach us that being number one is the most important goal of all.

One of the key diagnostic criteria for narcissistic personality disorder, interpersonal exploitiveness, is highly adaptive in our society. Indeed, the very fabric of our economic system is based on rewarding those who are able to talk others into buying a product (Maccoby 1976; Person 1986). In the corporate world, "making it" has become more important than values of commitment, loyalty, integrity, and interpersonal warmth. College athletic coaches can get away with outrageous treatment of their athletes as long as they continue to bring home conference titles. Winning forgives everything.

Given this cultural ambience, it is often problematic to determine which traits indicate a narcissistic personality disorder and which are simply adaptive cultural traits. Moreover, the difference between a healthy self-esteem and an artificially inflated self-esteem is often ambiguous. Let us visualize, for example, a mental health professional presenting a scientific paper to an audience of peers. The presenter notices that about half the audience are falling asleep during his presentation, while others are getting up and leaving. During the discussion period at the end of the presentation, the presenter is severely criticized for "muddy thinking," "insufficient familiarity with the literature," and "presenting nothing new." He responds to these criticisms by saying to himself, "No matter what they think, I know I'm competent anyway." How do we evaluate this response? Based on the information in this example, we could reach one of two conclusions: 1) this person has a healthy self-regard that does not collapse merely because of one untoward experience, or 2) the presenter's response is reflective of pathological narcissism in that it is a grandiose defensive reaction to compensate for a devastating injury to his self-esteem.

With such a bewildering array of varied usage, developmental differences, and cultural influences, what definitive criteria can be used to differentiate healthy from pathological narcissism? The time-honored criteria of psychological health—to love and to work—are only partly useful in answering this question. An individual's work history may provide little help in making the distinction. Highly disturbed narcissistic individuals may find extraordinary success in certain professions, such as big business, the arts, politics, the entertainment industry, athletics, and the televangelism field (Gabbard 1983; Rinsley 1985, 1989). In some cases, however, narcissistic pathology may be reflected in a superficial quality to one's professional interests (Kernberg 1970), as though achievement and acclaim are more important than mastery of the field itself.

Pathological forms of narcissism are more easily identified by the quality of the individual's relationships. One tragedy affecting these people is their inability to love. Healthy interpersonal relationships can be recognized by qualities such as empathy and concern for the feelings of others, a genuine interest in the ideas of others, the ability to tolerate ambivalence in long-term relationships without giving up, and a capacity to acknowledge one's own contribution to interpersonal conflicts. People whose relationships are characterized by these qualities may at times use others to gratify their own needs, but this tendency occurs in the broader context of sensitive interpersonal relatedness rather than as a pervasive style of dealing with other people. On the other hand, the person with a narcissistic personality disorder approaches people as objects to be used up and discarded according to his or her needs, without regard for their feelings. People are not viewed as having a separate existence or as having needs of their own. The individual with a narcissistic personality disorder frequently ends a relationship after a short time, usually when the other person begins to make demands stemming from his or her own needs. Most importantly, such relationships clearly do not "work" in terms of the narcissist's ability to maintain his or her own sense of self-esteem (Stolorow 1975).

Phenomenology of Narcissistic Personality Disorder

The psychodynamic literature on narcissistic personality disorder is somewhat confusing because the label seems to apply equally well to patients with quite different clinical pictures. DSM-IV (American Psychiatric Association 1994) lists nine criteria for the diagnosis of narcissistic personality disorder (Table 16–1).

These criteria identify a certain kind of narcissistic patient—specifically, the arrogant, boastful, "noisy" individual who demands to be in the spotlight. However, they fail to characterize the shy, quietly grandiose, narcissistic individual whose extreme sensitivity to slights leads to an assiduous avoidance of the spotlight (Cooper and Michels 1988).

DSM-III-R (American Psychiatric Association 1987) included a criterion, "reacts to criticism with feelings of rage, shame, or humiliation (even if not expressed)" (p. 250), that has since been deleted from the criteria in DSM-IV. Empirical studies designed to identify discriminating criteria of narcissistic personality disorder indicated that this criterion lacked specificity (Gunderson et al. 1991; Ronningstam and Gunderson 1990). Patients with borderline personality disorder and paranoid personality disorder showed similar sensitivity to criticism. On the other hand, the criterion of "arrogant, haughty behaviors or attitudes" has been shown to have considerable usefulness in differentiating narcissistic personality disorders from other Axis II diagnoses (Gunderson et al. 1991) and has been added to the DSM-IV criteria as a result.

The literature identifies something of a continuum of narcissistic personality disorder. Kernberg (1970, 1974a, 1974b) identified an envious, greedy type who demands the attention and acclaim of others, while Kohut (1971, 1977, 1984) described a narcissistically vulnerable type prone to self-fragmentation. Bursten (1973) divided narcissistic patients into four groups—the craving, the paranoid, the manipulative, and the phallic-narcissistic. The various types of narcissistic pa-

---

Table 16–1. DSM-IV criteria for narcissistic personality disorder

A pervasive pattern of grandiosity (in fantasy or behavior), need for admiration, and lack of empathy, beginning by early adulthood and present in a variety of contexts, as indicated by at least *five* of the following:

1. has a grandiose sense of self-importance (e.g., exaggerates achievements and talents, expects to be recognized as superior without commensurate achievements)

2. is preoccupied with fantasies of unlimited success, power, brilliance, beauty, or ideal love

3. believes that he or she is "special" and unique and can only be understood by, or should associate with, other special or high-status people (or institutions)

4. requires excessive admiration

5. has a sense of entitlement, i.e., has unreasonable expectations of especially favorable treatment or automatic compliance with his or her expectations

6. is interpersonally exploitative, i.e., takes advantage of others to achieve his or her own ends

7. lacks empathy: is unwilling to recognize or identify with the feelings and needs of others

8. is often envious of others or believes that others are envious of him or her

9. shows arrogant, haughty behaviors or attitudes

Source. DSM-IV. Because the criteria sets were not final at press time, the reader should consult DSM-IV for final criteria.

tients described by these authors may be conceptualized as falling between two poles on a continuum based on the typical style of interpersonal relatedness. From a descriptive standpoint, the two opposite extremes on this continuum may be labeled the *oblivious* narcissist and the *hypervigilant* narcissist (Gabbard 1989) (see Table 16–2). These terms specifically refer to the person's predominant style of interacting, both in transference relationships with a therapist and in social relationships in general.

Oblivious types appear to have no awareness whatsoever of their impact on others. They can often be observed in action at cocktail parties or in other social situations. They talk as though addressing a large audience, rarely establishing eye contact and generally looking over the heads of those around them. They talk "at" others, not "to" them. Persons of this type are oblivious to the fact that they are boring and that some people will therefore leave the conversation and seek companionship elsewhere. Their talk is replete with references to their own accomplishments, and they clearly need to be the center of attention. They are insensitive to the needs of others, even to the point that they do not allow others to contribute to the conversation. These people are often perceived as "having a sender but no receiver." The oblivious type of narcissistic personality disorder closely matches the clinical picture described in the DSM-IV criteria.

The narcissistic issues of the hypervigilant type, on the other hand, are manifested in starkly different ways. These people are exquisitely

Table 16–2. Two types of narcissistic personality disorder

The Oblivious Narcissist	The Hypervigilant Narcissist
1. Has no awareness of reactions of others	1. Is highly sensitive to reactions of others
2. Is arrogant and aggressive	2. Is inhibited, shy, or even self-effacing
3. Is self-absorbed	3. Directs attention more toward others than toward self
4. Needs to be the center of attention	4. Shuns being the center of attention
5. Has a "sender but no receiver"	5. Listens to others carefully for evidence of slights or criticisms
6. Is apparently impervious to having feelings hurt by others	6. Has easily hurt feelings; is prone to feeling ashamed or humiliated

sensitive to how others react to them. In fact, their attention is continually directed toward others, in contrast to the self-absorption of the oblivious narcissist. Like the paranoid patient, they listen to others carefully for evidence of any critical reaction, and they tend to feel slighted at every turn. One narcissistic patient was so attuned to his therapist's reactions that every time the therapist shifted position in his chair or cleared his throat, the patient viewed it as a sign of boredom. When this therapist removed a dead leaf from an office plant on his desk, the patient felt humiliated and demanded a new therapist. Patients of this type are shy and inhibited to the point of being self-effacing. They shun the limelight because they are convinced that they will be rejected and humiliated. At the core of their inner world is a deep sense of shame related to their secret wish to exhibit themselves in a grandiose manner.

Although both types struggle with maintaining their self-esteem, they deal with that issue in extremely different ways. Oblivious narcissists attempt to impress others with their accomplishments while insulating themselves from narcissistic injury by screening out the responses of others. Hypervigilant narcissists attempt to maintain their self-esteem by avoiding vulnerable situations and by intensely studying others to figure out how to behave. They projectively attribute their own disapproval of their grandiose fantasies onto others (Gabbard 1983). This typology is closely related to Rosenfeld's (1987) distinction between "thick-skinned" and "thin-skinned" narcissistic patients and to Broucek's (1982) categories of *egotistical* and *dissociative*. However, whereas the oblivious narcissist is virtually identical with the egotistical type, the hypervigilant patient does not project his or her grandiosity onto an idealized other, as is the case with Broucek's dissociative type, but instead retains it within and regards the other as a persecutor.

Despite the failure of the DSM-IV criteria to represent the hypervigilant variant of narcissistic personality disorder, there is empirical support for the oblivious-hypervigilant distinction. Wink (1991) performed a principal-components analysis of six Minnesota Multiphasic Personality Inventory (MMPI) narcissism scales and found two orthogonal factors: a Vulnerability-Sensitivity dimension and a Grandiosity-Exhibitionism aspect. He concluded that these two relatively uncorrelated sets, which he referred to as *covert* and *overt* narcissism, confirmed the existence of two distinct forms of pathological narcissism. Although both forms shared in common the features of disregard for others, self-indulgence, and conceit, the Vulnerability-Sensitivity group was characterized as introverted, defensive, anxious, and vulnerable to life's traumas, while the Grandiosity-Exhibitionism group was extraverted, self-assured, exhibitionistic, and aggressive.

Further empirical support for the two subtypes of narcissistic personality disorder has come from a study of 701 college students (Hibbard 1992). The subjects filled out questionnaires containing eight scales measuring narcissism, object relations, masochism, and shame. Narcissism formed two distinct subgroups, a narcissistically vulnerable style and a "phallic," grandiose style. The affect of shame was central in dividing these groups—it correlated positively with the vulnerable style and negatively with the grandiose style.

Although these two types may occur in pure form, many patients present with a mixture of phenomenological features from both types. Between these two endpoints on the continuum will be many narcissistic individuals who are much smoother socially and who possess a great deal of interpersonal charm.

Psychodynamic Understanding

For the past two decades, the principal controversy surrounding the theoretical understanding of narcissistic personality disorder has revolved around the models of Kohut and Kernberg (Adler 1986; Glassman 1988; Kernberg 1974a, 1974b; Ornstein 1974a). Because the self psychology theory of Kohut was covered in some detail in Chapter 2, it will be only schematically reviewed here.

Kohut (1971, 1977, 1984) believed that narcissistically disturbed individuals are developmentally arrested at a stage where they require specific responses from persons in their environment to maintain a cohesive self. When such responses are not forthcoming, these individuals are prone to fragmentations of the self. Kohut understood this state of affairs as the result of the parents' empathic failures. Specifically, the parents did not respond to the child's phase-appropriate displays of exhibitionism with validation and admiration, did not offer twinship experiences, and did not provide the child with models worthy of idealization. These failures manifest themselves in the patient's tendency to form a mirror, twinship, or idealizing transference.

Kohut postulated a double-axis theory (see Figure 2–5 in Chapter 2) to explain how both narcissistic needs and object-related needs can coexist in the same individual. Throughout our lives, Kohut argued, we are in need of selfobject responses from the people around us. In other words, at some level we all regard others not as separate persons but as sources of gratification for the self. A need for the soothing, validating functions of selfobjects is never outgrown. The goal of treatment is to move away from a need for archaic selfobjects toward an ability to use more mature and appropriate selfobjects.

A case example may help illustrate how the theory of self psychology manifests itself in a clinical situation.

> Ms. II was a 26-year-old, single woman who came to treatment after her 4-year relationship with her boyfriend ended. She indicated that his rejection of her had been "devastating." While she specifically denied any suicidal thoughts, she did say that she felt she was no longer alive without him. Although it had been a year since the breakup, she was unable to get her life back on track. She sat around feeling empty and lonely. She continued to go to work, but then would return home each evening and just sit in her apartment staring blankly or watching television. Throughout her day at work she felt detached from any activities she pursued, as if she was on "automatic pilot." She repeatedly spoke of needing to be "plugged in" to her boyfriend to feel alive. She desperately missed having him stroke her hair to calm her down when she came home anxious from work. She poignantly stated: "Without him, I am nothing. I can't soothe myself." She lacked the symptoms necessary for a diagnosis of Axis I major depressive episode, but she described herself as depressed and empty.
>
> She met with her therapist for several weeks and reported that she began to "feel alive again." Ms. II then stated that she felt "plugged in" to her therapist. She tended to misinterpret her therapist's comments to mean that he was about to reject her at any moment. She asked if her therapist would increase the number of sessions from two to five a week so she could see him every weekday. The therapist, on the other hand, believed that all he was doing was listening. He noted to his supervisor: "I don't think she is really interested in anything I say. She's perfectly content if I simply give her my undivided attention."

Kernberg's theoretical formulations (1970, 1974a, 1974b, 1984) differ sharply from those of Kohut (Table 16–3). The major theoretical differences in their conceptualizations of narcissistic personality disorder may well relate to the different populations of patients that they studied. Kohut's sample consisted of relatively well-functioning outpatients who could afford psychoanalysis. Typically, they were professional people who described vague feelings of emptiness and depression and particular problems in their relationships. They struggled to maintain their professional self-esteem, and they tended to feel slighted by others (Kohut 1971). Kernberg, on the other hand, has always worked in hospitals, and he based his conceptual framework on a mixture of inpatients and outpatients. His clinical descriptions portray patients who are more primitive, more arrogant, more aggressive

Table 16–3. Dynamic understanding of narcissistic personality disorder

Kohut	Kernberg
1. Based theory on relatively well-functioning people whose self-esteem is vulnerable to slights—all outpatients	1. Based theory on a mixture of inpatients and outpatients, most of whom are primitive, aggressive, and arrogant, with haughty grandiosity coexisting with shyness
2. Differentiates narcissistic personality from borderline states	2. Defines narcissistic personality as a strikingly similar subcategory of borderline personality (While most have better ego functioning than borderline patients, some function at an overt borderline level)
3. Does not define inner world of narcissistic personality because emphasis is on internalization of missing functions	3. Delineates primitive defenses and object relations typical of borderline personality disorder
4. Defines archaic "normal" self as one that is developmentally arrested	4. Defines self as a highly pathological structure composed of the fusion of the ideal self, the ideal object, and the real self
5. Views self as nondefensive	5. Views grandiose self as being *defensive* against investment or dependency on others
6. Focuses mainly on libidinal/ idealizing aspects with aggression conceptualized as *secondary* to narcissistic injury	6. Emphasizes envy and aggression
7. Accepts idealization at face value as a normal developmental phase making up for missing psychic structure	7. Views idealization as defensive against rage, envy, contempt, and devaluation

(often with antisocial features), and more overtly grandiose (although the grandiosity may alternate with shyness) than those depicted by Kohut.

Kohut (1971) differentiated narcissistic personality disorders from borderline conditions. He saw the borderline patient as not having achieved sufficient cohesiveness of the self to be analyzed. His diagnosis of narcissistic personality was based on the development of either the mirror or the idealizing transference in the context of a trial analysis. In contrast, Kernberg (1970) saw the defensive organization of narcissistic personality as strikingly similar to borderline personality disorder. In fact, he viewed it as one of several personality types that operate at a borderline level of personality organization (see Chapter 15). He differentiated narcissistic personality disorder from borderline personality on the basis of the narcissist's integrated but pathological grandiose self. This structure is a fusion of the ideal self, the ideal object, and the real self. This fusion results in the destructive devaluation of object-images. Patients with narcissistic personality disorder identify themselves with their idealized self-images in order to deny their dependency on external objects (other people) as well as on the inner images of those objects. At the same time, they deny the unacceptable features of their own self-images by projecting them onto others.

The pathological grandiose self explains the paradox of relatively good ego-functioning in the presence of the primitive defenses (splitting, projective identification, omnipotence, devaluation, idealization, and denial) typical of the borderline patient. In other words, whereas borderline patients tend to have alternating self-representations that make them look very different from day to day, narcissistic patients have a smoother, more consistent level of functioning based on an integrated pathological self. Also, the borderline personality is much more likely to have problems related to ego weaknesses, such as poor impulse control and poor anxiety tolerance. These ego weaknesses are much less common in narcissistic personalities because of the smooth-functioning self-structure. However, Kernberg also added that some narcissistic patients function at an overt borderline level. These patients have the grandiosity and haughtiness of the narcissistic personality with the poor impulse control and the kaleidoscopic object relations of borderline patients. It is this subgroup that occasionally requires hospitalization. (Hospital treatment for these patients is similar to that for borderline patients discussed in Chapter 15. Inpatient treatment of narcissistic patients with serious antisocial features is described in Chapter 17.)

The detailed description of the narcissistic patient's defensive constellation and internal object relations provided by Kernberg is in contrast with Kohut's tendency to leave undefined the inner world of the narcissistic patient. Kohut emphasized the internalization of missing functions from people in the environment and thus was less concerned about the patient's intrapsychic structure. He conceptualized the narcissistic self, however, as an archaic "normal" self that is simply frozen developmentally—in other words, the patient is a child in an adult's body. Unlike Kohut, Kernberg (1974a, 1974b) viewed the narcissistic self as a highly pathological structure that in no way resembles the normal developing self of children. He pointed out that the exhibitionistic self-display of children is charming and endearing, in contrast to the greed and demandingness of the narcissist's pathological self.

Another difference in their views of the self relates to the self's defensive functioning. Kohut saw the self as essentially nondefensive (i.e., a normally developing self that simply became stuck). Kernberg saw the pathologically grandiose self as defensive against investment in others, and specifically against dependency on others. This characteristic may manifest itself as a pseudo-self-sufficiency whereby the patient denies any need for nurturance while at the same time attempting to impress others and gain approval. Narcissistic patients frequently insist, for example, that they have no reactions to their therapists' vacations.

Kohut's view of the narcissistic personality is perhaps more charitable than Kernberg's. He focused mainly on the childhood longing for certain parental responses. Aggression is seen as a *secondary* phenomenon (i.e., narcissistic rage in reaction to not having one's needs for mirroring and idealizing gratified). In that sense, Kohut viewed aggression as an entirely understandable response to parental failures. Kernberg saw aggression as a more primary factor. Inordinately high levels of aggression cause the narcissistic patient to be destructive toward others. In Kernberg's (1970) view, the etiology of this aggression can be either constitutional or environmental. It was seen, however, as arising from within rather than as simply an understandable reaction to the external failures of others. One manifestation of the narcissistic patient's aggression is chronic intense envy (Kernberg 1974b), which causes the patient to want to spoil and destroy the good things of others. Although Kohut did not view envy as having a central role, Kernberg described these patients as constantly comparing themselves to others, only to find themselves tormented with feelings of inferiority and intense yearning to possess what others have.

Idealization was viewed quite differently by Kohut and Kernberg. Kohut viewed idealization in the transference as the recapitulation of a normal developmental phase. Rather than labeling it as a defensive posture, he saw it as a way to make up for missing psychic structure. Fundamental to Kohut's understanding is the notion that the narcissistic individual is incomplete without a selfobject. Kernberg viewed idealization as a defense against a variety of negative feelings, including rage, envy, contempt, and devaluation.

In light of these point-by-point differences between Kohut and Kernberg, it should be clear that Kernberg was describing patients who more closely approximate the oblivious type, while Kohut seemed to be writing about patients who are closer to the hypervigilant type. The narcissistic patients described by Kernberg frequently appear to have nothing but the most superficial forms of object relatedness. If the patient is male, he may have a "Don Juan" syndrome in which he systematically seduces women and discards them when his idealization of them turns to devaluation. Viewing women only as conquests, he has no capacity to empathize with their internal experience. Such a patient seems to have little interest in what others say unless the content is flattering. Although these patients are most commonly male, females may suffer from similar narcissistic pathology.

> Ms. JJ came to psychotherapy because of a vague sense of unhappiness and an inability to find satisfaction in any of her relationships. She was 28 years old, attractive and intelligent, but had never found a man who had particularly interested her. She described "numbness" and boredom in relationships. She said that when other people were talking to her, she simply waited impatiently for them to finish so that she could have the floor. Several months prior to her beginning therapy, Ms. JJ had been sexually assaulted in a parking lot by a man who forced her to perform fellatio on him. Attempting to empathize with the patient, the therapist said, "It must have been an awful experience for you." Ms. JJ responded, "No, I actually kind of enjoyed it. For once I actually felt something. I wasn't numb. I felt anger, humiliation, rage—and I actually cried!"

Ms. JJ had so numbed herself to experience that only an incident as shocking as the sexual assault could make her feel alive and related to others. The numbed state in which Ms. JJ lived her life is a reminder that the term *narcissism* is etymologically related to the Greek word *nark,* which means numbness. Indeed, part of the tragedy of this disorder is that these people seem to have never awakened to the possibilities of life.

The Kohut-Kernberg controversy continues to smolder, with proponents on each side claiming that clinical experience validates their own favorite theoretical perspective. In practice, some narcissistic patients seem to fit one framework better than the other. The broad range of patients encompassed by the term *narcissistic personality disorder* may demand more than one theoretical perspective for explanation. One research effort to validate the two constructs found data consistent with both theories but suggested that the most parsimonious explanation was to view Kohut's model as a special case of Kernberg's more general ego psychological–object relations theory (Glassman 1988).

The theoretical debate between Kohut and Kernberg often obscures other creative contributions to the understanding of narcissistic personality disorder. In a series of papers, Rinsley (1980, 1984, 1985, 1989) linked the origin of narcissistic personality disorder to Mahler's (1975) developmental framework. He postulated that whereas the borderline patient suffers from a developmental arrest of both separation and individuation subprocesses that reaches a peak during the rapprochement subphase (see Chapters 2 and 15), the narcissistic patient can be characterized as having a developmental *dissociation* of the two subprocesses—individuation was allowed to proceed while separation was arrested. This developmental scenario results in a "pseudo-mature" child who gets the message that he is allowed to separate psychologically from his mother only on the condition that all of his subsequent achievements are ultimately in relation to her. Rinsley's explanation resonates with Kernberg's observation that in certain areas the narcissistic patient may function smoothly and may even be able to achieve impressive gains at work, while still suffering from highly problematic object relations.

Rothstein (1984) attempted to understand the narcissistic personality disorder within the framework of the structural model (see Chapter 2). He defined narcissism as "a felt quality of perfection" that is a universal aspect of the human psyche. This perfect state can be integrated with either a healthy or a pathological ego—the nature of the ego determines whether the narcissism is pathological or healthy.

Modell (1976) used the metaphor of a cocoon to describe the narcissistic individual's sense of nonrelatedness to the environment. This cocoon is like an illusion of omnipotent self-sufficiency, reinforced by grandiose fantasies, which may be initiated by a mother who has an exaggerated grandiose view of her child's capabilities. Modell believed that the noncommunicative and nonrelated facade reflects a fear of merger that the patient must defend against. The therapist's task must be to create a holding environment (Winnicott 1965) to allow development to proceed, much as in the treatment of schizoid personality disorders (described in Chapter 14).

Individual Psychotherapy and Psychoanalysis

Both Kernberg and Kohut believed that psychoanalysis is the treatment of choice for most patients with narcissistic personality disorder. Because of practical limitations of time and money, many of these patients are also seen in expressive-supportive psychotherapy with a predominance of expressive techniques in once- or twice-weekly sessions. The specific technical suggestions of Kohut and Kernberg reflect their different theoretical conceptualizations.

For Kohut, empathy was the cornerstone of the technique (Ornstein 1974b). Treaters must empathize with the patient's attempt to reactivate a failed parental relationship by coercing the therapist into meeting the patient's need for affirmation (the mirror transference), for idealization (the idealizing transference), or for being like the therapist (the twinship transference). The emergence of these selfobject transferences should not be prematurely interpreted. Kohut's emphasis on empathizing with the patient as a victim of the empathic failures of others does not imply a predominantly supportive technique. He has stressed that the analyst or therapist should interpret—rather than actively gratify—the patient's yearning to be soothed (Kohut 1984). A typical intervention might sound like this: "It hurts when you are not treated the way you feel you deserve to be treated."

Despite Kohut's insistence that his technical approach did not depart radically from classical psychoanalytic technique, his suggestions as described by supervisees (Miller 1985) revealed fundamental differences from that technique. He advised analysts to always take analytic material in a "straight" manner, just as the patient experiences it. The therapist can thus avoid repeating the empathic failures of the parents, who often try to convince a child that his or her actual feelings are *different* from those the child describes. Kohut indicated that, if the face-value approach does not bear fruit, one could always invert material or look for hidden meanings beneath the "experience-near" feelings. This approach is intimately related to Kohut's view of "resistance" as a psychic activity that safeguards the cohesiveness of the self (see Chapter 2).

Kohut was acutely sensitive to evidence of a patient's self-fragmentation in the actual analytic or therapeutic session. When such fragmentations occur, the therapist must focus on the precipitating event rather than on the content of the fragmentation itself (Miller 1985; Ornstein 1974a). For example, after one of Kohut's supervisees sneezed in an analytic session and the patient found it difficult to continue, Kohut advised the analyst to focus on the naturalness of the patient's response to such an unexpected stimulus rather than on the patient's special sensitivity to the stimulus (Miller 1985). This focus is in keeping with a general premise of self psychology that therapists must be continually attuned to how they recapitulate infantile traumas with their patients. Kohut believed that the patient is always right; if the patient feels deflated or hurt, it is reasonable to assume that the analyst or therapist has made an error. He noted that patients frequently feel exposed and ashamed when the analyst calls attention to slips of the tongue, so he did not stress the interpretation of parapraxes. Kohut was always sensitive to the proneness of narcissistic patients to feel shame. The therapist must avoid bypassing the patient's conscious subjective experience to address unconscious material outside the patient's awareness. Interpretations of unconscious motives will only make the patient feel "caught," misunderstood, and ashamed.

Kohut stressed the importance of looking at the *positive* side of the patient's experience, and he scrupulously avoided comments that might be viewed as harshly critical. He called attention to the patient's progress and shunned the asking of questions. He believed that it was the therapist's job to understand, not the patient's (Miller 1985).

Kohut asserted that the goal of psychoanalytic and psychotherapeutic treatment of narcissistic personality disorder is to help the patient identify and seek out appropriate selfobjects. Kohut believed that mental health professionals tend to overvalue separation and autonomy. He was concerned that therapists might use a moralistic tone to convey to patients the expectation that they *should* become more independent.

Kohut's technical approach has been criticized on many counts. His refusal to integrate self psychology with more classical approaches has led to charges of isolationism (Wallerstein 1985). Similarly, his tendency to separate the development of the self from classical structural theory and from the vicissitudes of object relations has been criticized as artificial and needlessly polarizing (Kernberg 1974a, 1974b; Meissner 1986; Rangell 1982). Kohut's reduction of all psychopathology to empathic failures on the part of parents has been criticized as oversimplified "parent blaming" and as being out of keeping with the core psychoanalytic principle of overdetermination (Curtis 1985; Stein 1979). His emphasis on staying "experience near" in the therapeutic technique has also been challenged as having the potential to overlook important unconscious issues that should be addressed during treatment (Curtis 1985).

Kernberg (1974a, 1974b) observed some of the same transference phenomena as Kohut, but he believed that different technical approaches are indicated. For example, he conceptualized the mirror and idealizing transferences in a more parsimonious manner (see Table 16–4). Kernberg saw the patient's grandiose self as being alternately projected and reintrojected so that one idealized figure is always in the room while the other figure is devalued and in the shadow of the idealized person. He also viewed idealization as a frequent defensive operation that involves splitting. In other words, because idealization of the therapist may be the patient's way of defending against split-off feelings of contempt, envy, and rage, the therapist should interpret idealization as a defense rather than simply accepting it as a normal developmental need, as Kohut advocated.

Kernberg's approach in general is much more confrontational than Kohut's. Convinced that the greed and demandingness typical of the narcissistic personality disorder are not simply aspects of normal development, Kernberg believed that these traits must be confronted and examined from the standpoint of their impact on others. Whereas Kohut emphasized the positive side of the patient's experience, Kernberg believed that early, negative transference developments must be systematically examined and interpreted. Specifically, Kernberg stressed that the therapist must focus on envy and how it prevents the patient from receiving or acknowledging help. When patients receive something positive from their therapist, it often escalates their envy because it generates feelings of inadequacy or inferiority in response to the therapist's capacity for nurturing and understanding. A sample interpretation might sound like this: "To avoid painful feelings of envy, you may need to dismiss my comments as being ridiculous or meaningless."

Although Kernberg is often misconstrued as focusing exclusively on negative transference, he in fact advocated a systematic examination of both positive and negative transference developments (Kernberg 1974b). He warned that therapists who address only the positive aspects of the transference may unconsciously increase their patients' fear of their own envy or rage. A patient who believes that the therapist

Table 16–4.   Psychotherapeutic technique—Kohut versus Kernberg

Kohut	Kernberg
1. Views mirror and idealizing transferences as two different poles of bipolar (Kohut 1977) or tripolar (Kohut 1984) self	1. Views mirror and idealizing as aspects of transference related to projection and reintrojection of patient's grandiose self
2. Accepts idealization of patient as normal developmental need	2. Interprets idealization as a defense
3. Empathizes with patient's feeling as an understandable reaction to failures of parents and others	3. Helps patient see his or her own contribution to problems in relationships
4. Accepts patient's comments at face value, viewing resistances as healthy psychic activities that safeguard the self	4. Confronts and interprets resistances as defensive maneuvers
5. Looks at the positive side of patient's experience	5. Examines both positive and negative aspects of patient's experience (if only positive experiences are emphasized, the patient may develop an increased fear of internal envy and rage)
6. Calls attention to patient's progress	6. Focuses on envy and how it prevents patient from acknowledging and receiving help
7. Has treatment goal of helping patient acquire ability to identify and seek out appropriate selfobjects	7. Has treatment goal of helping patient to develop guilt and concern, and to integrate idealization and trust with rage and contempt

cannot handle those aspects of the patient may therefore split them off and keep them outside the therapeutic process.

Kernberg also differs significantly from Kohut in important ways regarding the goals of treatment. Whereas Kohut's technique implies that the essence of the cure is not in the cognitive sphere, Kernberg believed that a cognitive understanding via the interpretive process is crucial to therapeutic success. The goal of treatment for Kernberg (1970) included developing guilt and concern for others, as well as integrating idealization and trust with rage and contempt (i.e., integrating the "good" aspects of experience with the "bad").

Kernberg viewed persons with narcissistic personality disorder as among the most difficult patients to treat because much of their effort goes into trying to defeat the therapist. For the treatment and the therapist to be effective, these patients must deal with their intense feelings of envy that someone else has good qualities that they lack. The patient defensively uses devaluation and omnipotent control to keep the therapist at a distance. Kernberg believed that for the treatment to be viable, these defensive maneuvers must be continually confronted. A patient with significant antisocial features (which are common in narcissistic patients) may simply be untreatable. (The factors that determine the treatability of antisocial patients are discussed in Chapter 17 in some detail.) However, several factors suggest a favorable prognosis (Kernberg 1970): some ability to tolerate depression and mourning, more guilt than paranoid tendencies in the transference, some ability to sublimate primitive drives, relatively good impulse control, and good motivation. Patients who seek therapy or analysis simply for training purposes or because they think it will confer prestige on them in the eyes of others may present a formidable resistance that contributes to a less favorable prognosis.

In the subgroup of patients just mentioned who operate at an overtly borderline level, Kernberg (1984) suggested that a truly supportive psychotherapy is a much more effective treatment than expressive therapy or analysis. This approach should probably be combined with inpatient treatment if the ego weaknesses, such as lack of impulse control, are particularly severe. The indications for supportive therapy in narcissistic personality disorders include excessive cruelty and sadism, prominent antisocial features, virtually no involvement with other people, intense paranoid reactions to others, and a proneness to chronic rage that is always rationalized as someone else's fault. In these supportive processes, Kernberg (1984) suggested that patients may benefit from "stealing" positive qualities from their therapist. Because this identification with the therapist may help patients function better, the process is best left uninterpreted.

Critics of Kernberg's approach argue that it interferes with the natural development of selfobject transferences. Some have even suggested that aggressively confronting the oral aggression of patients may result in their deteriorated functioning (Brandschaft and Stolorow 1984). In this view, the borderline picture of rage, contempt, and devaluation is an artifact of the narcissistic injury induced by the therapist's "critical interventions." Thus the differences in the kinds of patients described by Kernberg and Kohut could be viewed as partially resulting from iatrogenic factors (Adler 1986).

Psychotherapists faced with the formidable task of treating narcissistic patients must avoid an "either/or" approach to the theories of Kernberg and Kohut. Rather than obsessing about which one is "right," therapists may more usefully apply themselves to listening carefully to their patients, observing the transference and countertransference developments, and particularly noting their responses to trial interventions. In this manner therapists will soon reach a tentative conclusion about which theoretical and technical model is the most helpful with the particular patient under consideration. Some patients will simply not tolerate anything but an empathic, experience-near approach based on Kohut's model. Any deviation from that pattern of interventions will be met with prolonged "shutdowns," with the patient refusing to talk and feeling misunderstood, or even abruptly deciding to quit therapy.

In other cases, the patient may feel understood by interpretations of envy and contempt and may therefore respond better to Kernberg's technique. Some narcissistic patients do not develop any of the selfobject transferences Kohut described, but instead present the therapist with continual devaluation and rage. In some instances, the therapist must interpret and confront these overt verbal attacks or the patient will find it difficult or impossible to persist in the treatment. Mitchell (1988) pointed out that it is erroneous to regard Kohut's approach as more empathic than Kernberg's. Both respond empathically to different dimensions of the patient.

Still other patients can benefit from a combination of technical strategies. Although purists would argue that the two theories are incompatible, the patient is not aware of theories. Moreover, the therapist treats patients, not theories. Many patients require the self psychological approach to technique early in their treatment because it helps build a therapeutic alliance based on a sense that the therapist understands and empathizes with the experience of victimization. After an alliance is established, the therapist may begin to confront patients with their own contributions to their interpersonal difficulties, such as inordinate expectations that others cannot fulfill. Practically speaking, narcissistic pathology can rarely be conceptualized as wholly the fault of either the parents or the patient. More commonly, both parties have contributed to the difficulty, and a comprehensive therapy should address these problems from both angles. Indeed, the majority of analysts and other dynamically oriented clinicians operate from some midpoint between the two extremes (Mitchell 1988).

Finally, we must not assume that the etiology and pathogenesis of narcissistic character pathology will always fit neatly into the theoretical frameworks of Kohut and Kernberg. In sharp contrast to the parent with empathic failures, some parents of narcissistic patients tend to be overly indulgent. They seem to encourage grandiosity through a pattern of excessive mirroring. Such parents shower their children with admiration and approval, making them feel truly special and gifted. When these children grow up, they are repeatedly shattered because others do not respond to them as their parents did. In other cases, mother-son incest or variants thereof may produce a narcissistic picture of the hypervigilant type (Gabbard and Twemlow 1994). These patients have a grandiose view of themselves as entitled to occupy a special position with others, combined with a paranoid tendency to anticipate retaliation or abandonment for perceived oedipal transgressions. Hence, therapists can benefit from taking a heuristic approach (see Chapter 4) with narcissistic patients; the therapy should be a collaborative effort in which patient and therapist together discover the origins of the patient's difficulties without rigidly forcing the material to fit one theory or another.

Countertransference

Regardless of a therapist's theoretical framework, certain predictable countertransference problems arise in the treatment of narcissistic patients. Some of these problems are of sufficient magnitude and intensity to undermine the treatment situation irrevocably. Hence the optimal management of countertransference patterns cannot be stressed enough.

There is little question that psychotherapy as a career provides an opportunity to gratify wishes to be loved, needed, and idealized (Finell 1985). The therapist in the throes of an idealizing transference from a narcissistic patient may enjoy basking in the glow of warmth and love to such an extent as to collude with the patient's wish to exclude hatred and anger from the therapy. A frequent development in the treatment of narcissistic patients is that they will initially idealize their current therapist while devaluing all previous treaters. Instead of viewing this process as a defensive maneuver, therapists who long for idealization may simply accept at face value the notion that they have unique gifts that were lacking in their patients' previous therapists.

Narcissistic issues are not the exclusive province of the narcissistic personality disorder. These issues reside in all patients and in all therapists. Therapists who cannot acknowledge and accept their own narcissistic needs, and then harness them in the service of delivering effective treatment, may instead disavow and externalize them. These defenses contribute to an erroneous view of the patient as the sole carrier of narcissism in the patient-therapist dyad.

Another countertransference problem that regularly surfaces in the treatment of narcissistic patients is boredom. This usually arises from a feeling that the patient is unaware of or oblivious to the therapist's presence. For prolonged periods, the therapist may have to tolerate a sense of being used as a sounding board by the patient. This pattern is particularly typical of the oblivious narcissistic patient who holds forth as though speaking to an audience, ignoring the therapist as a separate person with separate thoughts and feelings.

Mr. KK came to therapy after three previously failed attempts. His last treatment had lasted 3 years with a therapist in another city. Mr. KK denigrated that therapeutic experience as "a complete waste of time" and could not even recall his previous therapist's name. (These two signs, an inability to remember a previous therapist's name and a complete devaluation of the previous therapeutic experience, are often diagnostic clues to narcissistic character pathology.) He said that "doctor what's his name" interrupted him a lot and was not a good listener. Mr. KK talked at great length about his need for a really "special" therapist. He even speculated that there might not be anyone in the city who could really understand him.

As Mr. KK continued to ramble on at some length over many weeks, his therapist began to dread each session. The therapist found his thoughts wandering to his plans for the evening, his financial status, unfinished paperwork, and a variety of other matters with little bearing on Mr. KK and his problems. The therapist also found himself glancing at the clock more often than usual, eagerly awaiting the end of Mr. KK's session. When the therapist intervened, Mr. KK would often ignore his comments and say, "Just let me finish this train of thought first," or, "Oh, yes, I'm already aware of that."

After returning from a 3-week vacation, the therapist resumed his sessions with Mr. KK. In the first session, the patient picked right up where he had left off at the end of their last session, as though no time had elapsed. The therapist, exasperated by his sense that he had no importance whatsoever to Mr. KK, said, "You act as though we saw each other yesterday. Didn't the 3-week separation from me have any impact on you?" Mr. KK detected a critical, sarcastic tone in the therapist's voice and replied, "You have the same problem as my last therapist. You're always inserting yourself into this. I'm not paying you to talk about you or your feelings. I'm here to talk about myself."

All of us have a need to be needed, and it is therefore difficult for therapists to tolerate the "satellite existence" (Kernberg 1970) that many narcissistic patients assign them. This feeling of being excluded by the patient may represent a projective identification process (Adler 1986; Finell 1985) in which the patient excludes the therapist just as he was once excluded by his own parents. In other words, an aspect of the patient is projected onto the therapist, who identifies with that self before helping the patient to reintroject it. The containment of this projected aspect of the patient may be a major part of the psychotherapeutic treatment in narcissistic patients. Understanding this pattern may keep the therapist from withdrawing from the patient, from sadistically confronting the patient, or from feeling hurt and abused by the patient.

The hypervigilant variety of narcissistic personality leads the therapist to struggle with countertransference problems of feeling controlled. When the patient reads every movement as an indication of boredom or rejection, the therapist may feel coerced into sitting still and into focusing attention on the patient every moment. Interventions designed to address this interaction may deal productively with this countertransference development. A therapist working from Kernberg's perspective might say: "You seem to have an unrealistic expectation that you can control others and make them behave as extensions of yourself rather than allowing them to respond from within according to their own needs." A self psychological intervention might consist of

"It seems to hurt your feelings when I clear my throat or fidget in my seat because you feel I am not giving you my full attention." Regardless of the pros and cons of these two sample interventions, the main point is that such comments bring a behavioral interaction associated with a countertransference response into the verbal realm, where it can be discussed openly as an issue between therapist and patient.

Finally, the therapist will often have to struggle with countertransference feelings in response to intense devaluation by the patient.

> Ms. LL was a narcissistic patient functioning at an overtly borderline level who had been hospitalized for drug abuse. She demanded barbiturates for insomnia and became enraged when her hospital doctor refused to prescribe them. Each time the doctor made daily rounds, Ms. LL would recite her doctor's many shortcomings: "You're only a resident, so you don't understand how to relate to patients. When you try to go into practice after your residency, you won't have any patients because you don't know how to relate to people. Instead of listening to my needs, you practice psychiatry out of a book. You don't even know how to dress. You're a complete joke as a physician." The doctor asked, "Why is it that you feel such hatred for me?" Ms. LL responded, "Hatred? You're not worth hating! You're beneath contempt!"

These verbal barrages are all too common with narcissistic patients. When they go on at some length, the doctor feels useless and impotent, as well as hurt and angry. These patients engender strong countertransference hatred that can lead to vengeful comments or ill-advised management decisions as a way to get back at the patient. Although as therapists we can contain a certain amount of abuse, we all have a limit that only we can determine. When that line is crossed, the therapist may need to confront the patient's contempt forcefully by pointing out how the barrage is destroying the patient's chance of getting effective treatment.

Group Psychotherapy

Dynamic group psychotherapy with narcissistic personality disorders is fraught with difficulties if it is the only treatment used (Azima 1983; Horner 1975; Wong 1979, 1980; Yalom 1985). Oblivious narcissistic patients may enjoy the idea of having an audience in group psychotherapy, but they may also resent the fact that other people take some of the therapist's time and attention. One such patient quit group therapy because he never got enough "air time." The hypervigilant narcissistic patient may be injured at even the suggestion of group therapy. The referral itself is experienced as a rejection or as an indication that the therapist is not interested in the patient. Most narcissistic patients will see group psychotherapy as a situation in which their specialness and uniqueness will be overlooked. When narcissistic patients do enter group therapy, they often monopolize the group discussions or take on the role of "doctor's assistant," making observations about other people's problems but denying their own (Wong 1979).

Despite the problems inherent in group settings for narcissistic patients, there are clearly some advantages. In groups, narcissistic patients must confront and accept the fact that others have needs and that they themselves cannot expect to be the center of attention at all times. Moreover, narcissistic patients may also benefit from the feedback that others provide about the impact of their character traits on others. Narcissistic patients can have therapeutic effects on others in the group by activating latent feelings of envy and greed in patients with other forms of characterological disturbance (Azima 1983).

Some authors have suggested that combined individual and group psychotherapy may benefit narcissistic patients more than either approach alone (Horwitz 1977; Wong 1979, 1980). Few groups can absorb the narcissistic patient's intense demands for attention, but if an individual process is begun first, the patient may make fewer demands on the group. Wong (1979, 1980) specifically recommended a rather long preparatory period of individual therapy with a technical approach along the lines described by Kohut so that a solid therapeutic alliance exists by the time the patient enters the group. This preparatory period also gives the patient time to explore personal fantasies about group psychotherapy. Wong recommended using the same therapist for both individual and group psychotherapy. Even with the combination, however, the therapist must actively support the patient if the other group members begin to scapegoat the narcissistic member. The group therapist can help the other patients empathize with the narcissistic patient's need to be recognized and admired.

As discussed in Chapter 5, group psychotherapy can serve to dilute intense negative transferences. This principle is certainly applicable to narcissistic patients, and the other patients in the group are often helpful in pointing out the distortions involved in devaluing or idealizing the therapist. Similarly, the countertransference reactions that are so problematic in the treatment of narcissistic patients can also be diluted in group therapy (Wong 1979). However, it is advisable to have only one narcissistic patient at a time in a heterogeneous group, lest the impact of these patients' demandingness overwhelm the other members.

Narcissistic Personality Disorder Over the Course of the Life Cycle

Narcissistic patients who come to treatment as young adults often complain about the quality of their intimate relationships. They may have had repeated infatuations that are short-lived and unsatisfying. After the initial luster of the relationship wears off, idealization of the partner turns either to devaluation or to boredom, and they withdraw and seek new partners who can fulfill their needs for admiration, affirmation, unconditional love, and perfect attunement. This pattern of sucking people dry and discarding the empty shells may eventually become tiresome. These patients frequently settle down and marry in their 30s or 40s.

Not surprisingly, characteristic patterns of difficulty occur in the marriages of patients with narcissistic personality disorder. They may first seek marital therapy under the guise of sexual problems, depression, or impulsive behavior (Lansky 1982). Beneath the disguised presentation is often a dread of being shamed or humiliated by the marital partner (i.e., a fear of self-fragmentation, in self psychological terms). A narcissistic husband, for example, may blame his wife for deliberately trying to humiliate him rather than acknowledging that he has a problem with being excessively vulnerable, dependent, and extraordinarily needy of selfobject responses, such as mirroring, from his wife. This same husband may eventually reach a state of chronic narcissistic rage, in which he maintains an intractable resentment and bitterness toward his wife for not treating him in the manner to which he feels entitled. Such marriages may be highly refractory to marital therapy because the narcissistic spouse perceives the injury as so damaging that forgiveness is out of the question and nothing the offending spouse can do could possibly redress the grievances.

Regardless of whether narcissistic patients choose to marry as they travel through life, they are likely to find the aging process highly distressing. In many cases these patients are physically attractive or interpersonally charming and have achieved a certain degree of success during their young adult years. However, although they can postpone facing the emptiness at their core, they cannot ultimately escape it. Kernberg (1974b) noted:

> If we consider that throughout an ordinary life span most narcissistic gratifications occur in adolescence and early adulthood, and that even though the narcissistic triumphs and gratifications are achieved throughout adulthood, the individual must eventually face the basic conflicts around aging, chronic illness, physical and mental limitations, and above all, separations, loss, and loneliness—then we must conclude that the eventual confrontation of the grandiose self with the frail, limited, and transitory nature of human life is unavoidable. (p. 238)

Narcissistic patients do not age well. Their grandiose fantasies of unending youth and beauty are torn asunder by the vicissitudes of aging. To prove their youth and vigor, they may frantically seek extramarital affairs with partners half their age or take on ill-advised pursuits such as marathon running. Also common are dramatic religious conversions in which the narcissist avoids mourning by a manic flight into the shadow of an idealized object (God).

Much of the pleasure of midlife and old age involves vicarious enjoyment of the success of younger people, such as one's children (Kernberg 1974b). One of the tragedies facing persons who suffer from narcissistic personality disorder is that they are robbed of this source of pleasure because of their envy and despair. These feelings may bring patients to treatment for the first time when they are well into their 40s. Faced with a sense of having missed something and the feeling that their lives are on a faulty course, they may finally be amenable to treatment. They often find themselves lonely, without any supportive relationships, and with a devastating feeling of being unloved. They see themselves confirming the warning of Benjamin Franklin: "He who loves himself will have no rivals."

Narcissistic patients provide enormous challenges for therapists. Kernberg (1974b) argued that the effort is well worthwhile, however, because if even partially successful, it will help attenuate the ravages of the second half of life. If, through treatment, narcissistic patients can achieve some degree of empathy, can partially replace their envy with admiration, and can begin to accept others as separate individuals with their own needs, then they may be able to avoid ending their lives in embittered isolation.

References

Adler G: Psychotherapy of the narcissistic personality disorder patient: two contrasting approaches. Am J Psychiatry 143:430–436, 1986

American Psychiatric Association: Diagnostic and Statistical Manual of Mental Disorders, 3rd Edition, Revised. Washington, DC, American Psychiatric Association, 1987

American Psychiatric Association: Diagnostic and Statistical Manual of Mental Disorders, 4th Edition. Washington, DC, American Psychiatric Association, 1994

Azima FJC: Group psychotherapy with personality disorders, in Comprehensive Group Psychotherapy, 2nd Edition. Edited by Kaplan HI, Sadock BJ. Baltimore, MD, Williams & Wilkins, 1983, pp 262–268

Brandschaft B, Stolorow R: The borderline concept: pathological character or iatrogenic myth? In Empathy II. Edited by Lichtenberg J, Bornstein M, Silver D. Hillsdale, NJ, Analytic Press, 1984, pp 333–357

Broucek FJ: Shame and its relationship to early narcissistic developments. Int J Psychoanal 63:369–378, 1982

Bursten B: Some narcissistic personality types. Int J Psychoanal 54:287–300, 1973

Cooper AM, Michels R: Book review of *Diagnostic and Statistical Manual of Mental Disorders, 3rd Edition, Revised* (DSM-III-R by the American Psychiatric Association). Am J Psychiatry 145:1300–1301, 1988

Curtis HC: Clinical perspectives on self psychology. Psychoanal Q 54:339–378, 1985

Finell JS: Narcissistic problems in analysts. Int J Psychoanal 66:433–445, 1985

Gabbard GO: Further contributions to the understanding of stage fright: narcissistic issues. J Am Psychoanal Assoc 31:423–441, 1983

Gabbard GO: Two subtypes of narcissistic personality disorder. Bull Menninger Clin 53:527–532, 1989

Gabbard GO, Twemlow SW: The role of mother-son incest in the pathogenesis of narcissistic personality disorder. J Am Psychoanal Assoc 42:159–177, 1994

Glassman M: Kernberg and Kohut: a test of competing psychoanalytic models of narcissism. J Am Psychoanal Assoc 36:597–625, 1988

Gunderson JG, Ronningstam EF, Smith LE: Narcissistic personality disorder: a review of data on DSM-III-R descriptions. Journal of Personality Disorders 5:167–177, 1991

Hibbard S: Narcissism, shame, masochism, and object relations: an exploratory correlational study. Psychoanalytic Psychology 9:489–508, 1992

Horner AJ: A characterological contraindication for group psychotherapy. J Am Academy of Psychoanal 3:301–305, 1975

Horwitz L: Group psychotherapy of the borderline patient, in Borderline Personality Disorders: The Concept, the Syndrome, the Patient. Edited by Hartocollis PL. New York, International Universities Press, 1977, pp 399–422

Kernberg OF: Factors in the psychoanalytic treatment of narcissistic personalities. J Am Psychoanal Assoc 18:51–85, 1970

Kernberg OF: Contrasting viewpoints regarding the nature and psychoanalytic treatment of narcissistic personalities: a preliminary communication. J Am Psychoanal Assoc 22:255–267, 1974a

Kernberg OF: Further contributions to the treatment of narcissistic personalities. Int J Psychoanal 55:215–240, 1974b

Kernberg OF: Severe Personality Disorders: Psychotherapeutic Strategies. New Haven, CT, Yale University Press, 1984

Kohut H: The Analysis of the Self: A Systematic Approach to the Psychoanalytic Treatment of Narcissistic Personality Disorders. New York, International Universities Press, 1971

Kohut H: The Restoration of the Self. New York, International Universities Press, 1977

Kohut H: How Does Analysis Cure? Edited by Goldberg A. Chicago, IL, University of Chicago Press, 1984

Lansky MR: Masks of the narcissistically vulnerable marriage. International Journal of Family Psychiatry 3:439–449, 1982

Lasch C: The Culture of Narcissism: American Life in an Age of Diminishing Expectations. New York, WW Norton, 1979

Maccoby M: The Gamesman: The New Corporate Leaders. New York, Simon & Schuster, 1976

Mahler MS, Pine F, Bergman A: The Psychological Birth of the Human Infant: Symbiosis and Individuation. New York, Basic Books, 1975

Meissner WW: Can psychoanalysis find its self? J Am Psychoanal Assoc 34:379–400, 1986

Miller JP: How Kohut actually worked. Progress in Self Psychology 1:13–30, 1985

Mitchell SA: Relational Concepts in Psychoanalysis: An Integration. Cambridge, MA, Harvard University Press, 1988

Modell AH: "The holding environment" and the therapeutic action of psychoanalysis. J Am Psychoanal Assoc 24:285–307, 1976

Ornstein PH: A discussion of the paper by Otto F. Kernberg on "Further contributions to the treatment of narcissistic personalities." Int J Psychoanal 55:241–247, 1974a

Ornstein PH: On narcissism: beyond the introduction, highlights of Heinz Kohut's contributions to the psychoanalytic treatment of narcissistic personality disorders. Annual of Psychoanalysis 2:127–149, 1974b

Person ES: Manipulativeness in entrepreneurs and psychopaths, in Unmasking the Psychopath: Antisocial Personality and Related Syndromes. Edited by Reid WH, Dorr D, Walker JI, et al. New York, WW Norton, 1986, pp 256–273

Rangell L: The self in psychoanalytic theory. J Am Psychoanal Assoc 30:863–891, 1982

Rinsley DB: The developmental etiology of borderline and narcissistic disorders. Bull Menninger Clin 44:127–134, 1980

Rinsley DB: A comparison of borderline and narcissistic personality disorders. Bull Menninger Clin 48:1–9, 1984

Rinsley DB: Notes on the pathogenesis and nosology of borderline and narcissistic personality disorders. J Am Acad Psychoanal 13:317–328, 1985

Rinsley DB: The adolescent, the family, and the culture of narcissism: a psychosocial commentary. Adolesc Psychiatry 13:7–28, 1986

Rinsley DB: Notes on the developmental pathogenesis of narcissistic personality disorder. Psychiatric Clin North Am 12:695–707, 1989

Ronningstam E, Gunderson J: Identifying criteria for narcissistic personality disorder. Am J Psychiatry 147:918–922, 1990

Rosenfeld H: Impasse and Interpretation: Therapeutic and Anti-Therapeutic Factors in the Psychoanalytic Treatment of Psychotic, Borderline, and Neurotic Patients. Edited by Tuckett D. London, Tavistock, 1987

Rothstein A: The Narcissistic Pursuit of Perfection. New York, International Universities Press, 1984 (original work published 1980)

Stein MH: Book review of The Restoration of the Self by Heinz Kohut. J Am Psychoanal Assoc 27:665–680, 1979

Stolorow RD: Toward a functional definition of narcissism. Int J Psychoanal 56:179–185, 1975

Wallerstein RS: How does self psychology differ in practice? Int J Psychoanal 66:391–404, 1985

Wink P: Two faces of narcissism. J Pers Soc Psychol 61:590–597, 1991

Winnicott DW: Psychiatric disorder in terms of infantile maturational processes, in The Maturational Processes and the Facilitating Environment: Studies in the Theory of Emotional Development. New York, International Universities Press, 1965, pp 230–241

Wong N: Clinical considerations in group treatment of narcissistic disorders. Int J Group Psychother 29:325–345, 1979

Wong N: Combined group and individual treatment of borderline and narcissistic patients: heterogeneous versus homogeneous groups. Int J Group Psychother 30:389–404, 1980

Yalom ID: The Theory and Practice of Group Psychotherapy, 3rd Edition. New York, Basic Books, 1985

Chapter 17

Cluster B Personality Disorders: Antisocial

Antisocial patients are perhaps the most extensively studied of all those with personality disorders, but they are also the patients that clinicians tend to avoid the most. In the therapeutic situation, these patients may lie, cheat, steal, threaten, and otherwise act irresponsibly and deceptively. They have been referred to as "psychopaths," "sociopaths," and "character disorders"—terms that, in psychiatry, have traditionally been equated with being untreatable. Some might even argue that such patients should be regarded as "criminals" and should not be included under the purview of psychiatry. Clinical experience suggests, however, that the antisocial label is applied to a broad spectrum of patients, ranging from the totally untreatable to those who are treatable under certain conditions. The existence of this latter group warrants a detailed understanding of these patients so that those amenable to help can receive the best possible treatment.

In his classic work, *The Mask of Sanity,* Hervey Cleckley (1941/ 1976) provided the first comprehensive clinical description of these patients (Table 17–1). As his title implies, Cleckley viewed the psychopath as an individual who was not overtly psychotic but whose behavior was so chaotic and so poorly attuned to the demands of reality and society that it indicated a psychosis beneath the surface. Whereas psychopaths seemed to be able to relate superficially to other people, they were completely irresponsible in all their relationships and had no regard for the feelings or concerns of others. Moreover, they seemed utterly incapable of learning from experience. Cleckley believed that psychopaths lacked a fundamental humanness. Their irresponsibility and exploitativeness in relationships caused enormous distress among their family and friends. As a result of this observation, Cleckley saw the education of the psychopath's significant others as one of the major values of his work.

The term *psychopath* fell out of favor during the decades following the appearance of Cleckley's landmark work. *Sociopath* was used for a while, ostensibly as a reflection of the social rather than psychological origins of some of the difficulties faced by these individuals. By the time the American Psychiatric Association's second Diagnostic and Statistical Manual (DSM-II) was published in 1968, the term *antisocial personality* had become the preferred nomenclature. With the arrival of DSM-III in 1980, the antisocial personality disorder had been considerably altered from Cleckley's original description. Although the DSM-III criteria provided more diagnostic detail than those for any

---

Table 17–1. Cleckley's 1941 criteria for psychopathy

1. Superficial charm and good "intelligence"
2. Absence of delusions and other signs of irrational thinking
3. Absence of "nervousness" or psychoneurotic manifestations
4. Unreliability
5. Untruthfulness and insincerity
6. Lack of remorse or shame
7. Inadequately motivated antisocial behavior
8. Poor judgment and failure to learn from experience
9. Pathological egocentricity and incapacity for love
10. General poverty in major affective reactions
11. Specific loss of insight
12. Unresponsiveness in general interpersonal relations
13. Fantastic and uninviting behavior with drink and sometimes without
14. Suicide rarely carried out
15. Sex life impersonal, trivial, and poorly integrated
16. Failure to follow any life plan

Source. Based on Cleckley 1941/1976.

other personality disorder, they narrowed the focus of the disorder to a criminal population likely to be connected with oppressed and disadvantaged lower socioeconomic groups (Halleck 1981; Meloy 1988; Modlin 1983). Detailed studies of prison populations indicate that only 40%–50% of incarcerated criminals have antisocial personalities (Guze 1976; Hare 1983).

Another problem with the DSM-III criteria was that they were so atheoretical that they provided little more than behavioral descriptions of activities commonly found in criminals. Cleckley's description more closely approximated a true personality disorder in the sense that there were psychodynamic underpinnings to such qualities as incapacity for love, loss of insight, lack of remorse or shame, and failure to learn from experience (Meloy 1988; Modlin 1983). The authors of DSM-III-R (American Psychiatric Association 1987) attempted to respond to these criticisms by adding "lacks remorse" to the criteria.

The addition of one item did not appreciably alter the specific criticisms leveled at the diagnostic criteria. In addition to the concerns that the criteria were too closely tied to criminal activity and did not reflect trait constructs for psychopathy, some clinicians claimed that the sheer length and complexity of the criteria made their clinical utility somewhat problematic. A field trial was conducted to assess the feasibility both of simplifying the criteria set and of including additional features of psychopathy (Widiger 1992). The results of the field trial suggested that the criteria could be simplified, with more emphasis on psychopathic traits and less focus on criminal behavior. Hence, the DSM-IV (American Psychiatric Association 1994) criteria are more "user friendly" (see Table 17–2).

Despite improvements in the DSM-IV criteria, however, certain problems persist. Although psychopathy traits are somewhat more evident in the new set, the criteria still reflect behavioral rather than psychodynamic constructs. Some of the more dynamically oriented psychopathy items tested in the field trial, such as "inflated and arrogant self-appraisal" and "lacks empathy," did not make it into the final list. The term *psychopath* has grown in popularity in recent years as a diagnostic term that implies particular psychodynamic and even biological features that are not captured in the DSM-IV criteria of antisocial personality disorder (Meloy 1988; Person 1986; Reid et al. 1986). Meloy (1988) used this term to describe persons with a total absence of empathy and a sadomasochistic interactional style based on power rather than emotional attachment. Person (1986) viewed psychopathy as "an impulse disorder in which the short-term relief of anxiety is more important than any long-term consequence" (p. 266). These psychodynamic views are clinically useful because a person can be a psychopath without meeting DSM-IV criteria for an antisocial personality disorder. Conversely, a person can meet the DSM-IV criteria for antisocial personality disorder but not be a psychopath.

One final problem with the DSM-IV criteria is that they are not particularly useful in determining treatability. With antisocial patients, the clinician must determine first and foremost whether a particular patient is treatable under the circumstances. This dilemma can be conceptualized by viewing the antisocial patient as a subcategory of narcissistic personality disorder (Kernberg 1984; Meloy 1988; Reid 1985). Indeed, there is a narcissistic continuum of antisocial pathology ranging from the most primitive psychopath in its purest form, to narcissistic personality disorder with ego-syntonic antisocial features to narcissistic patients who are simply dishonest in the transference (Kernberg 1984).

Table 17–2.   DSM-IV criteria for antisocial personality disorder

A.   Current age at least 18 years.

B.   Evidence of conduct disorder with onset before age 15

C.   A pervasive pattern of disregard for and violation of the rights of others occurring since age 15, as indicated by at least *three* of the following:

  1.   failure to conform to social norms with respect to lawful behaviors as indicated by repeatedly performing acts that are grounds for arrest

  2.   deceitfulness, as indicated by repeated lying, use of aliases, or conning others for personal profit or pleasure

  3.   impulsivity or failure to plan ahead

  4.   irritability and aggressiveness, as indicated by repeated physical fights or assaults

  5.   reckless disregard for safety of self or others

  6.   consistent irresponsibility, as indicated by repeated failure to sustain consistent work behavior or honor financial obligations

  7.   lack of remorse, as indicated by being indifferent to or rationalizing having hurt, mistreated, or stolen from another

D.   Occurrence of antisocial behavior is not exclusively during the course of schizophrenia or a manic episode.

Source.   DSM-IV. Because the criteria sets were not final at press time, the reader should consult DSM-IV for final criteria.

Clinicians will encounter many patients with antisocial features. The dynamic psychiatrist should approach each patient with this narcissistic continuum in mind. Using the dynamic understanding (discussed later in this chapter) related to narcissistic and antisocial pathology, clinicians can make a dynamically informed decision about whether a patient is treatable and what conditions warrant a treatment effort. In this chapter, the term *psychopath* refers only to patients at the lower end of Kernberg's (1984) continuum (although he uses "antisocial personality" to describe such patients)—the subgroup that fits the clinical and dynamic descriptions of Meloy (1988) and Person (1986). "Antisocial patients" will be used generically to describe patients along the continuum who show varying degrees of antisocial behavior. In this sense, *psychopath* is viewed as a dynamic construct, whereas the DSM-IV category of antisocial personality disorder is primarily descriptive.

Epidemiology

A considerable body of knowledge has been accumulated regarding the epidemiology of antisocial personality disorder (Cadoret 1986), which has a 2%–3% lifetime prevalence in the United States population. Persons with this disorder are more commonly found in impoverished central city areas, and many of them drop out of high school before graduation. There is a downward drift in the lives of antisocial individuals (Person 1986), who tend to make and lose money cyclically until they "burn out" in middle age, often accompanied by severe alcoholism and debilitation (Halleck 1981).

There is a striking correlation between antisocial character pathology and substance abuse (Cadoret 1986; Halleck 1981; Meloy 1988; Modlin 1983; Reid 1985; Vaillant 1983). The current thinking on the interrelationship of the two is that they often coexist but that each has a separate etiology (Cadoret 1986; Reid 1985; Vaillant 1983). It is also well established, of course, that criminal activity is intimately tied to substance abuse (Holden 1986). Fifty-two percent to 65% of felons have also been found to be drug abusers.

Patients with antisocial problems are generally thought to be male, and indeed the male-to-female ratio among antisocial personality disorders varies from 4:1 to 7.8:1 (Cadoret 1986). Familial links between psychopathy and somatization disorder (hysteria) have been extensively documented (Cadoret 1978; Cloninger et al. 1984; Cloninger and Guze 1975; Woerner and Guze 1968). A recently proposed explanation for this correlation is that gender influences whether individuals with hysterical or histrionic personality tendencies will develop antisocial personality or somatization disorder (Lilienfeld et al. 1986).

Psychopathy can and does occur in female patients, despite its much more common occurrence among males. Clinicians may overlook the diagnosis in females because of sex role stereotypes. A seductive and manipulative woman who exhibits considerable antisocial activity is much more likely to be labeled hysterical, histrionic, or borderline. One 19-year-old hospitalized female patient had been involved in extensive antisocial behavior, including the murder of a man she had said was attempting to rape her, as well as stealing, lying, and undermining the treatment of other patients. At one point during her hospitalization, she convinced two male patients to take a crowbar to her window to help her escape. After flying across country with them (using her parents' credit cards), she abandoned them without money in an airport. Her treatment reached a turning point when she started a fire in her room that threatened the safety of everyone on her hospital unit. Because this patient was attractive, seductive, and not without interpersonal charm, her treaters kept giving her the benefit of the doubt. Some even viewed her behavior as reflecting "depression" rather than antisocial pathology. Yet she met both the DSM-IV criteria for antisocial personality disorder and the psychodynamic criteria for psychopathy.

This tendency to misdiagnose antisocial women may be changing (Reid 1985), however, as women gain increasing social freedom. As more women modify their life-styles in the direction of traditionally male patterns, more of them may be diagnosed with antisocial personality disorder.

Dynamic Understanding

A comprehensive understanding of the antisocial personality disorder must begin with recognition that biological factors clearly contribute to the etiology and pathogenesis of the disorder. Studies of twins offer convincing evidence that genetic factors influence the development of psychopathy (Cadoret 1986). The concordance for criminality, for example, is two to three times higher for monozygotic twins than it is for dizygotic twins (Christiansen 1977; Wilson and Herrnstein 1985). One study of psychopaths reported that 91% were neuropsychologically impaired (Yeudall 1977). Studies have also linked aggression to hormonal and neurochemical factors (Meloy 1988). Finally, antisocial individuals have been found to be autonomically hyporeactive, possibly because of their inability to learn from experience (Meloy 1988). A lesser degree of autonomic arousal in the face of adverse experience may be related to the dynamic inference that psychopaths have less anticipatory anxiety to deter them from ill-advised actions. Raine et al. (1990) related criminality status at age 24 to psychophysiological measures at age 15. Criminality was linked to underarousal in all three response systems measured—electrodermal, cardiovascular, and cortical.

Certain antisocial patients also apparently become violent during neurologically triggered episodes of dyscontrol. However, this subgroup of patients far more commonly uses such physical complaints as an *excuse* for violence (i.e., as a disavowal of any personal responsibility for causing harm to others) (Meloy 1988). Similarly, criminals will often use psychiatric constructs, such as dissociation or multiple personality, to avoid prosecution. A celebrated example of this deception was Kenneth Bianchi's attempt to convince authorities that he was suffering from multiple personality disorder when arrested in connection with the Hillside Strangler murders. Nearly two-thirds of all murderers claim that they are amnestic for the crime (Bradford and Smith 1979).

These biological factors may in turn contribute to early problems in the infant-mother relationship. Antisocial patients frequently have a history of childhood neglect or abuse by parental figures. Constitutional factors may make these infants particularly difficult to soothe and comfort and may interfere with the normal attachment process (Meloy 1988). Regardless of whether the responsibility belongs with the infant, the mother, or both, psychopaths clearly have not attained the developmental level of object constancy (Mahler et al. 1975). As a result they lack a soothing maternal introject (see Chapter 2). Like patients with narcissistic personality disorder, they form a pathological grandiose self. This structure differs, however, from that of the narcissistic patient in one important way. Kernberg (1975) described the narcissistic personality's grandiose self as a fusion of the real self, the ideal self, and the ideal internal object. In the psychopath, on the other hand, the "ideal object" is an *aggressive* introject, often referred to as the "stranger selfobject" (Grotstein 1982; Meloy 1988). Unlike the selfobjects of Kohut's self psychology (see Chapter 2), this version reflects an experience of the parent as a stranger who cannot be trusted and who harbors malevolence toward the infant. This threatening, internalized figure may derive from real experiences of parental cruelty and neglect.

Lack of basic trust, combined with the absence of loving experiences with a maternal figure, has grave implications for the psychopath's further development. The maturational process apparently reaches a stalemate before the completion of separation-individuation and the development of object constancy. At the same time, the infant's emotional attachment to the mother is derailed because the mother is experienced as a stranger or predator. In the child's subsequent development, two separate processes coexist (Meloy 1988). One is characterized by a profound detachment from all relationships and from affective experience, while the other is a more object-related path characterized by sadistic attempts to bond with others through the exercise of power and destructiveness.

Another implication of the child's early relationship with the mother is that the subsequent withdrawal from relatedness precludes a normal passage into the depressive position and the oedipal phase of development. The psychopathic patient never becomes aware of other people as separate individuals with feelings of their own. Hence these patients do not develop a capacity for depressive anxieties or for guilt stemming from concern that their actions can hurt others. A corollary of this fact is that psychopaths are incapable of true depression. When psychopaths refer to depression, they may actually be describing a state of rageful resentment at the world for not conforming to their wishes, a reaction accompanied by feelings of emptiness and boredom (Yochelson and Samenow 1977). Suicide attempts among these patients thus tend to grow out of narcissistic rage rather than out of genuine hopelessness and a wish to die, as in patients with affective disorders (Meloy 1988). The presence of an Axis I major depressive episode precludes the diagnosis of true psychopathy. However, a number of patients with antisocial behavior and even some meeting the DSM-III-R criteria for antisocial personality disorder will have a concomitant Axis I diagnosis of major depression (Gabbard and Coyne 1987; Woody et al. 1985).

The serious impairment of internalization in the psychopath obviously leads to a massive failure of superego development—the classical hallmark, in a dynamic sense, of the psychopath. The absence of any moral sense in these individuals is one of the chilling qualities that make them seem lacking in basic humanness. Their only value system of any consequence is the exercise of aggressive power, and their only trace of superego development may be the sadistic superego precursors (or stranger selfobjects) manifested by their sadistic and cruel behavior (Kernberg 1984).

Higher-level patients, who do not fit the category of the pure psychopath, may exhibit superego lacunae (Johnson 1949). These individuals, because of their relatively more favorable constitutional factors and environmental experiences with parenting, have some semblance of a conscience but with circumscribed areas in which the superego does not seem to operate. Some of these individuals have been subtly or not-so-subtly encouraged in their antisocial behavior by one or both parents.

> Allen was a 10-year-old boy who was admitted to the hospital by his parents. During the admission interview with the psychiatrist and social worker, his mother and father described a long history of aggressive behavior. Allen had repeatedly fought at school, engaged in minor acts of vandalism of neighbors' property, and refused to obey his parents. Allen's father described the incident that finally precipitated his son's admission to the hospital: "This old guy was driving by our house, and Allen was out in the yard with his bow and arrow. Even though the guy was driving 35 miles an hour, Allen was able to shoot an arrow through the car's windshield and hit the guy in the eye. You have to admit that it was a pretty good shot." As a smile flickered across Allen's father's lips, a confused look appeared on Allen's face.

White-collar criminals often fit this category of superego lacunae. Their narcissistic personality structure has allowed them to succeed, but certain defects in their conscience eventually become manifested in antisocial behaviors that are detected by others. It is important in this context to distinguish between antisocial *behavior* and true antisocial personality. Behavior of an antisocial nature may arise from peer pressure, from neurotic conflict, or from psychotic thinking. In these cases, it may bear no relation to antisocial personality disorder.

Another aspect of superego pathology more characteristic of the true psychopath than of the higher-level narcissistic variants is a complete lack of effort to morally justify or rationalize the antisocial behavior (Meloy 1988). When confronted with their antisocial behavior, psychopaths are likely to respond with self-righteousness, declaring that the victims of their antisocial acts deserved what they got. Psychopaths may also choose to lie and to avoid any responsibility for their behavior.

> Mr. MM was a 23-year-old man who had been involuntarily committed to long-term hospitalization by the court. Shortly after admission, he was seen by a consultant, and the following dialogue took place:
>
> Consultant: What brings you to the hospital?
> Patient: The court sent me.
> Consultant: How come?
> Patient: I was in a car accident, and my best friend was accidentally killed.
> Consultant: How did it happen?
> Patient: I was driving down the street, minding my own business, when the guy in front of me slams on his brakes. I plow into his rear end, and the gun in my glove compartment goes off and accidentally shoots my friend through the head.
> Consultant: Why did you have a gun in your glove compartment?
> Patient: You gotta have a gun in the neighborhood I come from. I gotta protect myself. There's all kinds of drug dealers around.
> Consultant: Why did the court commit you to a hospital as the result of an accident?
> Patient: Good question.
> Consultant: Do you have any emotional problems?
> Patient: No, I'm a pretty happy-go-lucky guy.
> Consultant: Have you had any other problems with the law?
> Patient: The only other thing that happened wasn't my fault either. These buddies of mine ripped off a dollar-changing machine from a laundromat and left it on my porch as a gag. The police thought I did it and arrested me.

Mr. MM's disavowal of responsibility shows his absence of concern about his "best friend" and his complete inability to acknowledge any of his own problems that might have contributed to his situation. This vignette underscores the difficulty therapists may have engaging antisocial patients in treatment because they externalize all problems.

Psychopathy is best understood as a primitive variant of the narcissistic personality disorder (see Chapter 16) described by Kernberg (1984; Meloy 1988; Reid 1985), with the same underlying borderline personality organization that relies on primitive defenses and highly pathological internal object relations (Kernberg 1975). There are five main differences between the psychopathic and the nonpsychopathic narcissistic personality disorders (see Table 17–3).

Both the narcissist and the psychopathic variant are plagued with boredom and emptiness because their envy precludes meaningful relationships with others. The psychopath simply manages these affects more aggressively than does the narcissistic personality. Both manipulate others with charm, but charm of the narcissistic patient is based more on stabilization of self-esteem, in contrast to the psychopath, whose primary motivation for manipulation is symbolic destruction, humiliation, and domination of the other person (Person 1986). Although the psychopath's object seeking may appear hedonistic, it is best understood as satisfying the aggressive need to dominate.

One form of splitting is particularly prominent in antisocial patients. The discontinuity in their self-representations often takes the form of disavowal of past behavior. A female antisocial patient, for example, who was asked about antisocial behavior on admission, denied having any problems. When she was confronted with having written bad checks that had resulted in her arrest, her response was, "That was over a month ago. What's that got to do with anything now?" Thus the same bland denial of contradictory self-representations common to borderline patients is also operative in antisocial patients.

Psychodynamically differentiating the treatable narcissistic patient from the pure psychopath may be difficult in many clinical situ-

Table 17–3. Features that distinguish the psychopathic variant from other forms of narcissistic personality disorder

1. All interactions with others are characterized by aggression and power rather than attachment.
2. The only evidence of superego development is the presence of sadistic superego precursors that are manifested by sadistic and cruel behavior toward others.
3. The internalized "ideal object" is a highly aggressive introject (the stranger selfobject) based on an abusive or neglectful parental figure.
4. No interest is shown in rationalizing or morally justifying one's behavior.
5. There is no adherence to any value system other than the exploitative, aggressive exercise of power.

Source. Based on Kernberg 1984 and Meloy 1988.

ations because antisocial patients tend to deceive clinicians. In the next section, I will examine more objective criteria for determining treatability.

Hospital Treatment

There is a broad consensus that patients with serious antisocial behavior are unlikely to benefit from a treatment approach characterized exclusively by outpatient psychotherapy (Frosch 1983; Gabbard and Coyne 1987; Person 1986; Reid 1985). Some form of institutional or residential setting is necessary for even modest improvement. If psychotherapy is employed as a treatment, it must begin while the antisocial patient is contained by the structure of a round-the-clock milieu. These action-oriented individuals will never get in touch with their affective states as long as they have the outlet of behavior to discharge their impulses. It is only when they are immobilized by an inpatient setting that the treatment staff will begin to see them display emotions such as anxiety and emptiness (Frosch 1983; Person 1986).

The decision to hospitalize an antisocial patient in a general psychiatry unit containing patients with a variety of diagnoses usually leads to regret. The psychopath's disruptive behavior may grossly interfere with the treatment of other patients and may bring all therapeutic programs in the milieu to a grinding halt. These patients will steal from, sexually exploit, and assault other patients; they will also lie to and ridicule staff members, smuggle drugs and alcohol into the unit, ridicule the treatment philosophy, and corrupt staff members into dishonest and unethical behavior. Some will systematically destroy any therapeutic alliance that other patients have developed with the treatment staff.

> Mr. NN was a 46-year-old clergyman forced into hospital treatment by his superiors in the church because his behavior was creating chaos in his congregation. He had seduced a number of women connected with his church and had delighted in "undermining their faith" by challenging the basic tenets of their beliefs. Similar patterns of behavior and object relations occurred in the hospital. Mr. NN was silent in most group meetings, but he insidiously "poisoned" the milieu by devaluing staff members in private one-to-one meetings with other patients and by systematically eroding other patients' faith that treatment could be helpful. He viewed all his relationships with fe-

male patients and female treaters as sexualized conquests, and even when his sexual acting out was blocked by the structure of the hospital unit, Mr. NN would find other ways to dominate and humiliate women. He often joked with other patients about the relative sexual merits of various female nurses and doctors on the unit, and he devalued the expertise of all staff members regardless of gender. His treatment ended when he planned and executed an elopement with a female inpatient. For several months after Mr. NN's departure, however, his impact on the unit was still felt in the patients' pervasive doubt about the value of treatment—a doubt that he had fueled by his comments and actions.

More sophisticated and intelligent psychopaths may present a different problem in the hospital milieu. Because they are aware that hospitalization is far more comfortable than prison, they may deceive the treatment staff into thinking that they are benefiting greatly from treatment. Such patients may be highly skilled charmers who convince the staff that they should be discharged sooner than initially expected. The behavioral changes of antisocial patients that occur during hospitalization, however, do not usually continue beyond discharge (Frosch 1983). These patients often just go through the motions of treatment without being touched by it. When they revert to their antisocial behavior after discharge, the hospital staff may feel outraged because they have been conned.

To avoid wasting an enormous investment of time, money, and energy, hospital clinicians must determine which antisocial patients warrant a trial of psychiatric hospitalization. There is a broad consensus that true psychopaths do not belong on general psychiatry units because they are unable to benefit from such treatment, perhaps because they tend to transform the experience into an exploitative situation of the proverbial "fox in the chicken coop." Specialized units, such as those in prison settings (Kiger 1967; Sturup 1968), nonmedical community residential programs (Reid and Solomon 1981), and wilderness programs (Reid 1985) have had somewhat better success with psychopathic patients and are generally viewed as the only hope for those in this diagnostic category.

In specialized institutional settings, such as the Patuxent Institution in Maryland or the Herstedvester Institution in Denmark, the treatment of the psychopath is enhanced by the homogeneous composition of the milieu. These programs rely heavily on group confrontation by peers. Other psychopaths are familiar with the "con artist" techniques of their cohorts; when these are consistently confronted, their effectiveness is neutralized. These programs also employ a tight structure with clear and rigidly enforced rules. The consequences for rule breaking of any kind are implemented swiftly without any allowance for bargaining or rationalizations on the part of the patients (Reid 1985; Yochelson and Samenow 1977).

Once these institutions have established control over the lives of the patients and have blocked their usual channels for discharging unpleasant affects through action, these patients may begin to come to terms with their anxiety and aggression. The staff's predictable and consistent responses to all breaks in structure frustrate the usual efforts to get around "the system." These programs depend on court-mandated treatment, however, because the patients may wish to leave the institution as soon as untoward feelings creep into awareness.

A small subsample of patients with antisocial features, usually those with borderline or narcissistic personality disorders, may benefit from voluntary hospitalization in a general psychiatry unit (Gabbard and Coyne 1987). However, differentiating these patients from the pure psychopath may be difficult because of the intense countertransference reactions evoked by antisocial patients. Mental health professionals, by the very nature of their career choice, are inclined to be charitable and kindly toward those they treat. They are prone to give patients the benefit of the doubt and to see them as somehow treatable no matter how resistant they may appear. This tendency may lead treaters to downplay the extent of ruthlessness in psychopathic patients and to assume that antisocial behavior is really a "cry for help." Hospital staff members in particular often have a deep-seated need to see themselves as capable of treating the untreatable patient. They may take extraordinary steps to connect with a patient who has no interest in meaningful human relationships. In reaching out to such patients, they may collude with the tendency of these patients to minimize the extent of their antisocial behavior and superego pathology. One aspect of this countertransference denial is that clinicians may underdiagnose psychopaths and thus view them as more treatable than they actually are. For example, in one study, only half the patients meeting DSM-III-R criteria for antisocial personality disorder were given that diagnosis (Gabbard and Coyne 1987).

Underdiagnosis may result in viewing the patient as simply narcissistic rather than psychopathic, as immature—with a character structure that is "not yet crystallized," or as primarily a substance abuser. In fact, substance abuse may be an excuse used by psychopaths themselves. In some cases, treatment staff collude with this excuse by arguing vehemently that a patient's crimes occurred only under the influence of drugs and alcohol so the patient should not be viewed as antisocial. These professionals will often argue that treating the patient's substance abuse will eliminate the problematic antisocial behavior. This point of view fails to consider the extensive overlap between psychopathy and drug abuse, which was described earlier in this chapter. Moreover, some studies have demonstrated that drug abuse in no way improves a psychopath's prospects for psychological change (Gabbard and Coyne 1987; Woody et al. 1985).

Because of countertransference contamination in distinguishing between the treatable antisocial patient and the pure psychopath, objective criteria are essential to such determinations. "Gut feelings" about particular patients are notoriously unreliable. The data from one study of hospitalized patients with antisocial features found that there are three predictors of a reasonably positive treatment outcome for these patients in a general psychiatry unit (Gabbard and Coyne 1987) (Table 17–4).

As explained earlier in this chapter, the presence of an Axis I diagnosis of a major depressive episode effectively rules out (by definition)

Table 17–4.   Predictors of positive and negative treatment response on a general psychiatric unit

Negative response
1. History of felony arrest
2. History of repeated lying, aliases, conning
3. Unresolved legal situation at admission
4. History of felony conviction
5. Hospitalization forced as an alternative to incarceration
6. History of violence toward others
7. Diagnosis on Axis I of organic brain impairment

Positive response
1. Presence of anxiety
2. Axis I diagnosis of depression
3. Axis I psychotic diagnosis other than depression or organic brain syndrome

---

Note.   Based on Gabbard and Coyne 1987.

the presence of true psychopathy. Patients who meet the Axis I criteria for depression have some superego development and some capacity, however minimal, for remorse. Similarly, the presence of anxiety represents some concern about one's behavior and its consequences. Finally, the presence of an Axis I psychotic diagnosis, such as mania, suggests that pharmacological treatment may improve the prognosis. It is certainly well known that individuals in the midst of a manic episode often exhibit antisocial behavior. Pharmacological treatment has not been particularly effective for the true psychopath (Halleck 1981).

The same study delineated several predictors of negative treatment response for the same population (see Table 17–4). When there is no other way to keep psychopathic patients involved in treatment, they may benefit from involuntary hospitalization in a specialized penal setting. Psychopaths who are forced to seek hospital treatment as an alternative to prison, however, will simply exploit the opportunity to con the staff of the unit, who are predisposed anyway to see such patients as "sick" or "disturbed" rather than as criminals in need of punishment. Under these conditions, the patients will either disrupt the unit or merely go through the motions of treatment. Many patients will use the hospital to "hide out" from an unresolved legal situation that requires a court appearance. A serious history of violence bodes poorly for treatment because, when these patients become frustrated, they may resort to violence, either against staff members or against other patients. Likewise, a serious organic brain impairment may interfere with a patient's ability to understand and benefit from the constructive feedback provided in a hospital milieu, which in turn may increase frustration.

Antisocial patients seldom have all the positive predictors and rarely lack any of the negative predictors in Table 17–4. Although there is no ideal antisocial patient, each additional positive predictor improves a patient's suitability for hospital treatment, and each negative predictor worsens the patient's amenability to hospital treatment (Gabbard and Coyne 1987).

Even with a relatively favorable profile, antisocial patients present a host of difficulties in a typical psychiatric milieu. Only long-term hospital treatment has a chance of producing any lasting change in these patients. They naturally attempt to continue their pattern of impulsively translating their feelings into actions. The cornerstone of treatment must therefore be a tightly controlled structure. From day one, treaters must anticipate and address likely forms of acting out in the hospital. Certain expectations must be spelled out at admission. For example, the patient must be told that substance abuse, violence, theft, and sexual relationships with other patients will not be tolerated. If the patient is a drug abuser, all mail must be opened in front of staff members to help prevent the smuggling in of drugs. Patients must be clearly told that they will be accompanied by staff whenever they leave the unit and that they will remain at that level of responsibility for a considerable time. Phone calls and access to cash and credit cards also must be restricted. The patient should be made aware that any breaks in structure will result in clear-cut consequences, such as room restriction. Treatment must be viewed initially as being conducted on a trial basis only—as a period of evaluation (usually of several weeks)—to determine the patient's suitability for treatment. All these conditions may be written out as a "contract" at the time of admission, so that the patient will have a copy for reference.

Staff members must scrupulously monitor their countertransference reactions, both as individuals and in the group context. Three common staff reactions are disbelief, collusion, and condemnation (Symington 1980). Disbelief may surface as denial that the patient is really "that bad." Rationalizing antisocial behavior as being due to such problems as drug abuse or adolescent rebellion may cause staff members to deny the presence of psychopathic features and to instead view the patient as depressed or misunderstood.

Collusion is one of the most problematic forms of countertransference. A common development in the hospital treatment of antisocial patients is for the patient to corrupt one or more staff members. In the belief that they are helping the patient, the staff members involved in such countertransference acting out may commit illegal acts or otherwise behave unethically. Staff members have been known to lie on behalf of such patients; they also have falsified records, been seduced into sexual relationships, and helped these patients to escape from the hospital. These countertransference developments can be understood as part of the projective identification process whereby a corrupt aspect of the patient's self enters the treater and transforms that individual's behavior. Staff members who are involved in such countertransference acting out often report that "I was not acting like myself."

Another way to conceptualize these countertransference collusions is that they are the result of what Meloy (1988) referred to as *malignant pseudo-identification*. In this process, "the psychopath consciously imitates or unconsciously simulates a certain behavior to foster the victim's identification with this individual, thus increasing the victim's vulnerability to exploitation" (p. 139). Through simulated tearfulness, remorse, or sadness, antisocial patients manipulate clinicians into empathizing with them. If only one clinician sees this simulated self-presentation of the patient, it can lead to splitting among the hospital staff. The staff member involved in the malignant pseudo-identification will adamantly defend the patient against the "attacks" of other staff members. Meloy points out that these simulated affects in the patient can often be identified by sadistic countertransference feelings in the face of the patient's outpouring of sadness and by the patient's apparently rapid recompensation, leaving observers with the impression that they have witnessed a performance.

Condemnation is a third common countertransference reaction. It is often manifested in expressions by hospital staff that a patient is totally untreatable and that no effort should be made to establish a treatment relationship. Such a decision can be made by rationally assessing objective factors, but it is more often a knee-jerk reaction to hearing some history of antisocial activity. This automatic reaction may be countertransference in the narrow sense, because it is based on the treater's past experience with similar individuals. Condemnation that stems from intensive work with the patient may be understood as a projective identification with the aggressive introject of the patient.

Other common countertransference reactions in the treatment of antisocial patients include feelings of helplessness and impotence in the face of a treatment-resistant patient, wishes to destroy the patient that grow out of anger, and feelings of invalidity and loss of identity (Strasberger 1986). The treatment staff may also fear an assault by these patients, who are often threatening and menacing. (Certain psychopathic patients evoke an intense fear of predation in treaters merely by looking at them [Meloy 1988].) Fear of assault may lead staff members to avoid implementing the firm structure that the patient so desperately needs. To avoid arousing the patient's anger or violence, staff members may rationalize their loose structure and indulgence of the patient. For example, although a muscular young man in a long-term hospital unit had beaten up other patients on several occasions, he was allowed to freely wander the grounds. His treatment team justified this loose structure by saying that they were not going to be provoked into responding punitively to the patient as his parents had.

A major aspect of the hospital treatment of antisocial patients must be the continual focus on their faulty thought processes (Yochelson and Samenow 1976). When they pose as the victim because of being held accountable for their behavior, they must be confronted with how they are responsible for what happens to them. Staff members must also function as auxiliary egos in terms of judgment. The staff must point out over and over how these patients fail to anticipate the consequences of their behavior.

The antisocial patient tends to move directly from impulse to action. The hospital staff must therefore help these patients insert *thought* between impulse and action. In other words, each time an antisocial patient has an impulse, the staff must encourage the patient to think about what may result from the action. In milieu treatment, patients must also learn that impulses and actions grow out of feelings. Often the language of emotions is so foreign to the patients that they cannot identify their internal states.

All these strategies focus on the "here and now" in the milieu, because exploring the childhood origins of such problems is often useless with antisocial patients. Any attempt by the antisocial patient to corrupt staff members must also be confronted *as it occurs*. If an intervention is not made immediately after the acting-out behavior, then the patient may dismiss it or forget it.

A case example of a treatable antisocial patient will illustrate many of the principles described here.

Mr. OO was a single 24-year-old who came to a long-term hospital unit after being released from prison, where he had served time for selling cocaine. The hospitalization was not a condition of parole, and Mr. OO was seeking admission voluntarily. He said that he needed to change his life-style so that he would stop abusing drugs and destroying any chance he had to become successful. In addition to a history of selling and abusing cocaine, Mr. OO also had a history of extensive antisocial behavior, including lying, cheating, stealing, and operating as a building contractor without a license. His object relations were characterized by exploitative and manipulative patterns. Despite this ominous-sounding history, Mr. OO experienced genuine anxiety about his destructive behavior and was motivated to change it. Moreover, because he was not under pressure to seek hospitalization, he was viewed as having a reasonable chance to improve. Diagnostically, Mr. OO was best described as having a narcissistic personality with antisocial features.

The cornerstone of Mr. OO's treatment plan was a contractual agreement between him and the treatment team. This contract stipulated that Mr. OO would have to adhere to a specific structure in order to be adequately treated. This structure included staff accompaniment to all activities and appointments outside the unit during the first 4 months of hospitalization, staff monitoring of telephone calls, a $25-per-week allowance and no access to credit cards, no visits from friends, attendance at all treatment activities and meetings, no violent behavior, no sexual behavior with other patients, no substance abuse, and no negotiation of this structure during the first 4 months of treatment. By frustrating the various outlets for impulses, the staff forced the patient to deal with his anxiety and internal emptiness rather than to discharge it through acting-out behavior.

The patient found this structure enormously frustrating and restricting, but he seemed to realize that it was necessary. Mr. OO was repeatedly confronted by staff members about his tendency to externalize problems that occurred in relationships on the unit. He was told that he was not a passive victim under the influence of others, but rather, an active contributor to the problems that occurred with other people on the unit. He was a handsome and charming man who behaved seductively toward a number of female patients but then complained that he could not possibly please them all.

Mr. OO also devalued the treatment structure, openly saying that it was ridiculous and that he did not require such restrictions. He aroused considerable sympathy from other patients by portraying himself as a victim of an extremely harsh and sadistic treatment team. The clinicians working to deal with this manipulation conducted a good deal of group work on the unit. In the group meetings, Mr. OO was confronted with his efforts to appear as a victim instead of as a manipulative patient whose history warranted such tight structure. Since he would not mention his antisocial behavior in the treatment meetings, the staff often had to remind him, and the other patients, of the reasons for Mr. OO's hospitalization. He had developed an artificial split between his "bad self," which he had left outside the hospital, and his "good self," which was in the hospital. He repeatedly minimized his antisocial past as being "past history." The treatment staff, on the other hand, confronted him with the reality that *he* had committed those antisocial acts and that he still had the potential for such behavior. Thus Mr. OO's splitting maneuvers were challenged, and his "good self" and "bad self" were brought together.

Early in the treatment, Mr. OO broke the established structure on several occasions by using the phone to call friends who might supply him with cocaine. Whenever this occurred, the staff immediately implemented further restrictions, such as unit confinement, without discussion or negotiation. Mr. OO also had to open all his mail in front of a staff member, who checked to be sure that no drugs or contraband were being mailed to him.

On one occasion Mr. OO was able to manipulate a female mental health technician (who found him charming and attractive) into loaning him a dollar to buy a Coke. After buying the Coke, he did not return any change to her. While the mental health technician dealt with her countertransference acting out in supervision, Mr. OO was confronted about his actions in a group treatment meeting. He went on at great length about how "totally ridiculous" it was to focus on such a small amount of money. He said that he had fully intended to return the change, but that he had simply forgotten. The treatment team confronted his minimization and denial and pointed out that his behavior outside the hospital was being repeated, only on a smaller scale.

Over several months, Mr. OO became increasingly psychologically minded. He was referred for twice-weekly psychotherapy after he began to show an ability to reflect on the staff's confrontations rather than to respond defensively and automatically. A turning point occurred when a female patient in his "harem" attempted suicide because she could not stand the way he was leading her on while simultaneously sharing his attention with several other women. Only then did Mr. OO begin to realize that his exploitative relationships with women could be highly destructive. He also eventually realized that he lacked empathy for others and was simply using women to gratify his own needs. By the time he left the hospital after 18 months of treatment, he had begun to piece together how internal anxiety states led him to drug abuse and other impulsive actions as a way to "treat" his anxiety. Specifically, he realized that he was extremely concerned about being rejected or abandoned by women, so he maintained several relationships at a time to reduce his vulnerability. He called this manipulation his "spare tire" strategy.

After discharge, Mr. OO continued psychotherapy and joined Narcotics Anonymous as well. In his final meeting with his hospital psychiatrist, Mr. OO noted that his inpatient experience was the first time that he had ever really felt understood. In his own words, "You guys knew what a con artist I was." At 4-year follow-up, Mr. OO had remained abstinent from cocaine and other drugs and was working full-time in a business-related field. He had become quite active in the stock market, where he was able to sublimate his thrill-seeking and risk-taking tendencies in a legal and socially acceptable manner.

Mr. OO is unusual among hospitalized antisocial patients. Many will leave treatment when the frustration becomes too great to bear. A small subgroup, however, can benefit from long-term hospitalization. As with borderline patients, milieu treatment combined with psychotherapy provides these patients with an opportunity to internalize new patterns of object relatedness. One reason for Mr. OO's improvement was the "softening" or modification of his aggressive self- and object-representations. Clearly, the enormous expense of such intensive treatment must not be squandered on patients who will misuse the treatment or who will not benefit from it.

Individual Psychotherapy

Outpatient individual psychotherapy of the severely antisocial patient is doomed to failure. Affects will be discharged through action because there is no contained environment in which to control such channeling. In addition, the patient's lies and deceptions are so pervasive that the therapist will have no idea what is really going on in the patient's life. In an institutional or hospital setting, there is some reason for guarded optimism about psychotherapy with a select subgroup of antisocial patients such as Mr. OO. As with hospital treatment, the clinician's task is to determine which patients are worth the time, energy, and money required by a long-term therapy process with an uncertain outcome. The pure psychopath, in the dynamic sense, will not respond to psychotherapy, and so it should not be attempted (Kernberg 1984; Meloy 1988; Woody et al. 1985). Further along the continuum, the patient who has a narcissistic personality disorder with severe antisocial features is somewhat more amenable to psychotherapy. These patients may subtly reveal dependency in the transference, their antisocial behavior may have an enraged quality about it, and their internal "ideal object" may be somewhat less aggressive than that of the pure psychopath (Kernberg 1984; Meloy 1988). Meloy (1988) has suggested that the superego pathology of these patients may be more related to environmental factors than is the biogenic etiology of the psychopath. They may attempt to rationalize or justify their behavior, thus reflecting some rudimentary value system. Their treatability will be essentially determined by their ability to form some semblance of an emotional attachment to others and to exercise some rudimentary superego functions.

Projective psychological testing may be extraordinarily helpful in assessing the antisocial patient's superego development and object relations. The Rorschach has been used, for example, to quantitatively evaluate the severity of the antisocial pathology (Exner and Weiner 1986). Although patients may successfully deceive clinicians during an interview by simulating guilt or concern for others, they have much more difficulty with the ambiguous stimuli of an inkblot, where there are no obviously "correct" answers.

The presence of bona fide depression appears to be a sign of amenability to psychotherapy just as it is a positive predictor of hospital treatment response. In a study of patients with antisocial personality disorder who were opiate addicts, the presence of depression appeared to indicate suitability for psychotherapy even if there continued to be behavioral manifestations of psychopathy (Woody et al. 1985). The antisocial patients in the study who were not depressed fared poorly in psychotherapy. In addition, the absence of relatedness to others was the most negative predictor of psychotherapy response.

Clinicians who evaluate antisocial patients must feel comfortable making a recommendation for no treatment. Such a decision may be a perfectly rational determination based on the patient's strengths and weaknesses and the danger that the patient might pose to those attempting to treat him. This manner of evaluating treatability differs greatly from the knee-jerk countertransference response described earlier. Meloy (1988), using his extensive experience in the psychotherapy of psychopaths, has identified five clinical features that absolutely contraindicate any attempt in psychotherapy (see Table 17–5). Sadistic cruelty toward others, total absence of remorse, and lack of emotional attachment are three key features that differentiate the psychopath from the more treatable narcissistic patient. The chilling countertrans-

---

Table 17–5. Clinical features that contraindicate psychotherapy of any kind

---

1. A history of sadistic, violent behavior toward others that resulted in serious injury or death
2. A total absence of remorse or rationalization for such behavior
3. Intelligence that is either in the very superior or mildly mentally retarded range
4. A historical incapacity to develop emotional attachments to others
5. An intense countertransference fear of predation on the part of experienced clinicians even without clear precipitating behavior on the part of the patient

---

Source. Based on Meloy 1988.

ference feelings that lead therapists to fear for their personal safety can paralyze them and preclude any constructive efforts at treatment. Finally, the paradoxical contraindications of both high and low intelligence reflect the extremely bright patient's adeptness at thwarting the process and the dull patient's cognitive inability to grasp the therapist's interventions.

Therapists who attempt psychotherapy with severely antisocial patients must be able to quickly confront their patients or they will be deceived again and again. For, while the therapist's goal is an unflinching search for truth, the patient's goal is deception. Therapists must also learn to accept the fact that they will be conned despite all their diligent efforts to avoid it. The therapeutic alliance is either completely absent or glimpsed only in brief, intermittent flashes of collaboration.

Deceiving or conning others is a way of life for antisocial patients. They experience a powerful sense of delight, or even exhilaration, whenever they "put something over" on their therapist (Bursten 1972; Meloy 1988). Unconscious envy of the therapist's positive qualities often leads to this repetitive cycle of deception. The exhilarating feeling of triumph at a successful con is laced with contempt, which serves as a defense against envy. The patient's avoidance of a meaningful relationship with the therapist also wards off feelings of envy, but leaves the patient feeling empty.

If therapists can accept the fact that these patients will practice deception, they can proceed with psychotherapy based on the recommendations of those therapists who have had extensive experience with this population (Adler and Shapiro 1969; Frosch 1983; Kernberg 1984; Lion 1978; Meloy 1988; Person 1986; Reid 1985; Strasberger 1986; Vaillant 1975). These recommendations can be distilled into six basic principles of technique:

1. *The therapist must be stable, persistent, and thoroughly incorruptible.* More than with any other patient group, the therapist must be absolutely scrupulous about maintaining normal procedures in therapy (Person 1986). Deviating from the structure and usual context of the hours is inadvisable. These patients will do whatever they can to corrupt the therapist into unethical or dishonest conduct. David Mamet's movie, *House of Games* (1987), portrays the perils of attempting to help the antisocial patient by departing from the role of therapist and becoming overinvolved in the patient's life.

2. *The therapist must repeatedly confront the patient's denial and minimization of antisocial behavior.* Pervasive denial even infiltrates the antisocial patient's choice of words. If the patient says, "I ripped off this guy," the therapist needs to clarify, "So, you are a thief." If the patient says, "I offed this dude," the therapist may confront the patient by responding, "So, you are a murderer then." This technique of repeated confrontation enables the therapist to help these patients become aware of their tendency to externalize all responsibility, and they can therefore begin to acknowledge and accept responsibility for their antisocial behavior.

3. *The therapist must help the patient connect actions with internal states.* Just as with antisocial patients undergoing hospital treatment, those in individual psychotherapy require education in this regard.

4. *Confrontations of here-and-now behavior are more effective than interpretations of unconscious material from the past.* In particular, the patient's denigration of the therapist and contemptuous devaluation of the process must be repeatedly challenged.

5. *Countertransference must be rigorously monitored to avoid acting out by the therapist.* Any collusion must also be carefully avoided, despite the tendency to "take the path of least resistance."

6. *The therapist must avoid having excessive expectations for improvement.* Antisocial patients will detect this *furor therapeuticus* and will take great delight in thwarting their therapist's wishes to change them. Therapists whose self-esteem depends on the improvement of their patients should not treat antisocial patients.

Progress is painstakingly slow with antisocial patients in psychotherapy. At some level, these patients experience therapy as a threat to the grandiose self. They will fight their therapist every step of the way to avoid giving up their cherished grandiosity. Therapists must therefore be cognizant of this resistance and must realize that the patient's internal cohesiveness depends on a grandiose self-concept (Reid 1985). For long periods in the therapy process, the therapist may feel paralyzed by the patient's overt or covert threats (Kernberg 1984). This intimidation may deskill therapists and effectively stalemate their efforts. To avoid becoming victimized by their patients, therapists must be constantly attuned to these attempts at control.

One final comment about neutrality is in order. Therapists treating antisocial patients cannot reasonably expect to maintain a neutral position regarding the patient's antisocial activities. Attempting to do so would be tantamount to a silent endorsement of or collusion with the patient's actions. More to the point, the therapist's moral outrage will be evident in a myriad of nonverbal communications and vocal intonations, so the patient will view any effort at neutrality as hypocritical. When therapists are shocked at a patient's antisocial behavior, they should simply say so (Gedo 1984). Empathy, in accord with the self psychological approach, is both misguided and collusive in such instances.

Even when therapists are capable of navigating the various obstacles of resistance presented by the antisocial patient, their attempts to be effective can still backfire. Competent therapists who are able to avoid being destroyed by the patient are the ones most likely to evoke intense envy, which may surface as hatred toward the loving or idealized object (i.e., the therapist), eventually leading to an intractable negative therapeutic reaction. Despite these pitfalls, however, many experienced clinicians believe that psychotherapeutic efforts with these patients pay off frequently enough to warrant such heroic treatment.

References

Adler G, Shapiro LN: Psychotherapy with prisoners. Curr Psychiatr Ther 9:99–105, 1969

American Psychiatric Association: Diagnostic and Statistical Manual of Mental Disorders, 2nd Edition. Washington, DC, American Psychiatric Association, 1968

American Psychiatric Association: Diagnostic and Statistical Manual of Mental Disorders, 3rd Edition. Washington, DC, American Psychiatric Association, 1980

American Psychiatric Association: Diagnostic and Statistical Manual of Mental Disorders, 3rd Edition, Revised. Washington, DC, American Psychiatric Association, 1987

American Psychiatric Association: Diagnostic and Statistical Manual of Mental Disorders, 4th Edition. Washington, DC, American Psychiatric Association, 1994

Bradford JMW, Smith SM: Amnesia and homicide: the Padola case and a study of thirty cases. Bull Am Acad Psychiatry Law 7:219–231, 1979

Bursten B: The manipulative personality. Arch Gen Psychiatry 26:318–321, 1972

Cadoret RJ: Psychopathology in the adopted-away offspring of biologic parents with antisocial behavior. Arch Gen Psychiatry 35:176–184, 1978

Cadoret RJ: Epidemiology of antisocial personality, in Unmasking the Psychopath: Antisocial Personality and Related Syndromes. Edited by Reid WH, Dorr D, Walker JI, et al. New York, WW Norton, 1986, pp 28–44

Christiansen KO: A preliminary study of criminality among twins, in Biosocial Bases of Criminal Behavior. Edited by Mednick SA, Christiansen KO. New York, Gardner Press, 1977, pp 89–108

Cleckley HM: The Mask of Sanity: An Attempt to Clarify Some Issues About the So-Called Psychopathic Personality, 5th Edition. St. Louis, MO, CV Mosby, 1976 (original work published 1941)

Cloninger CR, Guze SB: Hysteria and parental psychiatric illness. Psychol Med 5:27–31, 1975

Cloninger CR, Sigvardsson S, von Knorring A-L, et al: An adoption study of somatoform disorders, II: identification of two discrete somatoform disorders. Arch Gen Psychiatry 41:863–871, 1984

Exner JE, Jr, Weiner IB: The Rorschach: A Comprehensive System, Vol I: Basic Foundations, 2nd Edition. New York, Wiley, 1986

Frosch JP: The treatment of antisocial and borderline personality disorders. Hosp Community Psychiatry 34:243–248, 1983

Gabbard GO, Coyne L: Predictors of response of antisocial patients to hospital treatment. Hosp Community Psychiatry 38:1181–1185, 1987

Gedo JE: Psychoanalysis and Its Discontents. New York, Guilford, 1984

Grotstein JS: Newer perspectives in object relations theory. Contemporary Psychoanalysis 18:43–91, 1982

Guze SB: Criminality and Psychiatric Disorders. New York, Oxford University Press, 1976

Halleck SL: Sociopathy: ethical aspects of diagnosis and treatment. Curr Psychiatr Ther 20:167–176, 1981

Hare RD: Diagnosis of antisocial personality disorder in two prison populations. Am J Psychiatry 140:887–890, 1983

Holden C: Growing focus on criminal careers. Science 233:1377–1378, 1986

Johnson AM: Sanctions for superego lacunae of adolescents, in Searchlights on Delinquency: New Psychoanalytic Studies. Edited by Eissler KR. New York, International Universities Press, 1949, pp 225–245

Kernberg OF: Borderline Conditions and Pathological Narcissism. New York, Jason Aronson, 1975

Kernberg OF: Severe Personality Disorders: Psychotherapeutic Strategies. New Haven, CT, Yale University Press, 1984

Kiger RS: Treating the psychopathic patient in a therapeutic community. Hosp Community Psychiatry 18:191–196, 1967

Lilienfeld SO, VanValkenburg C, Larntz K, et al: The relationship of histrionic personality disorder to antisocial personality and somatization disorders. Am J Psychiatry 143:718–722, 1986

Lion JR: Outpatient treatment of psychopaths, in The Psychopath: A Comprehensive Study of Antisocial Disorders and Behaviors. Edited by Reid WH. New York, Brunner/Mazel, 1978, pp 286–300

Mahler MS, Pine F, Bergman A: The Psychological Birth of the Human Infant: Symbiosis and Individuation. New York, Basic Books, 1975

Meloy JR: The Psychopathic Mind: Origins, Dynamics, and Treatment. Northvale, NJ, Jason Aronson, 1988

Modlin HC: The antisocial personality. Bull Menninger Clin 47:129–144, 1983

Person ES: Manipulativeness in entrepreneurs and psychopaths, in Unmasking the Psychopath: Antisocial Personality and Related Syndromes. Edited by Reid WH, Dorr D, Walker JI, et al. New York, WW Norton, 1986, pp 256–273

Raine A, Venables PH, Williams M: Relationships between central and autonomic measures of arousal at age 15 years and criminality at age 24 years. Arch Gen Psychiatry 47:1003–1007, 1990

Reid WH: The antisocial personality: a review. Hosp Community Psychiatry 36:831–837, 1985

Reid WH, Solomon G: Community-based offender programs, in The Treatment of Antisocial Syndromes. Edited by Reid WH. New York, Van Nostrand Reinhold, 1981, pp 76–94

Reid WH, Dorr D, Walker JI, et al (eds): Unmasking the Psychopath: Antisocial Personality and Related Syndromes. New York, WW Norton, 1986

Strasberger LH: The treatment of antisocial syndromes: the therapist's feelings, in Unmasking the Psychopath: Antisocial Personality and Related Syndromes. Edited by Reid WH, Dorr D, Walker JI, et al. New York, WW Norton, 1986, pp 191–207

Sturup GK: Treating the Untreatable: Chronic Criminals at Herstedvester. Baltimore, MD, Johns Hopkins University Press, 1968

Symington N: The response aroused by the psychopath. Int Rev Psychoanal 7:291–298, 1980

Vaillant GE: Sociopathy as a human process: a viewpoint. Arch Gen Psychiatry 32:178–183, 1975

Vaillant GE: Natural history of male alcoholism, V: is alcoholism the cart or the horse to sociopathy? Br J Addict 78:317–326, 1983

Widiger TA: Antisocial personality disorder. Hosp Community Psychiatry 43:6–8, 1992

Wilson JQ, Herrnstein RJ: Crime and Human Nature. New York, Simon & Schuster, 1985

Woerner PI, Guze SB: A family and marital study of hysteria. Br J Psychiatry 114:161–168, 1968

Woody GE, McLellan AT, Luborsky L, et al: Sociopathy and psychotherapy outcome. Arch Gen Psychiatry 42:1081–1086, 1985

Yeudall LT: Neuropsychological assessment of forensic disorders. Canada's Mental Health 25(2):7–15, 1977

Yochelson S, Samenow SE: The Criminal Personality, Vol I: A Profile for Change. New York, Jason Aronson, 1976

Yochelson S, Samenow SE: The Criminal Personality, Vol II: The Treatment Process. New York, Jason Aronson, 1977

Chapter 18

Cluster B Personality Disorders: Hysterical and Histrionic

In the transition from DSM-II (American Psychiatric Association 1968) to DSM-III (American Psychiatric Association 1980), hysterical personality disorder disappeared from the official diagnostic nomenclature of American psychiatry. This change eliminated a diagnostic entity with a time-honored clinical tradition paralleled by few other psychiatric syndromes. DSM-III replaced it with histrionic personality disorder which, the manual suggests, is synonymous with hysterical personality disorder. In fact, the diagnostic criteria for DSM-III histrionic personality disorder described a much more primitive, much more impulsive, and much less stable variant that sounded remarkably like borderline personality disorder. Indeed, in one study, 74% of a sample of patients with borderline personality disorder also fulfilled DSM-III criteria for histrionic personality disorder (Pope et al. 1983).

Because of widespread criticism that the DSM-III entity of histrionic personality disorder overlapped too much with borderline personality disorder, the criteria were modified in DSM-III-R (American Psychiatric Association 1987) (Widiger et al. 1988). The criteria of angry outbursts and tantrums, as well as manipulative suicidal behavior, were deleted because they suggested borderline features. To make the characteristics of the diagnosis sound more like the classic hysterical personality disorder, the diagnostic criteria were emended to include "inappropriately sexually seductive in appearance or behavior" (p. 349).

Despite the DSM-III-R modifications, the diagnostic criteria for histrionic personality disorder still failed to capture the well-integrated and higher-functioning hysterical personality well known to dynamic clinicians for decades. Studies using DSM-III-R criteria continued to find overlap between histrionic and borderline personality diagnoses in the range of 44%–95% (Pfohl 1991). Two DSM-III-R criteria—"constantly seeks or demands reassurance, approval, or praise" and "is self-centered, actions being directed toward obtaining immediate satisfaction; has no tolerance for the frustration of delayed gratification"—had especially low specificity. More than 80% of borderline patients were also found to meet these criteria (Pfohl 1991). Both have been dropped from the DSM-IV criteria (American Psychiatric Association 1994).

The DSM-IV criteria (see Table 18–1) have added a new item, "considers relationships to be more intimate than they actually are," based on historical concepts and the favorable ratings of expert consultants (Pfohl 1991). The new criteria, however, still do not capture the well-integrated and higher-functioning hysterical personality. Because both

---

Table 18–1.   DSM-IV diagnostic criteria for histrionic personality disorder

A pervasive pattern of excessive emotionality and attention seeking, beginning by early adulthood and present in a variety of contexts, as indicated by at least *five* of the following:

1. is uncomfortable in situations in which he or she is not the center of attention
2. interaction with others is often characterized by inappropriate sexually seductive or provocative behavior
3. displays rapidly shifting and shallow expression of emotions
4. consistently uses physical appearance to draw attention to self
5. has style of speech that is excessively impressionistic and lacking in detail
6. shows self-dramatization, theatricality, and exaggerated expression of emotion
7. shows suggestibility, i.e., is easily influenced by others or circumstances
8. considers relationships to be more intimate than they actually are

---

Source.   DSM-IV. Because the criteria sets were not final at press time, the reader should consult DSM-IV for final criteria.

the high-level hysterical personality disorder and the more primitive histrionic personality disorder are commonly encountered in clinical practice, both will be considered in this chapter in an effort to make clinically useful distinctions.

Hysterical Versus Histrionic

The staunchly atheoretical nature of the personality disorder criteria in DSM-IV is particularly problematic when considering patients with hysterical or histrionic tendencies. To determine the appropriate treatment for this diverse group of patients, a careful psychodynamic assessment is far more crucial than a descriptive cataloging of overt behaviors. One primary source of confusion in the related literature has been a tendency to rely on behavioral characteristics instead of dynamic understanding.

A further source of confusion is that the term *hysterical* has been used not only to describe a personality disorder but also to refer to a disease largely of women, characterized by frequent surgeries and multiple somatic complaints, and to denote various conversion symptoms, such as paralysis or blindness, that have no organic basis. The former condition, known as Briquet's hysteria or Briquet's syndrome, is currently subsumed by somatoform disorder in DSM-IV. Conversion symptoms may now be found in Axis I under conversion disorder. Hysterical conversion symptomatology is what opened the gates of the unconscious to Freud and led to the development of psychoanalysis. Freud understood conversion symptoms as symbolic physical symptoms that represented displaced and repressed instinctual wishes. However, there is a broad consensus in modern psychiatry that hysterical conversion symptoms and hysterical personality disorder are not related either clinically or dynamically (Chodoff 1974). Although conversion symptoms can occur in patients with hysterical personality disorder, they also can occur across a wide variety of other character diagnoses.

During the first half of the century, the intrapsychic conflicts associated with the hysterical personality were thought to derive from genital-oedipal developmental issues. Part of the legacy of Freud's work with hysterical conversion symptoms was the more generalized view that repressed sexuality was of paramount importance in both character neuroses and neurotic symptoms. Clinically unsuccessful psychoanalytic efforts to treat these patients led some to question Freud's formulation. Beginning with Marmor's classic 1953 article, the psychiatric literature has strongly identified pregenital (particularly oral) issues as central to the pathogenesis of hysterical personality disorder (Chodoff 1974).

The literature of the last three decades has seen a convergence of opinion regarding the existence of both "healthy" and "sick" hysterical patients (Baumbacher and Amini 1980–81; Blacker and Tupin 1977; Chodoff 1974; Easser and Lesser 1965; Kernberg 1975; Lazare 1971; Sugarman 1979; Wallerstein 1980–81; Zetzel 1968). "Healthy" hysterical patients are referred to by a variety of names, including "good," "phallic," and "true." Even more labels have been applied to those in the latter group—"oral hysterics," "so-called good hysterics," "hysteroids," and "infantile personalities." For reasons of clarity, in this chapter I will refer to the healthier group as *hysterical personality disorders* and the more disturbed group as *histrionic personality disorders*.

Defining the exact interrelationship between the hysterical and the histrionic personality is a controversial process. While some have argued that the two are simply gradations along a continuum (Blacker and Tupin 1977; Lazare 1971; Wallerstein 1980–81; Zetzel 1968), others viewed the two groups as so different as to constitute sharply distinct entities (Baumbacher and Amini 1980–81; Sugarman 1979). What appears to link hysterical persons and histrionic persons is an overlap in overt behavioral characteristics, such as labile and shallow emotionality, attention seeking, disturbed sexual functioning, dependency and helplessness, and self-dramatization. These qualities have come to be associated with the use of "hysterical" by laypersons to mean *dramatic overreaction*. The paradox is that these characteristics are far more typical of histrionic patients than of hysterical patients. As Wallerstein (1980–81) noted: "Those who behaviorally look more hysterical in the sense of the dramatic or flamboyant hysterical character type are the very ones who look less hysterical in the sense of the dynamics of the 'good' or 'true' hysteric" (p. 540). Zetzel (1968) similarly observed that the "so-called good hysterics" who appear floridly hysterical are often mistaken for analyzable, high-level hysterical patients although they are actually primitively organized and unanalyzable— what I refer to here as *histrionic personalities*.

The literature distinguishing the two groups can be summarized by listing the characteristics that differentiate hysterical personality disorder from histrionic personality disorder (Easser and Lesser 1965;

Kernberg 1975; Lazare 1971; Sugarman 1979; Zetzel 1968) (see Table 18–2). The histrionic personality is more florid than the hysterical in virtually every way. All the DSM-IV criteria symptoms are more exaggerated in the histrionic person. Greater lability of affect, more impulsivity, and a more overt seductiveness are all hallmarks. The sexuality of these patients is often so direct and unmodulated that it may actually "turn off" members of the opposite sex. Their demanding, exhibitionistic need to be the center of attention may also fail to engage others because of its ruthless nature. In this regard, these patients clearly have much in common with persons who have narcissistic personality disorder.

By contrast, persons who have true hysterical personality disorder may be much more subtly dramatic and exhibitionistic, and their sexuality may be expressed more coyly and engagingly. In addition,

Table 18–2. Differentiation of hysterical personality disorder from histrionic personality disorder

Hysterical Personality Disorder	Histrionic Personality Disorder
1. Restrained and circumscribed emotionality	1. Florid and generalized emotionality
2. Sexualized exhibitionism and need to be loved	2. Greedy exhibitionism with a demanding, oral quality that is "cold" and less engaging
3. Good impulse control	3. Generalized impulsivity
4. Subtly appealing seductiveness.	4. Crude, inappropriate, and distancing seductiveness
5. Ambition and competitiveness	5. Aimlessness and helplessness
6. Mature, triangular object relations	6. Primitive, dyadic object relations, characterized by clinging, masochism, and paranoia
7. Separations from love objects can be tolerated	7. Overwhelming separation anxiety occurs when abandoned by love objects
8. Strict superego and some obsessional defenses	8. Lax superego and a predominance of primitive defenses, such as splitting and idealization
9. Sexualized transference wishes develop gradually and are viewed as unrealistic	9. Intense sexualized transference wishes develop rapidly and are viewed as realistic expectations

Wallerstein (1980–81) has suggested that a sizable group of high-level hysterics are not dramatic or flamboyant at all. He described these patients as "constricted wall flowers, shy and even tongue-tied in interpersonal encounter, at extremes mousy and totally inhibited in demeanor and interaction" (p. 540). He persuasively pointed out that a focus on overt behavior rather than underlying dynamics can result in a misdiagnosis.

Patients with hysterical personality disorder are often reasonably successful at work and demonstrate ambition as well as constructive competitiveness. This active mastery can be juxtaposed with the aimless, helpless, dependent quality that keeps histrionic patients from succeeding except in the sense of passively manipulating others to meet their needs. Whereas the true hysterical patient has attained mature whole-object relations characterized by triangular oedipal themes and has been able to form significant relationships with both parents, the histrionic patient is fixated at a more primitive dyadic level of object relations often characterized by clinging, masochism, and paranoia.

Hysterical patients can tolerate separation from their love objects even though they may identify those relationships as their main area of difficulty. Histrionic patients, on the other hand, are often overwhelmed with separation anxiety when apart from their love objects. The strict superego and other obsessional defenses of the hysterical patient contrast with the histrionic patient's typically lax superego and predominantly more primitive defenses, such as splitting and idealization.

When hysterical patients enter psychotherapy or psychoanalysis, sexualized transference wishes develop gradually over a considerable time and are generally viewed as unrealistic by the patients themselves. Histrionic patients, on the other hand, develop intense erotic transference wishes almost immediately and often view these wishes as realistic expectations. When the wishes are frustrated, the patient may become furious with the therapist for not being more gratifying. Zetzel (1968) has pointed out that the hysterical patient's capacity to differentiate the therapeutic alliance from transference feelings is intimately linked with the ability to separate internal from external reality, an ego function that is compromised in the histrionic patient.

The distinguishing features of the histrionic personality disorder highlight its close relationship with the borderline personality disorder. Kernberg (1975), for example, explicitly conceptualized the infantile personality as having an underlying borderline personality organization. These patients do not defend against genital sexuality so much as against passive and primitive orality (Lazare 1971).

Patients with hysterical personality disorder, on the other hand, usually present with problems that revolve either around genital sexuality per se or around difficulties with the sexual objects in their lives. Although the hysterical female has classically been described as "frigid" or anorgasmic, she may also be promiscuous or fully orgasmic but basically dissatisfied with her sexual relationships. She may be unable to make a romantic or sexual commitment to a man who is appropriate for her, instead falling hopelessly in love with an unavailable man. Another recurrent problem for the female hysterical patient is that men often misinterpret her actions as sexual advances, and she is continually surprised at this misunderstanding—a fact that reflects the *unconscious* nature of her seductiveness.

Gender and Diagnosis

The more flamboyant descriptive characteristics of the hysterical—and particularly the histrionic—personality disorder paint a picture that is often described as a caricature of femininity (Chodoff and Lyons 1958). These diagnoses are so commonly applied to women that some clinicians would regard the term *male hysteric* as an oxymoron. Throughout the history of psychiatry, the hysterical personality has been associated with the female gender. This tendency to think of the diagnosis only in relation to women probably relates more to cultural sex role stereotypes than to psychodynamics. Halleck (1967) has pointed out that deprived males in our society tend to deny their own needs and attack those they believe have rejected them. Women in our society, however, are not expected to deny their dependency needs and have "little opportunity to express aggression directly" (p. 753). Female children "are more likely to adapt to deprivation by seeking to bind people to . . . [them] through relationships in which . . . [the women assume] a highly dependent role" (p. 753). Others (Hollender 1971; Lerner 1974) have noted that the hysterical personality characteristics reflect cultural expectations of how women are supposed to adapt in American society. Another glaring contributor to the overwhelming tendency to view hysterical personality as a female disease is the fact that, with few exceptions, the literature on the disorder has been written entirely by men (Chodoff and Lyons 1958; Luisada et al. 1974).

Despite the predominant association between hysterical personality and femininity, hysterical personality disorder has been extensively documented in males (Blacker and Tupin 1977; Cleghorn 1969; Kolb 1968; Halleck 1967; Luisada et al. 1974; MacKinnon and Michels 1971; Malmquist 1971). The descriptions of male hysterical patients fall into two broad subtypes: the hypermasculine and the passive/effeminate. Those in the hypermasculine subtype are directly analogous to the classical female hysteric in that they are caricatures of masculinity. They may be "Don Juans" who act seductively toward all women and may even engage in antisocial behavior. The latter subtype of passive, effeminate males may be "foppish" (MacKinnon and Michels 1971), flamboyant homosexuals or passive, impotent heterosexuals who are fearful of women. The same distinction between the high-level hysterical personality and the lower-level histrionic personality can be made in male patients, based largely on the same criteria used to distinguish the two groups in females.

In a study of 27 male patients with hysterical personality disorder, Luisada et al. (1974) found that the vast majority were heterosexual, but that all had some form of disturbed sexual relationships. Antisocial behavior, such as lying and unreliability, were common problems in the group, as were alcohol and drug abuse. These investigators identified both effeminate and hypermasculine subtypes, with unstable relationships typical of both. Many of these patients would probably receive a diagnosis of narcissistic personality disorder, some with antisocial features, but as a group they tended to have much more warmth toward and empathy for others than the true narcissist.

Despite the overt differences in the behavior of the passive, effeminate subtype and the hypermasculine subtype, the underlying dynamics of these two variants of the male hysterical personality disorder are remarkably similar. These dynamics and their contribution to the behavioral facade of the male hysterical patient will be discussed later in this chapter.

Cognitive Style and Defense Mechanisms

One aspect of intrapsychic functioning that links the hysterical and the histrionic personality disorders is cognitive style. Shapiro (1965) has identified the cognitive style typical of these personality disorders as generally "global, relatively diffuse, and lacking in sharpness, particularly in sharp detail. In a word, it is *impressionistic*" (p. 111). When a therapist asks a patient with this cognitive style, "How was your weekend?" the response is likely to be along the lines of "just great" or "really awful," without any supportive detail. The same order of response is likely to apply to significant figures in the patient's life. When one hysterical patient was asked to describe her father, she responded, "He's just super!" Similarly, when patients with this form of cognitive style approach a task, such as psychological testing, they are inclined to avoid concentrating on facts and to instead respond with a hunch. The therapist may encounter considerable frustration, for example, in getting historical facts about a patient's family background.

This global, impressionistic cognitive style is complementary to two of the chief defense mechanisms of the hysterical personality: repression and denial (Horowitz 1977b). Repression is facilitated by this cognitive style (Shapiro 1965) because of the patient's sketchy original retention of facts and the patient's impressionistic and poorly focused subsequent recall of facts. Because of the distractible deployment of attention, aspects of reality are disavowed as well, in keeping with the defense mechanism of denial. In the early literature on hysteria, the patient's attitude was often described as *la belle indifference*, referring to the female patient's apparent lack of concern about her conversion symptoms. Although this phrase is rarely used in modern psychiatry, patients with hysterical personality disorder do manifest a blasé attitude about certain aspects of reality that they appear to scotomize. The hysterical cognitive style may account for this failure to integrate or recognize implications, consequences, and details of experience.

This same attitude of indifference occurs in patients with histrionic personality disorder after they have displayed intense emotions during an outburst. Like the borderline patient, the histrionic patient may react with bland denial to the contradiction between the self-representation associated with the outburst and the self-representation associated with calm, subdued functioning *after* the outburst. Kernberg (1975) has suggested that hysterical patients use repression as a predominant defense, while infantile patients (histrionic patients, for purposes of this discussion) use splitting instead of repression as their major defense. Recent research (Perry and Cooper 1986) suggests, however, that repression and splitting are not necessarily at opposite ends of the same continuum. Indeed, the two defenses commonly co-

exist in hysterical and histrionic patients. For example, histrionic patients who use splitting will often report pervasive amnesia (indicative
of repression) regarding early childhood experiences. Nevertheless,
Kernberg's distinction is useful in the sense that repression is probably
more prominent than splitting in most hysterical persons and vice
versa in histrionic persons.

Dissociative states, like conversion symptoms, have often been
classified as hysterical phenomena, even though they are found in patients with a variety of diagnoses. The most extreme manifestation of
dissociation is multiple personality disorder, which involves both splitting—in the sense that different self-representations are maintained
as separate—and repression—in the sense that the primary personality usually has no memory of the alters. The reactions of histrionic
patients to their emotional outbursts resemble dissociation and multiple personality disorder, albeit in attenuated form. These patients
often have poor recall of their actions, which they say seemed to be like
those of "someone else."

One histrionic patient who also suffered from dissociative symptoms discovered cuts on her left breast but could not explain how they
got there. Shortly after this discovery, her husband found her in the
bathroom at 3 A.M.; she was in a dissociated state and was cutting her
left breast lightly with a razor blade. Hypnotized for diagnostic purposes, the patient said, "I must suffer as my mother suffered." Her
mother had just undergone surgery for breast cancer. This patient also
illustrates the defense mechanism of identification, another common
hysterical defense (MacKinnon and Michels 1971).

One final defense mechanism that may be found in both hysterical
and histrionic patients is emotionality itself. Becoming intensely, yet
superficially and shallowly, emotional may defend against deeper,
more heartfelt affects that the patient wishes to avoid (MacKinnon and
Michels 1971). Knee-jerk emotionality in concert with the global, impressionistic cognitive style serves to keep the histrionic patient from
being in touch with any genuine affective states or attitudes toward
self and others.

Horowitz (1977b) has incorporated the hysterical defensive patterns and cognitive style into an operational definition of hysterical
personality based on long-range, medium-range, and short-range patterns. The short-range patterns involve the hysterical patient's infor-
mation-processing style. These patterns last only minutes or seconds
and include global deployment of attention and incomplete communi-

cations lacking in detail. The medium-range patterns, occurring over hours or days, are referred to as "traits." These include childlike behavior, suggestibility, fluid transitions from one mood or emotion to another, seductiveness, and attention-seeking behavior. Finally, the longer-range patterns, covering months to years, focus on interpersonal relationships. Typical stereotyped patterns for all three frames are victim-aggressor or child-parent interactions and rescue or rape themes.

Psychodynamic Understanding

Because a variety of overt behaviors in both genders are subsumed under the categories of hysterical and histrionic personality disorders, a careful psychodynamic assessment is crucial to the informed assignment of the appropriate type of psychotherapy. Female patients with hysterical or histrionic personality styles tend to encounter difficulties at two of the classical psychosexual stages of development: they experience relative maternal deprivation during the oral stage, and they have difficulty resolving the oedipal situation and emerging with a clear sexual identity (Blacker and Tupin 1977). Although both hysterical and histrionic patients have some difficulty with oral and phallic-oedipal issues, the histrionic patient obviously encounters greater difficulty at the earlier stage, whereas the hysteric is fixated primarily at the later stage.

In the case of the histrionic female patient, the lack of maternal nurturance leads her to turn to her father for the gratification of dependency needs (Blacker and Tupin 1977; Hollender 1971; MacKinnon and Michels 1971). She soon learns that flirtatiousness and dramatic exhibitionistic displays of emotion are required to gain her father's attention. As she matures, she learns that she must repress her genital sexuality to remain "daddy's little girl." When the little girl grows up, the primitive neediness characteristic of all her sexual relations may be termed the *breast-penis equation*. She often engages in promiscuous sexual behavior that is ultimately unsatisfying since the male penis only serves as a substitute for the maternal breast she unconsciously longs for.

The female with hysterical personality disorder has negotiated the oral stage of development with a reasonable degree of success. She, too, is disappointed with her mother, but the disappointment occurs at a more advanced stage of development. In the phallic stage of development directly preceding the full-blown oedipal situation, the little girl must come to terms with the fact that she cannot physically possess her mother as her father can. The narcissistic injury ensuing from this awareness of genital difference normally leads the little girl to transfer her libidinal phallic strivings from her mother to her father during the oedipal phase of development.

Some hysterical patients who have been unable to shift from mother to father maintain an unconscious phallic attachment to their mother (Baumbacher and Amini 1980–81). By maintaining this attachment, they ward off the narcissistic injury connected with their feelings of inadequacy. They also may displace their phallic strivings from the genitals to the entire body. The hyperfemininity that results is sometimes referred to as the *body phallus,* in the sense that the patient "adorns her body . . . makes herself and her presence intrusive, creates a stir wherever she goes, and in her childishness or naïveté . . . may be very aggressive" (Baumbacher and Amini 1980–81, p. 515). The patient thus defends against her anger and disappointment in her mother by forming a positive, even idealized attachment to her mother.

The end result of this developmental constellation is that the overtly heterosexual hysterical woman continues to have her mother as a (homosexual) unconscious love object. She lacks any real investment in male relationships, however, because no man can compete with her unconscious attachment to her mother. These patients have relatively good ego functioning, but their unconscious self-representations are inadequate because they lack a coherent sexual identity because of an inability to shift their attachment to their mother into a more oedipal attachment to their father.

Other hysterical patients are able to shift from their mother to their father but then cannot let go of the father. As little girls, these women often idealized their father, perhaps as the only man worth having. This intense attachment led to rivalrous feelings toward the mother and active wishes to replace her. In the course of therapy or analysis, many hysterical patients recover previously repressed fantasies of this nature. If they perceive that their brothers are granted special status with their fathers by virtue of their male gender, they also may develop deep resentment and may become highly competitive with men.

The common finding of anorgasmia in hysterical patients may be partly related to an unconscious wish to achieve power over men through the sexual act (MacKinnon and Michels 1971). Alternatively, all sexuality may be tinged with incestuous meanings because of the oedipal attachment to the father. These women also may choose inappropriate partners as a further defense against giving up oedipal longings. These dynamics are often covert, however, and often only become clear after a careful evaluation. While some hysterical patients may have overt, conscious attachments to their father, others will have repressed this dimension of development. Their conscious experience of their father may be tinged with anger as a defense against their underlying longing. Similarly, they may be unaware of their rivalrous feelings toward their mother, whom they consciously love. Evidence of hysterical dynamics in the female patient may come instead from persistent patterns of triangular relationships, such as falling in love with married men, or from slowly emerging developments in the transference, such as intense rivalry with other female patients. Whether or not the dynamics are repressed may depend on the father's response to his daughter's oedipal longings. If he views such feelings as unacceptable, he will convey this attitude to his daughter, who will then feel that she must repress them.

The developmental dynamics outlined for the female patient may be similarly applied to the male. The histrionic male patient will have experienced maternal deprivation and will have looked to his father for nurturance. If the father is absent or emotionally unavailable, the boy child is faced with two alternatives: he may model himself after his mother and develop a passive, effeminate identity, or (in the absence of a true masculine role model) he may mimic various cultural stereotypes of hypermasculinity to take flight from any anxiety about effeminacy and to counteract his regressive pull to be like his mother (Blacker and Tupin 1977).

The male patient with hysterical personality disorder resembles his female counterpart in that he enters the phallic stage intensely attached to his mother. He also experiences feelings of genital inadequacy when comparing himself to his father or other adult males. The narcissistic injury associated with greater genital awareness prevents him—just as it does some females—from entering the competitive arena of the Oedipus complex. He remains attached to his mother and may become passive and effeminate by identification (Baumbacher and Amini 1980–81). He does not become homosexual, but his heterosexual relationships are largely related to efforts to reassure himself about his underlying genital inadequacy. He is always disappointed in women, since none of them can measure up to his mother. Some men with this hysterical configuration will choose a celibate life-style, such as the priesthood, to unconsciously maintain unswerving loyalty to their mother. Other boys will deal with their perceived genital inadequacy by indulging in hypermasculine activities, such as bodybuilding and the compulsive seduction of women. Thus they can reassure themselves that they are "real men" with nothing to feel inferior about.

No discussion of female hysteria would be complete without reference to incest and childhood seduction. Freud originally believed that many of his hysterical patients had been seduced by their fathers because he so often heard such reports from his patients. He later became convinced that many of these reports were fantasies stemming from oedipal wishes. We now know that many little girls are indeed victims of actual incestuous sexuality with their fathers, stepfathers, or other male relatives. Amidst the furor over whether Freud's view was correct, many clinicians have adopted an either/or position. Either little girls are actually seduced, or they merely fantasize seduction. This dichotomy is further complicated by the fact that many women who have been victimized by incest nevertheless have powerful fantasies about and yearnings for the perpetrator of the incest. Even women who have never been violated by their father may still have powerful conscious or unconscious sexual wishes for him. Finally, there is considerable middle ground where erotized interactions occur that do *not* result in overt incest, but that *do* encourage fantasies.

In terms of the developmental pathogenesis of histrionic and hysterical personality disorder, a history of actual incest is much more likely to be found in the histrionic patient. These patients may go through their adult life repeating the original trauma by seeking out men who are forbidden in one way or another, such as therapists, married men, or bosses. They may be unconsciously attempting to actively master a passively experienced trauma by being the one to initiate it rather than the one to passively submit.

The higher-level hysterical patient is much less likely to have a history of overt incest but may have had what she perceived as a special relationship with her father. Hysterical patients frequently have a father who was unhappy with his wife and turned to the patient for fulfillment and gratification not possible in the marriage. The patient may receive an implicit message that she must remain loyal to her father forever to rescue him from an unhappy marriage. Fathers in this situation may give subtle or even overt signs of disapproval whenever their daughters show interest in other men. In this scenario, the hysterical patient will find herself surrounded with dynamics similar to incest, only in attenuated form. Hysterical patients with these dynamics and family constellations may find themselves unable to give up their dependency on their father and get on with their lives.

Individual Psychotherapy

Patients with hysterical personality disorder generally respond well to expressive individual psychotherapy or to psychoanalysis. The discussion here will focus on those patients, since therapeutic strategies appropriate to the lower-level histrionic patient are similar to those used in the treatment of the borderline personality disorder (Allen 1977) discussed earlier (see Chapter 15). Where appropriate, modifications of technique required for the treatment of histrionic personality disorders will be discussed.

Although some patients with hysterical personality disorder will present with a discrete symptom, such as sexual dysfunction, more commonly they enter psychotherapy because of a general dissatisfaction with their relationship patterns. The precipitating event may be the breakup of a marriage or a love relationship. They also may experience vague feelings of depression or anxiety related to disappointment with their current partner (MacKinnon and Michels 1971). Unlike many patients with the personality disorders in Clusters A and B of DSM-IV, the patient with hysterical personality disorder readily becomes attached to the therapist and quickly develops a therapeutic alliance in which the therapist is perceived as helpful. The psychotherapy process will generally go well if the therapist adheres to several general principles.

Principles of Technique

A rule of thumb in expressive work is to address resistance before attempting to interpret the underlying content. In the case of the hysterical patient, this axiom dictates that the patient's cognitive style must be dealt with first, since it is so intimately bound up with the patient's defensive configuration. Hysterical patients often begin psychotherapy with an unconscious expectation that the therapist should be able to understand them intuitively, nonverbally, and globally without details of their intrapsychic world (Allen 1977). Therapists confronting this expectation must matter-of-factly let their patients know that the only way they can develop understanding is if the patients provide a detailed account of their internal experience. Hence the initial approach must be geared to eliciting as much detail as possible from the patient (Allen 1977; Horowitz 1977a; MacKinnon and Michels 1971).

As soon as the therapist has established the need for detail, the patient is likely to struggle with compliance. Hysterical patients are not accustomed to thinking in such terms, and the therapist can expect responses along the lines of "I don't know." At this point in the process, therapists can gently encourage the patients with comments such as, "Let's not accept 'I don't know' and see what comes to mind as you reflect on it." Over and over again, the therapist must help the patient learn how to *reflect* instead of simply reporting an impressionistic feeling. Therapists may thus call the patient's attention to the vagueness of perception and interpret defensive reasons for not wanting to fully recognize certain thoughts or feelings (Horowitz 1977a).

The internal experience of the hysterical patient is often that of a leaf in the wind buffeted by powerful feeling states. There may be a complete repression of the ideas that connect one feeling with another. In urging the hysterical patient to reflect and to attend in detail to internal and external reality, the therapist helps the patient retrieve the ideational connections between feelings. As Allen (1977) has noted, part of this process involves teaching the hysterical person to feel with more depth and genuineness. Superficial and shallow feelings defend against more disturbing and more deeply experienced affects. As the patient's tolerance for these deeper feeling states increases, a concomitant increase occurs in the patient's ability to attend to details (Horowitz 1977a).

As hysterical patients become able to identify their feelings, attitudes, and ideational states, they develop a greater sense of self-as-agent in effective interaction with the environment rather than self-as-passive-victim of the environment (Horowitz 1977a). Hysterical patients often experience vivid visual images and fantasies, but they will not translate these into words unless the therapist assists in this process. Thus, therapists help their patients identify what they want and feel. Patients also learn that having certain thoughts or feelings is not dangerous.

When threatening thoughts and feelings emerge, hysterical patients frequently express a wish to know all about the therapist's life.

They are highly suggestible, and if therapists share a lot about their own life and beliefs, their patients will rapidly adopt similar qualities so as to please their therapists and to thereby avoid the arduous task of getting in touch with their own feelings and beliefs. A cardinal rule in the treatment of hysterical patients is to frustrate rather than gratify their wish for personal information about the therapist. Gratifying these demands leads to their becoming endless (Allen 1977). The wish to know about the therapist may be interpreted as a defensive maneuver to avoid anxiety about self-disclosure (Allen 1977). Therapists should similarly avoid giving advice to their hysterical patients, who need to learn that they have considerable resources within themselves with which to approach their problems.

Patients in long-term therapy will find that the process of modifying their cognitive style leads to a modification of object relatedness as well. As these patients begin to attend in more detail to self and others in interpersonal contexts, they develop new patterns of perceiving relationships (Horowitz 1977a). Instead of always seeing themselves as the victim of others, patients begin to understand that they play an active role in perpetuating certain patterns of relating to others. They develop a capacity to compare the actual facts of an interpersonal situation with the internal patterns often superimposed on external situations. Ultimately, the self-representation of the passive child so typical of the hysterical patient is replaced by a more mature representation involving activity and sexuality. This transition may take years, however, because patients frequently experience the loss of the hysterical cognitive style as a threat to a basic sense of identity.

In the psychotherapy of hysterical personality disorder, therapeutic work within the transference is the main vehicle for change. The problems that the patient encounters in relationships outside the therapy will be reproduced within the transference. Although psychotherapy can be effective and gratifying with hysterical patients, the mishandling of transference, particularly erotic transference, is probably the most frequent cause of therapeutic failure.

Management of Erotic Transference

Despite the pervasiveness of the phenomenon of erotic transference, not only in hysterical patients but also in others, many therapists do not receive adequate training in the effective and therapeutic management of transference feelings. One female psychiatry resident who was struggling with a male patient's sexual feelings toward her took the problem to her psychotherapy supervisor, an analyst. He responded by scratching his head and replying, "I don't know what you girls do about this problem." Historically, a subtle (or not-so-subtle) sexism has pervaded psychotherapy training programs. Because the vast majority of erotic transference reports in the literature, from Freud to the present, have been of female patients who have fallen in love with their male therapists or analysts, male supervisors have sometimes inadvertently promoted among their male supervisees a casual, denigrating attitude toward female patients who develop an erotic transference. One male resident who was beginning psychotherapy training told his male supervisor that he was uncertain about how to approach his first psychotherapy patient. His supervisor informed him, "It's really very simple. Do you know how to seduce a woman?" The supervisor went on to draw an analogy between "hooking" the patient in a psychotherapy process and seducing a woman. This unprofessional attitude typifies an unfortunate historical trend to "enjoy" the erotic transference rather than analyze and understand it.

Since the term is used loosely to describe a number of different transference developments, a clear definition of the phenomenon is relevant to a discussion of its management. Person (1985) provided a succinct definition that applies to psychotherapy as well as to psychoanalysis:

> The term *erotic transference* is used interchangeably with the term *transference love*. It refers to some mixture of tender, erotic, and sexual feelings that a patient experiences in reference to his or her analyst and, as such, forms part of a positive transference. Sexual transference components alone represent a truncated erotic transference, one that has not been fully developed or is not fully experienced. (p. 161)

In hysterical patients, the erotic transference usually develops gradually and with considerable shame and embarrassment. Sexual longings for the therapist are often experienced as ego-dystonic, and the patient knows that the fulfillment of these wishes would be inappropriate.

Histrionic and borderline patients may develop a subtype of erotic transference that Blum (1973) has termed the *erotized transference*. In contrast to ordinary transference love, the patient in the throes of an erotized transference makes a tenacious and ego-syntonic demand for sexual gratification. Because of ego impairments in these patients, their internal and external realities are blurred, and they view their expectation of sexual consummation with their therapist as reasonable and desirable. Their seeming obliviousness to the crossing of symbolically incestuous boundaries may stem from a childhood history of being victimized in actual sexual seductions by parents or parental figures (Blum 1973; Kumin 1985–86).

The spectrum of transferences ranging from the erotic to the erotized is aptly described by Person (1985) as "both gold mine and minefield" (p. 163). These transferences can set the scene for devastating countertransference acting out. Therapist-patient sex has severely stigmatized the mental health professions, has ruined the careers of a number of psychotherapists, and has caused severe psychological damage to the patients who are its victims (Gabbard 1989; Pope and Bouhoutsos 1986). Surveys reveal that as many as 10% of all male therapists have engaged in such behavior (Gabbard 1989), so it cannot be dismissed as an occasional aberration of only the seriously disturbed therapist. Many of these unfortunate therapists appear to be both seeking a cure for themselves and making a desperate attempt to cure their patients (Twemlow and Gabbard 1989).

The "gold mine" aspect of erotic transferences is that they provide the therapist with an in vivo recapitulation of a past relationship in the present situation of the transference relationship. Such patients show their therapists what contributions they bring to similar relationships outside the therapeutic situation. Thus a patient's problems with love and sexuality can be examined and understood as they develop in a safe relationship where the patient will not be exploited or abused. To mine the gold in the experience without being destroyed by the minefield requires therapists to adhere to four principles of technique (see Table 18–3). Although there are definite gender differences in the expression of erotic transference, I will first discuss the handling of erotic transference in general and then examine the specific gender-determined aspects of the phenomenon.

Examination of countertransference feelings. The therapist's countertransference reactions to erotic transference feelings in the patient may represent countertransference narrowly as a reactivation of a relationship in the therapist's past, broadly as an identification with a projected aspect of the patient, or as a mixture of both (Kumin 1985–

86; Sandler 1976). Although the patient may well represent a forbidden but sexually arousing object from the therapist's past, the therapist's desire for the patient may also be linked to the actual incestuous desire of a parental figure from the patient's oedipal phase of development. Thus the first step in monitoring countertransference, in keeping with the practice of dynamic psychiatry, is for therapists to assess the relative weight of their own contributions versus those of the patient. Therapists who attempt to manage erotic transference in intensive psychotherapy without a personal treatment experience, however, will be at a serious disadvantage.

Several common countertransference patterns relate to erotic transference. The first, common in male residents treating attractive female patients, is to see erotic transference where none exists. Male therapists may respond to their own sexual arousal by projectively disavowing it and instead seeing it in their patients, whom they label as "seductive." In these circumstances, the resident who is pressed for details about why the patient is seductive or why she is sexually interested in him is often at a loss to present convincing evidence. Because of anxieties about his own sexual feelings, he has avoided them, much as the hysterical patient attempts to avoid her sexual feelings. Although this avoidance may simply reflect beginner's anxiety about having sexual feelings in psychotherapy, it may also be a repetition of the patient's father's response to his own sexual desire for his daughter (Gorkin 1985). If beginning therapists ignore these feelings, they unconsciously act them out by making phallic, "penetrating" interpretations too often and too soon, another common pitfall of the new therapist.

A second countertransference reaction is cold aloofness in response to the patient's confessions of erotic longings for the therapist (MacKinnon and Michels 1971). To control any sexual countertransference

Table 18–3. Therapeutic management of erotic transference

1. Examination of countertransference feelings
2. Nonexploitative acceptance of erotic transference as important therapeutic material to be understood
3. Assessment of the multiple meanings of the transference in its function as a resistance to a deepening of the therapeutic process
4. Interpretation of connections between transference and both current and past relationships

reactions to the patient's feelings, the therapist may become more silent, less empathic, and more distant. This "straitjacketing" of all emotions helps to rigidly maintain control of sexual impulses that seem threatening.

A third common countertransference reaction is anxiety stemming from the fear that sexual feelings—either in the patient or in the therapist—will get out of control. This anxiety may lead the therapist to divert the conversation from the patient's expressions of love or sexual arousal, or to interpret such feelings prematurely as "resistance," a digression from the therapeutic task. When a male therapist inappropriately tells his female patient that he will not allow the therapy to be sidetracked by her feelings for him, he forces her to stick to the problems outside therapy that brought her to treatment. Such anxious attempts to eliminate erotic transference feelings may give patients the message that sexual feelings are unacceptable and possibly disgusting, a view that often mirrors feelings of these patients. The therapist's own underlying disgust relates to the covert message in intense erotic transference that therapy is useless—that only sex or "love" can cure (Gorkin 1985).

In the fourth countertransference pattern, which may be more insidious than the others, therapists may encourage and foster erotic feelings for their personal gratification. These therapists, who listen with voyeuristic delight to the details of their patient's sexual fantasies, may have been drawn to the profession because they long to be idealized and loved. Underneath this wish, they may gain sadistic pleasure from arousing their patients' futile sexual wishes. This pattern can often be traced to these therapists' childhood interactions, in which they felt they were aroused by the opposite-sex parent only to be frustrated. By practicing psychotherapy, these individuals may be trying to reverse that childhood situation. Thus therapists must be aware of their own desires in the therapeutic relationship. As Kumin (1985–86) noted, "Both the analyst's capacity and incapacity to interpret accurately the patient's wishes in the transference requires an appreciation of not only what and whom the patient desires but also what and whom the analyst desires" (p. 13). Kumin has also suggested that the desires of the therapist for the patient may present a more formidable resistance than do the patient's desires for the therapist. Numerous psychotherapy processes have become stalemated in the throes of intense erotic transference because the therapist has been too busy basking in the glow of sexual feelings.

Nonexploitative acceptance of erotic transference as important therapeutic material to be understood. After the therapist has carefully monitored countertransference feelings, the next step is to convey to the patient that sexual or loving feelings are acceptable aspects of the therapeutic experience. The therapist may make an educational comment such as "In psychotherapy you are likely to experience a broad range of feelings—hate, love, envy, sexual arousal, fear, anger, and joy—all of which must be dealt with as acceptable topics for discussion and as carriers of important information for the therapy." While it is true that erotic transference may serve as resistance to the emergence of other material in the therapy, it is a technical error to immediately interpret such feelings as resistance. To understand what is being repeated from the past, the erotic transference must be allowed to develop fully.

Freud (1914/1958) first used the term *acting out* to describe a patient's tendency to repeat in action something from the past rather than remember and verbalize it. Patients can be told that the feelings developing in the therapy will provide important information about feelings that develop in their other relationships, both past and present. If a patient insists on having the therapist gratify the transference wishes, the therapist can point out that not gratifying the wishes can lead to a better understanding of what happens in other relationships. The therapist should keep in mind that erotic transference may be intensely unpleasant for the patient (just as it may be for the therapist), not only because of the frustration it brings but also because it may be embarrassing. The therapist may wish to communicate an empathic understanding of the patient's shame: "I know it is difficult and painful for you to have these feelings without being able to gratify them, but if we can explore them together we may be able to help you understand more fully the problems that brought you here."

Assessment of the multiple meanings of the transference in its function as a resistance. Erotic transference is a resistance in the sense that something is being repeated rather than remembered and verbalized. Resistance should not be equated, however, with "something bad that must be removed immediately," as it often is by beginning therapists. As just noted, erotic transference is also an important communication that should be understood. Like all other mental phenomena, erotic transference is determined by the principle of multiple function. It should not be taken simply at face value, but rather should be explored via the patient's associations, dreams, and memories for all its multiple meanings, some of which may be unconscious. For example, a male patient's erotic transference to a female therapist may represent passive homosexual longings even though the therapist is of the opposite sex (Torras de Be 1987). Because erotic transference must also be understood in terms of its function at a particular moment in therapy, the therapist must assess what preceded its development and what follows its flourishing.

One male patient began his therapy session with his male therapist by saying that he had been helped enormously in the previous session by the therapist's explanation. After commenting on how much the therapist's interpretation had helped him at work, the patient began to contradict what he had just said by maintaining that his relationships were deteriorating. As he continued to talk, he revealed that he had been having sexual fantasies about the therapist and that he believed the therapist could only help him by ejaculating semen into his rectum to make him more masculine. The therapist pointed out that the patient was devaluing the help of the insights that he had received in the previous session by holding onto a magical belief that a sexual liaison was the only way to be helped. The patient acknowledged that he needed to devalue the therapist's help because he felt so inferior to the therapist, who he said was "on Mt. Olympus." The therapist then explained that the patient's envy had increased as he was helped, so he had sexualized the transference to devalue the help. (If the therapist's insights were not particularly effective or useful, there was much less to envy.) In response, the patient said that his liberating feelings of having been helped had alternated with feelings of humiliation because he had to acknowledge that the therapist knew something the patient did not know, which made him feel vulnerable.

In this instance, the patient's erotic transference was a way to defend against his envy of the therapist's competence by devaluing it. Sexualization in the transference may be a way to defend against other feelings as well.

A male patient was seeing his female therapist for the last time prior to her departure at the end of her residency training program. He told her that he had seen a movie the night before in which a female psychiatrist had kissed one of her male patients. He observed that the patient had seemed to benefit from the therapist's affection, and he asked his therapist if she might do the same with him. After an ini-

tially anxious reaction to the request, the therapist asked if the unexpected request might be related to the termination of the therapy. The
patient responded that he would rather not think about that subject.
The therapist then pointed out to the patient that his wish to sexual-
ize their relationship might be a defense against facing the grief associated with termination.

Sexualizing the end of a relationship is a common phenomenon (in
therapy and in life in general). It serves to avoid the mourning process
connected with loss of an important figure. In this vignette, the patient's wish to become physically involved with his therapist was also
a way to deny the definitive nature of termination: A kiss might lead
to a *beginning,* rather than an ending.

Therapists who view transference love as a natural and understandable response to their enormous sexual appeal are overlooking
the darker side of erotic transference. One of the many stories told
about Dr. Karl Menninger illustrates this dilemma:

> A somewhat depressed and hysterical 40-year-old woman was hospi-
> talized at the Menninger Clinic for over a year with essentially no
> change in her condition. She had developed an intense and intractable
> erotic transference toward her male psychotherapist. Dr. Menninger
> was asked to consult on the case because of the therapeutic stalemate
> that had been reached. Throughout much of the interview, the patient
> repeatedly commented on her great love for her therapist. After lis-
> tening to her protestations of love for several minutes, Dr. Menninger
> reportedly said, "You know, if you really loved him, you would get bet-
> ter for him."

Dr. Menninger was addressing the hostility that often lies just beneath the surface of a patient's transference love. Indeed, erotic transferences frequently mask considerable aggression and sadism, even to
the extent that an erotic transference might be considered a form of
negative transference (Kumin 1985–86). Exploration of transference
wishes for a sexual relationship regularly reveal wishes to hurt, embarrass, or destroy the therapist. A patient's demands for sexual
boundary crossing may be so tormenting, especially in instances of the
erotized variant typical of histrionic and borderline patients, that the
therapist dreads each session. The therapist may feel used and transformed into a need-gratifying object whose only function is to fulfill the
patient's inappropriate demands (Frayn and Silberfeld 1986).

Ms. PP was a 24-year-old homosexual histrionic patient functioning at a borderline level of ego organization who had a history of sexual abuse by male relatives. She formed an intense erotized transference to her female therapist almost immediately. She flirted with her provocatively in the sessions by touching the therapist's foot lightly with her own foot and asking, "Does this make you nervous?" Ms. PP steadfastly maintained that her therapist could only get to know her if she slept with her. She also demanded to know her therapist's sexual orientation. Although the therapist frustrated the patient's wish to destroy their professional relationship by transforming it into a sexual one, the patient continued her efforts at seduction.

The patient would regularly bring in explicit sexual fantasies about her therapist:

> I am caressing your body—your back, your hips, your thighs. I gently and quickly stroke my hand across your pussy. You moan softly and tighten your grip across my back. I kiss you and whisper softly in your ear that I'm going to make love to you. I softly massage your breasts and kiss them. I kiss your stomach and move down toward your pussy. I kiss the inside of your thighs while stroking your clitoris with my tongue. I continue to kiss, suck, and caress you with my tongue. You moan with pleasure as you have an orgasm. I kiss your thighs again and lightly squeeze your breasts and run my fingers down your sides to your hips. I begin to lick at your clitoris again and stick my tongue inside you. I then lick and suck on your clitoris while I gently ease one, then two of my fingers into you. You have a long, multiple, satisfying orgasm which ends with you stroking my hair and me lightly kissing your pussy.

Needless to say, the patient's expression of such fantasies made the therapist feel uncomfortable and anxious, as well as controlled. If she interrupted the fantasies, she felt that she was revealing her discomfort and disapproval of the patient's transference feelings. If she remained silent, she felt that she was colluding in an exhibitionist-voyeur pairing.

The patient finally revealed some of the underlying aggressive feelings that were masquerading as erotized transference. She commented to the therapist, "You know I'm aware of still wanting to piss you off. Probably force you into rejecting me. Make you hate me. Am I succeeding? I really want you to like me. But since I know that's out of the question, I'll just drive you away. It's the shits, isn't it? You see,

> I see our relationship in two ways: either we fuck, or I make you hate
> my guts."

To a large extent, Ms. PP had induced a paralysis in the therapist,
who felt cruel and sadistic by frustrating the patient's wishes. A consultation helped the therapist understand that she was being controlled by a projective identification process so that the normal,
professional limits of psychotherapy seemed ruthless and unreasonable. In other words, a cold, depriving object from the patient's past had
been projected onto the therapist, who unconsciously identified with
this projected material. Moreover, her own anger at the patient for her
relentless control of the therapy also contributed to her feeling that any
intervention would appear cold and ruthless. As the psychotherapy
continued, it became clearer that the overt sexual wish was only the
tip of an iceberg.

> During one session, Ms. PP reported a dream in which she was in a
> high-tech office. There was a machine that could translate the pa-
> tient's thoughts, so that she did not have to tell them to her therapist.
> In the patient's associations to the dream, she acknowledged that her
> longings for the therapist were not truly sexual, but rather a wish for
> her therapist to really know her intimately. The therapist eventually
> helped Ms. PP to see that her wish for sex was really a wish for
> merger—a wish that her therapist would know her thoughts without
> her having to voice them.

This regressive longing to return to the mother-infant symbiotic
state is often a powerful component of erotic or erotized transferences
in the female patient-female therapist dyad. The sexualized wish may
be preferable to the more threatening wish for merger.

**Interpretation of connections between transference and both
current and past relationships.** A correct interpretation of the
erotic transference will often reduce the desire and the resistance inherent in transference love (Kumin 1985–86). To avoid premature interpretation, the therapist may need to silently formulate the
interpretation to help with countertransference desires even before delivering the interpretation to the patient. The timing of transference
interpretations is a matter of judgment, but a rule of thumb is to not
interpret the transference until it becomes a resistance. Another guide-

line is to avoid interpreting it until the underlying linkages to past relationships and to current extratransference relationships are near conscious awareness. The therapist can use the model of the triangle of insight described in Chapter 4 to construct connections between the transference feelings and past relationships, as well as between the transference and current extratransference relationships. By pointing out that transference love is a repetition of something from the past, and by asking the patient if the situation is reminiscent of past situations, the therapist can lay the groundwork for interpretive interventions. An actual transcript of a psychotherapy session may illustrate some of the technical approaches to interpreting erotic transference.

Ms. QQ was a 26-year-old married patient with a diagnosis of hysterical personality disorder. She was seen twice weekly by a male therapist in expressive-supportive psychotherapy with a predominantly expressive emphasis. She began psychotherapy with complaints of anorgasmia, headaches, constant marital difficulties, fear of "standing on her own two feet," feelings of being unloved and unwanted, and a generalized concern that she was too dependent. Midway through the second year of treatment, the following interchange occurred in one session:

Patient: My husband and I haven't been getting along. We don't see each other much, and when we do, we argue. I wanted to make you a buddy again today, but when I walked in, something changed. I don't know what to say today. I'd like to get real mad at you, but I don't know why. Probably because I need attention and my husband's not giving me any. When I don't have anything to say, it's usually because I have feelings for you—I had butterflies just now when I said that. There are two kinds of feelings I get in here—one is when I feel that you're like my dad and I want you to cradle me and give me the pat on the back. The other is when I want you to hold me real tight . . . (patient stops)

Therapist: You had a feeling just now that stopped you in midsentence. What was it?

Patient: I don't want to say it. It's ridiculous. (with great hesitation) I can't just come in here . . . and look at you . . . and think, "I want to make love with you." I can't feel that way. That's not me.

Therapist: To think that you could have sexual feelings is so unacceptable to you that you cannot own the feelings as yours?

Patient: I'm just not like that. Not even with my husband. My subconscious wants to hang on to you and hold you tightly, but my conscious mind wants to pretend I don't have the feelings. I'd rather go back to just having the feeling that you were like my dad and I need a pat on the back.

Therapist: It's particularly unacceptable for you to have sexual feelings for someone that you also view as a dad. I wonder if the same thing happened as a little girl in your relationship with your father.

Patient: I was always very special to my dad. When he walked me down the aisle and gave me away at the wedding, he told me that I was always his favorite of his three daughters. I shouldn't be talking like this. I have to go out and get in the car with my husband and spend the evening with him, but my thoughts are going to be about you.

Therapist: It sounds like there is a similarity between your attachment to me and your attachment to your dad in that both make it difficult for you to invest emotionally in your husband.

In this vignette, the therapist draws a connection between the patient's erotic transference and her feelings for her father. Sexual feelings are forbidden in both relationships because she sees them as incompatible with her otherwise paternal view of the therapist and her father. After linking the transference feelings to the patient's past relationship with her father, the therapist connects these longings to her difficulty with her husband, a current extratransference relationship.

These four principles of technique may be helpful to the psychotherapist who is treating a patient struggling with erotic transference feelings. However, adherence to these principles requires rational, level-headed thinking. As poets have long known, passion clouds judgment. By their very nature, feelings of love and/or lust tend to evoke enactments in both patient and therapist (Gabbard, in press). In other words, both persons are prone to lose their reflective awareness of the transferential and countertransferential characteristics of the feelings because they seem so real and compelling. Therapists must carefully monitor deviations from their standard clinical practice as a way of alerting themselves to countertransference enactment. Several warning signs are particularly useful in this form of boundary monitoring: extending sessions beyond their usual length, reducing the fee or not charging the patient, self-disclosing about one's personal life to the patient, daydreaming constantly about the patient, paying careful attention to one's appearance on the day of the patient's appointment, hugging the patient or engaging in other forms of physical contact, wishing to meet the patient in a nonclinical setting, and imagining that one can rescue the patient from his or her misery (Gabbard and Wilkinson 1994; Gutheil and Gabbard 1993). When therapists begin to observe that they are deviating along these lines or being swept away by erotic feelings toward the patient, they would be wise to seek out consultation or supervision from a respected colleague.

Therapists must also be aware that all patients experiencing sexual feelings toward the therapist will not respond to interpretive efforts. Some histrionic and borderline patients may translate their feelings into action and throw themselves at the therapist's feet, sit on the therapist's lap, or passionately hug the therapist as they move toward the office door. In such cases, the therapist must set firm limits. Patients may need to be told that they must return to their chairs and that physical contact is off limits. Sometimes an educational comment is helpful as well: "Psychotherapy is a verbal treatment that can only work under certain circumstances. One of those circumstances is that you sit in your chair and I sit in mine."

Gender Differences in Erotic Transference

The overwhelming majority of case reports in the literature involving erotic or erotized transferences are of female patients with male therapists. Lester (1985) pointed out that the absence of reports involving male patients and female therapists may reflect the general rarity of transference love in those dyads. She speculated that the male patient's anxiety about the female analyst as a powerful preoedipal phallic mother, who makes "penetrating" interpretations, can overshadow and greatly inhibit his expression of sexual feelings toward the analyst as an oedipal mother. Lester also noted that the regressive passivity in analytic therapy goes against the grain of the traditional active male sexual role.

Lester's experience has not been corroborated by all female therapists. Gornick (1986) viewed Lester's scenario of the phallic mother as only applicable to some male patients working with female therapists. Other male patients, she asserted, find it much more unacceptable to be passive and dependent vis-à-vis a female than to express direct sexual feelings. The shame of being dependent may lead certain male patients to defend against such feelings by "turning the tables" and using sexual feelings in the transference to restore a sense of male dominance.

Because so many more case reports of female patients with erotic transference have appeared in the literature, Person (1985) has observed that clinicians might get the impression that sexual feelings in therapy are specifically and exclusively related to the psychology of women. However, while many male patients being treated by a male therapist may suppress or deny erotic transference because of homosexual anxieties, some do develop full-blown erotic or erotized transference to their male therapist that needs to be systematically understood and interpreted. In many cases, the sexualized transference is a defense against more uncomfortable feelings of love and longing that are difficult to express (Gabbard, in press).

Although male patients apparently experience a spectrum of erotic transference manifestations, these do not seem to be as intense, as prolonged, and as fully developed as the erotic transference that female patients in general experience. Person (1985) has related this variance to the differences in moral development between men and women (Gilligan 1982). While women are raised to define themselves more through affiliation and relationships, men are socialized to value autonomy over relatedness. As a result, men may feel that their masculinity is threatened by dependency, whereas women do not feel an analogous threat to their femininity. Person (1985) also suggested that erotic transference in women is more often a longing for love, while in men the feelings are more often specifically sexual.

Another distinction between male and female erotic transferences is that female patients more often use it as a resistance, while male patients display a resistance to the awareness of any erotic transference (Person 1985). Male patients will frequently displace erotic feelings for their therapist onto a woman outside the therapy, because acknowledging such longings for the therapist might threaten their sense of autonomy.

Group Psychotherapy

Clinicians have often noted that patients who are good candidates for dynamic individual psychotherapy are also good candidates for dynamic group psychotherapy. Such is the case with hysterical patients, who often become "stars" in their groups. They are highly valued by other group members for their ability to express feelings directly and for their care and concern about others in the group. The hysterical patient's cognitive style and its associated defenses of repression and denial can be dealt with quite effectively in group psychotherapy. Other patients in the group will help hysterical patients see how they tend to distort their view of self and others by omitting details from interactional situations. For example, when one female hysterical patient described how she was misunderstood as being seductive when she was simply being friendly with a man at work, male patients in the group pointed out that she might be overlooking what she had said (or how she had said it) in the interaction. Furthermore, they pointed out how this patient behaved similarly in the group itself and how she seemed oblivious to the flirtatious signals she gave men in the group as well.

Hysterical patients generally form a positive maternal transference to the group as a whole. They seize group therapy as an opportunity to receive some of the maternal nurturance that they believe they missed during childhood. They are therefore well motivated to attend group therapy and to encourage others to view it as a valuable resource. Histrionic patients, however, can be more problematic in groups, because they will often "upstage" other patients by demanding to be the center of attention through florid displays of emotionality. Such patients can be effectively treated in group psychotherapy only if they are also in individual psychotherapy, much as with group psychotherapy of borderline patients (see Chapter 15).

References

Allen DW: Basic treatment issues, in Hysterical Personality. Edited by Horowitz MJ. New York, Jason Aronson, 1977, pp 283–328

American Psychiatric Association: Diagnostic and Statistical Manual of Mental Disorders, 2nd Edition. Washington, DC, American Psychiatric Association, 1968

American Psychiatric Association: Diagnostic and Statistical Manual of Mental Disorders, 3rd Edition. Washington, DC, American Psychiatric Association, 1980

American Psychiatric Association: Diagnostic and Statistical Manual of Mental Disorders, 3rd Edition, Revised. Washington, DC, American Psychiatric Association, 1987

American Psychiatric Association: Diagnostic and Statistical Manual of Mental Disorders, 4th Edition. Washington, DC, American Psychiatric Association 1994

Baumbacher G, Amini F: The hysterical personality disorder: a proposed clarification of a diagnostic dilemma. International Journal of Psychoanalytic Psychotherapy 8:501–532, 1980–81

Blacker KH, Tupin JP: Hysteria and hysterical structures: developmental and social theories, in Hysterical Personality. Edited by Horowitz MJ. New York, Jason Aronson, 1977, pp 95–141

Blum HP: The concept of erotized transference. J Am Psychoanal Assoc 21:61–76, 1973

Chodoff P: The diagnosis of hysteria: an overview. Am J Psychiatry 131:1073–1078, 1974

Chodoff P, Lyons H: Hysteria, the hysterical personality and "hysterical" conversion. Am J Psychiatry 114:734–740, 1958

Cleghorn RA: Hysteria—multiple manifestations of semantic confusion. Canadian Psychiatry Association Journal 14:539–551, 1969

Easser BR, Lesser SR: Hysterical personality: a re-evaluation. Psychoanal Q 34:390–405, 1965

Frayn DH, Silberfeld M: Erotic transferences. Can J Psychiatry 31:323–327, 1986

Freud S: Remembering, repeating and working-through (further recommendations on the technique of psycho-analysis II) (1914), in The Standard Edition of the Complete Psychological Works of Sigmund Freud, Vol 12. Translated and edited by Strachey J. London, Hogarth Press, 1958, pp 145–156

Gabbard GO (ed): Sexual Exploitation in Professional Relationships. Washington, DC, American Psychiatric Press, 1989

Gabbard GO: On love and lust in erotic transference. J Am Psychoanal Assoc (in press)

Gabbard GO, Wilkinson SM: Management of Countertransference With Borderline Patients. Washington, DC, American Psychiatric Press, 1994

Gilligan C: In a Different Voice: Psychological Theory and Women's Development. Cambridge, MA, Harvard University Press, 1982

Gorkin M: Varieties of sexualized countertransference. Psychoanal Rev 72:421–440, 1985

Gornick LK: Developing a new narrative: the woman therapist and the male patient. Psychoanalytic Psychology 3:299–325, 1986

Gutheil TH, Gabbard GO: The concept of boundaries in clinical practice: theoretical and risk management dimensions. Am J Psychiatry 150:188–196, 1993

Halleck SL: Hysterical personality traits: psychological, social, and iatrogenic determinants. Arch Gen Psychiatry 16:750–757, 1967

Hollender M: Hysterical personality. Comment on Contemporary Psychiatry 1:17–24, 1971

Horowitz MJ: Structure and the processes of change, in Hysterical Personality. Edited by Horowitz MJ. New York, Jason Aronson, 1977a, pp 329–399

Horowitz MJ: The core characteristics of hysterical personality (Introduction), in Hysterical Personality. Edited by Horowitz MJ. New York, Jason Aronson, 1977b, pp 3–6

Kernberg OF: Borderline Conditions and Pathological Narcissism. New York, Jason Aronson, 1975

Kolb LC: Noyes' Modern Clinical Psychiatry, 7th Edition. Philadelphia, PA, WB Saunders, 1968

Kumin I: Erotic horror: desire and resistance in the psychoanalytic situation. International Journal of Psychoanalytic Psychotherapy 11:3–20, 1985–86

Lazare A: The hysterical character in psychoanalytic theory: evolution and confusion. Arch Gen Psychiatry 25:131–137, 1971

Lerner HE: The hysterical personality: a "woman's disease." Compr Psychiatry 15:157–164, 1974

Lester EP: The female analyst and the erotized transference. Int J Psychoanal 66:283–293, 1985

Luisada PV, Peele R, Pitard EA: The hysterical personality in men. Am J Psychiatry 131:518–521, 1974

MacKinnon RA, Michels R: The Psychiatric Interview in Clinical Practice. Philadelphia, PA, WB Saunders, 1971

Malmquist C: Hysteria in childhood. Postgrad Med 50:112–117, 1971

Marmor J: Orality in the hysterical personality. J Am Psychoanal Assoc 1:656–671, 1953

Perry JC, Cooper SH: A preliminary report on defenses and conflicts associated with borderline personality disorder. J Am Psychoanal Assoc 34:863–893, 1986

Person ES: The erotic transference in women and in men: differences and consequences. J Am Acad Psychoanal 13:159–180, 1985

Pfohl B: Histrionic personality disorder: a review of available data and recommendations for DSM-IV. Journal of Personality Disorders 5:150–166, 1991

Pope HG Jr, Jonas JM, Hudson JI, et al: The validity of DSM-III borderline personality disorder: a phenomenologic, family history, treatment response, and long-term follow-up study. Arch Gen Psychiatry 40:23–30, 1983

Pope KS, Bouhoutsos JC: Sexual intimacy between therapists and patients. New York, Praeger, 1986

Sandler J: Countertransference and role-responsiveness. International Review of Psychoanalysis 3:43–47, 1976

Shapiro D: Neurotic Styles. New York, Basic Books, 1965

Sugarman A: The infantile personality: orality in the hysteric revisited. Int J Psychoanal 60:501–513, 1979

Torras de Be E: A contribution to the papers on transference by Eva Lester and Marianne Goldberger and Dorothy Evans. Int J Psychoanal 68:63–67, 1987

Twemlow SW, Gabbard GO: The lovesick therapist, in Sexual Exploitation in Professional Relationships. Edited by Gabbard GO. Washington, DC, American Psychiatric Press, 1989, pp 71–87

Wallerstein RS: Diagnosis revisited (and revisited): the case of hysteria and the hysterical personality. International Journal of Psychoanalysis and Psychotherapy 8:533–547, 1980–81

Widiger TA, Frances A, Spitzer RL, et al: The DSM-III-R personality disorders: an overview. Am J Psychiatry 145:786–795, 1988

Zetzel ER: The so called good hysteric. Int J Psychoanal 49:256–260, 1968

Chapter 19

Cluster C Personality Disorders: Obsessive-Compulsive, Avoidant, and Dependent

The three personality disorders classified in Cluster C of DSM-IV (American Psychiatric Association 1994)—obsessive-compulsive, avoidant, and dependent—are grouped together because persons suffering from these disorders supposedly have anxiety or fear in common as a prominent characteristic. A long clinical-psychoanalytic tradition is associated with the obsessive-compulsive personality disorder, but no similar traditions exist for the other two characterological entities of Cluster C. The fact that all three personality disorders are considered here in one chapter reflects the paucity of contributions to the psychodynamic literature regarding avoidant and dependent personality disorders.

Obsessive-Compulsive Personality Disorder

The distinction between obsessive-compulsive disorder (or neurosis) and obsessive-compulsive personality disorder is based on the difference between symptoms and enduring character traits. As described in

Chapter 9, the patient suffering from obsessive-compulsive disorder is plagued with recurring unpleasant thoughts and is driven to perform ritualistic behaviors. These symptomatic manifestations are ego-dystonic in that the patient recognizes them as problems and ordinarily wishes to be rid of them. In contrast, the traits that constitute the DSM-IV diagnosis of obsessive-compulsive personality disorder (see Table 19–1) are lifelong patterns of behavior that are ego-syntonic. These traits seldom cause distress in the patients themselves and may even be regarded as highly adaptive. Indeed, studies of physicians suggest that certain obsessive-compulsive characteristics contribute significantly to success as a physician (Gabbard 1985; Krakowski 1982; Vaillant et al. 1972). The unswerving devotion to work typical of the obsessive-compulsive person also leads to high achievement in professions other than medicine where attention to detail is essential. However, success in the work sphere often comes at a high price to these people. Their significant others often find them difficult to live with

---

Table 19–1. DSM-IV criteria for obsessive-compulsive personality disorder

A pervasive pattern of preoccupation with orderliness, perfectionism, and mental and interpersonal control, at the expense of flexibility, openness, and efficiency, beginning by early adulthood, and present in a variety of contexts, as indicated by at least *four* of the following:

1. is preoccupied with details, rules, lists, order, organization, or schedules to the extent that the major point of the activity is lost
2. shows perfectionism that interferes with task completion (e.g., is unable to complete a project because his or her overly strict standards are not met)
3. shows excessive devotion to work and productivity to the exclusion of leisure activities and friendships (not accounted for by obvious economic necessity)
4. shows overconscientiousness, scrupulousness, and inflexibility about matters of morality, ethics, or values (not accounted for by cultural or religious identification)
5. is unable to discard worn-out or worthless objects even when they have no sentimental value
6. is reluctant to delegate tasks or to work with others unless they submit to exactly his or her way of doing things
7. adopts a miserly spending style toward both self and others; money is viewed as something to be hoarded for future catastrophes
8. shows rigidity and stubbornness

Source. DSM-IV. Because the criteria sets were not final at press time, the reader should consult DSM-IV for final criteria.

and frequently instigate their coming to psychiatric attention.

Although the distinctions between obsessive-compulsive disorder and obsessive-compulsive personality disorder in DSM-IV are clear and useful, there is some controversy over the extent of the overlap between these two diagnostic entities. Psychodynamic clinicians, noting the similarities in the psychodynamic basis of both disorders, have observed that many individuals with obsessive-compulsive neurotic symptoms also have an underlying obsessive-compulsive character structure (Nemiah 1980). Symptoms of an obsessive-compulsive nature have also been reported as transitory occurrences during the psychoanalytic treatment of patients with obsessive-compulsive personality disorder (Munich 1986). However, nondynamic empirical studies indicate that a wide range of personality disorders may occur in patients with obsessive-compulsive disorder. In one study, less than half of the patients with obsessive-compulsive disorder satisfied the criteria for obsessive-compulsive personality disorder (Rasmussen and Tsuang 1986). Another investigation of 23 patients with obsessive-compulsive disorder found that only one subject also suffered from obsessive-compulsive personality disorder (Joffe et al. 1988). In fact, the most common characterological diagnosis in this sample was a mixed personality disorder with avoidant, dependent, and passive-aggressive features. In a recent study (Baer et al. 1990) that assessed 96 patients with obsessive-compulsive disorder, only 6% had an Axis II diagnosis of obsessive-compulsive personality disorder. Mixed, dependent, and histrionic personality disorders were those most frequently diagnosed.

The relatively minor changes in the criteria for the DSM-IV diagnosis of obsessive-compulsive personality disorder were designed to improve the discrimination of the diagnosis from other personality disorders and to increase compatibility with the International Classification of Diseases (ICD). One criterion from DSM-III-R (American Psychiatric Association 1987) involving indecisiveness was deleted because of its low specificity and lack of clustering with other items. DSM-IV criterion 8, "rigidity and stubbornness," has been added, but it has long been a classical feature of obsessive-compulsive disorder and does not add any significant new dimension to the diagnosis.

Psychodynamic Understanding

Early psychoanalytic contributions (Abraham 1921/1942; Freud 1908/1959; Jones 1948; Menninger 1943) connected certain character traits—particularly obstinacy, parsimony, and orderliness—with the anal phase of psychosexual development. Patients with these personality features were viewed as having regressed from the castration anxiety associated with the oedipal phase of development to the relative safety of the anal period. Driven by a punitive superego, they presumably employed characteristic defensive operations of the ego, including isolation of affect, intellectualization, reaction formation, undoing, and displacement (see Chapter 2). Their obsessive orderliness, for example, was conceptualized as a reaction formation against an underlying wish to engage in anal messiness and its derivatives. The considerable difficulty that the obsessive-compulsive personality has expressing aggression was related to early power struggles with maternal figures around toilet training. The stubbornness of the obsessive individual could also be viewed as an outgrowth of those same struggles.

More recent contributions (Gabbard 1985; Gabbard and Menninger 1988; Horowitz 1988; Salzman 1968, 1980, 1983; Shapiro 1965) have gone beyond the vicissitudes of the anal phase to focus on interpersonal elements, self-esteem, management of anger and dependency, cognitive style, and the problems of balancing work and emotional relationships. Individuals with obsessive-compulsive personality disorder suffer from a good deal of self-doubt. Their experience as children was that they were not sufficiently valued or loved by their parents. In some cases, this perception may relate to actual coldness or distance in parental figures, while in others the children may simply have required more reassurance and affection than the ordinary child to feel a sense of parental approval. Psychodynamic treatment of these patients reveals strong unfulfilled dependent yearnings and a reservoir of rage directed at the parents for not being more emotionally available. Since obsessive-compulsive patients find both anger and dependency consciously unacceptable, they defend against those feelings with defenses such as reaction formation and isolation of affect. In a counterdependent effort to deny any dependency on anyone, many obsessive-compulsive persons go to great lengths to demonstrate their independence and their "rugged individualism." Similarly, they strive for complete control over all anger, and they may even appear deferential and obsequious to avoid any impression of harboring angry feelings.

Intimate relationships pose a significant problem to the obsessive-compulsive patient. Intimacy raises the possibility of being overwhelmed by powerful wishes to be taken care of, with the concomitant potential for frustration of those wishes, resulting in feelings of hatred and resentment, and a desire for revenge. The feelings inherent to intimate relationships are threatening because they have the potential for becoming "out of control," one of the fundamental fears of the obsessive-compulsive person. Significant others frequently complain that their obsessive-compulsive loved one is too controlling. Stalemates and impasses often occur in such relationships because obsessive-compulsive persons refuse to acknowledge that anyone else might have a better way to do things. This need to control others often stems from a fundamental concern that sources of nurturance in the environment are highly tenuous and may disappear at any moment. Somewhere in every obsessive-compulsive person is a child who feels unloved. The low self-esteem connected with this childhood sense of not being valued often leads to an assumption that others would prefer not to put up with obsessive-compulsive persons. The high level of aggression and the intense destructive wishes lurking in the unconscious of the obsessive-compulsive person may also contribute to this fear of losing others. These patients often fear that their destructiveness will drive others away or that it will lead to counteraggression, a projection of their own rage.

Obsessive-compulsive persons are also characterized by a quest for perfection. They seem to harbor a secret belief that if they can only reach a transcendent stage of flawlessness, they will finally receive the parental approval and esteem they missed as children. These children often grow up with the conviction that they simply did not try hard enough, and as adults, they chronically feel that they are "not doing enough." The parent who seems never satisfied is internalized as a harsh superego that expects more and more from the patient. Many obsessive-compulsive individuals become workaholics because they are unconsciously driven by this conviction that love and approval can be obtained only through heroic efforts to achieve extraordinary heights in their chosen profession. The irony in this striving for perfection, however, is that obsessive-compulsive persons rarely seem satisfied with any of their achievements. They appear driven more by a wish to gain relief from their tormenting superego than by a genuine wish for pleasure.

These dynamic underpinnings lead to a characteristic cognitive style (Horowitz 1988; Shapiro 1965). Whereas hysterical and histrionic patients tend to overvalue affective states at the expense of careful thought, the reverse is true for obsessive-compulsive persons. Not unlike Mr. Spock of *Star Trek* fame, obsessive-compulsive individuals seek to be thoroughly rational and logical in every endeavor. They dread any situation of uncontrolled emotion, and their mechanistic tendency to be totally without affect may drive those around them to distraction. Moreover, their thinking is logical only within certain narrow parameters. Their thought patterns can be characterized as rigid and dogmatic (Shapiro 1965). Dynamically, these qualities can be understood as compensatory for the underlying self-doubt and ambivalence that plague the obsessive-compulsive person.

In contrast with the cognitive style of the hysterical patient, that of the obsessive-compulsive individual involves careful attention to detail but an almost complete lack of spontaneity or flexibility, with impressionistic hunches being automatically dismissed as "illogical." Obsessive-compulsive persons expend extraordinary energy to maintain their rigid cognitive and attentional styles, so that absolutely nothing they do is without effort. Taking vacations, or even relaxing, generally hold no allure whatsoever for the true obsessive-compulsive person. In one survey of 100 self-professed obsessive-compulsive physicians (Krakowski 1982), only 11% took vacations exclusively for the sake of a vacation and only 10% regularly took time away from work to relax.

Although many of these individuals are high achievers, some find that their character style impairs their ability to succeed at work. Obsessive-compulsive persons may ruminate endlessly about small decisions, exasperating those around them. They often get bogged down in details and lose track of the main purpose of the task at hand. Their indecision may be dynamically related to deep feelings of self-doubt. They may feel that the risk of making a mistake is so great as to preclude a definite decision one way or another. Similarly, their concern that the final outcome of a project may be less than perfect may contribute to their indecisiveness. Many obsessive-compulsive persons are extraordinarily articulate verbally but encounter major psychological obstacles in their writing because of this concern that the end result will not be flawless.

The "driven" quality inherent in the actions of the obsessive-compulsive person has been well described by Shapiro (1965) as having "the appearance of being pressed or motivated by something beyond the interest of the acting person. He does not seem that enthusiastic. His genuine interest in the activity, in other words, does not seem to account for the intensity with which he pursues it" (p. 33). These patients are always driven by their own internal overseer who issues commands about what they "should" or "ought to" do. Dynamically speaking, they have little autonomy from their own superego injunctions. They behave the way they do because they must, regardless of how their behavior impinges on others.

The hypertrophied superego of the obsessive-compulsive patient is relentless in its demands for perfection. When those demands are not satisfied over a long period, depression may set in. This dynamic link between the obsessive-compulsive character and depression has been observed by clinicians for many years. The obsessive-compulsive person may be at particularly high risk for depression in middle age, when the idealistic dreams of youth are shattered by the reality of time running out with advancing age. These patients may become suicidal at this point in their life cycle and may require hospitalization, despite a long history of functioning reasonably well in a work situation.

Psychotherapeutic Considerations

In contrast with the refractory nature of the obsessive-compulsive disorder, obsessive-compulsive personality disorder is often greatly improved by psychoanalysis or individual psychotherapy with an expressive emphasis (Gunderson 1988; Horowitz 1988; Munich 1986; Salzman 1980). Dynamic group psychotherapy may also be effective for patients with obsessive-compulsive personality disorder. Whether individual or group psychotherapy is chosen, similar therapeutic problems arise, requiring similar approaches.

In considering the resistances commonly encountered in the psychotherapy of obsessive-compulsive patients, one must first empathize with the implications that dynamic psychotherapy has for such patients. The very idea of the unconscious threatens their sense of control. Psychodynamic theory teaches that we are unconsciously controlled and consciously confused. Hence, the typical obsessive-compulsive patient is going to resent the basic premise of dynamic therapy. To deal with the feeling of being threatened, the obsessive-compulsive person may discount all the therapist's insights as "nothing new." Obsessive-compulsive patients may at first be reluctant to admit that the therapist is saying anything that they are not already aware of (Salzman 1980). Resistance can be understood as a patient's typical defensive operations as manifested in the psychotherapeutic process.

Isolation of affect, then, may present itself as a lack of awareness of any feelings toward the therapist, particularly dependency or anger. The patient may talk at great length about factual information from both past and present situations, with no apparent emotional reaction to these events. When the therapist returns from a lengthy vacation, the obsessive-compulsive patient is likely to be reluctant to admit any emotional reaction to the separation. If reaction formation is a prominent defense, the patient will probably respond with: "Oh, no, I wasn't bothered by it. I just hope that you had a wonderful time and feel refreshed."

Obsessive-compulsive persons also respond to the threat of intense affect by obsessional rambling that serves as a smoke screen to mask their real feelings. More precisely, it may serve as an anesthetizing cloud that puts others to sleep. As the patient wanders farther and farther afield from the original point, the therapist may lose track of the thread that links the patient's associations and may begin to "tune out" the patient. Because these persons may experience thoughts as having as much power as actions, the patient may feel the need to undo what has already been said, as follows:

> During the weekend visit with my parents, I became somewhat irritated with my father. Well, I wouldn't really say that I was irritated, in the sense that I truly felt any anger toward him. It's just that he sat and watched TV and seemed to have no interest in speaking to me. At one point, I had the thought of turning the TV off and confronting him, but of course I didn't really do that. I would never actually be that rude to anyone.

The rambling speech pattern typical of the obsessive-compulsive patient in psychotherapy features the frequent canceling of thoughts or wishes that have just been verbalized. In addition, an overinclusiveness of thinking leads the patient to bring in peripheral events that take the content of the rambling progressively further from the main theme of the session.

Many obsessive-compulsive patients will attempt to become the "perfect patient." They may try to produce exactly what they think the therapist wants to hear, with the unconscious fantasy that they will finally get the love and esteem they feel they missed as children. Because they are certain that any expression of anger will result in disapproval, they may consciously experience no anger while unconsciously expressing it by completely monopolizing the session. One obsessive-compulsive patient talked nonstop for 50 minutes, only to cease exactly on time, without ever letting the therapist get a word in edgewise. In this manner, the patient was able to express his anger without having to acknowledge any angry feelings.

Other obsessive-compulsive patients will manifest their resistance by re-creating in the transference relationship with the therapist their power struggle with their mother.

> Mr. RR was an obsessive-compulsive printer who came to psychoanalytic therapy twice a week. He initially presented as a rather submissive and passive "good boy," who was completely unable to express any anger within the therapy sessions. However, he developed a pattern of not speaking for approximately half the 50-minute session and of not paying his bill. Although he denied any anger toward the therapist when this behavior was brought out in the open, he developed a pattern of ventilating his anger with an exit line. One day, after failing to voice anger about the therapist "staring" at him during the session, he strode to the door and said, "I guess you didn't catch my cold," referring to a previously expressed concern that he might give his therapist his cold. On another occasion, after he was confronted about his failure to pay his bill, he exited with the following comment: "Don't freeze to death!" Shortly thereafter, another session ended with, "Don't slip on the ice!"
>
> One of Mr. RR's most remarkable exit lines occurred after a session where he was largely silent except for an occasional comment on the failure to pay his bill. The therapist connected his failure to produce payment for the bill with his failure to produce verbal material for the sessions. After a prolonged silence, Mr. RR was informed that the time was up. As he went to the door, he turned to the therapist and said, "I almost bought you a book at a sale yesterday. It was by a physician and was entitled *Thirty Years of Rectal Practice*." Then he rapidly left the room and slammed the door. During the next session, his therapist brought up this comment about his seemingly benevolent wish to buy him a gift. Mr. RR was able to explore his feeling that the therapist's attempt to extract money and words was comparable to an intrusive finger in his anus attempting to extract feces.

In the transference, Mr. RR had re-created a highly ambivalent relationship with his mother, which involved issues of withholding and control. He experienced his therapist as a mother who was demanding that he produce his feces (words and money) when and where she ordered him to. To defy what he felt as a sadistic and unreasonable command, he withheld his productions until the last moment, then let them go under his own control. In so doing, he attempted to make active what was passively experienced, ventilating his sadistic aggression in angry comments. However, as these examples illustrate, his characterological defense of reaction formation got the best of him in each exit line. Seeing through the reaction formation, the exit lines can be heard as follows: "Don't slip on the ice!" would be "I hope you slip on the ice." "Don't freeze to death!" would mean "I wish you would freeze to death." Even Mr. RR's attempt to equate his therapist with a sadistic and intrusive mother who was forcibly extracting his bodily contents had to be cloaked in the thought of buying him a gift. Despite the reaction formation, the anger in these exit lines still came through to the therapist. Because of Mr. RR's omnipotent concerns about the devastating power of his anger, he had to exit immediately after any hostile expression. He feared that his therapist would be so profoundly affected by these comments that he would retaliate in a massive and destructive fashion. Hence Mr. RR could only express his anger as he left the office, out of danger from retaliation (Gabbard 1982).

Therapeutic approaches to address these characteristic resistances of obsessive-compulsive patients begin with careful attention to countertransference. The therapist may feel a strong pull to disengage from the rambling, mechanistic presentation of factual material. Therapists may begin to isolate affect just as the patient does rather than experience the irritation and anger as an important part of the process that needs to be interpreted to the patient. For example, when the therapist begins to feel bored and distanced by the material, a useful comment might be "Is it possible that you are presenting all this factual material as a way of keeping emotionally distant from me?" Another countertransference pitfall is for the therapist to scotomize certain aspects of the patient's psychopathology because of the therapist's own obsessive-compulsive tendencies. Because obsessive-compulsive traits are highly adaptive in getting through medical school and psychiatry residency training (Gabbard 1985), therapists may be prone to overlook how these same traits might negatively affect a patient's relationships. To acknowledge the relational consequences of obsessive-compulsive tendencies may make therapists feel uncomfortable because the patient's situation may resonate with similar trends in the therapist's own personal relationships.

One effective strategy in the psychotherapeutic treatment of patients with obsessive-compulsive character structure is to cut through the smoke screen of words to go directly after feelings. The therapy process will frequently get bogged down in the patient's search for facts to avoid feelings, as in the following example:

> Mr. SS was a 29-year-old graduate student who sought psychotherapy with the chief complaint of not being able to complete his dissertation. His therapist was a psychiatry resident slightly younger than him. In the first few sessions, the patient struggled with his concern about the therapist's age by attempting to establish certain facts.

> Mr. SS: You look like you're probably not old enough to be a fully trained psychiatrist. I would guess you're approximately the same age as me. Is that correct?
> Therapist: Yes. I'm approximately the same age as you.
> Mr. SS: I assume, of course, that you've had considerable training in psychotherapy. Isn't that correct?
> Therapist: Yes, I have.
> Mr. SS: How long is a psychiatry residency anyway?
> Therapist: Four years.
> Mr. SS: And what year are you in?
> Therapist: I'm in my third year.
> Mr. SS: I guess you probably have a supervisor, though, don't you?

> At this point, the resident became aware that this question-and-answer approach was bypassing the patient's feelings. Instead of merely answering all the patient's factual questions, the therapist chose to address the process itself.

> Therapist: Mr. SS, it seems to me that this attempt to establish the facts of my training is a way of not addressing the feelings you're having about seeing a therapist who is approximately your own age and who is in training. I wonder if there isn't some anger and possibly even a bit of humiliation about having been assigned to a resident.

This vignette illustrates how the therapist should aggressively address the patient's feelings even when the patient is denying their existence. Obsessive-compulsive patients will also flee from transference feelings by retreating into long discourses about historically distant events. The therapist may have to bring the patient back to the here and now in the transference and attempt to establish what is going on in the present situation that caused the patient to seek refuge in the past (Salzman 1980, 1983). By keeping certain overarching themes and goals of the treatment in mind, often those with which the patient originally came to treatment, the therapist can maintain anchoring points for the process (Salzman 1980, 1983). When the patient endlessly ruminates about seemingly irrelevant minutiae, the therapist may have to interrupt the ruminations and bring the patient back to the central theme or issue that began the session. Group psychotherapy is often highly effective in dealing with this problem, because the patient may accept such feedback from peers without the same power struggle that accompanies feedback from the therapist.

An overall goal in the psychotherapeutic treatment of the obsessive-compulsive patient is superego modification. In the simplest terms, this means that these patients must accept their humanness. They must accept that their wish to transcend feelings of anger, hatred, lust, dependency, and so forth is doomed to failure. Feelings must finally be embraced as part of the human condition. They must be integrated as part of the person's self-experience rather than suppressed, denied, repressed, or disavowed as belonging to someone else. To accomplish this goal of making the superego a more benign structure, reassurance is rarely useful. Comments such as "You're not really as bad as you think you are" or "You're much too hard on yourself " will sound hollow to the patient.

Superego changes are more likely to occur through detailed interpretation of the patient's conflicts around dependency, aggression, and sexuality, in concert with the therapist's stable neutrality over time. By remaining nonjudgmental and equidistant from the superego, the ego, and the id, the therapist helps the patient discover that his or her perceptions of the therapist are distorted according to templates forged by past relationships. Although the patient will repeatedly try to view the therapist as critical and judgmental, the therapist can facilitate recognition that the patient is attributing his or her own critical, judgmental attitude to the therapist.

As these patients begin to understand that others are not nearly as critical as they themselves are, their self-esteem may correspondingly increase. They realize that others have accepted them all along much more than they had imagined. As they experience their therapist's acceptance of them for who they are, they also gain an increasing self-acceptance. As they learn that their conflicts over aggression and dependency stem from childhood situations, they gain greater mastery over these feelings and accept them as part of being human. The therapist can use periodic confrontations about the unrealistic expectations these patients so frequently harbor about themselves. One patient, for example, berated himself in a psychotherapy session over his feelings of rivalry with his older brother at a Christmas family gathering. The therapist commented, "You seem to believe that you should be able to transcend all feelings of competition with your brother and that you're a failure if you don't."

As in the psychotherapy of most patients, resistances are interpreted before underlying content. Defenses against anger, such as reaction formation, may have to be addressed for some time before the patient can see the defensive pattern clearly enough to relate it to underlying anger. For example, the therapist might have to deliver an interpretation such as the following: "Each time I announce a vacation, I notice that you say, 'No problem!' I wonder if that response covers up some other feelings that are more unacceptable." When obsessive-compulsive patients can finally experience and express undisguised anger toward the therapist, they learn that it is not nearly as destructive as they had thought. The therapist is a consistent, durable figure who is there week after week, clearly unscathed by expressions of anger. Similarly, these patients discover that they themselves are not transformed by their anger into monsters—like David Banner's metamorphosis into the Incredible Hulk.

To the obsessive-compulsive patient, sexual feelings are frequently just as unacceptable as anger or dependency. Again, the transference will reenact the childhood situation in which the patient sees the therapist as a parent who disapproves of sexuality. By maintaining a position of concerned neutrality, the therapist allows the patient to eventually see that such prohibitions are internal, not external. The threat (of castration or loss of love) attributed to the therapist can be understood, then, as an illusory one emanating from within the patient.

Avoidant Personality Disorder

This controversial disorder was designed to characterize a group of socially withdrawn individuals distinct from schizoid patients. As discussed in Chapter 14, the avoidant patient, unlike the schizoid patient, longs for close interpersonal relationships but is also afraid of them.

These individuals avoid relationships and social situations because they fear the humiliation connected with failure and the pain connected with rejection. Their desire for relationships may not be readily apparent because of their shy, self-effacing self-presentation.

The distinction between avoidant and schizoid personality disorders has been criticized on several grounds: for having no "clinical, empirical, or even widely accepted theoretical rationale" (Gunderson 1983, p. 23), for impoverishing the historical concept of schizoid personality disorder by obscuring some of its key features (Livesley et al. 1985; Livesley and West 1986), and for not adequately differentiating the two groups of patients (Reich and Noyes 1986). In a study of 82 psychiatric outpatients, Reich and Noyes (1986) found that a large percentage of those with schizoid personality disorder also met the diagnostic criteria for avoidant personality disorder. Their data suggested that schizoid personality might actually be a variant of avoidant personality disorder.

The data on diagnostic overlap, however, are contradictory. Two studies (Kass et al. 1985; Trull et al. 1987) found that whereas avoidant and schizoid diagnoses had a very low correlation, dependent personality disorder had considerable overlap with avoidant personality disorder. Trull et al. (1987) argued that in actual practice the diagnosis of schizoid personality disorder is rare, so that the overlap of avoidant and schizoid disorders has little clinical significance. They suggested that much more concern should be directed at the overlap between avoidant and dependent personality disorders.

In response to these criticisms, the DSM-III-R criteria for avoidant personality disorder were modified from those in the DSM-III (American Psychiatric Association 1980) version. Nonspecific criteria, such as "low self-esteem" and "desire for affection and acceptance," were deleted because these features apply to many other personality disorders. Also, new features, including an exaggeration of the risks in everyday life and an inordinate fear of being embarrassed, were added to bring the entity more in line with the psychoanalytic concept of the phobic character (Widiger et al. 1988). The DSM-III-R definition was also expanded to encompass avoidance of situations as well as interpersonal relationships. Although this revision of the diagnostic category was still somewhat problematic, it provided clear gains from a psychodynamic perspective because it was more closely linked with the psychoanalytic tradition of the phobic personality described by Fenichel (1945). Moreover, this improvement further defined the avoidant personality disorder as a neurotic character rather than a more primitive one. A number of authors (Akhtar 1986; Kernberg 1975; Meissner 1988) view the schizoid personality disorder as part of the borderline spectrum because identity diffusion and splitting are prominent features. In contrast, the avoidant personality disorder may be neurotic in the sense that identity diffusion is not present, and repression and other high-level defense mechanisms are much more prominent than splitting. Akhtar (1986) noted: "Avoidant personality is an ego-syntonic characterological counterpart of the phobic neurosis, just as obsessional personality is an ego-syntonic characterological counterpart of obsessional neurosis" (p. 1061).

Because of continued concern about the overlap between avoidant personality disorder and other Axis II diagnoses, the criteria in DSM-IV are more specific than those in DSM-III-R (see Table 19–2). While patients with dependent and avoidant personality disorders have some characteristics in common, fear of humiliation and rejection that results in withdrawal and social timidity is the key feature of avoidant personality disorder. Submissive, clinging behavior related to an excessive need for attachment is at the heart of dependent personality disorder (Hirschfeld et al. 1991). The new criteria reflect this distinction by placing greater emphasis on fears of humiliation, embarrassment, and rejection.

Table 19–2. DSM-IV criteria for avoidant personality disorder

A pervasive pattern of social inhibition, feelings of inadequacy, and hypersensitivity to negative evaluation, beginning by early adulthood and present in a variety of contexts, as indicated by at least *four* of the following:

1. avoids occupational activities that involve significant interpersonal contact, because of fears of criticism, disapproval, or rejection
2. is unwilling to get involved with people unless certain of being liked
3. shows restraint within intimate relationships due to the fear of being shamed or ridiculed
4. is preoccupied with being criticized or rejected in social situations
5. shows inhibition in new interpersonal situations because of feelings of inadequacy
6. views self as socially inept, personally unappealing, or inferior to others
7. is unusually reluctant to take personal risks or to engage in any new activities because they may prove embarrassing

Source. DSM-IV. Because the criteria sets were not final at press time, the reader should consult DSM-IV for final criteria.

The criteria for avoidant personality disorder are frequently present in clinical populations. However, the disorder is rarely the primary or sole diagnosis in clinical practice (Gunderson 1988). It is most commonly a supplementary diagnosis to another personality disorder or is used in conjunction with an Axis I diagnosis. The centrality of shame in the avoidant patient provides a psychodynamic link with certain types of narcissistic patients (particularly the phenomenologically hypervigilant type and some of those described by Kohut). Both narcissistic and avoidant patients may be prone to shame, but the former are also often characterized by a sense of entitlement and a quiet grandiosity.

Psychodynamic Understanding

People can be shy and avoidant for a variety of reasons. They may have a constitutional predisposition to avoid stressful situations based on inborn temperament that is secondarily elaborated into their entire personality style (Gunderson 1988). Some research data suggest that the trait of shyness is of genetic-constitutional origin but that it requires a specific environmental experience to develop into a full-blown trait (Kagan et al. 1988). Shyness or avoidance defends against embarrassment, humiliation, rejection, and failure. As with any other form of anxiety, the psychodynamic meaning of the anxiety must be explored to understand fully its origins with each individual patient. However, the psychotherapeutic and psychoanalytic treatment of individuals with these concerns often uncovers shame as a central affective experience.

Shame and self-exposure are intimately connected. What avoidant patients generally fear is any situation in which they must reveal aspects of themselves that leave them vulnerable. While guilt involves concerns about punishment for having violated some internal rule, shame relates more to an assessment of the self as somehow inadequate, as not measuring up to an internal standard. In this sense, guilt is more closely related to the superego in the structural model, whereas shame is more closely connected to the ego ideal (see Chapter 2).

Individuals with avoidant personality disorder may feel that social situations must be avoided because they allow their inadequacies to be displayed for all to see. They may feel ashamed about many different aspects of themselves; for instance, they may perceive themselves as weak, as unable to compete, as physically or mentally defective, as messy and disgusting, as unable to control bodily functions, or as exhibitionistic (Wurmser 1981).

Shame is etymologically derived from the verb "to hide" (Nathanson 1987), and the avoidant patient often withdraws from interpersonal relationships and situations of exposure out of a wish to "hide out" from the highly unpleasant affect of shame. Shame cannot be reductionistically linked with one developmental moment in the life of the child, but seems instead to evolve from many different developmental experiences at various ages (Nathanson 1987). Apparently present from very early in life, shame certainly is evident at the onset of stranger anxiety around 8 months of age (Broucek 1982). It is also connected with feelings that arise from bladder and bowel accidents and from an internalization of the parental reprimands often associated with those accidents. The 2-year-old child who is exhilarated by romping in the buff may also develop shame when a stern parent stops such activity by insisting that the child get dressed (Gabbard 1983). All these developmental experiences may be reactivated in the avoidant patient upon exposure to a group of people or an individual who matters a great deal to the patient.

Psychotherapeutic Approaches

Both individual and group expressive-supportive psychotherapy can be highly effective with patients suffering from avoidant personality disorder. Supportive elements involve an empathic appreciation of the embarrassment and humiliation associated with exposure, coupled with a firm encouragement to nevertheless expose oneself to the feared situations. The expressive elements of the psychotherapy involve exploring the underlying causes of shame and their linkages to past developmental experiences. The expressive aspect of therapy is greatly enhanced if the patient is willing to risk confronting the feared situations. More of the anxieties and fantasies will be activated in the actual situation of exposure than in the defensive posture of withdrawal. This fact can be explained to these patients in an educational intervention to help them see the value of actively seeking out the feared situations.

Initial exploratory efforts may be frustrating because avoidant patients will not be entirely sure what it is that they fear. Avoidant patients often resort to psychiatric clichés, such as "rejection." The therapist must seek more detail of actual situations to help the patient move beyond such vague explanations for avoidance. The therapist may ask, "What was your actual fantasy of what your co-workers might think of you when you sat in the lunch room with them yesterday?" Similarly, specific fantasies can be explored in the context of the transference. Avoidant patients usually have a good deal of anxiety about the exposure inherent in psychotherapy. When a patient blushes about something that has been verbalized, the therapist might ask, "Can you share with me what's embarrassing you right now? Is there some reaction that you imagine I'm having to what you just said?" By pursuing the details of specific situations, the patient will develop a greater awareness of the cognitive correlates of the shame affect.

> Ms. TT was a 24-year-old nursing student who came to psychotherapy because she felt dissatisfied with her life, had difficulty establishing heterosexual relationships, and experienced anxiety in social situations. She described chronic problems with feeling timid and shy around men. Since she was exceptionally attractive, she was frequently asked out, but her anxiety about each date would escalate to the point where she had to drink alcohol to relax. She told her therapist that she felt at risk for developing a dependence on alcohol, because she was only able to "open up" to men when she was under the influence. Ms. TT also noted the same experience of anxiety when she found herself "loosening up" with other people, such as peers in nursing school.
>
> She had tried group psychotherapy for several months, but found herself tongue-tied and self-conscious in the group. She would rarely speak for fear of "saying the wrong thing." When she began missing group psychotherapy sessions, she rationalized her absence by saying that it did not matter since she was not participating anyway. Ms. TT decided to seek individual psychotherapy because she thought it would be easier to open up to one person instead of eight.
>
> In her third session in psychotherapy, she began to fall silent frequently. The therapist was patient during these silences, but after a few more sessions, he noted that her silences seemed to occur when she was about to experience strong feelings. She acknowledged that she was terribly afraid of losing control when she became emotional. The therapist asked Ms. TT if she were concerned about his response to her expression of emotion. Ms. TT said that she felt certain he would criticize her and "shame" her for "acting like a baby."
>
> At this point the therapist asked Ms. TT if this fear was based on any similar past experiences. She launched into an extensive description of how her father had treated her as a child. She said that he was "a big man who couldn't take criticism but could deal it out." Each

time she brought home a report card, he would yell at her, demanding, "Why didn't you get an A?" She also remembered spilling her milk at the supper table and being severely reprimanded by her father, who railed at her, "Why can't you be more like your sister?" With considerable embarrassment, she said her father had never made her feel comfortable about being female. He teased her on the day of her first period by telling her she now had an excuse for being "bad" once a month. She recalled being extraordinarily mortified and crying in her room for hours. When she came home one day full of excitement because she had been selected as a cheerleader, her father called her "conceited and spoiled." She held a strong conviction that she would never be able to measure up to her father's expectations.

At one point in the therapy, Ms. TT was talking about her difficulty in attending parties or other social situations. Again the therapist asked about past situations that might be related to this fear. Ms. TT remembered that when she had been a little girl, her mother would dress her up and take her over to a friend's house, and everyone would always comment on how "cute" she was. She remembered her sense of embarrassment at these compliments, as though she had been "showing off." As the therapist helped her explore that feeling further, she realized that to some extent she had enjoyed the exposure because she had received such positive feedback in contrast to the constant criticism from her father. The therapist encouraged her to attend some of the social functions to which she was invited to see what other associations came to mind during an anxiety attack.

When Ms. TT began socializing more without first becoming inebriated, she realized that she feared enjoying herself. If she enjoyed the compliments of the men who hovered around her at a social gathering, then she was convinced that she was "conceited and spoiled," just as her father had used to say. This conviction made her feel that she was a "bad girl."

The case of Ms. TT illustrates that success in interpersonal situations often may be feared every bit as much as failure. The thrill of an exhibitionistic display may automatically trigger earlier parental reprimands about "showing off." Many individuals with avoidant personality disorder fear that they will become intoxicated with themselves when they are in the spotlight. This dynamic is central to the experience of stage fright (Gabbard 1979, 1983). Coexisting with Ms. TT's fear of enjoying her moment at center stage was another fear that she would fall short of the high expectations she had set for herself. These expectations were internalized by living with a father who had excessively high expectations. In the therapy, she was eventually able to acknowledge her intense anger at her father for repeatedly shaming her and making her feel so conflicted about her sexuality and her femaleness. Miller (1985) has noted a consistent connection between the inhibition of anger and the shame experience. Ms. TT could never freely express her anger at her father, and she felt ashamed of even having such feelings.

Dependent Personality Disorder

Dependency, like rejection, has become something of a psychiatric cliché. Everyone is dependent to some degree, and most patients in a clinical setting will have some conflict over their feelings of dependency. Particularly in American culture, where a powerful myth centers on rugged individualism and independence, the word "dependency" is often used pejoratively. Yet self psychologists would argue that true independence is neither possible nor desirable (see Chapter 2). We are all in need of various selfobject functions, such as approval, empathy, validation, and admiration, to sustain us and to regulate our self-esteem.

The DSM-IV category of dependent personality disorder is meant to capture a dependency so extreme as to be pathological. These individuals are unable to make decisions for themselves, are unusually submissive, are always in need of reassurance, and cannot function well without someone else to take care of them. Dependent personality disorder was not listed in DSM-II (American Psychiatric Association 1968) and was added to DSM-III only because some contributors were convinced that a "passive-dependent" type of personality disorder was needed as a counterpart to the "active-dependent" type characterized by the criteria for histrionic personality disorder (Gunderson 1983). Although the category is somewhat related to the traditional "oral character" identified in psychoanalytic writings, there are no empirical data to support the active-dependent and passive-dependent distinction.

The DSM-III version of dependent personality disorder was criticized for being too vague—it had only three diagnostic criteria—and for being too gender biased in its examples, which suggested that women were more likely to suffer from the disorder (Widiger et al. 1988). The revised category expanded the criteria to nine items and, to some extent, corrected the gender bias by changing the examples. Although the diagnosis may actually be applied more frequently to women (Gunderson 1988), this fact may be related to entrenched sexual stereotypes in our culture, which allow women to be more dependent than men.

The principal changes in the DSM-IV criteria for dependent personality disorder were designed to reduce overlap with other Axis II diagnoses such as avoidant personality disorder and borderline personality disorder (see Table 19–3). The emphasis in the new criteria is on these patients' excessive need to be taken care of and their clinging and submissive behavior in the service of maintaining attachment. The DSM-III-R criterion "is easily hurt by criticism or disapproval" was omitted because of its lack of specificity. Criterion 3 has shifted its emphasis from the fear of rejection to the fear that the other person will become unsupportive, reflecting the paramount importance of maintaining a connection and further differentiating this disorder from

---

Table 19–3. DSM-IV criteria for dependent personality disorder

---

A pervasive and excessive need to be taken care of, leading to submissive and clinging behavior and fears of separation, beginning by early adulthood and present in a variety of contexts, as indicated by at least *five* of the following:

1. is unable to make everyday decisions without an excessive amount of advice and reassurance from others

2. needs others to assume responsibility for major areas of his or her life

3. has difficulty expressing disagreement with others because of fear of loss of support or approval (Note: Do not include realistic fears of retribution)

4. has difficulty initiating projects or in doing things on his or her own (due to a lack of self-confidence in judgment or abilities rather than to a lack of motivation or energy)

5. goes to excessive lengths to obtain nurturance and support from others, to the point of volunteering to do things that are unpleasant

6. feels uncomfortable or helpless when alone, because of exaggerated fears of being unable to care for himself or herself

7. urgently seeks another relationship as a source of care and support when a close relationship ends

8. is unrealistically preoccupied with fears of being left to take care of himself or herself

---

Source. DSM-IV. Because the criteria sets were not final at press time, the reader should consult DSM-IV for final criteria.

avoidant personality disorder (Hirschfeld et al. 1991). Criterion 6 was revised to emphasize the exaggerated fear of being unable to take care of oneself as a way of differentiating this feature more fully from the borderline patient's intense anxiety about being abandoned. Similar changes were made in criterion 8.

Dependent personality disorder, like avoidant personality disorder, is rarely used as a principal or single diagnosis. It is often associated with dysthymic disorder, with depression, and with anxiety. It is also commonly diagnosed in conjunction with other personality disorders, such as borderline, histrionic, and avoidant. While more than 50% of patients diagnosed with dependent personality disorder also receive the diagnosis of borderline personality disorder, the two diagnoses can be differentiated based on key aspects of relationship patterns. Borderline patients react to abandonment with rage and manipulation, whereas dependent patients become submissive and clinging (Hirschfeld et al. 1991). Moreover, the intense and unstable quality of the borderline patient's relationships is not found in the relationships of persons with dependent personality disorder.

Psychodynamic Understanding

Many patients with dependent personality have grown up in households where the parents have communicated in one way or another that independence is fraught with danger. Overinvolved and overintrusive mothers are common to this group of patients. Like many histrionic and borderline patients, dependent patients have a history of being subtly rewarded for maintaining loyalty to their parents, who subtly reject them in the face of any move toward separation and independence.

Despite this similarity to patients with borderline personality disorder, the patient with dependent personality does not react to separation exactly like the borderline individual does. Both may dread abandonment, both may cling to the significant other, and both may feel lost in the absence of the significant other. Borderline patients commonly react to separation with a sense of panic, leading to impulsive, self-destructive behavior. Such dramatic reactions in those with dependent personality disorder are uncommon—the dependent patient is much more likely to simply sit and cry. This difference might be related to greater object constancy in the developmental histories of those with dependent personality disorder. An alternative hypothesis would be that dependent patients lack the genetic-constitutional predisposition to the flamboyant, self-destructive behavior characteristic of borderline patients.

Although early psychoanalytic writers believed that problems with dependency were connected with disturbances during the oral phase of psychosexual development, this view is not widely held today (Gunderson 1988). Such a formulation has the same problem as other phase-specific explanations for psychopathology. A pervasive pattern of parental reinforcement for dependency throughout all phases of development is more likely to be operative in the backgrounds of patients with dependent personality disorder. One empirical study (Head et al. 1991) found that families of persons with dependent personality disorder were characterized by low expressiveness and high control, in contrast with families in a clinical control group and a normal control group.

A submissive stance toward others may have a myriad of meanings. Just as the avoidant patient shuns exposure as a result of multiply determined unconscious factors, the dependent patient seeks caretaking because of anxieties that lie beneath the surface. The clinician should ask each individual, "What is it about independence or separation that is frightening?" Dependent clinging often masks aggression. It may be viewed as a compromise formation in the sense that it defends against hostility that is also concomitantly expressed. As many mental health professionals know from firsthand experience, the person who is the object of the dependent patient's clinging may experience the patient's demands as hostile and tormenting.

Dependent behavior may also be a way to avoid the reactivation of past traumatic experiences. The therapist should explore with the patient any memories of past separations and their impact.

Mr. UU was a 29-year-old married postal clerk. He had a long-standing dysthymic disorder and chronically complained of insomnia, lack of energy, difficulty making decisions, and anxiety. Nevertheless, he managed to show up at his job conscientiously, even though he found it difficult to take any initiative when it was expected of him. Prior to his psychiatric hospitalization for suicidal thoughts and wishes, Mr. UU had broken down in tears in front of his supervisor when he was told he was not doing his job properly.

During the admission interview, Mr. UU expressed extreme concern about being away from his wife during the hospitalization, even though he realized that his suicidal wishes were dangerous enough to necessitate inpatient treatment. Mrs. UU explained that her husband had never liked to be away from her. He relied on her to make all decisions in the home, and he could not function very well without her. Almost immediately after being admitted, Mr. UU latched onto a female patient approximately his age and looked to her for guidance in the same way he had related to his wife. He ate all his meals with her and spent all his leisure time with her when he was not involved in treatment activities. He made no sexual overtures toward this other patient but simply reported that he felt safe in her company.

Mr. UU's history revealed a lifelong pattern of anxious dependency. He had always experienced considerable anxiety at the prospect of doing something alone or upon initiating any plan of action without consulting others. He had school phobia when he started elementary school, and his mother reported that he had cried until she would take him home. Similarly, at the age of 10, he had been sent to visit his uncle overnight and had cried so hard that his mother had to return to the uncle's house and bring him home. When he graduated from high school, all of his friends in his peer group enlisted in the service, so he followed suit. Upon discharge from the service, they went to work for the post office, so he applied along with them. Any independent action on his part seemed to reactivate the painful anxiety associated with early separations. He behaved as though convinced that he would be abandoned for any autonomous behavior.

The origins of Mr. UU's dependency and separation anxiety became clearer when his mother began to call him in the hospital. She complained about his decision to enter the hospital: "How can you justify being away from us like this? Your condition can't be that bad. What if we need you to do something and you're not available?" The patient explained that even as an adult, he had responded to his mother's call to come over to her house each week to do various menial jobs. He went on to say that his parents were virtually noncommunicative and that his mother had relied on him for conversation. Mr. UU had grown up in a household where his mother had conveyed a powerful message—namely, that she needed him as a stand-in for her emotionally estranged husband. Independence was thus regarded as an aggressive and disloyal act that would lead to the loss of his mother's love.

Psychotherapeutic Considerations

The psychotherapy of patients with dependent personality disorder presents an immediate therapeutic dilemma—for these patients to overcome their problems with dependency, they must first develop dependency on their therapist. This dilemma often becomes elaborated into a specific form of resistance in which the patient sees dependency on the therapist as an end in itself rather than as a means to an end. After a period in therapy, these patients may forget the nature of the complaint that brought them to treatment, and their only purpose becomes the maintenance of their attachment to the therapist. Dreading termination, they may repeatedly remind their therapist of how awful they feel to assure continuation of the treatment. If the therapist comments on any improvement whatsoever, the patient may paradoxically worsen since the thought of improvement is equated with termination.

One rule of thumb in treating dependent patients is to remember that what they say they want is probably not what they need. They will attempt to get the therapist to tell them what to do, to allow them to continue their dependency, and to collude in the avoidance of making decisions or asserting their own wishes. The therapist must feel comfortable in frustrating these wishes and instead promoting independent thinking and action in the patient. The therapist must convey that the anxiety produced by this frustration is tolerable and also productive in that it may lead to associations about the origins of the dependency and the fears associated with it.

Time-limited dynamic psychotherapy has been successful with a number of these patients (Gunderson 1988). Knowing from the beginning of the psychotherapy that the patient-therapist relationship will end after 12, 16, or 20 sessions forces these patients to confront their deepest anxieties about loss and independence. Moreover, this approach also helps patients address powerful fantasies involving the never-ending availability of nurturing figures. When long-term, open-ended therapy reaches something of a stalemate, a modification of the time-limited technique can be utilized by setting a deadline for termination. Anxieties that may have lain dormant will be brought rapidly to the surface when the end of therapy is in sight.

A subgroup of dependent patients are simply unable or unwilling to make use of the framework of brief psychotherapy. The prospect of losing the therapist after "just getting started" creates too much anxiety. Because of lesser amounts of ego strength or greater degrees of separation anxiety, these patients need to develop a positive dependent transference to a therapist over a long time. Nevertheless, considerable therapeutic gains are possible with this supportive strategy, as documented by Wallerstein's (1986) research (discussed in Chapter 4).

Some patients change as part of a "transference trade" (Wallerstein, p. 690) with the therapist. They are willing to make certain alterations in their lives in return for the therapist's approval. Others may become "lifers" who can maintain change as long as they know that the therapist will always be there for them. These patients may do well even when the therapist tapers down the sessions to one every few months, provided there is no threat of termination.

Patients with dependent personality disorder commonly create countertransference problems related to dependency conflicts in their treaters. Physicians in general, and psychiatrists in particular, may feel conflicted about their own dependency (Gabbard 1985; Gabbard and Menninger 1988; Vaillant et al. 1972). Psychotherapists must be wary of countertransference contempt or disdain toward the dependent patient. The longings of the patient may resonate with the unconscious longings of the therapist, and an empathic attunement with such dependency wishes may be acutely uncomfortable. Therapists who repudiate their patient's longings may be repudiating their own longings as well.

Personality Disorder Not Otherwise Specified

Having completed our survey of the DSM-IV personality disorders, it is worth noting that patients generally do not present themselves as "pure cultures" of any one personality disorder. DSM-IV has an extra category of *personality disorder not otherwise specified* to acknowledge this fact. This category can be used for personality disorders that are "mixed" and for those in the Appendix, such as passive-aggressive personality disorder. Passive-aggressive personality disorder, which was included in DSM-III-R, was relegated to the Appendix in the transition to DSM-IV because the diagnosis was considered too situation-specific, too narrowly defined, too redundant, and too reflective of a symptom cluster rather than a personality disorder.

The uniqueness of each individual is a source of continued delight and challenge for the dynamic psychiatrist. In Chapter 1 we noted that the dynamic psychiatrist is more interested in how patients differ from one another than in how they are similar. Nowhere in psychiatry is this axiom more relevant than in the treatment of personality disorders.

References

Abraham K: Contributions to the theory of the anal character (1921), in Selected Papers of Karl Abraham, M.D. London, Hogarth Press, 1942, pp 370–392

Akhtar S: Differentiating schizoid and avoidant personality disorders (letter). Am J Psychiatry 143:1061–1062, 1986

American Psychiatric Association: Diagnostic and Statistical Manual of Mental Disorders, 2nd Edition. Washington, DC, American Psychiatric Association, 1968

American Psychiatric Association: Diagnostic and Statistical Manual of Mental Disorders, 3rd Edition. Washington, DC, American Psychiatric Association, 1980

American Psychiatric Association: Diagnostic and Statistical Manual of Mental Disorders, 3rd Edition, Revised. Washington, DC, American Psychiatric Association, 1987

American Psychiatric Association: Diagnostic and Statistical Manual of Mental Disorders, 4th Edition. Washington, DC, American Psychiatric Association 1994

Baer L, Jenike MA, Ricciardi JN, et al: Standardized assessment of personality disorders in obsessive-compulsive disorder. Arch Gen Psychiatry 47:826–830, 1990

Broucek FJ: Shame and its relationship to early narcissistic developments. Int J Psychoanal 63:369–378, 1982

Fenichel O: The Psychoanalytic Theory of the Neurosis. New York, WW Norton, 1945

Freud S: Character and anal erotism (1908), in The Standard Edition of the Complete Psychological Works of Sigmund Freud, Vol 9. Translated and edited by Strachey J. London, Hogarth Press, 1959, pp 167–175

Gabbard GO: Stage fright. Int J Psychoanal 60:383–392, 1979

Gabbard GO: The exit line: heightened transference-countertransference manifestations at the end of the hour. J Am Psychoanal Assoc 30:579–598, 1982

Gabbard GO: Further contributions to the understanding of stage fright: narcissistic issues. J Am Psychoanal Assoc 31:423–441, 1983

Gabbard GO: The role of compulsiveness in the normal physician. JAMA 254:2926–2929, 1985

Gabbard GO, Menninger RW: The psychology of the physician, in Medical Marriages. Edited by Gabbard GO, Menninger RW. Washington, DC, American Psychiatric Press, 1988, pp 23–38

Gunderson JG: DSM-III diagnoses of personality disorders, in Current Perspectives on Personality Disorders. Edited by Frosch JP. Washington, DC, American Psychiatric Press, 1983, pp 20–39

Gunderson JG: Personality disorders, in The New Harvard Guide to Psychiatry. Edited by Nicholi AM Jr. Cambridge, MA, Belknap Press of Harvard University Press, 1988, pp 337–357

Head SB, Baker JD, Williamson DA: Family environment characteristics and dependent personality disorder. Journal of Personality Disorders 5:256–263, 1991

Hirschfeld RMA, Shea MT, Weise R: Dependent personality disorder: perspectives for DSM-IV. Journal of Personality Disorders 5:135–149, 1991

Horowitz MJ: Introduction to Psychodynamics: A New Synthesis. New York, Basic Books, 1988

Joffe RT, Swinson RP, Regan JJ: Personality features of obsessive-compulsive disorder. Am J Psychiatry 145:1127–1129, 1988

Jones E: Anal-erotic character traits, in Papers on Psycho-Analysis, 5th Edition. Baltimore, MD, Williams & Wilkins, 1948, pp 413–437

Kagan J, Reznick JS, Snidman N: Biological bases of childhood shyness. Science 240:167–171, 1988

Kass F, Skodol AE, Charles E, et al: Scaled ratings of DSM-III personality disorders. Am J Psychiatry 142:627–630, 1985

Kernberg OF: Borderline Conditions and Pathological Narcissism. New York, Jason Aronson, 1975

Krakowski AJ: Stress and the practice of medicine, II: stressors, stresses, and strains. Psychother Psychosom 38:11–23, 1982

Livesley WJ, West M: The DSM-III distinction between schizoid and avoidant personality disorders. Can J Psychiatry 31:59–62, 1986

Livesley WJ, West M, Tanney A: Historical comment on DSM-III schizoid and avoidant personality disorders. Am J Psychiatry 142:1344–1347, 1985

Meissner WW: Treatment of Patients in the Borderline Spectrum. Northvale, NJ, Jason Aronson, 1988

Menninger WC: Characterologic and symptomatic expressions related to the anal phase of psychosexual development. Psychoanal Q 12:161–193, 1943

Miller S: The Shame Experience. Hillsdale, NJ, Analytic Press, 1985

Munich RL: Transitory symptom formation in the analysis of an obsessional character. Psychoanal Study Child 41:515–535, 1986

Nathanson DL: A timetable for shame, in The Many Faces of Shame. Edited by Nathanson DL. New York, Guilford, 1987, pp 1–63

Nemiah JC: Obsessive-compulsive disorder (obsessive-compulsive neurosis), in Comprehensive Textbook of Psychiatry, 3rd Edition, Vol 2. Edited by Kaplan HI, Freedman AM, Sadock BJ. Baltimore, MD, Williams & Wilkins, 1980, pp 1504–1517

Rasmussen SA, Tsuang MT: Clinical characteristics and family history in DSM-III obsessive-compulsive disorder. Am J Psychiatry 143:317–322, 1986

Reich J, Noyes R Jr: Differentiating schizoid and avoidant personality disorders (letter). Am J Psychiatry 143:1062, 1986

Salzman L: The Obsessive Personality: Origins, Dynamics, and Therapy. New York, Science House, 1968

Salzman L: Treatment of the Obsessive Personality. New York, Jason Aronson, 1980

Salzman L: Psychoanalytic therapy of the obsessional patient. Current Psychiatric Therapies 22:53–59, 1983

Shapiro D: Neurotic Styles. New York, Basic Books, 1965

Trull TJ, Widiger TA, Frances A: Covariation of criteria sets for avoidant, schizoid, and dependent personality disorders. Am J Psychiatry 144:767–771, 1987

Vaillant GE, Sobowale NC, McArthur C: Some psychologic vulnerabilities of physicians. N Engl J Med 287:372–375, 1972

Wallerstein RS: Forty-Two Lives in Treatment: A Study of Psychoanalysis and Psychotherapy. New York, Guilford, 1986

Widiger TA, Frances A, Spitzer RL, et al: The DSM-III-R personality disorders: an overview. Am J Psychiatry 145:786–795, 1988

Wurmser L: The Mask of Shame. Baltimore, MD, Johns Hopkins University Press, 1981

Index

*Page numbers printed in **boldface** type refer to tables or figures.*

Alternate personalities. *See* Alters
Alters, amnesia and, 298–299, 302
  multiple personality disorder and,
    296–297, 297–298, 302,
    304–305, 306, 314–315
  hospital treatment and, 314–315
  integration of, 304–305, 306
  multiple personality disorder and,
    296–297, 297–299, 302, 303,
    304–305, 314–315
  resolution of, 304–305
  therapeutic alliance and, 303
Altruism. *See* Defense mechanisms
Alzheimer's disease, 406–407,
  410–413. *See also* Cognitive
  disorders
  case example of, 414–412
Amini, F., 559, 566
Amnesia, alters and, 298–299, 302
  dissociation and, 295, 302
  dissociative type, 292–293, 295
  multiple personality disorder and,
    295, 297, **298,** 298–299, 302,
    304–305
Anal phase. *See* Developmental
  phases
Anonymity, of therapist, 96–97
Anorexia nervosa, 373–380
  borderline pathology and, 374
  bulimia nervosa and, 380–381,
    381–382
  countertransference and, 379–380
  family therapy and, 367–377,
    377–378
  hospital treatment for, 377–378
  individual psychotherapy and,
    376–377
  interpretation and, 379
  mother-child relationship and, 374
  obsessive-compulsive behavior
    and, 476
  projective identification and,
    378–379

  psychodynamic understanding of,
    373–376
  psychotherapy and, 377–380
  resistance in, 378–380
  self psychology and, 375–376
  treatment approaches for, 376–380
Antisocial personality disorder,
  527–554, **528, 530, 541, 549**
  antisocial behavior and, 536–537,
    538–359, 540–541, 543, 551,
    551–552
  case examples of, 535, 536,
    538–539, 545–548
  confrontation and, 539–540, 551
  countertransference and,
    543–544, 551
  depression and, 534, 549
  drug abuse and, 369, 531, 540–541
  DSM-III and, 528–529
  DSM-III-R and, 529
  DSM-IV and, 529–530, **530**
  epidemiology of, 531–532
  hospital treatment for, 538–548,
    541
  hysterical personality disorder
    and, 562
  individual psychotherapy and,
    548–542
  mother-child relationship and,
    533–534
  narcissistic personality disorder
    and, 533–534, 535–536, **537,**
    540
  neutrality and, 551–552
  object relations and, 533–534,
    536–537
  paraphilias and, 332
  pharmacotherapy and, 542–543
  predictors of treatability and, **541,**
    541–542, 552
  projective identification and, 533
  psychodynamic understanding of,
    532–538